The Camelot General Chemistry Primer

by
Dwight Wayne Coop

Camelot/Hellenic Series

KENNDON, KRASTINS & GOULD, PUBLISHERS

i

The Camelot General Chemistry Primer
(A Scientific Drama...)

All inquiries should be addressed to:

Kenndon, Krastins & Gould
Camelot/Hellenic College Series
P.O. Box 732
Temecula CA 92593
United States of America

Cataloging and Publication Data

Library of Congress Card Number: Pending

International Standard Book Number: 1-883316-19-7

Coop, Dwight Wayne

The Camelot General Chemistry Primer

416 pp.
Includes Index

Preface

If you read nothing else in this book, read this!

I'M THE 1-MINUTE CHEMISTRY ACE!!

I
𝔖tatement of 𝔓urpose

𝔗he author's intent was to provide a self-taught course in general chemistry to (1) complement standard textbooks and lectures and/or (2) impart considerable readiness, in both skill and confidence, to the student who works through the primer in anticipation of taking college general chemistry or high school chemistry.

On a more private level, the author, a generalist with no graduate background in the sciences, wrote the book to end his tutoring career while continuing to satisfy the demands made on it (e.g. "Just get me through this [expletive] test!"). It incorporates the methods developed in his experience and reflects his familiarity with the most common ambiguities and patterns of error.

For less than the cost of two hours of tutored assistance, an unlimited access to the same methods becomes available; it is the 24-hour portable general chemistry tutor, to the limited but still considerable extent that a such a book can be designed take the place of a person.

II
𝔚arning/𝔇isclaimer

𝔍f you are willing to do all the work in this book in addition to later or concurrent classwork, you can reasonably set for yourself a grade objective one letter higher than what you would otherwise expect to achieve. Along these lines, there is, for the moment, no guarantee. However, if you do buy the book and succeed (or fail) in such an objective, please inform the publisher. Please also send along any suggestions; if enough are received, the book will be revised.

The Camelot Primer, in spite of its deliberately novel approach, is not a "gimmick" nor is it "dumbed-down." The idea was to make chemistry clearer, not "easier," as the material must be learned in one way or another.

This is explained in more detail in the Introduction, should you choose to read it.

111
Is this book for you?

Yes...if now or later you will enroll in general college chemistry. General chemistry, by any name (e.g. Chem. 1-2-3, Chem. 101-102-103), is the first stage of the chemistry sequence for majors in engineering, medicine, dentistry, chiropractic, nutrition, pharmacology, science education, etc., and all the natural sciences.

    The Primer is specifically a general chemistry lecture (not lab) text, skills manual, and workbook.

Yes...if you are taking or will take prep or high-school chemistry. The lecture material of such a one-year course is treated to a comparable degree (or beyond) in this work.

Maybe...if your chemistry is that needed by allied health majors (nursing, dietetics, etc.), which is less in depth and greater in breadth than general chemistry (but about equally challenging). You might find that the Primer over- or underemphasizes most class topics.

    One suggestion would be to compare the table of contents with your class syllabus or to consult your academic advisor. Another book, the Camelot Allied Health Sciences Chemistry Primer is being written for this chemistry sequence and is due out in 1993.

No...if your chemistry course is a one-term survey for nonscience majors, the kind of class you take to meet a general education requirement for the physical sciences. The class will be interesting, but not very hard. You will not, in any case, need *this* book (although the publisher will not object if you buy it!).

Maybe...if you are not (in the finite sense) a student, but are nevertheless inclined towards chemistry for esthetic reasons.

    Because, even as you read this, chemical mechanisms between your brain's synapses are the very medium of your thoughts.

    The Primer could indeed teach chemistry for its own sake; however, for fairness, some alternatives are described in the back of the book (see "Further Reading").

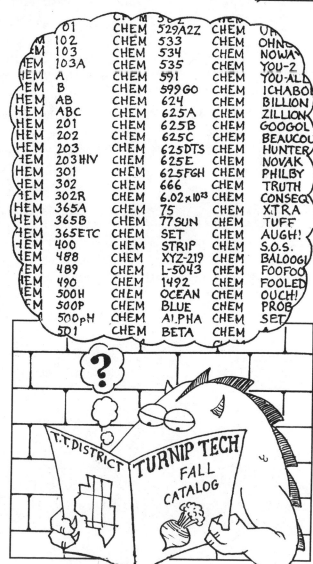

"It seems probable
to me that God in
the beginning formed
matter in solid,
massy, hard, impenitrable,
movable particles, so very hard
as to never wear out
nor break in pieces,
no ordinary power
being able to divide
what God Himself
made in
the First Creation."

---Newton
(a devout atomist)

Foreword

Anyone who is enrolled in or plans to enroll in a general chemistry course, a prep or high school chemistry course, or is required to take chemistry for a health major, would greatly profit from studying Dwight Wayne Coop's *The Camelot General Chemistry Primer*. This study would be especially valuable to those who have experienced, or fear they will experience, difficulty in understanding general chemical principles and their applications. While not diluting the knowledge, principles, and practical applications employed in general chemistry courses, Coop presents the material in a way that is both easily understood and entertaining. His approach, while novel, is thorough and accomplishes the goal he has set forth—to provide a self-taught course in general chemistry that will enable the user to acquire skill and confidence in mastering such a course. For many students, his book will help to convert a course in chemistry from a study that may seem both dull and difficult to one which is actually exciting and easy to master.

A brief examination of the contents of this book will serve to convince any reader that Coop has covered his subject in sufficient scope and depth to satisfy the student's needs. At last, prospective chemistry students have the help they require in a way that will be a delight to employ.

Duane T. Gish, Ph. D.
El Cajon, California

Table of Contents

Seven: Concerning Energy And The States   243

Eight: Concerning The Equilibria   283

Nine: Concerning The Acids And Bases   315

Ten: Concerning Oxidation And Reduction   345

Epilogue: Concerning The Full Circle   377

Introduction

I. Why Was This Book Written?

As noted, this is a self-teaching manual for use prior to or concurrent with general or high-school chemistry. A general chemistry sequence takes about a year and a half to complete, and is prerequisite to more advanced study. This Primer covers the first 35-40% of general chemistry, or a year of honors high school chemistry. It was designed using syllabi from such courses.

Experienced chemistry students will testify that your grade in first-term chemistry has a way of repeating itself. You can confidently expect the Primer to improve your performance in the first two courses in the sequence; however, it is also hoped that through this grade-rut phenomenon that the benefit will accrue to subsequent courses.

"Chemistry 1" (or 101, etc.), occupies a toll position in Academe. All science and some nonscience majors must take it. This book was written for them. It anticipates the usual (and certain unusual) patterns of error. It might also inculcate an appreciation for chemistry's origins, its place among the great liberal disciplines, and its platonic beauty.

II. What Are The Primer's Features?

The Camelot Primer differs from other chemistry texts (although not necessarily to their discredit). It is deficient, for example, in its lack of entire chapters on the elements and the element families. Instead, there are quickie profiles of selected elements. These snapshots are intended to enhance *skills* introduced in earlier sections, ahead of *knowledge* of the elements themselves, which can easily be found in your regular textbook. To have included such material here, then, would have been unneeded duplication. This accounts for the Primer's brevity yet allows its completeness as a skills-oriented manual. The lecture (not lab) skills that you will encounter in "Chem. 1" are covered here to the same depth.

The most important, if least visible, of the Primer's features is its inductive/deductive presentation. The angle of most science texts is nearly wholly deductive. The idea here was to harness both the student's logical facilities as an adult and his or her ability to learn passively and from recurring specifics. Of the latter, all adults retain a degree from childhood.

Among the other features, which were rarely or never uncovered in the author's research, are comics and hundreds of other aids: original mnemonic devices, puns, analogies, error analyses, overlearning techniques, and the "color refresher" (see p. xv). None of these elements are present to make the material *easier*, but, rather, to make it *clearer*, or to otherwise edify the reader.

Also, each chapter ends not with a page-filling summary but a synthesis with its own problem set. Here, especially, associative mechanisms were worked in.

There is also a "story line" with characters and the denouement of a bit of mystery. The student/reader participates vicariously, as it were, through one of these characters, as both pupil and protagonist.

The other three main characters, based on historical people, are in fact abbreviated caricatures of their actual personalities and appearances. The auditioning for the three "apprentice" roles saw worthy takes by Pauling, Gay-Lussac, Mendeleev, and others. The three finally chosen were picked not only for their provision of a spectrum of scientific stereotypes---the nerdy, the sanguine, the perfectionist---but because their contributions were (1) as vital as those of any other to the evolution of general chemistry, and (2) they provided a workable literary and historical substrate in which to spin what there is of a "plot."

III. Is The Primer "Dumbed-Down"?

None of these features is gimmickry, so the title "The One-Minute Chemistry Ace" (as one cynical suggestion went) was never seriously considered, although it made marketing "sense."

While it is not gimmickry, neither is the Primer a product of "dumbing down." This wretched current---the dilution of curricula, textbooks, objectives, and teacher credentialing to condescend to scholastic decline---is an easier response to the problem than doing whatever is needed to return to the older, better standards that were once de rigeur for graduation.

One consequence of dumbing down is that hypothesizing and causal analysis are being replaced by mere description. This takes place from the earliest grades, such that "science books" have become little more than gold-plated compilations of pictures and captions assembled with truncated vocabularies. Study questions *by design* no longer test the grasp of concepts, but mere reading comprehension. This is dumbing-down at its subtlest, and it sneaks past almost everyone who is charged with textbook selection these days.

Dumbing down has gone unchecked for so long that its first generation of "laureates" include a class of smug semi-literates that, irony of ironies, are administering public schools in the US. The early benefit of science education is the practical application of cause-and-effect thinking. The ultimate benefit is the academic and social application of the same (e.g., voter informedness on ecological issues). If such people cannot reason causally at any level, how can they pass it on to others?

In Iowa, perhaps the most literate and numerate of the United States, one must still work for a high school diploma, but the same document from the Los Angeles Unified Schools has become a proverb of cultural decline. "Self-esteem needs" must then be ground into the official curriculum and added to the teachers' already impossible burden. Since everything beyond the three Rs (and much of what was traditionally part of them) has been abandoned, the students will need this extra "self-esteem," as they will end up knowing nothing else and become the homeless of the job market.

For all these reasons, no apologies are made for the preference of erudite over common or cliché language in this book. This work, in spite of its appearance, is a humbly scholarly one, though by no means esoteric. Again, clarity, not some chimerical easiness, was the goal. Precise language is clearer than dumbed-down language (with its inevitable ambiguities) to the student willing to practice and master its usage. It is clearer still to the student with a broad latitude of preparation. If you study Kafka, Descartes, Aquinas, and Plato, will you have an edge in chemistry (and elsewhere) over the student who has slept through empty-calorie courses in elementary education? Yes!

It is almost certain that the sacrifice of precision for ease---another albatross of the dumbing-down syndrome---has contributed to chemistry's "hardness." Confusion can only proliferate as useful old words tumble into the maw of Orwell's Memory Hole.

IV. What Else Do You Need?

If you have been a victim of dumbing-down, there is hope yet, and it may begin here. Get a good dictionary---one providing notes on etymology and context---and develop, like A.G. Draggin' does, a sensitivity to words and look them up even when you know their meanings.

You also need a little algebra, although even logarithms are indirectly taught in this book as they relate to chemistry. And, if you hate algebra, know that extreme efforts were made on your behalf.

Certain demands, therefore, may be made on you by the Camelot General Chemistry Primer, depending on the degree of educational deprivation that your system imposed on you. If it did not so limit you, great. If so, then rise to the challenge.

'Please send your comments to me, via the publisher, so that I can refine future editions. I will respond personally to detailed commentary, if requested.

A,C&D Brand
Black India Ink

On Color

Color is rich in therapeutic and contemplative applications, and there will be abundant opportunity to use it in this book. To do so is most appropriate.

For one thing, chemistry, as the medium of color, is worthy of it; and the study of the subject will bring you into contact with much more color than you will find in the pages of standard textbooks (unless your textbook has one of those price-doubling stacks of glossy plates in the middle).

Yet even a typical textbook has one color, often blue or orange, to enhance in many hues its black and white. This book, however, lacks even this mono-chromism; it is all black and white.

Why not, then, *add* the color yourself? Whenever you see the color wheel motif, ⊕, coloring will be part of an exercise or the exercise itself.

Otherwise, take "color-refreshers" at will to animate the line art. As you do, ponder the current topic of study, and it may be then that a breakthough in understanding comes. It is not for nothing that the margins of used textbooks are often rife with doodling. The color refresher is a legitimization and an extension of this.

Any medium (except heavy markers) will do: colored pencils, felt pens, even pastels or tempera. My favorite is crayons, and a 48- or 64-color set, with its many intermediate and metallic colors, comes recommended. Most of the time, a light, even shading will be best.

Here is a sample refresher to get started; it concerns the colors of the Family 7A elements (the halogens). You will have to assume, for expediency's sake, that the vessel holding the fluorine is made with some special new glass that resists the gas.   DWC

⊕ Color the chlorine gas green-yellow (GY); the bromine, reddish brown or rust; the sublimated iodine crystals, purple; and the fluorine gas, yellow.

Acknowledgements

The author owes a debt to the following individuals.

The first to be mentioned must be Antonio Toscana, who elevates desktop pagemaking to the level of fine art. As dextrous with a keyboard as was Dürer with a wood chisel, Mr. Toscana wrought a miracle by raising in stages a hand-drawn manuscript to a masterpiece of eye-friendly precision. Further, he demonstrated a perfectionist zeal and an enthusiasm for the project that rivaled even my own, not to mention the high premium he put on customer satisfaction. Doing business with him was advantageous not only for his competence and good faith, but for practical reasons as well, such as his full bilingualism and his full range of desktop cabapabilities. I recommennd him to anyone needing such services. Potential clients in the US and other nearby countries may wish to contact him at: Ruta 4 7-57 Z.4, Ciudad de Guatemala, Central America.

Nor could this project have reached fruition without the help of several talented editors, including my longtime friend Shailaja Reddy; who spent some of her vacation time with the MS; and my onetime tutees, Barry Fortney and Luz Carmen Contreras. Another good friend, Franco Nanartonis of Antigua Guatemala, was always available to critique my own rather plebian artwork, which is no small thing considering his fifty-plus years as a professional (and, it should be added, highly talented) artist.

Two exceptional professors from El Camino College in Torrance, CA, deserve special mention. Dr. Richard Zuck stands out from other chemistry professors for many reasons, not the least of which is his policy of letting students call him at home when they are stuck. This primer's error-analysis feature is dedicated to him. To Dr. Robert Long, a friend and intellectual mentor, is dedicated the ecological tidbits found here and there in the book. He retired before I could take his class, but he was (and is) a help to others, not only in chemistry but in even better things.

Another chemistry professor, and a rather famous one at that, Dr. Duane Gish of San Diego's Creation Research Institute, contributed both the foreword to the Camelot Primer and some right ideas to its author. Dr. Gish is himself an author and internationally known lecturer.

The other major influence was my brother, Mr. Gordon Coop. A punster extraordinaire and an inimitasble marvel of cleverness, he contributed in two ways. First, he provided the original inspiration for a thematic and funny chemistry book by making me and everyone else around him endure decades of his relentless "PUNishment." Second, a few of his gems have found their way into the Primer itself.

Significant support of one kind or another came from my parents, Don and Jennean Coop; my sister, Melody Myrick; my fiancée, María González; my grandmother, Opal Allred; and my former employer, Jaqueline Pilcher. There were also many nonchemistry professors, such as the erudite and original Dr. Charles Leyba and several of his colleagues at Cal State L.A., notably Dr. Allen Freedman, a brilliant lecturer; and Drs. Stahl, Nicholas Beck and Roger Beck, A. R. Fellow, and "Hap" Holladay. Also, Drs. David Pierce, Warren Hirt, John Hartley, Charles Donovan, and Richard Sherman, all of El Camino; Dra. Reina Sánchez de Soto of the Autonomous University of Nuevo León, Monterrey, N.L.

Five selfless and kind administrators provided encouragement, something that few members of their profession are capable of, and so merit mention. They are Dr. William Taylor and Dr. Juanita Mantovanni, Cal State's finest; Mr. Roy Duplessix, principal of Ascot Elementary School in East Los Angeles; Mrs. Delois Carruth of Loma Vista Elementary in Maywood, CA; and Dr. Roscoe Cook of the L.A. County Juvenile Court Schools.

Several former colleagues from Loma Vista YA School in Maywood, CA, provided encouragement: Margie Jo Powell, Joan Harmon, Judy Dieter, John Slane, Valerie Gallinger, Linda Schuckman, Lorelei Reuter, Ron Clark, Carli Simons, Pam Greene, Pam O'Neil, Gloria Acosta, Richard Valdez, Sarai Rodriguez. Of Rolling Hills High School, John Hunt, Ralph Porter, Wes Snively, Cliff Birrell, Billy Kramer, Jerry Kestenberg, John Brueckner, David Medved. Of Dapplegray Intermediate, Jackie Meredith, Mildred Lamb, Bob DiJune, Carter Smart, and the lovely Irma Ruiz.

Finally, there is Mrs. Dorothy Corliss, who inculcated in me and generations of other schoolchildren, a love of learning and a reverence both for books and people.

Other supporters who fit no particular category are Bill and Joanne Click of Sacramento; Ron and Lisa Stinnett of Petaluma; Jack Funk of Malibu; Karen Owsley of New York City; Dr.Taylor Mack of the University of Louisiana

Of Riverside County, Ted Lawler, Ed Anderson, Joyce Bohannon, Pattie Lou Powers, Beth Platner de Castañeda, Bonnie McCarthy; Jeffrey and Genevieve Coleman, Christina McCabe, and Richard and Jackie Pilcher; Hugh Brom; Dick, Francine, Rod, Jamie, Tiffany, and Deanna Walden of Online International; Natividad Hernández; Joe, Kathi and Michelle Fox, Eileen Parlee, Susan Dencklau; Jeff, Jim, and Travis of Jeff Hardy and Associates, Architects; the reference librarians at Temecula Library; Hang and Shanna "Rose" Coop, Rita Cox, Gene Riddle, Dick Guffey, Dick Johnson. Of San Luis Obispo County, Steven and "Moose" Myrick, Ricardo and Alexander González, Cathy and Peter Fagin, Delphia Conella. Of San Diego, Laurence Taylor, MD, and Cal Evans of the Banta Company.

Of Guatemala City, Luis, Mary, Mónica, Ana Luisa, Gustavo Adolfo, and Sofía Pérez; Ana María Valenzuela, Josefina López, and Estela of the Fuente de Salud "Aurora"; Gladis Ramos, Jaqueline Ramos, and Paulino Reyes; Clara Alvarado, Eric Duarte, Rodolfo and Ana Oseida, Dr. Roberto Gil, Patricia Aldana Maglioli, Edgar Chavez, Dorcas de León and María Victoria López; Sergio and Orfelina Gutierrez, and Raquel Rosales of the Children's International Office; Pablo, Ruth, and Angela Hernández; Elsi Calderón; Pepe, Mary, José Carlos, Ana María, and Geisha de León; Eddy Ruiz Umana; Carlos Rodríguez; Doña Silvia and her crew of occasionally useful librarians at Instituto Guatemalteco Americano; the poet Edgar Arrévalo; María Luisa Morales Guerra, Alicia Ochoa, María Feldman, Dr. Otto Hernández, Mike Smith, Telma Melgaraje, Carmen and Elsa Valenzuela; Steven, Hilsa, and "Harvito" King; the Arriaga family: Marta, Carlos, Helen, Rosa María, Cristina, and Olga; Beverly Virgil of the Policía Nacional; Leti Gallardo, Marleni Avilás Soto, Mercedes Godínez and her niece, Lesley Jennifer, Maribel Barrera of Casa Plástica; Doña Antonia of Pan Iberia; the crew at Pastelería Lins: Lesvia, Lilian, María Antonia, Mirna, Olga, and Beatriz.; of the Hogar Campestre Los Pinos, Laura Galvez and Abigail Diaz, and Doñas Marta and Francisca, who can really cook.

Of El Progreso Department, Guatemala, the González Boch family: Zenón, Feliciana, "Arturo," Ismael, Miriam, Elizabeth, Carmen, Basilio, Iginio, "la Negra" María Romelia, Mayra, Alba, David, etc.

Of Tegucigalpa, Honduras, Don Dany and María Encarnación Baca Fúnez, of the Picadilly Restaurant, and my librarian, Raquel de Acosta. In Querétaro, Mexico, Mary Lugo Ramos; in Monterrey, Fidel Sagastume; in the Federal District, Benedicto Navarro.

Prologue:
Concerning Some Chemical Fundaments

Trismagistus Merlinus

Daltonius Manchestus

Curious Slovodiscus

Avogadrus Avicennus

Dramatis Personae

Now introducing the players in our scientific drama...

Merlin, the royal alchemist, on his way to discovering chemistry and (maybe) gold, with the assistance of his three able prodigies, Dalton, Curie, and Avogadro...also debuting is Mantissa the cat, whose existence has been experimentally confirmed, and Pollynomial the parrot...only rumored to exist, however, is an irksome kobald, by the name Al, and a faerie who shares his mischievous proclivities, Kimmie...also of doubtful being are uncountable moles of atoms, molecules, and ions, as well as someone crazed enough to become the first victim of a dreadful phenomenon known as...

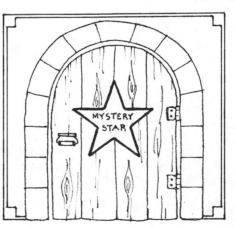

Chemistry Anxiety!

In Aristotle's day, when science and philosophy were one and inseparable, there were only four elements...

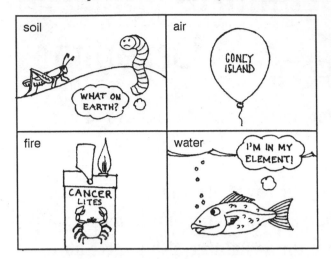

...which, by definition, could not be broken into simpler substances but were, rather, the ingredients of all other matter. The elements could, however, be divided *ad infinitum* into ittier and bittier parts. That is, they were not made of discrete particles, as a dissenting minority then held.

Democritus, in the fifth century before Christ, was among the dissenters. He spoke of the smallest bits of an element as *a-tomos* ("uncut"), whence comes Dalton's word, *atom*. The atom, however, did not again see the philosophical light of day for almost two millenia.

Meanwhile, in the Middle Ages, the alchemists kept air and water in the element club and correctly added sulfur, arsenic, and the seven known metals, each of which was ruled by a major celestial body. This was due to a lingering astrological influence.

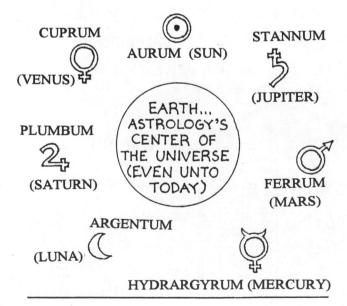

So the alchemists, until Boyle, were unable to isolate chemistry from its mystical underpinnings. Indeed, the four-element system was not fully laid to rest until the late eighteenth century, when it was found that water was not one element, but a compound of two. Air and soil were mixtures of unrelated substances, and fire—alas Aristotelians— was in fact not a substance at all but a process.

Molecules are particles that are *chemically* divisible into atoms. For the next few pages, we can also think of atoms as being to elements what molecules are to compounds.

Until molecules break into atoms and/or re-combine (*chemical change*), they remain particles of compounds, even though their relation to other particles of the same substance may undergo alteration by heat transfer (*physical change*).

Physical changes, then, concern the "altered states" of matter. Steam, water, and ice are the states of the substance H_2O. Except for ionized noble gases—such as in neon signs—all matter on Earth belongs to one of three physical states. Let us consider, cursorily, these states at the particle level:

In the *solid* state, particles of the compounds and elements more-or-less stick together and vibrate...

In the more energetic *liquid* state, they are (as Democritus posited) like marbles rolling over each other in a bag...

As a *gas*, an even more energetic state, the particles have almost no attraction for each other, but often collide...

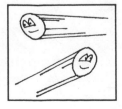

By the late twentieth century, 100-plus elements were known and arranged in a Periodic Table...*periodic* because there are periodic recurrences of certain properties as you trail your finger (from left to right, top to bottom, as in a book) from the lightest element (H) to the heaviest (beyond Ha). This recurrence is said to obey a *Periodic Law*, and the trend itself is called *periodicity*. The German physicist Meyer and and the Russian chemist Mendeleev sorted the elements of like properties into vertical families with names like 1A and 3B. The seven horizontal rows are the periods. After several decades of experimental tailoring, the Periodic Table "shaped-up" like this:

REVEALED IN ITS TRUE SHAPE FOR THE FIRST TIME EVER...

THE PERIODIC TABLE OF ELEMENTS!

At right is a modernized version of one of Mendeleev's early periodic table models. He took the first 20 elements and numbered them in order of their weights, beginning with 1. This is the *atomic number*, or Z, of hydrogen.

This little table shows only members of what would become the "A families" or *representative elements*, and none of the "B families" or *transition elements*, all of which are metals.

Examine carefully the irregular shape of both the true and abbreviated tables. Note how the latter derives from the former; it is largely the first three periods. The Periodic Table is not a normal rectangular grid for reasons which Mendeleev had no data, but for which we *do* have, and which will be looked at in Chap. 3.

Nonetheless, there is a pattern (that needs now only be noted, not memorized). Period One is uniquely only two elements long, but Periods Two and Three both have a width of eight elements; Periods Four and Five have 18; and Period Six and (potentially) Period Seven both have 32. All of these period-widths are even numbers.

Eventually, chemists sawed off the *lanthanides* and the *actinides* to more conveniently display the elements, as shown at right. For other periodic tables, see p. 375.

⊛ Look at the true Table, at the top of the page. Color the elements left of the "stairs" (the metals) one color and the nonmetals, another. Do not color Family 8A, the noble gases (He, Ne, Ar, etc.). Next, color in the corresponding sections of the other tables on this page in the same colors.

PERIODS	1A	2A	3A	4A	5A	6A	7A	8A
I	1 H							2 He
II	3 Li	4 Be	5 B	6 C	7 N	8 O	9 F	10 Ne
III	11 Na	12 Mg	13 Al	14 Si	15 P	16 S	17 Cl	18 Ar
IV	19 K	20 Ca	FAMILIES					

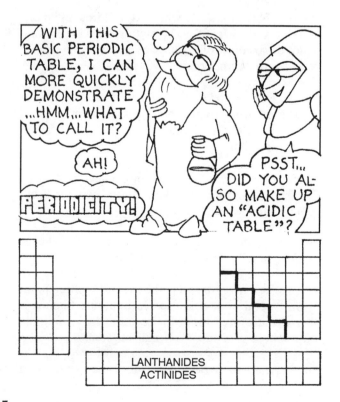

LANTHANIDES
ACTINIDES

We will be concerned with only half of the elements, for which the symbols must be learned. The modern system, an "alphabet" developed by the Swedish scientist Berzelius, replaces Dalton's older and quainter pictographic system. Most of the new symbols are initials from the elements' names. For now, get started on learning these:

H hydrogen	He helium	Li lithium	Be beryllium	B boron	C carbon
N nitrogen	O oxygen	F fluorine	Ne neon	Na sodium	Mg magnesium
Al aluminum	Si silicon	P phosphorus	S sulfur	Cl chlorine	Ar argon
K potassium	Ca calcium	Ti titanium	Cr chromium	Mn manganese	Fe iron
Co cobalt	Ni nickel	Cu copper	Zn zinc	As arsenic	Se selenium
Br bromine	Sr strontium	Mo molybdenum	Ag silver	Cd cadmium	Sn tin
Sb antimony	I iodine	Cs cesium	Ba barium	W tungsten	Pt platinum
Au gold	Hg mercury	Pb lead	Bi bismuth	Ra radium	U uranium

Some element symbols, however, reflect their Latin or Germanic roots, or are otherwise confusing. Fortunately, there are mnemonic approaches to learning them...

Ag silver (*argentum*) is Above gold in the Table. This is no surprise, considering its association with...

Au gold (*aurum*). Autumn leaves and one's Autumnal years are "golden." Ag and Au form a familiar triad with...

Cu copper (*cuprum*), which is Colored uniquely. Only Cu and Au, among the metals, have a color that is not a variation of Ag's. There is also the useful bogus word, "Cupper."

Na sodium (*natrium*). Na could well stand for "Nastium," owing to its blood-pressure toxicity. Still, it is necessary for living things, as is its heavier, pot-bellied sibling...

K potassium (*karium*). The K might have come from the Teutonic *kettelassium*, so chemists kept the K but replaced the kettle with a pot.

Fe iron (*ferrum*) is the stuff of Fenders, Ferris Wheels, Fencing swords, and, in Mexico, *Ferrocarriles*.

W tungsten (*wolfram*) has the highest melting point of any metal and so is used in lightbulb filaments. The W, therefore, stands for both the dimension, the Watt, and its medium, Wolfram/tungsten.

Sn tin (*stannum*). Both the symbol and name end in *n*, and *S* preceeds *t*, alphabetically and in *stannum*..

Hg mercury (*hydrargyrum*) is a Heavy goo, a thermal Heat gauge, or a cause of madness: Hatters' glue.

Sb antimony (*stibium*). To be "anti-money," you must be a Successful barterer.

Ar/As argon/arsenic. Both start with *ar*, but argon is first, both in the dictionary and in the Table.

Mg/Mn magnesium/manganese. Both start with *ma*, so they compromised and now go by their first and third initials. This, by the way, was one of Berzelius' spelling rules.

Co cobalt (*kobold*). Although copper begins with these letters, cobalt begins with this *syllable*.

Ti titanium. Although tin begins with these letters, titanium begins with this *syllable*.

WITH MY FAIL-SAFE YOYO SYSTEM, YOU CAN LEARN THE OTHER 60-ODD ELEMENT SYMBOLS!

HOW?

YER ON YER OWN, THAT'S HOW!

OF COURSE. OF LATE, I HAVE THOUGHT ABUNDANTLY OF THE LAWS OF DEFINITE COMPOSITION AND CONSERVATION OF MASS.

Definite Composition

...the weight percentage of elements in a compound is always the same, regardless of its source or how it was prepared.

Conservation of Mass

...in any chemical change, mass—the "material"—is conserved; it is neither created nor destroyed.

Definite Composition means that a water molecule from the Thames is identical in composition to one from the Tigris...and that a cheap sugar molecule from a humble Ukrainian beet is absolutely indistinguishable from a sugar molecule of Pure Cane Sugar from Hawaii.

Conservation of Mass simply means that the weight of the particles entering into a reaction will equal the weight of the particles resulting from it. This is common sense.

SO WHAT'S THE DIFFERENCE BETWEEN MASS AND WEIGHT?

FOR OUR PURPOSES...

...NOTHING, UNLESS WE DECIDE TO MOVE OUR LAB TO OUTER SPACE, WHERE THERE IS MASS (MATERIAL), BUT NO WEIGHT...

YOU WON'T LATER, GODZILLA-BREATH!

SO TELL US SOMETHING WE DO NOT KNOW...

FASCINATING! I GET IT!

QUAKER OATS

VERY WELL. HERE BE THE 5 POSTULATES OF MY THEORY.

(1) Every element is made of discrete particles...

(2) ...that are indivisible (we cannot maketh nor breaketh them; they are uncut).

(3) All atoms of the same element are alike (in mass)...

(4) ...but different (in mass) from atoms of all other elements.

(5) Atoms of one element combineth with atoms of other elements in whole-number ratios.

How is the Law of Multiple Proportions entailed by Dalton's fourth and fifth postulates? This rhetorical proof is offered:

Postulate 4: Atoms of each element are different. The specific difference that Dalton has in mind is mass/weight. Each element's atom, he believes, has its own atomic weight.

Postulate 5: One element's atoms mix with atoms of other elements in whole-number ratios.

The "unique weights" part (Post.4) and the "whole-number ratios" part (Post. 5) together make up Dalton's new law, namely Multiple Proportions.

The Law becomes relevant when we consider combinations of elements that can form *more than one compound*, as can, for instance, oxygen and nitrogen. One nitrogen atom can combine with one, two, or three oxygen atoms (to form NO, NO_2, or NO_3^-) or two nitrogens can bond to one, three, or even five oxygens (N_2O, N_2O_3, N_2O_5). Thus nitrogen, in two fixed proportions (1 and 2) can combine with two sets of multiple proportions (1, 2 , and 3; and 1,3, and 5) of oxygen.

The possible nitrogen-to-oxygen ratios, then, are 1:1, 1:2, and 1:3; and 2:1, 2:3, and 2:5. Nitrogen and oxygen therefore have multiple "mating" possibilities.

Consider this analogy. Let oxygen atoms be men, and nitrogen atoms, women, with respective weights of 16 and 14. The compound NO is a monogamous arrangement, but NO_2 and N_2O are polygamous.

This whole-atom-to-whole-atom circumstance necessarily expresses itself in any quantity of the compound in question. Thus, as the 14 from one nitrogen atom combines with the 16 of one oxygen atom to make the 30 of one NO molecule, 14 grams (or tons) of nitrogen combine with 16 grams (or tons)—no more nor less—of oxygen to make 30 grams (or tons) of NO. The 14 grams of nitrogen could no more combine fully with, say, 11.3 grams of oxygen than could one woman with 64.7% of a man. Dalton accepted some experimental evidence of this as support for his, Newton's, and Democritus' theory of matter (atomism) over that of Aristotle (continuity).

	ratio	analogy		mass
NO	1:1	Nitric oxide is monogamous. Note that there is conservation of mass because 14 + 16 = 30.		14 16 ― 30
NO₂	1:2	Nitrogen dioxide is "polyandrous" —a woman with more than one husband. As always, mass is conserved.	2(16) =	14 32 ― 46
N₂O	2:1	In "polygynous" nitrous oxide, it is nitrogen that now differs in weight, but in a precise multiple of 14.	2(14) =	28 16 ― 44

Take two elements, say carbon, C, for the fixed proportion, and oxygen, O_2, for the multiple ones. We must write oxygen with the "two" subscript because oxygen atoms travel in pairs—they are *diatomic*.

Carbon is *oxidized* (more on this in Chaps. 4 and 10) if air and sufficient heat are present. If the air is limited, then there will only be enough oxygen atoms to combine with carbon atoms in a 1:1 ratio, as in Act I, below.

⊛ Color all of the oxygen atoms on this page light blue and lightly shade the carbons dark gray.

Act I: This is the reaction: $O_2 + 2C \rightarrow 2CO$

This chemical change is the incomplete "burning" of carbon to form the poisonous gas, carbon monoxide, CO.

If this is the incomplete burning, then what is the complete burning of carbon? If sufficient air (that is, oxygen) is present, then each carbon atom can combine with not just one but two oxygen atoms, to form the rather inert gas, carbon dioxide, CO_2. (⊛ Keep coloring!)

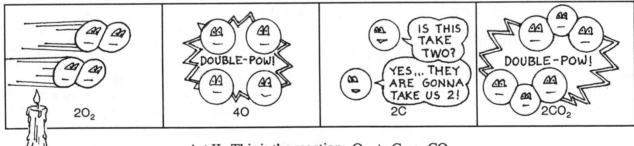

Act II: This is the reaction: $O_2 + C \rightarrow CO_2$

If you thought it was $2O_2 + 2C \rightarrow 2CO_2$, then you were correct, but you were not thinking in terms of simplest ratios (so you do not need the coefficients, the big twos), in which two oxygen atoms (O_2) combine with one carbon atom (C). In the case of the above two reactions, the fixed weight is that of carbon (12) and the differing weights are of oxygen (16, 32). Therefore, oxygen exhibits *multiple* proportions with carbon.

Because we are showing oxygen and carbon in multiple proportions, namely 1:1 and 1:2. However, both of the above illustrations were made with two—not one—carbon atoms because the oxygen atoms they combined with came in pairs. There are no single oxygen atoms floating about unattached, so they cannot enter a reaction that way. Take note of the *ratios* of the elements in the resulting molecules, and forget about the *pairs*, and it will be clear.

10

Diatomic Elements

In hydrogen, nitrogen, oxygen, and the elements of Family 7A (the *halogens*, or "salt formers"), the atoms are paired. This is the case under most familiar circumstances and in the three basic earthly states of matter (solids, liquids, and gases). This fact has some important consequences, as you will discover.

It is true. The particles of these seven elements are, in fact, the most molecular of all molecules even though they are particles not of compounds but of elements (this will be explained in Chap. 3).

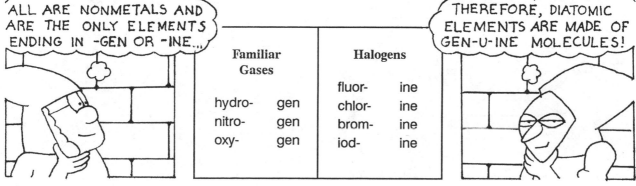

Familiar Gases		Halogens	
hydro-	gen	fluor-	ine
nitro-	gen	chlor-	ine
oxy-	gen	brom-	ine
		iod-	ine

And so commenced one of natural philosophy's most important experiments: the teaching of a new empirical discipline to a scientific neophyte. What would be the final result?

1. Match the following:

_____Avogadro	a. least bit of a compound or (for us) of seven special elements
_____CO	b. vertical series in the Periodic Table
_____atom	c. a substance that is not a compound
_____family	d. scientist who pioneered periodicity and its table
_____Meyer or Mendeleev	e. the recombination of different particles
_____chemical change	f. product of the incomplete burning of carbon
_____molecule	g. "altered states"
_____Aristotle	h. scientist who developed the modern chemical alphabet
_____element	i. horizontal series in the Periodic Table
_____period	j. scientist who first described "a" (above)
_____physical change	k. product of the "burning in air" of carbon
_____CO_2	l. least bit of an element
_____Berzelius	m. scientist who believed in the infinite divisibility of matter

2. Name the seven diatomic elements. Refer to the Periodic Table inside the back cover, if you wish.

1_____   2_____   3_____   4_____

5_____   6_____   7_____

3. Now match these chemical principles to their circumlocuted descriptions, below:

_____Law of Multiple Proportions   _____Law of Definite Composition

_____Periodicity (Periodic Law)   _____Law of Conservation of Mass

_____Dalton's First (or Democritus') Postulate

a. The percentage of an element in a given compound never varies.

b. When atoms of one element can form more than one compound with another element, the combinations are whole-number ratios.

c. Matter is not infinitely divisible into smaller and smaller bits.

d. Certain properties appear and disappear at predictable intervals as we go from the lightest element to the heaviest.

e. While atoms "change partners" or lose them altogether, the total weight of all the atoms involved in a reaction remains constant.

4. Chemical symbols are to formulae (plural of formula) as letters are to words. Some chemical words you already know: NaCl (sodium chloride), CO_2 (carbon dioxide), etc. The "spelling" of formulae is easy. For instance, whenever O, F, or Cl combine with another element (to form its oxides, fluorides, or chlorides), the other element's symbol is written first. The formulae have subscripts to indicate the whole-number ratios of the elements that make up the compounds. In this way, we can write octane as C_8H_{18} instead of CCCCCCCCHHHHHHHHHHHHHHHHHH. If the number *1* is part of the ratio, it does not appear as a subscript; it is omitted (e.g., CO_2, not C_1O_2).

Complete this table using the infromation on p. 6 (and note the several examples of multiple proportions).

SiO	1 silicon, 1 oxygen	Fe_2O_3	2 irons, 3 oxygens
	1 silicon, 2 oxygens		2 arsenics, 5 oxygens
	1 boron, 3 fluorines		2 manganeses, 7 oxygens
	1 potassium, 1 chlorine		1 manganese, 7 chlorines
	1 calcium, 2 chlorines	CoO	
	1 lead, 2 fluorines	Co_2O_3	
	1 lead, 4 fluorines	SCl_6	

5. Curie has intuited that Dalton's Second and Third Postulates may fall. Reread the former (p. 8) and explain why, if it does *not* fall, that the alchemists (Merlin and Co.) will be unable to produce gold from "baser" metals:

——— Across ———

1. 4th Century B.C. Greek philosopher/scientist
6. Atomic no. 73
7. Element named for two continents
8. No. 50
10. Sibling of chromium, tungsten
12. Periodic theory chemist
15. Ultra-alkaline cleaning agent
16. Chem. or Phys.
19. No. 68
20. Atom creator, as per Newton
21. Noble gas
22. No. 96
24. Light metal
26. Compound atoms

——— Down ———

1. Democritus' concept (adj.)
2. No. 88
3. Powdered SiO_2
4. Follows 19A
5. No. 65
8. Jovian metal
9. Sibling of 24A
10. Periodic theory physicist
11. Lanthanides, to actinides (prep.)
13. Nos. 63, 64
14. __ement or __ectron
17. A coinage metal
18. Number of elements not containing atoms
21. Portion of B-family elements that are metals
22. Named for a great Polish-French scientist
23. No. 42
24. Alchemical objective
25. Sibling of N, P, etc.

14

80
Hg
200.59

Profile: Mercury

Mercury was the Roman god of commerce. A planet and a metal are named for him.

Mercury is unreactive enough to exist naturally in elemental form, and so was known to the ancients, who were the first to call it quicksilver. The alchemists, later on, believed that with sulfur and an elusive third factor (the "philosopher's stone"), mercury could be transmuted to gold.

It is the only metal that is a liquid at room temperature (although gallium melts in the hand) and, in fact, it remains in the liquid state until well below the freezing point of water. The range of volume in the liquid state is what makes mercury practical as a thermometer.

Liquid mercury has a surface tension six times that of water and, for this, it does not "wet" the surfaces that it comes in contact with. Solid mercury is as soft and pliable as lead at room temperature.

Alloys containing mercury have their own name: *amalgams*. They are used in the refining of other metals, for mercury readily bonds with most other metallic elements. After the amalgam is formed, impurities are removed and the amalgam is converted back to mercury and the sought metal by electrolysis. Amalgams have an end in their own as tooth fillings.

Mercury compounds have abundant industrial, agricultural, and pharmaceutical applications. One is even used in laxative preparations.

Most of them, however, are highly toxic. The methyls—CH_3Hg and $(CH_3)_2Hg_2$—are perhaps the deadliest of all, and are said to liquefy brain and nervous tissue. Some organic mercury compounds have made their way into the supermarket, via the aquatic food chain, where they concentrate in large predatory fish such as tuna. Minamata disease, in Japan, was linked conclusively to mercury

contamination of a nearby bay by factories.

In spite of all this notoriety, the elemental liquid is fairly harmless, but its gas phase—the bits of vapor that escape the liquid— is not. When the English hatmakers used mercury as a felting agent, there was some real truth to the stereotype of the mad hatter.

Biochemists doubt that mercury is a necessary trace element for living things, and none of its salts have any known biological function.

The commonest compound is cinnabar, which is the actual product of mercury and sulfur. Very unlike gold, it is a chalky, reddish mineral that is easily reduced by coking.

Mercury has a common monatomic cation, Hg^{2+}, but also a unique polyatomic elemental cation, Hg_2^{2+}. They are called mercury (II) and mercury (I), respectively, and each forms a separate series of salts. Mercury (II) salts are more soluble, as a group, than mercury (I) salts.

Because of its high electronegativity for a transition element, mercury forms numerous covalent compounds, with even chlorine, with which it forms two salts —$HgCl_2$ and Hg_2Cl_2—with the above-mentioned ions.

Of mercury's two lighter sisters in Family 2B, only zinc is essential for living tissues. It is also employed in the galvanization of corrodible metallic surfaces. Cadmium, like mercury, is a heavy-metal toxin and pollutant, but finds application as rods used to control reactions in nuclear power facilities.

1. j f l b d e a m c i g k h 3. b d c a e

2. hydrogen, nitrogen, oxygen, fluorine, chlorine, bromine, iodine

4.

SiO	1 silicon, 1 oxygen	Fe_2O_3	2 irons, 3 oxygens
SiO_2	1 silicon, 2 oxygens	As_2O_5	2 arsenics, 5 oxygens
BF_3	1 boron, three fluorines	Mn_2O_7	2 manganeses, 7 oxygens
KCL	1 potassium, 1 chlorine	$MnCl_2$	1 manganese, 2 chlorines
$CaCl_2$	1 calcium, 2 chlorines	CoO	1 cobalt, 1 oxygen
PbF_2	1 lead, 2 fluorines	Co_2O_3	2 cobalts, 3 oxygens
PbF_4	1 lead, 4 fluorines	SCl_6	1 sulfur, six chlorines

5. The atoms of each element are unique (Fourth Postulate) and discrete (First Postulate). To change their identities from, say, Pb to Au, the atoms would have to be altered by making and/or breaking them, and this is contrary to the Second Postulate. Nevertheless, Curie suspects that it is possible. Your own answer to this question may have been worded much differently yet still be correct.

1.1 Dimensional Analysis

A dimension is something that is added to a number to give it meaning and magnitude:

$$50 + grams = 50\ grams$$

In chemistry, we must often label dimensions in order to quantify a particular substance:

$$50\ grams\ O_2\ (or)\ 50g\ O_2$$

The dimension here is grams (g) and the label is O_2.

It was thus that alchemic labors evolved into a demystified "natural philosophy" (the Renaissance term for science. This implies that, by this time, science had become distinct from, but not wholly independent, of philosophy). The actions—and of course, the reactions—of this new discipline could be described in terms of *dimensional analysis*.

Boyle, working in Ireland in the 17th century, was himself the last of the alchemists and the first of the true chemists. He believed in atoms or, as he called them, "corpuscles."

Dimensional analysis, or "DA," despite its quite formidable name, is merely a problem-solving method that may take on apparent complications; in fact, it is only a series of steps—ranging from the absurdly easy to the not-very-hard—by which we design an arithmetical jumping-board to reason our way through chemisty problems.

Dimensional analysis was not used in classical alchemy which, unlike modern chemistry, was not a quantitative discipline.

Here is an example: use dimensional analysis to determine the number of hours in a week:

$$?\ hours = 1\ week\ \times\ \frac{7\ days}{week}\ \times\ \frac{24\ hours}{day}\ =\ 168\ hours$$

Conversion Factors

Conversion factors are fractions that always equal one, but which contain different dimensions and—usually—different numbers in the top and bottom parts of the fraction. In the example from p. 18, there were two conversion factors:

$$\frac{7\ \text{days}}{\text{week}} \qquad \frac{24\ \text{hours}}{\text{day}}$$

In each, the denominator equals the numerator as surely as in each of the following:

$$\frac{3}{3} \qquad \frac{28}{28} \qquad \frac{d}{d} \qquad \frac{165.04}{165.04} \qquad \frac{57xy^2z^3}{57xy^2z^3}$$

Some conversion factors—such as the two from the example—are familiar and understood and so are often unstated as well. Others must be given in a problem or looked up.

Below are some expressions that are not conversion factors, because the top and bottom are not equal, and so they cannot equal 1:

$$\frac{6\ \text{days}}{\text{week}} \qquad \frac{\text{horse}}{3\ \text{legs}} \qquad \frac{34\ \text{hours}}{\text{day}}$$

We can also flip-flop a conversion factor to its reciprocal when we need to. Either way, it equals 1:

I

A fraction in which the denominator equals the numerator has a value of 1.

II

If you multiply this same 1 by some other thing (or number), the answer is that other thing (or number).

III

We can "cancel" dimensions that appear in both a numerator and in a denominator.

$$\frac{7\ \text{days}}{\text{week}} \qquad \frac{\text{week}}{7\ \text{days}}$$

19

Given and Wanted

In the example (p. 18) the *given* was "1 week" and the *wanted* was "? hours." Both the given and the wanted quantities of a dimensional analysis problem contain a number and a dimension, and may also have labels. At the beginning of a DA problem, we luckily have in our posession both parts of the given and one part of the wanted. The other part of the wanted, which is a number, is itself the answer.

Do Have: **Don't Have:**

given number   wanted number
given dimension
wanted dimension

Analogy

Think of the wanted and the given as two places on a map such as the one below. The former is the destination, and the latter is the starting point. Let the dimensions be latitude, and the numbers, longitude.

If you prefer geometry to geography you can, of course, think of them as the x- and y-axes (and if you do not know geometry from geography, you had better forget science and change your major to Education Administration).

The conversion factors make up the route you take to get from the given coordinates to the wanted coordinates.

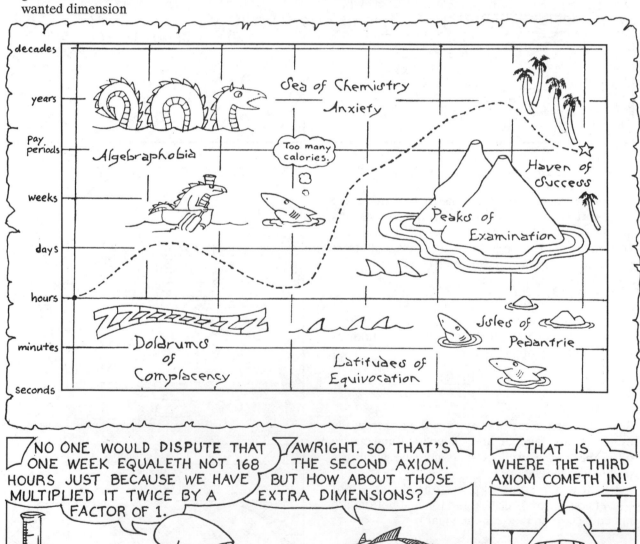

NO ONE WOULD DISPUTE THAT ONE WEEK EQUALETH NOT 168 HOURS JUST BECAUSE WE HAVE MULTIPLIED IT TWICE BY A FACTOR OF 1.

AWRIGHT. SO THAT'S THE SECOND AXIOM. BUT HOW ABOUT THOSE EXTRA DIMENSIONS?

THAT IS WHERE THE THIRD AXIOM COMETH IN!

Dimensions, like numbers in a fraction, can be cancelled, no matter whether there are two or 22 conversion factors. As with pure numbers, you may cancel one dimension found among the numerators for every identical dimension in the denominators. Here, again, is the original example, but with the appropriate cancellations.

$$? \text{ hours} = 1 \text{ week} \times \frac{7 \text{ days}}{\text{week}} \times \frac{24 \text{ hours}}{\text{day}} = 168 \text{ hours}$$

Without the extra dimensions, the problem becomes 1 x 7 x 24 hours =. Notice that when a conversion-factor number is 1, it is not written with the dimension; as with formula subscripts, it is unstated and understood.

Once the dimensional-analysis "bridge" (as some instructors like to call it) is constructed, one only has to push the "x" key on the calculator for each x (multiplication symbol) while working laterally across the numerator (or upstairs) level, and then switch to pushing the "÷" key (again, for each x) to work through the denominator (or downstairs) level.

In short, you multiply the numerators in sequence, then divide their product by the sequence of denominators. The resulting quotient will be the answer.

Having discussed the charting of a path (or, if you prefer, a route or a bridge) from a given quantity to a wanted one by way of conversion factors, we can now consider the actual steps involved in the construction of a DA set-up. There are three of them.

STEP ONE Identify and write down all the conversion factors.

STEP TWO Make a simple equation, showing the relation of the wanted to the given. An ordinary question mark will stand for the "don't have."

STEP THREE Join the conversion factors to the equation, making a numerator reappear as the next link's denominator, and calculate.

Now, a problem. A quail hen lays an average of 1.89 eggs in a 48-hour period. How many will she lay over her egg-laying life of three years?

First, get the conversion factors (next column):

$$\frac{1.89 \text{ eggs}}{48 \text{ hours}} \qquad \frac{52 \text{ weeks}}{\text{year}} \qquad \frac{168 \text{ hours}}{\text{week}}$$

The first of these was explicitly stated, and the others, while unstated, were already known to you. Now that we have identified the conversion factors (Step 1) by pairing together stated or known quantities, the odd, remaining quantity is the given.

We can now go on to Step 2:

$$\begin{array}{ccc} ? \text{ eggs} & = & 3 \text{ years} \\ (\text{wanted}) & & (\text{given}) \end{array}$$

THAT WAS THE HARDEST PART...

...BUT STILL EASY!

AND NOW FOR THAT THIRD STEP...

I'M KINDA CURIOUS...

Finally, stick on the conversion factors (Step 3), cancel, and calculate:

$$? \text{ egg} = 3 \text{ yrs.} \times \frac{52 \text{ wks.}}{\text{year}} \times \frac{186 \text{ hrs.}}{\text{week}} \times \frac{1.89 \text{ eggs}}{48 \text{ hrs.}} =$$

Without the now excess dimensions, the problem really boils down to...

$$? \text{ egg} = 3 \times \frac{52}{1} \times \frac{186}{1} \times \frac{1.89 \text{ eggs}}{48} = 1031.94 \text{ eggs}$$

...or, when all of the calculating is done, 1032 eggs (which, though it is not the "eggsact" result of the calculation, is rounded to the nearest whole egg).

I NOTICE THAT THE FIRST DIMENSION THAT WE CANCEL IS THE GIVEN ONE OF THE EQUATION...

...OF COURSE! IT'S A NUMERATOR!

21

1.2 DA Troubleshooting

The more you study dimensional analyis, the easier it gets, even as the problems grow ever more complicated. Does this sound like a contradiction? It is not.

Sufficient practice offsets the complications that gradually and cumulatively introduce themselves into the study of dimensional analysis. In fact, all of the DA problems in this book—save for a few in Chap. 6, which differ only slightly—use more or less the same pattern as the examples in Sect. 1.1, but with more (and often even less) detail. Even the most nonmathematically inclined students often find that, after awhile, dimensional analysis problems become so easy that they cannot be written down quickly enough.

With this growing facility, however, comes a danger. One must keep in mind, while constructing a DA bridge, that the process involves only concrete, possible relations. Because of this, some answers (that is, some resulting quotients) will be, on the face of it, ridiculous. If you fall into a habit of mechanical, nonthinking problem-solving, you may be unable to avoid this kind of error.

For instance, in a lab exercise in which atomic weight is used to identify an unknown metal, you get an answer of 244. Looking up this weight on a Periodic Table, you discover it to be the mass of plutonium, a very rare and extremely radiotoxic metal.

Unless you have become a Mindless Robotic Dimensional-analysis Zombie, this will cause you to think again. Checking your calculations, you find an error in place value—perhaps due to a misplaced decimal—and realize that the real answer is 24.4, the weight of common, benign magnesium.

Often, avoiding error is a matter of doing a little qualitative thinking before the quantitative work. If, for instance, you are asked to determine the volume of a gas sample that has undergone an increase in temperature, you would expect the new value to be more than the old value, for volume increases with temperature, as you may already know.

Another good habit is to mentally estimate what an answer will be, when you can see that far ahead. This may be no more than predicting what power of ten the answer will be in.

Aside from DA Zombieism there are several other types of errors that students new to dimensional analysis are prone to commit. They are analyzed on p. 23 and identified by their results:

Bizarre and Undesirable Ending Quantities	Chinese tea costs 90 cents a kilo and Bengali tea is 70 cents. How many kilos of Bengali tea can one buy with five bucks?	Solution: the price of tea in China is completely irrelevant. Given information often contains superfluous data.

$$? \text{ kilos } = \$5.00 \times \frac{100 \text{ cents}}{\$} \times \frac{\text{kilo tea}}{90 \text{ cents}} \times \frac{70 \text{ cents}}{\text{kilo tea}}$$

$$= 388.9$$

More Bizarrities, but with Wierd Exponent-Containing Fractions	How many pints are there in six gallons of any liquid (as you know, the conversion factors are 4 quarts/gallon and 2 pints/quart)?	Solution: a conversion factor must be inverted to its reciprocal:

$$\frac{\text{quart}}{2 \text{ pts}} = \frac{2 \text{ pts.}}{\text{quart}}$$

$$? \text{ pts } = 6 \text{ gals.} \times \frac{4 \text{ qts}}{\text{gal}} \times \frac{\text{quart}}{2 \text{ pints}} = \frac{12 \text{ quart}^2}{\text{pint}}$$

Unwanted Labels in the Answer (Qualitative Error)	One thousand grams of table salt, NaCl, yield 393 grams of sodium. How much sodium is present in 650 grams of salt (g = grams)?	Solution: the same dimension can have look-alike but different labels in the same problem. The labels should be...

$$393\text{g } Na/1000\text{g } NaCl$$

$$? \text{ grams Na } = 650\text{g NaCl} \times \frac{393 \text{ grams NaCl}}{1000 \text{ grams NaCl}}$$

$$= 255.5\text{g NaCl}$$

Conversion Factors Without n:1 Ratios Where n = Any Number	A chartered flight from Houston to Monterrey costs a group of 60 passengers $3670. How many pesos will each flyer pay if there were 2900 pesos to the dollar?	Solution: such conversion factors are not only acceptable, but common. This problem now only lacks the factor...

$$2900 \text{ pesos/dollar}$$

YOU COULDN'T EVEN ANSWER THIS ONE!

$$? \text{ pesos } = \text{ passenger } \times \frac{\$3670}{60 \text{ passengers}}$$

1.3 Temperature Conversions

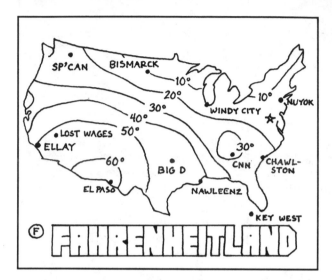

FAHRENHEITLAND

An example: the average temperature in Bismarck, North Dakota, is 58°F. What is this in °C?

(1) $58 - 32 = 26$ (2) $\dfrac{26}{1.8} = 14.44°C$

The answer, in what we call *signicant figures*, is 14°C.

The boiling and freezing points of water, in °F, are 212° and 32° respectively. Use the two steps as a proof and convert these two values to celsius (at right). Your results should be 0°C and 100°C.

IN CHEMISTRY, HOWEVER, ANOTHER DEGREE IS USED... THE KELVIN. IT'S THE SAME SIZE AS THE CELSIUS DEGREE.

HE'S GIVING US THE THIRD DEGREE!

The degree of temperature (°) is a dimension that comes in two sizes. The Celsius (°C) is the larger and also the more sensible of the two because it uses the freezing point of water as its zero value (0°) and the boiling point of water as its centennial value (100°).

The Kelvin (K) degree belongs to a separate scale, but it is "Celsius–sized."

Lamentably, a certain backward New World society clings unregenerately to the aging Fahrenheit (°F) size. For this reason, chemists in that country must know how to convert °F to °C. It involves two easy steps:

STEP ONE   Subtract 32 from the number of °F.

STEP TWO   Divide the difference by 1.8.

Convert 32°F to °C
Convert 212°F to °C

One advantage of the Kelvin Scale is that all measurements are positive. Water is frozen at 0°C, but *everything* is frozen at 0 K (no degree symbol), which is called *absolute zero* because below it there is *absolutely* no heat to be measured. Therefore, negative K values are impossible.

Another advantage of the Kelvin over the Celsius is that relative temperature changes, or temperature comparisons, are clearer. 300 K is obviously 50% warmer than 200 K, but with the corresponding Celsius values—27°C and −73°C—this is far from obvious. Still, in some types of calculations, °C and K are interchangeable because they are the same size.

To convert °C to K, just add 273; K to °C, subtract 273. For example, ethyl ether boils at 77°.

What is the K?

$77 + 273 = 350$

1. Match the following (use deduction to match any unfamiliar term):

_____dimension   a. a sometimes-detailed fraction that nevertheless only equals 1

_____label   b. that which gives a number meaning

_____equation   c. in dimensional analysis, the wanted/given relationship

_____conversion factor   d. contains a number and something to give it meaning

_____quantity   e. the turning of a fraction upside-down

_____reciprocals   f. that which identifies the thing or substance measured

_____defined relation   g. an invariable something that does not affect sigfigs

Do the following dimensional-analysis problems. First, write down all the conversion factors. Then, write the simple equation. Finally, add on the conversion factors, cancel the excess dimensions, and calculate.

2. How many ounces are in 25 tons if a ton has 2000 pounds and a pound, 16 ounces?

3. Give the number of feet in 9.4 nautical miles (one naut = 6076 feet).

4. How many seconds are in a nonleap year? In addition to several known but unstated conversion factors, use...

$$\frac{\text{pay period}}{\text{4 weeks}} \quad \text{and} \quad \frac{\text{13 pay periods}}{\text{year}}$$

5. A nog recipe calls for two fifths of rum to make a gallon of the beverage. Three fifths costs $7.00. How much money (? $) will have to be spent on the rum needed to prepare eight gallons of nog?

6. Spain's monetary system has four units. One real is worth 25 centimos; a duro equals five pesetas; and four reales make up a peseta. How many centimos are in 14 duros?

7. Convert these Fahrenheit readings to (a) Celsius and then to (b) Kelvins:

258°F		°C		K
−522.7°F		°C		K
6170°F		°C		K

8. On the Kelvin Scale, 0 degrees is *absolute* zero. Explain:

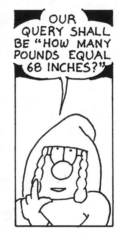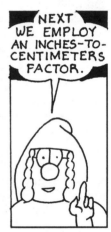

$$? \text{ pounds} = 68 \text{ in} \times \frac{2.54 \text{ cm}}{\text{inch}} \times \frac{\text{kilo}}{4.93 \text{ cm}} \times \frac{2.2 \text{ lbs.}}{\text{kilo}} = 77 \text{ pounds}$$

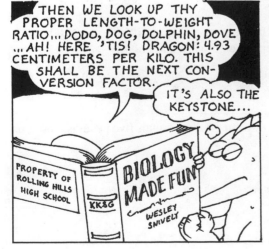

1.4 Length, Volume, & Mass

NOW WE'LL BEGIN LOOKING AT DIMENSIONS THAT HAVE SPECIFIC APPLICATIONS TO OUR NEW DISCIPLINE. THEY INCLUDE DIMENSIONS OF LENGTH, MASS, AND VOLUME...

LATER, WE'LL LOOK AT PRESSURE, HEAT, AND OTHERS.

Length

The most useful unit of length, for chemists, is the *angstrom* (Å). There are ten billion of them in a meter. They must be small, for this number is double the world's population (circa 1980s). This tininess makes the angstrom practical for studying things like atomic radii, bond lengths, intermolecular distances, and so forth.

Mass

The basic dimension for mass and weight in chemistry is the gram (g). There are about 454 of them to the pound. Two other chemically useful units, that you are no doubt familiiar with and which derive from the gram, are the milligram and the kilo.

While these two units are the respective tools of the pharmacist and the metallurgist—two specialized types of chemists—general chemists (that's us) have endless need of all three. In dimensional analysis, their abbreviations, as you probably already know, are *mg*, *g*, and *kg.*

Volume

$\mathbb{T}$o measure the space occupied by a sample—its volume—we favor the milliliter (ml), which is interchangeble in all calculations with a cubed unit of length, the cubic centimeter (cm^3). We prefer the former, not only because *ml* is visually cleaner than cm^3, but because it is related to the volume dimension that we use when dealing with samples of gases, the liter (L), which, of course, is 1000 ml. When a liquid or solid sample vaporizes and, in so doing, increases its volume several magnitudes, we have an appropriate unit, in the liter, to deal with it.

Atomic Mass

To review a distinction mentioned in the Prologue, the *mass* of a particle is a measure of its matter. The *weight* of that particle, which corresponds precisely to its mass, is the measure of the force of the Earth's gravity on it. On the Earth's surface, these two terms are interchangeable for all our purposes.

Individual particles, however, are far too small to be measured (weighed), so an arbitrary dimension, the *amu*, or *atomic mass unit,* is used to give *relative* weight values to atoms and molecules.

Hydrogen has a value of about 1 (1.008 amu, to be exact); nitrogen, as you by now know, has 14 (14.0067 amu); and chlorine, 35.5 (35.453 amu). Hydrogen chloride, then, has about 36.5 (one Cl plus one H); and ammonia, NH_3, about 17; and so on.

Avogadro is developing a way to make these quantities meaningful, that is, useful for the weighing and comparing of meaningful quantities of sustances (of which single particles are not). He will reveal it in the next chapter.

Dimension Conversion Factors

YOU WILL NOT UTILIZE ALL OF THESE IN THIS BOOK, YET THOSE SHOWN ARE INCLUDED TO AUGMENT YOUR COGNIZANCE OF [1] CONVERSION FACTORS AND [2] DIMENSIONS GENERALLY.

$$\frac{meter}{1.0 \times 10^{10} Å}$$

$$\frac{liter}{1.0 \times 10^3 ml}$$

$$\frac{gram}{1.0 \times 10^3 mg}$$

$$\frac{kilo}{1.0 \times 10^3 g}$$

1. b   f   c   a   d   e   g

2. ? ounces = 25 tons x $\dfrac{2000 \text{ lbs.}}{\text{ton}}$ x $\dfrac{16 \text{ oz.}}{\text{lb.}}$ = 800,000 oz. (8.0×10^5 oz.)

3. ? feet = 9.4 nauts x $\dfrac{6076 \text{ ft.}}{\text{naut}}$ = 57,114.4 feet (5.7×10^4 feet)

4. ? seconds = year x $\dfrac{13 \text{ pay periods}}{\text{year}}$ x $\dfrac{4 \text{ wks.}}{\text{pay pd.}}$ x $\dfrac{7 \text{ day}}{\text{week}}$ x $\dfrac{24 \text{ hrs.}}{\text{day}}$ x $\dfrac{60 \text{ mins}}{\text{hour}}$ x $\dfrac{60 \text{ secs}}{\text{minute}}$

    = 31,449,960 seconds

5. ? dollars = 8 gals nog x $\dfrac{2 \text{ fifths rum}}{\text{gal nog}}$ x $\dfrac{\$7.00}{3 \text{ fifths rum}}$ = $37.33

6. ? céntimos = 14 duros x $\dfrac{5 \text{ pesetas}}{\text{duro}}$ x $\dfrac{4 \text{ reales}}{\text{peseta}}$ x $\dfrac{25 \text{ céntimos}}{\text{real}}$ = 7000 céntimos

7. 258°F = 126°C = 399 K   (boiling point of octane)

    –522.7°F = –272.6°C = 0.4 K   (theoretical freezing point of helium)

    6170°F = 3410°C = 3683 K   (melting point of tungsten)

8. Scientifically speaking, there is no such thing as "coldness." There is only the presence—in measurable degree—or the absence, of heat. Zero Kelvin is the absolute absence of heat, the point at which all extra-molecular and extra-atomic activity ceases.

Interestingly, an upper limit for temperatures is not known, and the apparent range of heat values can be represented geometrically:

0 K ———————————————————→ ∞

A noon, midsummers day on the sun-facing surface of the Neptunian moon Triton is thought to be about 38 K, making it the coldest world in the solar system visited by manmade probes.

1.5 Significant Figures

WHEN WE RE-CORD A MEASURE-MENT, WE SHOULD INCLUDE ONE UN-CERTAIN (PROBABLE) DIGIT AND NONE BEYOND IT...

𝔄 *defined relation* is a type of conversion factor in which the denominator and the numerator never vary with respect to each other. The days/week conversion factor is such a one, for a week is defined (not *measured*) by seven days. Thus, *defined relations are invariable conversion factors.* Except for those in problem 5, all the factors you used in the previous problem set were defined relations, and we are never uncertain as to their digits.

In measurements, on the other hand, which can be precise but never perfect, we record only those digits which are significant. Whether we are putting together a conversion factor to use in a DA problem or dealing with the excess digits in the result of the calculation, we need a way to keep only the *significant figures* and dump the insignificant ones.

In 25 words or less, the practice of "counting" significant figures is (1) the inclusion of all digits that, according to our measurements, are certain, and (2) the first *uncertain* one, which is an estimate.

⊛ Color the liquid in the graduated cylinder (right) any light color, up to the mark indicated.

Now let us suppose that this cylinder contained somewhere in the neigborhood of 37.632885094-67381007725163333333 milliliters. But, having only the cylinder to measure with, what do we record? 3 and 7, of course, for they are certain, and 6, because, though not certain, it is probable (within the limits of our ability to estimate). None of the other digits is significant; those that are, the first three, would be the only ones used in a calculation.

ONLY 37.6 IS SIGNIFICANT!

50ml

40ml

30ml

20ml

10ml

Paracelsus

LAUSD X-107

OK. WHEN WE LOOK AT A GRADUATE OR OTHER MEASURING DEVICE, WE CAN PHYSICALLY INFER WHAT IS SIGNIFICANT. BUT HOW 'BOUT RECORDED MEASUREMENTS OR THE PRODUCTS OF CALCULATIONS?

ELEMENTARY. WE COUNT ONLY SIGFIGS WHICH COUNT.

Chemists must perform many calculations for which they have not personally taken measurement (as you will also do in the problem sets ahead). Nevertheless, they need to know which digits are worth keeping and which are not. They need a theoretical system of estimation in place of physical devices such as the graduated cylinder on p. 29. This theoretical system is known in general chemistry parlance as the "counting" of significant figures.

Counting, in this context, does not mean enumeration (1, 2, 3...); rather, it is the identifying of those digits which "count" (have import) and the discarding of those digits that do not count.

Be on the lookout for this unconscious equivocation when sigfigs, as they are also called, are being discussed or taught.

This counting begins with the first nonzero digit on the left and continues to the last "includable" one, which is also the first uncertain one.

Often, however, we see numbers that contain insignificant zeros. In order to count/identify the significant figures in such numbers, we use certain conventions to determine which zeros are significant and which are not. Consider the four possible cases:

Case	Purport	Examples	
Zeros between other significant digits are significant.	They are like any other numeral in the number.	405	3
		13,067	5
		2,000,619	7
		807.105	6
Zeros on the right of the last nonzero are significant.	They would not otherwise be recorded. If the cylinder had held 50.02375 ml then, to the chemist's eye, it would be 50.0 ml.	3.6	2
		3.60	3
		0.03600	4
		3,600,000	7
Zeros on the left of the first nonzero digit are not significant.	They only show us the position of the decimal, or the magnitude of the measurement, but they do not indicate which figures are significant to the measurement.	0.006	1
		0.352	3
		0.077854	5
		0.000006	1
Zeros on the right of the last nonzero but left of the decimal, are ambiguous, but can be clarified with scientific notation.	If, in a measurement of 47,000 in which the first zero is the uncertain sigfig, the answer is 4.70×10^4; if the second zero is the uncertain one, 4.700×10^4, etc.	47,000	2-5
		360	2-3
		1,000,000	1-7
		1.00×10^7	3

HEY... LOOK AT HIM! WHO? THAT NINE. HE'S SMALL! WE'RE PROOF OF THAT! AT LEAST I'M SIGNIFICANT! AND PRECISE! AS WE PROVE! SIGNIFICANTLY!

0.0000009000

We use all of the digits in numbers provided in a problem (that is, those that are known to be significant) to do our calculation, but we eliminate some of them from our answer, once we get it. Failure to do so can cause you to lose points on a test. Below are the conventions for each arithmetical operation.

Before discarding the unwanted digits however, we use them to round off the answer, using the same three rules (bottom) that are taught in pre-algebra classes everywhere, and which apply to mathematics in general.

In ADDITION, a sum of sigfigs will have no more digits to the right of the decimal than does any addend; likewise...	$\begin{array}{r} 126.7 \\ 7439.575 \\ \underline{8.33} \\ 7574.605 \end{array}$ $\rightarrow$ 7574.6
In SUBTRACTION, a difference is limited in its right-of-decimal digits by the number in the calculation with the fewest right-of-decimal digits.	$\begin{array}{r} 4639.753 \\ \underline{-1542.61} \\ 3097.143 \end{array}$ $\rightarrow$ 3097.14
In MULTIPLICATION, the *product* will have no more sigfigs than any factor used in the calculation (except for defined relations); similarly...	87.1 x 2.6666 x 32 = 7432.3475 $\rightarrow$ 7.4×10^3
In DIVISION, the *quotient* will have no more sigfigs than any divisior used in the calculation (except for defined relations).	$\dfrac{167.90}{22}$ = 7.6318181818 $\rightarrow$ 7.6
When the unwanted digits are more than five, round upwards (add 1 to the previous digit).	(to 3 sigfigs) 2.45633 $\rightarrow$ 2.46
If they are less than five, round downwards (add nothing to the previous digit).	(to 4 sigfigs) 37,913 $\rightarrow$ 37,910 $\rightarrow$ 3.791×10^4
If exactly five, round down if the previous digit is even, and up if odd (make the answer even).	(to 5 sigfigs) 58.0115 $\rightarrow$ 58.012

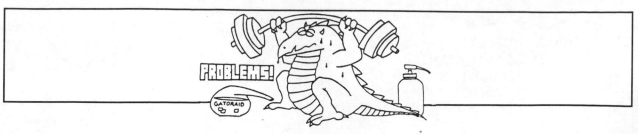

PUSH IN CASE OF DIRE EMERGENCY!

Namely, of not understanding all there is to understand about sigfigs...did you push it? Here's what to do: first, do the problem set, ready or not; then, check out the good news at the end of the set on p. 33.

OH, TO BE WINGED!!

1.   Match:

_____significant 0   a. zero below which no temperature readings are possible

_____precision   b. the volume dimension favored for most liquid samples

_____factor   c. the mass/weight dimension used for comparisons of elements or compounds

_____angstrom   d. a characteristic of the penultimate signifciant figure

_____absolute 0   e. zero left of a decimal, following another number

_____uncertainty   f. a length dimension used in the physical sciences at the particle level

_____liter   g. that which limits a product's significant figures

_____insignificant 0   h. zero between nonzero sigfigs, right or left of decimal

_____amu   i. the volume dimension favored for most gas samples

_____ambiguous 0   j. our best substitute for perfection in measurement

_____certainty   k. zero right of decimal, followed by nonzero sigfigs

_____divisor   l. a characteristic of the final significant figure

_____milliliter   m. that which limits a quotient's significant figures

HEY! WHADDYA DOIN'!? COME BACK W'THAT!!

2.   Measure the jousting lance with a metric ruler an answer to four significant figures:

Answer:_____cm

James 4:7

3. How many significant figures are in each of the following numbers? "Count" them.

____ a. 26	____ g. 5.50	____ m. 0.9	____ s. 9,380
____ b. 1314	____ h. 0.06667	____ n. 1×10^4	____ t. 2,600,000
____ c. 8.6	____ i. 2.600	____ o. 2600	____ u. 30
____ d. 26.0	____ j. 1.9070	____ p. 556.094	____ v. 3.0×10^1
____ e. 0.99	____ k. 0.05040	____ q. 2.6000×10^7	____ w. 7.4×10^{-4}
____ f. 0.0260	____ l. 2600.0	____ r. 6.02×10^{23}	____ x. 8.0808×10^{-16}

After solving these problems with a calculator, trim the answers to sigfigs:

4.   37.
     + 9.83
	5. 123.1
	     + 56.245
		6. 324.8
		     - 11.
			7. 163.2
			      717.631
			      532.0
			   + 13.82065

8.   160.
     x 12.
	9. 290.800
	     - 71.30
		10.
		 $13 \overline{)424}$
			11.
			
			 $173.96 \times 22 =$

12. $\dfrac{80}{5} \times \dfrac{1.6}{40} =$		13. $\dfrac{5.00 \times 10^{-4}}{625} \times \dfrac{0.0820}{1.57 \times 10^{-4}} =$	

DID YOU PUSH IT?

Here's the good news. First, there are no tests in this book to fail.

Also, you need not worry, because just by working through the Primer, you will pick up a mastery of sigfigs inductively, by noting patterns.

As in dimensional analysis, practice makes...well, better.

> SO WHO NEEDS WINGS? I'LL JUST KEEP DOING THE PROBLEMS AND I'LL GET IT AS WE GO ALONG..., BUT, COME TO THINK OF IT,... THERE'S NOT THAT MUCH TO IT...

(The answers to this problem set can be found on p. 38.)

1.6 Chemical Density

Density $= \dfrac{\text{mass}}{\text{volume}}$

...or, in chemically relevant dimensions...

Density $= \dfrac{\text{grams}}{\text{milliliter}}$

To determine the density (D), of a substance, therefore, we must measure both the weight (m, for mass) and the volume (v) of a sample.

While the liter will be the unit we use when studying gas densities (and gas properties in general) in Chap. 5, we are right now concerned mainly with liquid and solid samples, and thus with milliliters.

Because density combines two measurements, its dimension resembles a fraction; it is two-storied. Recall, however (from Curie's thought balloon), that density—according to its complete definition—is mass per *unit* of volume (mass per *one* ml or *one* L). This simplifies things so much that density determinations are ordinary simple divisions that do not even require a dimensional-analysis bridge for their execution.

The "multiple dimension" of density is indeed a conversion factor, one that equals 1 for the substance in question.

Density has many applications in and out of the laboratory and this book, including metal assays, jewelry appraisals, buoyancies, construction, the preparation of solutions (as we will see in Chap. 6), and the determination of weights or volumes of samples *using* density as a conversion factor.

But first, let us look at some examples of the reverse: how density is determined from a given mass or volumes...

Problem (What D?)	given m	given v	calculation	answer (unreduced)	answer (sigfigs)
A block of mahogany weighs 578 g and displaces 624.1 ml	578 g	624.1 ml	$? D = \dfrac{578 \text{ g}}{624.1 \text{ m}}$	0.9261336 g/ml	0.926 g/ml
An alchemic elixir fills a cylinder to 70 ml and weighs 84.13 g	84.13 g	70 ml	$? D = \dfrac{84.13}{70 \text{ ml}}$	1.2018571 g/ml	1.2 g/ml

This very simple algebraic equation can be manipulated to provide any of the three values that make it up whenever the other two are known.

We have just seen how to determine density when mass or volume are the givens. How, then, can we use given densities (looked up, say, in the Handbook of Chemistry and Physics) to determine the mass or the volume of a sample?

Imagine that we were missing, from the examples just examined, the mass of the mahogany block and the volume of the elixir. It would be (literally) easier to calculate them, using their known densities, than to even bother with measurements.

The givens are 624.1 grams for the hardwood sample and 84.13 milliliters for the mysterious elixir. Looking up their densities in the Handbook (or the medieval equivalent), we can solve the problems (as worded) and, as we already know what to expect (for having done the same problems in the reverse direction), we have proofs of the density equation.

(1) Determine the weight (the mass in grams) of the block of mahogany (density, 0.926 g/ml) that has a volume of 624.1.

$$?g\ wood = 624.1\ ml \times \frac{0.926\ g\ wood}{[one]\ ml\ wood} = 578\ g\ wood$$

(2) Now, suppose we have a scale in the lab but no clean beakers or marked cylinders with which to measure a liquid's volume. The first thing to do is weigh the elixir to get the given: 84.13 g. We know that its density—our conversion factor—is 1.2 g/ml. What, then, is its volume?

$$?ml\ elix = 84.13\ g\ elix \times = \frac{ml\ elix}{1.2\ g\ elix} = 70\ ml\ elix$$

All that remains, in either problem, is to cancel the excess dimensions and calculate. As you may have noticed, when density is the conversion factor and one of the givens, instead of the wanted, a miniature, ready-to-assemble DA problem is our method.

Here are some further examples of how density can be used as a conversion factor. It is DA as usual.

Problem (What m/v?)	given (m/v)	conv. factor	DA calculation	answer (sigfigs)
How much of a 500 ml beaker will one kilo of mercury (13.6 g/ml) fill?	1 kg (1000 g)	$\frac{13.6\ g}{ml}$	$?\ ml\ Hg = 1000\ g\ Hg \times \frac{ml\ Hg}{13.6\ g\ Hg} = 73.5\ ml\ Hg$	
What is the wieght of 360 ml of ethanol (0.791 g/ml)?	360 ml	$\frac{0.791\ g}{ml}$	$?\ g\ eth = 360\ ml\ eth \times \frac{0.791\ g\ eth}{ml\ eth} = 285\ g\ eth$	

To simplify something we will gradually look at in more complexity in Chaps. 2 and 3, atoms—alone or combined, neutral or charged—are basically very dense, very tiny nuclei surrounded by "clouds" of whizzing, orbiting electrons. The nucleus of an atom accounts for virtually all of its mass, while the clouds of electrons make up its volume. The hydrogen ion, H^+, is an exception, for it lacks electrons, and, therefore, has no volume to speak of; it is in fact nothing more than a bare proton.

Hence, masses of particles with relatively small electron clouds or relatively hefty nuclei tend towards greater density, although, as we will see in Chap. 3, there are other factors that contribute to an element's density.

In 1911, the Englishmen (Ernest) Rutherford developed this atomic model after his famous experiment in which he fired alpha particles (helium nuclei) at a thin gold foil. He expected all of them to penetrate the foil, as the contemporary atomic model likened nuclei to raisins in a sort of "electron pudding."

He was quite surprised, then, when a few alpha particles bounced off the foil and into a capture medium. From such evidence, Rutherford correctly inferred that atoms were almost all space with dinky nuclei at their centers which were dense enough to deflect the alpha particles.

Below is a function of the densities of all the Period 4 metals, beginning with potassium and ending with germanium. The two metals at either end are A-familiy elements, and all those in between are B-family, or transition, elements. What does the function say about the size of B-family electron clouds relative to A-family electron clouds, and, by extension, the density of the metals themselves?

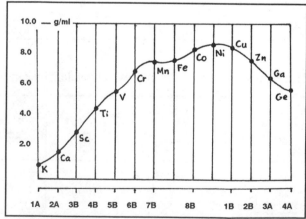

Answer: family-B metals have smaller electron clouds, for their masses, than family-A metals. The transition metals thus have denser atoms making up denser metals.

ℌroíile: ℌulfur

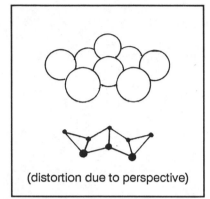

Sulfur crystal are made of octatomic molecules, as shown in this diagram.

(distortion due to perspective)

The alchemists believed that mercury imparted to gold its malleability and luster, and sulfur, its yellowness. This is because sulfur's two crystal allotropes (crystal-lattice geometries) are deeply yellow.

Sulfur occurs by itself in nature in vast underground beds or as parts of countless minerals, such as the already mentioned cinnabar (HgS), pyrite (FeS_2), barite ($BaSO_4$), and the dihydrate, gypsum ($CaSO_4 \cdot 2H_2O$). The first two are sulfides, meaning that they are formed with the sulfide ion (S^{2-}) and the others are sulfates, formed with the sulfate ion (SO_4^{2-}).

Elemental sulfur is often extracted from underground deposits with the Frasch Process. Very hot water is forced down a tube to melt it; then, hot air is pumped in to displace it and force it up another tube and into large pools on the surface, where it dries and crystallizes.

Sulfur is quarried, and has been for centuries, for many uses. One of the first things that Hernán Cortés did when he landed in the New World was to look for sulfur to make gunpowder for his four cannons, which he would use to decisive psychological, if not tactical, advantage.

Many pharmaceuticals, among them the sulfa drugs, contain sulfur, as do a great deal of organic substances, including some proteins. Needless to say, life could not exist without it, and it is the seventh most present element in living tissues. By weight, the human body is a few tenths of a percent sulfur.

Selenium, just below sulfur in the Periodic Table, is also necessary to life, but in trace amounts, and can be bought in dietary supplements. Under it is tellurium, a metalloid with curious properties, and polonium, a true (and very radiocative) metal.

It is sometimes said that a nation's wealth can be informally measured by its supply of sulfuric acid (H_2SO_4). This is due to the technical complexity of its preparation and the value of the industrial products made with the colorless, greasy acid, which the alchemists called *oil of vitriol*. It is among the strongest of acids—that is, it is extremely prone to shoot a hydrogen ion at a passing metal (or, among other things, fingers and nasal passages).

The burning of bituminous coal and some fireworks, which are high in sulfur compounds, releases the pollutants SO_2 (which has the rotten-egg smell) and SO_3, which go on to contribute to acid rain.

The trioxide is the anhydride of oil of vitriol. When a molecule of the gas is added to one of water, we get the acid:

$$SO_3 + H_2O \rightarrow H_2SO_4$$

Unlike its lighter Family-6A sibling, oxygen, sulfur's polyatomic nature does not not affect reaction ratios; so, while its proper formula is S_8, a simple S can be used in equations involving elemental sulfur, and its polyatomism, unlike that of oxygen (O_2) can usually be ignored.

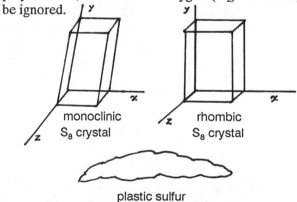

monoclinic S_8 crystal

rhombic S_8 crystal

plastic sulfur

The S_8 molecule, however, does express itself at the macromolecular level in two crystalline forms. An unusual third allotrope, called plastic sulfur, is a reddish-brown rubbery stuff made up of long chains of sulfur atoms and is not crystalline at all, but amorphous.

⊛ Color the three allotropes. Rhombic sulfur is a slightly fainter yellow than monoclinic sulfur.

1. h j g f a l i k c e d m b

2. 11.67 centimeters; the 7, the uncertain digit, is an estimate. Anything from 11.65 to 11.69 is probably correct.

3.
a. 2	b. 4	c. 2	d. 3	e. 2	f. 3	g. 3	h. 4	i. 4	j. 5	k. 4	l. 5
m. 1	n. 1	o. 2/4	p. 6	q. 5	r. 3	s. 3/4	t. 2/7	u. 1/2	v. 2	w. 2	x. 5

4. 47

5. 179.3

6. 314

7. 1426.7

8. 1.9×10^3

9. 219.50

10. 33

11. 3.8×10^3

12. 0.6

13. 4.18×10^{-4}

38

1.7 Specific Gravity

VERY WELL. DENSITY IS HOW MUCH MASS THERE IS IN A MILLILITER OF SOMETHING. BUT HOW'D WE GET THE ONE MILLILITER AND THE ONE GRAM...AND ISN'T THERE SOME WAY TO INDEX **RELATIVE** DENSITIES, USING JUST A NUMBER WITHOUT MESSY DIMENSIONS?

THY QUERY IS MOST SPECIFIC!

NOT TO MENTION ONE OF GRAVITY, NO LESS!

Water, by dint of its simplicity and ubiquity, was the substance chosen to become the arbitrary one-gram/one-milliliter standard. All substances are thus heavier (denser, in this context) than water—more than a gram per milliliter—or lighter (less than a gram).

Because volumes change with temperature, we say, as a convention, that it is water at 4°C (277 K) that is exactly 1.0 g/ml. This is water's *specific gravity,* and that of any other substance (nickel, for instance) is merely its density expressed as a ratio of its own g/ml to that of water:

$$\text{specific gravity (Ni)} = \frac{1 \text{ gram of nickel}}{1 \text{ gram of } H_2O \text{ at } 4°C}$$

The gram dimension cancels out of this expression, and the ones are omitted; they are understood. Replace the labels "nickel" and "H_2O at 4°C" with their respective values (8.9 and 1.0). Then, because (1) any number divided by one is that same number, and because (2) the dimensions canceled, we can express the ratio as a simple, dimensionless number (specific gravity), rather than as a conversion factor (density):

$$\frac{8.9 \text{ g/ml}}{1.0 \text{ g/ml}} = 8.9$$

Nickel, then, is amost nine times as dense as water. Anything with an overall specific gravity below 1.0 will be buoyant; it will float on pure water.

The standard for gases, which we will not worry about in this book, is dry air.

Archimedes' Principle

...AN OBJECT THAT IS IMMERSED IN A FLUID IS BUOYED UP BY A FORCE EQUAL TO THE MASS OF THE DISPLACED FLUID. BUOYANCY (THIS PRESSURE) IS THEREFORE THE DIFFERENCE BETWEEN AN OBJECT'S WEIGHT IN WATER AND ITS WEIGHT IN AIR...

Archimedes used this idea to prove that a crown of "pure" gold ordered by the king of Syracusa had been alloyed with another metal, because the crown was more buoyant than pure gold.

The hull of a luxury liner is mostly iron (specific gravity 7.9) with coatings of paint and noncorrosive alloys. Nevertheless, it floats, for its specific gravity *as an entire object*—open spaces, ballast, and all—is less than 1.0. Therefore, it has sufficient buoyancy to float (not to mention that saline water is more supportive).

LUV BOAT

1. Some matching:

_____nucleus   a. heaviness as a quotient of volume and mass

_____A-family metals   b. difference between a thing's apparent weight in water and in air

_____density   c. a group of relatively dense solid elements

_____alpha particles   d. helium atom cores

_____electrons   e. hydrogen atom cores

_____transition metals   f. that which is responsible for an atom's volume

_____specific gravity   g. that which is responsible for an atom's mass

_____buoyancy   h. a thing's heaviness, relative to water's heaviness

_____protons   i. a group of relatively light (low density) solid elements

Here are some density-equation problems ($D = m/v$) and more space than you will need in which to solve them. Keep in mind their extreme simplicity: if a value for density is the wanted, a single division operation, no more, is all that is called for. If, on the other hand, a volume or mass value is the wanted quantity, and density is among the givens, it is only a matter of multiplying the density (a conversion factor) by the other given. Make sure that your answer is in significant figures.

2. A rod of osmium (the densest of all metals) weighs 862.2 grams and displaces 38 milliliters. What is its density?

3. Red Dye No. 2 has a density of 0.569 g/ml. What is the volume of a sample weighing 500 grams?

4. Solid gold, an alloy with 10% copper (to harden it) is 18.7 g/ml. How many grams will an ingot that is 12 x 3 x 15 centimeters weigh (v = width x heighth x length; one cm^3 = one ml)?

5. Give the specific gravities for:

osmium   _____

Red Dye No. 2   _____

solid gold   _____

6. Using the appendix "Densities of Elements at STP," plot the specific gravities (or densities in g/ml) of the Period 5 metals from rubidium to tin. Label each dot with the appropriate symbol and connect them with a curve (not line segments) as in Sect. 1.6

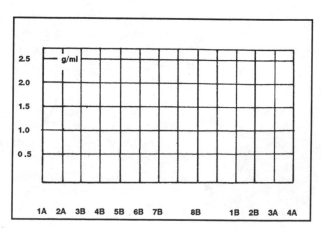

1.8 Chapter Synthesis

THOSE STUDENTS PUT OFF BY MATH WILL BE PLEASED TO LEARN THAT, DESPITE APPEARANCES, D.A. PROBLEMS ARE MAINLY CREATURES NOT OF MATH BUT RATHER OF LANGUAGE.

... SOME REQUIRE ANCILLARY CALCULATIONS IN ALGEBRA OR LOGARITHMS, BUT THE BASIC IDEA IS THE SAME.

WE ARE NOW READY TO STUDY D.A. INCORPORATING THE OTHER TOPICS OF CHAPTER 1.

THESAURUS ROGET & BOGUE

Keep in mind that the given is the key to a DA set-up, or "question." It is unique to the problem and, therefore, has no "per" to connect it to some other quantity. At first, one can simply deduce the given by pairing the other quantities in the problem into conversion factors (which are then listed, as Step 1).

Often, problems will have unstated conversion factors, which are like the missing links of a chain. The denominator of the previous link will be your clue to the numerator of the unstated link which, when you have it, will connect with the numerator of the next link.

Eventually and with practice, givens will leap from their respective problems and declare themselves as such. Then, after writing the given as part of the question (Step 2), you stitch in the listed conversion factors (Step 3) by making a numerator in one reappear as the denominator in the next. The great majority of DA problems obey this simple pattern; the only common complication is that some have more conversion factors than others.

The word *per* may well not appear even once in the wording of a problem. Become adept at recognizing its synonyms and circumlocutions ("to a," "for each/every," etc.). *Per* and its many forms always wind up being expressed by that little line that separates a numerator from a denominator and translates mathematically as *divided by*.

Here is a dimensional analysis problem that is a bit "complex" (but only in the sense mentioned above) for this stage, but there is nothing in it that we have not looked at separately in this chapter. See that you understand how each conversion factor is derived (one is from the table on p. 42) before going on to the problem set and the next chapter (which is about half-devoted to dimensional analysis).

A factory buys mercury by the kilogram at 7°C and warms it to 24° to manufacture thermometers, with each getting 2.09 milliliters of the warmed Hg. When purchased, the metal thus has a different density than when it is added to the thermometers. How many kilograms must be bought to make ten gross (one gross = 144) thermometers (note: convert the temperatures from °C to K before putting them into any conversion factor)?

$$?\text{kg Hg (280K)} = 10\text{ gross therms} \times \frac{144\text{ therms}}{\text{gross therms}} \times \frac{2.09\text{ ml Hg (297K)}}{\text{therm}} \times \frac{13.5782\text{ ml Hg (280K)}}{13.5364\text{ ml Hg (297K)}}$$

$$\times \frac{\text{kg Hg (280K)}}{1000\text{g Hg (280K)}} = 3.0188936\text{ kg Hg} = 3.0\text{ kg Hg (280K)}$$

The answer is 3.0 kg Hg at 7°C. A gross = 144 is a defined relation, so the 1 does not affect sigfigs, which instead are limited by the 10 in the question set-up. You need not have been able to do this problem on your own yet, but you will be doing "harder" ones before you finish Chap. 2. Note the importance of precise labeling.

1. g i a d f c h b e

2.

$$? \frac{g}{ml} = \frac{862.2\,g}{38ml} = 23\,g/ml$$

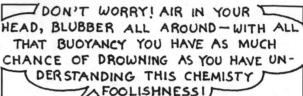

DON'T WORRY! AIR IN YOUR HEAD, BLUBBER ALL AROUND—WITH ALL THAT BUOYANCY YOU HAVE AS MUCH CHANCE OF DROWNING AS YOU HAVE UNDERSTANDING THIS CHEMISTY FOOLISHNESS!

3.

$$?\,ml\,dye = 500\,g\,dye \times = \frac{ml\,dye}{0.569\,g\,dye}$$

$$= 879\,ml\,dye$$

4.

$$(12\,cm)(3\,cm)(15\,cm) = 540\,cm^3 = 540\,ml$$

$$?g\,solid\,Au = 540\,ml\,solid\,Au \times$$

$$\frac{18.7\,g\,solid\,Au}{ml\,solid\,Au} = 1.01 \times 10^4\,g$$

5. Osmium is 23 (times as "heavy" as water); red dye no. 2, 6.9; and solid gold, 18.7.

6.

Volume of Mercury at Various Temperatures			
°C	ml/g	°C	ml/g
-3	13.6029	19	13.5487
-2	6004	20	5462
-1	5979	21	5438
0	5955	22	5413
1	5930	23	5389
2	5906	24	5364
3	5881	25	5340
4	5856	26	5315
5	5832	27	5291
6	5807	28	5266
7	5782	29	5242
8	5758	30	5217
9	5733	31	5193
10	5708	32	5168
11	5684	33	5144
12	5659	34	5119
13	5634	35	5095
14	5610	36	5070
15	5585	37	5046
16	5561	38	5021
17	5536	39	4997
18	13.5512	40	13.4973

Do these dimensional-analysis problems by identifying the given quantity—that having a number unique to the problem—and making it into a question with the wanted dimension. Then add on the stated and unstated conversion factors. This is the most direct way to do dimensional analysis, and the way you will sooner or later be using with experience. If you do not feel completely confidant with DA at this point, use the comprehensive 3-step procedure.

Reduce all answers to sigfigs. Do not allow numbers in defined relations to affect your sigfig counts. Also, beware of quantities that are not relevant to the arithmetic of the problem (Sect. 1.2).

1. How many seconds are in three hours (this problem will require the use of two unstated but very familiar defined relations as conversion factors)?

2. What number of spokes do 80 bicycles have if each wheel has 32 spokes and each handlebar has three black, white, and yellow Bardahl decals (one unstated conversion factor)?

3. What is the density of brass, a copper-zinc alloy, if a block displacing 40.8 cm^3 weighs 324 grams? What is its specific gravity?

4. A Klingon destroyer uses 7.67 kg of dilithium (Li$^{\pm}_{2}$) to travel one lightyear. How much of this fuel will be needed to get from Beta-Negri 4 to Epsilon-Zuck 34B, a distance of 10.7 parsecs (one parsec = 3.27 lightyears)?

5. The density of milk is about 1.07 g/ml. How many gallons weigh 5.00 kilograms, if there are 0.946 liters in a quart (two unstated conversion factors, both defined relations)?

6. At a doohickey factory, 14.5 gallons of joy juice go into the production of 100 pounds of Q powder, of which 9.6 ounces are needed to glaze one thingumbob. How many doohickeys can be made with 75 gallons of joy juice (there is one unstated but familiar conversion factor) if each doohickey takes 36 thingumbobs?

7. Some concentrated nitric acid, $HNO_3(l)$, density 1.21 g/ml, fills a beaker to the 760 ml mark. The beaker weighs 211 g. How much does the solution weigh? What is the specific gravity of the acid?

8. To "afterburn" 100 g of CO to CO_2 in a platinum-palladium catalyic honeycomb requires the consumption of 57.2 grams of O_2. How many *kilo*grams of O_2 is needed to afterburn 85 grams of CO?

9. Density, as you know, is mass per unit of volume. Using the Earth's mass and volume as dimensions ("earthvolume" or EV, and "earthmass" or EM), determine the densities of Saturn (95 EM, 835 EV) and Mars (0.107 EM, 0.151 EV). Only the unquantified unit, EV, will be in the denominator.

10. To produce 100 g of carbon disulfide, CS_2, 84.3 grams of sulfur is expended. How many liters of CS_2 can be made from 950 grams of sulfur, if the density of the mineral is 0.67 g/ml (one unstated conversion factor)?

...AND AFTER I EFFORTLESSLY BLAZED THRU THE FIRST DENSITY PROBLEM, I DID THE TREKKIE ONE, WHICH WAS NO SWEAT!

Interpolation: Phlogiston

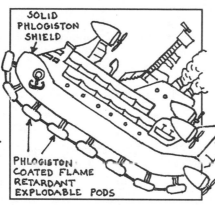

SOLID PHLOGISTON SHIELD

PHLOGISTON COATED FLAME RETARDANT EXPLODABLE PODS

The gravity shield on a Jules Verne flying machine is made of solid phlogistion.

Phlogiston is an element that never graduated from theory to the Periodic Table. And yet, the idea was a post-alchemic one.

It was a neat and, for some time, a reasonable way of explaining combustion. Meaning, literally, "firestuff," phlogiston (flow-JIS-tun) was said to be the flammable essence that escaped as flame from any material that could be burned. Ashes could be remade into the original substance if the phlogiston were somehow returned to them. In fact, some experiments in which lead and tin ashes were reduced by roasting over a phlogiston "source" (such as charcoal) seemed to bear this out. That some things were more easily combusted than others simply meant that they contained more of this substance.

Up until a few years before the French Revolution, no one could be blamed for believing this, until it was noticed that the ashes often weighed *more* than the original fuel, at which time the theory gained a bizarre corollary.

Phlogiston, it was now posited, was the only element having the property of "levity," the opposite of a certain other property had by all the other elements, namely gravity. This roundly violated the Law of Conservation of Mass; nonetheless, it was defended by some of the otherwise best scientists of the day (not least among them Cavendish and Priestly), even when the theory could not even begin to explain why at other times the ashes weighed *less* than the fuel.

In 1785, Lavoissier complained that "chemists have made phlogiston a vague principle [which] consequently fits all the explanations demanded of it. Sometimes it has weight, sometimes it has not; sometimes it is free fire, sometimes it is fire combined

with an earth; sometimes it passes through...vessels, sometimes they are impenetrable to it. It explains at once caustisity and non-caustisity, transparency and opacity, color and [colorlessness]. It is a veritable Proteus [changing form at] every instant!"

Finally, Lavoissier cooked some pure mercury for 12 days in a sealed container and discovered that the metal had formed a heavier, red ash, and that the air in the container was proportionately lighter.

From this, he concluded that combustion was in fact the reaction of a substance with a gas. In this and in most such cases, that gas is oxygen.

Many science historians mark the birth of modern chemistry—from the ashes of phlogiston, so to speak—with this event. Just the same, it still remained, in Lavoissier's time, for several other nonelements—including heat, light, and various compounds—to be removed from the element club, which, over 24 centuries has grown in membership from four to over a hundred (and counting).

As late as 1801, Priestly published a treatise defending phlogiston. His refusal to part with the idea was probably due in some degree to his hatred for Lavoissier, who attempted to steal from him the credit for the discovery of oxygen. In any case, he remained pro-phlogiston until his death, rejecting prima faciae evidence to the contrary.

Today making fun of the pro-phlogiston school for their parochialism and obstinacy in the face of incontrovertible findings is an almost obligatory anecdotal footnote of modern chemistry study. Their arguments, however, were as good or better than some "arguments" used by some *modern* scientists to defend evolution, which, like geocentrism and phlogiston, did made sense—once.

I WONDER HOW THE PHLOGISTONISTES WILL EXPLAIN THIS! PERHAPS THEY'LL SAY THAT SOME TIMES THERE IS LEVITY AND AT OTHER TIMES, NO...

1. ? secs. = 3hrs. x $\dfrac{60 \text{ mins.}}{\text{hr.}}$ x $\dfrac{60 \text{ secs.}}{\text{min.}}$ = 1×10^4 (10,800 rounded to significant figures)

2. ? spokes = 80 bikes x $\dfrac{2 \text{ wheels}}{\text{bike}}$ x $\dfrac{32 \text{ spokes}}{\text{wheel}}$ = 5.1×10^3 spokes

3. ? D$\left(=\dfrac{m}{v}\right)$ = $\dfrac{324 \text{ g}}{40.8 \text{ cm}^3}$ $\left(=\dfrac{324 \text{ g}}{40.8 \text{ ml}}\right)$ = 7.94 g/ml; spec. gravity: 7.94

4. ? kg $Li_2^\pm$ = 10.7 parsecs x $\dfrac{3.27 \text{ ltyrs.}}{\text{parsec}}$ x $\dfrac{7.67 \text{ kg } Li_2^\pm}{\text{lightyear}}$ = 268 kg $Li_2^\pm$

5. ? gals. milk = 5.00 kg milk x $\dfrac{1000 \text{ g milk}}{\text{kg milk}}$ x $\dfrac{\text{ml milk}}{1.07 \text{ g milk}}$ x $\dfrac{\text{L milk}}{1000 \text{ ml milk}}$

   $\dfrac{0.946 \text{ qt. milk}}{\text{L milk}}$ x $\dfrac{\text{gal. milk}}{4 \text{ qts. milk}}$ = 1.11 gals. milk

6. ? doohickeys = 75 gals. joy juice x $\dfrac{100 \text{ lbs. Q pdr.}}{14.5 \text{ gals. jj.}}$ x $\dfrac{16 \text{ oz. Q pdr.}}{\text{lb Q pdr.}}$ x $\dfrac{\text{thingambob}}{9.6 \text{ oz. Q pdr.}}$

   x $\dfrac{\text{doohickey}}{36 \text{ th' bobs}}$ = 23 (complete) doohickeys

7. ? g HNO_3 soln. = 760 ml HNO_3 soln x $\dfrac{1.21 \text{ g } HNO_3 \text{ soln}}{\text{ml } HNO_3 \text{ soln}}$ = 920 g (acid) + 211 g (beaker)

   = 1131 g; spec. gravity, HNO_3 soln : 1.21

8. ? g O_2 = 85.0 kg CO x $\dfrac{100 \text{ g CO}}{\text{kg CO}}$ x $\dfrac{57.2 \text{ g } O_2}{100 \text{ g CO}}$ = 2.1×10^3 g O_2 (2.1 kg)

9. ? D_{saturn} = $\dfrac{95 \text{ Em}}{835 \text{ Ev}}$ = $\dfrac{0.11 \text{ Em}}{\text{Ev}}$; ? D_{Mars} = $\dfrac{0.107 \text{ Em}}{0.151 \text{ Ev}}$ = $\dfrac{0.709 \text{ Em}}{\text{Ev}}$

   spec. gravity, such that Earth = 1.0 : Saturn : 0.11 ; Mars : 0.709

10. ? L CS_2 = 950 g S x $\dfrac{100 \text{ g } CS_2}{84.3 \text{ g S}}$ x $\dfrac{\text{ml } CS_2}{0.67 \text{ g } CS_2}$ x $\dfrac{\text{L } CS_2}{1000 \text{ ml } CS_2}$ = 1.7 L CS_2

Note: in DA problems with "1000" in both a numerator and a denominator, we can simplify the calculation by not figuring them in, as they mutually cancel.

Two: Concerning Chemical Composition

2.1 Chemical Bond Types

FIRST WE LEARN THAT THE ELEMENTS ARE MADE OF ATOMS, AND COMPOUNDS, OF MOLECULES; THEN THAT ELEMENTS LIKE N_2, Cl_2, AND S_8 ARE MADE OF MOLECULES. NOW YOU TELL ME THAT SOME COMPOUNDS DON'T EVEN HAVE MOLECULES. SO WHY AREN'T THE BITS OF SO-CALLED IONIC COMPOUNDS PROPER MOLECULES?

MAYBE THEY NEVER READ EMILY POST'S MANUAL OF ETIQUETTE!

Atoms are are attached to one another by any of three types of bonds.

Only one of these, the *covalent bond*, is the coupling force in true molecules; among chemists, in fact, the adjectives "covalent" and "molecular" are virtual synonyms. The other main type of chemical glue, the *ionic bond*, joins not neutral atoms *per se*, but charged ones. There are gradations between covalent and ionic, as we will see in Chap. 3. The third type is the *metallic bond*, which we will examine only cursorily in this book.

A key generalization is that most metal-nonmetal bonds are ionic, while most nonmetal-nonmetal bonds are covalent.

The Covalent Roommates

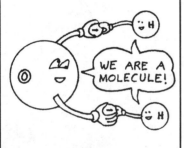

WE ARE A MOLECULE!

In covalent bonding, neutral or largely neutral atoms are roommates with shared responsibilities, namely electrons, which they co-possess (as in H_2O). The more equal the sharing, the more covalent (molecular) the particle; hence, particles of the seven diatomic elements are the most molecular of all, for their sharing is fully equal. Molecules are discrete (individual) particles which can stick to other molecules through the action of intermolecular forces that we will look at in Chaps. 3 and 7.

All substances that are gases at normal temperatures are covalent, even, in effect, the few that are composed of nonbonded atoms (the noble gases), because they *behave* as molecules (i.e., are discrete and uncharged).

The Ionic Communalists

WE COULD BE A FORMULA UNIT!

In ionic bonding, charged particles (ions) form communes of positive and negative ions. Some ions are charged atoms; others are charged molecules that *contain* covalent bonds but, externally, form ionic ones. Ions do not form molecules because each ion has a competing affinity for every nearby, oppositely charged ion. The formula NaCl, for instance, indicates a sodium ion and a chloride ion (Na^+, Cl^-). So, for calculation purposes only, we have a "molecule equivalent", the *formula unit*.

Only by understanding the difference between covalent and ionic can you know whether a formula stands for a molecule or a formula unit.

The Metallic Brave New World

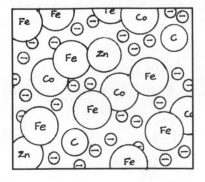

In metallic bonding, there are different ideas of the role of electrons. One is that the electron clouds of metal atoms overlap. Another is that metal is a mass of spaced nuclei in a lake of electrons. That the lake can become a river, or a current, in two senses of the word, explains the electrical conductivity of metals.

Alloys are combinations of metals with other metals, although some alloys, such as the iron/chromium steels, contain some carbon.

2.2 Binary Formulae

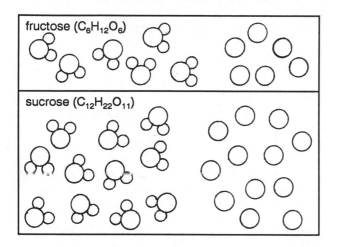

fructose ($C_6H_{12}O_6$)

sucrose ($C_{12}H_{22}O_{11}$)

All carbohydrates, "hydrated carbons," were once thought to have the molecular formula $C_x(H_2O)_y$, such as these two simple sugars. When metabolized, they yield about 4 kcal/g.

Recall Dalton's Law of Multiple Proportions and how carbon and oxygen formed CO and CO_2. The Law also applies to compounds of three or more elements, indeed more so, as the multiplicity of possible proportions increases rapidly with the addition of more elements.

Within carbohydrates, hydrogen and oxygen are combined in a fixed ratio of 2:1, but in differing ratios with carbon. (Note: do not infer from the illustrations at left that these sugars result from the direct reaction of carbon and water).

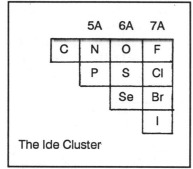

	5A	6A	7A
C	N	O	F
	P	S	Cl
		Se	Br
			I

The Ide Cluster

Ide Cluster Roots

carb-	ide	sulf-	ide
nitr-	ide	chlor-	ide
ox-	ide	selen-	ide
fluor-	ide	brom-	ide
phosph-	ide	iod-	ide

Some Binary Molecular Compounds

CO	carbon monoxide
SiO_2	silicon dioxide
SF_6	sulfur hexafluoride
CCl_4	carbon tetrachloride
C_6H_6	benzene

——————Binary Molecular Compounds——————

Berzelius gave us the current and universal method for writing formulae, a system that in its efficient beauty is faithful to The Law of Multiple Proportions and, at the same time, easy to use in constructing formulae. The logical starting point for the study of formulae is the simple *binary compound*, that is, a compound of two elements.

Binary *molecular* compounds, as opposed to binary *ionic* compounds, are made of true molecules and are usually formed from two nonmetals.

In both the binary formula and in the spelled-out name, that element which is leftmost in the Periodic Table will normally be the left, or first-written, half of the formula. Also, it will retain its name when spoken or spelled out.

Obviously, then, it is up to the rightmost element (on the Table) to make up the right side of the formula, although its name is altered by the *-ide* suffix being added to its root. The important exceptions are mostly hydrogen-containing binaries, but you will learn them effortlessly as you go along. The "ide cluster" (an unscientific mnemonic device) includes the "true ides" (oxygen and the halogens), which are practically always on the right side of a binary formula. They can be thought of as the True Ide-side elements. The "semi-ides" (carbon, nitrogen, phosphorus, sulfur, and selenium) are very often on the right, but can just as easily be on the left and going by their usual, unmodified names. Carbon in particular tends to be on the left, and carbides are comparatively rare.

❀ Color the true ides in the cluster diagram above, left, yellow, and the semi-ides, light green.

The roots of the ide-cluster will be useful again when we study the formulae of polyatomic ions, acids, and the ionic compounds.

In addition to the symbols which we use to spell compound formulae, Berzelius also came up with a way to quantify elements—by atom or ratio (not by weight)—within the formula…

49

Berzelius introduced subscripts into formulae to show how many atoms of each element were contained in a molecule (ionic binary compounds are named in an altogether different fashion, as will be seen in Sect. 2.6). He did not use subscripts of 1; nor, of course, will we.

When spoken or spelled out, Greek prefixes are used to quantify atoms in a formula. The prefix for 1—*mono*—is usually omitted for the same reason that 1 is not used as a subscript in formulae or a coefficient in equations (it is understood as being *one*). The best known exception is carbon monoxide (CO) which would sound too much like carbon dioxide (CO_2) without the *mono-*.

Notice that except for *di-* and *tri-*, the prefixes drop their final vowel if the root they are modifying begins with a vowel (oxide, iodide, etc.):

$$P_2O_5 = \text{diphosphorus pentoxide}$$
$$\text{(not "pentaoxide")}$$

A few very important chemicals go only by their common names. NH_3 is always ammonia, and its ion (NH_4^+) is ammonium. The same goes for water, for even the stuffiest chemist does not want to drink or swim in dihydrogen oxide.

No.	prefix		examples
1	mono-	CO	carbon monoxide
2	di-	SiO_2	silicon dioxide
3	tri-	NF_3	nitrogen trifluoride
4	tetra-	CCl_4	carbon tetrachloride
5	penta	P_2O_5	diphosphorus pentoxide
6	hexa-	SBr_6	sulfur hexabromide
7	hepta-	IF_7	iodine heptafluoride
8	octa-	C_8H_{18}	octane

The names of some more complex chemicals are inflected according to their class of chemical. For example: dimethyl hydrazine is $(CH_3)_2N_2H_4$. Some simpler organic binaries are named with roots that are unrelated to their formulae such as *meth*ane, CH_4; and *benz*ene, C_6H_6 (organic binaries are carbon-hydrogen compounds).

Atomic and Molecular Weight

As you by now know, the nucleus has practically all of an atom's mass. How much that nucleus weighs (in atomic mass units) depends on its number of *nucleons*. One nucleon weighs one amu.

A common hydrogen atom has only one nucleon, so its atomic weight is also 1. A common nitrogen atom has 14 of these subatomic particles. A molecule of ammonia (NH_3), therefore, will have a *molecular weight* of 17.

In the same way that molecules are made up of whole numbers of atoms, nuclei are made up of whole numbers of nucleons. The heaviest naturally-occurring element (plutonium) has a whopping 242 nucleons. The upper limit for artificially produced elements is around 300.

Since ionic compounds are not made up of molecules, we speak of the mass of a formula unit in terms of *formula weight*. The concept is otherwise identical to molecular weight. For instance, a formula unit of potassium fluoride (KF) would have a weight of 58 amu, because a typical potassium atom contributes 39 nucleons while the fluorine puts in 19.

If you read an article that mentions uranium-235 (which is fissionable) and uranium-238 (which is nonfissionable), you will know that the numbers refer to the nucleon count. Both nuclei have 92 protons, but one isotope has three more neutrons than the other.

THE PROBLEM IS THAT WE CHEMISTS CANNOT WEIGH A SAMPLE OF AN ELEMENT OR A COMPOUND ONE PARTICLE AT A TIME...

...WE NEED SOME WAY TO MEASURE AN **EQUAL** NUMBER OF PARTICLES FROM **DIFFERENT** SUBSTANCES USING A PRACTICAL DIMENSION (LIKE THE GRAM) AND A RELATIVE ONE (LIKE THE AMU).

2.3 Isotopes and Nucleons

I'VE GOT A QUESTION. IF THE NUCLEI ARE MADE UP OF WHOLE NUMBERS OF NUCLEONS, THEN WHY DOES CHLORINE HAVE AN ATOMIC WEIGHT OF 35.45 AND NICKEL 58.70? THEY MUST HAVE FRACTIONAL NUCLEONS.

NAY. 'TIS LIKE THIS: A SAMPLE OF MOST ELEMENTS WILL HAVE ATOMS WITH DIFFERENT NUMBERS OF NUCLEONS. EACH POSSIBLE QUANTITY...

...IS AN ISOTOPE.

Two Types of Nucleons

Each of the three basic subatomic particles makes its own contributions to an atom's character.

Electrons—the negatively charged particles—are responsible for an atom's volume, its charge, and, very importantly, its valency (more on this later).

Protons and neutrons are the two types of nucleons. Both weigh about one amu **and**, as electrons weigh only about 0.0005 amu apiece, they are together responsible for an atom's mass (atomic weight). Each, however, makes an additional contribution. Protons—the positively charged particles—determine, by their number, an atom's elemental identity (e.g., an atom with five protons can only be boron). Neutrons—which have no charge— determine, also by the number present, to which isotope the atom belongs.

Isotopes

If the neutron population of an element's atoms varies from one atom to the next, then that element has multiple *isotopes*. Beryllium invariably has five neutrons (to go with its four protons) and phosphorus always has 16. Therefore, these two elements, and a half-dozen or so others, have only one isotope (beryllium-9, phosphorus-31, etc.).

Chlorine atoms, however, have two possible neutron counts: 18 and 20 (but only one possible proton count, 17). Hydrogen has three, sulfur has four, while tin memorably *has ten naturally* occuring isotopes.

Each Sn atom, however, must at the same time have exactly 50 protons or it would not, by definition, be tin. But the atom may have as few as 62 neutrons or as many as 76; the average for all tin atoms is about 69. This is why the average atomic weight of tin atoms is approximately 119 (50 protons + 69 neutrons = 119 nucleons = 119 amu).

Happily, the isotopes of all elements are more-or-less uniformly distributed, so we can expect a sample to always weigh about the same, regardless of its source. This means that the weights of the Periodic Table, while not values for individual particles, are still adequate constants. For example,

a sample of chlorine, no matter where it came from, will likely be 75.5% chlorine-35 and 24.5% chlorine-37:

$$^{35}Cl \ (0.7553)(34.97 \text{ amu}) = 26.41 \text{ amu}$$
$$^{37}Cl \ (0.2447)(36.95 \text{ amu}) = \underline{9.04 \text{ amu}}$$
$$(\text{and so...}) \qquad\qquad\quad 35.45 \text{ amu}$$

The H Nucleus: Three's a Crowd

Simple hydrogen can be slightly more complex with the addition of neutrons, but 99.985% of all H atoms are still "protium." Deuterium is a stable isotope accounting for the other 0.015%, and radioactive tritium decays when a neutron leaves. It exists naturally only in trace quantities.

⊕ Color the protons red and the neutrons, tan or grey.

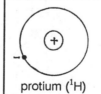

protium (^{1}H)

deuterium (D)

tritium (T)

Ye "Basic" Periodic Table

1A	2A	3A	4A	5A	6A	7A	8A
1 H 1.008							2 He 4.003
3 Li 6.939	4 Be 9.012	5 B 10.81	6 C 12.01	7 N 14.01	8 O 16.00	9 F 19.00	10 Ne 20.18
11 Na 22.90	12 Mg 24.31	13 Al 26.92	14 Si 28.09	15 P 30.97	16 S 32.06	17 Cl 35.45	18 Ar 39.95
19 K 39.10	20 Ca 40.08						

21 Sc	22 Ti	23 V	24 Cr	25 Mn	26 Fe	27 Co	28 Ni	29 Cu	30 Zn

It is not atomic weight that determines an element's position in the Table, but, rather, its atomic number (Z), which is also its proton census.

At one time, however, cobalt (Z = 27) and nickel (Z = 28) were wrongly put in each other's place because chemists discovered that cobalt atoms were heavier than nickel atoms.

Outside of the nuclear and physical branches of chemistry, it is only the electrons and the protons that really matter most of the time, because the protons define an atom's identity and the electrons, its behavior.

For us, then, neutrons are not greatly important. If we were to let them determine the order of elements in the Table because of their effect on atomic weight, we would have to put volatile, ultra-metallic potassium between inert, gaseous neon and krypton. Staid, invisible argon would be equally out of place among the alkalai metals.

In sum, atomic weight is not a consistent periodic function because there are no less than three pairs of elements in which the element with one fewer proton has more than enough neutrons to outweigh its neighbor.

It would be advisable at this point (before going on) to commit to memory any of the symbols of the first twenty elements and those of the first row of transition elements—or at least those with atomic numbers 24 to 30—that you do not yet know.

⊛ In the table above, color the alkalai metals (Li, Na, K) green; hydrogen, blue-violet; the alkaline earths (Be, Mg, Ca), green-yellow; the metalloids (B, Si), orange; aluminum, yellow; the halogens, red; the remaining nonmetals, red-orange; and the bar of transition metals, yellow-green. Do not color the noble gases.

1. Identify the bond type associated with the following (I = ionic; C = covalent; M = metallic):

_____joins formula units   _____exists between charged particles

_____most crystal lattices   _____alloys

_____gases   _____joins neutral atoms

_____synonymous with "molecular," especially before the word "bond."

2. Spell out the prefixes corresponding to each number:

1_____   2_____   3_____   4_____   5_____

6_____   7_____   8_____   9 *mona-*   10 *deca-*

3. Complete the chart, using the Periodic Table (T = true ide, S = semi-ide):

Z	symb.	family	atomic wt.	element	"ide" form	T/S
	C					
			14.01			S
					oxide	
9						
	P					
				sulfur		
			35.45			T
	34					
		7A			bromide	
	I					

4. The weight of a nucleon, for all intents and purposes, is 1 amu; that of an electron is so minute (5.45×10^{-4}) that its contribution to an atom's weight is negligible. Therefore, atomic weights should be nearly exact whole-number values. Often, however, they are not. Explain:

5. When chemists like Mendeleev (and physicists like Meyer) began assembling the Periodic Table, they ordered the elements by weight. Why is this an unreliable criterion?

6. Some more matching:

_____neutrons   a. protium, deuterium, tritium

_____isotopes   b. fluorine, chlorine, bromine

_____alkalai metals   c. subatomic particles that determine an atom's identity and its mass

_____electrons   d. boron, silicon, arsenic

_____halogens   e. subatomic particles that determine an atom's isotopism and its mass

_____nucleons   f. lithium, sodium, potassium

_____alkaline earths   g. generic name for all subatomic particles with a mass of 1 amu

_____metalloids   h. subatomic particles that determine an atom's charge, volume, and valency

_____transition elements   i. beryllium, magnesium, calcium

_____protons   j. titanium, manganese, zinc

7. Spell out the name of each binary molecular formula or write the formula where the name is given. Note: when elements of the same family combine, the heavier one is written first and the lighter one is the "ide."):

CO			diiodine hexafluoride	NF_3	
H_2O		$SiBr_4$			dichlorine oxide
NH_3		H_2S		XeF_6	
CH_4		C_6H_6		I_2O_5	
	sulfur trioxide	NO_2			(di)hydrogen selenide
As_2S_5			carbon tetrafluoride	N_2F_4	
	(di)nitrogen pentoxide	IF_7		CS_2	
PF_3		SiO_2		C_3O_2	

In some of compounds above (and below), the di- prefix is extraneous, although you may continue to use it until you are aware that there is no such thing, for instance, as "mononitrogen pentoxide" or "NO_5" (why this and certain other combinations are not possible will gradually become clear). Chemists are thus free to use the unaffixed form, even though the formulae indicate that two hydrogen atoms are present.

Of the nitrogen oxides, two have exceptional names; the rest follow standard nomenclature rules:

N_2O *nitrous* oxide
NO *nitric* oxide
NO_2 nitrogen dioxide
N_2O_3 nitrogen trioxide
N_2O_5 nitrogen pentoxide

⊛ At right, color the nitrogen atoms violet and the oxygen atoms light blue.

54

2.4 The Mole

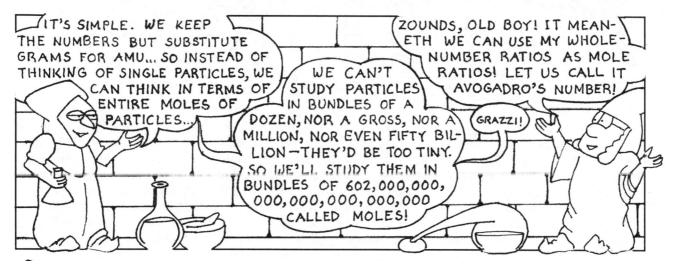

One mole is like one dozen, one score, or one gross, only much bigger. A dozen only has 12 eggs, but a mole has 602,000,000,000,000,000,000,000 eggs. A dozen eggs, end-to-end, stretch about half of a meter, but a mole of eggs could make 161 million round trips to Alpha Centauri (or, for that matter, a hefty omelette). As you can see, a mole is a humongous quantity; it is, in fact, the largest quantity with a name.

The familiar weights of the Periodic Table give us the weights in amu of single atoms, but the same numbers also tell us the weight in grams of one mole of any element's atoms. This is the element's *molar weight*.

However, the fact that we now have a tangible way to quantify the particles does not, obviously, mean that atoms, molecules, and formula units lose their peculiar properties.

For this reason, we will continue to use the terms atomic weight, molecular weight, and formula weight, but with the understanding that (henceforth) they stand for grams, not atomic mass units.

Specifically, *molar weights*—of any of the three categories—*are the number of grams in one mole* (6.02 x 10^{23} particles) of any substance. Here are a few examples:

mass of boron atom	10.81 amu
atomic weight of boron	10.81 grams
mass of H_2O molecule	18.02 amu
molecular weight of H_2O	18.02 grams
mass of NaCl form. unit	58.45 amu
formula weight of NaCl	58.45 grams

$$23.00 + 35.45 = 58.45 (NaCl)$$

... AND, IF A COMPOUND HATH MULTIPLE ATOMS OF AN ELEMENT, A LITTLE MULTIPLICATION IS ENTAILED. A MOLE OF TABLE SUGAR HATH 12 MOLES OF CARBON, 22 OF HYDROGEN, AND 11 MORE OF OXYGEN...

$$C: 12(12.01) = 144.12$$
$$H: 22(1.008) = 22.18$$
$$O: 11(16.00) = \underline{176.00}$$
$$342.30$$

The formula for sucrose, $C_{12}H_{22}O_{11}$, indicates the numbers of moles of atoms of each element in one mole of the compound. The recipe (for indeed that is what a formula is) calls for 12 moles of carbon, 22 moles of hydrogen, and 11 moles of oxygen.

In chemistry, however, a mole of hydrogen or oxygen is not a mole of *atoms* but a mole of *molecules*. A molecule of either element, as you know, contains two atoms, not one. It is as though the seven diatomic elements came only in quarts while all other elements were available in pints. So, to whip up a batch of sucrose, we need 12 pints of carbon, but 11 quarts of hydrogen and 51/2 quarts of oxygen:

$$12 \text{ mols C} \quad \rightarrow \quad 12 \text{ mols C}$$

$$11 \text{ mols } H_2 \quad \rightarrow \quad 22 \text{ mols H}$$

$$5\tfrac{1}{2} \text{ moles } O_2 \quad \rightarrow \quad 11 \text{ mols O}$$

Therefore, while the atomic weights of hydrogen and oxygen are one and 16 grams, respectively, their moles will weigh two and 32 grams, because they and five other elements that you can name are diatomic.

So when a mole of any of these seven elements is spoken of, it is understood that a mole of molecules is being referred to, unless otherwise indicated. These moles weigh *double* the number from the Periodic Table because they are *di*atomic.

Do not be confused by the fraction in $5\tfrac{1}{2}$ O_2. A mole, after all, is not a single particle, but septillions of them. Moles, and parts of moles, then, can obviously combine in fractions, becasue the *ratios* of the combining substances will always be in whole numbers.

For instance, 1.44 moles of carbon sulfide result from the reaction of carbon and sulfur in a 1:2 ratio:

$$1.44 \text{ mols C} + 2.88 \text{ mols S} = 1.44 \text{ mols CS}_2$$

We use molar (atomic, formula, or molecular) weights to count or measure moles of a substance with the *molar conversion factor*:

$$\frac{\text{grams X}}{\text{mol X}} \quad \text{...and its reciprocal...} \quad \frac{\text{mol X}}{\text{grams X}}$$

This is the single most important conversion factor in chemistry. With it, we can determine the number of moles that are in a sample simply by weighing it. Or, we can find out how many grams we need to get a wanted quantity (weight) of moles. In short, we can convert grams to moles and back, using dimensional analysis.

Now we are ready to consider some samples of substances. To start, we need only one bit of data: the molar weight; our source is the ever versatile Periodic Table.

56

Ni 500 grams	Ar 0.10 mol	SiO_2 97 grams	Br_2 32.9 mols	$KMnO_4$ 221.7 grams

No arithmetic. The value comes right from the Table.	Again, no figuring to be done; it's another element.	Si: 1(28.09) = 28.09 O: 2(16.00) = 32.00	An element, but a diatomic one, so... Br: 2(79.90) = 159.8	K: 1(39.10) = 39.10 Mn: 1(54.94) = 54.94 O: 4(16.00) = 64.00
atomic wt: 58.71	atomic wt: 39.95	molecular wt: 60.09	molecular wt: 159.8	formula wt: 158.0

The molar conversion factor varies from substance to substance, depending on the weight of the substance.

Each of the above samples has a given number and a given dimension, grams or moles. To get the molar conversion factor we need for a monatomic element, we just look at the Periodic Table. If the sample is a diatomic element, we simply double the atomic weight. If it is a compound, then a little arithmetic is in order.

Now to the dimensional analysis, and the application of the molar conversion factor.

If the given is in grams, the wanted will be in moles; if moles are given, then grams will be wanted.

To find out how many moles of nickel we have, the question is "? mols Ni = 500 g Ni." As the dimension in the given is grams, so also, then, must be the dimension in the following denominator of the conversion factor:

$$?\text{mols Ni} = 500\text{ g Ni} \times \frac{\text{mol Ni}}{58.71\text{ g Ni}}$$

Cancelling the grams leaves us with the wanted dimension (moles) and, in effect, with nothing more to do than a single division operation, for the given (as in any DA problem) is a numerator. The answer, in sigfigs, is 8.52 moles.

The advantage of performing the calculation *procedurally* using DA, over just writing one number over the other and dividing, is that we are left with the correct dimension. Eventually, you will do such problems in your head, aided only by a calculator; still, this sort of problem is a foretaste of longer problems that will always have to be written out.

The given quantity of the argon sample is 0.10 moles, so we want, to two sigfigs, the mass in grams:

$$?\text{ grams Ar} = 0.10\text{ mol Ar} \times \frac{39.95\text{ g Ar}}{\text{mol Ar}}$$

The answer is 4.0 grams Ar. Now try the next three.

In this problem, complete the "bridge" (what there is of one) by filling in the molar conversion factor, and solve: how many moles of quartz (SiO_2) are in 97 grams of it?

$$?\text{ mol }SiO_2 = 97\text{ g }SiO_2 \times \frac{1\,mol\,SiO_2}{60\,g\,SiO_2} =$$

Ans. 1.6 mol

This time, you will construct the question, then solve. How many grams will 32.9 moles of bromine weigh?

$$3.29\,mol\,Br \times \frac{159.8\text{ g }Br_2}{\text{mol }Br_2} =$$

Ans. 5.26×10^2 g Br_2

Now, do both the question and the conversion factor. If there are 221.7 grams of Potassium permanganate ($KMnO_4$), how many moles will there be?

$$221.7\,g\,KMnO_4 \times \frac{1\,mol}{158\,g} =$$

Ans. 1.403 mol $KMnO_4$

(Answers on p. 69).

Applications for Abogadro's Number

6.02×10^{23} is the lucky number that happens to equal a mole, but the number itself is useful only in illustrating the enormity of a mole; and, for chemistry teachers, in reviewing scientific notation.

For these reasons, there will be a few exercises in the following problem sets that use it in conversion factors.

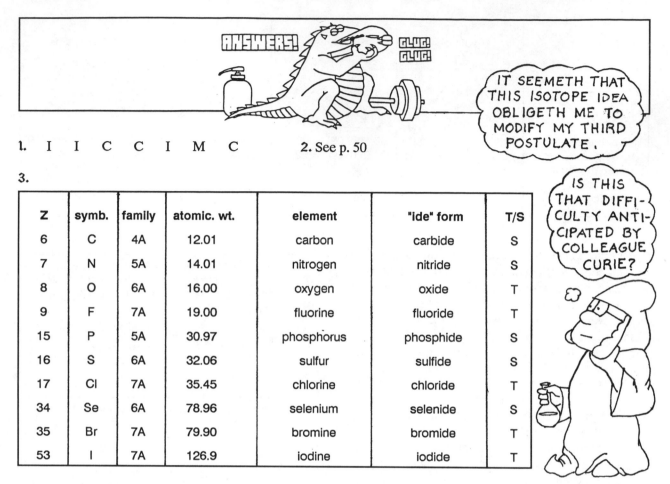

1. I I C C I M C   2. See p. 50

2. See p. 50

IT SEEMETH THAT THIS ISOTOPE IDEA OBLIGETH ME TO MODIFY MY THIRD POSTULATE.

IS THIS THAT DIFFICULTY ANTICIPATED BY COLLEAGUE CURIE?

3.

Z	symb.	family	atomic. wt.	element	"ide" form	T/S
6	C	4A	12.01	carbon	carbide	S
7	N	5A	14.01	nitrogen	nitride	S
8	O	6A	16.00	oxygen	oxide	T
9	F	7A	19.00	fluorine	fluoride	T
15	P	5A	30.97	phosphorus	phosphide	S
16	S	6A	32.06	sulfur	sulfide	S
17	Cl	7A	35.45	chlorine	chloride	T
34	Se	6A	78.96	selenium	selenide	S
35	Br	7A	79.90	bromine	bromide	T
53	I	7A	126.9	iodine	iodide	T

4. Most elements have particles of different weights; each possible weight is an isotope. A sample of any of these elements will contain atoms of every naturally occurring isotope and, therefore, have nonwhole-number mass (weight) values.

5. Weight is an unreliable way to order the elements because an element with fewer protons than another may more than make up for it in neutrons.

6.   e   a   f   h   b   g   i   d   j   c

7.

CO	carbon monoxide	I_2F_6	diiodine hexafluoride	NF_3	nitrogen trifluoride
H_2O	water	$SiBr_4$	silicon tetrabromide	Cl_2O	dichlorine oxide
NH_3	ammonia	H_2S	(di)hydrogen sulfide	XeF_6	xenon hexafluoride
CH_4	methane	C_6H_6	benzene	I_2O_5	diiodine pentoxide
SO_3	sulfur trioxide	NO_2	nitrogen dioxide	H_2Se	(di)hydrogen selenide
As_2S	(di)arsenic sulfide	CF_4	carbon tetrafluoride	N_2F_4	(di)nitrogen tetrafluoride
N_2O_5	(di)nitrogen pentoxide	IF_7	iodine heptafluroide	CS_2	carbon disulfide
PF_3	phosphorus trifluoride	SiO_2	silicon dioxide	C_3O_2	tricarbon dioxide

2.5 % Composition I: Compounds

SO WHAT ELSE CAN WE USE MOLAR CONVERSION FACTORS FOR?

STOICHIOMETRY, EMPIRICAL FORMULAE, SOLUTION CONCENTRATIONS, % COMPOSITIONS...

WHAT KIND OF % COMPOSITIONS?

ELEMENTS IN A COMPOUND, FOR ONE.

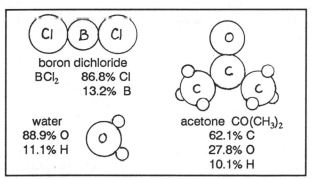

boron dichloride
BCl_2 86.8% Cl
            13.2% B

water
88.9% O
11.1% H

acetone $CO(CH_3)_2$
62.1% C
27.8% O
10.1% H

⊛ Pictured above are some molecules, the units of covalent compounds. Color the boron atom brown; the chlorines, green-yellow; the carbons, dark gray; the oxygens, light blue; and the tiny hydrogens, red.

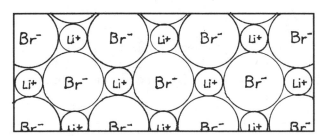

⊛ In this diagram is a section of the lattice of an ionic compound, the salt lithium bromide, which by weight is 92.1% bromine and 7.9% lithium. Color a single bromide ion red-orange and one adjoining lithium, blue-grey. This is a LiBr formula unit.

Percent means, literally, parts per one hundred.

At times, we may need to know the percentage—by weight—of a particular compound. All we require is the compound's formula and the Periodic Table—which is the immediate or ultimate source of all molar weights—and, of course, the symbols used to spell formulae.

Dimensional analysis problems with answers in percentages are extremely easy to perform because the set-up is simple and invariable, and the given number is always 100.

Apart from failing to label the dimensions, mistakes are all but inconceivable. Here are the simple mechanics of the percentage problem:

I
The given number is always 100.

II
Both the given and the wanted dimensions will be the same, usually grams.

...but watch out! In percentage problems, *you must pay close attention to labels*. This is the only potential pitfall if you have learned to avoid other types of DA errors; so the dimensions—grams or moles—must be assiduously labeled at all times with the formulae of the elements and compounds in question.

Any percent-composition problem, then, will *always* start like this:

$$?g\,X \;=\; 100\,g\,XY$$

...where X is the element, and XY a compound that contains it. Of course, the compound could just as easily be X_2YZ_5, or something even more complex, as we shall see. This, however, would only entail a little more simple arithmetic, like that in Sect. 2.4.

-------------------- **Error Analysis** --------------------

There is a confusion to be avoided here. Although we use molar weights, we shall actually be referring to individual particles; let it be understood that these particles are in very deed *models* of the compound, duplicated 6.02×10^{23} times by the mole.

WE ARE GOING TO EMPLOY MOLES IN WHOLE-NUMBER RATIOS. EACH MOLE OF CO HATH EXACTLY 1 MOLE OF OXYGEN. EACH MOLE OF CO_2 HATH EXACTLY TWO MOLES OF OXYGEN...BECAUSE CO AND CO_2 MOLECULES CAN HAVE NO MORE NOR LESS THAN 1 AND 2 OXYGEN ATOMS!

LAW OF MULTIPLE PROPORTIONS

THEN WHAT'S THE % WEIGHT IN, SAY, CO?

The simplest type of compound, obviously, is a binary with a 1:1 ratio of elements. The wanted element and the given compound are different substances, so a special conversion factor, a *keystone*, will be used to show their quantity relationship. Most keystones used in Chem. 1 and beyond are ordinary mole ratios.

Now, to Draggin's' question. First, we need the weights: oxygen is 16.00 and CO, 28.01 (in percent problems, unlike in some other DA problems, we use the elemental weight of *all* elements, including the the diatomic ones).

This step—getting the weights—is ludicrously easy, as is the next, because it is always the same:

$$? \text{ g (element)} = 100 \text{ g (compound)}$$

And now, the DA bridge (with the answer in sigfigs)...

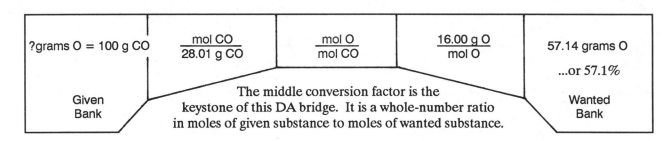

?grams O = 100 g CO	$\dfrac{\text{mol CO}}{28.01 \text{ g CO}}$	$\dfrac{\text{mol O}}{\text{mol CO}}$	$\dfrac{16.00 \text{ g O}}{\text{mol O}}$	57.14 grams O ...or 57.1%
Given Bank		The middle conversion factor is the keystone of this DA bridge. It is a whole-number ratio in moles of given substance to moles of wanted substance.		Wanted Bank

Notice the memorable and, therefore, helpful symmetry of this problem. The first conversion factor is grams-to-moles; the middle one—the keystone—is moles-to-moles; and the last one is moles *back* to grams.

After you have written the set-up (or question) which, remember, never varies in percent problems except as to labels, all you do is stick on the conversion factors that are dictated by this symmetry. Note that each labeled dimension in a numerator—beginning with that of the given (in this case, grams of CO)—reappears as the following denominator. Here it will hint—if you recall the simple symmetry just discussed (and perhaps even if you do not, as eventually you will not have to)—at the numerator to be written above it (in this case, mol CO). Then, write the keystone and the other molar conversion factor, to get back to the wanted dimension.

When the wanted dimension—labeled with the wanted substance—pops up in the last numerator, it is time to cancel everything else out, and calculate:

$$? \text{ g O} = 100 \text{ g CO} \times \frac{\text{mol CO}}{28.01 \text{ g CO}} \times \frac{\text{mol O}}{\text{mol CO}} \times \frac{16.00 \text{ g O}}{\text{mol O}} = 57.13 \text{ grams O}$$

Carbon, of course, combines with oxygen in not just one but multiple proportions— four, in fact—to form the gases CO, CO_2, and C_3O_2 and the ion, CO_3^{2-} (the carbon/oxygen ratios are clearly 1:1, 1:2, 3:2, and 1:3). Each C_3O_2 molecule, then, has three carbon atoms (note, below, the keystone). What is the percentage of carbon in C_3O_2? The weights for this problem are water under the bridge.

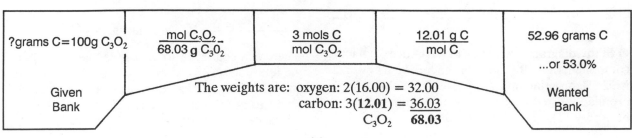

?grams C=100g C_3O_2	$\dfrac{\text{mol } C_3O_2}{68.03 \text{ g } C_3O_2}$	$\dfrac{3 \text{ mols C}}{\text{mol } C_3O_2}$	$\dfrac{12.01 \text{ g C}}{\text{mol C}}$	52.96 grams C ...or 53.0%
Given Bank		The weights are: oxygen: 2(16.00) = 32.00 carbon: 3(**12.01**) = 36.03 C_3O_2 **68.03**		Wanted Bank

To determine the percent-weight of an element in a more complex compound, such as a hydrate or a large radical, we do exactly the same thing as before. However, computing the compound's weight this time will require a little more fifth-grade arithmetic; refer back to the example of sucrose—$C_{12}H_{22}O_{11}$—in Sect. 2.3.

It's that simple!

In the case of a hydrate, we will often need to know the percent-weight of water in the compound.

Even so, it is still only a matter of basic arithmetic, and we treat the water just as though it were an element, with an "atomic weight" of 18.01.

Radicals

...for our purposes (for there is a bit more to the formal definition) are polyatomic ions that usually participate in reactions as such, rather than as elemental particles. Sometimes, however, they do break up. Being ions does not appreciably change their masses, so we still use the Periodic Table as our source of information on molar weights.

We are not yet concerned with ionic charges, and so can ignore, for now, the charge superscripts in, for example, sulfate (SO_4^{2-}) and hydronium (H_3O^+). In the case of sulfate, we add one sulfur (32.064) to four oxygens (64.000) to get a molar weight of 96.064. To find sulfur's percent-weight in a compound, we merely proceed as before, but we substitute the molar weight of a radical for that of an element.

Write in the molar weights of these radicals:

NO_3^-	nitrate	_____
CO_3^{2-}	carbonate	_____
PO_4^{3-}	phosphate	_____
OH^-	hydroxide	_____
NH_4^+	ammonium	_____

Hydrates

...are compounds that crystallized in a watery solution and, as they did, gathered some water molecules into their structures; they are *hydrated*.

If the water were heated off, an *anhydrous* substance—usually the original compounds would remain.

The name of a hydrate includes the name of the compound and the word "hydrate" modified with the appropriate Greek numerical prefix. The formula is made up of that of the anhydrous compound's formula, a dot, and "H_2O" with a coefficient.

Adding the weight of the water to the total is very easy; it is always a multiple of 18.01, the molar weight of water.

Now, determine these weights (answers on p. 69):

copper sulfate pentahydrate _____
($CuSO_4 \cdot 5H_2O$)

sodium carbonate octahydrate _____
($Na_2CO_3 \cdot 8H_2O$)

iron (II) dichloride hexahydrate _____
($FeCl_2 \cdot 6H_2O$)

An example: what is the percent weight of sulfate in copper sulfate pentahydrate?

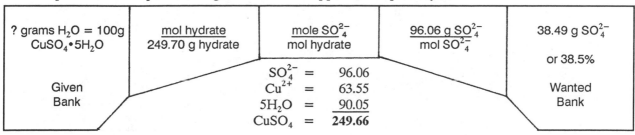

1. Match:

_____ mols/mols   a. a polyatomic particle with a charge

_____ molecule   b. the density conversion factor

_____ radical   c. the keystone conversion factor

_____ grams/mls   d. a polyatomic particle containing water molecules

_____ grams/mols   e. a neutral and discrete polyatomic particle

_____ hydrate   f. the molar conversion factor

2. What two quantities do the weight values of the Periodic Table represent? Include dimensions in the answers.

3. Give the number of moles of each element that would result from the breakup of one mole of the following compounds (Careful! It might not be as simple as it looks...)

a. NO: (N)_____(O)_____   b. $CuCl_2$: (Cu)_____(Cl)_____   c. $KMnO_4$ (K)_____(Mn)_____(O)_____

d. $C_{10}H_{22}$ (C)_____(H)_____   e. BaI_2 (Ba)_____(I)_____   f. $C_2H_3O_2^-$ (C)_____(H)_____(O)_____

4. Atoms combine only in whole numbers, but moles do not, necessarily. Why is this so?

5. Calculate and answer, to four significant figures, the molecular weights of the following substances:

a. I_2 _____   b. MgS _____   c. $MgSO_4$ _____   d. $C_6H_{12}O_6$ _____   e. $Mn(CN)_3$ _____

1. The boiling range of kerosene-derived fuels is 200-315°C. What is this range in Kelvins?

2. How much does one liter of metallic hydrogen—H(s)—found in the core of the Sun, weigh if its specific gravity is 1.08×10^5?

3. How many lugnuts, if four to a wheel (including the spare), are on 759 automobiles? Use dimensional analysis.

For the next six problems, you will (1) determine molar weights arithmetically (using the Periodic Table), and then (2) construct a dimensional analysis bridge, using a single conversion factor—the *molar* one. Review Sects. 1.1 and 1.2 as needed and label carefully(!).

6. How many moles of phosphorus are in a 160-gram sample of the element?

$$160 \, g \, P \times \frac{1 \, mol \, P}{31 \, g \, P} = 5.16 \, mol \, P$$

7. How many moles of the salt magnesium sulfide (MgS) are in a 500 grams of it?

8. How many moles of glucose are in 41.7 grams, if this sugar's formula is $C_6H_{12}O_6$?

9. Determine the weight in grams of 72 moles of pure elemental silicon.

10. At room temperature how much nitrogen gas (N_2) is in a room that contains 933 moles of it?

11. How much $MgSO_4$ is in a 10.1-mole sample of this anhydrous salt?

$$10.1 \, mol \, MgSO_4 \times \frac{120.3 \, g \, MgSO_4}{1 \, mol \, MgSO_4} = 1.22 \times 10^3 \, g \, MgSO_4$$

----- Across -----

1. Math skill used for getting molar wts.
9. Oc___ (gasoline)
10. Organic suffix
11. 3 lightest from Fam. 6A (not in order)
13. Commonest metal
14. Length dim. (pl.)
17. Prefix: three
18. The three physical states
19. Carbon monoxide
22. Aristotle was ANTI; Democritus was ___

24. Hahn, Roentgen, Geiger, Kekule, etc.
27. Liquid halogen
28. Coinage metal
29. Z = 19, 20
31. Prefix: opposite of *cath-* or *cat-*
33. 2 nonmetals
35. Prefix in SO_3
37. Adj. for mole
38. Prefix: six

----- Down -----

1. Elementary bit
2. Z = 88
3. Atomic wt. 114.8
4. 2 Fam. 6A middleweights

5. Weight, practically speaking
6. Organic suffix
7. Fam. 6A metalloid
8. Where Berkeley, Livermore, are
12. Type of impurity
13. Noble gas
15. *exempli gratis* and *id est*
16. Atomic wt. 204.38
17. Period 1, to rest of Table
20. 3 from Period 3 (first letter may vary)
21. 2 noble gases
23. An alkalai metal
24. Weight/mass unit
25. Radioactive Fam. 2A member

26. Z = 21
30. Ionic suffix
32. Nitric oxide
34. Fam. 7A member
36. Pharmacists' logo

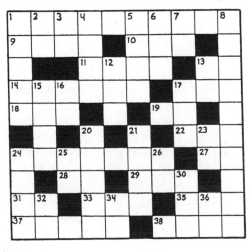

63

In these percent-weight problems, keep in mind that the given will *necessarily* be 100. After writing the simple wanted/given equation (the set-up), you will use a molar conversion factor, a keystone, and then another molar conversion. After that, you just cancel and compute.

12. What is the percent-weight of beryllium in beryllium oxide (BeO)?

13. When silver oxide (Ag_2O) is reduced, what percentage of it will be pure metal?

14. The formula $Mn(CN)_3$ indicates three cyanide radicals in manganese (III) cyanide. Determine the percent-weight of cyanide in this compound.

15. If barium sulfate pentahydrate crystals are melted, what pecentage of the total weight will be lost as the water is liberated and evaporates?

16. What is the percent-weight of lithium in lithium fluoride if the the fluorine is 72%? Do not use DA.

17. This problem, which will require you to use a conversion factor containing Avogadro's Number, is optional; but it is not hard if you know the defined relation for a mole (and are not put off by exponents): how many moles of lead atoms can be made from 3.61×10^{25} atoms?

2.6 Ions and Ionization

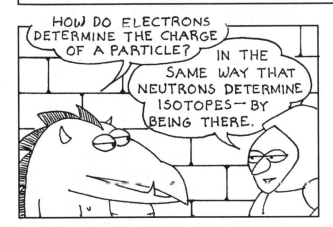

Any particle with an equal number of protons and electrons is electrically neutral. Any particle with an excess of either is an ion.

A particle with one extra electron has a charge of $1-$; two extra electrons, or bits of negativeness, $2-$; and so on. The minus symbol, then, means that as an ion it is quantitatively something a wee bit more than it would be as a neutral particle; *qualitatively*, however, it has very different properties.

Conversely, a particle that is short one electron has a charge of $1+$, expressing the electrical primacy, to one degree, of the protons. A charge of $2+$ means that two electrons are lacking, and so on. A positive ion is therefore very slightly lighter (and often considerably smaller) than its neutral counterpart.

The change of a neutral particle to a charged one is called *ionization*. Most particles, including all atoms, ionize by losing or gaining electrons. Two special classes of molecules, however—acids and bases—ionize by losing or gaining protons.

Negative ions are called *anions*. There are six common monatomic anions, namely, those of the five "true ides" and of sulfur. You know (Sect. 2.2) that these elements, when they form the second part of molecular binaries (and in other compounds, as we will see later), end in *-ide*. This is also true of their ions. The name consists in the inflected form and the word, *ion*. For example:

$$\text{sulfur (S)} + 2e^- \rightarrow \text{sulfide ion (S}^{2-})$$

There are many polyatomic anions, with names ending in *-ide*, *-ite*, or *-ate*. Most of those we will study contain oxygen *(oxyanions)* and some contain metal.

Positive ions are called *cations*. The cations you will meet in Chem. 1 are metallic, with two very important exceptions (ammonium, NH_4^+; and hydronium, H_3O^+). Most of these cations are also monatomic, with three important exceptions: the two nonmetallic cations just mentioned, and mercury (I), or Hg_2^{2+}.

The formula of all ions of every category *must* include the charge superscripts to be correct, unless that formula appears in part of a compound's formula unit.

For instance, silver oxide (Ag_2O) is an ionic formula containing two silver ions ($2Ag^+$) and a single oxide ion (O^{2-}).

e substances are happier being ions than the neutral substances they correspond to. Coral reef skeletons, rls, the chalk cliffs of Dover, and limestone deposits are all nothing more than enormous lattices of ionically ded calcium ions (Ca^{2+}) and carbonate ions (CO_3^{2-}); the formula is $CaCO_3$, and the formula unit has one each ion. Neutral calcium metal is very reactive and so gladly gives up its two outermost (valence) electrons to become an ion. Carbonate does not have a neutral counterpart, because "carbonic acid" is not a naturally occurring chemical. But the carbonate radical is found in an abundance of compounds, notably in a series of largely insoluble salts.

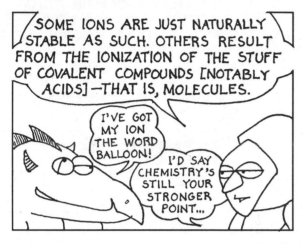

SOME IONS ARE JUST NATURALLY STABLE AS SUCH. OTHERS RESULT FROM THE IONIZATION OF THE STUFF OF COVALENT COMPOUNDS [NOTABLY ACIDS]—THAT IS, MOLECULES.

I'VE GOT MY ION THE WORD BALLOON!

I'D SAY CHEMISTRY'S STILL YOUR STRONGER POINT...

Ionization of Be to Be^{2+}

Be^0 Be^{2+}

$Be - (-2) = Be^{2+}$

Ionization of O_2 to $2O^{2-}$

O^0 O^{2-}

$O_2 + (2-) = 2O^{2-}$

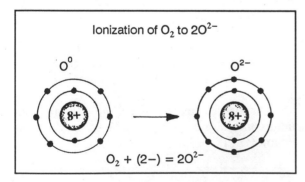

The BeO formula unit, expressed diagramatically as a molecule (when, in fact the two ions would be part of an ionic continuity, as described in Sect. 2.1).

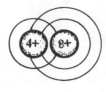

When a compound ionizes in water—forming a new compound with the water itself, or just breaking up—ions are in a free state, and we write the special state designation "(aq)" after their formulae. Covalent substances that dissolve in water (become *aqueous solutions*) without ionizing are also designated as such, although they leave molecules, not ions, in solution.

Ionization, like all chemical changes, involves heat transfer; thus, a solution in which an ionization is taking place can get very hot or very cold; in any case, it will show *some* change in temperature, if only imperceptibly.

Elements, it has been pointed out, ionize by gaining or losing electrons. Nonmetals tend to gain them because they are more *electronegative*; they have more relative ability to capture electrons. Metals are less able to hold onto their outer electrons, and so tend to lose them.

Compounds can also ionize by gaining or losing electrons when one of their component elements gains or loses. When this happens, though, the compound normally goes through other changes as well, such as disinitegrating fully to recombine anew. Neutral acids and bases on the other hand, which are covalent substances, become ions by gaining or losing protons, rather than electrons.

When the anion chlorite (ClO_2^-) gains a proton (H^+), it becomes chlorous acid ($HClO_2$). Conversely, an acid becomes an anion by giving up protons while keeping the electrons that compensated for the protons' charges. If an acid has multiple protons to spare but does not give up all of them, it is said to be *partially ionized* or to have undergone stewpwise ionization, to form an acid ion (more on this in Chaps. 6 and 9).

If some beryllium is left "exposed to the elements," so to speak, one of them, highly electronegative oxygen, attacks, stripping the metal of its two outer electrons to become oxide (O^{2-}) in ionic combination with beryllium ion (Be^{2+}). These two half-reactions (more on this in Chap. 10) are illustrated here. The formula unit is BeO.

Acids can ionize by reacting with and in water to form solutions of hydronium and the resultant anion. In the case of most soluble salts (which we may roughly define as mineral compounds that are usually—not always—ionic), the ions are hydrated with water molecules that are drawn to them by their charges (specifically, by their polarities).

Use this Table only to observe the pattern. Some of these elements can form more than one elemental ion. Hydrogen sometimes forms the 1- ion (in metal hydrides) and so is shown twice.

1A	2A	3A	4A	5A	6A	7A	8A
H^+							H^-
Li^+	Be^{2+}			N^{3-}	O^{2-}	F^-	
Na^+	Mg^{2+}	Al^{3+}		P^{3-}	S^{2-}	Cl^-	
K^+	Ca^{2+}	Ga^{3+}	Ge^{4+}	As^{3-}	Se^{2-}	Br^-	
Rb^+	Sr^{2+}	In^{3+}	Sn^{4+}		Te^{2-}	I^-	
Cs^+	Ba^{2+}	Tl^{3+}	Pb^{4+}				

ANIONS

charge of 1−

_____ permanganate

_____ nitrate*

_____ hydroxide

_____ cyanide*

charge of 2−

_____ sulfate*

_____ carbonate

charge of 3−

_____ phosphate*

CATIONS

charge of 1+

_____ hydronium

_____ ammonium

Note a periodic pattern in this table of the A families, which is the same Mini (or "basic") Table from the Prologue, but extended downwards.

The Family-1A metals form ions with a 1+ charge, because they have only one *valence electron* to lose. The 2A metals form 2+ ions, for they lose two electrons upon ionizing; and the 3A metals form 3+ ions for reasons that you can probably by now guess. The lightest 4A elements, however, seldom form elemental ions, preferring instead to help form molecules; yet the three metals beneath them, not surprisingly, form 4+ ions by giving up all four of their valence electrons. Tin and lead can also shed just two, though, to form 2+ ions. In this ability to form multiple ions, they are like the transition metals.

Then, starting with the 5A nonmetals, we count towards, not away from, zero. Family 5A elements *have room* for three more valence electrons, and so they most commonly form 3− ions; the 6A elements can accommodate two to form 2− ions; and the 7A elements, just one to form 1− ions.

At left are the names of the polyatomic ions that have been mentioned so far. Some (*) result from the total ionization of acids, and their charge is equal to the number of protons, or hydrogen ions (H^+) that were ionized from them. Write in the formula for each one, using the preceding pages if necessary.

⊛ Color, in the Mini-Table, Family 1A, violet; 2A, blue; 3A, indigo; 4A, green; 5A, yellow; 6A, orange; 7A, red. Do not color the unmarked squares.

First Energy of Ionization Periodicity

In the phrase "energy of ionization", the latter word has a more precise denotation than when used alone: it refers to the *work needed to pull an electron from the positively charged remainder of the atom of any element when excited to the gas state.* Do not confuse it with ionization itself, which can also come about through a gain in electrons or a gain or loss in protons.

The alkali metals give up an electron without much trouble, so the energy needed to ionize, in their cases, is low.

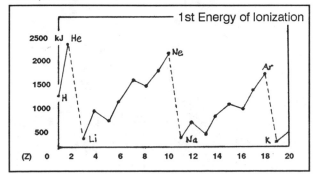

Moving across the Periodic Table towards the nonmetals, or from a period's lighter elements to its heavier ones, we see an increase in the energy of ionization; this lateral trend is a periodic function. Find cesium on a larger Periodic Table. A mole of this metal needs only 376 kilojoules (a kJ is a heat dimension) to ionize. Helium, at the extreme opposite corner, is so stable that it takes over 2400 kJ. Note the periodicity of the 20 elements from the original Mini-table: each period starts in a gully and ends in a peak.

In determining ionization energy values, the heat that is absorbed must be measured. Since this type of change absorbs heat, it is given a positive value and is said to be an *endothermic* change. Chemical changes such as combustion and the majority of reactions you will study in Chem. 1 liberate (or lose) heat, and so are given negative values to quantify heat loss; such changes are called *exothermic* (Greek, "heat outside"). More on all this in Chap. 7.

1. c   e   a   b   f   d

2. atomic weight, in amu; and molar weight, in grams

3. a. ½ N_2 ½ O_2 b. 1 Cu 1 Cl_2 c. 1 K 1 Mn 2 O_2

d. 10 C 11 H_2 e. 1 Ba 1 I_2 f. 2 C 1½ H_2 1 O_2

4. Atoms are discrete and, for our purposes at this point, indivisible; moles—which are 6.02 x 10^{23} atoms (or other particles), grains of sand, specimens of *Euglena coli*, or Brazilian bureaucrats—are indeed divisible. One can break this huge number into many smaller ones.

5. a. 253.8 grams   b. 56.36 grams   c. 120.4 grams   d. 180.2 grams   e. 132.9 grams

6. ? mols P = 160 g P x $\dfrac{\text{mol P}}{31.0 \text{ g P}}$ = 5.16 mols P

7. ? moles MgS = 500 g MgS x $\dfrac{\text{mol MgS}}{56.36 \text{ g MgS}}$ = 8.87 mols MgS

8. ? moles $C_6H_{12}O_6$ = 41.7 g $C_6H_{12}O_6$ x $\dfrac{\text{mol } C_6H_{12}O_6}{180 \text{ g } C_6H_{12}O_6}$ = 0.232 mols $C_6H_{12}O_6$

9. ? grams Si = 72 mols Si x $\dfrac{28.09 \text{ g Si}}{\text{mol Si}}$ = 2.0 x 10^3 g Si

10. ? grams N_2 = 933 mols x $\dfrac{28.01 \text{ g } N_2}{\text{mol } N_2}$ = 2.61 x 10^4 g N_2

11. ? grams $MgSO_4$ = 10.1 mols $MgSO_4$ x $\dfrac{120.4 \text{ g } MgSO_4}{\text{mol } MgSO_4}$ = 1.22 x 10^4 g $MgSO_4$

12. ? grams Be = 100 g BeO x $\dfrac{\text{mol BeO}}{25.01 \text{ g BeO}}$ x $\dfrac{\text{mol Be}}{\text{mol BeO}}$ x $\dfrac{9.012 \text{ g Be}}{\text{mol Be}}$ = 36.0 g Be = 36.0%

13. ? grams Ag = 100 g Ag_2O x $\dfrac{\text{mol } Ag_2O}{231.7 \text{ g } Ag_2O}$ x

$\dfrac{2 \text{ mols Ag}}{\text{mol } Ag_2O}$ x $\dfrac{107.9 \text{ g Ag}}{\text{mol Ag}}$ = 93.1 g Ag = 93.1%

14. A cyanide radical weighs 26.01 amu, so a mole of it must weigh 26.01 grams, so...

? grams CN^- = 100 g $Mn(CN)_3$ x $\dfrac{\text{mol } Mn(CN)_3}{132.9 \text{ g } Mn(CN)_3}$ x

$\dfrac{3 \text{ mols CN}}{\text{mol } Mn(CN)_3}$ x $\dfrac{26.01 \text{ g CN}}{\text{mol } CN^-}$ = 58.7 g CN^- = 58.7%

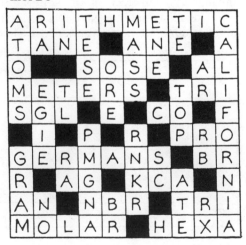

15. ? grams H_2O = 100 g $BaSO_4 \cdot 5H_2O$ x $\dfrac{\text{mol } BaSO_4 \cdot 5H_2O}{323.4 \text{ g } BaSO_4 \cdot 5H_2O}$ x $\dfrac{5 \text{ mols } H_2O}{\text{mol } BaSO_4 \cdot 5H_2O}$

x $\dfrac{18.00 \text{g } H_2O}{\text{mol } H_2O}$ x = 27.8 g H_2O = 27.8%

16. $100 - 72_F = 28_{Li}$

17. ? mols Pb atoms = 3.62×10^{25} Pb atoms x $\dfrac{\text{mol Pb atoms}}{6.02 \times 10^{23} \text{ Pb atoms}}$ = 50.0 mols Pb atoms

Answers, p. 58

1.6 mols SiO_2
5.26×10^3 g Br_2
(or 5.26 kg)
1.403 mols $KMnO_4$

Answers, p. 61

NO_3^-	62.01
CO_3^{2-}	60.01
PO_4^{3-}	94.97
OH^-	17.01
NH_4^+	19.05
$CuSO_4 \cdot 5H_2O$	251.0
$Na_2CO_3 \cdot 8H_2O$	250.1
$FeCl_2 \cdot 6H_2O$	234.8

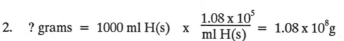

1. $(200-315) + 273 = 473-588K$

2. ? grams = 1000 ml H(s) x $\dfrac{1.08 \times 10^5}{\text{ml H(s)}}$ = 1.08×10^8 g

3. ? lugnuts = 759 cars x $\dfrac{5 \text{ wheels}}{\text{car}}$ x $\dfrac{4 \text{ lugnuts}}{\text{wheel}}$
   = 1.52×10^4 lugnuts

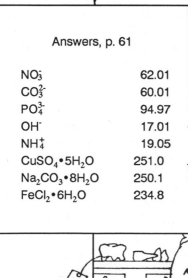

2.7 Ionic Combinations

DON'T THE TRANSITION METALS FORM IONS? AND WHAT ABOUT THE ELEMENTS THAT FORM MORE THAN JUST ONE ION?

I HAVE DEVELOPED A MNEMONIC SYSTEM TO LEARN THEM ALL.

In the first place, all the transition elements are metals, so they form only cations (with extremely rare exceptions). We do not need, at this or any point, to learn every elemental ion that there is; those that appear in this and in the previous section will suffice for now, and a few more will be introduced later.

The pattern shown on p. 69—which is essentially counting from 1 to 4 and then back to 1—shows us the charges, for the most part, of the A Families. Recall, though, that tin and lead also form 2+ ions. Just remember that $2 + 2 = 4$ and that there are 2 metals in Family 4A that both form 2+ and 4+ ions.

® Do not color the blank squares. Choose a light color for each group, coloring both the squares and the tiles in the legend (below) that identify them. Copper, the inter-section of two, will be striped.

Legend:
- 1A cations
- 2A cations
- Cr to Co
- mercury
- NCZ
- coinage ions
- 3-4A cations
- 5-6A anions
- halides

1A	2A	3B	4B	5B	6B	7B	8B	8B	8B	1B	2B	3A	4A	5A	6A	7A	8A
H^+																H^-	
Li^+	Be^{2+}													N^{3-}	O^{2-} O_2^{2-}	F^-	
Na^+	Mg^{2+}											Al^{3+}		P^{3-}	S^{2-}	Cl^-	
K^+	Ca^{2+}				Cr^{2+} Cr^{3+}	Mn^{2+} Mn^{3+}	Fe^{2+} Fe^{3+}	Co^{2+} Co^{3+}	Ni^{2+}	Cu^+ Cu^{2+}	Zn^{2+}					Br^-	
										Ag^+			Sn^{2+} Sn^{4+}			I^-	
	Ba^{2+}							Au^+	Hg^{2+} Hg_2^{2+}		Pb^{2+} Pb^{4+}						

Now look at the four metals beginning with chromium and think of "2 or 3 Cringing Matrons Fearing Cobwebs" (some of these form still more ions, but you need not worry about them for now). The next three Period 4 metals are the "Nickel-Copper Zone," a region of 2+ ions. The NCZ intersects the 1+ region, the coinage metals. This leaves only one oddball, mercury, whose atoms form 2+ ions, but singly or in pairs.

Note that among elemental anions that oxygen does the same thing as mercury, although its ions are negatively charged (are anions). The system of naming multiple elemental ions and writing their formulae is easy. We use the name of the metal with a Roman numeral in parentheses that identifies the charge. Thus, Cu^+ is copper (I) ion and pronounced "copper one," while Cu^{2+} is "copper two." K^+ and Al^{3+} are simply called potassium ion and aluminum ion, because they can be said to form no others (the word "ion" is therefore obligatory).

Again, the oddball is mercury. Hg^{2+} is, naturally, mercury (II) ion, but Hg_2^{2+} is mercury (I) ion. The way to learn these is to think of each atom in mercury (I) contributing *one* charge to the ion, while the lone atom in mercury (II) contributes *two* charges. Like all elemental anions, H^- and O_2^{2-} contain the -ide suffix. Their names are hydride ion and peroxide ion.

Fill in the names and formulae

O_2^{2-}	_____	_____ mercury (II)
Cr^{2+}	_____	_____ nickel ion
Zn^{2+}	_____	_____ hydroxide
Fe^{3+}	_____	_____ lead (IV)
Hg_2^{2+}	_____	_____ cobalt (III)
P^{3-}	_____	_____ oxide
Sn^{4+}	_____	_____ iron (II)
Ag^+	_____	_____ sodium ion

-ate = O_3; charge = 1-			
ClO_4^-	*per-*	chlor	*-ate*
ClO_3^-		chlor	*-ate*
ClO_2^-		chlor	*-ite*
ClO^-	*hypo-*	chlor	*-ite*
BrO_3^-		brom	*-ate*
BrO_2^-		brom	*-ite*
BrO^-	*hypo-*	brom	*-ite*
IO_4^-	*per-*	iod	*-ate*
IO_3^-		iod	*-ate*
NO_3^-		nitr	*-ate*
NO_2^-		nitr	*-ite*
MnO_4^-	*per-*	mangan	*-ate*
O_2^{2-}	*per-*	ox	*-ide*

-ate = O_4; charge = 2-			
CO_3^{2-}		carbon	*-ate*
$C_2O_4^{2-}$		oxal	*-ate*
SO_4^{2-}		sulf	*-ate*
SO_3^{2-}		sulf	*-ite*
CrO_4^{2-}		chrom	*-ate*
$Cr_2O_7^{2-}$	*di-*	chrom	*-ate*

-ate = O_4; charge = 3-			
PO_4^{3-}		phosph	*-ate*
PO_3^{3-}		phosph	*-ite*

oxyanions with no pattern			
OH^-		hydrox	*-ide*
$C_2H_3O_2^-$		acet-	*-ate*
$S_2O_3^{2-}$	*thio-*	sulf-	*-ate*

There is a hierarchy of affixes in the naming of oxyanions that we use to name ions from their formulae, not only for these but others you will encounter later on. A parallel system for naming acids will be examined in Chap. 9.

per-	root	*-ate*	stuffed and saturated with oxygen
	root	*-ate*	full, no more, no less, with oxygen
	root	*-ite*	somewhat oxygen anemic
hypo-	root	*-ite:*	severely oxygen-anemic; suffocating

After reading each of the following "rules," ponder the chart and the affix explanations until you understand the point.

(1) The "root-*ate*" combination is the one from which the others derive: *per*-root-*ate* means one more oxygen; root-*ite* means one less oxygen; and *hypo*-root-*ite* means two less.

(2) When root-*ate* means three oxygens, it also means a charge of 1−, unless the ion has carbon.

(3) When root-*ate* has one more oxygen, it also has one more charge (O_4, 2−) unless the ion has phosphorus.

The six common 2− oxyanions shown above are a "soccer" (SCCr) team; they contain sulfur, carbon, or chromium. Oxalate, sulfate, and chromate are all team players to the full. So is sulfite, for it is anemic sulfate. Dichromate, the Siamese twins, try to be, but between them they only "ate" seven oxygens, not eight, as the two chromiums might seem to indicate. Carbon, in the form of CO_3^{2-}, is again the exception, but only halfway (in number of oxygens, but not charge) and so spends half its time in the penalty box.

(4) Look at the elemental anions on p. 70. They happen to have the same charges as do the oxyanions they are part of; memorize them together. The halogen oxyanions have a charge of 1−. The sulfur-containing oxyanions have 2−. The phosphorus-containing ones have 3−.

But do the nitrogen-containing oxyanions follow this pattern? Read their formulae as if they were words: NO!

Three other oxyanions—hydroxide, acetate, and thiosulfate—and two important polyatomic anions without oxygen—cyanide (CN^-) and thiocyanate (SCN^-)—fit no pattern and must therefore be learned by rote.

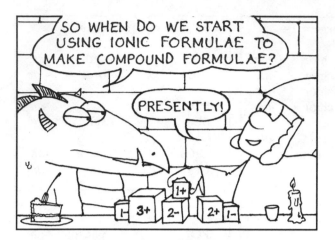

Ions, as we know, are charged particles that can form neutral compounds, some of which are covalent. The key to ion combining is the equality between the negative charges and the positive ones.

For example, lithium ion (1+) and chloride ion (1−) have equal and commensurate charges and form the salt lithium chloride:

$$Li^+ + Cl^- \rightarrow LiCl$$

The same is true of calcium ion and sulfate:

$$Ca^{2+} + SO_4^{2-} \rightarrow CaSO_4$$

What if the charges are unequal? Highly reactive lithium can also bond with nitrogen, but, as always, its ions have a charge of 1+ while nitride has 3−. To create a stable, neutral compound therefore, three lithium ions are needed for each nitride:

$$3Li^+ + N^{3-} \rightarrow Li_3N$$

Now, let us go on to radicals. In most reactions, they remain intact, retaining their charges and identities just like the simple elemental ions. Note how nitrite (1−) combines with sodium and magnesium. With sodium, it is one-on-one:

$$Na^+ + NO_2^- \rightarrow NaNO_2$$

...but two nitrites are needed to balance the double charge of the magnesium:

$$Mg^{2+} + 2NO_2^- \rightarrow Mg(NO_2)_2$$

Remember that nitrite will (in most cases) keep its identity. If the compound contains more than one nitrite, the radical's formula must be parenthetically separated from the subscript that quantifies it. Otherwise, we would have, in the current example, "$MgNO_{22}$," which not only does not exist, but it violates both the Law of Conservation of Mass and common sense.

Look again at the formula for lithium nitride (not *tri*lithium nitride, for lithium does not bond in multiple proportions with nitrogen, so there is no other lithium/nitrogen compound to confuse it with). The charge superscripts have disappeared and the three lithiums are quantified in the formula by a subscript that comes from the coefficient in the equation.

In the diagram below, highly electronegative nitrogen strips three lithium atoms of their single valence electrons, becoming in the process a nitride ion. As such, it has a strong mutual attraction for the now positive lithiums, and so bonds with them. While there will be little actual sharing of the electrons, molecules nevertheless result for reasons of bonding geometry that will be discussed in Chap. 3.

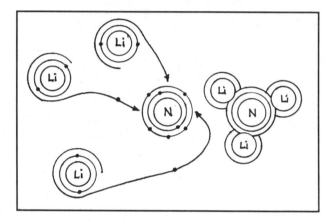

Parentheses are needed even when the multiplied radical has no subscripts of its own:

$$K^+ + OH^- \rightarrow KOH$$

(but...) $$Al^{3+} + 3OH^- \rightarrow Al(OH)_3$$

and not, to be sure, "$AlOH_3$."

When ammonium radicals bond with a polyatomic anion, they, like other cations, are written first in the formula. If there is more than one of them, they, too, are put in parentheses:

$$NH_4^+ + C_2H_3O_2^- \rightarrow NH_4C_2H_3O_2$$

(but...) $$3NH_4^+ + PO_4^{3-} \rightarrow (NH_4)_3PO_4$$

Incidentally, the first of these two products (ammonium acetate) has one nitrogen atom and seven hydrogen atoms (count them and see for yourself); but ammonium phosphate has three nitrogens and 12 hydrogens, for the subscript outside of the radical (3) acts as a multiplier of the subscripts within the parentheses (1,4).

If we know the formulae of ions, including their charges, we can name ionic compounds from their formulae or do the reverse and spell the formulae from the names.

We know that oxide always carries a charge of 2−, but that iron has multiple possibilities: iron (II) and iron (III). Oxide and iron (II), then, are balanced, and combine neatly and simply:

$$Fe^{2+} + O^{2-} \rightarrow FeO$$

Since the product contains the iron (II) ion, the name of the compound is iron (II) oxide ("iron-two-oxide"). The formula, with its subscripts, is Fe_1O_1.

These subscripts will have to be adjusted, however, if oxide combines with iron (III), for the charges do not balance. We look, then, for the lowest common multiple of 2 and 3 which, of course, is 6.

This means that there must be enough of each ion present to contribute six equal, opposing charges. Oxide has a charge of 2−, so three of them are needed; but only two iron (III) ions are required, for they have a treble charge.

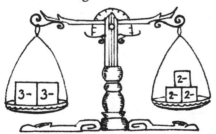

In other words, it takes two Fe^{3+} ions to offset, neutralize, or compensate for—however you wish to think of it—the three O^{2-} ions.

$$2Fe^{3+} + 3O^{2-} \rightarrow Fe_2O_3$$

Do not read this formula as "iron-two-oxide" just because the subscript is 2; the charge of the iron ion is 3+, so its name is iron (III) oxide.

Now we can look at some formulae. Lead has two ions, Pb^{2+} and Pb^{4+}. Fluorine has but one ion, fluoride, F^-. By knowing the invariability of ionic fluorine (1−), the charges of the lead ions in PbF_2 and PbF_4 are easily deduced. The compounds can then be named: lead (II) and lead (IV) fluoride. These are lead's multiple proportions with fluorine.

These lead ions can also bond with sulfate to form $PbSO_4$ and $Pb(SO_4)_2$. How can these be named from their formulae? In the same way as the others.

Ask yourself this: what is the negative, and invariable charge of the anion compound (the radical)? Sulfate contributes 2−, so the lead in $PbSO_4$ must put in 2+; together, then, they form lead (II) sulfate. The total charge of the two sulfates in the other formula is 4−, so a lead (IV) ion is needed to balance them, and the product is lead (IV) sulfate.

Error Analysis

There are three common types of errors in formula literacy; two have already been warned against.

(1) Failure to isolate and quantify radicals with parentheses when there is more than one of the same species.

(2) Confusing the *charge* of a cation in a formula with its *number*, as indicated by the subscript.

(3) Applying covalent nomenclature to ionic compounds, or the reverse. Cobalt (III) oxide cannot be "dicobalt trioxide" or some such thing. As Co_2O_3 is made up of ions, so, too, must its name be.

Covalent compounds are molecular individualists and, therefore, Greek in nature. Ionic compounds, on the other hand, are orderly and regimented, and so are Roman. The Greek prefixes and the Roman numerals in their spelled out names are thus a sure clue to their bonding identities (and you can forget all about Greek capitals).

1. Match these:

_____anion	a. element that forms both a monatomic and a poyatomic elemental cation
_____hydrate	b. polyatomic ion corresponding to oxygen-containing acids
_____mercury	c. element that forms two monatomic cations
_____exothermic	d. chemical change that absorbs heat
_____neutral atom	e. an ion with more electrons than protons
_____carbon	f. element that almost always forms covalent bonds
_____radical	g. has equal numbers of protons and electrons
_____iron	h. element that forms both a monatomic anion and a monatomic cation
_____oxyanion	i. chemical change that liberates heat
_____valence electron	j. element that forms both a monatomic and a polyatomic elemental anion
_____hydrogen	k. the general name, in this book, for polyatomic anions
_____cation	l. ion with more protons than electrons
_____oxygen	m. an entity that, when lost or gained, results in an ion
_____endothermic	n. polyatomic particle containing whole water molecules

2. Now match these. There are a few that will be unfamiliar (have not been seen in this book); but using elimination and deduction, they, too, can be matched.

_____PO_4^{3-}	_____$H_2C_2O_4$	_____HCO_3^-	a. oxalic acid	d. phosphite	g. iodic acid
_____HIO_3	_____C^{4-}	_____AsO_3^{3-}	b. arsenite	e. arsenate	h. phosphate
_____AsO_4^{3-}	_____PO_3^{3-}	_____HIO_4	c. periodic acid	f. methanide	i. hydrogen carbonate

3. Write out the full names of these ionic formulae:

BeS	_____	$Zn_3(PO_4)_2$	_____
NaH	_____	HgI_2	_____
CuF_2	_____	CoO	_____
Hg_2I_2	_____	$AgBrO_3$	_____
$KMnO_4$	_____	Na_2SO_3	_____
FeS_2O_3	_____	$Pb(ClO_4)_4$	_____
$Al(ClO)_3$	_____	NH_4SCN	_____

Cr_2O_3	_____
$(NH_4)_2Cr_2O_7$	_____
Li_2CO_3	_____
$Ni(IO_4)_2$	_____
$KClO_2$	_____
$Hg(C_2H_3O_2)_2$	_____
CrO	_____

$SnF_4 \cdot 4H_2O$ _____ $MnSO_4 \cdot 8H_2O$ _____

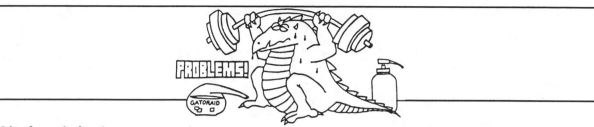

4. Write formula for these compounds:

_____barium bromide   _____calcium nitrate   _____sodium cyanide

_____antimony hydride   _____chromium (II) sulfate   _____mangan. (III) chlorate

_____nickel chloride   _____tin (II) phosphate   _____beryllium phosphate

_____iron (III) sulfide   _____silver nitrate   _____sodium chromate

_____sodium peroxide   _____ammonium chlorate   _____iron (II) hypobromite

_____cobalt (II) chlorite   _____potassium iodate   _____calcium oxalate

_____boron perchlorate trihydrate   _____lead (II) nitrite pentahydrate

(The answers to this problem set are on p. 80.)

1. What is the molar weight of acetic acid ($HC_2H_3O_2$)?

2. Name the following covalent compounds: SO_2, SiF_4, As_2O_5

3. Give the percent weight of element in $(NH_4)_2S$. Use dimensional analysis to get the percentages for hydrogen and nitrogen, and (then) subtraction to get the sulfur percentage.

LET'S LUNCH BEFORE LAUNCH, AVO. THEN WE'LL HAVE A BLAST, BUT ON A FULL STOMACH.

1
H
1.0079

$\mathfrak{Profile:}$ $\mathfrak{Hydrogen}$

Information from Pioneer II suggests that the giant planets are vast hydrogen seas with some CH_4 and NH_3.

Hydrogen is the ultimate element, for all others are theoretically fissionable to it. It is, further, the commonest element in the universe, accounting for well over 90% of all matter. It is the nuclear fusion of hydrogen atoms into helium atoms that fuels the stars.

On Earth, however, hydrogen makes up something less than one percent of the total mass of the Earth's crust, and, in its elemental form, is a diatomic gas that does not liquify until its temperature is brought down to 20 K; it only solidifies at 13 K. It has no odor or color, but it is very flammable, reacting with oxygen to yield steam. It was for this that the famous German airship, the *Hindenburg*, exploded in 1939. Since then, heavier but fully inert helium has been used as the lift medium.

Hydrogen was isolated by Cavendish in 1783 when he was testing acids on metals. All acids contain hydrogen and, when they are able, react with (or oxidize, to be specific) metal. Ions of the metal substitute themselves in the acid for the hydrogen ions, which then pick up the electrons left behind by the ionizing metal and vaporize. The reaction of nitric acid with zinc, for example, produces the diatomic gas and the salt, zinc nitrate:

$$Zn + 2HNO_3 \rightarrow H_2{\uparrow} + Zn(NO_3)_2$$

The hydrogen ion (H^+) is important in chemistry because it makes a solution acidic in proportion to its presence. This ion does not exist as a stable pure substance; rather, it is always part of something else or on its way to becoming a part. In water solutions, it is hydrated as the hydronium ion (H_3O^+) and can be written this way or as H^+(aq), even though hydro-

nium is a true radical. The "sourness" of acids is a rain of these ions on the olfactory receptors of the tongue and the nose. So, for all their invisibility, hydrogen ions—mere hydrated protons, in deed—can be literally tasted.

The most important hydrogen compound is water, and so it is not for nothing that the element's name means "water-former." While water is clearly covalent, it can both form from ions (such as in an acid/base neutralization), or yield them (as in electrolysis). In either case, the ions are H^+ and hydroxide, OH^-, which is to another class of chemicals—the bases—what hydrogen ion is to the acids. The rare hydride ion (H^-), a proton with two electrons, is found only in combination with certain weakly electronegative metals.

In the hydrogenation process, hydrogen is added to oils and other carbon compounds to render them fully or partially hydrogenated (the former of these is saturation). This is how margerine is made from oil.

The detonation of a hydrogen warhead is the actualization of three nuclear reactions. First, a conventional, uranium-fueled fission bomb is exploded as a trigger, releasing excess neutrons and a temperature of a few million Kelvins:

$$^{235}U_{critical} \rightarrow {}^{84}Kr + {}^{138}Ba + 2n + \triangle$$

This is only fission; things are cool yet. The neutrons strike a lithium-6 target, producing tritium:

$$n + {}^6Li \rightarrow He + T + \triangle$$

At the peak temperature, which lasts only a nanosecond, the fresh tritium undergoes fusion with a deuterium source, and...well, they don't call it thermonuclear for nothing!

2.8 Empirical Formulae

THE CHUNK OF SODIUM YOU LEFT OUT REACTED WITH OXYGEN FROM THE AIR. YOU KNEW THIS WOULD HAPPEN.

OF COURSE... BUT ALL THIS FORMULA THEORY MADE ME DESIRE TO TEST THE DATA PERSONALLY. I AM AN EMPIRICIST.

THE 300-GRAM SAMPLE OF SODIUM METAL HAS CONVERTED TO A HOARY WHITE OXIDE WEIGHING 404 GRAMS... THEREFORE, THE OXYGEN ADDED 104 GRAMS.

By knowing the weight of each element in a sample, Curie can determine a formula, first by converting the grams of each component into moles (Sect. 2.4) and then by reducing the mole ratios to the simplest whole-number ratios. Here are the grams-to-moles conversions:

$$? \text{ mols Na} = 300 \text{ g Na} \times \frac{\text{mol Na}}{23.00 \text{ g Na}} = 13 \text{ moles Na}$$

$$? \text{ mols O} = 104 \text{ g O} \times \frac{\text{mol O}}{16.00 \text{ g O}} = 6.5 \text{ mols O}$$

From this, we know that 6.5 moles of oxygen atoms are bonded to 13 moles of sodium atoms. To get the ratio we want, we simply divide both answers by the least of the two:

$$(\text{O}) \ \frac{6.5}{6.5} = 1 \qquad (\text{Na}) \ \frac{13}{6.5} = 2$$

The simplest whole-number ratio, therefore, is 2:1. From it comes Na_2O, the *empirical formula*; empirical because it can be determined using only atomic weights and simple experimentation.

The empirical formula may or may not also be the *actual* formula for the compound; sodium oxide might just as well be Na_4O_2 or even $Na_{700}O_{350}$. To make this further determination would require more information, but the empirical formula brings us at least half the distance by limiting the possible formulae to the ratio that we calculated, as shown, from empirical data.

If nothing else, we know that Na_2O—because it is ionic—will have one oxide for every two sodium ions (recall that ions weigh virtually the same as their neutral counterparts, and so the Periodic Table weights apply fully to them).

Here are some examples of true, or actual, formulae reduced to their empirical formulae:

compound	true	empirical
hydrogen peroxide	H_2O_2	HO
decene	$C_{10}H_{20}$	CH_2
dinitrogen tetroxide	N_2O_4	NO_2
fructose	$C_6H_{12}O_6$	CH_2O
sucrose	$C_{12}H_{22}O_{11}$	$C_{12}H_{22}O_{11}$
boric acid	H_3BO_3	H_3BO_3
manganese (II) sulfide	MnS	MnS

N_2O_4 AND NO_2 ARE TRUE COMPOUNDS, BUT NOT HO AND CH_2!

AUGH!

THIS IS OF NO CONSEQUENCE. SOME EMPIRICAL FORMULAE ARE NOT ACTUAL COMPOUNDS.

77

Normally, the given data will be in percentages. This is no problem; we just act as if the percentages were instead given in grams, as in this example:

A salt is 25.7% calcium, 33.3% chromium, and the remainder is oxygen (if you do not know how to get the oxygen, you could be suffering from the onset of Mindless Robotic Zombieism; check problem 16, in the problem set on pp. 62-64 as a last resort). What is the empirical formula of the salt?

grams	Ca 25.7g	Cr 33.3g	O 16 g
moles	Ca .641	Cr .641	O 2.56
ratio	Ca 1	Cr 1	O 3.98

This is the GamMa Ray system. Grams, moles, and the whole-number ratio each have a line in the grid, and a syllable beginning with its initial, in correct order, in the phrase.

The first line is for the given information, so, right now, fill it in (25.7 for Ca, etc.).

Now do the first "row of arithmetic" in which we change those grams into moles, as in the examples on p. 77 and in Sect. 2.4:

$$? \text{ mols Ca } = 25.7 \text{ g Ca} \times \frac{\text{mol Ca}}{40.08 \text{ g Ca}} = .641 \text{ mols Ca}$$

$$? \text{ mols Cr} = 33.3 \text{ g Cr} \times \frac{\text{mol Cr}}{51.966 \text{ g Cr}} = .641 \text{ mols Cr}$$

$$? \text{ mols O } = 41.0 \text{ g O} \times \frac{\text{mol O}}{16.00 \text{ g O}} = 2.56 \text{ mols O}$$

Now, write these answers on the mole line, above. The second—and often last—row of arithmetic is to divide each of these answers by the least of them, as in the example with Na_2O:

$$(Ca) \ \frac{.644}{.644} = 1 \ \ (Cr) \ \frac{.644}{.644} = 1 \ \ (O) \ \frac{2.56}{.644} = 3.98$$

The answer for oxygen, as you can see, is really only a close approximation of a whole number. This does not matter. In fact, this is even to be expected for one or more such quotients in each problem, because the percentages whence they came were also inexact.

Write these answers—the *rounded* simple whole numbers—on the ratio line. The empirical formula comes directly from these; they are the very subscripts in the formula, which is $CaCrO_4$ ($Ca_1Cr_1O_4$).

The salt is calcium chromate and, as the ratio is already at its simplest, the empirical formula is also the true one.

Empirical formulae are easy. If you can write the GamMa Ray grid, you almost cannot fail to recall the steps.

In some cases, though, getting an empirical formula for a relatively complex compound will require an extra step—an algebraic adjustment.

An example: give the empirical formula of cortizone, if it is 60.3% carbon, 5.64% hydrogen, 22.3% oxygen, and 11.7% nitrogen.

grams	C $60.3g$	H $5.64g$	O $22.3g$	N $11.7g$
moles	C 5.01	H 5.58	O 1.39	N 0.835
ratio	C 6.00	H 6.68	O 1.66	N 1
adj.	C 18.00	H 20.04	O 4.99	N 3

ONE Begin, as before, by filling in the blanks with the given information and do the first step: the grams-to-moles conversion. If your conversions are correct, you should get 5.01 moles of carbon, 5.58 moles hydrogen, 1.39 moles of oxygen, and 0.835 mols of nitrogen. Write these on the mole line, above.

TWO Do the second step by dividing all the mole values by the smallest of them. This time, you should get 6.00 for oxygen, 6.68 for hydrogen, and, 1.67 for oxygen, and 1.00 for nitrogen.

THREE Unlike in the two previous examples, the resulting ratio is not, as you can see, made up entirely of whole numbers. The way out of this problem is to multiply all of them by another whole number, namely the smallest number that will make the other numbers whole. At worst this may take a little trial and error, while at other times it will probably occur to you immediately. In the above example, it is three. Multiplying the ratio line by three gives us the formula's subscripts on the adjustment line and, therefore, the forumla itself: $C_{18}H_{20}O_5N_3$. Curiously, this last step is no problem for many students, until they realize that it is algebra (at which time they develop an unreasoning terror of it).

—The "Grid-Only" GamMa Ray System—

grams	C $\dfrac{60.3}{12.01}$	H $\dfrac{5.64}{1.008}$	O $\dfrac{22.3}{16.00}$	N $\dfrac{11.7}{14.00}$
moles	C $\dfrac{5.01}{.835}$	H $\dfrac{5.58}{.835}$	O $\dfrac{1.39}{.835}$	N $\dfrac{.835}{.835}$
ratio	C $\dfrac{6.00}{3x}$	H $\dfrac{6.68}{3x}$	O $\dfrac{1.67}{3x}$	N $\dfrac{1.00}{3x}$
adj.	C 18	H 20	O 5	N 3

With the Grid-Only GamMa Ray tour de force, you need never even lift your pencil from the grid. Instead of a DA bridge for each molar conversion, just write the atomic weight directly under the gram quantities and perform an ordinary division operation.

Then, when you get your row of quotients on the moles line, just write the smallest of them under each of these, and do the second row of automatically set-up division operations.

Finally, if the results are not whole, write the multiplier under each line, and multiply. If you cannot master this shortcut, you do not *deserve* to pass chemistry.

1. e n a i g f k c b m h l j d **2.** h g e a f d i b c **3. (and) 4.**

BeS	beryllium sulfide	$Zn_3(PO_4)_2$ zinc phosphate	Cr_2O_3 chromium (III) oxide
NaN	sodium hydride	HgI_2 mercury (II) iodide	$(NH_4)_2Cr_2O_7$ ammon. dichromate
CuF_2	copper (II) fluoride	CoO cobalt (II) oxide	Li_2CO_3 lithium carbonate
Hg_2I_2	mercury (I) iodide	$AgBrO_3$ silver bromate	$Ni(IO_4)_2$ nickel periodate
$KMnO_4$	potassium permanganate	Na_2SO_3 sodium sulfite	$KClO_2$ potassium chlorite
FeS_2O_3	iron (II) thiosulfate	$Pb(ClO_4)_4$ lead (IV) perchlorate	$Hg(C_2H_3O_2)_2$ mercury (II) acetate
$Al(ClO)_3$	aluminum hypochlorite	NH_4SCN ammonium thiocyanate	CrO chromium (II) oxide

$SnF_4 \cdot 4H_2O$ tin (IV) fluoride tetrahydrate $MnSO_4 \cdot 8H_2O$ manganese (II) sulfate octahydrate

$BaBr_2$	barium bromide	$Ca(NO_3)_2$ calcium nitrate	NaCN sodium cyanide
SbH_3	antimony hydride	$CrSO_4$ chromium (II) sulfate	$Mn(ClO_3)_3$ mangan. (III) chlorate
$NiCl_2$	nickel chloride	$Sn_3(PO_4)_2$ tin (II) phosphate	$Be_3(PO_4)_2$ beryllium phosphate
Fe_2S_3	iron (III) sulfide	$AgNO_3$ silver nitrate	Na_2CrO_4 sodium chromate
Na_2O_2	sodium peroxide	$NHClO_3$ ammonium chlorate	$Fe(BrO)_2$ iron (II) hypobromite
$Co(ClO_2)_2$	cobalt (II) chlorite	KIO_3 potassium iodate	CaC_2O_4 calcium oxalate

$B(ClO_4)_3 \cdot 3H_2O$ boron perchlorate trihydrate $Pb(NO_3)_2 \cdot 5H_2O$ lead (II) nitrate pentahydrate

1. $\quad$ H 4(1.008) = 4.032
    $\quad$ C 2(12.01) = 24.02
    $\quad$ O 2(16.00) = 32.00
    $\qquad\qquad\qquad$ 60.05

2. sulfur dioxide
    silicon tetrafluoride
    diarsenic pentoxide

3. $? \, g \, N = 100 \, g \, (NH_4)_2S \times \dfrac{mol \, (NH_4)_2S}{68.09 \, g \, (NH_4)_2S} \times \dfrac{2 \, mols \, N}{mol \, (NH_4)_2S} \times \dfrac{14.01 \, g \, N}{mol \, N} = 41.2 \, g \, N = 41.2\%$

$\quad$ $? \, g \, H = 100 \, g \, (NH_4)_2S \times \dfrac{mol \, (NH_4)_2S}{68.09 \, g \, (NH_4)_2S} \times \dfrac{8 \, mols \, H}{mol \, (NH_4)_2S} \times \dfrac{1.008 \, g \, H}{mol \, H} = 11.9 \, g \, H = 11.9\%$

For sulfur: 100 − 41.2 − 11.9 = 46.9%

2.9 % Composition II Impurities

WE SHOULD BE ABLE TO EXPRESS THE COMPONENTS OF IMPURE OR MIXED SAMPLES AS PERCENTAGES...

PITCHBLENDE PROVIDED COURTESY OF THE GOVERNMENT OF AUSTRIA AND HUNGARY

U_3O_8 (imp.)

...HMM. THIS BOHEMIAN PITCH-BLENDE IS MOST HETEROGENEOUS... BITS OF IT GLOW IN THE DARK...

In Sect. 2.5, we studied percentages of elements in compounds, using particles as models. The same principles apply to using dimensional analysis to determine percent compositions of impure substances.

As before, the given number is always 100. The given and wanted dimensions will also be the same and, in general chemistry, they will usually be grams. A familiar peril is carried over from those problems, however, for labeling is of paramount import.

There are two classes of pure substances. The elements are those which *cannot* be broken down into other pure substances, and the compounds—as you also know—are those that *can* be broken down into others, namely elements and/or other compounds. In any case, a compound is a chemical combination.

A *mixture*, on the other hand, is a physical combination of pure substances. For chemists, then, mixtures are impure substances, particularly when a certain component, a *purity,* is sought or must be quantified within the sample.

Think of pencils and erasers as elements that can bond chemically. Together, they form a compound, but together or separate, they are pure substances.

Toasters and blenders, however, can also combine, but they obviously cannot bond. In other words, they can form a mixture but not a compound. If the appliances are stored together in unmarked boxes, they are a *homogeneous* mixture, one that is *apparently* the same throughout. If removed from the boxes and piled up, they are a *heterogeneous* mixture, one that is obviously made up of distinct and unrelated parts.

Raw milk is a heterogeneous mixture of cream and milk, for one of these can be seen floating on top of the other. Homogenization, then, is so-called because it agitates the cream and milk to the point where, as a mixture, they appear to be a single substance.

Solutions in which the components are not chemically bonded are homogeneous mixtures.

If water is the solvent, then we have an aqueous solution.

Pure Substances

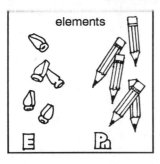

elements

compound

Mixtures

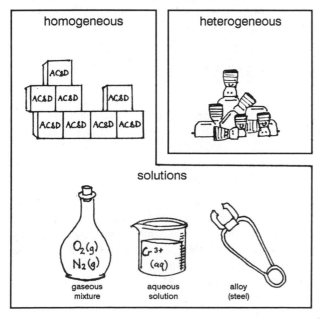

homogeneous

heterogeneous

solutions

O_2(g) N_2(g)
gaseous mixture

Cr^{3+} (aq)
aqueous solution

alloy (steel)

If you can determine the percentage of an element in a compound, you can just as easily determine the percentage of a purity in an impurity. *The purity*, for the sake of dimensional analysis, *is the wanted*, and *the impurity is the given.*

Beyond that, the definition of an impurity, even when limited to chemical contexts, is many-faceted. It may be an ore, an alloy, an aqueous solution, or even a gaseous one. An ore contains one or more metal compounds—often oxides—and other substances, and so is a mixture. Most other impurities that chemists are familiar with are of the homogeneous type. This includes samples of air, although the air over Milan, a very large sample of a gaseous solution, is infamously heterogeneous, what with its layers of contamination. On the whole, however, the atmosphere of the Earth may be thought of as impure nitrogen, or an impure solution of N_2 and O_2.

For our examples, let us begin with ores. A mining concern is testing ore samples to see if they contain sufficient metal to be commercially worthwhile. They do this by reducing completely a 30.0-gram sample of copper ore. If the sample yields 5.80 grams of pure copper, what is the percent weight of the copper in the ore? The set-up and solution are like those of any other percent-weight problem:

$$? \text{ grams Cu } = 100 \text{ g Cu imp } \times \frac{5.80 \text{ g Cu}}{30.0 \text{ g Cu imp}} = 19.3 \text{ g Cu } = 19.3\%$$

This problem is very simple. The only conversion factor is the keystone itself (a keystone, you will recall, is that conversion factor which gets us from the given quantity to the wanted quantity). Suppose, though, that the mining company came across some platinum ore. The pure metal, because it is so rare, will probably be measured in milligrams rather than grams when they finally isolate it. If another 30.0-gram sample is analyzed, this time for platinum, and 76 milligrams are yielded, what percentage of the ore is this? Because the purity is in milligrams, so also must be the impurity. Therefore, after we write our set-up, we need to convert the impurity's dimension (grams) to the purity's dimension with a conversion factor. This conversion will connect us to the keystone, and another will take us from it (with its unwanted dimension), back to grams (the wanted dimension), and the answer:

$$? \text{ g Pt } = 100 \text{ g Pt imp } \times \frac{1.0 \times 10^3 \text{ mg Pt imp}}{\text{g Pt imp}} \times \frac{76 \text{ mg Pt}}{3.0 \times 10^4 \text{ mg Pt imp}} \times \frac{\text{g Pt}}{1.0 \times 10^3 \text{ mg Pt imp}}$$
$$= 2.53 \text{ g Pt } = 2.53\%$$

...but here is a shortcut: by remembering that a gram is equal to 1000 milligrams, you can move the decimal for the purity quantity three places to the left. This way, you will not have to bother with milligrams in the first place, because 76 mg = 0.076 g. There is no need, then, to convert back and forth:

$$? \text{ g Pt } = 100 \text{ g Pt imp } \times \frac{0.076 \text{ g Pt}}{30.0 \text{ g Pt imp}} = 2.53 \text{ g Pt}$$

Another common application of percent-weight calculations is the determination of the weight of a dissolved substance in an aqueous solution. For this, we will need the density of the solution, which we get by measuring the two parameters that make up density—mass and volume—and writing them as a conversion factor. We will also need the density of the dissolved substance, or solute. Since it is already part of the solution in question, however, we must depend on another source of information, such as the Handbook of Chemistry and Physics or, in the case of a test, the problem itself.

If all this seems like a lot to remember, then do not try to memorize it all at once (it will eventually, with practice, be mastered instinctively). For now, just recall that all the conversion factors relevant to a problem should be written down prior to the set up. Then, as always, you will find the given, and make it into a question relating it to the wanted, and then join the conversion factors to it in standard DA fashion (by making a numerator reappear in the denominator of the next segment of the bridge). And, of course, expect unstated conversion factors. Most of the language in DA problems is really only elaborate circumlocution of the word *per*. Think of it as reducing, as it were, a "complicated" problem from its impurities.

In fact, a percent-weight problem involving a solution turns out to be quite simpler than its *description* (bottom of p. 82) would lead you to believe. As the next example will show, such a problem has the same "symmetry" that was explained in Sect. 2.5, only this time you will use the given densities (instead of molar conversions) to make bookends for the keystone.

What, for instance, is the percent-weight of sulfuric acid (H_2SO_4) in a 250-milliliter aqueous solution with a density of 1.05 g/ml, if the solution contains 40 milliliters of the acid, which we know has a density of 1.30 g/ml? Use the density of the impurity (in this case, a solution) to connect the set-up to the keystone, and the density of the purity, the wanted, to connect the keystone to the answer:

$$?g\ H_2SO_4(l) = 100\ g\ H_2SO_4(aq) \times \frac{ml\ H_2SO_4(aq)}{1.05\ g\ H_2SO_4(aq)} \times \frac{40\ ml\ H_2SO_4(l)}{250\ ml\ H_2SO_4(aq)} \times \frac{1.30\ g\ H_2SO_4(l)}{ml\ H_2SO_4(l)} = 1.98\ g\ H_2SO_4(l)$$

...or, expressed as a percentage in sigfigs, 20%. Notice the similarity between the pure and impure substances in this problem. There is nothing to distinguish them save for the abbreviations for *liquid* (the purity) and *aqueous* (the impurity). There are no set rules governing the kinds of labeling that you use in dimensional analysis; use what you like. But whatever happens, see that you do not lose track of which is which, or you will walk into quicksand. Once you commit this error, your struggle to undo it may only take you in deeper. Again, watch those labels in percent-weight problems.

Now let us move on to a related type of problem. Imagine that the mining company gives up on platinum and copper, but discovers that their stake is rich in aluminum. So they take a 30.0-gram sample of bauxite (an aluminum ore) and, after the lab work and the percent-weight calculation, find it to be 61.7% alumina (Al_2O_3). They have found a lode of bauxite that they estimate at 425 metric tons (1000 kg). What do they do next?

They use the percent-weight itself as a conversion factor (that's what) to estimate the amount of oxide in the ore. The question, then, is How much alumina is present in 425 metric tons of bauxite?

$$?\ MT\ alumina = 425\ MT\ bauxite \times \frac{61.7\ MT\ alumina}{100\ MT\ bauxite} = 262\ MT\ alumina$$

All that was needed here was the given and the keystone; no extra conversion factors were in order. Because even in this type of problem, which *uses* (rather than *seeks*) a percentage, the wanted and given dimensions are identical (61.7 g, like 61.7 MT, would still equal 61.7%).

Now, suppose we wanted to know the weight of a solid that is dissolved in a solution of known density. In such a problem, the density of the solution and the percent-weight are given and ready-made conversion factors. For example: how much potassium chloride is in 750 milliliters of a solution that is 31.0% KCl and has a density of 1.35 g/ml?

$$?\ grams\ KCl = 750\ ml\ KCl(aq) \times \frac{1.35\ g\ KCl(aq)}{ml\ KCl(aq)} \times \frac{31.0\ g\ KCl}{100\ g\ KCl(aq)} = 314\ g\ KCl$$

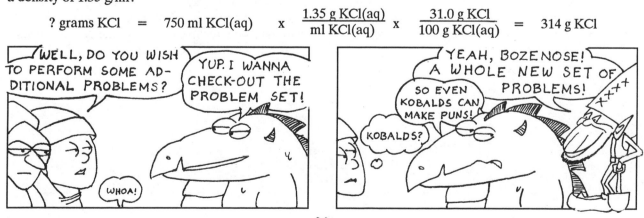

1. Match these:

_____pure substance   a. a type of impurity

_____heterogeneous sample   b. indicates number of atoms of each element

_____ore   c. an element or compound

_____solution   d. a "physical compound"

_____empirical formula   e. something visibly having different components

_____homogeneous sample   f. indicates ratio of atoms of each element

_____mixture   g. alloys, air, amalgams, etc.

_____true formula   h. something that is visibly alike throughout

2. Write the empirical formulae for the following "true" formulae:

a. CO_2 _____   b. P_2O_4 _____   c. $Na_2S_2O_4$ _____   d. $C_6H_3N_3O_6$ _____

e. $(NH_4)_2Br_2$ _____   f. $K_2Cl_2O_4$ _____   g. $Ba(ClO_4)_2 \cdot 4H_2O$ _____

h. $Al_2(SO_3)_3 \cdot 4H_2O$ _____   i. $G_2(XO_3)_4 \cdot 6H_2O$ _____

Figure the next four problems using the GamMa Ray system. Then, write the correct empirical formulae for each below, at the bottom of the page.

3. What is the empirical formula of a compound that is 63.4% cobalt, 34.4% oxygen, and 2.20% hydrogen?

4. Feldspar is 14.0% potassium, 9.7% aluminum, 30.3% silicon, and 46.0% oxygen. What is its empirical formula?

5. Determine the empirical formula of a compound that is 53.7% iron, with the remainder, sulfur.

6. A certain ammonium salt is 11.1% nitrogen, 3.2% hydrogen, 41.2% chromium, and the rest is oxygen. What is its empirical formula?

Answers: (3)_____   (4)_____   (5)_____   (6)_____

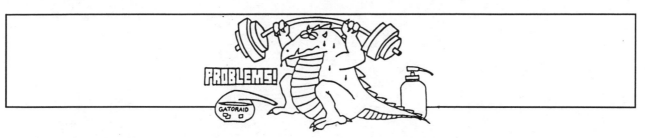

7. A 60.0-gram sample of wolframite, a tungsten ore, yields 41.9 grams of tungsten (V) oxide, W_2O_5. What is the percent-weight of the oxide?

8. What is the percent-weight of zinc in a zinc impurity if, when 325 grams of impurity is added to acid, 4.33 grams of hydrogen evolve, and it is known that it takes 31.8 grams of zinc to displace a gram of H_2?

9. A 500-milliliter solution of the salt phlogiston exate has a density of 1.21 g/ml. It contains 167 milliliters of dissolved Fl_2XO_3, which has a density of 1.63 g/ml. What is the percent-weight of the compound in the solution?

10. What is the proof (twice the percent-weight) of a rum if its density is 1.19 g/ml and a fifth contains 320 milliliters of alcohol, which has a specific gravity of 0.790 (one fifth = 757 ml)? Use "alcohol" or its formula, C_2H_5OH, whichever you prefer, as a label.

11. The density of air at sea level on the planet Urras is 1.26 g/L and is 5.50% argon (same density). If this gas could be removed from the air with perfect efficiency, how many liters of it would 70.0 liters of air yield?

12. This problem contains a red herring. A sugar solution that is 21.8% sugar has a density of 1.10 g/ml. How much anhydrous sugar would result if 650 milliliters of the solution were completely dehydrated? The density of glucose is ($C_6H_{10}O_5$) is 1.92 g/ml.

1. c   e   a   g   f   h   d   b   2. a. CO_2 b. PO_2 c. $NaSO_2$ d. C_2HNO_2

    e. NH_4Br f. $KClO_2$ g. $Ba(ClO_4)_2 \bullet 4H_2O$ h. $Al_2(SO_3)_3 \bullet 4H_2O$ i. $G(XO_3)_2 \bullet 3H_2O$

3.   Co <u>63.4</u>   O <u>34.4</u>   H <u>2.20</u>   4.   K <u>14.0</u>   Al <u>9.7</u>   Si <u>30.3</u>   O <u>46.0</u>

        Co <u>1.08</u>   O <u>2.15</u>   H <u>2.18</u>   K <u>.358</u>   Al <u>.360</u>   Si <u>1.08</u>   O <u>2.88</u>

        Co <u>1</u>   O <u>2</u>   H <u>2</u>   K <u>1</u>   Al <u>1</u>   Si <u>3</u>   O <u>8</u>

5.   Fe <u>53.7</u>   S <u>46.3</u>   6.   N <u>11.1</u>   H <u>3.2</u>   Cr <u>41.2</u>   O <u>44.5</u>

        Fe <u>.962</u>   S <u>1.44</u>   N <u>.792</u>   H <u>3.17</u>   Cr <u>.793</u>   O <u>2.78</u>

        Fe <u>1</u>   S <u>1.5</u>   N <u>1</u>   H <u>4.00</u>   Cr <u>1.00</u>   O <u>3.51</u>

        Fe <u>2</u>   S <u>3</u>   N <u>2</u>   H <u>8</u>   Cr <u>2</u>   O <u>7</u>

Answers: (3) CoO_2H_2 (4) $KAlSi_3O_8$ (5) Fe_2O_3 (6) $N_2H_8Cr_2O_7$

7. ? grams W_2O_5 = 100 W_2O_5 imp x $\dfrac{41.9 \text{ g } W_2O_5}{60.0 \text{ g imp}}$ = 69.8 g W_2O_5 = 69.8%

8. ? grams zinc + 100 g Zn imp x $\dfrac{4.33 \text{ g } H_2}{325 \text{ g imp}}$ x $\dfrac{31.8 \text{ g Zn}}{1.00 \text{ g } H_2}$ = 42.4 g Zn = 42.4%

9. ? grams Fl_2XO_3 = 100 g Fl_2XO_3(aq) x $\dfrac{\text{ml } Fl_2XO_3(aq)}{1.21 \text{ g } Fl_2XO_3(aq)}$ x $\dfrac{167 \text{ ml } Fl_2XO_3}{500 \text{ ml } Fl_2XO_3(aq)}$

    x $\dfrac{1.63 \text{ g } Fl_2XO_3}{\text{ml } Fl_2XO_3}$ = 45.0 g Fl_2XO_3 = 45.0%

10. ? g C_2H_5OH = 100 g rum x $\dfrac{\text{ml rum}}{1.19 \text{ g rum}}$ x $\dfrac{\text{fifth rum}}{757 \text{ ml rum}}$ x $\dfrac{320 \text{ ml } C_2H_5OH}{\text{fifth rum}}$

    x $\dfrac{0.790 \text{ g } C_2H_5OH}{\text{ml } C_2H_5OH}$ = 28.1 g C_2H_5OH (2x) = 56.2 proof

11. ? grams Ar = 70.0 L air x $\dfrac{1.26 \text{ g air}}{\text{L air}}$ x $\dfrac{5.50 \text{ g Ar}}{100 \text{ g air}}$ x $\dfrac{\text{L Ar}}{1.26 \text{ g Ar}}$ = 3.85 g Ar

12. ? grams sugar = 650 ml sugar(aq) x $\dfrac{1.10 \text{ g sugar(aq)}}{\text{ml sugar}}$ x $\dfrac{21.8 \text{ g sugar}}{100 \text{ g sugar(aq)}}$ = 156 g sugar

In problem 12, the formula and density for glucose is completely irrelevant to the solution; the sugar in question is not explicitly specified. You can see, in any case, that a density for the sugar was not needed (although the density for *a* sugar was given), because the other conversion factors sufficed by themselves to get you from the given to the wanted.

2.10 Chapter Synthesis

THE COMMON THREAD IN CHAPTER 2 IS THE TENDANCY OF PURE SUBSTANCES TO FORM "UNITIES" IN WHOLE-NUMBER RATIOS, REGARDLESS OF THE QUANTITY OF PARTICLES INVOLVED...

TEN-FOUR!

When you encounter, for instance, unfamiliar and relatively uncommon ions such as thiosulfate, $S_2O_3^{2-}$, and chromium (VI), Cr^{6+}, and it is your job to combine their formulae into a compound, you will know what to do.

To form a neutral compound, the chromium (VI) and thiosulfate ions must be balanced in their charges. You can do a little mental aglebra by taking the ion with the larger charge and asking yourself, "how many ions with the smaller charge will be needed to offset it?"

$$\_\_ Cr^{6+} + \_\_ S_2O_3^{2-} \rightarrow _____$$

If you can divide 6 by 2 to get 3, you can write the coefficients—whence come the subscripts—and, therefore, the answer to the above equation:

$$1Cr^{6+} + 3S_2O_3^{2-} \rightarrow Cr_1(S_2O_3)_3$$

...or $Cr(S_2O_3)_3$, the formula for the salt chromium (VI) thiosulfate. The arrow, while it means "equals," also indicates the direction of the reaction (in this case, the formation, rather than the decomposition, of a compound).

Were thiosulfate to combine with vanadium (V), a little more algebra, but still only mental algebra, would be called for, because the ratio of thiosulfate to vanadium is two *and a half* to one. But since you know that in chemistry only whole-numbers of atoms go to make up compounds, you look for the lowest

whole multiple of 2 ½ which, of course, is 5. But five thiosulfates together have ten negative charges, which is too much for one vanadium (V) with its five positives, but just right for two of these cations:

$$2V^{5+} + 5S_2O_3^{2-} \rightarrow V_2(S_2O_3)_5$$

Determination of empirical formulae, while practical, also helps satisfy an historical desire for unity and simplicity dating from the seventh century B.C. in Greece and India. Philosophers (the earliest chemists) and mathematicians, then as now, have always sought a oneness, a commonality, or a convergence wherever they perceive a divergence. When unable to uncover a unity, they have settled for a duality, or a triplicity, etc., but they have never been happy with fractions in such matters.

So while the true formula C_5H_{10} can be reduced to CH_2, fractional and even decimal results can be made pleasantly unified and scientifically acurate with only bits of algebra:

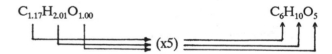

$$C_{1.17}H_{2.01}O_{1.00} \qquad\qquad C_6H_{10}O_5$$

$$(\times 5)$$

Another useful and beautiful unity is 100 percent. Chemists must often seek its parts by applying its whole, and any chemist worth his NaCl should not be satisfied unless a chemical unity he is dealing with is also satisfied—that is, if it is 100 parts making up a whole.

You must habitually ask yourself, on seeing any percentages, "do they make 100?" If not, you must account for the difference.

Here is a unity for a compound represented as a pie graph. What is the "size" in percentage, of the piece that will satisfy it? Use addition, then subtraction, to get the answer.

87

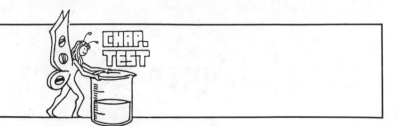

1. The nuclear formula for sodium, an element with one isotope, can be written $^{23}_{11}Na$. The subscript is its Z (number of protons), and the superscript, its mass number (number of nucleons). Write the nuclear formula for each of these one-isotope elements. Use the Periodic Table.

_____fluorine   _____beryllium

_____aluminum   _____phosphorus

2. If the formula for stibate is SbO_4^{3-}, then that for stibite must be (a, below); if selenate is SeO_3^{2-}, then perselenate must be (b); if borate is BO_3^{3-}, then "hypoborite," if it existed, would be (c); if "astatite" were AtO_2^-, then "perastatate" would be (d)

a. _____   b. _____

c. _____   d. _____

3. What charges have the monatomic (next column) elemental ions that are formed by the elements of these families?

1A_____   2A_____   3A_____

5A_____   6A_____   7A_____

4. What are the molar weights of these elemental and compound species to four sigfigs (Some figgerin' space, compliments of the producers, is below)?

B _____ O _____ Cl _____ Mn _____ I _____

Ag _____ O_2 _____ I_2 _____ RbBr _____

HNO_3 _____ C_2H_5OH _____ $CaSO_4 \cdot 2H_2O$ _____

$C_{63}H_{90}O_{14}N_{14}PCo_3$ (cyanocobalamin)_____

5. Use dimensional analysis to determine the percent-weight of calcium in lime, CaO.

6. How many grams of calcium could be produced from the decomposition of 65.8 grams of lime?

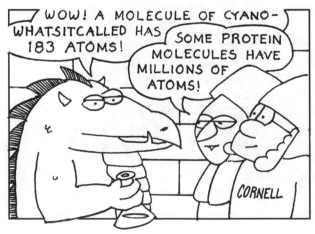

88

7. Cobalt, as part of vitamin B-12, is a necessary trace element. Just how small, in micrograms (106 mcg = 1 g) is that trace, if the recommended daily allowance for cyanocobalamin is 3.00 micrograms?

8. What is the empirical formula of a compound which is 9.9% carbon, 58.7% chlorine, and the rest, fluorine? Use the GamMa Ray system.

9. A manganese ion with a charge other than 2+ or 3+ forms a compound that is 49.5% manganese and 50.5% oxygen. Determine the empirical formula and name the compound.

10. How much elemental tungsten can be produced from 168.3 grams of tungsten (V) oxide?

11. Invar, a steel, has a density of 11.3 g/ml. Six liters of molten invar holds 2.37 liters of nickel (specific gravity, 8.9). Find the percent-weight of nickel in invar:

1. $^{19}_{9}F$ $^{9}_{4}Be$ $^{27}_{13}Al$ $^{31}_{15}P$

2. (1A) 1+ (2A) 2+ (3A) 3+ (5A) 3- (6A) 2- (7A) 1-

3. a. SbO_3^{2-} b. SeO_4^{2-} c. BO^{3-} d. AtO_4^{-}

4. (B) 10.81   (O) 16.00   (Cl) 35.45   (Mn) 54.94   (Ag) 107.9   (I) 126.9 (O_2) 32.00 (I_2) 253.8

   (RbBr) 165.4 (HNO_3) 63.01 (C_2H_5OH) 46.07

   $(CaSO_4 \cdot 2H_2O)$ 172.2   (B-12) 1.475×10^3

5. ? grams Ca = 100 g CaO $\times \dfrac{\text{mol CaO}}{56.08 \text{ g CaO}} \times \dfrac{\text{mol Ca}}{\text{mol CaO}} \times \dfrac{40.08 \text{ g Ca}}{\text{mol Ca}}$ = 71.5 g Ca = 71.5%

6. ? grams Ca = 65.8 g CaO $\times \dfrac{71.5 \text{ g Ca}}{100 \text{ g CaO}}$ = 47.0 g Ca (conversion factor is from previous problem)

7. ? mcg Co = 3.00 mcg B-12 $\times \dfrac{\text{g B-12}}{1.00 \times 10^6 \text{ mcg B-12}} \times \dfrac{\text{mol B-12}}{1475 \text{ g B-12}} \times \dfrac{\text{mol Co}}{\text{mol B-12}} \times \dfrac{58.93 \text{ g Co}}{\text{mol Co}}$

   $\times \dfrac{1.00 \times 10^6 \text{ mcg Co}}{\text{g Co}}$ = 0.120 mcg Co

8. C 9.9   Cl 58.7   F 31.4
   C .824   Cl 1.66   F 1.65
   C 1   Cl 2.01   F 2.00

   Answer: CCl_2F_2

9. Mn 49.5   O 50.5
   Mn .901   O 3.16
   Mn 1   O 3.52
   Mn 2   O 7

   Answer: Mn_2O_7, manganese (VII) oxide, which contains the Mn^{7+} ion

10. ? grams W = 168.3 g W_2O_5 $\times \dfrac{\text{mol } W_2O_5}{447.7 \text{ g } W_2O_5} \times \dfrac{2 \text{ mols W}}{\text{mol } W_2O_5} \times \dfrac{183.85 \text{ g W}}{\text{mol W}}$ = 138.2 g W

11. ? grams Ni = 100 g Inv $\times \dfrac{\text{ml Inv}}{11.3 \text{ g Inv}} \times \dfrac{2370 \text{ ml Ni}}{6000 \text{ ml Inv}} \times \dfrac{8.9 \text{ g Ni}}{\text{ml Ni}}$ = 31.1 g Ni = 31.1%

Three: Concerning the Nature of Particles

3.1 The Hydrogen Atom

OH! WE'RE GONNA GET "PHYSICAL"!

NOW, WHAT DO ELECTRONS DO IN THEIR SHELLS? I CAN NAME AND COMBINE FORMULAE, BUT I ALSO WANT TO KNOW WHAT ATOMS AND MOLECULES ACTUALLY LOOK LIKE.

FOR THAT WE SHALL REQUIRE A PHYSICIST!

PRECISELY!

I KNOW JUST THE MAN... BUT HE'S A "BOHR-ING" FELLOW!

THAT DOES IT!

LOUISVILLE SLUGGER

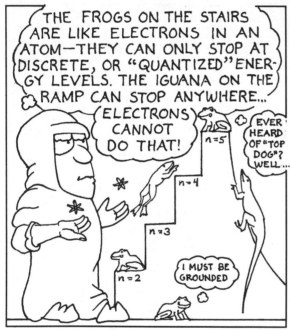

THE FROGS ON THE STAIRS ARE LIKE ELECTRONS IN AN ATOM—THEY CAN ONLY STOP AT DISCRETE, OR "QUANTIZED" ENERGY LEVELS. THE IGUANA ON THE RAMP CAN STOP ANYWHERE...

ELECTRONS CANNOT DO THAT!

EVER HEARD OF "TOP DOG"? WELL...

$n = 5$

$n = 4$

$n = 3$

$n = 2$

I MUST BE GROUNDED

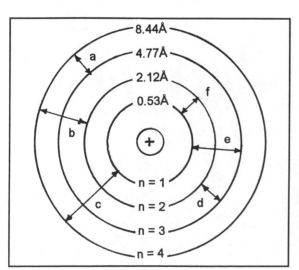

8.44Å

4.77Å

2.12Å

0.53Å

a

f

b

e

+

c

d

$n = 1$

$n = 2$

$n = 3$

$n = 4$

The frog at the top level has the most energy, as he would quickly discover were he to leap all the way to the bottom. The energy he would lose would precisely equal that which he gained by making a series of "quantum leaps" on his way to the highest energy level. (The word *energy*, elsewhere in this book, is often synonymous with heat, but not for the sake of this analogy).

The Danish physicist Bohr assigned simple integers to the energy levels which he believed the electron in a hydrogen atom could rise or fall to. We call these *Principle Energy Levels*, *n*. PEL 1 is *ground state*, and all the PELs above it are *excited states*. An electron—in a hydrogen atom or any other—will remain in a ground state unless it absorbs some energy from an outside source.

By exciting a sample of neutral hydrogen (H_2) with electric arcing, we can energize its electrons, which then leap to the higher states. But they are unstable in these higher Principle Energy Levels, and fall back to ground state as soon as they can, releasing the energy they temporarily held as light, or photons. Each possible jump releases light, but on a different wavelength, λ (lambda).

The diagram at left is a cross-section of a hydrogen atom, showing the radii of the PELs and the possible quantum jumps. An electron may leap 1, 2, or 3 steps at once (but, never, for example, one and two-ninths).

Jumps that produce visible light occur only over certain distances (measured in angstroms) from the nucleus. In the case of the hydrogen atom, only jumps (b) and (d), as shown, do this. The infrared light waves that jump (a) releases are too long to be seen (do not confuse the length of the jump with the wavelength of the light it produces). The ultraviolet waves that the other three jumps produce are too short to be visible (the PELs in the diagram, which appear as concentric rings, are not drawn to scale, for in reality, PELs are not spaced at the perfect intervals suggested).

92

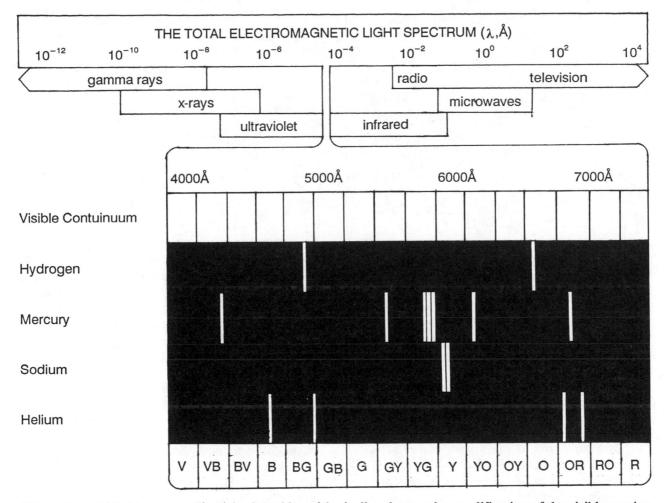

THE TOTAL ELECTROMAGNETIC LIGHT SPECTRUM (λ,Å)

[Note: the total light spectrum (top) is plotted logarithmically, whereas the amplification of the visible portion of the above spectrum (above) is not; the visible spectrum—the "continuum"—is actually vastly tinier than even the dinky slice of the total spectrum shown (top)].

⊛ Color the five spectra: the visible light continuum, above and below the darkened area, and the four elemental spectra within it. Use the guides above and below to align your ruler so as to color 16 vertical columns. Also, color the guide bar at the bottom in a way that reflects the continuum. Avoid making permanent pencil marks; rather, make the colors merge gently (V = violet, VB = violet-blue, BV = blue-violet, etc.).

Without an involved discussion of wave mechanics, let it be understood that there are several types of light, and that most of them cannot be seen by corporeal eyes.

Radio and television—or Hertzian—waves are very long and of very low frequency, ν (nu); in other words, relatively few pass a given point during a second. At the other extreme are the high-energy gamma and X-rays, which have very short λ but very high ν.

A few of the wavelengths of light given off by electrons plunging back to their ground states —which can be higher than (n =) 1 in elements other than hydrogen—are in the visible range. This is quite fortunate, for otherwise we would all be blind.

Look at the hydrogen spectrum. Recall that two of the electron jumps that take place in the hydrogen atom produce visible-light. This is because their wavelengths are (about) 4900Å and 6600Å (within the visible range) and so they leave their signatures whenever a sample of hydrogen is excited.

In case you are interested, or might already have inferred, the relation between frequency and wavelenght is an inverse one: $c = \nu\lambda$, where the constant, c, is the speed of light, 3.0 x 106 km/sec.

⊛ Look at the colors of the two visible hydrogen lines. Trace their corresponding jumps on the diagram on p. 92 in the same colors: blue-green for jump (d) orange-red for jump (b).

The Bohr Model of the hydrogen atom, then, is a monoprotic nucleus with an electron in spherical (not circular) orbit, forming a "shell" or "cloud" around the nucleus. This electron moves tirelessly and very fast. With the addition of energy, the electron cloud can expand from the ground state ($n = 1$) to any of the discrete, or quantized, radii corresponding to the excited states (Principle Energy Levels 2, 3, and 4). The electron can remain there for as long as the hydrogen atom is in the path of the energy source. The energy is conserved, though transformed into light, when the energy source is removed.

Two diagrams of electron-cloud models for hydrogen appear on this page (Keep in mind, however, that they are only models, and are not necessarily *spatially* accurate; our problem is that no one has yet seen a hydrogen atom or an H_2 molecule with everyday vision.).

Diagram (1) shows the spherical atomic model on which the foregoing discussion has been based. Unfortunately, it is limited by the fact that there are no single, neutral hydrogen atoms anywhere, any more than there could be a magnet in a box of nails not attached to a nail. Such a magnet could, however, be attached to another magnet, and this is is why we need a model of the diatomic hydrogen molecule (2). Unlike the atomic model, which is geometric for the sake of the quantized PELs within it, this model represents the electrons as dots showing the probability of the electrons' positions (as if it were possible to pinpoint them a few hundred or thousand times in a fixed period).

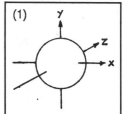

To paraphrase Heisenberg's Uncertainty Principle, it is not, nor will it ever be, possible to both determine the location of a wavelike particle at any instant and know its velocity. We can thus only think of the electrons as being "everywhere" at once.

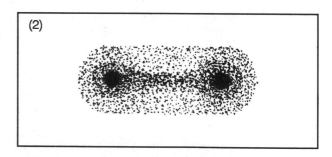

20
Ca
40.08

Profile: Calcium

A dinosaur skeleton is mostly calcium phosphate.

Calcium is a soft, silvery-white metal that never occurs uncombined in nature. Virtually all of its compounds are ionic, owing to its rather low electronegativity (1.0).

This alkaline earth metal's high reactivity is due to its two valance electrons. Instead of filling the 3d sublevel (the d-sublevel of n = 3), these frontier-minded electrons live by themselves out on the 4s sublevel and readily jump ship in the presence of most nonmetals.

Calcium, despite its importance, was neither isolated nor even known until 1807, when Davy electrolyzed some pulverized ore. In this experiment, the wayward 4s electrons joined calcium *cat*ions (Ca^{2+}) at the *cat*hode of Davy's voltage cell, while the *an*ions that had been bonded to the calcium ions flocked to the other pole, the *an*ode.

By weight, calcium is the fifth most abundant metal in the human body, outweighing many times over all other metals and minerals combined. The nonliving bulk of most vertebrate skeletons is mostly the phosphate salt, Ca_3PO_4. If it were not for the insolubility (in water) of this salt, we would not have fossil and skeletal records of most prehistoric fauna.

Another calcium salt, the carbonate, $CaCO_3$, is the answer of many invertebrate phyla to the problem of skeleton-building. Mollusk shells, squid combs, polyp reefs, echinoderm spines, and diatom skeletons are all examples. The deposits of the latter are "diatomaceous earth" pressed into limestone by slow geologic processes. Limestone, in all, is the second most abundant mineral on Earth. Even marble was once "alive," for it is really only the result of limestone lattices that collapsed under great pressure.

Calcium deficiency has legion consequences. At the systemic level, there is a weakening of the bones, teeth, skin, membranes, and connective tissues; nervous dysfunction; and acidification of the blood and lymphatic fluid. The specific functions of the brain, heart, liver, spleen, kidneys, and immune and endocrine systems depend on calcium salts at all times.

Fortunately, there are many good sources: onions, potatoes, cabbage, spinach, dates, pears, figs, peaches, and the white residue that settles from freshly pressed carrot juice (shake well!).

Commercial milk is also a "good" source, but this is a theoretical half-truth, for most dairy calcium is denatured and unhealthful, and contributes to arthritis and other infirmities ("Milk has something for everybody," as the PR saying goes).

Of calcium's siblings, strontium is probably best-known for its own connection with milk, which contains "safe" amounts of radioactive strontium-90. Magnesium is also necessary for living things, but hard and comparatively unreactive beryllium is not, and is indeed poisonous. Barium has many useful salts that find applications from X-ray diagnoses to producing a green flame in flares and fireworks.

Many synthetic fertilizers are now made with calcium. One of them, calcium cyanamide, is made in two steps:

$$CaO + 3C \rightarrow CaC_2 + CO\uparrow$$

$$CaC_2 + N_2 \rightarrow Ca(CN)_2$$

Spectral analysis of the Sun's solar flares reveals the presence of calcium, in highly ionized and attenuated form.

3.2 Quantum Numbers

Whereas an electron in the n = 2 and higher Principle Energy Levels is unstable in hydrogen, electrons in larger atoms can and do *remain* in higher PELs, without the introduction of energy. What are excited states for hydrogen-bound electrons are regular ground states for the great majority of electrons in other elements.

These electrons, too, can be excited to even higher states, up to n = 7 in fact. Each higher level, however, is also a ground state. This includes even the seventh level, for the representative elements of Period 7 (wouldn't you know it?).

As the electrons excited to these (even) higher states lose some or all of their temporary energy, they, like the electron in hydrogen, fall to (or at least *towards*) their ground states, releasing photons.

There is an easy way—hinted at above—to know how many ground states an element has under ordinary conditions. Look at the Periodic Table. For all A-family elements, the number of the Period is—plain and simple—the number of Principal Energy Levels. For the transition elements, you subtract 1 to get the number of PELs. For the lanthanides and actinides, subtract 2.

―――――――――― Sublevels ――――――――――

If to you the phrase Principle Energy Level implies the existence of subordinate levels, you are quite correct. These energy *sublevels*, as they are termed, are not named with integers but with a series of letters: *s*, *p*, *d*, and *f*. This order is important, because it goes from the lowest (in energy) sublevel, *s*, to the highest, *f*.

If the idea of sublevels seems to be a contradiction of the concept of quantized (principle) energy levels—that is, If the PELs are divided, then how can they at the same time be quantized?—then you have to realize that, for atoms more complex that hydrogen or helium, a more comprehensive numbering system is needed.

The energies at the principal levels are still quantized, but the PELs, while discrete, are themselves divided into *equally* discrete sublevels.

The Principle Energy Level, n, which can be any integer from 1 to 7, is said to be the *first quantum number*, or the most general and inclusive part of an electron's address; the sublevels, though labeled with letters instead of integers, are nonetheless also a quantum *number*, the *second* one, to be exact. They are slightly more specific than the first, n.

The Principle Energy Level is the state or province of an electron's address; the sublevel is the city. To repeat, they are the first and second quantum numbers.

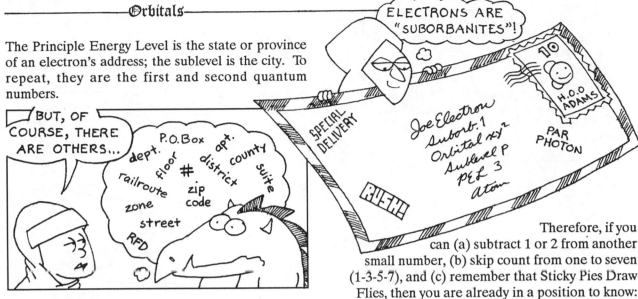

Orbitals are an electron's street address, and are the third quantum number.

Let us return for a moment to the sublevels, s, p, d, and f. The higher (in energy) the sublevel, the more orbitals it will contain. The quantities contained by each form a simple and regular progression: the s-sublevel holds one orbital; the p-sublevel has three; the d-sublevel has five; and (as you may have guessed), the f-sublevel contains seven.

Therefore, if you can (a) subtract 1 or 2 from another small number, (b) skip count from one to seven (1-3-5-7), and (c) remember that Sticky Pies Draw Flies, then you are already in a position to know:

(1) how many ground states an element has (by looking at the Periodic Table);

(2) the labels of the sublevels; and

(3) their order, in relative energy; and finally,

(4) the number of orbitals in each sublevel.

As for the orbitals' shapes, an atom with only the lone s-sublevel orbital found in the hydrogen atom or at the core of a larger atom, is a theoretical sphere, as per the Bohr and Quantum Mechanical Models, and the H_2 molecule is a fuzzy dumbbell. Helium, while not otherwise fully conforming to Bohr's Model (in ways we will

not go into), could also be represented as a sphere, because it has no sublevel beyond s. Indeed, it is more likely than hydrogen to be truly sperical, because helium atoms do not bond to others of their kind (nor to anything else). Things begin to get complicated with the eight Period 2 elements, for they not only have the single orbital in their first PEL (1s), but also the orbitals in the sublevels of their second PEL: 2s and 2p (The number before the letter stands for a PEL.).The 2p sublevel, because it is a p-sublevel, necessarily contains three orbitals.

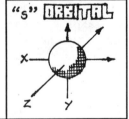

"s" ORBITAL

A p orbital is made of two opposing "lobes." Despite this bizarre (and theoretical) shape, each orbital in a p-sublevel, if it is home to an electron or two, is every bit as much an electron cloud as the plain old sphere of an s-sublevel orbital. If no electrons are in it, it can be thought of abstractly (as if we have not had enough abstraction already)

"P" ORBITALS

as the spatial entity wherein the electron(s) would live, if present. In the analogy, then, empty orbitals are vacant electron houses.

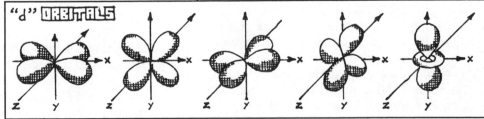

"d" ORBITALS

So what does an atom look like? Ask this question, and you may wind up sorry for having asked, for it is virtually unanswerable (although there are now photographs of excited atoms). The Quantum Mechanical Model—which tries to do for the other elements what the Bohr Model does for hydrogen—provides only this mathematical and abstract vision of an atom, rather than a finite, concrete picture.

An obvious difficulty to our way of thinking is that the orbitals of the p- and d-sublevels and, therefore, the electrons themselves, *seem* to collide with the nucleus and even penetrate it, although we know the nucleus to be very dense and, to boot, oppositely charged. How can this be?

De Broglie posited, by way of partial explanation, that , while the electrons have a very tiny bit of mass, they are also small enough to be wavelike, and so have properties such as λ and ν and the ability to penetrate certain media.

As confusing or contradictory as this might sound, the Quantum Mechanical Model has proven to be experimentally accurate in the case of every element. The explanation given here is an expedient and superficial treatment, but it is all you will need in Chem. 1. It may also be said that this affair is a good example of scientists wisely accepting, as a working hypothesis, something they know is not completely true.

A happy corollary of Quantum Mechanics is that, as already implied, an orbital—no matter the sublevel to which it belongs nor how strange its apparent shape—can have only 0, 1, or 2 electrons in it; no other circumstance is possible. This restriction on the nature of of all orbitals—giving them one thing, at least, in common—is the *Pauli Exclusion Principle.*

The orbitals, being the third quantum number, do—like the PELs and sublevels—have a numbering system of their own. With it, we can distinguish, for instance, one orbital in a 4d sublevel from another.

In this book, however, we are concerned only with the (1) quantities of orbitals in a sublevel and (2) the number of electrons that each orbital may contain (which, again, is 0, 1, or 2).

Suborbitals

Orbitals are quite specific parts of the electronic addressing system, being rather like the house number and street. Yet even they are not the electrons themselves.

The *fourth* quantum number, the *suborbital,* corresponds to the individual electrons, but we will not study it here to any real depth.

Pauli believed that each of an orbital's two possible electrons constituted a suborbital in its own right, and that each had the property of "spin" in either the "−" direction or the "+" direction. These are analogous to clockwise and counterclockwise motion and, although mere signs, are yet a quantum number.

Recapitulation

The key things to remember about quantum numbers in Chem. 1 are the *order* and *identities* of the first two (1, 2, 3, 4, 5, 6, 7; and s, p, d, and f) and the *quantities* of the last two (1, 3, 5, 7; and 0, 1, or 2) within their respective groupings.

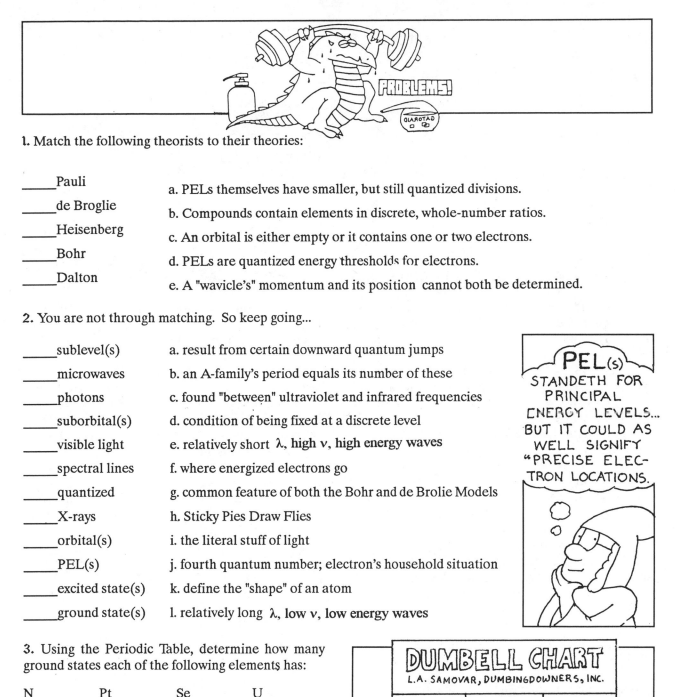

1. Match the following theorists to their theories:

_____ Pauli

_____ de Broglie

_____ Heisenberg

_____ Bohr

_____ Dalton

a. PELs themselves have smaller, but still quantized divisions.

b. Compounds contain elements in discrete, whole-number ratios.

c. An orbital is either empty or it contains one or two electrons.

d. PELs are quantized energy thresholds for electrons.

e. A "wavicle's" momentum and its position cannot both be determined.

2. You are not through matching. So keep going...

_____ sublevel(s)

_____ microwaves

_____ photons

_____ suborbital(s)

_____ visible light

_____ spectral lines

_____ quantized

_____ X-rays

_____ orbital(s)

_____ PEL(s)

_____ excited state(s)

_____ ground state(s)

a. result from certain downward quantum jumps

b. an A-family's period equals its number of these

c. found "between" ultraviolet and infrared frequencies

d. condition of being fixed at a discrete level

e. relatively short λ, high ν, high energy waves

f. where energized electrons go

g. common feature of both the Bohr and de Brolie Models

h. Sticky Pies Draw Flies

i. the literal stuff of light

j. fourth quantum number; electron's household situation

k. define the "shape" of an atom

l. relatively long λ, low ν, low energy waves

3. Using the Periodic Table, determine how many ground states each of the following elements has:

N _____   Pt _____   Se _____   U _____

Bi _____   Xe _____   Al _____   Gd _____

Cd _____   In _____   Rn _____   Ti _____

4. An s-sublevel in any Principle Energy Level has but one orbital; a p-sublevel has three. Given that an orbital can hold no more than two electrons, what is the maximum number of electrons that could be found in each sublevel (s, p, d, f)?

s _____   p _____   d _____   f _____

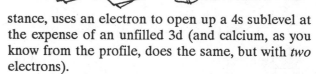

1. c a e d b

2. h l i j c a d e k g f b

3. (N) 2 (Pt) 5 (Se) 4 (U) 5 (Bi) 6 (Xe) 5

   (Al) 3 (Gd) 4 (Cd) 4 (In) 5 (Ti) 4 (Rn) 7

4. An s-sublevel (1s, 2s, 3s, 4s, 5s, 6s, 7s) can have no more than two electrons (1 x 2); a p-sublevel (2p, 3p, 4p, 5p, 6p, 7p) can have up to three filled sublevels and, therefore, up to six electrons (3 x 2). A d-sublevel (3d, 4d, 5d, 6d) can have as many as ten electrons (5 x 2). You might by now have figured out, then, that f-sublevels (4f and 5f) can have as many as 14 electrons (7 x 2). There are no d-sublevels above 6d nor f-sublevel above 5f in any element discovered to date.

Look at the diagram below. It shows the electron distribution of the ten lightest elements in an unexcited state (all electrons are in their ground states). Since they are of the first and second periods only, all of their electrons are found in either n =1 or n = 2, the two lowest PELs. The blanks represent orbitals containing 0, 1, or 2 electrons (suborbitals), shown here as arrows. The up-or-down direction of the orbitals is arbitrary, but it serves to remind you of the opposite spin of two electrons within an orbital.

The elements are labeled with their atomic numbers. With an increase in atomic number (Z), the three following trends are observed:

(1) the lower Principle Energy Levels **fill up first**;

(2) within a PEL with multiple sublevels (of which only n = 2 is shown here), the lower ones will fill entirely before the next higher levels get any electrons; and

(3) all the orbitals within a sublevel are half-filled (get one electron) before any other is filled (gets two).

The third rule is infallible, but the other two begin to fail among the heavier elements; Potassium, for in-

stance, uses an electron to open up a 4s sublevel at the expense of an unfilled 3d (and calcium, as you know from the profile, does the same, but with *two* electrons).

The essence of these three trends, of which the last should be learned by heart—is that—in general, there is a priority for the filling of lower PELs and lower sublevels first, and also an "equitable -as-possible" division of electrons within a sublevel.

The notations on the right of the diagram are the subject of the next section; but, before you go on to the next section, notice how the superscripts for the sublevels are derived, and how their total equals the elements' Z. Electrons, after all, equal protons in a neutral atom.

Z	$n = 1$	$n = 2$				
	1s	2s	2p			
$_1$H	↑					$1s^1$
$_2$He	↑↓					$1s^2$
$_3$Li	↑↓	↑				$1s^2 2s^1$
$_4$Be	↑↓	↑↓				$1s^2 2s^2$
$_5$B	↑↓	↑↓	↑			$1s^2 2s^2 2p^1$
$_6$C	↑↓	↑↓	↑	↑		$1s^2 2s^2 2p^2$
$_7$N	↑↓	↑↓	↑	↑	↑	$1s^2 2s^2 2p^3$
$_8$O	↑↓	↑↓	↑↓	↑	↑	$1s^2 2s^2 2p^4$
$_9$F	↑↓	↑↓	↑↓	↑↓	↑	$1s^2 2s^2 2p^5$
$_{10}$Ne	↑↓	↑↓	↑↓	↑↓	↑↓	$1s^2 2s^2 2p^6$

3.3 Electron Configurations

HE KEEPS ASKING ABOUT THE IRREGULAR SHAPE OF OUR PERIODIC TABLE...

HOW COME IT'S NOT JUST AN ORDINARY RECTANGLE?

'TIS HIGH TIME THAT WE TAUGHT THE OLD BOY TO WRITE ELECTRON NOTATIONS EMPLOYING THE TABLE...

Early versions of the Periodic Table were in fact rectangular matrices of elements arranged horizontally by increasing weight and vertically by shared properties. The periods at the top, however, turned out to be briefer than those below them; that is, the recurring propeties that define periodicity recurred at shorter intervals. It was this circumstance that dictated the historic evolution of the Table's shape, even before there was a good understanding of *why* some periods were longer than others. As it turns out, this unevenness (and the properties of the elements themselves) has to do with the filling of Principal Energy Levels and their subdivisions as the Table progresses from the lightest element, hydrogen,

to hahnium (which, for no better reason than alliteration, we will pretend is the heaviest).

It is the electrons in the outermost PEL that are, in every element, the valence electrons.

Additionally, some of the electrons in the next-to-outermost PEL of the transition metals also qualify as valance electrons. They, too, can be lost or gained by the atom and (therefore) determine the properties that periodically recur and (therefore) decide the shape of the Periodic Table.

Only the noble gases succeed in completely filling their outer levels with electrons, and for this reason their atoms are chemically indifferent, even to each other. Helium is full with only two, because its only PEL is n = 1, and this PEL has only one sublevel, s, which has only one orbital, 1s, which, like any other s-sublevel, holds a maximum of two electrons. The other noble gases are full with eight because their outermost PEL (no mater the *n*) has only an s- and a p-sublevel (2 from *n*s and 6 from *n*p). Look at the electron distribution of neon (p. 100), with its full highest PEL. Its heavier siblings, the other noble gases, also follow this pattern.

You know that PELs are ordered from 1 to 7, and sublevels, from s to f. But the PELs overlap in their energies such that, for instance, a 4f sublevel is more energetic than a 5s and even a 5p sublevel, as can be seen.

These overlaps must be known in order to write an element's electronic configuration (that is, its succession of sublevels) and to be able to express this configuration in notation, as shown in the diagram on p.100.

Happily, the Periodic Table, by dint of its unusual shape, provides a simple, painless way to know this...

EACH BAR IS A SUBLEVEL; EACH LITTLE BOX, AN ORBITAL.

101

Periodic table with cartoon speech bubbles: "ALRIGHT..." / "...SO JUST WHAT IS THIS SIMPLE, PAINLESS WAY TO WRITE ELECTRON NOTATIONS?" / "READING THE TABLE—AS THOU WOULD A BOOK!"

H 1																	He 2
Li 3	Be 4											B 5	C 6	N 7	O 8	F 9	Ne 10
Na 11	Mg 12											Al 13	Si 14	P 15	S 16	Cl 17	Ar 18
K 19	Ca 20	Sc 21	Ti 22	V 23	Cr 24	Mn 25	Fe 26	Co 27	Ni 28	Cu 29	Zn 30	Ga 31	Ge 32	As 33	Se 34	Br 35	Kr 36
Rb 37	Sr 38	Y 39	Zr 40	Nb 41	Mo 42	Tc 43	Ru 44	Rh 45	Pd 46	Ag 47	Cd 48	In 49	Sn 50	Sb 51	Te 52	I 53	Xe 54
Cs 55	Ba 56	La 57	Hf 72	Ta 73	W 74	Re 75	Os 76	Ir 77	Pt 78	Au 79	Hg 80	Tl 81	Pb 82	Bi 83	Po 84	At 85	Rn 86
Fr 87	Ra 88	Ac 89	Rf 104	Ha 105													

LANTHANIDES • ACTINIDES • TRANSITION ELEMENTS • 3A – 8A

Ce 58	Pr 59	Nd 60	Pm 61	Sm 62	Eu 63	Gd 64	Tb 65	Dy 66	Ho 67	Er 68	Tm 69	Yb 70	Lu 71
Th 90	Pa 91	U 92	Np 93	Pu 94	Am 95	Cm 96	Bk 97	Cf 98	Es 99	Fm 100	Md 101	No 102	Lr 103

Legend

☐ s orbitals ☐ p orbitals
☐ d orbitals ☐ f orbitals

® Color the alkali metals, the alkaline earths, and helium, light blue. Color the transition metals, including Family 3B—the single group to the immediate right of the alkaline earths—yellow-orange. Color the lanthanides and actinides—both the elements themselves and their place holder between the transition elements—pink. Color the "3A-8A" region tan. Finally, color the legend, using this clue: the blue block is two elements wide and the total electron capacity of the s-sublevel, with its single orbital, is two, so you will color the "s orbital" tile the same color. Now, measure (by counting) the widths of the other three blocks (ignoring the gap in the transition elements) and use your knowledge of the total electron capacities of the other three sublevels to color the other three tiles (if you cannot do this right away, see "Error Analysis" on p. 103).

A *neutral* atom, as you know, has as many electrons as it has protons and, therefore, an electron population equal to its Z. Element number 74, therefore, has 74 electrons.

As we move laterally from one element to the next, the electrons are added one-by-one and, in this way, the configuration very gradually becomes more complex. An *electron notation* is the listing of this configuration's sublevels in their order of energy and indicating—with superscripts—how many electrons are in each orbital.

That of fluorine (Z = 9) is $1s^2 2s^2 2p^5$. This means that two of the orbitals of the 2p sublevel are full, and one is half-full ($2 \times 2 + 1 = 5$); in all, the sublevel is one electron away from being full. The next element, neon (Z = 10) has that additional electron, and so its notation (or written configuration) is $1s^2 2s^2 2p^6$. All the sublevels are full, so if we want to keep going, we will have to know where to put the eleventh electron of sodium (Z = 11). This element is in the s block, which you colored blue, and in Period 3. Now we know the notation: $1s^2 2s^2 2p^6 3s^1$. Magnesium (Z = 12), with one more 3s electron than sodium, will be $1s^2 2s^2 2p^6 3s^2$. Aluminum (Z = 13) has still one more electron, but look: it is over in the p block, so its final valence electron will be in a p-sublevel orbital: $1s^2 2s^2 2p^6 3s^2 3p^1$. And so on.

You can readily see, then, that if you can identify the four divisions of the Periodic Table, you are not only freed from having to memorize the order of the sublevels, but you are all but *practically prevented* from mistaking it. As you write a notation, you just add, as we just did, one electron for each successive element.

The location of the element in the Periodic Table will give you the sublevel of that electron, and the Period will give you the PEL integer (although *for transition elements* you must subtract one from the period number to get the PEL; finally, the lanthanides and actinides we can forget).

1s	H		→
2s→			2p ————
3s→			3p ————
4s→	3d ————————→		4p ————
5s→	4d ————————→		5p ————
6s→	5d ————————→		6p ————
7s→	6d Ha		
		4f ————————————	
		5f ————————————	

⊛ Color the Periodic Table on this page in identical fashion as the one on the previous page (by block).

As you write an electronic notation, use the Periodic Table to remember the order of the sublevels for you. Move your eye from left to right, top to bottom, until you get to the destination element. For each "passage" through a block (see arrows, above right), you will write three things: the (1) PEL (1, 2, 3, 4....), the (2) sublevel (s, p, d, f), and (3) the width of the block (or sublevel) as a superscript. You have already seen several examples of this on previous pages.

As you can see from the Periodic Table, only four widths are possible (and only three, 2, 6, and 10, are dealt with in this book). Further, each of these widths is associated with its own sublevel letter (s^2, p^6, d^{10}). All, or all but one, of the superscripts in a notation, then, will be one of these because they represent full sublevels. Only the last superscript may be different. If your element is in the middle of a block instead of on its leading edge, the "passage" will be incomplete and the last width less; as each passage corresponds to a sublevel, this means an incompletely filled sublevel. To get this final superscript, then, you need only count the width of the incomplete passage.

An example: write the electronic notation for manganese.

The three "things" for the first complete passage are $1s^2$; so you write this and do the same for the other full passages up to the last one, which, because it does not stop at the end of a block, is incomplete. Manganese is five electrons, or squares, wide; thus:

$$1s^2 2s^2 2p^6 3s^2 3p^6 4s^2 3d^5$$

After writing an electronic notation, you can check its accuracy by adding the superscripts. Their sum must equal the element's Z. The total in the above notation is 25, which is the atomic number of manganese, so the notation is correct.

Now, then, where can one go wrong? In three places, really.

Error Analysis

The first you might already know about: it has to do with the failure to subtract 1 from the Period to get the n of a passage through the transition metals, or the d-block.

So think of it like this: blocks of *representative* elements always correctly *represent* the PEL with their period number. Transition elements are more *conservative*; they want to conserve the electrons they have and so fill the d-sublevel of the lower PEL instead of putting them out on an s-sublevel in the next highest PEL. So, for *d*-block passages, you "*d*-duct" 1 from the period number. For their *conservatism*, transition metals are called "inner-building."

The second type of error is the failure to automatically associate 2 with s, 6 with p, etc., in all but the last part of a notation.

Finally, there is a semantic confusion. As adjectives modifying the noun "electron(s)," the words "s-sublevel" (or *p*- or *d*- or *f*-) and "s-orbital" and "s-block" all mean the same thing.

103

3.4 Valence Electrons

1A	2A	3A	4A	5A	6A	7A	8A
H 1	valence electrons						He 2
Li 1	Be 2	B 3	C 4	N 5	O 6	F 7	Ne 8
Na 1	Mg 2	Al 3	Si 4	P 5	S 6	Cl 7	Ar 8
K 1	Ca 2			As 5	Se 6	Br 7	Kr 8

⊕ s-orbitals light green; p, light blue

The term "valence electrons" refers to those outermost electrons that—by their number and the strength of their attachment to their atoms—determine the peculiar behavior of each element.

Aside from the nuclear branch of chemistry, valence electrons are responsible for most of what an atom does, even though they average only about 1.0 $\times 10^{-4}$ of the atom's mass.

In the representative elements, the valence electrons are those that compose the entire top PEL. This limits s-block elements to a maximum of two valence electrons, and p-block elements, to eight (six from the p-sublevel and two from the s-sublevel).

In transition elements, the valence electrons come not only from the highest PEL, but also from the highest *sublevel* which, as indicated by the Table, is *not* in the highest PEL, but in the next highest. This means that when, say, manganese ionizes, it can lose electrons from both the 4s and 3d sublevels. Specifically, it can lose 2, 3, 4, 6, or even 7 (which is all the electrons in both top sublevels). Thus it has *valencies* of 2, 3, 4, 6, and 7, and so can form the ions Mn^{2+}, Mn^{3+}, Mn^{4+}, Mn^{6+}, and Mn^{7+}. A transition metal is not, however, always at risk of losing all its valence electrons. Iron, for instance, has even one valence electron *more* than manganese, but it only loses 2 or 3, and so it has only these valencies.

Chlorine's only valency is 1, because it has 7 *valence electrons*, and so room for only one more (so it forms only the Cl^- ion). In the Table (left) note that, in A-family elements, the number of valence electrons increases from one to eight within a period. All members of these families have the same number of valence electrons, although some have *multiple*

valencies (e.g., tin and lead: 2+ and 4+). Note the correlation between valence electrons and family number.

The noble gases have a full set, or *octet* [from Latin, "eight"] of electrons, except helium, which is full with a *duet*. These two arrangements, especially the former, are *noble-gas configurations*. A-family elements ionize because they, too, want these noble-gas configurations, which they obtain by gaining or losing valence electrons.

How many? This you already know. Calcium and its siblings lose two ($4s^2$) to present an octet to the world. Lithium loses its single valence electron ($2s^1$) to form a duet as the ion, Li^+. Arsenic must gain three ($3p^3 \to 3p^6$) and become arsenide, As^{3-}, to get an octet.

Do not confuse noble-gas configurations with the noble gases themselves. Acquiring the former does not affect an atom's proton count, nor, therefore, its elemental identity, even though its properties are radically altered (and in *no* case will it behave like a noble gas). Nor must you confuse valency (which can vary) with an element's number of valence electrons (which is fixed for each).

Elements such as boron, carbon, and silicon rarely form elemental ions, but their valencies are still relevant to the concept of oxidation numbers, as we will see in Chap. 10.

3.5 Electronegativity

H 2.1									He –
Li 1.0	Be 1.5	**PAULING**		B 2.0	C 2.5	N 3.0	O 3.5	F 4.0	Ne –
Na 0.9	Mg 1.2	**SCALE**		Al 1.5	Si 1.8	P 2.1	S 2.5	Cl 3.0	Ar –
K 0.8	Ca 1.0		Mn 1.5	Ga 1.6	Ge 1.8	As 2.0	Se 2.4	Br 2.8	Kr –
Rb 0.8	Sr 1.0	Y 1.2		In 1.7	Sn 1.8	Sb 1.9	Te 2.1	I 2.5	Xe –
Cs 0.7	Ba 0.9		Hg 1.9	Tl 1.8	Pb 1.8	Bi 1.9	Po 2.0	At 2.2	Rn –

Electronegativity is the relative ability of a neutral atom to capture valence electrons from other atoms. The more highly electronegative elements become anions by taking electrons from less electronegative atoms which, in the same process, become cations. Ideally, both come away from the experience with a noble-gas configuration.

Being relative, the electronegativity values do not derive from direct measurements, which are impossible. Pauling got the value for each element by measuring the energy needed to break its bonds with other elements (bond energies). He discovered, however, that an element's (or an atom's) electronegativity is not constant because it can be affected by the number and properties of the other elements in the compound.

Yet, while the Pauling Scale values may not be precise, electronegativity is nevertheless useful in predicting whether a compound will be covalent, ionic, or have characteristics of both; for while most compounds (excepting the all-metal ones) are demonstrably one or the other, a great many belong to a range of gradations in between ionic and covalent, as we will see presently.

To make such a prediction for a binary compound is easy: merely calculate (if it can be called that) the difference in the two elements' electronegativities. If the difference is under 1.7, we consider the compound covalent (molecular). If it is over 1.9, we put it in the ionic category.

For instance, carbon dioxide is covalent, because $3.5 - 2.5 = 1.0$. Nitric oxide is even more covalent, for $3.5 - 3.0 = 0.5$. Potassium oxide, though, is truly ionic, as $3.5 - 0.8 = 2.7$. But when magnesium and chlorine get together, we have a borderline case. Check the electronegativities shown above and perform the subtraction, and you will see why.

Notice the periodicity of electronegativity. Allowing for the imprecise and arbitrary nature of the values, the Period 2 elements—lithium to fluorine—increase at regular intervals (of 0.5) as does most of Period 3 (0.3). Roughly speaking, the more heavy and metallic an element is, the less electronegative it will be, and vice versa. The noble gases, with their full outer PELs, are completely uninterested in other atoms' electrons, and so have no Pauling Scale values.

A *noble gas core* is something which has nothing whatsoever to do with the noble gases. It is a shorthand device for abbreviating electron notations, and consists in a noble gas' symbol in brackets ([He], [Ne], [Ar], etc.) and stands for all the electrons included in the gas' configuration. Thus, potassium, for instance, can be written $[Ar]4s^1$ instead of $1s^22s^22p^63s^23p^64s^1$. It signifies only electrons and does not, of course, suggest that there is also an argon nucleus at the center of a potassium atom.

9
F
18.998

𝕻rofile: 𝕱luorine

F_2 is used as an oxidizing agent to combust rocket fuels such as hydrazine (N_2H_4).

More than one early discovery attempt of element number nine went like this: a caustic gas with an apocalyptic color evolved, attacking everything in its path, including the discoverer's own spectacles and then even killing him. It is not for nothing that chemistry teachers often call fluorine the "meanest element."

There are other, less anthropomorphic superlatives that help explain fluorine's bad disposition. Of all the elements, it is the most reactive, the most nonmetallic, the strongest oxidizer, and the most electronegative (with a Pauling Scale value of 4; think of "four-ine"). Ironically, in spite of (and even because of) all this malevolence, fluorine compounds are among the most stable and inert substances known.

The tenacity with which this element holds onto other elements is the reason for the exceptional stability of such compounds as teflon (C_2F_2), the familiar pan coating, and the refrigerant, freon ($C_2Cl_2F_2$). In both, the element's active nature is fully tamed.

A salt, tin (II) fluoride (or "stannous fluoride" by an older system of nomenclature) is the active ingredient in most commercial toothpastes sold in the U.S. and India. Some water supplies in the former country were fluoridated (to 1 ppm) in a broad effort to fight tooth decay after it was found that residents of Deaf Smith County, Texas, enjoyed exceptional dental health, and that the local water supplies were naturally fluoridated. The salt is thought to undergo a replacement reaction with the surface of the teeth themselves, leaving fluoride ions (which act very differently from fluorine atoms) in the enamel. Fluoridation has been debated but rejected in the United Kingdom, although fears that the ion was a carcinogen seem unfounded. It is a virtual certainty however, that fluorine is not a necessary trace element for living tissues.

Only 0.1% of the Earth's crust is fluorine, if that. Obviously, it is never found uncombined, but instead in minerals such as fluorspar (CaF_2) and cryolite (Na_3AlF_2). It can be isolated by electrolyzing anhydrous salts such as potassium fluoride. Isolation by chemical means is literally impossible, because fluorine will either combine with any agent used to obtain it or it will resist being uncombined with what it is already bonded to.

The gas hydrofluoric acid is a weak acid and so reacts poorly with metals and bases; but it reacts vigorously with glass, and so is used in glass-etching. It is also the closest thing we have to an "ionic gas," as will be explained in the following section.

Fluorine's oxidizing potential enables it to displace chlorine from its salts. Oxidizing strengths decrease with an increase of atomic weight in the halogen family. Chlorine can likewise displace bromine from its salts, as bromine can replace iodine.

Not surprisingly, fluorine was the first element to be reacted with a noble gas (but under only under some pretty extenuated laboratory conditions).

With the promotion, in xenon, of a 5p and a 5s electron to an artificially created 5d sublevel, four electrons are left unpaired to bond with four fluorine atoms, to form XeF_4 (1962).

5s	5p		5s	5p		5d	
⇅	⇅ ⇅ ⇅	△→	↓	⇅ ⇅ ↓	↑	↑ ⇅ ⇅	
			F	F F			

In this way, xenon is made to have four, rather than eight, valence electrons, each of which are snapped up by an octet-seeking fluorine atom.

More recently fluorine was combined with krypton, and oxygen with xenon.

ACTIVE INGREDIENT: STANNOUS FLUORIDE

1. Fill in the blanks with "duet" or "octet" according to the description:

_____ configuration for hydride (H^-), helium, beryllium ion (Be^{2+}), etc.

_____ an s-orbital plus a p-orbital

_____ full outermost PEL for all Period 1 elements

_____ full outermost PEL for all Period 2, 3, 4, 5, 6, and 7 elements

_____ configuration for krypton, oxide, arsenide, sodium ion, barium ion, etc.

2. Explain briefly how the number of electrons "holdable" by each sublevel determines the shape of the Periodic Table:

3. Identify the sublevel block (s, p, d, f) of each of the following using a standard Periodic Table (one not from this chapter)(hint below if needed):

_____ alkali metals   _____ halogens   _____ Family 4A

_____ coinage metals   _____ helium   _____ actinides

_____ lanthanides   _____ other noble gases   _____ Cringing Matrons

_____ all but two nonmetals   _____ Family 4B   Fear Cobwebs

(hint: what orbitals are being filled as we pass through each group on the way from hydrogen to Hahnium, adding an electron with each square?)

4. Using a standard Periodic Table, write the electron notations for:

H _____   O _____

Mg _____   Cl _____

Sc _____

Fe _____

Zn _____

Kr _____

Rb _____

Now, continue, using not the Table, but the notation you have just done for rubidium (Z = 37) to do notations for strontium (Z = 38) and yttrium (Z = 39):

Sr _____

Y _____

5. Identify this element using the Periodic Table:

$$1s^2 2s^2 2p^6 3s^2 3p^6 4s^2 3d^{10} 4p^6 5s^2 4d^{10} 5p^6 6s^2 5d^1$$

Answer: _____

6. List in order the electronegativities for (a) Period 2 elements up to fluorine and (b) Period 3 elements up to phophorus:

Li to F: _____

Na to P: _____

7. Using electronegativity disparities, predict the bond nature of these binary possibilites (C = covalent; I = ionic; B = border line):

C,S ____   Ca,O ____   C,H ____   Mn,O ____

Sn,F ____   C,O ____   Na,Cl ____   K,I ____

Pb,O ____   Si,Cl ____   Br,N ____   P,H ____

Ba,Br ____   Mg,N ____   Hg,S ____   Cs,F ____

3.6 Covalency

IN COVALENT COMPOUNDS, THE ATOMS ARE LIKE OVERLAPPING PUZZLE PIECES.

YES!

THEY'RE PUZZLING!

The theory of ionic bonding is older than that of covalent bonding. It was once believed that all atoms had to become ions to form compounds.

But while some compounds had properties that clearly revealed their ionic pedigrees—such as good electrical conductivity—other compounds did not. For this, chemists began to suspect that compounds might somehow be made up of neutral atoms. In 1916, Lewis proposed that in such substances neutral atoms were joined by shared electrons rather than the opposite charges that resulted from the transfer of electrons (as is still believed to be the case for *ionic* compounds). These shared electrons are, of course, valence electrons, and this is how we get "co-valent."

The *co-* prefix means shared, while the root word (valent) reminds us just which electrons are involved.

Covalent also means molecular. An ion's charge can be felt by any nearby and oppositely charged ion, whereas in a covalent species the bonding medium is an actual particle—the electron. These electrons, in pairs, fasten neutral or relatively neutral atoms into larger discrete particles—molecules. In covalent, as well as in ionic bonding, atoms seek duets or octets. But if the electrons are truly shared by two atoms, the atoms will not themselves be charged and, therefore, not pulled every which way by other particles. They are "free" and, therefore, molecules rather than formula units. There are, by the way, inter*molecular* forces which are like the inter*ionic* forces that hold lattices together. They differ primarily only in degree, with molecules having the weaker attractions for each other, such that they are discrete particles.

To demonstrate covalency, Lewis used the symbols of the elements surrounded by dots representing their valence electrons.

Family	1A	2A	3A	4A	5A	6A	7A	8A
Period 2	• Li	:Be	:B•	:C••	:N•• •	:O: ••	• :F: ••	•• :Ne: ••
Period 3	•Na	:Mg	:Al•	:Si••	:P•• •	:S: ••	• :Cl: ••	•• :Ar: ••

This chart is not for memorizing; use it to observe the pattern. By now, though, you should be used to the number of valence electrons in at least a few of the elements (H, C, N, O, Na, Cl, Ca, for instance). If you know the numbers, you will be able to do your own Lewis, or dot, diagrams. For heavier A-family elements, it is only a matter of looking at the Periodic Table to find (if you do not already know) the family that the element belongs to.

The number of the A-family, **remember**, is also the number of valence electrons.

Fluorine (Family 7A) has seven, and so iodine, far (but directly) below it, will also have seven. Like fluorine, then, iodine will also have a **valency** of 1 (iodine also has other valencies, for it can lose some of its valence electrons; fluorine is invariable because it cannot). This valency of 1 is accounted for by the fact that, with just one more electron, either element can form an octet.

It will not matter, when you draw Lewis diagrams, how you arrange the dots; the only important thing is having the right number of them.

SO HOW DOES AN ATOM'S VALENCY DERIVE FROM ITS NUMBER OF VALENCE ELECTRONS?

THERE ARE EITHER TOO FEW OR TOO MANY VALENCE ELECTRONS IN MOST NEUTRAL ATOMS FOR OCTETS AND DUETS. THE NUMBER OF ELECTRON(S) THEY MUST SNARE, SPARE OR SHARE TO HAVE AN OCTET OR DUET WITHIN A COMPOUND ARE VALENCIES...

I'LL BE BACK!

An atom's valency is its "snare, spare, or share" number, the quantity of electrons that it must share with another atom (covalency) *or* snare from/spare to another atom (ionism) to get a noble-gas configuration.

You already know some of these as ionic charges. Magnesium has a charge of 2+ and (therefore) a valency of 2; it has two electrons to *spare* in an ionic combination or to *share* in a covalent one (it is not electronegative enough to ever *snare* any). Fluorine is different. It's charge is always 1− and (so) its valency, as you know, is always 1. This time, however, the number is usually the snare kind, although it can occasionally share (but it *never* spares).

Recall that many elements, notably the transition metals, have multiple valencies. In other words, they can share different numbers of electrons when they form covalent compounds, or snare-or-spare different numbers when they form ionic compounds. As some elements have intermediate Pauling Scale values and therefore seldom form elemental ions, most or nearly all of their compounds are covalent.

Carbon has four valence electrons to share, and so is able to bond with up to four other atoms that have electrons to share. When any two atoms join covalently, each contributes an electron to the bond. *Covalent bonds*, then, *are composed of two electrons, a shared pair.*

Hydrogen atoms can form only one bond, because they cannot hold enough electrons—neither valently nor covalently—to form more. A single hydrogen atom has a single valence electron, but when bonded to another hydrogen (fig. a) it has two valence electrons through sharing.

(The "kcals" label is included here only to remind you that chemical reactions involve heat transfer. The reaction in (a) happens to be exothermic, giving off 104 kilocalories for each mole of H_2 formed from hydrogen atoms breaking off of acid molecules.)

(a)

$$H\cdot \ + \ \cdot H \ \rightarrow \ H\overset{\bullet}{\cdot}H \ + \ 104 \text{ kcals}$$

(b)

$$K\cdot \ + \ \cdot\ddot{Cl}\colon \ \rightarrow \ K\overset{\bullet}{\cdot}\ddot{Cl}\colon \ + \ 192 \text{ kcals}$$

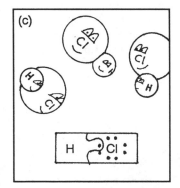

(c)

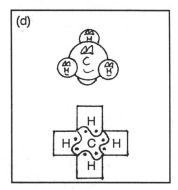

(d)

Potassium and chlorine also form from only one bond, because their number of valence electrons (7 and 1, respectively) is such that whenever they share, snare, or spare, only one electron is involved, so both have a valency of 1. When these two get together, chlorine snares and potassium spares (b) because their electronegativity disparity is fairly high (2.2).

Hydrogen and chlorine, with their rather low difference (0.9), form a covalent compound (c), one made of molecules.

A solution of KCl (a salt) will conduct electricity because it is an ionic compound, whereas pure HCl, an acid, will not (although it *will* in aqueous solution, but only because the water causes it to ionize).

Finally, hydrogen and carbon in a 1:4 ratio form methane, which is so covalent (disparity of 0.4) that its molecules are gaseous at normal temperatures because they have too little of the intermolecular attraction (caused by unequal sharing) to stick together (d).

109

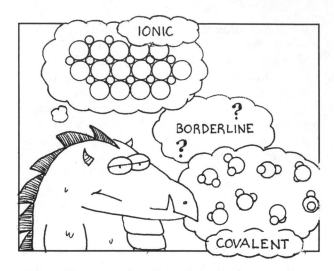

Borderline cases—those compounds between elements with electronegativity disparities from 1.7 to 1.9—are molecular, but they are said to have *strong ionic character.*

Indeed, bonds between elements with differences as low as 0.5 exhibit *some* partial ionic character, such that the nature of chemical bonds, like spectral lines, expresses itself as a continuum of differences. The extremes of the bonding continuum, as it were, are (1) those compounds that are highly ionic and those that are (2) highly covalent.

Hydrofluoric acid (hydrogen fluoride) is an example of a compound right in the middle, one with partial ionic character. The Pauling Scale difference between its two components is 1.9. If we were to test some liquefied HF, we would observe both ionic and covalent properties.

Its character is covalent because the electrons are shared, but it is also ionic because the sharing is so unequal as to make one component (the fluorine atom) into a negatively charged region within the molecule, and the other component (the hydrogen atom) into a positively charged region.

Since the fluorine hogs the electron cloud, it seems (and is) more negative and is therefore attracted to the positive regions ("the hydrogen ends") of *other* HF molecules. These other hydrogen atoms naturally reciprocate the attraction. In this way, a semi-ionic bond is formed *between* atoms of different molecules, while a somewhat covalent bond continues to exist *within* the molecules.

The hydrogen fluoride particle, then, is still a molecule, but—as a consequence of very unequal electron sharing—it is an exceedingly polar one. It has a positive pole (hydrogen) and a negative pole (fluoride) that cause it to link up with other such molecules, forming something that is perfectly analogous to a chain of joined bar magnets.

Just a little more polarity, however, would blur the distinction between the weakly covalent bonds inside the molecules and the nearly ionic bonds outside of them. It would cause the molecules to lose their discreteness, or individuality, and HF would just be a formula unit. Then, each atom would be joined to no one (oppositely charged) neighboring atom in particular, but to all.

Electron distribution in a HF molecule

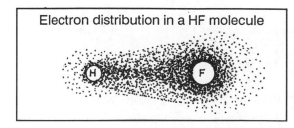

Quasi-ionic chain of polar HF molecules

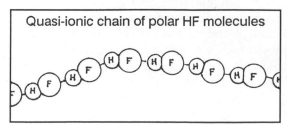

110

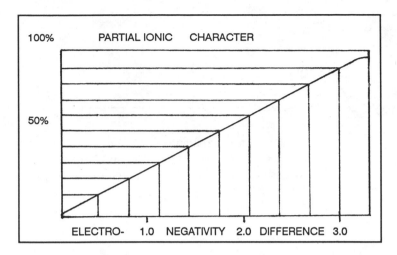

Polar covalent compounds result from the bonding of elements with an electronegativity difference between 0.5 and the 1.7-1.9 borderline range. They have positive and negative poles due to an asymmetric distribution of electrons in the molecule, such as that just described for hydrogen fluoride. As this sharing becomes more equitable, however, the compounds are more and more like what we think of as truly molecular.

If the electronegativity difference is very low—under 0.5—then the electrons will be so evenly shared and distributed that the molecule will have no poles to speak of; it will be *nonpolar*. Hence, the comparison of (1) nonpolar covalent, (2) polar covalent, and (3) primarily ionic can be defined by a parallel continuum based on the degree of electron sharing:

nonpolar covalent ‹ › polar covalent ‹ › primarily ionic

equal sharing ⟵⟶ unequal sharing ⟵⟶ nonsharing

Compare the electron cloud of hydrogen fluoride, on p. 110 with that of H_2 on p. 97. The respective differences in Pauling Scale values are 1.9 and 0. HF is very polar and asymmetrical while H_2 has perfect symmetry and, therefore, no poles whatsoever. This is to be expected for molecules of diatomic elements, because the electronegativity difference between the bonding atoms—which are identical, according to Dalton's third postulate—is 0 (a difference of 2.1 − 2.1), and this is why elemental molecules are the most molecular of all.

The molecules of a few combinations of elements also achieve this extreme covalency, such as in the case of carbon disulfide, made up of two elements with equal electronegativity, and so also have a difference of 0.

⊛ Color the rectangle in the lower left corner of the above chart, violet. This is the nonpolar covalent region. Then color the next four (the polar covalent area) in order, VB, BV, B, and BG. Lastly, color the ionic zone GB, G, GY, YG and, finally, yellow. Try to make the colors merge as you did when coloring the visible light continuum in Sect. 3.1.

1. duet, octet, duet, octet, octet

2. The electron capacity of a sublevel equals the number of element-squares that make up a period (this answer could be phrased much differently and still be correct).

3. (by columns :)

s	p	p
d	s	f
f	p	d
p	d	

4.

(H) $1s^1$

(O) $1s^22s^226^4$

(Mg) $1s^22s^22p^63s^2$

(Cl) $1s^22s^22p^63s^23p^5$

(Sr) $1s^22s^22p^63s^23p^64s^23d^{10}4p^65s^2$

(Sc) $1s^22s^22p^63s^23p^64s^23d^1$

(Fe) $1s^22s^22p^63s^23p^64s^23d^6$

(Zn) $1s^22s^22p^63s^23p^64s^23d^{10}$

(Kr) $1s^22s^22p^63s^23p^64s^23d^{10}4p^6$

(Rb) $1s^22s^22p^63s^23p^64s^23d^{10}4p^65s^1$

(Y) $1s^22s^22p^63s^23p^64s^23d^{10}4p^65s^24d^1$

5. Lanthanum (Z = 57); Did you count the subscripts? That is the easier way.

6. 1.0, 1.5, 2.0, 2.5, 3.0, 3.5, 4.0 (count by fives)   0.9, 1.2, 1.5, 1.8, 2.1 (count by threes)

7. (C,S) C (Ca,O) I (C,H) C (Mn,O) I (Sn,F) I (C,O) C (Na,Cl) I (K,I) B (Pb,O) B (Si,Cl) C (Br,N) C (P,H) C (Ba,Br) I (Mg,N) B (Hg,S) C (Cs,F) I

112

3.7 Dot Diagrams

The tendency of A-family elements (except hydrogen and a few others) to seek complete eight-electron noble gas configurations is called, appropriately enough, the *octet rule*.

Carbon and silicon each have four valence electrons, so they seek four more through sharing (both have middling electronegativities and so form mostly covalent compounds). In ethane, C_2H_6, (as in methane), each carbon atom gets these four electrons from four other atoms; in this case, they are another carbon and three hydrogens. We can represent each bonding pair (of shared electrons) as a coupling dash:

$$
\begin{array}{ccc}
\overset{\displaystyle H}{\underset{\displaystyle H}{H\!:\!C\!:}} \overset{\displaystyle H}{\underset{\displaystyle H}{C\!:\!H}} & \text{becomes} & \overset{\displaystyle H \;\; H}{\underset{\displaystyle H \;\; H}{H-C-C-H}}
\end{array}
$$

Ethane and methane (p. 109), then , are very happy arrangements, for, through sharing, each hydrogen atom has its duet, or two valence electrons, and each carbon atom, its octet.

methane	ethane
$\overset{\displaystyle H}{\underset{\displaystyle H}{H-C-H}}$	$\overset{\displaystyle H \;\; H}{\underset{\displaystyle H \;\; H}{H-C-C-H}}$
ethene	ethyne
$\overset{H\qquad\quad H}{\underset{H\qquad\quad H}{C=C}}$	$H-C\equiv C-H$

If, however, when these gases form from decomposing organic matter, there is not enough hydrogen to go around, no problem; the atoms still manage to find a way. If only four (rather than six) hydrogens are available for every two carbons, then each carbon has only three other atoms to bond with, but it needs to form four bonds for an octet. So, the two carbons share their leftover electrons with each other:

$$
\overset{\displaystyle H}{\underset{\displaystyle H \;\; H}{H-C\text{-}C-H}} \quad \text{becomes} \quad \overset{H\qquad\quad H}{\underset{H\qquad\quad H}{C=C}}
$$

Ethene, C_2H_4, then, has a *double covalent bond.*

If still less hydrogen were around, such that each carbon would have still one bonding partner fewer and, consequently, two excess electrons, it does the same thing as before: it shares with the other carbon to form, in ethyne, C_2C_2, a *triple covalent bond:*

$$
H-C\text{-}C-H \quad \text{becomes} \quad H-C\equiv C-H
$$

A multiple bond, a triple one in particular, has a higher bond energy value than a single bond; that is, more energy is required to break it than to break a single bond. This fact explains the stability of the nitrogen molecule, N_2:

$$:N\equiv N:$$

...although even this triple bond can be broken by the pressures and temperatures inside the internal combustion engine, which combine N_2 into oxide pollutants.

The halogen atoms, such as F_2 and Br_2, are more weakly bonded to each other, having only one shared pair:

$$:\ddot{F}-\ddot{F}: \qquad :\ddot{Br}-\ddot{Br}:$$

This fact goes a long way towards explaining the eager reactivity of this family. That they form just one bond, remember, is due to their valency (1); their octets lack one electron, while nitrogen (whose valency is usually three) lacks three.

Count the dots around the atoms in the diatomic and organic molecules above, letting each bond count as *two* dots for *both* of the atoms it touches, and you will see that the octet rule is satisfied in each case.

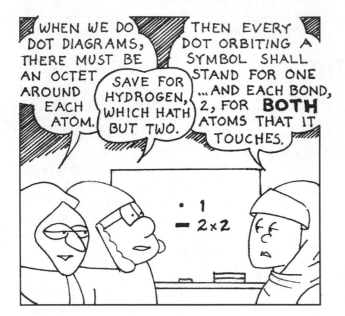

WHEN WE DO DOT DIAGRAMS, THERE MUST BE AN OCTET AROUND EACH ATOM.

SAVE FOR HYDROGEN, WHICH HATH BUT TWO.

THEN EVERY DOT ORBITING A SYMBOL SHALL STAND FOR ONE ...AND EACH BOND, 2, FOR **BOTH** ATOMS THAT IT TOUCHES.

Whenever we do Lewis, or "dot" diagrams, we are aided by the stalwart reliability of four important nonmetals:

Hydrogen always forms *one* bond.

Fluorine always forms *one* bond.

Carbon and *silicon* nearly always form four bonds.

If you know the valencies of these elements (and by now you should), then there is nothing more to memorize. In nonmetals, specifically, valency most of the time refers to the number of electrons that an element's octet *lacks*. The valency of nonmetals, in most cases (and in all cases for H, F, C, and Si) is the same as the number of bonds they form because they try, at every opportunity, to satisfy their electron appetites with the same number of electrons.

To go with the engraved-in-stone rules for the four above-mentioned elements are two generalizations, one for oxygen and another for a grab-bag of other elements, including some metals that can form true radicals and molecules.

The oxygen generalization is that, due to its valency, oxygen usually forms two bonds, but it sometimes forms only one. The other elements also follow the valency/bond number correlation, unless they bond with a more electronegative element than themselves. Since chlorine (3.0), for instance, seeks only one more valence electron —and, therefore, to form only one bond—and since it already has seven valence electrons, it can be forced to share those it already has with oxygen (3.5). Together, the two gases only form one or two marginally stable neutral compounds, but they do form a series of important and very stable ions (figs. a-d) and, by extension, a series of acids.

The second generalization, which springs from these circumstances, is this: in an oxyanion or oxyacid or certain non-oxygen-containing atoms, *the central atom will be surrounded by its more electronegative partners*

(unless it is hydrogen, which can only surround and not *be surrounded by* others). In most oxygen-containing dot diagrams which you will see and do in Chem. 1, oxygen will be surrounding the other elements.

One more important fact, about acids. Acids, as you know, are a large class of covalent hydrogen compounds. When ionized, they lose all or some of their hydrogen as protons (H^+). But while hydrogen is covalently part of an acid molecule, *the hydrogen is typically bonded to an oxygen atom* (fig. e).

There are, of course, a few common acids without oxygen, and some are shown (fig. f).

Note the relation between the oxyanion, chlorate (fig. c), and its conjugate oxyacid, chloric acid (fig. e). In the former, there are three oxygens, each having one bond and six nonbonding valence electrons. In the **ion's acid** *conjugate*, a proton is attached to one of the oxygens, so that that oxygen has two bonds and only four nonbonding electrons.

We will not be concerned, at this level, with acids corresponding to ions more complex than those introduced in Sect. 2.6.

(a) hypochorite (ClO^-)	(b) chlorite (ClO_2^-)
(c) chlorate (ClO_3^-)	(d) hypochlorite (ClO_4^-)
(e) chloric acid ($HClO_3$)	(f) acids without oxygen

NO SWEAT. ALL I HAFTA DO IS RECALL VALENCIES AND RELATIVE ELECTRONEGATIVITIES, AND THAT HYDROGEN USUALLY STICKS TO OXYGEN, AND OXYGEN TO EVERYTHING ELSE... BUT WHAT'S THE FIRST STEP IN DRAWING A DOT DIAGRAM?

COUNTING THE AVAILABLE VALENCE ELECTRONS.

STEP ONE Add up the valence electrons of all the elements present.

STEP TWO Arrange the Lewis symbols according to the rules and generalizations from p. 114. Put (at first) single bonds between the atoms, and dots outside of them. Give each atom (except H) an octet's worth of bonds and dots.

STEP THREE Add up the valence electrons represented in your drawing (a dot = 1; a bond = 2). If this second addition equals the first addition, you are done; no fourth step is needed. But...

STEP FOUR ...if your new count is overmuch by 2, then there will be a double bond somewhere. If there are four too many, then there will be a triple bond or two double bonds. And so on.

For each extra two electrons, there will be an additional bond forming part of a multiple—double or triple—bond. By making multiple bonds in your diagrams, you can reduce the electron count to the original, correct sum. This is becuse, while a bond only counts for two electrons in the addition, it is like two electrons to *both* of the atoms it touches. In this way, one bond is made of *two* valence electrons but it substitutes for *four* valence electrons. Now, some examples.

Draw the dot diagram of hydrobromic acid, HBr. You know that hydrogen will form only one bond, and you might remember that bromine—as a halogen—has seven valence electrons, so it, too, will form one bond (at least in this and most other cases). First, you add the valence electrons (fig. 1a), then draw the diagram to give hydrogen its two electrons, and iodine its eight (1b). Counting the new total (1c) you get the original total, and so you are done.

Another example. Sulfur dioxide (2a-d) has 18 valence electrons in all, six from each atom (they are all Family-6A atoms). Draw the diagram and count in the usual way. The new total is 20, so you must add a bond (2 electrons) somewhere and remove an electron pair from both atoms that the bond joins. Arithmetically, this is 20 + 2 − 4 = 18.

The inequality of the two S−O bonds, by the way, is not real; the extra bond "resonates" or is distributed in some way between the two otherwise single bonds. Just the same, it is alright to draw the bonds in this fashion (What choice do you have?).

Organic molecules are characterized by chains of carbon atoms with other atoms attached. Draw the carbon "skeleton" first, with single bonds, then add on the rest. At left is propyl bromide. Its empirical formula is C_3H_7Br and its structural formula is $CH_3CH_2CH_2Br$. Can you see how?

(1a)	(1b)	(1c)
H 1 Br 7 ——— 8	H−Br:	dots 6 bonds 2 ——— 8

(2a)	(2b)
S 6 O (2 x 6) 12 ——— 18	:S−O: | :O:

(2c)	(2d)
dots 16 bonds 4 ——— 20	·S=O: | :O:

carbon chain	saturation
−C−C−C−	H H H | | | H−C−C−C−Br | | | H H H

(1)	(2a)	(2b)	(2c)	(2d)
$\left[:\ddot{O}-S-\ddot{O}:\right]^{2-}$ with $:\ddot{O}:$ below	C (2 x 4) = 8 H (3 x 1) = 3 O (2 x 6) = 12 Charge = 1 —— 24	$\left[\begin{array}{c}H\\H-C-C\\H\end{array}\right]^{-}$ with two O's	dots 14 bonds 12 —— 26	$\left[\begin{array}{c}H\\H-C-C\\H\end{array}\right]^{-}$ with two O's

To diagram a radical, or compound ion, you follow the same steps as before, but you *let the charge account for part of the electron total.* You should also bracket the diagram and label it with its charge. In sulfite (fig.1), for instance, the sulfur atom contributes six; each of the three oxygens also puts in six, and the charge adds two to the first, pre-diagramming sum. Conveniently, this sum will be the same number you get by giving each atom an octet. Think, then, of the charge not as a complication, but instead as a conspicuous, known discrepancy that you, as a bookkeeper, know will balance the accounts. Note that it is *not* figured into the second addition.

Acetate (figs. 2a-d), whose structural formula is CH_3COO^-, is the conjugate of acetic acid, which gives vinegar its sourness. It (acetate) is a particle with the works: multiple bonding, organic character, and charge. Study each of the above steps (the same four described on p. 115). When you understand completely, good. It is more difficult than most or all of the problems in the problem set and on Chem. 1 tests.

Error Analysis

There is a common confusion in diagramming polyatomic ions like sulfite and acetate: substracting, rather than adding electrons because the charge has a negative (−) sign. Electrons, keep in mind, increase an ion's "negativeness."

Another problem, and not just with ions, is the fault of the atoms themselves. Not all have to form octets when they combine; there are exceptions to the octet rule. These atoms can, however, form stable compounds in which they have not eight shared valence electrons, but 3, 5, 6, 7, 10, 12, and even 14. So, if on a test you cannot make an octet each time, you are not automatically wrong.

Hydrogen, which is inherently unable to form octets, is the exception you already know. But neither can lithium and beryllium form octets, for their two s-sublevels do not have room. Boron almost never does. Nitrogen, while it usually does form octets, cannot do so with oxygen. Try as you may, you cannot take nitrogen's odd (in more ways than one) number of valence electrons (5) and make octet-containing oxides with them (although the oxygen atoms in these compounds will have *their* octets).

Many flourine (and, less frequently, chlorine) compounds are exceptional because fluorine atoms, with their extreme electronegativity can snare just about any other atom's valence electrons and, in doing so, form as many bonds as the other atom has valence electrons. The other exceptions cannot obey the octet rule; fluorine can ignore it. Some examples of these "metoctets" are below.

Beryllium and boron, while they cannot gather octets, can bond with fluorine in such a way that they have no unpaired electrons remaining (figs. a-b). We would expect these compounds to be ionic, due to the high electronegativity differences. In fact, they are molecules and thus (unlike formula units) diagrammable. In the next section, we will see why.

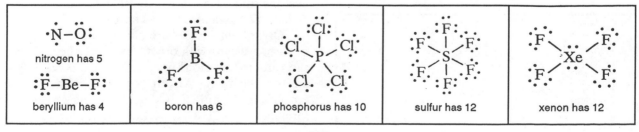

$\cdot N-\ddot{O}:$ nitrogen has 5 $:\ddot{F}-Be-\ddot{F}:$ beryllium has 4	$:\ddot{F}:$ B $:\ddot{F}:\quad:\ddot{F}:$ boron has 6	$:\ddot{Cl}:$ $Cl-P-Cl$ $Cl\quad Cl$ phosphorus has 10	$:\ddot{F}:$ $F-S-F$ $F\quad F$ $:\ddot{F}:$ sulfur has 12	$:\ddot{F}:\quad:\ddot{F}:$ Xe $:\ddot{F}:\quad:\ddot{F}:$ xenon has 12

1. Matching; connect the rows (as shown between the third and fourth columns).

bond type	Pauling Scale difference	examples	degree of sharing	bonding medium
polar	0-0.5	As-H	nonshared	e⁻ pair
nonpolar	18+	Cl-K	equal	charge
ionic	0.5-1.8	C-O	unequal	both

2. What generalizations can be made about the nature of metal/nonmetal bonds on the one hand and, on the other, those between two nonmetals?

3. Short answer: the gas N_2 is very stable due to its _____ _____.

4. Match these elements to their bonding patterns:

_____silicon   a. normally forms three bonds; sometimes more or less

_____nitrogen   b. never forms any bonds whatsoever

_____fluorine   c. always forms a single bond

_____sulfur   d. usually forms four bonds, potentially in long chains

_____neon   e. can form up to seven bonds

_____oxygen   f. can form up to six bonds

_____iodine   g. usually forms two bonds, sometimes only one

5. Boron does not form elemental ions. Why?

6. Do a dot diagram of each species, and name as many as you can:

a. I_2	b. O_2	c. O_3	d. O_2^{2-}	e. P^{3-}
f. PH_3	g. HCl	h. CO_2	i. CO	j. SiO_2
k. SeF_6	l. $SnCl_4$		m. BF_3	n. OH^-
o. NO_3^-	p. $AsCl_3$	q. H_3O^+	r. BrO_2^-	s. PO_3^{3-}
t. H_3PO_3	u. NH_4^+	v. H_2SO_4	w. CH_3Cl	x. CH_3CH_2OH

3.8 Molecular Geometry

To constuct ye basick tetrahedral moddell:
I. Connecte tentackles to the central atom.
II. Attache the repulsor paires as shown. They will maintaine precise 109.3° angles twixt. the tentackles.
III. Adde remaining atoms.

READY WHEN YOU ARE.

ELECTRONS REALLY ARE NEGATIVE!

WE HATE YOU!

WE HATE YOU, TOO!

Anyone who can do a molecule's dot diagram can predict its geometry. Most simple molecules without multiple bonds are of three types: (1) *linear*, (2) *tetrahedral*, and (3) modified tetrahedral.

A *tetrahedron,* geometrically speaking, is a shape with four equilateral triangles as its sides.

Methane (illustrated, below) is a tetrahedron. If you were to connect its four hydrogen atoms with imaginary lines, the lines would define the triangles, while the hydrogen atoms themselves (the tetrahedron's points) would define the tetrahedron's external angles. In the middle is a carbon atom. The hydrogen atoms are attached to it at angles of 109.3° with respect to each other. In this way, the four hydrogen atoms are as far from each other as they can possibly be.

This perfect spacing is caused by the *Electron Pair Repulsion Principle*, which states that *electron pairs around a central atom*—whether they are bond-forming electron pairs or no*t—will keep their mutual distance*. In this way, valence electrons determine the positions of atoms within molecules and, therefore, the molecules' geometries.

If one of the hydrogen atoms in methane is displaced by a chlorine atom, the resulting methyl chloride molecule (see below) would still be a true

(if not quite perfect) tetrahedon, for only a tiny distortion of the 109.3° angle would result from this change.

The simplest molecules, of course have only two atoms, and all of them (such as N_2 or HF) are linear; geometrically, they are mere line segments.

A few linear molecules, however, are triatomic. Recall that BeF_2 is an exception to the octet rule, because the beryllium atom is two electron pairs short of being able to form an octet. When a beryllium atom combines with two atoms of any element with a valency of 1 (H, F, Cl, Br, I), a triatomic particle results in which the two pairs of electrons—the only two present—repulse each other (and the molecule) into a straight line. We can call this special geometry *triatomic linear* (as opposed to plain old *ordinary diatomic linear*) which is everywhere.

Boron also has an octet deficiency, but of only one pair (not two, like beryllium) and is therefore responsible for another special geometry. The three electron pairs repulse each other into a triangle to form the *planar triangular* geometry.

There are triatomic linear and planar triangular molecules that do not contain (respectively) beryllium and boron, but they need multiple bonds to be that way.

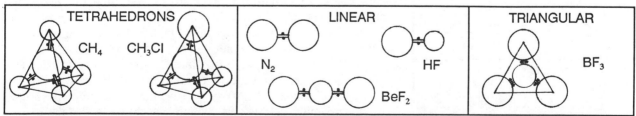

TETRAHEDRONS — CH_4 CH_3Cl

LINEAR — N_2 HF BeF_2

TRIANGULAR — BF_3

⊛ Color the carbon atoms dark gray; the hydrogen atoms, red; and the chlorine, green-yellow. In the linear molecules, color nitrogen blue-violet; fluorine, yellow; hydrogen, red again; and beryllium, light gray. In boron trifluoride, the boron is brown and the fluorine is again yellow.

A central atom with an octet is one surrounded by four electron pairs (4 pairs = 1 octet). This is how compounds whose dot diagrams follow the octet rule can form both true and modified (or "degenerate") tetrahedrons. The exceptions to the octet rule do not form tetrahedrons of any kind—neither true nor modified—because the central atom is surrounded by more or less than the four pairs and/or bonds needed to make an octet. Tetrahedrons are associated only with octets.

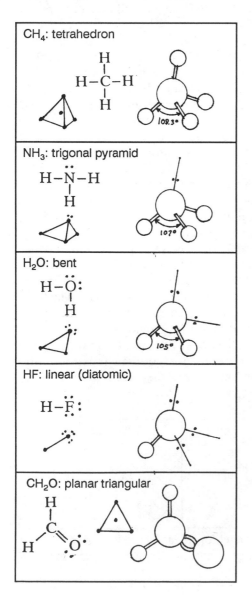

CH_4: tetrahedron

NH_3: trigonal pyramid

H_2O: bent

HF: linear (diatomic)

CH_2O: planar triangular

Methane is a true tetrahedron. Its central atom has a valence of 4, and so it can bond to four atoms of hydrogen (or other element). The mutually repulsive electron pairs maintain the maximum angle (109.3°) between the peripheral atoms, as explained on p. 119.

To illustrate the modified forms of the tetrahedron, let us look at ammonia. We remove a hydrogen from the tetrahedron and, of course, change the central atom to nitrogen, which has a valency of 3. But the central atom is still surrounded by four electron pairs, so a planar triangular geometry is precluded; the nonbonding pair repulses the other three pairs. The result is the *trigonal pyramid* geometry. The angles between the hydrogens are now about 107°. As this is still approximately 109.3°, the electrons, among themselves, still form a rough tetrahedon relative to the central atom.

By taking off another hydrogen and making the central atom oxygen (valence of 2), we get a water molecule. But , again, there are still four electron pairs, an octet. The angle between the hydrogens is now down to about 105°. As this is still not much different from the true tetrahedral angle, *we can still think of the electron pairs as forming their own tetrahedron*, while forcing the molecule into the V-shaped geometry we call *bent*.

Fluorine will bond to only one hydrogen. With yet one fewer outer atom, we finally have a diatomic molecule and, therefore, a linear one. Just the same, there are still a total of four electron pairs comprising their own tetrahedron. But the actual geometry no longer resembles a tetrahedron in any way; it is a mere line segment that is *geometrically* indistinguishable from any linear molecule that is not a degenerate tetrahedron (e.g., N_2, CO).

Multiple bonds make it possible for species that do obey the octet rule to form the special geometries of those species that do not. Formaldehyde (CH_2O) for one, is planar triangular, as shown.

Surprisingly, double and triple bonds do not affect the angles differently than do single bonds. Thus, the outer molecules in both formaldehyde and boron trifluoride are all 120° apart, even though the former contains a multiple bond and the latter does not.

The tetrahedron and its degenerations—through (1) trigonal pyramid, to (2) bent, to (3) linear—and the trigonal planar and regular linear molecular geometries exhaust the possibilities for molecules and ions in which a central atom is surrounded by an octet of electrons, or less. Each one of these geometries can be predicted from its dot diagram; so if you can do the diagram, you can identify the molecular geometry.

Yet molecular geometry can also be used to confirm polarity or nonpolarity. We can already predict this using electronegativity differences: the greater the difference, the less symmetrical (and, therefore) the more polar will be the molecule.

There are a few cases, however, in which we would expect high polarity—even an ionic compound—due to high Pauling Scale disparities; but in fact we find completely nonpolar molecules. The reason is simple and straightforward, and geometry provides the answer.

Look again at the beryllium fluoride molecule diagram (p. 119). The electronegativity disparity is so great (2.5), that we would not expect this compound to be even remotely molecular, much less nonploar.

The two fluorines in this molecule indeed hog the electrons, and so are negative regions (while the beryllium is a positive region); *but they are equally negative.* The distribution of charge within the molecule, then, is symmetrical and the molecule, therefore, is nonpolar. Electronegativity disparities suggest that boron fluoride or silicon tetrafluoride are also ionic; in reality they are a planar triangular molecule and a tetrahedron, respectively.

Now look again at the methyl chloride molecule (p. 119). Methane has four identical outer parts (hydrogen) but if one of these is taken away and a more electronegative chlorine atom put in its place, then the molecule is slightly polar, with the chlorine atom making up the negative pole and the three hydrogen atoms, the positive pole.

At right are some examples of a form that is slightly more complex than, but analogous to, a tetrahedron. This is the octahedron (Greek, "eight-based"), shown here with two of its degenerate forms. Octahedrons are possible when a central atom is surrounded by six pairs of electrons. By connecting the outer atoms with lines, we would define, in a true octahedron (e.g., SCl_6), a geometric form made up of eight equilateral triangles. Removing one outer atom would give us a *square pyramid* geometry; remove two and we would have *planar square*. Note that with or without outer atoms the mutually repulsing electrons maintain their own octahedron, as those in an octet maintain their own tetrahedron.

Can you see how the *Electron Pair Repulsion Principle* explains these molecular geometries as well as it explains the others? Further, do you fully understand the connection between dot diagrams and molecular geometry?

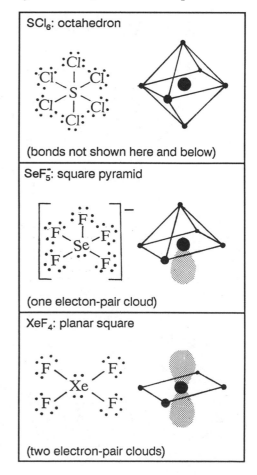

SCl_6: octahedron

(bonds not shown here and below)

SeF_5^-: square pyramid

(one electon-pair cloud)

XeF_4: planar square

(two electron-pair clouds)

121

1.

2. Most bonds between a metal and a nonmetal are ionic; those between two nonmetals are molecular (though they may have partial ionic character).

3. triple bond

4. d a c f b g e

5. Boron, like silicon, carbon, arsenic, and phosphorus, has a very intermediate (if that makes sense) Pauling Scale value, and so its compounds are nonpolar or relatively nonpolar.

6.

a. iodine	b. oxygen	c. ozone	d. oxide	e. phosphide	f. phosphine
:Ï–Ï:	:Ö=Ö:	:Ö=Ö–Ö: (or) :Ö–Ö=Ö:	[:Ö–Ö:]²⁻	[:P:]³⁻	H–P̈–H H
g. hydrochloric acid	h. carbon dioxide	i. carbon monoxide	j. silica (quartz, etc.)	k. selenium hexafluoride	l. tin tetrachloride
H–C̈l:	:Ö=C=Ö:	:O≡C:	:Ö=Si=Ö:	F/F–Se–F/F (F above and below)	Cl Cl Sn Cl Cl
m. boron trifluoride	n. hydroxide	o. nitrate	p. arsenic trichloride	q. hydronium	r. bromite
:F: B :F: :F:	[:Ö–H]⁻	[:Ö–N–Ö: :Ö:]⁻	:Cl–As–Cl: :Cl:	[H–Ö–H H]⁺	[:Ö: :Ö–Br:]⁻
s. phosphite	t. phosphorus acid	u. ammonium	v. sulfuric acid	w. methyl chloride	x. ethyl alcohol
[:Ö–P–Ö: :Ö:]³⁻	H–Ö–P–Ö–H :Ö: H	[H H–N–H H]⁺	H :Ö: H–Ö–S–Ö: :Ö:	H H–C–Cl: H	H H H–C–C–Ö–H H H

3.9 Atomic Radii

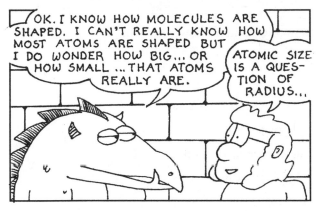

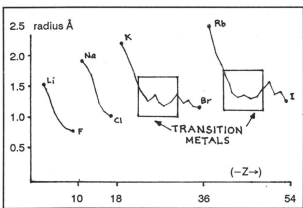

We have spoken of the exterior of atoms as "electron clouds." They are indeed cloudlike, in that even if we had a ruler dinky enough to measure the diameter of atoms, we could not do so, for their parameters (and, for that matter, their perimeters) are not well defined.

Instead, we measure the space that atoms occupy when they are bonded to other atoms; that is, the distance between the nuclei of two like, joined atoms. Half that distance is the atomic radius. In a bromine molecule, for example, the nuclei are 2.28° apart, so the radius assigned to the bromine atom is 1.14°.

The chart at left shows atomic radius as a function of atomic number. As we go *from left to right* (from the lightest to the heaviest element) in a Period, the *atoms generally get smaller, even as they get heavier* (although the transition metals depart from this trend for special reasons of their own that are related to their inner-building natures).

There is also a vertical trend within the families, and one which we find less surprising than the vertical one: *the heavier the atom, the larger it is.*

These two periodic trends result from the interplay of three factors.

The latter trend, an increase of radius with a *vertical* increase in weight is due entirely to the increase in occupied Principle Energy Levels (n). The more PELs the atom has, the more space it will take up, compared to its lighter siblings.

The horizontal decrease in radius with increasing weight is mostly explained by *nuclear charge*. The more protons there are in the nucleus, the more positive it will be (quantitatively speaking). Therefore, the nucleus will pull harder on the orbiting electrons; it is as though the electrons had more "gravity." Nuclear charge thus reduces the area of the electron clouds and, by extension, the atomic radius.

This phenomenon, however, is offset to some small to middling degree by the *shielding affect*. The outermost electrons, it is believed, are "shielded" from the full attractive force of the nucleus by the inner electron shells (Principal Energy Levels).

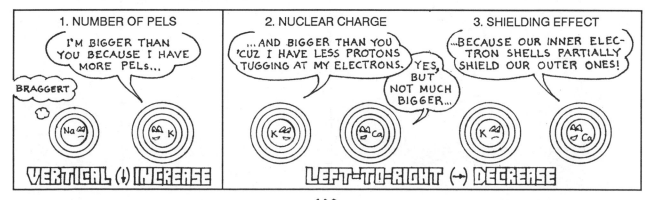

1. Compounds following the octet rule have four potentially bonding electron pairs, and so can form tetrahedrons. What is the tetrahedral angle?

Answer: _____

2. Match these molecular geometries to their descriptions:

_____planar triangular   a. central atom has four pairs, four bonds

_____tetrahedron   b. central atom has six pairs, four bonds

_____linear, diatomic   c. central atom has four pairs, two bonds

_____octahedron   d. central atoms has four pairs, three bonds

_____trigonal pyramid   e. a molecule with two atoms, any number of bonds

_____square pyramid   f. central atom has six pairs, six bonds

_____bent   g. central atom has three pairs, three bonds

_____linear, triatomic   h. central atom has two pairs, two bonds

_____planar square   i. central atom has six pairs, five bonds

3. Keep matching...

_____nuclear charge   a. reduces nuclear attraction for some electrons

_____symmetry   b. keeps electron clouds small by pulling them inward

_____geometry   c. that which is used to determine atomic radius or "size"

_____shielding effect   d. accounts for increase in radii, with weight, in a family

_____number of PELs   e. from the Greek words meaning "Earth measure"

_____intermolecular distance   f. imparts a nonpolar character to a molecule

4. Diagram the following and predict (1) their molecular geometries and (2) whether they are polar or nonpolar. You might also wish to name as many as you can, although not all have been named in the book so far.

a. SiH_4	b. RaO	c. H_2S	d. $BeCl_2$	e. SF_6	f. SF_5^-

124

g. SF_4^{2-}	h. SO_2	i. NH_4^+	j. CS_2	k. AsO_4^{3-}	l. CO_3^{2-}

5. Arrange the elements in these two groups in order from the smallest atomic radius to the largest:

a.   K   Na   Cs   Li   H   Fr   Rb   b.   S   Na   Cl   Mg   Al   P   Si

_____   _____

6. Atomic size cannot be derived from actual diameters. So what is it?

7. Explain how the Electron Pair Repulsion Principle governs molecular geometry:

1. What is the empirical formula of uranium oxide if it is 84.8% uranium?

2. Some ptichblende is 87.7% uranium oxide, 0.109% polonium oxide, and 0.0000450% radium oxide. How much uranium can come from 25 grams of pitchblende?

1. 109.3°   2. g a e f d i c h b   3. b f e a c d

4.

a. silane	b. radium oxide	c. hydrosulfuric acid	d. beryllium chloride	e. sulfur hexafluoride	f. sulfur penta-fluoride ion
H–Si–H with H above and below	:Ra=O:	:S–H with H below	:Cl–Be–Cl:	F₆ around S	[F₅ around S]⁻
tetrahedron nonpolar	linear polar	bent polar	linear polar	octahedron nonpolar	square pyramid polar
g. sulfur tetra-fluoride ion	h. sulfur dioxide	i. ammonium	j. carbon disulfide	k. arsenate	l. carbonate
[F₄ around S]²⁻	:S–O: with O below	[H–N–H with H above and below]⁻	:S=C=S:	[:O–As–O: with O below]⁴⁻	[O₃ around C]²⁻
planar square nonpolar	bent polar	tetrahedron nonpolar	linear nonpolar	trigonal pyramid polar	planar triangular polar

5. (a) H Li Na K Rb Cs Fr   (b) Cl S P Si Al Mg Na

6. An atom's exterior is too cloudy and nebulous to define, much less to measure. Radii are (therefore) considered to be half the distance between the nuclei of two joined atoms.

7. Electron pairs repulse each other due to like charge; they splay the molecule in as many directions as the central atom has pairs. Each pair, whether it forms a bond or not, is aimed by the repulsion of the other electron pairs in a direction where there may or may not be another atom.

1.

grams	84.8	15.2
moles	.356	0.95
ratio	1.00	.267
adj. (x3)	3	8

ans. U_3O_8

2.

$$? \, gU = 25 \, g \, U_3O_8 \, imp \times \frac{84.8 \, g \, U_3O_8}{100 \, g \, U_3O_8} \times \frac{mol \, U_3O_8}{842 \, g \, U_3O_8} \times \frac{3 \, mols \, U}{mol \, U_3O_8} \times \frac{238 \, g \, U}{mol \, U} = 18.0 \, gU$$

3.10 Chapter Synthesis

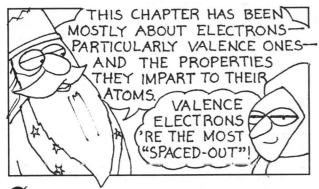

Any discussion of atomic structure is really a discussion of two arrangements: that of (1) electrons within the atom and of (2) elements within the Periodic Table. They are mutually explanatory.

Sect. 3.2 ends with a summary of the identities and orders of the four quantum numbers (not all of which are "numbers" per se). An element's position in the table is determined by how many Principal Energy Levels it has and by its highest (and usually unfilled) sublevel. These first two quantum numbers, because they collectively describe the distribution and population of electrons (in general) and valence electrons (in particular) within an atom, are the key to not only understanding where an element is found in the Table, but also to many chemical and physical properties. Among them are its atomic radius, stability, bonding patterns, metallic/nonmetallic character, and electronegativity. All of these are controlled by an element's valency or valencies—the share, spare, or snare potential(s) of its atoms.

Never forget that electrons repulse each other. This even goes for those sharing an orbit. Therefore, when you diagram an atom, you must give its valence electrons as much space as you can. When doing electronic notations, this same principle—the mutual repulsion of electrons—translates into half-filling all the orbitals before completely filling any.

Orbitals that are only half-filled (or even empty), however, can become full, to an atom's satisfaction, when covalent bonds are formed. An electron pair, while it is internally repulsive, also repulses other pairs, and this governs a molecule's geometric shape. We can predict this geometry from dot diagrams that, in their own turn, we were able to do with our knowledge of valence electrons (which in A-family elements neatly correspond to the family number).

The shape of a simple molecule can be understood by counting the electron pairs around the central atom. Each represents a direction, terminating in a theoretical point, and lines between these points make a shape.

Fluorine and chlorine atoms, with their high electronegativities *and* a valence of 1, are able to split electron pairs taken from other atoms and, with these "depaired atoms", can form more than the usual four bonds (an octet) around a central atom.

Intermediate electronegativity disparities between elements in a binary are expressed as intermediate bonding character. A lopsided distribution of electrons leads to a lopsided distribution of charge which in turn leads to polarity. A binary with a moderate disparity may still be made of molecules, but only barely. If, however, the more electronegative element surrounds the less electronegative one (e.g. BCl_3, CO_2, NH_4^+) there will be no polarity because of the perfect symmetry of electron-pair distribution. Since the atoms of the same element are alike (Dalton' third postulate), they enjoy perfect symmetry and so form perfect molecules.

Cesium has the largest radius and lowest electronegativity of any atom yet "measured" in these respects, because it has very many PELs and a single valence electron that is highly shielded from and independent of the nucleus, big as it is. This is why this most metallic of all elements ionizes so readily.

Finally, the unreactivity of the noble gases is explained by their 8 valence electrons. All have a full p-sublevel at the top of their energy hierarchies.

1. Fill in, using a Periodic Table showing only symbols, atomic weights, and Z. If you do not know the Pauling values (electronegativities) of all the elements, no problem; but you should know enough of the periodic *trend* in electronegativities to guide you to the approximate place on the Table. Then, deduce the element's identity, using the other data. All are A-family elements, and only one has multiple valencies.

element	Z	PELs	family/ # valence e⁻s	valency	Pauling Scale	electron notation
			8A/	–	–	$1s^2$
		4	/		2.8	
			5A/5	3,5		
		3	/	–	–	
		2	/	3	2.0	
			/3		1.5	
		1	/		2.1	
			/		1.0	$1s^2 2s^2 2p^6 3s^2 3p^6 4s^2$
		4	/		3.5	

2. Order these binary compounds from the most covalent to the most ionic, using Pauling Scale disparities:

(a) CH_4 SiO_2 MgO CsF H_2O _____

(b) BeF_2 BaI_2 NaI $SnBr_2$ PCl_3 _____

3. Circle the molecules and underline the formula units in problem 2.

Across

1. Type of ion (pl.)
9. Continent of Meyer, Curie, Cavendish, etc.
10. Ribonucleic acid
11. Sibling of 17D
12. $1s^2 2s^2 2p^6 3s^2...4d^{10}5p^1$
13. Draggin's' is at stake
14. $H_2O(s)$
16. A nonmetric unit (pl.)
18. $1s^2 2s^2 2p^6 3s^1$
20. Adenosine triphosphate
22. Negative particle
23. Num. prefix
24. Named for Curie's native land
25. CoS: cobalt (?) sulfide
26. $1s^2 2s^2 2p^6 3s^2...5s^2 4d^1$
31. Suffix for 30D

32. Adj. for SiO_2 beach
34. Has 10+ isotopes
35. A cluster
37. $1s^2 2s^2 2p^6 3s^2 3p^2$
38. High T, low H_2O (climate)
39. Four nonmetals
41. $1s^2 2s^2 2p^1$
43. Manganese sibling
44. $1s^2 2s^2 2p^6 3s^2...5p^6 6s^1$
45. $1s^2 2s^2 2p^6$
46. Suffix: "maker"

Down

2. Rare elemental gas
3. Two metals
4. Acids _____ (to be + adj.)
5. $1s^2 2s^2 2p^6 3s^2 3p^6 4s^2 3d^6$
6. Two gases

7. Sodium iodide
8. Nuke reactor controller
11. Type of lab dish
12. Avogadro's homeland
15. Positively charged
17. $1s^2 2s^2 2p^6 3s^2 3p^6 4s^2 3d^8$
19. Uncuttables
21. Uranium neighbor
24. Named for underworld god
27. A metal
28. Manganese sibling
29. A halogen
30. Root of CN^-
33. ...33, 34...
34. Three non-ion-formers
35. The ferrous metal
36. Horse that never took chemistry
38. $1s^2 2s^2 2p^6 3s^2 3p^6$

40. Water below 0°C   42. Densest metal
43. $1s^2 2s^2 2p^6 3s^2...5d^{10}6p^6$

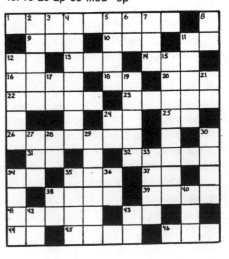

14
Si
28.086

Profile: Silicon

Pyrex is a borosilicate, a glass containing boron and silicon, which have a lot in common.

Silicon is a metalloid. As has been noted, it is semiconductive and lustrous. Yet, it is demonstrably more a nonmetal than a metal: elemental silicon is crystalline and brittle and virtually all of its binaries are covalent.

While silicon does not occur uncombined, it is, practically speaking, everywhere, making up about 28%, by weight, of the Earth's crust. Minerals containing it comprise at least 87% of all the material available to us (the Earth's crust and the atmosphere). The feldspars alone account for about one half of all rock.

The single commonest compound, which is often part of more complex aggregates, is silica, SiO_2. Its most familiar form is pure quartz. This mineral is so abundant that there is more of it than all other Earthly compounds combined; the crust is in fact a huge sample of it adulterated with human beings and other impurities. Quartz is a major ingredient of glass and can itself be molded into goblets and dinnerware marketed as "crystal," which, in fact, it is (glass, on the other hand, is by definition a hard, noncrystalline solid).

Some gemstones---which are ironically precious--- are nothing other than quartz colored by impurities of metal ions, notably those of titanium, iron, and magnesium. Among these are the purple amethysts and yellow citrines. Opal is hydrated silica with coloring admixtures. Agates are banded, multicolored, and opaque, while onyx is translucent. All are very hard. There is also a diamond-like allotrope of pure silicon, but it is not as tough as the carbon diamond.

Most building materials are silicon-containing. The glass and usually the masonry are silicate-based, while the steel reinforcement often contains silicon as an alloying agent. Carborundum (SiC), discovered by accident, was the hardest synthetic substance known until the 1930s.

The synthetic silicones (note the spelling) are a huge class of synthetic polymers. A polymer is a large molecule built up from chains or matrices of smaller molecules. As with carbon compounds, two or more polymers may have the same empirical formula while having radically different properties, owing to the dissimilar arrangement of their atoms. Among the applications for silicones are enamels, resins, varnishes, hydraulic fluids, lubricants (such as the near miraculous WD-40), strengtheners, and water-repellent coatings for stocks and textiles.

It is silicon's tendency to form four bonds that make not only all this polymerization possible but also its use as the base for artificial intelligence. This same property is why silicon's organic sibling, carbon, is---at the molecular level---the chain former for living things and why another sibling, germanium, finds employment in transistors. Tin and lead, however, form fewer such chains because, in addition to their second valence (2), many or most of their binaries are ionic.

San Jose, California, is not called the Silicon Valley because the element is quarried there (for indeed this can be done literally anywhere), but because it is a center for the design and manufacture of silicon-based technology (computer chips, semiconductors, etc.).

Silicon was isolated and identified as an element by Berzelius in 1824.

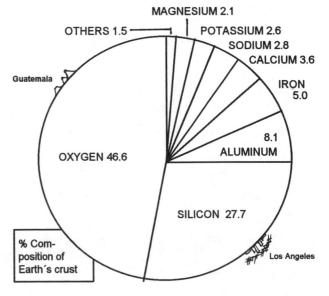

% Composition of Earth's crust

OTHERS 1.5
MAGNESIUM 2.1
POTASSIUM 2.6
SODIUM 2.8
CALCIUM 3.6
IRON 5.0
ALUMINUM 8.1
OXYGEN 46.6
SILICON 27.7

1.

He	2	1	8A/2	–	–	$1s^2$
Br	35	4	7A/7	1	2.8	$1s^2 2s^2 2p^6 3s^2 3p^6 4s^2 3d^{10} 4p^5$
P	15	3	5A/5	3	2.1	$1s^2 2s^2 2p^6 3s^2 3p^3$
Ar	18	3	8A/8	–	–	$1s^2 2s^2 2p^6 3s^2 3p^6$
B	5	2	3A/3	3	2.0	$1s^2 2s^2 2p^1$
Al	13	3	3A/3	3	1.5	$1s^2 2s^2 2p^6 3s^2 3p^1$
H	1	1	1A/1	1	2.1	$1s^1$
Ca	20	4	2A/a	2	1.0	$1s^2 2s^2 2p^6 3s^2 3p^6 4s^2$
O	8	2	6A/6	2	3.5	$1s^2 2s^2 2p^4$

2.   (a) CH_4 H_2O SiO_2 MgO CsF (b) PCl_3 $SnBr_2$ NaI BaO BeF_2

3. All are molecular except MgO (2.3), CsF (3.3), and BaO (2.6). BeF_2 is a molecule due to its special geometry and in spite of its high Pauling Scale difference (2.5).

𝕭𝖊𝖓𝖟𝖊𝖓𝖊: 𝕸𝖔𝖑𝖊𝖈𝖚𝖑𝖆𝖗 𝕾𝖓𝖔𝖜𝖋𝖑𝖆𝖐𝖊

There are two classes of organic (carbon) compounds: the *aliphatic*, based on carbon chain-links, and the *aromatic*, based on the *benzene ring*, a planar hexagonal molecule with the formula C_6H_6.

In the Lewis diagrams at right, there appear to be alternating single and double bonds; in fact, each carbon/carbon bond is intermediate, or *resonant*. The structure can be represented by either of the diagrams alone. Together, the two (or any other such set) are called *resonance structures* (as though the geometry were something that resonated between two molecular structures). You can see that the octet rule is clearly at work here.

Innumerable compounds can be synthesized by substituting radicals for one or more of the hydrogen atoms. Among them (the benzene "rings" are shown as hexagons):

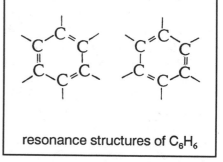

resonance structures of C_6H_6

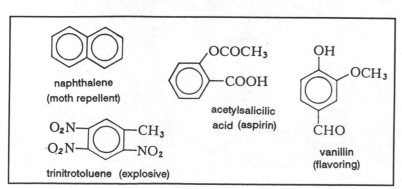

naphthalene
(moth repellent)

acetylsalicilic
acid (aspirin)

vanillin
(flavoring)

trinitrotoluene (explosive)

4.1 The Chemical Equation

I DROPPED 2 MOLES OF QUICKSILVER INTO ONE MOLE OF DILUTED OIL OF VITRIOL. ERE LONG, A MOLE OF MERCUROUS SULFIDE PRECIPITATED AND ANOTHER OF WATER-FORMER EVOLVED, WHILST THE CALORIMETER WAS EXCITED TO NIGH 600!

$$2Hg(l) + H_2SO_4(aq) \rightarrow Hg_2SO_4(s) + H_2(g) + 588kJ$$

A chemical equation (or sentence) is a shorthand system for describing reactions. Like any other shorthand, it is composed of symbols.

You already know (or should know) the symbols for the important elements and many compounds, but there are other types of symbols used in chemical equations, some of which we have already used here and there.

In Dalton's experiment, a mole of mercury (I) sulfate is formed. The arrow, like an equal sign (=), separates the reactants and the products, but it also reminds us of the direction of the reaction (what is becoming what). It is the "verb" of the equation. More on this in Chap. 8.

There are three other important classes of symbols that are germane to this level of the study of chemistry.

1. State Designations

The three earthly states of matter, when participants in a reaction, can be labeled (s) for the solid, (l) for the liquid, and (g) for the gaseous. Since most laboratory reactions take place in water solutions, chemistry has a "fourth state of matter", the *aqueous*, which, as you know, is symbolized (aq).

A solid which forms in a solution is called a precipitate, and it can alternately be symbolized ↓, for it falls out of (precipitates from) the solution. A gas that forms during a reaction can be indicated by ↑, because it rises from (evolves from) the solution. The above equation, with this alternative labeling, would look like this:

$$2Hg + H_2SO_4 \rightarrow Hg_2SO_4\downarrow + H_2\uparrow + 588kJ$$

These vertical arrows are used only for gases and solids that are the results (or products) of reactions; they can therefore only appear on the right side of the equation, when used at all. In this book, we will favor the letter designations for most purposes.

State designations, while often optional, are obligatory in certain equations. For example, if water is steam rather than in its liquid state, it must be written $H_2O(g)$ rather than $H_2O(l)$. State designations, needed or not, will be used throughout this chapter for practice.

2. Coefficients

Coefficients, as you know, are the "big" numbers in front of some of the formulae in an equation but which are never *part* of the formulae. Dalton did not, of course, add two mercury atoms to one molecule of sulfuric acid; rather, he used the measurable quantity, the mole (two moles of mercury, one of acid). While coefficients indicate the actual whole-number *ratios* in which discrete particles combine, they always quantify *moles*, such that

$$2Hg(l) \text{ is really } 2 \times 6.02 \times 10^{23} \text{ Hg atoms}$$

3. Heat Transfer

When the reactants in the above example recombined into products, they lost some energy as heat; the reaction, then, was exothermic.

This heat is "subtracted," as it were, from the equation. One mole of mercury (II) sulfate is formed and 588 kilojoules of energy evolves; this is the *molar heat of formation* for the Hg_2SO_4.

Heat transfer values (which are positive for reactions that absorb energy and negative for those that lose it) are usually omitted even though virtually all reactions have heat transfer, but sometimes (as will be seen in Chap. 7) they must be included. As a convention, they are written as a product.

4.2 Balancing Equations

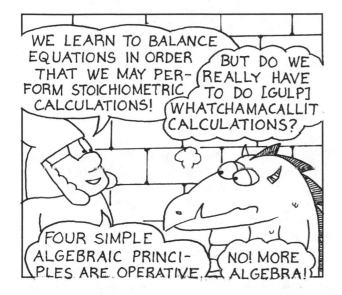

You are already familiar—whether or not you know it—with stoichiometric calculations and their algebraic manipulations.

On p. 19 you were reminded that we can cancel out anything that appears in both a numerator and a denominator. You have already applied this principle in solving dimensional analysis problems, and you will be able to use it further for the elimination of fractional coefficients. For instance

$$\tfrac{3}{2}N_2 \quad \text{really means} \quad \tfrac{3}{2} \times 2 \text{ nitrogen atoms}$$

(the subscript 2 after nitrogen is really a numerator, because 2 = 2/1). The two 2s, then, cancel each other out, leaving us with 3N.

Recall from the prologue, however, that some elements (such as nitrogen) are diatomic when uncombined. Therefore, we cannot write "3N," but neither can we write $\tfrac{3}{2}N_2$. In the former case, the species is unacceptable, and in the the latter case, the coefficient is unacceptable; we want only integers in the equation.

A second algebraic principle, which you used to solve empirical formulae, now comes into play. Look at the adjustment step in the example on p. 79, in which each part of the formula was multiplied by the same number. The difference is that with empirical formulae we had to do this to eliminate messy deci-

mals, whereas with equations we are only doing it to dispose of mere fractions.

A third mathematical tool for equation balancing is second-grade multiplication. We employ it to determine, for example, that in three molecules of phosphoric acid—$3H_3PO_4(aq)$ in chemical shorthand—there are nine atoms of hydrogen (3×3), three atoms of phosphorous (3×1), and 12 atoms of oxygen (3×4). It is simply a matter of multiplying subscripts by coefficients.

The remaining "principle" involved is kindergarten arithmetic: counting.

Suppose that you have to balance the equation for the formation of carbon monoxide. The unbalanced equation is (a), in the box below. Check it out: count the carbon and oxygen atoms on each side.

Your objective is to have the same number of atoms of each element on both sides of the equation without chemically altering the formulae (*that* would be rilly stoopid). Adjust only with coefficients. The carbon is already balanced (most unbalanced equations will contain at least one already-balanced element or ion) and, with the insertion of the coefficient ½, the oxygen is also balanced (b). The entire equation is now in balance and technically correct, but it contains a fraction. So, you multiply *everything* by 2—the denominator of the fraction—to eliminate it (c), then omit the coefficient of "1" for reasons discussed previously, and you are done (d).

In this way, all the mathematics so copiously reviewed above are applied in quick, easy succession and with a minimum of effort.

(a) $C + O_2 \rightarrow CO$

(b) $C + \tfrac{1}{2}O_2 \rightarrow CO$

(c) $2C + 1O_2 \rightarrow 2CO$

(d) $2C + O_2 \rightarrow 2CO$

If carbon burns in air, there will be enough oxygen present to form carbon dioxide, rather than carbon monoxide, according to the reaction.

$$C + O_2 \rightarrow CO_2$$

Notice that this equation needs no balancing. After translating the words into chemical shorthand, we count the atoms and realize that no adjustments with coefficients are necessary. More than a few equations are like this.

Both of the above reactions are of the *combination* variety, in which two or more reactants combine to form a single product. Here is another combination reaction: if potassium is exposed to chlorine gas, a binary salt results. First of all, write the translation from the verbal to the shorthand; that is, write the unbalanced equation:

$$K + Cl_2 \rightarrow KCl$$

Your knowledge of the chemical formulae, valencies, and ionic charges now comes into play. It will enable you to ascertain the product, even when it is not explicitly stated (as is often the case). You would know better than to write, say, "Cl" for elemental chlorine (which is diatomic) or "KCl_2," for potassium chloride.

In this unbalanced equation, potassium is already balanced, but chorine is not; giving the product a coefficient of 2 brings it into balance:

$$K + Cl_2 \rightarrow 2KCl$$

But now potassium is suddenly unbalanced. Do not panic. This is easily rectified by also giving it a 2; at which point everything is balanced:

$$2K + Cl_2 \rightarrow 2KCl$$

The salt KCl is thus the product of a combination reaction, but it could also be gotten in the reverse type, namely a *decomposition* reaction, wherein a compound—through heating, electrolysis, decay, whatever—disintegrates into simpler substances.

If we heat potassium chlorate—another salt—in a crucible for a long enough period, the chlorate ion itself will break up and the salt will lose all of its oxygen, becoming in the process potassium chloride. The unbalanced equation is

$$KClO_3 \xrightarrow{\triangle} KCl + O_2$$

(the triangle indicates catalysis by heat). This time, both potassium and chlorine are balanced; only the oxygen is not. We cannot change the oxygen subscript from 2 to 3, but we can multiply it with a fractional co-efficient:

$$KClO_3 \rightarrow KCl + \tfrac{3}{2} O_2$$

Now we have balance. To discard the fraction, we multiply *all* the coefficients in the equation by the denominator:

$$2KClO_3 \rightarrow 2KCl + 3O_2$$

This is the same procedure outlined on p. 133.

To be sure that this is the correct result, we count the atoms of each element. As each side has two potassiums, two chlorines, and six oxygens, we are done.

In this example, the only unbalanced element was an uncombined one, oxygen. *Whenever the only unbalanced species—reactant or product—is uncombined, then it may be the only one needing an adjustment.* This hint will be very useful in balancing more complex equations that are less immediately obvious in their solution.

134

Sucrose, $C_{12}H_{22}O_{11}$, can also be decomposed by heating into a black mass of elemental carbon and steam, $H_2O(g)$:

$$C_{12}H_{22}O_{11} \rightarrow C + H_2O$$

In this case, we need only to take the coefficients directly (or almost directly) from the reactants' subscripts: 12 carbons and enough water molecules to equal 11 oxygens and 22 hydrogens:

$$C_{12}H_{22}O_{11} \rightarrow 12C + 11H_2O$$

This water, escaping as steam, can be caught, condensed, and in its turn be decomposed into its component gases in another reaction:

$$H_2O \rightarrow H_2 + O_2$$

Oxygen, now out of balance, must be adjusted:

$$H_2O \rightarrow H_2 + \tfrac{1}{2}O_2$$

And the fraction removed algebraically:

$$2H_2O \rightarrow 2H_2 + O_2$$

IN REACTIONS WITH MULTIPLE REACTANTS AND MULTIPLE PRODUCTS, THE "OHO" SEQUENCE—WHERE PRACTICABLE—IS MOST USEFUL. CASE IN POINT: WHEN ORGANIC COMPOUNDS OXIDIZE...

OTHER ELEMENTS
HYDROGEN
OXYGEN

...BE IT GRADUALLY OR SPONTANEOUSLY (i.e., BY BURNING), THEY IDEALLY YIELD ONLY CARBON DIOXIDE AND WATER—AS WITH METHANE BURNING IN AIR.

3. ORGANIC OXIDATION

$C_nH_n + O_2 \rightarrow CO_2 + H_2O$

(n = any integer)

PASCAL

In *organic oxidation* reactions, a third type of reaction, a carbon compound combines with oxygen to yield, in ideal circumstances, only H_2O and CO_2 as products, as in the combustion of methane:

$$CH_4 + O_2 \rightarrow CO_2 + H_2O$$

The OHO sequence works like this: balance first the Other element(s); then Hydrogen (if present); and lastly, Oxygen (if present). Oxygen is often found to be already balanced by the time you get to it.

In most organic oxidations carbon will be the one to balance first (usually it is the only Other in an organic compound; if there are Others than carbon, however—notably nitrogen—then balance this "other Other" element before even carbon). As carbon is already balanced in the above equation, we do hydrogen (a) and then oxygen (b):

(a) $CH_4 + O_2 \rightarrow CO_2 + 2H_2O$

(b) $CH_4 + 2O_2 \rightarrow CO_2 + 2H_2O$

Note that we had to count and add the atoms of an element (oxygen in this case) from not one but *two* substances on one side of the equation to equal those in only *one* substance on the other side. (Did you also notice how adjusting the uncombined, elemental substance balanced the rest of the equation?)

Were the internal combustion engine able to perform a perfectly complete oxidation of gasoline, the unbalanced equation for the reaction would be:

$$C_8H_{18} + O_2 \rightarrow CO_2 + H_2O$$

Balancing for carbon and hydrogen, we get:

$$C_8H_{18} + O_2 \rightarrow 8CO_2 + 9H_2O$$

There are a total of 25 oxygen atoms in the products, so there must be 25 on the other side as well:

$$C_8H_{18} + \tfrac{25}{2}O_2 \rightarrow 8CO_2 + 9H_2O$$

...and, finally, by multiplying everything (all coefficients) by the denominator, we have the answer:

$$2C_8H_{18} + 25O_2 \rightarrow 16CO_2 + 18H_2O$$

In reality, of course, the engine also produces CO, as well as NO, which goes on to become the haze that is NO_2. CO, because it is relatively unstable, quickly becomes CO_2; thus, the burning is completed externally. The NO however, is catalyzed by sunlight into the coppery NO_2 (hence, "photochemical" smog).

Now let us consider the burning in air of isopropyl alcohol, $C_2H_5CH_2OH$. Setting up the unbalanced equation, using the empirical formula (which is derived by counting from the structural one), we have

$$C_3H_8O + O_2 \rightarrow CO_2 + H_2O$$

The Other and Hydrogen are then easily balanced:

$$C_3H_8O + O_2 \rightarrow 3CO_2 + 4H_2O$$

...but there are now 10 oxygens among the products. The alcohol molecule accounts for one of them, so nine must come from elemental oxygen:

$$C_3H_8O + \tfrac{9}{2}O_2 \rightarrow 3CO_2 + 4H_2O$$

Multiplying everything by the fraction's denominator provides the finished equation:

$$2C_3H_8O + 9O_2 \rightarrow 6CO_2 + 8H_2O$$

(Now recheck with one further count!)

Another major category is the *replacement* reaction. It is what takes place when, say, some zinc is dropped into a concentrated solution of hydrochloic acid:

$$Zn(s) + HCl(aq) \rightarrow ZnCl_2(aq) + H_2(g)$$

State designations are obligatory in this solution reaction because $HCl(l)$ and $HCl(aq)$ are not only different states but distinct chemical species as well, for reasons that will be explained later.

An arbitrary but generally useful rule is to balance first the element(s) you are *least* used to seeing, then those a little less exotic, then hydrogen next-to-last and oxygen last, as per the OHO sequence. As zinc is already balanced in this replacement reaction, you can balance the next Other:

$$Zn(s) + 2HCl(aq) \rightarrow ZnCl_2 + H_2(g)$$

Then, counting the hydrogens and finding them already balanced for this reaction, you recheck the whole equation by checking each element.

A complication to balancing this and other kinds of equations is that when radicals are present, they usually behave as atoms; that is, they leave and/or form compounds as atoms and elemental ions do. The good news is that this slight complication is more than offset by the tedium we avoid in only having to balance the whole radical, rather than each of its component atoms.

Do not get *too* used to balancing whole radicals, however; remember how chlorate broke up in an earlier example. On the whole, though, radicals usually hold together in reactions occurring *in solution*. Nitrate, for one, does so when nickel is added to silver nitrate solution to form aqueous nickel nitrate:

$$Ni(s) + AgNO_3(aq) \rightarrow Ni(NO_3)_2(aq) + Ag(s)$$

The OHO sequence hardly applies here; but no matter. A little trial and error will do the trick. In any event, only the radical in this equation remains unbalanced. So...

$$Ni(s) + 2AgNO_3(aq) \rightarrow Ni(NO_3)_2(aq) + Ag(s)$$

But look: this throws silver, which had been balanced in the original equation, out of whack. As with oxygen in two previous examples, though, it is the sole unbalanced species remaining and is elemental in form. Ergo, its adjustment balances the whole equation:

$$Ni(s) + 2AgNO_3(aq) \rightarrow Ni(NO_3)_2(aq) + 2Ag(s)$$

The lesson of this example is that by balancing one species, you may cause another to be unbalanced. That is why you do the overall check before going on.

136

Exchange reactions are also called double-replacement or metathesis reactions. They are unique in involving neither the transfer of electrons (as with the already-mentioned types of reactions) nor of protons (as the next category does).

Here is the exchange reaction in which another silver salt, this one insoluble, precipitates when we mix solutions of silver sulfate and potassium chloride:

$$Ag_2SO_4(aq) + NaCl(aq) \rightarrow Na_2SO_4(aq) + AgCl(s)$$

When the equation has radicals, deal with them first. Then, take care of the least frequently encountered elements (e.g., silver) and then the commoner ones (chlorine, sodium, etc.). In the above equation, sulfate is already balanced, but silver is not; so...

$$Ag_2SO_4 + NaCl \rightarrow Na_2SO_4 + 2AgCl$$

Now you must rebalance chlorine. This automatically also fixes the sodium and, with it, the whole equation:

$$Ag_2SO_3 + 2NaCl \rightarrow Na_2SO_3 + 2AgCl$$

An exchange may involve several radicals, such as that between tin (II) acetate and ammonium sulfate:

$$Sn(C_2H_3O_2)_2 + (NH_4)_2SO_4 \rightarrow SnSO_4 + NH_4C_2H_3O_2$$

First, balance any radical that requires it. In this case, only acetate and ammonium do, as indicated by the subscripts. Both are together in a compound on the right. On the left, however, both are doubly present in their respective reactants. Stick a 2 in front of the ammonium acetate and no further adjustments are needed for, in doing this, you have not unbalanced tin or sulfate:

$$Sn(C_2H_3O_2)_2 + (NH_4)_2SO_4 \rightarrow SnSO_4 + 2NH_4C_2H_3O_2$$

Balancing this equation did not even require algebra!

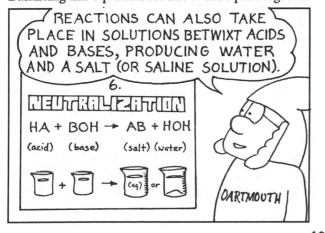

In a *neutralization* reaction, an acid is ionized by reacting it with a base which, by one definition, is a soluble metal hydroxide. In this way, ionic material (a precipitated salt or an ionic soup) results from the breakup of covalent material (acid). The reverse can also happen: covalent water results from H^+ ions coming from the acid and OH^- ions from the base.

A better and more specific definition of a neutralization is an acid/base reaction going to completion rather than to equilibrium (more on this later, of course).

The OHO sequence can be used to balance neutralization equations such as that for the reaction of hydroiodic acid and aluminum hydroxide:

$$Al(OH)_3 + HI \rightarrow AlI_3 + H_2O$$

First, balance the Others (i.e., aluminum and iodine):

$$Al(OH)_3 + 3HI \rightarrow AlI_3 + H_2O$$

And then balance water and its ionic components:

$$Al(OH)_3 + 3HI \rightarrow AlI_3 + 3H_2O$$

The majority of chemical changes that you will study at this or any level will belong to one of these six categories; however, a few in the problem set belong to none of them.

Whenever you get stalled while trying to balance an equation, it often helps to write out the equation on another part of the page you are using and start afresh. Do not beat to death an equation that seems to be a row of square pegs.

By the way, do you wonder how water could form from two ions and still be molecular? Once the hydrogen ion joins the hydroxide ion, the oxygen atom in the latter cannot tell the two hydrogens apart.

The electronegativity disparity between the two elements (1.4), while not great enough to keep these ions ionic, nevertheless entails that water molecules have partial ionic character.

4.3 Equation Troubleshooting

THERE'S GOTTA BE ANOTHER WAY!

BONK!

NEW!! CHEATIES

STERNO

Several things can go wrong when you balance equations, although this in itself does not make them difficult. Rather than attempting to memorize this guide, refer back to it as needed, as you have perhaps been doing with Sect. 1.2. It might also help to review this section before a test on equation writing.

1. Incorrect Formulae

When you rewrote the formulae from the unbalanced equation to the scratchwork area, you inadvertently caused one (or more) of them to reincarnate as something else.

In most cases, this is the omission of a subscript.

2. Counting Error

You failed to count all the atoms (or radicals) of a particular element because it was present in more than one species on the same side of the equation.

In equation (h) in problem 2 of the following problem set, you must insure that the carbon atoms on the left equal the collective total of the carbon atoms in both carbon-containing species on the right. In (k), oxygen appears three times and in (d) it is present in every species participating in the reaction. Watch out!

3. Subscript Adjustment

You were a real Numbnerd and tried to balance an equation by adjusting the subscripts when you are only allowed to adjust coefficients. The former, keep in mind, is part of the formula; the latter is not. By altering the subscripts, you alter the ratio of elements in the compound. A big No-No. If you want to learn this lesson indelibly, stick one hand into a beaker of HNO_2(aq) and the other hand in one of HNO_3(aq).

4. Algebraic Error

You violated the Distributive Property by not multiplying (or not multiplying *correctly*) subscripts inside parentheses by those outside of them.

Or, when you multiplied the coefficients by the denominator of a fractional coefficient, you failed to multiply all of them.

5. Sequence Error

The palindromic OHO sequence stands for Other/ Hydrogen/Oxygen, not the reverse. Later, you will transpose hydrogen and oxygen for a new mnemonic sequence (OOH!), but you do not need to worry about this until Chap. 10.

6. Symbol Confusion

Perhaps from fatigue, you mixed up look-alike formulae beginning with or containing the same letters (e.g., Co, CO, Ca, CaO, CoO).

Or, you forgot a lower case letter in a two-letter symbol and transmuted, for instance, Sn to S, something that even the best Chem. 1 student has no business doing.

7. Mindless Robotic Zombieism

This danger, often due to recklessness, overconfidence, or caffeine, was described in relation to dimensional analysis in Sect. 1.2.

1. Match these:

_____ CO_2 a. a product of confined combustion reactions

_____ fractional coefficients   b. something we use to quantify moles in equations

_____ whole coefficients   c. component of a base

_____ OH^- d. values are molar (for one mole)

_____ H^+ e. a product of combustion in air

_____ CO f. something which must be changed to integers

_____ HOH   g. a product of all neutralizations and organic oxidations

_____ heat of formation   h. component of an acid (H_3O^+ in solutions)

2. Balance each of these equations, using only coefficients to make the adjustments. State designations are not needed in this exercise (Note: not all of these reactions would really take place).

a. $Cu + S \rightarrow Cu_2S$

b. $Mg + HCl \rightarrow MgCl_2 + H_2$

c. $NaBr + Cl_2 \rightarrow NaCl + Br_2$

d. $HC_2H_3O_2 + O_2 \rightarrow CO_2 + H_2O$

e. $AsI_3 \rightarrow As + I_2$

f. $Hg + O_2 \rightarrow HgO$

g. $Ra(OH)_2 + HF \rightarrow RaF_2 + H_2O$

h. $SiO_2 + C \rightarrow SiC + CO$

i. $HNO_3 + Ag_2S \rightarrow AgNO_3 + H_2S$

j. $KNO_3 \rightarrow KNO_2 + O_2$

k. $C_3H_8 + O_2 \rightarrow CO_2 + H_2O$

l. $Li_2Se + HClO_4 \rightarrow LiClO_4 + H_2Se$

m. $P + O_2 \rightarrow P_2O_5$

n. $FeS + O_2 \rightarrow Fe_2O_3 + SO_2$

o. $Pb(NO_3)_2 \rightarrow PbO + O_2 + NO_2$

p. $Ba(OH)_2 + HI \rightarrow BaI_2 + H_2O$

q. $Cu(C_2H_3O_2) + Mg \rightarrow Mg(C_2H_3O_2)_2 + Cu$

r. $CaO + CO_2 \rightarrow CaCO_3$

s. $FeCl_2 + Na_3PO_4 \rightarrow Fe_3(PO_4)_2 + NaCl$

t. $C_2H_2 + O_2 \rightarrow CO_2 + H_2O$

u. $MnO_2 + HCl \rightarrow MnCl_2 + Cl_2 + H_2O$

v. $KHF_2 \rightarrow H_2 + F_2 + KF$

w. $B(OH)_3 + H_2SO_4 \rightarrow B_2(SO_4)_3 + H_2O$

x. $WO_3 + H_2 \rightarrow W + H_2O$

y. $Co_2(SO_4)_3 + Ba(OH)_2 \rightarrow Co(OH)_3 + BaSO_4$

z. $C_6H_{12}O_6 + O_2 \rightarrow CO_2 + H_2O$

I. $NH_3 + H_2SO_4 \rightarrow (NH_4)_2SO_4$

II. $SO_3 + KOH \rightarrow K_2SO_4 + H_2O$

III. $Sr(OH)_2 + H_3AsO_3 \rightarrow Sr_3(AsO_3) + H_2O$

IV. $Al + H_2SeO_4 + Al_2(SeO_4)_3 + H_2$

V. $C_{10}H_{22} + O_2 \rightarrow CO_2 + H_2O$

VI. $^{210}Po \rightarrow ^{206}Pb + He$ (optional)

3. Classify the above reactions as   (D) decomposition;   (C) combinations;   (O) organic oxidation;
(R) replacement;   (E) exchange;   (N) neutralization;   (X) none of the above.

a._____ b._____ c._____ d._____ e._____ f._____ g._____ h._____ i._____ j._____ k._____

l._____ m._____ n._____ o._____ p._____ q._____ r._____ s._____ t._____ u._____ v._____

w._____ x._____ y._____ z._____ I._____ II._____ III._____ IV._____ V._____ VI._____

140

4.4 Stoichiometric Relations

Stoichiometry (from the Greek for "element measure") is nothing more than the dimensional analysis we do after balancing an equation. Structurally, it is identical in principle to the percentage composition problems you did in Chap. 2.

In fact, some chemistry professors call those other DA calculations "formula stoichiometry" and the ones we are about to do "reaction stoichiometry."

They are really only different in that, in this case, we will take the whole-number ratios for the keystone from the equation's coefficients instead of from the chemical formulae themselves. If you can do one, you can surely do the other.

The keystone of both the above-mentioned stoichiometries is based on mole ratios that come from formulae in one case and from balanced equations in the other. We know, for instance, that the formula $Fe_3(PO_4)_2$ indicates three moles of iron, two moles of phosphorus, and eight moles of oxygen. Now consider this reaction, the burning in air of pentane:

$$2C_5H_{12}(l) + 16O_2(g) \rightarrow 10CO_2(s) + 12H_2O(l)$$

The ratio of the product and reactants to each other is 2:16:10:12; this information comes directly from the equation's coefficients. We can use it to construct a keystone of any possible combination of two species from the equation. With such a keystone, we can do any of the following:

1. We can determine how much of one reactant is needed to completely consume a given quantity of another reactant. If, say, we had 37 moles of pentane, how much oxygen would we need to burn it completely?

$$? \text{ moles } O_2 = 37 \text{ mols } C_5H_{12} \times \frac{16 \text{ mols } O_2}{2 \text{ mols } C_5H_{12}} = 3.0 \times 10^2 \text{ mols } O_2$$

2. We can know how much of a particular product is possible from a stated quantity of reactant. Suppose we needed to know the yield of carbon dioxide from the burning of the above 37 moles of pentane:

$$? \text{ moles } CO_2 = 37 \text{ mols } C_5H_{12} \times \frac{5 \text{ mols } CO_2}{\text{mol } C_5H_{12}} = 1.8 \times 10^2 \text{ mols } CO_2$$

3. We can also do the reverse, and know how much of a reactant is needed to get a stated quantity of a product. How much pentane, for instance, must be reacted for 4.50 moles of water (as steam) to evolve?

$$? \text{ moles } C_5H_{12} = 4.50 \text{ mols } H_2O \times \frac{\text{mol } C_5H_{12}}{6 \text{ mols } H_2O} = 0.75 \text{ mols } C_5H_{12}$$

It is hardly necessary to memorize these three applications as though they were rules (they are not). They are only a list of stoichiometric applications. In sum, stoichiometry *shows the quantitative relation between one substance and another* in a reaction. You will be able to use the above applications and take for granted that they even exist, if you think, again, in terms of given and wanted species. Simply take their numbers from an equation, in the same way that you already know how to take them from a formula, and make a keystone. That is all there is to it.

141

1. e f b c h a g d

You may prefer to use, when balancing neutralization reactions, the alternate formula "HOH" instead of H_2O. It implies a hydrogen ion attached to a hydroxide ion, and may make both the origin and the amount of the water produced easier to read, as shown:

$$Ba(OH)_2 + 2HCl \rightarrow BaCl_2 + 2HOH$$

⊛ With any light color, smudge the "OH" on both sides of the above equation; with another color, do the same for the "H" on both sides.

2., 3.

a. $2Cu + S \rightarrow Cu_2S$ (C)

b. $Mg + 2HCl \rightarrow MgCl_2 + H_2$ (R)

c. $2NaBr + Cl_2 \rightarrow 2NaCl + Br_2$ (R)

d. $HC_2H_3O_2 + 2O_2 \rightarrow 2CO_2 + 2H_2O$ (O)

e. $2AsI_3 \rightarrow 2As + 3I_2$ (D)

f. $2Hg + O_2 \rightarrow 2HgO$ (C)

g. $Ra(OH)_2 + 2HF \rightarrow RaF_2 + 2H_2O$ (N)

h. $SiO_2 + 3C \rightarrow SiC + 2CO$ (R)

i. $2HNO_3 + Ag_2S \rightarrow 2AgNO_3 + H_2S$ (E)

j. $2KNO_3 \rightarrow 2KNO_2 + O_2$ (D)

k. $C_3H_8 + 5O_2 \rightarrow 3CO_2 + 4H_2O$ (O)

l. $Li_2Se + 2HClO_4 \rightarrow 2LiClO_4 + H_2Se$ (E)

m. $4P + 5O_2 \rightarrow 2P_2O_5$ (C)

n. $4FeS + 7O_2 \rightarrow 2Fe_2O_3 + 4SO_2$ (X)

o. $2Pb(NO_3)_2 \rightarrow 2PbO + O_2 + 4NO_2$ (D)

p. $Ba(OH)_2 + 2HI \rightarrow BaI_2 + 2H_2O$ (N)

q. $2CuC_2H_3O_2 + Mg \rightarrow Mg(C_2H_3O_2)_2 + 2Cu$ (R)

r. $CaO + CO_2 \rightarrow CaCO_3$ (already balanced) (C)

s. $3FeCl_2 + 2Na_3PO_4 \rightarrow Fe_3(PO_4)_2 + 6NaCl$ (E)

t. $2C_2H_2 + 5O_2 \rightarrow 4CO_2 + 2H_2O$ (O)

u. $MnO_2 + 4HCl \rightarrow MnCl_2 + Cl_2 + 2H_2O$ (X)

v. $2KHF_2 \rightarrow H_2 + F_2 + 2KF$ (D)

w. $2B(OH)_3 + 3H_2SO_4 \rightarrow B_2(SO_4)_3 + 6H_2O$ (N)

x. $WO_3 + 3H_2 \rightarrow W + 3H_2O$ (R)

y. $Co_2(SO_4)_3 + 3Ba(OH)_2 \rightarrow 2Co(OH)_3 + 3BaSO_4$ (E)

z. $C_6H_{12}O_6 + 6O_2 \rightarrow 6CO_2 + 6H_2O$ (O)

I. $2NH_3 + H_2SO_4 \rightarrow (NH_4)_2SO_4$ (C)

II. $SO_3 + 2KOH \rightarrow K_2SO_4 + H_2O$ (X)

III. $3Sr(OH)_2 + 2H_3AsO_3 \rightarrow Sr_3(AsO_3)_2 + 6H_2O$ (N)

IV. $2Al + 3H_2SeO_4 \rightarrow Al_2(SeO_4)_3 + 6H_2$ (R)

V. $2C_{10}H_{22} + 31O_2 \rightarrow 20CO_2 + 22H_2O$ (O)

VI. $^{210}Po \rightarrow {}^{206}Pb + {}^4He$ (nuclear decomposition) (D)

4.5 Stoichiometry

As is true of percent-composition problems, real stoichiometry calculations seldom contain only a keystone and no other conversion factors. Happily, the two types differ only as to function, not form.

The everyday stoichiometric DA bridge takes us from a given quantity in grams to a wanted quantity, also in grams. Therefore, we build it by inserting two molar conversion factors around the mole/mole keystone:

$$\frac{\text{mols Z}}{\text{grams Z}} \ \text{x} \ \frac{\text{mols Y}}{\text{mols Z}} \ \text{x} \ \frac{\text{grams Y}}{\text{mols Y}}$$

This is in no way dissimilar to the bridges you built in Chap. 2. Note that the same "pieces" are present and that they form the same memorable symmetry.

Stoichiometry problems are solved in the usual DA manner (Sects. 1.1, 1.2) but can also be thought of as a "core" having those elements described in Sect. 4.4 (question, keystone, answer) which is clothed in conversion factors.

Remember, though, that, for all their similarities, percent composition problems and stoichiometric problems have an important difference. The former is concerned with ingredients, and the latter, with a recipe.

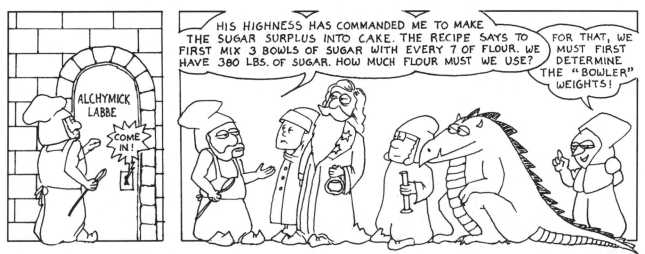

The balanced equation for this reaction is $3Su + 7Fl \rightarrow Su_3Fl_7$. Suppose that a bowl of each were weighed, and it was found that sugar had a "bowler weight" of 6.20 pounds, and flour, 4.45 pounds. With this, we have all the information: the ratio of bowls (moles) and the bowler (molar) weights. We can now solve:

$$? \text{ pounds flour} = 380 \text{ lbs Su} \ \text{x} \ \frac{\text{bol Su}}{6.20 \text{ lbs Su}} \ \text{x} \ \frac{7 \text{ bols Fl}}{3 \text{ bols Su}} \ \text{x} \ \frac{4.45 \text{ lbs Fl}}{\text{bol Fl}} = 636 \text{ lbs Fl}$$

Stoichiometry does the very same thing in chemistry for us, but with rather more practical dimensions.

Stoichiometry, because it is dimensional analysis, is largely linguistic rather than mathematical. Setting up a problem is mostly just a question of summarizing its language. You do, however, have to write a balanced equation before you do the stoichiometry, as you will certainly find yourself being reminded if you attempt to start without the balanced equation.

When you have a balanced equation—and as often as not this will be provided on, say, a test—then you follow the usual steps: write down the conversion factors, isolate the given, make a question from the wanted quantity, and link the conversion factors by making a dimension in a numerator reappear in the denominator of the next conversion factor. And, of course, cancel out and calculate.

Here is an example: how much oxygen is needed for the complete burning in air of 75.0 grams of butane? The balanced equation is:

$$2C_4H_{10}(g) + 13O_2 \rightarrow 8CO_2(g) + 10H_2O(l)$$

Only the molar weights of the substances mentioned in the problem are relevant to the calculation. You already know how to determine these (Sect. 2.4). Butane is 58.12 grams/mole and oxygen is 32.00 grams/mole.

The only other conversion factor is the keystone, which will move us from the given substance (C_4H_{10}) to the wanted substance (O_2). Its ratio comes directly from the coefficients. The stoichiometric bridge, then, is:

$$? \text{ grams } O_2 = 75.0 \text{ g } C_4H_{10} \times \frac{\text{mol } C_4H_{10}}{58.12 \text{ g } C_4H_{10}} \times \frac{13 \text{ mols } O_2}{2 \text{ mols } C_4H_{10}} \times \frac{32 \text{ g } O_2}{\text{mol } O_2} = 268 \text{ g } O$$

(As always, the keystone does not affect significant figures; it is a defined relation.)

Weight relations between reactants can be determined in this way, but so can those between a reactant and a product. If a toothpaste manufacturer reacts 640 grams of pulverized tin with fluorine gas, how much tin (II) fluoride is produced? First, the balanced equation...

$$Sn(s) + F_2(g) \rightarrow SnF_2(s)$$

Now, of course, you need the molar weights. Tin comes directly from the Periodic Table, and the value for fluorine is only double its elemental value. It so happens that these two elements form this compound, a salt, in the same ratio (1:2), so these elemental weights are added. The coefficient of both the given and the wanted is one. This does not mean, though, that you do not need the keystone; you *do* need it, in order to change substances:

$$? \text{ grams } SnF_2 = 640 \text{ g } Sn \times \frac{\text{mol } Sn}{118.7 \text{ g } Sn} \times \frac{\text{mol } SnF_2}{\text{mol } Sn} \times \frac{156.7 \text{ g } SnF_2}{\text{mol } SnF_2} = 845 \text{ g } SnF_2$$

These two examples are what might be called basic or plain ol' everyday stoichiometry problems. We will now broach some of the dreaded miscellaneous complications, which are really only conversion factors that are added to this basic stoichiometric core.

At any rate—whether simple or pseudo-complicated—every stoichiometry problem does the same thing: it takes us from the given amount of one substance to the wanted amount of another.

In most general chemistry classes, much shrift is given to the conversion of quantities with nonmetric dimensions to those having metric ones (and the reverse). This has not been, nor will it become to any important degree, the case in this book, because such converting back and forth does not represent any new principle in dimensional analysis and because it is not specifically related to chemistry as a science.

Nevertheless, conversions of this sort are included in all curricula and indeed have—along with Avogadro's number—one useful purpose, and that is practice in the construction of longer DA bridges. You shall, in any event, probably be provided with the necessary conversion factors, even on lecture examinations.

Here is an example: the toothpaste factory of the previous problem manufactures 2.40 tons of SnF_2 annually. How many kilograms of tin does this require? The bridge will have three more conversion factors. These will make it lengthier, but not in principle more complex.

$$? \text{ kg Sn} = 2.40 \text{ tons } SnF_2 \quad \text{x} \quad \frac{2000 \text{ lbs } SnF_2}{\text{ton } SnF_2} \quad \text{x} \quad \frac{454 \text{ g } SnF_2}{\text{lb } SnF_2} \quad \text{x} \quad \frac{\text{mol } SnF_2}{156.7 \text{ g } SnF_2} \quad \text{x}$$

$$\frac{\text{mol Sn}}{\text{mol } SnF_2} \quad \text{x} \quad \frac{118.7 \text{ g Sn}}{\text{mol Sn}} \quad \text{x} \quad \frac{\text{Kg Sn}}{1000 \text{ g Sn}} \quad = \quad 1.65 \times 10^3 \text{ kg Sn}$$

The final conversion factor is, of course, a metric-to-metric one, and it is called for by the question expression. The core problem, with the keystone at its center, is clearly visible within the expanded problem.

The number of substances in an equation does not in any way complicate stoichiometric calculations, which only show the relation between *two* species at a time. Here is a balanced equation with seven species:

$$2KMnO_4(s) + 5H_2C_2O_4(aq) + 6HCl(aq) \rightarrow 2MnCl_2(s) + 10CO_2(g) + 8H_2O(l) + 2KCl(aq)$$

Here is a problem based on it: how much oxalic acid (remember its conjugate, $C_2O_4^{2-}$?) will be needed to react fully with 19.4 pounds of potassium permanganate in an excess of hydrochloric acid? If your molar weight calculations are on target, you will get 158.0 grams/mole for the salt and 90.04 for the acid. Now, here is the DA bridge, with its nonmetric-to-metric conversion factor:

$$?\text{grams } H_2C_2O_4 = 19.4 \text{ lbs } KMnO_4 \quad \text{x} \quad \frac{454 \text{ g } KMnO_4}{\text{lb } KMnO_4} \quad \text{x} \quad \frac{\text{mol } KMnO_4}{158.0 \text{ g } KMnO_4} \quad \text{x}$$

$$\frac{5 \text{ mols } H_2C_2O_4}{2 \text{ mols } KMnO_4} \quad \text{x} \quad \frac{90.04 \text{ g } H_2C_2O_4}{\text{mol } H_2C_2O_4} \quad = \quad 1.25 \times 10^4 \text{g}$$

Do not worry about the word "excess" before HCl. Limiting and excess reactants are what Sect. 4.7 is made of.

In Sect. 2.9, we dealt with the dimensional analysis, in percentages, of impure substances. Now we will examine impurities within the context of stoichiometric calculations.

Most of the time, only a single additional conversion factor is entailed, and it will necessarily be provided in the problem. It may be made up from the weight of the purity and that of the whole impure sample (as in the first example below), or it may be a mere percentage (as in the second example).

As with other dimensional-analysis calculations involving impurities, however, these carry the caveat that cannot be overemphasized: label the dimensions completely. Now, to the examples.

A sample of chromium ore from Zimbabwe weighing 30.0 grams is assayed and found to contain 21.8 grams of the metal. How much hydrochloric acid will be required to react with 800 grams of the impurity to produce the chloride (from which the metal will itself be extracted later)? First, the balanced equation, which is...

$$2Cr(s) + 6HCl \rightarrow 2CrCl_3 + 3H_2$$

The first conversion factor is the "extra" one; once you have it in place, the rest of the bridge is like that of any other stoichiometric calculation:

$$? \text{ g HCl} = 800 \text{ g ore} \quad \times \quad \frac{21.8 \text{ g Cr}}{30.0 \text{ g ore}} \quad \times \quad \frac{\text{mol Cr}}{51.97 \text{g Cr}} \quad \times \quad \frac{6 \text{ mols HCl}}{2 \text{ mols Cr}} \quad \times \quad \frac{36.46 \text{ g HCl}}{\text{mol HCl}} \quad =$$

$$1.22 \times 10^3 \text{ g HCl}$$

It is somewhat commoner, however, for a sample's purity to be given as a percentage, as in the following example.

In a hermetically sealed container, a slab of white phosphorus (a waxy, very flammable allotrope) ignites and burns in ordinary air, which is 21.0% oxygen. If 8.7 grams of phosphorus pentoxide result, how much air was used up?

$$4P(s) + 5O_2(g) \rightarrow 2P_2O_5(s)$$

The impurity here is air itself; for the sake of this problem, it is (in effect) impure oxygen, and so might be labeled "air" or "O_2 imp." *But it must be labeled.* In solving the problem, then, just set up the question and write down the impurity conversion factor so that it will be in front of you when you need it (this time it comes in as nothing more than an appendage or an afterthought of the stoichiometric core).

$$? \text{ grams air} = 8.7 \text{ g } P_2O_5 \quad \times \quad \frac{\text{mol } P_2O_5}{141.9 \text{ g } P_2O_5} \quad \times \quad \frac{5 \text{ mols } O_2}{\text{mol } P_2O_5} \quad \times \quad \frac{32.0 \text{ g } O_2}{\text{mol } O_2} \quad \times \quad \frac{100 \text{ g air}}{21.0 \text{ g } O_2} \quad = \quad 46.7 \text{ g air}$$

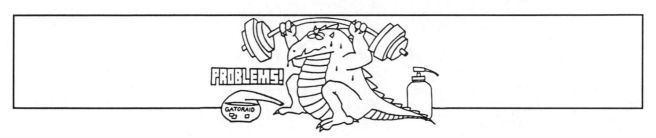

1. Mercury is most often obtained by roasting cinnabar. How many grams of this mineral are required for a yield of 165 grams of pure mercury?

$$HgS + O_2 \rightarrow Hg + SO_2$$

2. A sample of copper (II) oxide is heated in a crucible until only copper (I) oxide remains. If the original sample wieghed 34.9 grams, what will the resulting sample weigh?

$$4CuO \rightarrow 2Cu_2O + O_2$$

3. The alkene, nonene, is hydrogenated (saturated with hydrogen) to form the alkane, nonane. How much nonene will be needed to produce 250 grams of nonane?

$$C_9H_{18} + H_2 \rightarrow C_9H_{20}$$

4. How many milligrams of pure radium would we need to obtain 35.0 milligrams of radium nitride? The atomic weight of radium is estimated at 226.

$$3Ra + N_2 \rightarrow Ra_3N_2$$

5. The explosion of nitroglycerine is, chemically speaking, an instantaneous decomposition of a fairly complex compound into several gases, including nitrogen and water vapor. How much nitrogen will result from the explosion of 29.0 kg of nitroglycerine?

$$4C_3H_5(NO_3)_3 \rightarrow 12CO_2 + 6N_2 + O_2 + 10H_2O$$

6. In an exchange, or metathesis, reaction of tricalcium diphosphorus with hydrobromic acid, 144 grams of phosphine gas evolve. How much Ca_3P_2 was consumed by this reaction?

$$Ca_3P_2 + 6HBr \rightarrow 3CaBr_2 + 2PH_3$$

7. In the replacement reaction that began the iron age, carbon (in the form of hot coals) was used as a reducing agent on the oxide Fe_2O_3. An ore sample weighing 23.5 grams is found to contain 17.0 grams of the oxide. How much carbon went into the reduction of 2.5 kilograms of this impurity to elemental iron (Fe)?

$$Fe_2O_3 + 3C \rightarrow 3CO + 2Fe$$

8. How many tons of elemental silicon must be fully reacted with 6.00 tons of carbon to yield carbarundum?

$$C + Si \rightarrow SiC$$

9. In the roasting of galena, PbS, the compound is converted to lead (II) oxide and sulfur dioxide. How much oxygen will be consumed in the extraction of 1265 pounds of ore from a lode that is 84.0% galena?

$$PbS + 2O_2 \rightarrow PbO_2 + SO_2$$

(The answers to this problem set are found on p. 154)

DRAG·O·PLEX

VITAMINS

1. A compound is 74.1% oxygen and 25.9% nitrogen. What is its empirical formula?

2. A mineral is 37.7% sodium, 23.0% silicon, and the rest, oxygen. What is the empirical formula?

3. Name the compound in problem 1.

148

15
P
30.973

𝕻rofile: 𝕻hosphorus

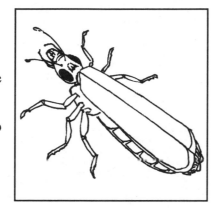

The firefly is really a beetle that uses the slow burn of phosphorus to "light up."

Phosphorus is truly unique. It is physically and chemically very unlike any other element, unlike even its neighbors in the Periodic Table.

Its discovery was fittingly bizarre. In 1669, when the remaining years of the alchemic era were numbered, a German alchemist named Brand was seeking gold from any substance of the same color. It was inevitable, then, that he would experiment with urine. Among the numerous substances that he isolated from this was a volatile, waxy yellow-white solid.

We now know that the body excretes phosphorus compounds that result from the metabolism of certain proteins. The human body is itself about 1% phosphorus. Most of it is insolubly locked into the bones as calcium phosphate, but the compound adenosine triphosphate (ATP) is the energy-reserve mechanism of animal tissues. Energy is released every time the compound releases one of its phosphate radicals to become adenosine diphosphate (ADP). It is thus an understatement to say that the element is needed for life.

The white allotrope is unstable and poisonous. Between 40°C and 44°C it explodes in air; above that, it melts. At lower temperatures it is slowly oxidized to a yellowish oxide. It is this reaction that produces the steady glow that gives phosphorus its name, which means "light-bearer."

When cooked in a vacuum, white phophorus is changed into gentler red phophorus. Either of these allotropes can be made into a third, even more stable allotrope, the flaky black phosphorus, by subjecting them to extreme pressures.

Phosphine gas, PH_3, forms under water from the phosphorus compounds in decaying organic matter. It ignites spontaneously in air and at night can be seen as the "will o' the wisp," the dim blue flame that is visible over marshes.

Another compound (this one a salt) is phosphorus trisulfide. P_4S_3 is the ignition medium used in matches. The heat of friction, from striking, ignites it; other compounds in the match head then sustain the flame. In several languages, the name of the element and the word for match is the same (New World Castilian, *fósforo*).

Phosphates (compounds containing the PO_4^{3-} radical) find their most important commercial application in fertilizers. Morocco is the world's largest exporter of phosphates, and this resource was the primary economic impetus for that country's annexation of its neighbor, Western Sahara, in the 1970s. Phosphate-enriched fertilizers can also be synthesized.

Asimov, himself a chemist, has noted that, in effect, phosphorus is the "limiting reactant" in the production of the Earth's biomass. Put another way, the dynamic totality of all life on Earth is prevented from further growth, in terms of sheer bulk, by the limited availability of phosphorus.

The Family 5A elements are the most physically dissimilar of all element families. Nitrogen is an invisible gas; phosphorus is a triallotropic nonmetal; arsenic is a metalloid with crystalline gray and amorphous black and yellow allotropes. Antimony is more metallic than nonmetallic, but bismuth is wholly metallic. It is the heaviest nonradioactive element. All three heavier siblings are used in alloying.

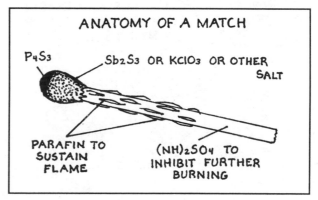

ANATOMY OF A MATCH

P_4S_3

Sb_2S_3 OR $KClO_3$ OR OTHER SALT

PARAFIN TO SUSTAIN FLAME

$(NH)_2SO_4$ TO INHIBIT FURTHER BURNING

149

4.6 Percentage Yield

When we perform a stoichiometric calculation to determine the amount of product that will result, we are in fact only determining the theoretical maximum that *could* result. In the real (i.e., untheoretical) world, all reactions come up short—if only to a negligible degree most of the time—of the quantity we expect from the calculation.

What we actually get is called, not surprisingly, the *actual yield*; we represent it as a percentage of the *theoretical yield*. Hence, the equation (if it is not too silly to call something like this an equation) is this:

$$\frac{\text{actual yield}}{\text{theoretical yield}} \times 100 = \text{percentage yield}$$

The determination of the cook's percentage yield, then, is...

$$\frac{898 \text{ lbs}}{926 \text{ lbs}} \times 100 = 97.0\%$$

If the terms are a bother to remember, just recall that the lesser quantity is also the shorter word (numerator) and the larger quantity, the longer word (denominator), and you cannot go wrong.

If, for some reason, you do in fact go wrong, you will know it right away because your actual yield will be *more* than 100. This will mean one of two things: either that (a) you goofed, or that (b) you will be the first beginning chemistry student ever to win a Nobel Prize, by virtue of your having created matter *ex nihilo*.

The dimensions make no difference, and so need no converting, provided they are the same (tons over tons, grams over grams, etc.).

In problem 2 of the previous problem set, the theoretical yield for Cu_2O was 27.9 grams. But, for one or more of the reasons mentioned by Dalton, let us assume that the product only weighs 27.3 grams. What is the percentage yield?

Write the actual yield over the theoretical one and multiply by 100:

$$\frac{27.3}{27.9} \times 100 = 98.2$$

While not all Chem. 1 lab reactions will require percent-yield determinations, those that do only entail this brief and uncomplicated pocket-calculator operation.

For reactions that go to completion, the yield should approach 100% (mid nineties, at least). If not, you should suspect an error in previous calculations.

4.7 Limiting Reactants

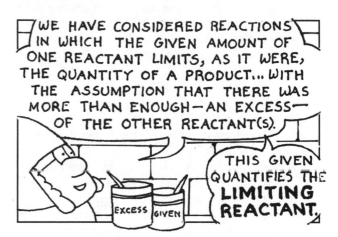

When the study of stoichiometry is first introduced, the student only encounters problems in which the quantity of a single reactant is given (unless, of course, a product quantity is the given). The other reactants are explicitly or implicitly unlimited by the wording of the problem. They are said to be "in excess."

Chemistry professors and textbooks must allow this in order that stoichiometry can be taught independently.

Under the real circumstances of the lab, however, we would have to measure each reactant, and the quantities we get for each are all potentially the given. What separates the true given from the pretenders?

It is the quantity of that reactant which would be the first to be used up in a reaction. All other quantities—including those of the products—are thus dependent on and limited by this reactant.

Therefore, we require a way to identify the reactant. After that, it is nothing more than stoichiometry as usual, because that which we must do to determine the *limiting reactant* does in no mean complicate the dimensional-analysis calculations that follow.

--------------------Analogy--------------------

A tricycle factory takes inventory and finds it has 142 assembled frames (a frame being an "uncuttable" aggregate of elements such as seats, chains, etc.), 479 wheels, and 280 pedals. The only model that the factory produces uses the same wheels in front as in back. How many trikes can they produce, according to the following balanced equation?

$$2P + F + 3W \rightarrow P_2FW_3$$

Divide the quantities by the coefficients:

(P) $\frac{280}{2} = 140$ (F) $\frac{142}{1} = 142$ (W) $\frac{479}{3} = 159$

The lowest result is for the pedals: therefore, pedals limit the amount of the product—they are the limiting reactant—while frames and wheels are in excess. The quantity of the limiting reactant is the one used as the given in the dimensional analysis question which will begin the stoichiometry:

? trikes = 280 pedals

Continuing with the analogy, the formula of the tricycle is P_2FW_3. Substituting hydrogen for the pedals, sulfur for the frame, and oxygen for the wheels gives us the formula of sulfurous acid, H_2SO_3.

Let us say that the formation of this compound were represented by the equation shown at right (in reality, it is erroneous; it is even questionable whether this acid actually exists; but the equation *does* show the molar relationship between the equation and any problem that might be based on it):

$$2H + S + 3O \rightarrow H_2SO_3$$

In the tricycle, numbers of parts were considered; in chemical equations, it is the numbers of *moles of parts* that are in question.

Suppose that we had 11.2 moles of sulfur (atoms), 33.4 moles of oxygen (atoms), and 26.7 moles of hydrogen (atoms) available for a reaction to produce molecules—or tricycles—of sulfurous acid. Which of these three elements is the limiting reactant?

First of all, we divide the number of moles of each part, or reactant, by their respective coefficients:

$$(H)\ \frac{26.7}{2} = 13.4 \quad (S)\ \frac{11.2}{1} = 11.2 \quad (O)\ \frac{33.4}{3} = 11.1$$

Oxygen is the limiting reactant because its *quotient* is the lowest. It limits both (1) the amount of the other reactants that the reaction will consume and also (2) the amount of product that the reaction will yield.

Now, only the quantity of the limiting reactant, and not its quotient, will be used from this point on. Ignore every other number as if it never existed.

$$(H)\ \frac{26.7}{2} = 13.4 \quad (S)\ \frac{11.2}{1} = 11.2 \quad (O)\ \frac{33.4}{3} = 11.1$$

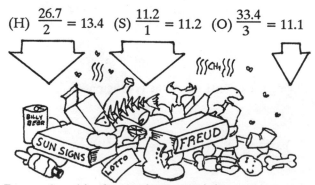

Remember this: the numbers pertaining to the excess reactants are themselves excess and must be discarded, lest they insidiously find their way into further calculations. When this happens, there is Hell to pay for it: you will descend deeper and deeper into a conundrum of numbers and angst and you may even fail to complete the problem, much less pull it off correctly.

The same goes for the quotient of the operation of the limiting reactant itself. Once it declares itself to be the smallest quotient, it is of no further use; its purpose is to point not to itself but to the limiting quantity. Trash it!

Do not worry about also ignoring the coefficients—they will wait for you in the balanced equation for when you need them (which you will, later, to make the keystone).

Finding the limiting reactant, then, is a potentially hazardous side-trip between the balanced equation and the stoichiometric work.

The pitfall does not come from any inherent complexity in the procedure so much as from the frightful slew of numbers that the determination seems to generate. You can avoid this hazard by conscientiously anticipating it and developing the habit, early, of highlighting the given (33.4 in the above example) the moment you get it, perhaps by circling it.

So far in our discussion, finding the limiting reactant has only involved dividing the reactants' molar quantities by molar coefficients and then knowing what number *not* to throw away.

In the lab, however, the samples of the reactants will not be conveniently marked with their molar quantities; instead, we will have to weigh them and convert the grams to moles. This means even more numbers, but there is no cause for alarm.

The GamMa Delta system, which is uncannily similar to the GamMa Ray system for empirical formulae (Sect. 2.8), will be useful in sorting through and controlling the morass of numbers. Its initials stand for Grams, Moles, and the second of two series (or "rows") of ordinary Divisions. If you mastered the GamMa Ray system, then the GamMa Delta system (which is slightly simpler) will be a piece of Viennese Torte.

Here is an example: a 63.0-gram sample of beryllium cyanide is added to a solution containing 59.7 grams of hydrochloric acid. How much beryllium chloride will precipitate?

$$Be(CN)_2 + 2HCl \rightarrow 2HCN + BeCl_2$$

Begin by simply filling in the grams line with the given data. Then, if you have written down the GamMa Delta chart correctly (which, unlike the GamMa Ray grid, will usually have only two columns), you cannot fail to remember what to do next: convert grams to moles. Once the mole line is filled in, the next step promptly presents itself: divide. But by what?

By the only other numbers around—the coefficients from the equation (see the GamMa Delta grid, above right).

Now that we know the limiting reactant, we can make up the question: how much $BeCl_2$ equals 63.0 grams of $Be(CN)_2$? By this point, you will have already begun the stoichiometry.

Let us go through another example (at right): how much silver chloride will result from the reaction of 150 grams of potassium chloride and 564 grams of silver nitrate?

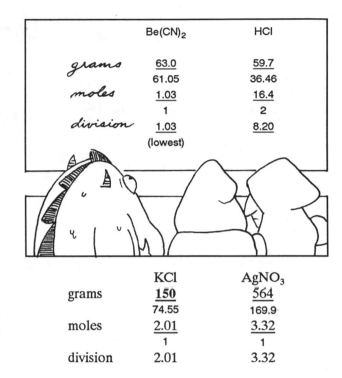

	Be(CN)$_2$	HCl
grams	63.0	59.7
	61.05	36.46
moles	1.03	16.4
	1	2
division	1.03	8.20
	(lowest)	

	KCl	AgNO$_3$
grams	**150**	**564**
	74.55	169.9
moles	2.01	3.32
	1	1
division	2.01	3.32

$$AgNO_3 + KCl \rightarrow AgCl + KNO_3$$

Make a column for each reactant. The grams come straight from the problem. In the first division, divide the grams by the molar weights. Then—in the second division—divide what you get from the first division by the coefficients (which in this case are all 1, so the limiting reactant will immediately be obvious). As with empirical formulae, you can use the one-grid, no-messy-figuring shortcut of writing the divisors underneath the gram and mole lines.

Since the reactants are given in grams rather than in moles, you will, as in the above example, circle the gram quantity of the limiting reactant. Do this *now*. On your own, you may wish to do the stoichiometry that this determination makes possible. Begin, of course, with the shorthand for the question, How much AgCl equals 15.0 grams of KCl? Then do the DA bridge. If you do it correctly, your answer will be 28.8 g AgCl.

Here is another example; this time fully worked out: How much anhydrous barium arsenite can be removed from a solution in which 722 grams of barium hydroxide were reacted with 690 grams of arsenious acid?

$$3Ba(OH)_2 + 2H_3AsO_3 \rightarrow Ba_3(AsO_3)_2 + 6H_2O$$

Fill in the grams line. Determine the molar weights:

$Ba(OH)_2$: $1(137.34) + 2(17.01) = 171.4$

H_3AsO_3: $3(1.008) + (74.922) + 3(16.00) = 125.9$

	Ba(OH)$_2$	H$_3$AsO$_3$
grams	**722**	690
	171.4	125.9
moles	7.41	5.48
	3	2
division	2.47	2.74

Now you can fill in the mole line by dividing the available grams by these weights; then, fill in the "Delta" line by dividing the available moles by the coefficients. Finally, circle the grams of the now-known limiting reactant, and use it and the substance it quantifies in the stoichiometric calculation:

$$? \text{ g Ba}_3(AsO_3)_2 = 722 \text{ g Ba(OH)}_2 \times \frac{\text{mol Ba(OH)}_2}{171.4 \text{ g Ba(OH)}_2} \times \frac{\text{mol Ba}_3(AsO_3)_2}{3 \text{ mols Ba(OH)}_2} \times \frac{657.9 \text{ g Ba}_3(AsO_3)_2}{\text{mol Ba}_3(AsO_3)_2}$$

(Note: the two arithmetical steps are the two divisions *between* the lines. The final line is named Delta to remind you that a division, not a multiplication (as in GamMa Ray) is the last operation. It could also be thought of, perhaps more accurately, as the "final quotient line," but, of course, this does not begin with D. If you do the above stoichiometry just for fun, you should get 924 g $Ba_3(AsO_3)_3$.

1. $? \text{ grams HgS} = 165 \text{ g Hg} \times \dfrac{\text{mol Hg}}{200.1 \text{ g Hg}} \times \dfrac{\text{mol HgS}}{\text{mol Hg}} \times \dfrac{233 \text{ g HgS}}{\text{mol HgS}} = 192 \text{ g HgS}$

2. $? \text{ grams Cu}_2\text{O} = 34.9 \text{ g CuO} \times \dfrac{\text{mol CuO}}{79.54 \text{ g CuO}} \times \dfrac{2 \text{ mols Cu}_2\text{O}}{4 \text{ mols CuO}} \times \dfrac{143.1 \text{ g Cu}_2\text{O}}{\text{mol Cu}_2\text{O}} = 31.4 \text{ g Cu}_2\text{O}$

3. $? \text{ grams C}_9\text{H}_{18} = 250 \text{ g C}_9\text{H}_{20} \times \dfrac{\text{mol C}_9\text{H}_{20}}{128.2 \text{ g C}_9\text{H}_{20}} \times \dfrac{\text{mol C}_9\text{H}_{18}}{\text{mol C}_9\text{H}_{20}} \times \dfrac{126.2 \text{ g C}_9\text{H}_{18}}{\text{mol C}_9\text{H}_{18}} = 246.1 \text{ g C}_9\text{H}_{18}$

4. $? \text{ milligrams Ra} = 35.0 \text{ mg Ra}_3\text{N}_2 \times \dfrac{\text{g Ra}_3\text{N}_2}{1000 \text{ mg Ra}_3\text{N}_2} \times \dfrac{\text{mol Ra}_3\text{N}_2}{706 \text{ g Ra}_3\text{N}_2} \times \dfrac{3 \text{ mols Ra}}{\text{mol Ra}_3\text{N}_2}$

$\times \dfrac{226 \text{ g Ra}}{\text{mol Ra}} \times \dfrac{1000 \text{ mg Ra}}{\text{g Ra}} = 33.6 \text{ mg Ra}$

5. $? \text{ grams N}_2 = 29.0 \text{ kg Nitro} \times \dfrac{1000 \text{ g Nitro}}{\text{kg Nitro}} \times \dfrac{\text{mol Nitro}}{227.2 \text{ g Nitro}} \times \dfrac{6 \text{ mols N}_2}{4 \text{ mols Nitro}} \times \dfrac{28.01 \text{ g N}_2}{\text{mol N}_2}$

$= 5.36 \times 10^3 \text{ g N}_2$

6. $? \text{ grams Ca}_3\text{P}_2 = 144 \text{ g PH}_3 \times \dfrac{\text{mol PH}_3}{33.99 \text{ g PH}_3} \times \dfrac{\text{mol Ca}_3\text{P}_2}{2 \text{ mols PH}_3} \times \dfrac{182.2 \text{ g Ca}_3\text{P}_2}{\text{mol Ca}_3\text{P}_2} = 386 \text{ g Ca}_3\text{P}_2$

7. $? \text{ grams Fe} = 25.0 \text{ g Fe}_2\text{O}_3 \times \dfrac{1000 \text{ g imp}}{\text{kg imp}} \times \dfrac{17.0 \text{ g Fe}_2\text{O}_3}{23.5 \text{ g imp}} \times \dfrac{\text{mol Fe}_2\text{O}_3}{159.7 \text{ g Fe}_2\text{O}_3} \times \dfrac{2 \text{ mols Fe}}{\text{mol Fe}_2\text{O}_3}$

$\times \dfrac{55.85 \text{ g Fe}}{\text{mol Fe}} = 1.26 \times 10^4 \text{ g Fe}$

8. $? \text{ tons Si} = 6.00 \text{ tons C} \times \dfrac{2000 \text{ lbs C}}{\text{ton C}} \times \dfrac{454 \text{ g C}}{\text{lb C}} \times \dfrac{\text{mol C}}{12.01 \text{ g C}} \times \dfrac{\text{mol Si}}{\text{mol C}} \times \dfrac{28.09 \text{ g Si}}{\text{mol Si}} \times \dfrac{\text{lb Si}}{454 \text{ g Si}}$

$\times \dfrac{\text{ton Si}}{2000 \text{ lbs Si}} = 14.0 \text{ tons Si}$

9. $? \text{ grams O}_2 = 1265 \text{ grams PbS imp} \times \dfrac{84.0 \text{ g PbS}}{100 \text{ g PbS imp}} \times \dfrac{\text{mol PbS}}{239.3 \text{ g PbS}} \times \dfrac{2 \text{ mols O}_2}{\text{mol PbS}} \times \dfrac{32.00 \text{ g O}_2}{\text{mol O}_2}$

$= 2.84 \times 10^2 \text{ g O}_2$

It is often expedient to substitute initials or abbreviated words for long formulae, as in problem 5.

In some problems, there are numbers which appear in both a numerator and a denominator. They need not, therefore, necessarily be used in the calculation. Examples are the 2s in problem 2, the 1000s in problem 4, and the 2000s in problem 6. The danger is in *habitually* excluding such numbers when, for instance, they appear once in the numerators but twice in the denominators.

Naturally, fractions such as 6/4 (problem 5) can be reduced to simplest terms; an advantage in not doing so is that their connection with the equation remains clear. This clarity is very helpful if an error is made elsewhere in the problem.

In these problems, you will use atomic weights in the limited-reactant determinations for all elements, including diatomic ones (Note: do not let differences in wording stop you from seeing similarities in problems).

1. A reaction from which 641 pounds of barium bromate (for which you must be able to write the formula) is expected yields only 622 pounds. "Calculate" the percentage yield.

2. When 400 grams of phosphorus pentoxide (which is named for its empirical formula rather than its true one) is reacted in an experiment with water, only 544 grams of phosphoric acid is actually produced. Perform the stoichiometry and, from the answer, determine the percentage yield.

$$P_4O_{10}(s) + 6H_2O(l) \rightarrow 4H_3PO_4(s)$$

3. If 70 tons of carbon are added to 100 tons of quartz to produce carborundum, which is the limiting reactant (remember that any dimension can also substitute for grams)?

$$SiO_2(s) + 3C(s) \rightarrow SiC(s) + 2CO(g)$$

4. In the production of some potassium hydrogen fluoride, the quantities of the reactants are 274 grams of KF; 44.5 grams of F_2; and 2.37 grams of H_2. Find the limiting reactant.

$$KF(s) + 2F_2(g) + H_2(g) \rightarrow KHF_2(s)$$

5a. Determine the limiting reactant in the formation of the salt $CaCl_2$ from 500 grams of calcium and 900 grams of chlorine (space provided at right).

$$Ca(s) + Cl_2(g) \rightarrow CaCl_2(s)$$

5b. What will be the maximum *theoretical* yield of $CaCl_2$ from this reaction?

5c. If 1.25 kilograms of $CaCl_2$ result from the reaction, what is the percentage yield?

6a. If 33.0 grams of the salt $FeCl_2$ is added to a solution containing 38.5 grams of Na_3PO_4, iron (II) phosphate will precipitate, leaving a new solution of NaCl. Determine the limiting reactant.

$$3FeCl_2 + 2Na_3PO_4 \rightarrow Fe_3(PO_4)_2 + 6NaCl$$

6b. What is the theoretical yield of iron (II) phosphate?

6c. All due care is taken in separating the precipitate from the solution and in drying it. Nevertheless, when measured, it is found to weigh 29.1 grams. What is the pecentage yield?

7. Soduim cyanide is a salt that you would never use to season your vegetables, but it has industrial applications. What is the percentage yield if 411 grams of NaCN is the actual yield from the reaction of 64.5 grams of nitrogen, 203 grams of carbon and 463 grams of sodium carbonate (Note: this is not a percentage-yield problem alone).

$$Na_2CO_3 + 4C + N_2 \rightarrow 2NaCN + 3CO$$

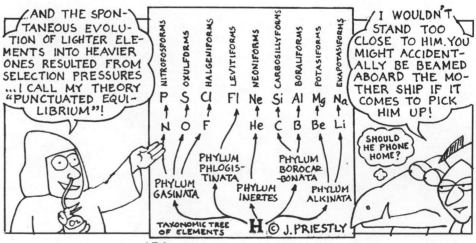

4.8 Chapter Synthesis

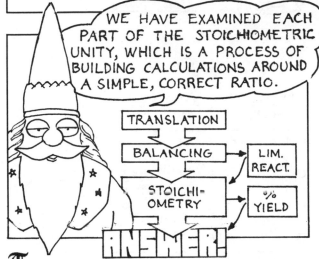

WE HAVE EXAMINED EACH PART OF THE STOICHIOMETRIC UNITY, WHICH IS A PROCESS OF BUILDING CALCULATIONS AROUND A SIMPLE, CORRECT RATIO.

This chapter has been all about what might be called the "stoichiometric unity." A section or two was devoted to each part of the unity, and each part follows in logical order, from its predecessor.

The first part is translation (Sect. 4.1). Obviously, the first thing you must do with any chemistry problem is render its words into the shorthand that makes up your equation.

Then, when that equation is written down, what is there to do next but balance it with coefficients (4.2, 4.3)? Two of these coefficients will make up a stoichiometric keystone, and where else could you use such a keystone if not in a stoichiometric calculation (4.4, 4.5)? The keystone connects the balanced equation (one step) with the stoichiometry (another step). The calculation itself is then only a matter of adding molar conversion factors and others—if impurities or nonmetrics are involved—to a question which is itself part of the shorthand work you already did while translating the problem. In any case, that keystone will be in the "middle" and will take you from the given substance to the wanted one.

Because chemistry is a laboratory-practical science, the stoichiometric unity has a few side trips, or, if you prefer, accessories. In the lab, we weigh reactants, and, in so doing, have more than one given.

For this, we must determine which one we will use, namely the one for the limiting reactant (4.7). We will automatically know when to make this pre-stoichiometry excursion, because it would be a jolly sight impossible to start the stoichiometry calculation with two givens, when the question expression only has room for one. In some theory problems, or problems unrelated to your labwork, the presence of the word *excess* in the problem all but assures that you will not need this step. But there will be less and less such problems as you go along; besides, limiting reactant calculations are almost fun when you have mastered the GamMa Delta system.

Finally, since laboratory yields can very nearly approach but never fulfill the theoretical maximum, a single calculator division (and the moving of a decimal two places) gives you the actual yield (4.6). This step will not implicitly always declare itself (like the others do), but someday it will be habit and, at worst, it is only the answer itself, with a very slight modification.

Here is a comprehensive problem, solved by the stoichiometric unity: the salt sodium sulfate can be formed by neutralizing sulfuric acid with the powerful base, sodium hydroxide. In a reaction of 85.0 grams of the base with 194 grams of the acid, how much salt will (theoretically) result? What is the percent yield if we wind up with 148.3 grams of salt (Note:both reactants are in the aqueous state)?:

1. TRANSLATION

$NaOH + H_2SO_4 \rightarrow Na_2SO_4 + H_2O$

2. BALANCING

$2NaOH + H_2SO_4 \rightarrow Na_2SO_4 + 2H_2O$

4. STOICHIOMETRY

$$? \text{ g } Na_2SO_4 = 85.0 \text{ g NaOH} \times \frac{\text{mol NaOH}}{40.0 \text{ g NaOH}} \times \frac{\text{mol } Na_2SO_4}{2 \text{ mols NaOH}} \times \frac{142.0 \text{ g } Na_2SO_4}{\text{mol } Na_2SO_4} = 150 \text{ g } Na_2SO_4$$

3. LIMITING REACTANT

	H_2SO_4	NaOH
G	194.0	85.0
	98.08	40.00
M	1.98	2.12
	1	2
D	1.98	1.06

5. % YIELD $\quad \dfrac{149 \text{ g}}{150 \text{ g}} \times 100 = 99.3\%$

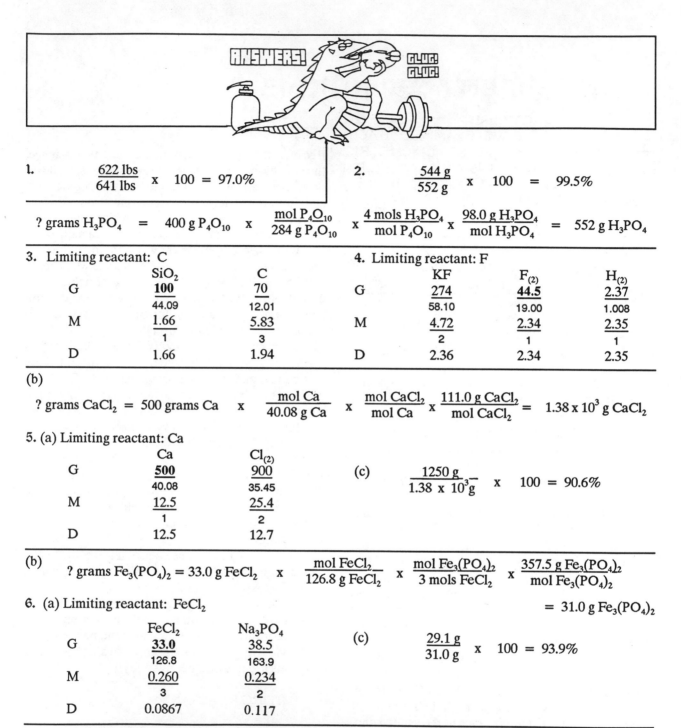

1.

$$\frac{622 \text{ lbs}}{641 \text{ lbs}} \times 100 = 97.0\%$$

2.

$$\frac{544 \text{ g}}{552 \text{ g}} \times 100 = 99.5\%$$

$$? \text{ grams } H_3PO_4 = 400 \text{ g } P_4O_{10} \times \frac{\text{mol } P_4O_{10}}{284 \text{ g } P_4O_{10}} \times \frac{4 \text{ mols } H_3PO_4}{\text{mol } P_4O_{10}} \times \frac{98.0 \text{ g } H_3PO_4}{\text{mol } H_3PO_4} = 552 \text{ g } H_3PO_4$$

3. Limiting reactant: C

	SiO_2	C
G	**100**	70
	44.09	12.01
M	1.66	5.83
	1	3
D	1.66	1.94

4. Limiting reactant: F

	KF	$F_{(2)}$	$H_{(2)}$
G	274	**44.5**	2.37
	58.10	19.00	1.008
M	4.72	2.34	2.35
	2	1	1
D	2.36	2.34	2.35

(b)

$$? \text{ grams } CaCl_2 = 500 \text{ grams Ca} \times \frac{\text{mol Ca}}{40.08 \text{ g Ca}} \times \frac{\text{mol } CaCl_2}{\text{mol Ca}} \times \frac{111.0 \text{ g } CaCl_2}{\text{mol } CaCl_2} = 1.38 \times 10^3 \text{ g } CaCl_2$$

5. (a) Limiting reactant: Ca

	Ca	$Cl_{(2)}$
G	**500**	900
	40.08	35.45
M	12.5	25.4
	1	2
D	12.5	12.7

(c)

$$\frac{1250 \text{ g}}{1.38 \times 10^3 \text{ g}} \times 100 = 90.6\%$$

(b)

$$? \text{ grams } Fe_3(PO_4)_2 = 33.0 \text{ g } FeCl_2 \times \frac{\text{mol } FeCl_2}{126.8 \text{ g } FeCl_2} \times \frac{\text{mol } Fe_3(PO_4)_2}{3 \text{ mols } FeCl_2} \times \frac{357.5 \text{ g } Fe_3(PO_4)_2}{\text{mol } Fe_3(PO_4)_2}$$

$$= 31.0 \text{ g } Fe_3(PO_4)_2$$

6. (a) Limiting reactant: $FeCl_2$

	$FeCl_2$	Na_3PO_4
G	**33.0**	38.5
	126.8	163.9
M	0.260	0.234
	3	2
D	0.0867	0.117

(c)

$$\frac{29.1 \text{ g}}{31.0 \text{ g}} \times 100 = 93.9\%$$

7. Though this problem only asked for a percentage yield, it was also implicitly a stoichiometry and limiting reactant problem as well, because those steps were needed for the ultimate calculation.

$$? \text{ grams } NaCN = 203 \text{ g C} \times \frac{\text{mol C}}{12.01 \text{ g C}} \times \frac{2 \text{ mols } NaCN}{4 \text{ mols C}} \times \frac{49.01 \text{ g } NaCN}{\text{mol } NaCN} = 414 \text{ g NaC}$$

	$N_{(2)}$	C	Na_2CO_3
G	64.5	**203**	463
	14.01	12.01	106.0
M	4.60	16.9	4.37
	1	4	1
D	4.60	4.22	4.37

$$\frac{411 \text{ g}}{414 \text{ g}} \times 100 = 99.3\%$$

The answer, from this *series* of calculations is 99.3%.

In doing these problems, you will use your knowledge of formulae to write the chemical species. Then, you will arrange them—as products and reactants—into an equation, according to the language of the problem. Next, balance the equation to get the coefficients needed for the keystone and do the stoichiometry, unless you must first determine the limiting reactant. This will be necessary *if more than one reactant is quantified* in the problem.

Keep in mind the principles discussed in Sects. 1.2 and 4.3. Finally, determine the percentage yield, if asked for. While this may be the only thing explicitly asked for, in this problem set or elsewhere, you know by now that it can also be the last in the series of calculations that make up the stoichiometric unity (and that there is other work to be done first).

1. How much magnesium oxide, combined with excess CO_2, is needed to get 500 grams of magnesium carbonate?

2. Arsine gas (AsH_3) is an analog of phosphine (PH_3) as can clearly be seen by comparing their formulae. In the Marsh Test for arsenic poisoning, forensic examiners or coroners react suspect substances (collected from tissues) with hydrochloric acid. The test is positive if arsine evolves. If calcium arsenide (the actual poison) is so tested, it yields arsine and a residue of calcium chloride. How much poison (Ca_3As_2) is indicated by the evolution of 1.17 grams of arsine?

3. The commercial production of sulfuric acid involves several steps ("consecutive reactions"), the final of which is the addition of water to pyrosulfuric acid ($H_2S_2O_7$) to get sulfuric acid. How much H_2SO_4 can be produced from 83.3 grams of pyrosulfuric acid and 8.50 grams of water?

4. Manganese (II) oxide, like most other transition-element oxides, yields pure metal and carbon monoxide when reduced with carbon. How much carbon is needed to react fully with 650 pounds of oxide that is 93.7% pure (lb = 454 g)?

5. 495 grams of chlorine gas is used to oxidize 173 grams of carbon disulfide (CS_2) in the production of two other gases: the solvent carbon tetrachloride (CCl_4) and disulfur chloride (S_2Cl_2). If the solvent produced in the reaction is condensed and found to weigh 341 grams, what is the percent yield?

6. A match factory bubbles 550 grams of hydrosulfuric acid (H_2S) into a solution containing 966 grams of (mon-)antimony trichloride. What percentage yield do you calculate if 718 grams of Sb_2S_3 result (and the other product is hydrochloric acid)?

In the next two problems, the products are unmentioned, so you will have to infer them to get your beginning, unbalanced equation. (some hints: problem 7 is an organic oxidation, and 8 is a neutralization).

7. How much oxygen will be consumed in the burning of 12 pounds of pentanol ($C_5H_{11}OH$) in air? The empirical formula of this alcohol is $C_5H_{12}O$.

8. The salt strontium phosphate, $Sr_3(PO_4)_2$, precipitates from the reaction of 63.5 grams of strontium hydroxide and 32.9 grams of phosphoric acid, $H_3PO_4(aq)$. The precipitate is then removed from the solution and weighed. If there are 74.9 grams, what is the percentage yield (Note: strontium, because it is an alkaline earth metal, necessarily has a valency of 2)?

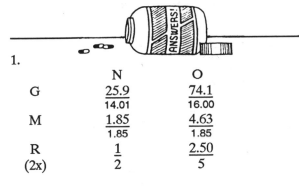

1.

	N	O
G	$\frac{25.9}{14.01}$	$\frac{74.1}{16.00}$
M	$\frac{1.85}{1.85}$	$\frac{4.63}{1.85}$
R (2x)	$\frac{1}{2}$	$\frac{2.50}{5}$

Empirical formula: N_2O_5

2. Sodium and silicon collectively account for 60.7% (23 + 37.7), so oxygen makes up the rest:

(100 − 60.7 = 39.3)

	Na	Si	O
G	$\frac{37.7}{22.99}$	$\frac{23}{28.09}$	$\frac{39.3}{16.00}$
M	$\frac{1.64}{.819}$	$\frac{.819}{.819}$	$\frac{2.46}{.819}$
R	2	1	3

Empirical formula: Na_2SiO_3

3. Dinitrogen pentoxide

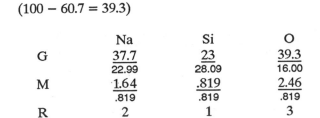

1. $MgO(s) + CO_2(g) \rightarrow MgCO_3(s)$

? grams MgO = 500 g MgCO$_3$ x $\dfrac{\text{mol MgCO}_3}{84.32 \text{ g MgCO}_3}$ x $\dfrac{\text{mol MgO}}{\text{mol MgCO}_3}$ x $\dfrac{40.31 \text{ g MgO}}{\text{mol MgO}}$ = 239 g MgO

2. $Ca_3As_2(s) + 6HCl(g) \rightarrow 2AsH_3(g) + 3CaCl_2(s)$

? grams Ca$_3$As$_2$ = 1.17 g AsH$_3$ x $\dfrac{\text{mol AsH}_3}{77.95 \text{ g AsH}_3}$ x $\dfrac{\text{mol Ca}_3\text{As}_2}{2 \text{ mols AsH}_3}$ x $\dfrac{270.1 \text{ g Ca}_3\text{As}_2}{\text{mol Ca}_3\text{As}_2}$ = 2.03 g Ca$_3$As$_2$

---

3. $H_2S_2O_7(l) + H_2O(l) \rightarrow 2H_2SO_4$

(next, you determined the limiting reactant:)

	H$_2$S$_2$O$_7$	H$_2$O
G	**83.3** / 178.1	8.50 / 18.01
M	0.468 / 1	0.472 / 1
D	0.468	0.472

? grams H$_2$SO$_4$ = 83.3 g H$_2$S$_2$O$_7$ x $\dfrac{\text{mol H}_2\text{S}_2\text{O}_7}{178.1 \text{ g H}_2\text{S}_2\text{O}_7}$ x $\dfrac{2 \text{ mols H}_2\text{SO}_4}{\text{mol H}_2\text{S}_2\text{O}_7}$ x $\dfrac{98.08 \text{ g H}_2\text{SO}_4}{\text{mol H}_2\text{SO}_4}$ = 91.8 g H$_2$SO$_4$

---

4. $Mn_2O_3(s) + 3C(l)^* \rightarrow 2Mn(s) + 3CO(g)$

? grams C = 650 lbs Mn$_2$O$_3$ imp x $\dfrac{454 \text{ g Mn}_2\text{O}_3 \text{ imp}}{\text{lb Mn}_2\text{O}_3 \text{ imp}}$ x $\dfrac{93.7 \text{ g Mn}_2\text{O}_3}{100 \text{ g Mn}_2\text{O}_3 \text{ imp}}$ x $\dfrac{\text{mol Mn}_2\text{O}_3}{157.9 \text{ g Mn}_2\text{O}_3}$

x $\dfrac{3 \text{ mols C}}{\text{mol Mn}_2\text{O}_3}$ x $\dfrac{12.01 \text{ g C}}{\text{mol C}}$ = 6.31 x 10^4 g C

---

5. $CS_2(s) + 3Cl_2(g) \rightarrow CCl_4(g) + S_2Cl_2(g)$

(two reactants are quantified, so...)

	CS$_2$	Cl$_2$
G	**173** / 76.14	495 / 70.91
M	2.27 / 1	6.98 / 3
D	2.27	2.33

? grams CCl$_4$ = 173 g CS$_2$ x $\dfrac{\text{mol CS}_2}{76.14 \text{ g CS}_2}$ x $\dfrac{\text{mol CCl}_4}{\text{mol CS}_2}$ x $\dfrac{153.8 \text{ g CCl}_4}{\text{mol CCl}_4}$ = 349 g CCl$_4$

---

6. $2SbCl_3(s) + 3H_2S(g) \rightarrow Sb_2S_3(s) + 6HCl(g)$

(again, more than one reactant is quantified...)

	H$_2$S	SbCl$_3$
G	550 / 34.08	**966** / 228.1
M	16.1 / 3	4.23 / 2
D	5.36	2.12

*(problem 4) The state designation is (l) because only molten carbon (coke, basically) is hot enough to react with the oxide.

6. (continued)

$$? \text{ grams } Sb_2S_3 = 966 \text{ g } SbCl_3 \times \frac{\text{mol } SbCl_3}{228.1 \text{ g } SbCl_3} \times \frac{\text{mol } Sb_2S_3}{2 \text{ mols } SbCl_3} \times \frac{339.7 \text{ g } Sb_2S_3}{\text{mol } Sb_2S_3} = 719 \text{ g } Sb_2S_3$$

(now you can determine percentage yield:) $\frac{718 \text{ g } Sb_2S_3}{719 \text{ g } Sb_2S_3} \times 100 = 99.9\%$

In metathesis reactions, of which problem 6 is an example, the reaction goes all the way, rather than part of the way and stopping at equilibrium. Put another way, all of the limited reactant is consumed along with corresponding amounts of the other and excess reactant(s). For this reason, you should be suspicious of any percentage yield from a metathesis (exchange) reaction that is not 100% (when rounded) or something very near it. A significantly lower percentage signals an error, either in the laboratory or in calculation.

In percentage-yield calculations, remember that the dimension and the label (grams and Sb_2S_3 in the above problem) cancel out and are therefore not part of the answer.

7. $2C_5H_{12}O(l) + 15O_2(g) \rightarrow 10CO_2(g) + 12H_2O(g)$

(In this problem, you had to recall that, in the complete and ideal burning of such a compound, the only products are water and carbon dioxide.)

$$? \text{ grams } O_2 = 12 \text{ lbs } C_5H_{12}O \times \frac{454 \text{ g } C_5H_{12}O}{\text{lb } C_5H_{12}O} \times \frac{\text{mol } C_5H_{12}O}{88.15 \text{ g } C_5H_{12}O} \times \frac{15 \text{ mols } O_2}{2 \text{ mols } C_5H_{12}O} \times \frac{32.00 \text{ g } O_2}{\text{mol } O_2}$$

$$= 1.5 \times 10^4 \text{ g } O_2$$

8. $3Sr(OH)_2(s) + 2H_3PO_4(aq) \rightarrow Sr_3(PO_4)_2(s) + 6H_2O(l)$

(A salt precipitate and water, or a dissolved salt and water, are the products of a neutralization.)

		$Sr(OH)_2$	H_3PO_4
(Once more, you have to find the limiting reactant...)	G	63.5	32.9
		121.6	98.00
	M	0.522	0.336
		3	2
	D	0.174	0.168

$$? \text{ grams } Sr_3(PO_4)_2 = 32.9 \text{ g } H_3PO_4 \times \frac{\text{mol } H_3PO_4}{98.00 \text{ g } H_3PO_4} \times \frac{\text{mol } Sr_3(PO_4)_2}{2 \text{ mols } H_3PO_4} \times \frac{452.9 \text{ g } Sr_3(PO_4)_2}{\text{mol } Sr_3(PO_4)_2}$$

$$= 76.0 \text{ g } Sr_3(PO_4)_2$$

(And finally, the percentage yield...) $\frac{74.9 \text{ g } Sr_3(PO_4)_2}{76.0 \text{ g } Sr_3(PO_4)_2} \times 100 = 98.6\%$

26	
Fe	# ℱrofile: Iron
55.847	

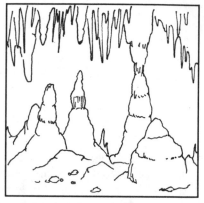

Some stalagmites and stalactites are brilliantly colored by iron salts.

Iron is probably the closest thing we have to "generic metal." More of it, as steel, is used in industry than all other metals combined. It is less abundant in the Earth's crust than aluminum, but it is much less costly to extract from its ores. The Earth's core, however, and perhaps the cores of other planets, is thought to be mostly iron and nickel. For this, and for iron's magnetism, the Earth itself is a sort of giant magnet, complete with poles. Thus, Earth's rotation generates a huge magnetic field.

Magnetism is a field that properly belongs to physics, but it can be noted here that only iron, its harder relatives nickel and cobalt, and the lanthanide gadolinium have this property; no other element is attracted to magnets.

Spectroanalysis of sunlight shows that iron is also present in the sun, where it is formed by the nuclear fusion of simpler elements. Iron, however, is the first element for which more energy must be spent in its stellar production than is released by it (compare this with the production of helium, in the hydrogen profile). Hence the solar genesis of heavier elements than iron, while it does happen, is not very frugal, energy-wise, for a star.

The element is so common on the Martian surface that its oxides give Mars its distinctive red-orange complexion.

Iron—which is fairly reactive by transition-metal standards—is uncombined in nature only as meteorites yet, as its ores are easily reduced with coals, it has been known for millenia. The iron age really began when the Hittites (and a little later the Assyrians) forged weapons and, with these, empires, from iron. The bronze age ended at the same time, for the bronze armor of these nations' opponents

became decisively obsolete.

Pure iron is a silvery-gray metal of only intermediate hardness that reacts easily, if undramatically, with moist air to form the hydrate $Fe_2O_3 \cdot 2H_2O$. Unlike most metal oxides, which form a protective coating, "rust" flakes off and the metal can completely corrode out.

The solution to rust is alloying. Pig iron is produced in blast furnaces, in which hot air reacts with coke to fuel the ore reduction (limestone is also added to remove silicates). Most pig iron (so-called because an older style of catch basins formed ingots that reminded someone of a row of suckling piglets) is then refined by the open-hearth process, during which time the carbon impurity is adjusted to an advantageous proportion, and other elements are added for specific desired properties. Nickel and manganese steels are very tough; cobalt and tungsten varieties stay hard at red-hot temperatures; vanadium imparts resiliency; and chromium, stainlessness.

While iron is commercially the cheapest metal, it is infinitely more precious than gold; life could not exist without it. The proteins hemoglobin (which colors the blood red) and fibrogen (which makes clotting possible) are both iron compounds. In several countries, highly processed foods are "enriched" with iron.

Cutaway Schematic of Blast Furnace

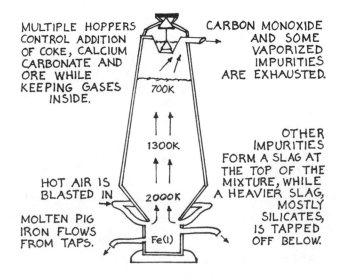

MULTIPLE HOPPERS CONTROL ADDITION OF COKE, CALCIUM CARBONATE AND ORE WHILE KEEPING GASES INSIDE.

CARBON MONOXIDE AND SOME VAPORIZED IMPURITIES ARE EXHAUSTED.

700K

1300K

OTHER IMPURITIES FORM A SLAG AT THE TOP OF THE MIXTURE, WHILE A HEAVIER SLAG, MOSTLY SILICATES, IS TAPPED OFF BELOW.

HOT AIR IS BLASTED IN

2000K

MOLTEN PIG IRON FLOWS FROM TAPS.

Fe(l)

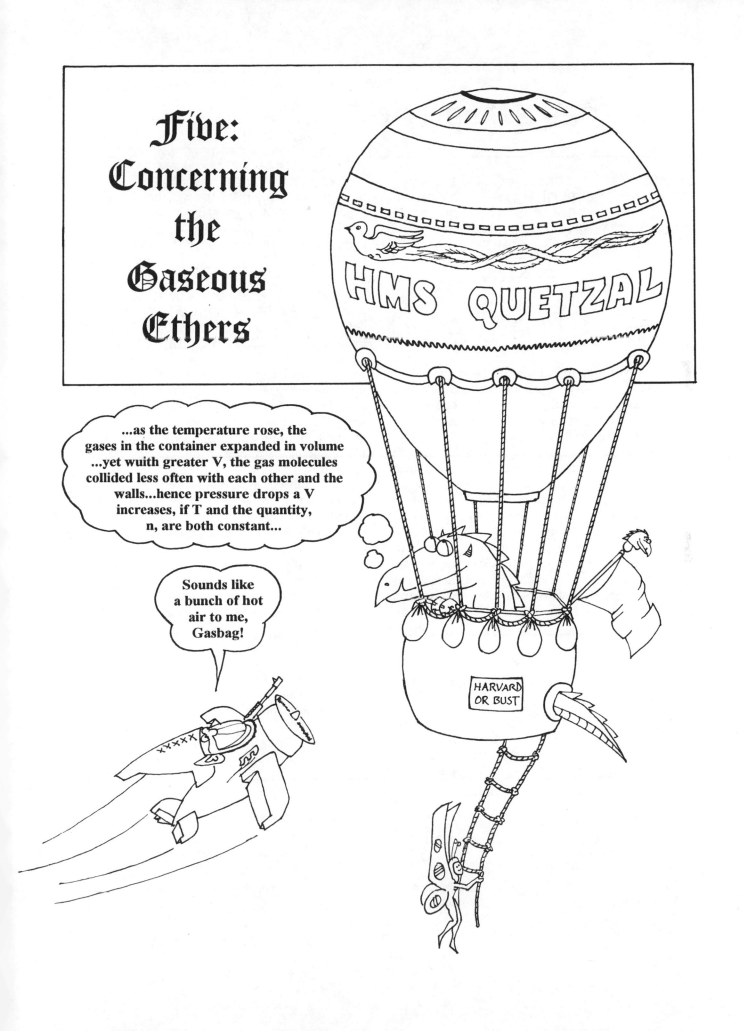

5.1 Gas Properties

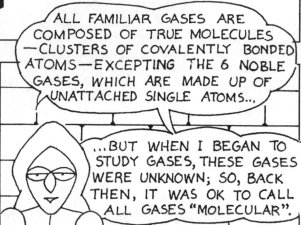

The convention of calling all gases *molecular* survived the discovery of the noble gases, to the extent that chemists even speak of "molecules" of argon or helium, though in fact the particles of the noble gases are necessarily monatomic.

All other gases—those belonging to the somewhat larger category of gases that participate in chemical changes—are made up of molecules. A handful are elemental: H_2, N_2, F_2, Cl_2, O_2, and O_3 (ozone). The remainder are compounds, such as CO, SO_2, SO_3, HF, B_2H_6, HI, NO_2, AsH_3, SiH_4, and CN.

The word *molecule* was first used (c. 1811) to denote a particle of any gas. A hundred or so years later, the term was extended to those nongaseous substances that proved to be covalent. Gases can also be ionic, but only at temperatures so high that

they are no longer even considered to be in the gaseous state (g) but, rather, in the plasmic state (p).

The physical properties of gases differ very markedly from those of liquids and solids. A gas is (1) easily compressed; (2) has very low density; and (3) can be mixed fully with another gas. Further, a sample of gas (4) fills its container—bottle or blimp—uniformly and completely; and therefore (5) exerts a pressure that is uniform (that is, equally-spaced-out) and constant on the container walls. The Earth's atmosphere, while seldom thought of as a "container" is nevertheless a system in which gases exhibit each of these properties.

These properties are explained by the Ideal Gas Model, which relates to gas samples and systems at the molecular level. It has five parts:

I

Gas molecules move about only in straight lines.

This is a manifestation of Newton's First Law; it is inertia at the particle level.

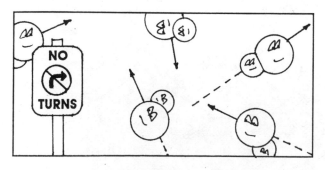

II

Gas molecules collide with each other and with the walls of their containers without a loss of energy (that is, without slowing down). The result of all these little collisions is pressure.

III

Gas molecules, unlike the component particles of a liquid or a solid, *have only a negligible attraction for each other...*

IV

...and because they are not strongly drawn together, *gas molecules are very widely spaced.*

V

(In fact, they are so spaced-out that) *the volume of the gas molecules themselves is almost nothing compared to the volume they occupy* with their energetic wandering. It is akin to the volume of a nucleus vis-a-vis that of its electron cloud, but more variable (because, remember, a gas is highly compressible).

All of this wandering is the reason that gas samples are able to fill their containers fully, and at all points exert the same pressure on its walls. Intermolecular forces are weak not only because of the distances between the particles (this weakness increases as the square of the distance), but also because of the nature of the particles themselves.

Because all gases (except mercury vapor) are covalent substances (or the completely inert elements of Family 8A), one of the forces that binds particles to each other—ionic charge—is not present to any appreciable degree, if at all (more on this in Chap. 7).

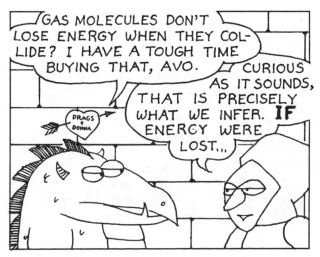

5.2 Gas Dimensions

Pressure

Pressure is defined as the *force exerted on a unit of area,* such as pounds per (one) square inch (note its analogy with the definition of density, Sect. 1.6).

There are at least a half-dozen pressure expressions—every one of which contains two dimensions—in use because chemists, engineers, meteorologists, etc., all have their own.

For chemists, the *torr* is the favored unit. One torr (1.00 torr) is the pressure needed to force a column of mercury to rise one millimeter in a barometer; that is, it is a single increment of barometric pressure. This dimension was named for Toricelli, who invented the barometer.

Another common unit, one often seen in Chem. 1, is the *atmosphere,* which equals 760 torr, or 760 millimeters of mercury, or (nonmetrically) 14.7 pounds to the square inch. Atmospheric pressure on Earth at sea level fluctuates around 1.000 atmosphere (though it is notably lower just before a storm).

Quantity

A quantity of gas may be expressed in grams or in kilograms, but precise weighings of substances in the gaseous state can be logistically difficult.

Fortunately, we can often express gas quantities (grams or moles, *n*, of particles) directly in liters, thanks to Gay-Lussac's Law.

Volume and Temperature

Because of the low density, or high spaced-outedness, of gases, the liter (L), as you already know, is preferred to the milliliter for gas volume (V) measurements and calculations.

The most practical unit for temperature (T) is the Kelvin (*K*, not "°K"), because measurements in Kelvins are always positive. You can expect, however, to see both °C and K used in your passage through general chemistry. Absolute temperature and conversions between these two units were covered in Sect. 1.3.

The Kelvin was named for the British scientist Thompson (Lord Kelvin), who first described the neutron.

Gay-Lussac's Law

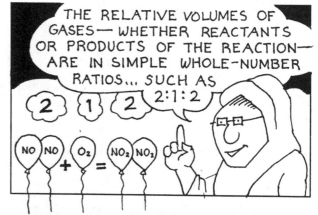

Just *why* this is so will be discussed a little later. For now, though, it is enough to know that this principle has some manifestly happy consequences.

For one thing, it underlines a consistency among all gases without regard to the peculiar properties of each. Take any two gases whatsoever, and the same volume (V) will hold the same number of moles (n) of each gas at the same temperature (T) and pressure (P). This constancy can be expressed mathematically and usefully, as we will see in Sect. 5.8.

It also means that one kind of stoichiometric calculation—that which involves only gases—can incredibly be performed *without* molar conversion factors.

5.3 Molecular Theory of Gases

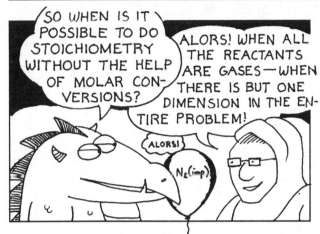

SO WHEN IS IT POSSIBLE TO DO STOICHIOMETRY WITHOUT THE HELP OF MOLAR CONVERSIONS?

ALORS! WHEN ALL THE REACTANTS ARE GASES—WHEN THERE IS BUT ONE DIMENSION IN THE ENTIRE PROBLEM!

One characteristic of gases is that they can be fullly and physically mixed with other gases; they are said to be *miscible*. Ordinary air is an example of such a solution.

Many gas combinations, however, can be mixed chemically: they react, often with the help of a catalyst, to produce new gases and/or nongaseous products.

Thanks to Gay-Lussac's principle, we can do an entire gas-to-gas stoichiometric calculation (one in which the problem both gives and asks for a quantity of a gas) with a single conversion factor: the keystone itself, which is expressed in ratios of liters rather than ratios of moles. Since both the given and wanted quantities are in liters, no molar conversions are required.

Here is an example: hydrogen and chlorine, when mixed in darkness, are as miscible as any other nonreactive blend of gases; but when they are exposed to sunlight (which acts as a catalyst), they react. How much hydrogen chloride gas will result from the reaction of 4.5 liters of chlorine and an excess of hydrogen? First, we write the balanced equation; then, we construct the DA bridge (what little there is of one) from it:

$$H_2(g) + Cl_2(g) \rightarrow 2HCl(g)$$

$$? \text{ liters HCl} = 4.5 \text{ L Cl}_2 \times \frac{2\text{L HCl}}{\text{L Cl}_2} = 9.0 \text{ L HCl}$$

This problem assumes the same temperature and pressure for each of the three gases. When these conditions vary for the two gases in the actual stoichiometric calculation, some simple adjustments are made to the calculation. These, however, will be treated later in this chapter.

Here, then, is another example. Do not worry that one of the products is not designated a gas; all the reactants, including the given and the wanted species, are. How much oxygen is required for the complete burning (or the burning in air) of 37.8 liters of butane?

$$2C_4H_{10}(g) + 13O_2(g) \rightarrow 8CO_2(g) + 10H_2O(l)$$

$$? \text{ liters O}_2 = 37.8 \text{ L C}_4\text{H}_{10} \times \frac{13 \text{ L O}_2}{2 \text{ L C}_4\text{H}_{10}} = 246 \text{ L O}_2$$

(You still remember, of course, that keystones are defined relations and so do not affect significant figures.)

Note in both of the above examples (and also in the following one) how liters replace moles, both as coefficients in the equations and, therefore, as ratios in the keystone.

Now for a further example, one using a dimension that is obsolete in the chem lab but which occasionally shows up on tests: how many imperial gallons of carbon monoxide will react with 200 imperial gallons of oxygen to form carbon dioxide? There are 4.55 liters in an imperial gallon.

$$2CO(g) + O_2(g) \rightarrow 2CO_2(g)$$

$$? \text{ imp. gallons CO}_2 = 200 \text{ IG O}_2 \times \frac{2 \text{ IG CO}_2}{\text{IG O}_2} = 400 \text{ IG CO}_2$$

If, on a test, you had attempted to work in an extra conversion factor or two (such as liters/imperial gallons or its reciprocal), you would have taken the bait and fallen into the trap. *Any* unit of volume can be substituted for moles—liters, cubic inches, imperial gallons, plain old everyday gallons, pint-sized peanut-butter jars, or petroleum barrels—with the proviso that the same volume dimension is used *throughout* the calculation (and, of course, that both the wanted and the given are gases). This, then, is stoichiometry at is utter simplest.

"Gay-Lussac made water from one volume of oxygen and two volumes of hydrogen. I already knew that the whole-number ratio of oxygen to hydrogen was 1:2. However, the water that results from this reaction, if prevented from condensing [kept in its gaseous state] fills two volumes, not one.

"This meant one of two things. Either [a] water vapor—a gas—was exactly twice as voluminous as any other gas, or [b] that particles of hydrogen and oxygen were diatomic; that they were molecules—or paired atoms—of elements.

"I dismissed the first possibility because it violated Gay-Lussac's Law and my own intuition. Hence, the elemental formulae for oxygen and hydrogen had to be O_2 and H_2."

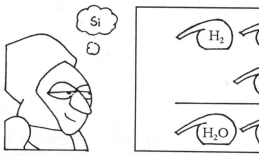

It is from Avogadro's Hypothesis—that identical volumes of gases contain identical numbers of molecules—and from his and Gay-Lussac's experiments (showing that gas volumes combine in whole-number ratios) that Avogadro correctly inferred the molecular (or "compound-atom" nature of all the elemental gases then known and successfully isolated (hydrogen, nitrogen, oxygen, and chlorine).

Only the noble gases are literally atomic in composition, but nobody knew about them until Ramsey came across argon in 1984 and neon, krypton, and xenon four years later.

SO, YOU SEE, WE NEVER REALLY CHANGED THE DEFINITION OF A MOLECULE AS A POLYATOMIC PARTICLE. BUT IN A CONTEXT OF GASES, IT MEANS ANY GAS PARTICLE.

1. Match these terms to that which defines or exemplifies them:

_____molecules   a. a function of the speed of a gas' particle

_____temperature   b. nitrogen, ozone, fluorine, sulfur dioxide, phosphine, steam

_____volume   c. a measurement of the force on a given unit of surface

_____atoms   d. helium, argon, xenon, krypton, neon, radon

_____pressure   e. quantifies a gas—both its space and particle content

2. Now match these concepts to their definitions (below):

_____Avogadro's Hypothesis   _____Gay-Lussac's Law

_____Ideal Gas Law (part)   _____Dalton's Atomic Theory (part)

a. Atoms that combine chemically do so only in whole-number ratios.

b. Equal volumes of all gases will contain the same number of particles if their pressure and temperature values are the same.

c. Gases that combine chemically do so only in whole-number ratios (of volume).

d. Gas particles, because they are nonionic, have little mutual attraction.

3. Explain why it is possible to perform gas-to-gas stoichiometry without the use of molar conversion factors:

4. In one step of the Ostwald Process for the manufacture of nitric acid (HNO_3), platinum catalyzes the burning of ammonia in oxygen to form nitric oxide (NO) and water. How much NO (a gas) will result if 24.0 liters of NH_3 (another gas) is consumed in the reaction (first, write the balanced equation)?

5. Diborane (B_2H_6) is an analog of ethane (C_2H_6), as is immediately clear from a comparison of their formulae. This gas is spontaneously flammable in air, reacting with oxygen to form crystalline boric acid (H_3BO_3). How much O_2 at 23°C and 1.00 atmosphere will react with 3.57 liters of B_2H_6 at 296 K and 760 torr (again, start with a balanced equation)? This is a "trick" question that appears, at first glance, more complex than it really is.

1. b   a   e   d   c

2. b   c   d   a

3. Because the ratios of the volumes equal the ratios of the **moles**. So, **we can** make up the keystone directly from the volume measurements (this is an accurate, if perhaps unrecognizable, paraphase of Gay-Lussac's Law, Sect. 5.2).

4. $4NH_3(g) + 5O_2(g) \rightarrow 4NO(g) + 6H_2O(l)$

$$? \text{ liters NO} = 24.0 \text{ L NH}_3 \times \frac{4 \text{ L NO}}{4 \text{ L NH}_3} = 24.0 \text{ L NO}$$

5. $B_2H_6(g) + 3O_2(g) \rightarrow 2H_3BO_3(s)$

$$? \text{ liters O}_2 = 3.57 \text{ L B}_2H_6 \times \frac{3 \text{ L O}_2}{\text{L B}_2H_6} = 10.7 \text{ L O}_2$$

Historical Note

Modern molecular theory evolved by way of the independent research of several scientists on gases. Dalton theorized that gases were composed of particles—which he named atoms—which combined in whole-number ratios. This idea was merely the expression of his atomic theory (Prologue) as it related to gases. Gay-Lussac proved, in the same year (1808) that gas *volumes*, in any case, *do* combine in whole-number ratios; this complemented and supported Dalton's belief. Avogadro, who understood English and French, read the published findings of Dalton and Gay-Lussac and surmised that equal volumes of gases were in fact equal volumes of particles, but that these particles were not atoms, but compound atoms or, as he preferred to call

them, *molecules* (a word which comes from the Latin diminutive for *mass*; thus meaning "tiny mass").

With some careful thought, you will realize that Gay-Lussac's Law and Avogadro's Hypothesis are more nearly the same thing than their wording and separate origins suggest. Basically, the former proves and the latter explains the same phenomenon.

They are alike in permitting us to do the same thing conceptually (both confirm Dalton's Atomic Theory and his Law of Multiple Proportions) and quantitatively (both allow us to do all-gas stoichiometry without molar conversions).

Because of this apparent duplication, one or the other is almost always excluded from Chem. 1 curricula or textbook contents. Both are included in this work not only for their complementarity, but for their historical significance and for their provision of alternative routes to the same learning objective.

Indeed, Gay-Lussac himself arrived by deduction, whereas Avogadro's conclusion was largely a result of induction.

5.4 Boyle's Law

CONFINE A SAMPLE OF ANY GAS. ITS PRESSURE IS THE INVERSE OF ITS VOLUME...THE HIGHER THE ONE, THE LOWER THE OTHER. THE P/V RELATION IS THUS A SIMPLE ALGEBRAIC ONE.

ALGEBRAIC!

$P \propto V$

n = 3.4 million

Lebanon
1.04×10^4 km^2

N.Z.
2.69×10^5 km^2

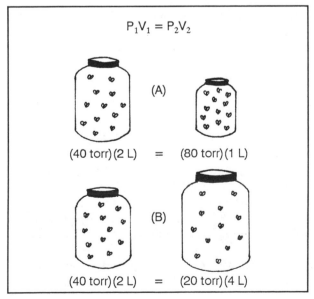

$P_1V_1 = P_2V_2$

(A)

(40 torr)(2 L) = (80 torr)(1 L)

(B)

(40 torr)(2 L) = (20 torr)(4 L)

Boyle, in the late 1600s, demonstrated this relation using a manometer, a device he coinvented, and a series of cylinders and pistons lubricated with mercury to prevent gases from escaping and to keep friction at a minimum.

With such variable-volume cylinders, we, like Boyle, can observe an increase in pressure as we decrease the volume, and visa-versa. The ability to manipulate volumes in this way also lets us observe concomitant temperature changes (Sect. 5.5) and, on top of everything, the interplay among volume, temperature, *and* pressure (Sect. 5.6).

Boyle's Law is neither difficult qualitatively nor mathematically. It is expressed by this equation:

$$P_1V_1 = P_2V_2$$

Analogies

Here is a purely metaphorical analogy, but a reliable one if you accept the (debatable) premise that population *pressures* are the ultimate cause of all war. New Zealand and Lebanon have the same population (constant n) and similar climates (constant T). But their areas (V) are very different, by a factor of 26. So, apparently, are their pressures (P), but inversely.

Here is another analogy, one dealing with changes (in volume) in both directions. Two "experiments" are conducted in a room that is thermostatically maintained at 68°C (constant T).

(A) A dozen flies are put into a two-liter jar (V_1 or "volume-one"). Then, the collisions of the flies with each other and with the walls of the jar are counted over a specific period; this is recorded as the first pressure measurement (P_1). Next, the flies are put in a one-liter jar (V_2) and the collisions are again counted. (P_2). The product of the first set of measurements will equal that of the second.

(B) This time, as before, there are a dozen flies in a two-liter jar, with the measurements V_1 and P_1. Then, the flies are put in a four-liter jar and the collisions counted (V_2, P_2). That which you expect to happen, happens: there are fewer collisions at an inverse proportion to the volume of the smaller jar. Again, P_1V_1 equals P_2V_2. Boyle's Law is mathematical common sense.

Now, in your own mind, substitute Boyle's cylinders for the jars and gas particles for the flies.

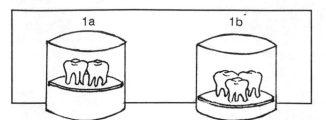
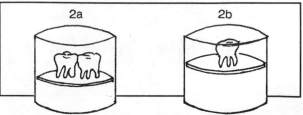

⊛ Color the gas (under the molar weights) in cylinders 1a and 2a with a medium shading of blue or brown; then do the gas in cylinder 1b with a somewhat heavier shading; and the gas in cylinder 2b, a very light shading.

In Boyle's Law problems, you will always have as givens the first set of measurements (P_1 and V_1) and one or the other of the second set (P_2 or V_2). With these three givens, you can find the missing fourth value.

As you read the problem, label each measurement as if making proofreading marks with the symbols P_1, V_1, and either P_2 or V_2. Then, substitute the numbers from the problem (with their dimensions) into Boyle's equation.

Next, divide the (arithmetical) product of the "ones" side by the only thing you have on the "twos" side. Nothing could be easier, although algebraphobes would do well to forget that this is, in fact, algebra, and to just follow the directions as just given. Algebraphiles, however, will want the equations, so...

$$\frac{P_1 V_1}{V_2} = P_2 \left(\text{because } \underline{P_1 V_1} = P_2 V_2 \right) \qquad \frac{P_1 V_1}{P_2} = V_2 \left(\text{because } \underline{P_1 V_1} = P_2 V_2 \right)$$

The first equation (left) shows the algebraic maneuvre used in a pressure determination, and the second is for a volume determination. Now, for a complete example. Again, you will probably wish to mark the givens, as suggested above. In the examples on this page, they are highlighted by a bracketed parameter.

A 6.00-liter (V_1) sample of some gas with a pressure reading of 1000 torr (P_1) is compressed to 3.60 liters (V_2). What will the pressure become? The wanted can only be what is left over (P_2), so...

$$(1000 \text{ torr}) (6.00 \text{ L}) = (P_2)(3.60 \text{ L}) \rightarrow \frac{(1000 \text{ torr})(6.00 \text{ L})}{(3.60 \text{ L})} = P_2 = 1.67 \times 10^3 \text{ torr}$$

Notice how the unneeded dimension (in the above example, L) happily cancels out. Now, we shall consider another example, this time one with a wanted volume.

To what volume must 2.54 moles of N_2 be brought to make the pressure fall to 355 torr (P_1) if 1.53×10^{24} nitrogen molecules are in a tank with a capacity of 9.00 liters (V_1) and a pressure gauge reading of 3800 torr (P_2)?

$$(3800 \text{ torr})(9.00 \text{ L}) = (V_2)(355 \text{ torr}) \rightarrow \frac{(3800 \text{ torr})(9.00 \text{ L})}{(355 \text{ torr})} = V_2 = 96.3 \text{ L}$$

On completing such a calculation, use a little post-calculation logic (Sect. 1.2). In the case of Boyle's Law problems, you should ask yourself if the increase or decrease in volume or pressure had the reverse and, therefore, the appropriate effect on the other. If not, an error is indicated. An even better **idea** is to apply such qualitative thinking *before* the mathwork. Ask yourself: will this change in P (or V) cause an increase or a decrease in V (or P)? Know what to expect!

5.5 Charles' Law

SO MUCH FOR THE RELATION BETWEEN VOLUME AND PRESSURE. BUT WHAT OF THE RELATION BETWEEN VOLUME AND TEMPERATURE?

Y'COULDN'T HANDLE THE PRESSURE, HUH?

YOU'RE BACK.

DID I LEAVE?

⊛ There are two cylinders at left, below. Do them in the same color (any of your choosing), but color cylinder 3a more densely than 3b.

If we heat a gas sample in a variable-volume cylinder without doing anything to alter the pressure (that is, keeping P constant), the gas will expand and force the piston upwards.

Conversely, cooling the gas sample (again, while observing constant pressure) will cause the piston to fall.

Thus, the volume-to-temperature relation—like the volume-to-pressure relation—is simple and predictable: the volume of a gas goes up or down with temperature. This is Charles' Law, and it is expressed:

$$\frac{V_1}{T_1} = \frac{V_2}{T_2} \qquad \left(\text{as, e.g., } \frac{10}{20} = \frac{15}{30} \text{ or } \frac{4}{8} \right)$$

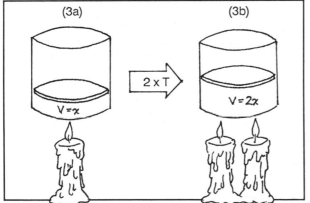

(3a)   (3b)

2 x T

V = x

V = 2x

Unlike Boyle's Law problems, in which either P_2 or V_2 is the sought parameter, only one measurement, V_2, is normally wanted because in the laboratory temperature is used to manipulate volume, but the reverse seldom takes place.

Therefore, you will probably always use this version of Charles' equation:

$$V_2 = V_1 \times \frac{T_2}{T_1}$$

The unalgebraically inclined student can recall this arrangement by thinking of the two Ts as being on the fraction's first and second "floors." As with a Boyle's Law problem, you just substitute the measurements (that you identified when you read the problem) into the equation. You will have recorded these measurements during a lab exercise, or you will have identified and highlighted them in a problem. In any case, they are your three givens, in precisely the same way that you had three givens in a Boyle's Law problem.

As always, keep in mind the caveat on p. 22. Common sense—and the Law itself—dictate that at constant P (and n) that the new volume (V_2) will be higher if the new temperature (T_2) is also higher and lower if T_2 is lower. *Volume increases or decreases in proportion to temperature.* Take a moment, then, to consider a problem qualitatively (Will V_2 be more or less that V_1?) *before* doing the calculation. Now for an example:

A sample of carbon dioxide fills a cylinder to 4.00 liters [V_1]. If it is cooled from 310 K [T_1] to 281 K [T_2], what volume will it occupy (first, the qualitative question: More or less?)?

$$V_2 = 4.00 \, L \times \frac{281 \, K}{310 \, K} = 3.63 \, L$$

5.6 The Combined Gas Law

IN REALITY, AREN'T WE CONCERNED WITH THE EFFECTS OF BOTH TEMPERATURE **AND** PRESSURE CHANGES ON A GIVEN VOLUME OF A GAS?

OUI... AND THE SOLUTION IS TO COMBINE BOYLE'S AND CHARLES' LAW. COMPRENDES-TU?

$\mathbb{I}$t is true. In general chemistry, it is commoner to encounter problems—especially in connection with labwork—in which the relation of volume with *both* pressure and temperature is the concern, rather than with just one of them.

For such real-world problems, Boyle's Law and Charles' Law are easily interwoven into the *Combined Gas Law:*

$$P_1V_1 = P_2V_2$$

$$\frac{T_1}{V_1} = \frac{T_2}{V_2} \quad \Longrightarrow \quad \frac{P_1V_1}{T_1} = \frac{P_2V_2}{T_2}$$

Notice that the Ps are next to the Vs, according to Boyle's Law, and that the Ts are under the Vs, according to Charles' Law. Therefore, if you know the simple equations from which the Combined Law clearly derives, you can construct its equation as well.

Notice further that two sets of *three* (not two) conditions are involved (rather than two sets of two), making a total of six. Later, in Chem. 2, you might be asked to use this equation to find T_2 or P_2; or—with each set representing a different gas—to determine any of the six conditions when given the other five. There are other possible applications besides these; none is difficult to master.

At this point, however, we are interested only in how a volume of a single sample is affected—changed from V_1 to V_2—by a change in both pressure *and* temperature.

The wanted variable, as in a Charles' Law calculation, is V_2. Solving for this algebraically, we come up with

$$V_2 = V_1 \ \text{x} \ \frac{T_2}{T_1} \ \text{x} \ \frac{P_1}{P_2}$$

Here is a memory crutch for those who would use it: set up for a Charles' Law problem. You already have a way to remember to put T_2 over T_1 (p. 175). Then, write the pressure fraction, remembering that changes in pressure have the reverse effect on a gas volume than changes in temperature, so you will reverse the subscripts in the pressure fraction. Use your grasp of this concept (with the mnemonic device) to remember the equation.

Otherwise, you will solve as before: label all the given conditions (of which there will be five rather than three) as you read them in the problem; substitute these into the equation, and calculate.

Here is an example: some dinitrogen oxide occupying 1.70 liters [V_1] of a 4.80-liter cylinder is at 64°C [T_1] and 675 torr [P_1]. If cooled to 25°C [T_2], yet compressed to 950 torr [P_2], what will the new volume [V_2] be?

(Warning: Non-Kelvin temperature measurements—°F and °C—must always be converted to Kelvins before doing anything else. Failure to do so will lead to error.)

64°C = 337 K
25°C = 298 K

$$V_2 = 1.70 \, \text{L} \ \text{x} \ \frac{298 \, \text{K}}{337 \, \text{K}} \ \text{x} \ \frac{675 \, \text{torr}}{950 \, \text{torr}} = 1.07 \, \text{L}$$

PROBLEMS!

1. Convert these temperatures to Kelvins.

a. 136°C_____   b. -136°C_____   c. 0°C_____   d. 4564°C_____   e. 10°F_____   f. -317°F_____

2. Match:

_____Avogadro's Hypothesis   _____Boyle's Law

_____Charles' Law   _____Combined Gas Law

a. The volume of the same gas sample is lowered with an increase in pressure and a decrease in temperature.

b. Equal volumes of different gas samples without differences in temperature or pressure hold equivalent amounts of their respective gases.

c. Changing the pressure of a gas while maintaining its temperature changes its volume inversely.

d. The volume of any gas increases with temperature if pressure is neither increased nor decreased.

3. Some CO_2 fills 450 milliliters (0.450 L) of a cylinder at 700 torr. What will be the new volume if it is decompressed to 540 torr (first, predict whether the volume will be more or less)?

4. To what volume will some ozone occupying 5.00 liters at 293 K change if it is heated to 313 K (first, more or less)?

5. Some gas filling 2.18 liters at 123 torr is put into a 6.55-liter container. What will the new pressure reading be (again, first predict whether it will be more or less)?

6. A gas takes up 4.98 liters of a 9.96-liter cylinder with a frictionless piston at 760 torr and 237 K. If both P and T are doubled, indicate separately the affect of both changes on the volume (this problem is qualitative and involves no math):

7. What new volume do you calculate for prob. 6?

8. A balloon expands to 7.00 liters at 752 torr and 66°F and is then tethered. That night, the temperature inside the balloon falls to 54°F while the pressure rises to 785 torr. To what volume will the balloon have expanded or shrunk to, assuming it has perfect elasticity (the equivalent of no friction in a cylinder)?

1. a. 409 K   b. 137 K   c. 273 K   d. 4837 K   e. 261 K   f. -194 K

2. (b) Avogadro's Hypothesis   (c) Boyle's Law
    (d) Charles' Law   (a) Combined Gas Law

3. more; $V_2 = \dfrac{(700 \text{ torr})(0.450 \text{ L})}{(540 \text{ torr})} = 0.583 \text{ L}$

4. more; $V_2 = 5.00 \text{ L} \times \dfrac{313 \text{ K}}{293 \text{ K}} = 5.34 \text{ L}$

5. less; $P_2 = \dfrac{(123 \text{ torr})(2.18 \text{ L})}{(6.55 \text{ L})} = 40.9 \text{ torr}$

6. This pressure change attends a smaller volume; this temperature change, a larger volume.

7. $V_2 = 4.98 \text{ L} \times \dfrac{760 \text{ torr}}{1520 \text{ torr}} \times \dfrac{546 \text{ K}}{273 \text{ K}} = 4.98 \text{ L}$

8. $V_2 = 7.00 \text{ L} \times \dfrac{752 \text{ torr}}{785 \text{ torr}} \times \dfrac{285 \text{ K}}{292 \text{ K}} = 6.54 \text{ L}$

5.7 Standard T & P

ONCE CHEMISTS REALIZED THAT THE QUANTITY OF **ANY** GAS FILLS THE SAME VOLUME AT THE SAME PRESSURE ~8 TEMPERATURE...

1 mol Cl₂ 70.9 g

...IT BECAME POSSIBLE TO DETERMINE THE RELATIVE MOLECULAR WEIGHTS OF EACH GAS, BY WEIGHING IDENTICAL [IN P 8 T] SAMPLES OF DIFFERENT GASES.

1 mol He 4 g

SO, TO RECORD THE WEIGHTS, WE AGREED ON A STANDARD PRESSURE AND TEMPERATURE AT WHICH TO WEIGH THE IDENTICAL VOLUMES.

1 mol NO 30 g

COULDN'T WE HAVE PICKED A WARMER TEMPERATURE FOR STP?

We have seen how volumes can substitute for moles in the quantifying of gas samples.

However, you also know that volumes are subject to changes in temperature and pressure. Therefore, for volumes to be reliable as a quantity unit, we must select a standard set of T and P conditions.

Identical volumes of all gases, at the same T and P, will contain the same number of molecules, though they will weigh differently because the molecules themselves weigh differently. In the same way, a mole of a heavier element weighs more than a mole of a lighter element, because the former's atoms are heavier. Thus, a volume of nitrogen (28.01 g/mol) outweighs helium (4 g/mol) seven to one.

The arbitrary standard used by chemists and physicists is 760 torr (1 atmosphere) and 273 K (0°C), the freezing point of pure water. Together, the two values are *Standard Temperature and Pressure*, or *STP*.

If we add one mole of any gas whatsoever to a cylinder with a movable piston at STP, it will take up 22.4 liters. This is the *molar volume of gases*; it is the space occupied by any 6.02×10^{23} molecules of any gas or combinations of gases at STP.

It was from samples of different gases at identical conditions of volume, pressure, and temperature that the first molecular (and ultimately atomic) weights were first able to be estimated.

179

5.8 The Ideal Gas Equation

The adjective *ideal* modifies the substantive *gas*, not model (the notion of an "ideal model" is contradictory). The model is of a gas that, if it existed, would be ideal (or, rather, absolute) in its conformity to the five postulates outlined in Sect. 5.1. No real gas succeeds in this for two reasons.

First of all, the molecules in a gas sample must themselves take up a miniscule bit of space, thereby restricting, if only infinitesimally, the space in which other molecules can move. This adds to volume, if not by much.

Secondly, there are very slight intermolecular attractions, *Van der Waals Forces*, that preclude the total independence of the molecules from each other, especially when those molecules have some polarity (due to partial ionic character). These weak electrostatic forces cause, as you would expect, a slight decrease in volume under most conditions.

Fortunately, the effect of both of these factors, in gases, is so negligible that significant deviation from the Ideal Gas Model is only observed at very high pressures or very low temperatures. In any event, they offset each other somewhat. We need not worry about them most of the time, for the fact remains that all gases, given identical, normal parameters (P, V, n, T) are capable of very closely approximating the ideal of the Model.

The Universal Gas Constant

This sameness is expressed by the *Universal Gas Constant*, R, which is the number 62.4. It derives from four other and by now familiar numbers (equation a). (When atmospheres are used instead or torr for pressure, the same constant is 0.0820.)

The T and P are from standard temperature and pressure (273 K and 760 torr); this much is obvious. But the n and the V are also from STP, for 1.00 mole of any gas *at STP* fills 22.4 liters of a variable volume-cylinder. In this way, the constant R—6.24—equals all of them collectively, as a quotient (b).

Equation (c) is the most familiar and versatile form of the *Ideal Gas Equation* (a), which is the mathematical proof of the Model of the same name. We use it to determine moles from a given volume, or volume from given moles, in a gas sample at STP.

(a) $$R = \frac{PV}{nT}$$

(b) $$R = \frac{(760 \text{ torr})(22.4 \text{ L})}{(1.00 \text{ mol})(273 \text{ K})} = 62.4$$

(c) $$PV = nRT$$

With the Ideal Gas Equation, we can determine how many moles (n) are in a given volume of gas (at a given temperature and pressure); or, we can do the reverse determination, and find out how much volume a given quantity of moles will occupy (again, at a given P and T).

To set such a problem up, we (algebraically) isolate the wanted variable (n or V) from the rest of the basic linear equation, which could also stand for "Poor Vagrants never Rent Tuxedos."

$$PV = nRT$$

If we are seeking a volume, we divide both sides of the equation by P to get a new equation, one that defines V (α, below). If it is moles we want, the algebraic permutation that defines n is (β).

$$(\alpha)\ V = \frac{nRT}{P} \qquad (\beta)\ n = \frac{PV}{RT}$$

If you have difficulty solving the linear equation for n to get equation (β), then just remember to put the "RooT" underground where it belongs and "Pole Vault" over it (and *into* an algebra class!). One other potential algebraic pitfall is the constant, R. It is a compound expression consisting of the constant itself, 62.4, with the dimensions "(L)" and "(torr)" always next to the number, and the dimensions "(K)" and "(mol)" always above or below it, as seen in the examples worked out below.

Next, as with the other types of gas-law problems with which you are familiar, just substitute the given numbers, with their dimensions, into the equation. Then cancel and do your calculator operations.

Let us consider an example: what volume will 0.720 moles of methane fill at 310 K and 500 torr? Volume is sought, so you will first write down the equation that solves the Ideal Gas Equation for V. From that, you will plug in the givens and solve.

$$V = \frac{nRT}{P} \qquad ?\ \text{liters CH}_4 = \frac{0.720\ \text{mols}\ \times\ 62.4\ (L)(torr)\ \times\ 310\ K}{500\ \text{torr}\ \times\ (K)(mol)} = 27.9\ L\ \text{CH}_4$$

Now, examine this example closely, comparing it to the equation used to set it up (left). The constant, 62.4, is in the numerator because the R is there as well. Notice that every one of the unneeded dimensions cancel out.

Right now, with your own pencil, cross out those that appear in both the numerator and in the denominator, and you will see that this is so. Therein lies the beauty of the Universal Gas Constant.

Now we will try a problem of the other sort, in which moles are sought: how many moles of hydrogen sulfide occupy 3.60 L at −23 °C and 912 torr (as with other gas-law problems, you must first convert nonkelvin temperature units to Kelvins)? The first thing to do is take the Ideal Gas Equation and solve for n (or use the mnemonic device). Then, as before, plug in the given numbers, cancel out the undesired dimensions, and calculate. Easy!

$$n = \frac{PV}{RT} \qquad ?\ \text{mols H}_2\text{S} = \frac{912\ \text{torr}\ \times\ (K)(mol)\ \times\ 3.60\ L}{62.4\ (L)(torr)\ \times\ 250\ K} = 0.210\ \text{mols H}_2\text{S}$$

The 250 K, of course, comes from 273 + (−23). Note that the entire expression for R—constant and dimensions—is inverted (to the reciprocal of the R expression in the previous example). We can do this because R is a type of conversion factor.

It is difficult to imagine how chemistry, molecular theory in particular, could have progressed without the providential sameness expressed by the Universal Gas Constant. Without the relative weights, which were first inferred from experiments on gases, the idea of combinations in whole-number ratios would have been far from certain (although Dalton had found a way, without using gases, that strongly supported the idea).

By expressing n (for moles, of course) as grams over molecular weight (g/MW), we can do as the early researchers did and get the "MW" of any gas by weighing a sample and measuring P, V, and T.

The needed equation derives from the basic PV = nRT. If, of course, you prefer the mnemonic to the algebraic, think of our being able to determine MW in this way as being a gift from "**gReaT ProVidence.**"

(i) $PV = nRT$　　　　(iii) $MWPV = gRT$

(ii) $PV = \dfrac{g}{MW}RT$　　　(iv) $MW = \dfrac{gRT}{PV}$

Here is an example of how to determine the molecular weight of an unknown gas in a lab exercise, or a known gas for which you do not know the molar weight (you could easily find out using a Periodic Table, but that is beside the point): find the molecular weight of sulfur dioxide if a sample weighing 1.27 grams fills 0.600 liters at 843 torr and 409 K. Solve for MW and then draw the one long line and put everything in its place.

$$MW = \frac{gRT}{PV} \qquad MW = \frac{1.27\ g \quad \times \quad 62.4\ (L)(torr) \quad \times \quad 409\ K}{843\ torr \quad \times \quad (K)(mol) \quad \times \quad 0.600\ L} = 64.1\ g/mol$$

Cross out all the dimensions that cancel and you will discover that only g and mol—the wanted dimensions—not only survive, but that they conveniently end up in just the right places. The constant is on top because the R is in the infinitive equation (left) which you wrote first.

Here is another example. In a lab experiment, you are given a sample of a colorless, odorless gas and told to identify it (using its molecular weight) from a list of gases that include CO_2, N_2, Ar, O_2, Ne, CO, NO, H_2, and C_3O_2. As with the previous gas-law problems considered in this chapter, you may wish to mark the given quantities in the problem, although they will be even more obvious than before.

The sample of gas is at 23°C and has a mass of 5.15 grams. It occupies 2.50 liters of a 3.50-liter cylinder that weighs 5.15 grams. If a reading of 864 torr is taken, can you identify the gas?

$$MW = \frac{gRT}{PV} \qquad MW = \frac{5.15\ g \quad \times \quad 62.4\ (L)(torr) \quad \times \quad 296\ K}{864\ torr \quad \times \quad (K)(mol) \quad \times \quad 2.50\ L} = 44.0\ g/mol$$

The only gas in the above list with this weight is carbon dioxide. Cross out all the cancelable dimensions in the calculation, and see that you understand whence came the "g/mol" in the answer.

⊛ For the two examples from p. 181, choose any five distinct colors and smudge the variables P, V, n, and T, and the constant, R, in the equations (α) and (β) and their corresponding areas in the examples on that page. The "R" part of the examples will of course dwarf the others and spill over the line, as well it should.

Then, take any six colors (but including the four already used for P, V, R, and T) and do the same thing (for P, V, R, T, g, and MW) in all the equations that appear on this page. Both ends of each of the four worked-out example equations will by necessity be the same color.

<table>
<tr><td>2
He
4.0026</td><td># Profile: Helium</td></tr>
</table>

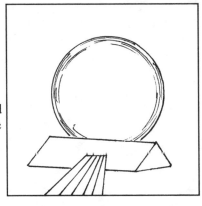

Helium, the "ideal gas," was first detected in the sun, where it is abundant.

While helium never participates in conventional (valence-electron) chemical reactions, it is of particular interest to astronomers and nuclear chemists because it is the product of stellar fusion, the primary source of energy in the universe.

In fact, it is the only element discovered away from the Earth. In 1868, Lockyer noticed some unfamiliar spectral lines while he was examining a spectrum of sunlight. For this reason, it was named helium, or "sun metal," although its properties are hardly metallic.

Although helium is common in the stars, it is somewhat rare on Earth. Its lightness makes it relatively free of the same gravity that traps other, heavier gases into the atmosphere. Moreover, its hermetic character—it is the most inert substance in Creation—prevents it from being locked up in compounds. When it is found, it is usually in the company of uranium ores, from which it springs as the product of the decay of heavy radioactive elements.

Helium should, however, be of some interest to general chemists (like us). Its atom is smaller than any other gas particle (although the hydrogen molecule is lighter) and Van der Waals attraction is virtually nonexistent. Hence, the element is so nearly ideal in its behavior that it can be considered *the* Ideal Gas; that is, the one gas that is able to conform very nearly perfectly to this model.

Only at a chilly 4 K (the lowest boiling point known) does it condense, and to solidify (freeze), it must be brought to below 1 K. Liquid helium is used as a coolant for superconductive materials, but it is tricky and potentially dangerous to handle because,

as the least little heat causes it to vaporize, the pressure it exerts as a gas can come about with frightening suddenness.

Though twice as heavy as hydrogen, helium nevertheless has about 93% of the former's lifting power. It can also substitute for another elemental gas, nitrogen, in diving equipment. Nitrogen, which is far more soluble in the blood than helium, forms bubbles on sudden decompression and causes the painful and crippling (and sometimes fatal) "bends."

Argon, on Earth, is many times more abundant than all the other noble gases combined. It is used in lightbulbs to create a "chemical vacuum" around the filaments and maintain an internal pressure (so that the external 760 or so torr will not crush the bulbs). It is also used by welders to protect hot metals from oxygen.

When neon, another helium sibling, is ionized by high alternating current, it gives off a red-orange light, whereas argon emits a purple one and krypton and xenon each give a type of blue. Radon is used to treat cancer by releasing helium nuclei (alpha particles).

Radon and helium—two gases—are themselves the products of the nuclear decomposition of radium:

$$^{226}_{88}\text{Ra(s)} \rightarrow \,^{222}_{86}\text{Rd(g)} + \,^{4}_{2}\text{He(g)}$$

This reaction, which to a theoretical observer would be the disappearance of a metal (radium) into "thin air," in reality produces radon anions and helium cations (alpha particles, again), but electrons are quickly lost or gained, as the case may be, and neutral atoms are the ultimate result. Note the conservation of mass, as indicated by the mass numbers.

WE'RE IDEAL!

5.9 Molar Volume and Density

By now you know that a mole of any gas—6.02×10^{23} airborne particles—at STP will measure 22.4 liters in a variable-volume cylinder. This circumstance provides us with a special conversion factor for doing certain very basic dimensional analysis calculations and, more specifically, gas stoichiometry problems beyond the all-gas type that was briefly considered in Sect. 5.3. The *molar volume conversion factor* and its reciprocal are:

$$\frac{22.4 \text{ L gas}}{\text{mol gas}} \quad \text{and} \quad \frac{\text{mol gas}}{22.4 \text{ L gas}}$$

...where *gas* is any gas at STP. Obviously, this conversion factor applies only to gases at standard temperature and pressure and (further) it has nothing whatsoever to do with liquids and solids (for which molar volumes would, in any case, be measured in milliliters or cubic centimeters, respectively).

Since (in our era) molecular weights have become known, determining a gas' density at STP is no problem, as long as you can remember the definition of density: "weight (or mass) per unit of volume."

Here is an example: what is the density of nitrous oxide at STP?

$$\frac{46.01 \text{ g}}{22.4 \text{ L}} = 2.05 \text{ g/L}$$

This kind of problem—because it is a density problem—is so simple that you need not even bother using dimensional analysis; just divide the molecular weight by 22.4 L. That is all. Note the dimensions of the answer: weight (grams) per unit (liter) of volume.

If the molecular weight of a gas is the wanted quantity (in the DA-sense of the word *wanted*) and density is the given, all we have to do is multiply this given density by the molar volume conversion factor, as in the following example.

What is the molecular weight of a gas that, at STP, has a density of 1.25 g/L?

$$\frac{1.25 \text{ g}}{\text{L}} \times \frac{22.4 \text{ L}}{\text{mol}} = 28.0 \text{ g/mol}$$

With your pencil, cancel out the unneeded dimension in this calculation.

Unknown samples, of course, cannot be labeled. But can you identify this gas from the list of colorless gases in the second example on p. 182? No, not quite, but only because two of them coincidentally have this particular weight. Thus, a little qualitative analysis is needed to reveal its identity (but don't use your nose—one of them is poisonous).

The molar volume conversion factor can also be used in more standard dimensional analysis bridges to predict the volume that a given quantity of moles will take up.

For instance, what will be the volume of 1.65 moles of phosphine (or xenon or oxygen or hydrogen iodide, *ad infinitum*) at STP? Set this problem up in the same way you would any other DA problem...

$$? \text{ liters } PH_3 = 1.65 \text{ mols } PH_3 \times \frac{22.4 \text{ L } PH_3}{\text{mol } PH_3} = 37.0 \text{ L } PH_3$$

Suppose, however, that the given quantity were in grams instead of moles. This would not cause you any difficulty, unless you had somehow forgotten how to convert grams to moles (Sect. 2.5, etc).

An example: what volume will 57.4 grams of ozone, O_3, occupy at STP? Knowing the formula and weight of atomic oxygen, you get a molecular weight of 48.00 (3 x 16.00) for ozone, and with this you can perform the dimensional analysis:

$$? \text{ L } O_3 = 57.4 \text{ g } O_3 \times \frac{\text{mol } O_3}{48.00 \text{ g } O_3} \times \frac{22.4 \text{ L } O_3}{\text{mol } O_3} = 26.8 \text{ L } O_3$$

You will see more of the molar volume conversion factor in the following two sections on gas stoichiometry.

Look at the vessels below. Assume that the pressure in each is 760 torr and that they are in a room with a temperature of 273 K and that this is also their temperature inside. Estimate—do *not* calculate—the number of moles in each one and (®) lightly shade the NO_2 brown and the Cl_2 green-yellow. Answers, to two sigfigs, are found on p. 200.

Cl_2_____ SO_3_____ H_2S_____ O_2_____ He_____ NO_2_____

1. Give the four parameters (P, V, n, T)—both number and dimension—associated with the molar volume of gas at STP; also, provide the number of the dimensionless constant (R) that derives from the four parameters:

P_____ V_____ n_____ R_____ T_____

2. Under what two special circumstances does the Ideal Gas Model begin to break down?

3. Even under ideal conditions of temperature and pressure, there is nevertheless a slight (indeed, negligible) deviation from the Ideal Gas Model. Give both reasons. Also, name the gas that deviates the least of all, based on these reasons.

4. What will be the new volume of 2.59 liters of chlorine brought to STP if the initial conditions were 203 K and 1168 torr (did you recognize this as a Combined Gas Law problem?)?

5. How many moles of sulfur dioxide are there in a 2.50-liter pyrex™ container at 300 K and 152 torr?

6. What volume will the combination of 2.00 moles of argon and 1.75 moles of nitrogen take up at −40°C and 830 torr?

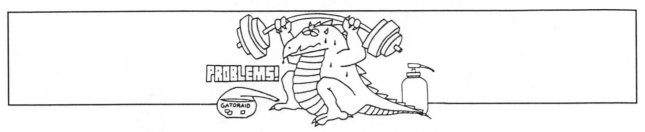

7. A 3.6-liter bathyscaph helium canister is filled with a compressed solution of oxygen (32.00 g/mol) and helium (4.0026 g/mol) at a temperature of 295 K and a pressure of 9500 torr. How many moles of gas does it contain?

8. 187 moles of hot gas causes a hot-air balloon to expand fully at 771 torr and 59°F and provide lift. What is the balloon's volume?

9. Determine the molecular weight of an unknown gas for which a 1.61-gram sample fills 17.9 liters at standard temperature and pressure.

10. Which of the 11 elemental gases occupies 12.1 liters of a cylinder with a movable piston and weighs 17.3 grams at STP (the molecular weight will identify the gas)?

11. What is the density at STP of (a) diatomic oxygen and of (b) the chemical weapon phosgene ($COCl_2$)?

12. What is the molecular weight (g/mol) of a compound gas that has a density of 3.22 g/L at STP?

13. How much volume will 0.140 of any gas occupy at standard temperature and pressure?

14. What volume of a stainless-steel variable-volume cylinder made in Pittsburgh (as opposed to Youngstown) will 19.2 grams of a hypothetical gas with a molecular weight (mass) of 20.0 fill at 760 torr and 273 K?

15. Identify, by circling, the unknown gases from problems 9, 12, and 14 from among the possibilities at right:

N_2O	CO	SbH_3	HF	Cl_2	Ne
C_5H_{12}	SO_2	H_2	O_3	CH_4	Ar
PH_3	NO	H_2S	Xe	NH_3	C_4H_{10}

1. The Amazon forests are by one estimate being decimated at an rate of 38 acres per minute.

How many years, then, will Brazil and the International Monetary Fund need to destroy the remaining 2.03 million acres if one km^2 = 247 acres (there are several unstated conversion factors here)?

2. Use the Table to write electronic notations for (a) Si (b) Mn (c) Kr.

3. How much calcium nitrate can be made with 100 grams of calcium hydroxide and 150 grams of nitric acid? Start by writing a GamMa Delta grid. The equation:

$$Ca(OH)_2 + 2HNO_3 \rightarrow Ca(NO_3)_2 + 2H_2O$$

5.10 Gas/Gas Stoichiometry

A gas produced by a reaction will not be at the same temperature and pressure as one that was reacted in it. These differences in temperature entail different volumes (Charles' Law). The explosion in a gun or an internal combustion engine demonstrates this principle. In both cases, a highly exothermic reaction occurs and hot, newly formed gases provide momentary high pressures which—according to Boyle's Law—just as suddenly *decrease* as the bullet or piston gets out of the way.

In other words, in a stoichiometric relation between two gases—whether both are reactants or only one is a reactant and the other, a product—we have two sets of conditions and so we use the Combined Gas Law to help us get from the given gas (described by P_1, V_1, and T_1) to the wanted gas (P_2, V_2, and T_2).

Another thing to remember about a stoichiometry problem in which *both* the given and wanted substances are gases is that molar conversions are not needed; only a keystone is required (Sect. 5.3).

Now, an example: how much hydrogen at 281 K and 690 torr is needed to react fully with 4.60 liters of nitrogen at STP to produce ammonia? You will begin, of course, with a balanced equation...

$$N_2(g) \; + \; 3H_2(g) \; \rightarrow \; 2NH_3(g) \quad so... \qquad ? \text{ liters } H_2 \; = \; 4.60\,L\,N_2 \; \times \; \frac{3\,L\,H_2}{L\,N_2} \; = \; 13.8\,L\,H_2$$

Then, using the Combined Gas Law, solve for V_2 and substitute the given information (V_1) into the equation to get...

$$V_2 \; = \; 13.8\,L \; \times \; \frac{273\,K}{281\,K} \; \times \; \frac{690\,torr}{760\,torr} \; = \; 12.2\,L$$

Does this look complicated? It can all be done in *one step* by putting the Combined Gas Law adjustments directly into **a single** stoichiometric bridge as two fractions (they do not equal 1, so we do not properly call them conversion factors). This can be seen in the following example. Note that both calculations—Combined Gas Law and gas/gas stoichiometry—seek a wanted quantity in liters from another such quantity, the given. This is why you can combine them into a single step without a hitch. An example: how much CO_2, at 985 torr and 476 K will result from the complete burning of 8.20 liters of methane at 764 torr and 292 K?

$$CH_4(g) \; + \; 2O_2(g) \; \rightarrow \; CO_2(g) \; + \; 2H_2O(g) \quad so...$$

$$? \text{ liters } CO_2 \; = \; 8.20\,L\,CH_4 \; \times \; \frac{L\,CO_2}{L\,CH_4} \; \times \; \frac{476\,K}{292\,K} \; \times \; \frac{764\,torr}{985\,torr} \; = \; 10.4\,L\,CO_2$$

The T and P adjustments (the Combined Gas Law equation inserted into a DA bridge) can be put anywhere in the bridge without risk of error because their dimensions cancel out internally; they do not need be joined to any other factor (or link) in particular (although it is advisable to lump them at one end or another so as not to split up the interlocking, true conversion factors).

189

ANSWERS! GLUG! GLUG!

1. (P) 760 torr   (V) 22.4 liters   (n) 1.00 mole   (R) 62.4   (T) 273 K

2. Very low temperatures or very high pressures

3. (a) Gas molecules themsleves occupy a very tiny amount of space and (b) there are extremely slight (in the gaseous state, anyway) electrostatic attractions among them (Van der Waals forces).   Helium.

4. V_2 = 2.59 liters Cl_2 x $\dfrac{273\ K}{203\ K}$ x $\dfrac{1168\ torr}{760\ torr}$ = 5.35 L Cl_2

5. n = $\dfrac{152\ torr\ \ x\ \ 2.50\ L\ x\ \ (K)(mol)}{300\ K\ \ x\ \ 62.4\ (L)(torr)}$ = 0.0203   (or 2.03 x 10^{-2})   mols SO_2

6. V = $\dfrac{3.75\ mols\ \ x\ \ 62.4\ (L)(torr)\ \ x\ \ 233\ K}{830\ torr\ \ x\ \ (K)(mol)}$ = 65.7 L Ar

7. n = $\dfrac{9500\ torr\ \ x\ \ 3.6\ L\ \ x\ \ (K)(mol)}{295\ K\ \ x\ \ 62.4\ (L)(torr)}$ = 1.9 mols He and O_2 (Watch those sigfigs!)

8. V = $\dfrac{187\ mols\ \ x\ \ 62.4\ (L)(torr)\ \ x\ \ 288\ K}{771\ torr\ \ x\ \ (K)(mol)}$ = 4.36 x 10^3 L hot gas

9. MW = $\dfrac{1.61\ g\ \ x\ \ 62.4\ (L)(torr)\ \ x\ \ 273\ K}{760\ torr\ \ x\ \ (K)(mol)\ \ x\ \ 17.9\ L}$ = 2.02 g/mol

10. MW = $\dfrac{17.3\ g\ \ x\ \ 62.4\ (L)(torr)\ \ x\ \ 273\ K}{760\ torr\ \ x\ \ (K)(mol)\ \ x\ \ 12.1\ L}$ = 32.0 g/mol (therefore, O_2)

11. a. $\dfrac{32.00\ g}{22.4\ L}$ = 1.43 g/L   b. $\dfrac{98.92\ g}{22.4\ L}$ = 4.42 g/L

12. $\dfrac{3.22\ g}{L}$ x $\dfrac{22.4\ L}{mol}$ = 72.1 g/mol

13. ? liters gas = 0.140 mols x $\dfrac{22.4\ L}{mol}$ = 3.14 L gas

14. ? liters gas = 19.2 g x $\dfrac{mol}{20.0\ g}$ x $\dfrac{22.4\ L}{mol}$ = 21.5 L gas

15. (9) hydrogen   (12) pentane, C_5H_{12} (14) hydrogen fluoride

...n IS FOR MOLES ...o IS FOR DEPHLO-GISTICATED AIR... p IS FOR ACID CONCENTRA-TIONS...q IS FOR HEAT EXCHANGE... r IS FOR 62.4...

5.11 Gas/Nongas Stoichiometry

Indeed, if you can do this much, you will not have to fish around for the needed conversion factors. By connecting them like polar molecules—but linking numerators and denominators (of different conversion factors) instead of positive and negative poles (of different molecules)—gas/nongas stoichiometry problems will practically write themselves down in as little time as it takes you to get them on paper.

Use each conversion factor as a clue to its successor and remember, too, that P and T adjustments are not true conversion factors and have no truck with the dimensions in the real conversion factors; it matters not where you put them in the bridge, provided that they are included at some point.

The *apparent* confusion is that quantities of gases are measured in volumes, whereas quantities of liquids and solids are weighed; it is liters in the former case and grams in the latter. The question set-up will therefore have grams as the wanted dimension if the problem is in the gas-to-nongas direction, and liters if you are going from a given nongas to a wanted gas. Stoichiometry between a gas and a nongas thus has two "directions."

This is no real buggaboo, however, since the problem will give you the dimensions of both the given and the wanted. With that information, you just set up the problem in the usual fashion and add the conversion factors until you arrive at the wanted substance in the appropriate dimension. It is recognizably stoichiometry as usual, with a keystone in or near the middle and conversion factors on either side. With the given data, you know where to begin. And, if your own answer to Dalton's query is in the affirmative, you will also know what to do next, up through to the end.

For instance, oxygen can be collected by roasting the salt potassium chlorate (as shown, above). How many liters of O_2 (a gas) will result from the decomposition of 45.0 grams of $KClO_3$ (a nongas)?

$$2KClO_3(s) \rightarrow 3O_2(g) + 2KCl(s)$$

$$? \text{ liters } O_2 = 45.0 \text{ g } KClO_3 \times \frac{\text{mol } KClO_3}{122.6 \text{ g } KClO_3} \times \frac{3 \text{ mols } O_2}{2 \text{ mols } KClO_3} \times \frac{22.4 \text{ L } O_2}{\text{mol } O_2} = 12.3 \text{ L } O_2$$

As you can see, the molar volume conversion factor has taken the place of one of the regular grams-to-moles factors. This stoichiometric pattern does not otherwise differ from that introduced in Sect. 4.5 for nongas/nongas stoichiometry. The same familiar symmetry is seen: a keystone sheathed between two molar conversions (of which one is slightly specialized).

To go from a given gas to a wanted solid or liquid, just reverse the order. You need not even be conscious of this fact to use it (but if you are conceptually aware of it, you have a little extra insurance against Mindless Robotic Zombieism). As always, the language of the problem will tell you what dimensions to begin and end with. If you can link up conversion factors (and, in most cases, slip in P and T adjustments), then it is a cinch.

Here is an example of a nongas-to-gas (or weight-to-volume) problem, the reverse of the above example: how much liquid water must be electrolyzed for a yield of 30.0 liters of oxygen at standard temperature and pressure?

$$2H_2O(l) \xrightarrow{\text{e}} O_2(g) + 2H_2(g)$$

$$? \text{ grams } H_2O(l) = 30.0 \text{ L } O_2 \times \frac{\text{mol } O_2}{22.4 \text{ L } O_2} \times \frac{2 \text{ mols } H_2O}{\text{mol } O_2} \times \frac{18.01 \text{ g } H_2O}{\text{mol } H_2O} = 48.2 \text{ g } H_2O$$

You almost cannot go wrong once you have set up the question, and the wording of the problem itself tells you what that is.

Obviously, gaseous reactants and products are not conveniently going to be at STP for our sake, so in gas/nongas stoichiometry, the Combined Gas Law also comes into play.

This time, however, we use it to adjust the volume of a single gas within the reaction *to* STP if it is a reactant ($T_1P_1 \to$ STP) or *from* STP if it is a product (STP $\to T_2P_2$).

Imagine that in the collection of oxygen in the first example (p. 191) that the gas produced was at 1025 torr and 314 K. What would its new volume (V_2) be? Instead of an initial volume (V_1), a weight is given, as are the initial temperature and pressure (T_1 and P_1). T_2 and P_2, then, are the other set and, automatically, STP. So, we just construct the stoichiometric bridge, slip in the P and T adjustments, tap a few calculator keys and *voilà!* Compare the bridge below with the same, but unadjusted, bridge on p. 191.

$$? \text{ liters } O_2 = 45.0 \text{ g } KClO_3 \times \frac{\text{mol } KClO_3}{122.6 \text{ g } KClO_3} \times \frac{3 \text{ mols } O_2}{2 \text{ mols } KClO_3} \times \frac{22.4 \text{ L } O_2}{\text{mol } O_2} \times \frac{314 \text{ K}}{273 \text{ K}} \times \frac{760 \text{ torr}}{1025 \text{ torr}} = 10.5 \text{ L } O_2$$

Here is a further example, one entailing additional conversion factors (in addition to P and T adjustments), but not *in principle* more complicated than the foregoing examples: how many ounces of octane (l), burned in air, will yield 6.40 gallons of CO_2 at 174° and 235 torr (1 oz = 28.3 g; 1 gal = 3.79 L)? Read the worked-out solution link-by-link, making sure that you understand whence each link comes and what it does in the calculation.

$$2C_8H_{18}(l) + 25O_2(g) \to 16CO_2(g) + 18H_2O(g)$$

$$? \text{ ounces } C_8H_{18} = 6.40 \text{ gals } CO_2 \times \frac{3.79 \text{ L } CO_2}{\text{gal } CO_2} \times \frac{\text{mol } CO_2}{22.4 \text{ L } CO_2} \times \frac{2 \text{ mols } C_8H_{18}}{16 \text{ mols } CO_2}$$

$$\frac{114.2 \text{ g } C_8H_{18}}{\text{mol } C_8H_{18}} \times \frac{\text{oz } C_8H_{18}}{28.3 \text{ g } C_8H_{18}} \times \frac{760 \text{ torr}}{735 \text{ torr}} \times \frac{447 \text{ K}}{273 \text{ K}} = 0.922 \text{ oz } C_8H_{18}$$

Error Analysis

Error results when (1) the wrong measurements are substituted into the P and T adjustments or (2) the adjustments are themselves absent-mindedly inverted (e.g., T_1 over T_2). The rest is just stoichiometry, in accordance with ordinary DA procedure. Here is what you can do to avoid these errors...

(1) Learn to count, both ordinally and cardinally, to two (that's right, *two*; that was not a typo). In gas/gas stoichiometry, the *one* and *two* sets of conditions correspond, respectively, to the *first* (given) gas and *second* (wanted) gas that you have *in order* as you work through and complete the problem.

In gas/nongas stoichiometry, you have only one gas, so the *one* set is for the gas if you have it *first* (reactant) and the *two* set is for the gas if you have it *second* (product). The leftover set of P and T is automatically STP.

(2) Memorize the two simple adjustments, T_2/T_1 and P_1/P_2. There is a mnemonic tip in Sect. 5.5 for T; and P is the inverse of T, as you already know.

5.12 Dalton's Law of Partial Ps

$$P_{\text{Total}} = p_1 + p_2 + p_3 + (p_4...)$$

According to the Kinetic Theory (of which the Ideal Gas Model is a part), molecules of all gases have the same energy if they are at the same temperature. For this reason, mixing them does not change the pressure that each of them exerts singly (unless, of course, they react).

Therefore, a liter of gas in a container is unaffected in the pressure it causes by the presence of other gases in the container. A liter of one gas exerts the same pressure as a liter of any other gas; if one gas is responsible for more pressure in a system than another, this simply means that there is proportionately more of it.

The Earth's atmosphere is such a blend of gases, and a sample of ordinary dry air is thus an appropriate sample for this topic. What is the *total* pressure of some dry air if nitrogen exerts a *partial* pressure of 602 torr; oxygen, of 155 torr; argon, of 9.16 torr; and all others, 7.35 torr? Can you add? If so, you can solve this problem:

$$p_{\text{Nitrogen}} + p_{\text{Oxygen}} + p_{\text{Argon}} + p_{\text{Etc}} = P_T$$
$$(602) \qquad (155) \qquad (9.16) \qquad (7.35) \qquad (774)$$

In the lab, gases are often collected by bubbling them through water and into an inverted container (p. 191) in which the gas displaces the water. As a result, there will always be some water vapor mixed in with the collected gas, and this bit of steam will be exerting its own (partial) pressure. Just *how* much is a function of temperature; the higher the T, the more water molecules will vaporize to produce pressure-causing collisions. The partial pressure of water vapor, which is constant with T, is looked up in a handbook or in a table such as that found in Appendix II of this book. This looked-up value is subtracted from the total pressure in the collecting vessel, and we are left with the partial pressure of the other gas.

Consider this example: what is the partial pressure of nitrous dioxide collected over water (as the lab parlance goes) at 298 K if the total pressure is 820 torr? Write the partial-pressure equation and find the water vapor value which, in this case, is 24.

$$p_{NO_2} + p_{H_2O} = P_T$$

$$p_{NO_2} + 24 = 820 \text{ (so...)}$$

$$820 - 24 = 796$$

(Algebraically, this result could be gotten by subtracting 24 from both sides of the equation; however, solving such a problem really requires nothing more than an understanding of the relation of the sum to its addends.)

⊛ Color the "molecules" and the "molar weights" of the CO_2 cylinder (below) green; the corresponding parts of the neon cylinder, orange-red; and of the hydrogen cylinder, purple. Color the same weights over the mixed cylinder, the same colors; underneath them, in the solution cylinder, color 12 molecules green; four, orange-red; and and eight, purple.

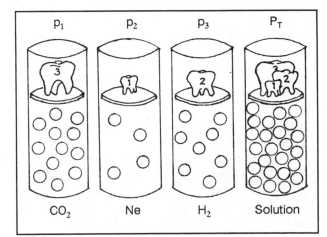

193

5.13 Graham's Law of Diffusion

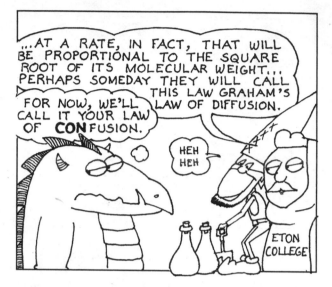

If you free a mole each of two gases in the same room, which of them will be the first to spread out, occupy the room, and form a fully mixed, gaseous solution with the air?

Under these implied conditions—identical P and T—the lighter gas will be the first to fully diffuse within a room, container, planetary atmosphere, or other system.

So sayeth Graham's Law, which is not concerned with absolute values but with relative ones (between any two gases). Remember that.

With it, we can predict how much faster a lighter gas will diffuse than a heavier one, and represent the comparison as a ratio of two values, one for each gas. Graham's Law problems, then, are necessarily concerned with only two gases at a time.

The ratio is determined by plugging the two relevant molecular weights into a brief equation and doing a little calculator work:

$$\frac{R_L}{R_H} = \frac{\sqrt{MW_H}}{\sqrt{MW_L}} = \sqrt{\frac{MW_H}{MW_L}}$$

...where R_L is the molecular weight of the lighter gas and R_H, that of the heavier one. Note that they are inverted and bracketted with the square-root symbol; hence the language "...inversely proportional to the square root of..."

However, this type of problem can be greatly simplified and then quickly solved using only the final expression in the equation just shown. How?

ONE Write the heavier weight as a numerator and the lighter one as a denominator.

TWO Follow the conventional order of operations ($\div$ key then $\sqrt{}$ key).

An example: hydrogen will diffuse more quickly than oxygen because it is lighter (this is pre-calculation qualitative logic, Sect. 1.2), but how much faster?

$$\frac{MW_{O_2}}{MW_{H_2}} = \sqrt{\frac{32}{2}} = \sqrt{16} = 4$$

Hydrogen diffuses four times as quickly as oxygen, or at a ratio of 4:1 (the molecular weights in this example were rounded for the sake of a simplified illustration).

Graham's Law may be the only topic in Chem. 1 in which ratios are seldom if ever true whole-number ratios. Consider Graham's own example of chloroform (119.4 g/mol) and laughing gas (44.02 g/mol):

$$\frac{MW_{CHCl_3}}{MW_{N_2O}} = \frac{\sqrt{119.4}}{\sqrt{44.02}} \boxed{\div} \sqrt{2.712} \boxed{\sqrt{}} \quad 1.647$$

Therefore, the rate of N_2O to that of $CHCl_3$ is a ratio of 1.647:1. The lighter gas thus diffuses about two-thirds again faster than the heavier one (so first the yuks, then the Zs).

194

THE COMBINED GAS LAW IS MOST VERSA-TILE—IT HAS MANY APPLICATIONS!

Among the applications we have considered for this law are calculations involving (1) a single gas at two sets of P and T (Sect. 5.6); (2) stoichiometry between a given gas and a wanted one, each with its own P and T (5.10); and (3) stoichiometry between a gas and a nongas, in which the gas has two set of conditions: its own and STP (Sect. 5.11). In the first case, we saw that the Law tells us how changes in P and T affect volume; in the other two, we used the Law to adjust volume and—because gas volumes are also gas quantities—to know the amount of a gas sample, with the help of the molar volume conversion factor.

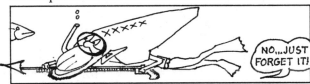

NO...JUST FORGET IT!

In each of the first nine problems in this set, you must begin by balancing the given equation.

1. How many liters of oxygen will be consumed in the complete burning of 1.48 liters of propane if both gases are at STP?

$$C_3H_8(g) + O_2(g) \rightarrow CO_2(g) + H_2O(g)$$

2. What quantity of carbon dioxide at 766 torr and 273 K will result from the reaction of 3.43 liters of carbon monoxide at 860 torr and 340 K?

$$CO(g) + O_2(g) \rightarrow CO_2(g)$$

3. How much chlorine at STP will be needed for the complete reaction of 1.40 liters of ammonia at 758 torr and 23°C (Balance hydrogen first this time)?

$$Cl_2(g) + NH_3(g) \rightarrow HCl(g) + N_2(g)$$

4. What quantity of oxygen at 35°C and 787 torr must be expended in order to obtain 4.65 liters of sulfur dioxide at 798 torr and 45°C?

$$H_2S(g) + O_2(g) \rightarrow SO_2(g) + H_2O(g)$$

5. How much fluorine at standard temperature and pressure will be needed to fully combust 7.5 kilograms of the liquid propellant hydrazine?

$$F_2(g) + N_2H_4(g) \rightarrow HF(g) + N_2(g)$$

6. The gas bismuthine quickly decomposes to its elements at room temperature. How much metallic (that is to say, elemental) bismuth would come of the breakdown of 10.0 liters of this gas at 21°F and 760 torr?

$$BiH_3(g) \rightarrow Bi(s) + H_2(g)$$

7. In one step of the Mond Process for removing nickel from a mixture of molten metals, carbon monoxide, and other ingredients, nickel carboxyl forms, only to **decompose** later and liberate pure cooled nickel. What **volume of carbon monoxide at 2100 torr and 302 K evolves with the production of a ton of nickel)to three sigfigs)?**

$$Ni(CO)_3(g) \rightarrow Ni(s) + CO(g)$$

8. The volcano show employed by classroom science teachers uses the brilliant orange salt ammonium dichromate soaked in ditto fluid (the oil of the teaching profession) which, when lit, heats the crystals to the point of ignition, resulting in a spectacular eruption. How much nitric oxide at 767 torr and 22°C will evolve from the burning of 5.40 grams of $(NH_4)_2Cr_2O_7$?

$$(NH_4)_2Cr_2O_7(s) + O_2(g) \rightarrow CrO_3(s) + NO(s) + H_2O(g)$$

9. What volume of hydrogen at standard temperature and pressure will be produced if 20.0 grams of dissolved sulfuric acid is reduced with 14.0 grams of zinc (note: you cannot go straight from the balanced equation to the stoichiometry)?

$$Zn(s) + H_2SO_4(aq) \rightarrow ZnSO_4(s) + H_2(g)$$

10. What is the total pressure on the surface of Venus if the partial pressure of carbon dioxide is 6.55×10^5; that of argon, 5.30×10^4; and that of helium, 2.10×10^4?

11. Exactly 18 grams of copper (I) oxide is roasted, yielding oxygen, which is meanwhile collected over water at 964 torr. Inside the container, the temperature is 28°C. From these data, determine the partial pressures of (a) the oxygen and (b) the water vapor (see the table in the appendix section).

12. Equal quantities of the following gases are released into separate chambers containing no other gas except helium, at one atmosphere and room temperature. Order the following from (1) the gas that will diffuse most quickly to (8) the slowest. Refer to the periodic table as needed.

_____ CH_4 _____ Ar _____ F_2 _____ CO

_____ NO _____ C_3O_2 _____ N_2O _____ AsH_3

13. How many times faster will Gas A diffuse than Gas B if their respective molecular weights are 151 g/mol and 6.20 g/mol?

14. What are the relative rates of diffusion for sulfur trioxide and carbon dioxide?

—— Across ——

1. Boyle's gadget
8. Prefix: same
9. Gas-group ending
10. Halogen heavyweight
11. Last lanthanide
13. 2 Period 6 d-blockers
14. Sea sire's metal
15. Ammonia derivative
17. Tinseltown twinkle
18. Aggressive acid
20. Predecessor of 11A
22. Hydrohalide
24. Fission fuel
26. Smell of SO_2
27. $1s^2 2s^2 ... 6s^2 5d^{10} 4f^1$
29. Large, lidded chemical container
31. Biochemical sensor
34. di_____ (B_2H_6)
35. Red_____ (subj. of Chap. 10)
36. 8B Element
37. 162.5 g/mol
38. named for Curie's adopted homeland
42. One of over 100
43. Lactose producer

—— Down ——

1. 6.02×10^{23} (adj.)
2. $1s^2 2s^2 ... 3p^6 4s^2 3d^8$
3. Top end of 6A
4. Gas corpuscle
5. Pressure "point"
6. Organic suffix
7. Double standard
10. Chemical suffix
12. Ending meaning "metal"
16. Hydrogen isotopes
17. Ends of Family 5A
19. Postcentenarian element
20. Organic suffix
21. Protein piece
22. Glass gasher
23. What gases are not made of
25. p_1 and p_2 do this for P_T
28. Anion angler
29. Not acidic
30. $1s^2 2s^2 ... 5s^2 4d^{10} 5p^1$
32. Nickel carb_____
33. ...99, 100...
34. Cereal cellulose
39. $1s^2 2s^2 ...$ $6s^2 4f^{14} 5d^5$
40. Pitchblende letters
41. n = g/?

197

5.14 Chapter Synthesis

THE RELE-VANT DETAIL IN THE STUDY OF GAS-ES IS THAT THE SAME QUANTITY OF ALL GASES FILLS THE SAME VOLUME WHEN AT THE EXACT SAME TEMPERATURE AND PRESSURE.

CH_4 IS NOT DIFFERENT FROM N_2 OR Xe OR O_2 OR O_3 OR Cl_2 OR HF OR PH_3 OR CO OR CO_2 OR N_2 OR...

All Earth-bound gases have a lot in common. All are molecular. All have low, if varying densities. And all take up the same amount of room.

Take a one-mole sample of two, three, ten, or 100 different gases at the same temperature and pressure. They will have different weights, different particle radii, different geometries, different colors and odors (if any), different points of condensation, different chemical properties, and the *same* volume. No inherent property or value affects the volume of any gas; only external conditions—pressure, temperature, and, of course, the quantity (n) itself—can do that.

Pressure is volume's inverse (Boyle's Law), because reducing a volume increases the frequency of molecular collision and, therefore, pressure. Temperature, on the other hand, rises and falls with volume (Charles' Law); this is evident from the tendency of a heated gas to expand and of a cooled one to contract until, ultimately, it condenses. Yet while a substance is in the gas state (in the normal range of P and T), however, its behavior is very nearly "ideal;" its particles act as if they had no volume of their own, nor any intermolecular attraction. All gases do, in fact, have a little of both. Helium, with the least of both volume and intermolecular attraction of these, is the most nearly ideal gas of all.

While individual gases do not have their own volumes, they do have their own masses. For this reason, our one-mole samples of different gases will have different densities, according to their molecular weights. Hydrogen, being the lightest of all gases, is accordingly the least dense.

At a standardized set of conditions—namely 760 torr and 273 K—each of the one-mole gas samples fills 22.4 liters of a variable-volume cylinder. A quotient of these four numbers—62.4—is accompanied, parenthetically, by the four dimensions of the four numbers, such that we are permitted to cancel out all dimensions that are not part of the wanted quantity, or answer, in calculations using this universal constant.

Stoichiometry, you will remember, is concerned with the quantitative relationship between two substances in a reaction, either as the reactants or as a reactant and a product. A gas can be related in this way to another gas or to a nongas (solid or liquid).

In the latter case, the first set of conditions (P_1T_1) apply to the gas if it is a reactant, and the second set is STP. If the gas is a product, it is the other way around with STP being the first set and the givens (P_2T_2), the second set.

Between two gases, the first set is, logically, for the given; the second set is for the wanted.

The consistency of volume among gases is a function of the sameness of pressure exerted by all of them at the same temperature. In a mixed sample (a gaseous solution), the pressure which governs volume is the same as if the sample were of a single gas.

When we prepare such a solution of, say, two gases, it is the lighter gas—the one with the lighter molecule—that will be the first to diffuse throughout the container if the gascocks are opened to the same degree for both.

YOU'RE QUITE A COOK, MONSIEUR. I PUT ON SIX KILOS DURING MY STAY!

ONE MORE WEEK AND WE'D HAVE TO CALL YOU GAY-TIGHTSAC!

TON POUR BOIRE.

MERCI.

BERKELEY · ITHACA · OXFORD · PARIS · UPPSALA · ALEXANDRIA

1. $C_3H_8 + 5O_2 \rightarrow 3CO_2 + 4H_2O$? liters O_2 = 1.48 L C_3H_8 x $\dfrac{5 \text{ mols } O_2}{\text{mol } C_3H_8}$ = 7.40 L O_2

2. $2CO + O_2 + 2CO_2$? liters CO_2 = 3.43 L CO x $\dfrac{2 \text{ L } CO_2}{2 \text{ L CO}}$ x $\dfrac{860 \text{ torr}}{766 \text{ torr}}$ x $\dfrac{273 \text{ K}}{340 \text{ K}}$ = 3.09 L CO_2

3. $3Cl_2 + 2NH_3 \rightarrow 6HCl + N_2$

    ? liters Cl_2 = 1.40 L NH_3 x $\dfrac{3 \text{ L } Cl_2}{2 \text{ L } NH_3}$ x $\dfrac{758 \text{ torr}}{760 \text{ torr}}$ x $\dfrac{273 \text{ K}}{296 \text{ K}}$ = 1.93 L Cl_2

4. $2H_2S + 3O_2 \rightarrow 2H_2O + 2SO_2$

    ? liters O_2 = 4.65 SO_2 x $\dfrac{3 \text{ L } O_2}{2 \text{ L } SO_2}$ x $\dfrac{787 \text{ torr}}{798 \text{ torr}}$ x $\dfrac{318 \text{ K}}{300 \text{ K}}$ = 7.10 L O_2

5. $2F_2 + N_2H_4 \rightarrow 4HF + N_2$? liters F_2 = 7.5 kg N_2H_4 x $\dfrac{1000 \text{ g } N_2H_4}{\text{kg } N_2H_4}$ x $\dfrac{\text{mol } N_2H_4}{32.31 \text{ g } N_2H_4}$

    x $\dfrac{2 \text{ mols } F_2}{\text{mol } N_2H_4}$ x $\dfrac{22.4 \text{ L } F_2}{\text{mol } F_2}$ = 1.0 x 10^4 L F_2

6. $2BiH_3 \rightarrow 2Bi + 3H_2$? grams Bi = 10.0 L BiH_3 x $\dfrac{\text{mol } BiH_3}{22.4 \text{ L}}$ x $\dfrac{2 \text{ mols Bi}}{2 \text{ mols } BiH_3}$ x $\dfrac{209.0 \text{ g Bi}}{\text{mol Bi}}$

    x $\dfrac{760 \text{ torr}}{760 \text{ torr}}$ x $\dfrac{273 \text{ K}}{267 \text{ K}}$ = 95.4 g Bi

7. $Ni(CO)_3 \rightarrow Ni + 3CO$? L CO = 1.00 TON Ni x $\dfrac{2000 \text{ lbs Ni}}{\text{TON Ni}}$ x $\dfrac{16 \text{ oz Ni}}{\text{lb Ni}}$ x $\dfrac{28.3 \text{ g Ni}}{\text{oz Ni}}$

    x $\dfrac{\text{mol Ni}}{58.71 \text{ g Ni}}$ x $\dfrac{3 \text{ mols CO}}{\text{mol Ni}}$ x $\dfrac{22.4 \text{ L CO}}{\text{mol CO}}$ x $\dfrac{760 \text{ torr}}{2100 \text{ torr}}$ x $\dfrac{302 \text{ K}}{273 \text{ K}}$ = 4.15 x 10^5 L CO

8. $2(NH_4)_2Cr_2O_7 + 5O_2 \rightarrow 4CrO_3 + 4NO + 8H_2O$? L NO = 5.40 g Comp x $\dfrac{\text{mol Comp}}{252.0 \text{ g Comp}}$

    x $\dfrac{4 \text{ mols NO}}{2 \text{ mols Comp.}}$ x $\dfrac{30.01 \text{ g NO}}{\text{mol NO}}$ x $\dfrac{295 \text{ K}}{273 \text{ K}}$ x $\dfrac{760 \text{ torr}}{767 \text{ torr}}$ = 1.38 L NO

9. In this problem, you had to determine the limiting reactant as soon as you had the coefficients from the balanced equation (both reactants are quantified in the problem). The equation, once you had written it down, was already balanced:

$$Zn + H_2SO_4 \rightarrow ZnSO_4 + H_2$$

	zinc	H_2SO_4
grams	14.0	**20.0**
	65.37	98.08
moles	0.214	0.204
	(1)	(1)
division	0.214	0.204

? liters H_2 = 20.0 g H_2SO_4 x $\dfrac{\text{mol } H_2SO_4}{98.08 \text{ g } H_2SO_4}$ x $\dfrac{\text{mol } H_2}{\text{mol } H_2SO_4}$ x $\dfrac{22.4 \text{ } H_2}{\text{mol } H_2}$ = 4.57 L H_2

ANSWERS! GLUG! GLUG!

10. $655,000 + 53,000 + 21,000 = 7.29 \times 10^5$

11. $964\,(P_T) - 28.3\,(p_{water}) = 936\,(p_{oxygen})\,(torr)$

12. (1) CH_4 (2) CO (3) NO (4) F_2
    (5) Ar (6) N_2O (7) C_3O_2 (8) AsH_3

13.
$$\sqrt{\frac{151}{6.20}} = \sqrt{24.4} = 4.94 \quad (4.94{:}1)$$

14.
$$\sqrt{\frac{80.06}{44.01}} = \sqrt{1.819} = 1.349 \quad (1.349{:}1)$$

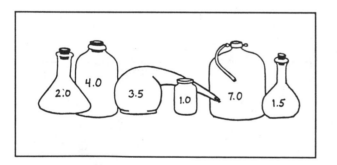

1. $\text{years} = 2.03 \times 10^6\ km^2 \times \dfrac{247\ acres}{km^2} \times \dfrac{minute}{38\ acres} \times \dfrac{hour}{60\ mins} \times \dfrac{week}{168\ hrs} \times \dfrac{year}{52\ weeks} = 25.2\ \text{years}$

2. (a) $1s^2 2s^2 2p^6 3s^2 3p^2$ (b) $1s^2 2s^2 2p^6 3s^2 3p^6 4s^2 3d^5$ (c) $1s^2 2s^2 2p^6 3s^2 3p^6 4s^2 3d^{10} 4p^6$

3.

	$Ca(OH)_2$	HNO_3
grams	$\dfrac{100}{(74.03)}$	$\dfrac{150}{(63.01)}$
moles	$\dfrac{1.35}{(1)}$	$\dfrac{2.38}{(2)}$
division	1.35	1.19

? grams $Ca(NO_3)_2 =$

$150\ g\ HNO_3 \times \dfrac{mol\ HNO_3}{63.08\ g\ HNO_3} \times \dfrac{mol\ Ca(NO_3)_2}{2\ mols\ HNO_3} \times \dfrac{164.1\ g\ Ca(NO_3)_2}{mol\ Ca(NO_3)_2} = 195\ g\ Ca(NO_3)_2$

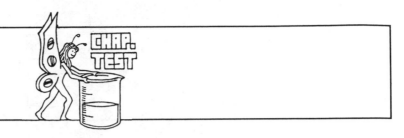

1. A 3.00-liter sample of argon at 865 torr is compressed to 1.81 liters. What is the new pressure?

2. A 4.64-liter sample of hydrogen is cooled from 27°C to 20°C. What is its volume?

3. Some CO_2 fills 2.40 liters of a 4.20-liter cylinder with a movable piston at 740 torr and 277 K. To what new volume will it rise or fall if the temperature is increased to 364 K and the ending pressure reading is 698 torr?

4. How many moles (n) of sulfur dioxide occupy 1.24 liters at 300 K and 770 torr?

5. What amount of space will 0.190 moles of phosphine (PH_3) take up at 3210 torr and 35°C?

6. If 58.9 grams of a certain elemental gas has a volume of 8.16 liters at 1512 torr and 238 K, can you name it?

7. Determine the density of pentane (C_5H_{12}) at STP:

8. How many liters will 2.50 moles of nitrogen fill at STP?

9. What will be the volume of 3.40 grams of laughing gas (N_2O) at STP?

THERE'S GOBS OF IRRELE-
VANT INFORMATION ON THESE
PAGES, BUT I'M GETTIN' SHARP AT SPOT-
TING IT... MAYBE MY NAME OUGHTA BE
"ZOOMIN" INSTEAD OF YOU-KNOW-
WHAT!

BRAGGART

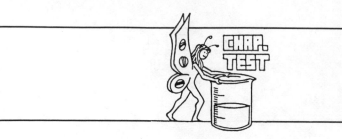

10. What volume of propene (C_3H_6) can be burned when reacted fully with 6.20 liters of oxygen, if both gases are at 24°C and 748 torr (first write a balanced organic oxidation reaction equation)?

11. How many liters of hydrogen bromide gas at 811 torr and 310 K will the reaction of 12.3 grams of elemental hydrogen yield at 726 torr and 291 K, according to the reaction shown (bromine is in excess):

$$H_2 + Br_2 \rightarrow 2HBr$$

12. How much of a variable-volume cylinder coated with teflon (C_2F_4) will be occupied by fluorine at 965 torr and 400 K resulting from the electrolysis of 64.0 grams of anhydrous potassium fluoride?

$$2KF \rightarrow F_2 + 2K$$

13. What weight of the salt ammonium sulfate, when reacted with the very strong base calcium hydroxide, will yield 15.0 grams of ammonia, among other products, at 792 torr and 35°C?

$$Ca(OH)_2 + (NH_4)_2SO_4 \rightarrow CaSO_4 + 2NH_3 + 2H_2O$$

14. Nitrogen is collected over water and into a container which then indicates a pressure of 906 torr at 21°C. Express the partial pressures of both the N_2 and the $H_2O(g)$ in an equation with the total pressure (again, you will use the table in the appendices).

15. How much more quickly can methane (CH_4) diffuse than sulfur dioxide under identical circumstances of P and T?

Answer to (a) four sigfigs, then to only (b) one.

8
O
15.999

Profile: Oxygen

The endothermy of birds, mammals, and some dinosaurs relies on the exothermy of oxidation.

Deinonychus

Oxygen enjoys a certain primacy among the elements for many reasons. For one thing, oxides are known for all but four or five naturally **occuring** elements. It also has a quantitative omnipresence, accounting for nearly half of the Earth's crust, one fifth of the atmosphere, about 60 percent of living tissues and 89 percent of water.

Atmospheric oxygen decreases dramatically with altitude, such that México (2640 meters), the world's largest city, has only about 40% of the oxygen that a sea-level town has.

The low bond energy of the O_2 molecule and the atom's high electronegativity also explain the element's wealth of compounds. Even so, most familiar reactions involving it require relatively high temperatures. In combustion, oxygen and a fuel must usually be primed with some heat in order to react; as the reaction begins, however, the reaction becomes self-sustaining because of the heat given off. Animal metabolism is a sort of combustion in slow motion; in a biological context, endothermy is the ability of some classes of vertebrates to maintain a constant body temperature (though at the cost of having to eat a great deal). Some evolutionists believe, paradoxically, that oxygen is a "toxic gas" that organisms adapted to the use of.

Medically, air mixtures with high O_2 concentrations are an aid to people with diminished ability to absorb the gas. Emphysema patients must use it because the internal surfaces of their lungs are critically reduced from smoking or air pollution.

Oxygen can be produced in several ways. One is by decomposing its compounds by heating. Another is the electrolysis of water into H_2 and O_2. Still another is the fractionation of liquefied air (made so by extreme cooling). As liquid air is slowly rewarmed, the nitrogen (which has a lower boiling point) bubbles away, leaving pale blue liquid oxygen, which itself vaporizes to an invisible gas around 90 K.

The allotrope ozone (O_3) is a vital part of the atmosphere, where it prevents excess ultraviolet radiation from striking the Earth. Certain chloro-fluorocarbons, used as refrigerants and atomizers for aerosols, reach the ozonosphere and cause the ozone layer to break up. A large hole is already known to be growing above Antarctica. These chemicals were restricted by international agreement in 1989, but the pact has many exemptions and manufacturers continue to "dump" the products into foreign markets where they are not yet prohibited, notably in the Third World.

Priestly discovered oxygen in 1774 and gave it the rather ironic christening, "dephlogisticated air." In his memoirs he described with obvious fondness the "high" he experienced from breathing pure oxygen.

Scheele came across the element even earlier, more appropriately calling it "fire air," but it was Lavoissier who first identified it as a chemical element and named it oxygen ("acid-former") because he believed (erroneously) that all acids contained it.

A branch of modern alchemy associates aging with "oxidation" at the cellular level. A swarm of dietary supplements called antioxidants has been developed and is sold in health-food stores.

1. $P_2 = \dfrac{(865 \text{ torr})(3.00 \text{ L})}{(1.81 \text{ L})} = 1.43 \times 10^3$ 2. $V_2 = 4.64 \text{ L} \times \dfrac{293 \text{ K}}{300 \text{ K}} \ x = 4.53 \text{ L}$

3. $V_2 = 2.40 \times \dfrac{364 \text{ K}}{277 \text{ K}} \times \dfrac{740 \text{ torr}}{698 \text{ torr}} = 3.34 \text{ L}$

4. $n = \dfrac{770 \text{ torr} \ \times \ 1.24 \text{ L} \ \text{(K)(mol)}}{300 \text{ K} \ \times \ 62.4 \text{(L)(torr)}} = 0.0510 \text{ mols} \ \ (5.10 \times 10^{-2} \text{ mols})$

5. $V = \dfrac{0.190 \text{ mols} \ \times \ 62.4 \text{ (L)(torr)} \ \times \ 308 \text{ K}}{3210 \text{ torr} \ \times \ \text{(K)(mol)}} = 1.14 \text{ L}$

6. $MW = \dfrac{58.9 \text{ g} \ \times \ 62.4 \text{ (L)(torr)} \ \times \ 238 \text{ K}}{1512 \text{ torr} \ \times \ 8.16 \text{ L}} = 70.9 \ \ (\text{the gas is chlorine})$

7. $\dfrac{g}{L} = \dfrac{72.15 \text{ g}}{22.4 \text{ L}} = 3.22 \text{ g/L}$ 8. $? \text{ L} = 2.50 \text{ mols} \times \dfrac{22.4 \text{ L}}{\text{mol}} = 56.0 \text{ L}$

9. $? \text{ L} = 3.40 \text{ g N}_2\text{O} \times \dfrac{\text{mol N}_2\text{O}}{44.01 \text{ g N}_2\text{O}} \times \dfrac{22.4 \text{ L N}_2\text{O}}{\text{mol N}_2\text{O}} = 1.73 \text{ L N}_2\text{O}$

(labelled because it contains a molar conversion)

10. $? \text{ L C}_3\text{H}_6 = 6.20 \text{ L O}_2 \times \dfrac{2 \text{ L C}_3\text{H}_6}{9 \text{ L O}_2} = 1.38 \text{ L C}_3\text{H}_6$ $(2\text{C}_3\text{H}_6 + 9\text{O}_2 \rightarrow 6\text{CO}_2 + 6\text{H}_2\text{O})$

11. $? \text{ L HBr} = 12.3 \text{ g H}_2 \times \dfrac{\text{mol H}_2}{2.016 \text{ g H}_2} \times \dfrac{2 \text{ mols HBr}}{\text{mol H}_2} \times \dfrac{22.4 \text{ L HBr}}{\text{mol HBr}} \times \dfrac{726 \text{ torr}}{811 \text{ torr}}$

$\times \dfrac{310 \text{ K}}{291 \text{ K}} = 26.1 \text{ L HBr}$

12. $? \text{ L F}_2 = 64.0 \text{ g KF} \times \dfrac{\text{mol KF}}{58.10 \text{ g KF}} \times \dfrac{\text{mol F}_2}{2 \text{ mols KF}} \times \dfrac{22.4 \text{ F}_2}{\text{mol F}_2} \times \dfrac{400 \text{ K}}{273 \text{ K}}$

$\dfrac{760 \text{ torr}}{965 \text{ torr}} \ x = 14.2 \text{ L F}_2$

13. $? \text{ g (NH}_4)_2\text{SO}_4 = 15.0 \text{ g NH}_3 \times \dfrac{\text{mol NH}_3}{17.0 \text{ g NH}_3} \times \dfrac{\text{mol (NH}_4)_2\text{SO}_4}{2 \text{ mols NH}_3} \times \dfrac{132.2 \text{ g (NH}_4)_2\text{SO}_4}{\text{mol (NH}_4)_2\text{SO}_4}$

$\times \dfrac{308 \text{ K}}{273 \text{ K}} \times \dfrac{760 \text{ torr}}{792 \text{ torr}} = 63.1 \text{ g (NH}_4)_2\text{SO}_4$

14. $906 \ (P_T) = 18.6 \ (p_{H2O}) + 887 \ (p_{N2})$

15. Optional part: $\left(\dfrac{R_L}{R_H} = \dfrac{\sqrt{64.06}}{\sqrt{16.04}} = \right) \ \sqrt{\dfrac{64.06}{16.04}} = \sqrt{3.994} = $ (a) 1.998 (b) 2

204

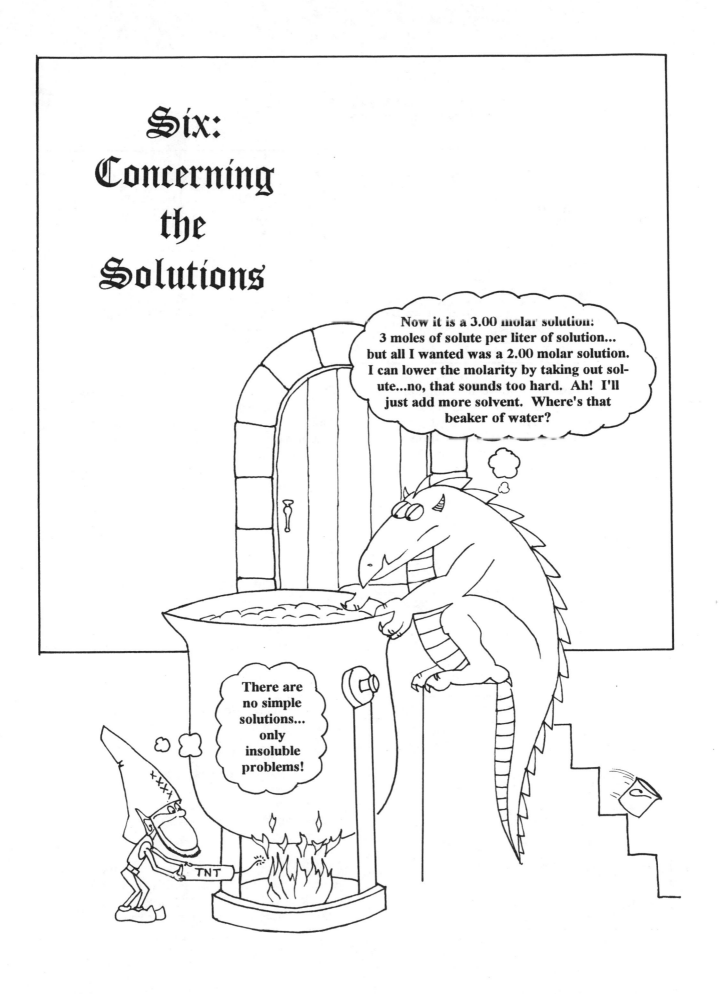

6.1 Solution Properties

While the distinction between a solution and a compound is important, it is the role of solutions in the formation, dispersion, and destruction of uncountable compounds that makes the study of solutions so central to chemistry; in very deed, the majority of Chem. 1 lab reactions take place in aqueous solutions, such that these are in effect the fourth state of matter as far as the chemist is concerned (g, s, l, aq). *Aqueous* is of Latin derivation for "water" and compares with *gaseous*, the adjective for another state.

As water is here the specified *solvent*—that in which other substances, *solutes*, are dissolved—it is called the "universal solvent" by dint of its ubiquity as a solution medium. The degree of a compound's solubility is always its particular solubility in water, unless another solvent is explicitly involved.

Still, solutions, as just defined, are a huge category including several classes of combinations among the three proper physical Earthly states. They are:

(a) Gases in gases. As you already know, air and planetary atmospheres are gas-in-gas solutions.

(b) Gases in liquids. A familiar example is carbonated water, which is dissolved, aqueous carbon dioxide.

(c) Liquids in liquids. Any combination of wholly miscible liquids—such as water and alcohol—is a solution. The different alcohol contents of intoxicating spirits underlines the variability of solution proportions. We are not bound to whole-number ratios here, and the multiplicity of proportions is all but literally infinite.

(d) Liquids in solids. This is a small category, but it includes the mercury amalgams.

(e) Solids in solids. Alloys other than amalgams can also be considered solutions if their components are fully and uniformly blended.

(f) Solids in liquids. This is the most studied type of solution in Chem. 1. Any powder or other material —be it a salt, a carbohydrate, a gem, or a metal tailing—forms a solution if it dissolves in a liquid.

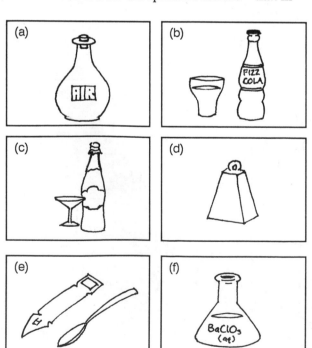

In a manner of speaking, solutions are combinations of two (or more) substances that have dissolved each other. By convention, though, the more (or most) abundant component is said to be the solvent and the the other(s), the solute(s).

This generalization is arbitrary in the case of two (or more) liquids, as either could be considered the solvent (depending on proportion); but we never have any trouble thinking of a gas or a solid as the solute when in combination with a liquid.

──────Dilute and Concentrated──────

A solution with a high proportion of solvent—and, therefore, a lower proportion of solute material—is dilute relative to another solution of the same substance with a higher proportion of solute, a concentrated one.

The terms *dilute* and *concentrated* are relative and qualitative; no particular level of concentration definitively separates one from the other.

──────Miscible and Immiscible──────

These terms are meaningful primarily in the context of liquid-in-liquid solutions. Most pairs of liquids in combination are clearly one or the other, but some partly miscible combinations exist (and so are poor examples of solutions). Combinations of gases, by their nature, are wholly miscible solutions.

──────Saturated and Unsaturated──────

A solution in which a solute dissolves to the limit of the solvent's capacity to hold it is a *saturated* solution, in which the solvent and the solute are in equilibrium.

If the concentration of the solute is below this solubility limit, the solution is an *unsaturated* one; it can dissolve and contain still more solute.

──────Supersaturated──────

Some saturated solutions, when kept very still and carefully cooled, can remain in solution somewhat beyond the normal solubility limit, forming a *supersaturated* solution. Such solutions are unstable: the addition of a tiny particle of solid solute (or the edge of a spoon) will cause the excess solute to immediately crystallize or, as it were, "undissolve."

If the tiny particle merely dissolves, however, this would mean that the solution was still unsaturated. If, on the other hand, nothing at all **happens**, a saturated solution is indicated.

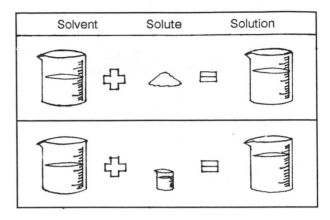

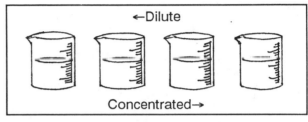

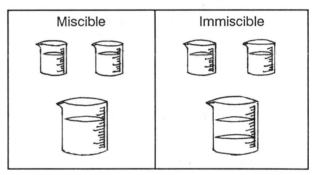

⊛ In the top frame, color the powdered solute red or maroon, and its solution, pink; color the solute in the little beaker dark blue and its solution, light blue. In the next frame, shade the most dilute solution very lightly brown, and the others, progressively darker. In the third frame, on the left, color one of the upper beakers orange, the other not at all, and the lower one, "dilute orange;" on the right, color the oil yellow, both in one of the upper beakers and the top half of the contents of the lower one (Note: not all solutes added to water retain their color in solution).

207

6.2 Solubility

Solubility is defined as the weight of a solute that is dissolved in a given weight or volume of solvent or solution.

The degree to which solute is dissolved in a solution is the solution's *concentration*. There are several ways to express concentrations, as we will see in Sect. 6.3. The commonest (molarity) is the amount (in moles) of solute in a liter of water (which is also a kilogram of water).

Practically every solid is soluble to some degree in water, though a compound that dissolves only negligibly may be considered insoluble.

In one liter of water at 25°C, no more than one thousandth of a gram of silver chloride, for example, will dissolve. But if *sodium* chloride is added to a liter of water, 350 grams of it dissolves; and almost two whole kilos of sucrose can dissolve in just one kilo of water. In this last instance, therefore, sugar is the technical solvent, and water, the solute.

Silver chloride, then, can definitely be classified as insoluble, whereas table sugar and table salt are demonstrably in the soluble category.

Solubility values in fact form a vast logarithmic scale from the extremely insoluble to the extremely soluble. Nonetheless, we are well served by the subsumation of potential solid solutes into soluble and insoluble classes. We say that if some solute—*no matter how big the quantity*—is added to a liter of pure water at 25°C and no more than one gram of the solute turns up dissolved, then that substance is insoluble. If the liter of water is found to hold more than ten grams of solute, we call the solute soluble. The relatively few (but in real terms, many) solutes with solubilities between one and ten grams per liter (1×10^0–10^1 g/L) may be called either slightly soluble or slightly insoluble in the same way that a glass may be half-full or half-empty. Some solids are so water-insoluble that their solubility values are not measurable and only theoretical.

Knowing what is soluble and what is not is vital to the preparation of solutions and in the prediction of reactions that may or may not take place in them. More on this in later sections.

In aqueous solutions, ionic and some covalent substances—*if soluble*—break into ions. These can recombine into new compounds (some of which are even molecular), both with the water itself and/or with other ions released by the dissolution. If no new compounds form, we are left with a chemical soup; but *if the components of an insoluble salt are made available in a solution, that same salt will form* and precipitate out.

Likewise, *a gas evolves if its molecules are liberated or formed in solution*. We can therefore predict the formation of gases, salts, and more in solutions by knowing something about solubilities.

Our study of solutions will emphasize—as do most Chem. 1 curricula—solutions of ionic species in general and those covalent species that form or are formed from ions in solution. In short, we will leave out the strictly covalent solutions (which, in any case, are rather boring as solutions go).

Solubility Rules for Salts, Oxides, and Hydroxides

Anion	Ammonium	Lithium	Sodium	Potassium	Magnesium	Calcium	Barium	Aluminum	Manganese (II)	Iron (II)	Iron (III)	Cobalt (II)	Nickel	Copper (II)	Zinc	Tin (II)	Lead (II)	Mercury (I)	Mercury (II)	Silver
Acetate								i												i
Nitrate																				
Nitrite														i						(i)
Chlorate																				
Chloride																	i	i		i
Bromide																	i	i	(i)	i
Iodide																	i	i	i	i
Sulfate						(i)	i										i	i		(i)

Anions Forming Mostly Soluble Compounds

Anion	Ammonium	Lithium	Sodium	Potassium	Magnesium	Calcium	Barium	Aluminum	Manganese (II)	Iron (II)	Iron (III)	Cobalt (II)	Nickel	Copper (II)	Zinc	Tin (II)	Lead (II)	Mercury (I)	Mercury (II)	Silver
Sulfite	s	s	s	s			s													
Phosphate	s		s	s																
Chromate	s	s	s	s	s	s												(s)		
Carbonate	s	s	s	s																
Sulfide	s	s	s	s	s	s	s	s												
Oxide	—	s	s	s		(s)	s													
Hydroxide	—	s	s	s		(s)	s													

Anions Forming Mostly Insoluble Compounds

There are, of course, a great many nonionic solutions because most covalent substances do not release ions in water, but only molecules. Sucrose is such a one.

This table shows most of the combinations that you are likely to come across in Chem 1; any others can be looked up in the Handbook. Only the exceptions to the "rules" are here marked so as to highlight them.

Parentheses signify slight (in)solubility (1 to 10 grams solute can saturate a liter of water at 25°C). Some possible combinations are unstable or do not even exist, but only a couple are so marked (−).

One bogus species is "$NH_4OH(aq)$" which, though not a true substance, is often seen on labels of dissolved ammonia. The true formula is $NH_3(aq)$.

Consider the following patterns and mnemonic clusters with respect to the solubility rules:

(1) Ammonium and Family 1A ions form the "crumbly compounds;" they always dissolve and ionize in water.

(2) Acetates, nitrates, nitrites, and chlorates Almost Never Cohere in solution.

(3) Halides—the salts of Cl^-, Br^-, and I^-—are insoluble only with a handfull of heavier metal ions.

(4) Sulfites, phosphates, chromates, and carbonates are Soluble Phor Crumbly Compounds.

(5) Sulfides, oxides, and hydroxides are the "insolublides" (ending in -ide). They dissolve only when their ions are part of crumbly compounds or some of the Family 2A salts. The soluble hydroxides form the strong bases when added to water.

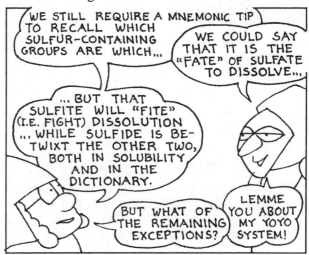

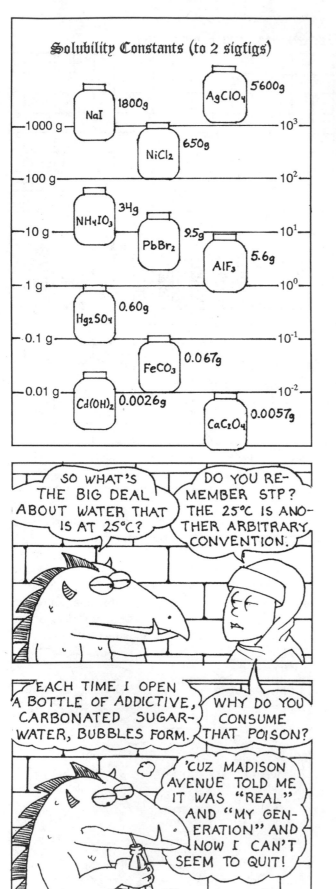

The amount of any solute that, if added to one liter of water (at 25°C), ends up in solution is that substance's *solubility constant*.

For instance, if we take three full one-liter flasks and pour 7.5 grams of the salt aluminum fluoride into the first, then 90 grams of it into the second, and 600 grams into the third, only 5.6 grams   each will be dissolved. The rest will just settle as dregs on the bottom. The solubility of this salt—and all others—is therefore "constant;" hence, it is called the solubility constant.

In the case of AlF_3, it is 5.6 grams per liter. We will return to solubility constants in Chap. 8. Start thinking about them now.

⊛ At left, color the reagent jars of the insoluble compounds pink; those of the soluble ones, light blue; and those in between, light purple or lavender.

Then, on the solubility rules chart on p. 209, color light purple all the squares with "(i)" or "(s)."

Next, color light blue (a) the first four columns of anions (the crumbly-compound formers), except the square for Li_3PO_4; and (b) all the other "s" squares on the bottom half of the chart and all the empty squares on the top half.

Finally, color pink what should be left: all the "i" squares above and all the blank ones below.

───────────Temperature and Solubility───────────

Temperature always has some affect—usually minor for our purposes—on solubility to a degree that varies from one solute to the next.

For this reason a temperature convention, ideally in the tepid range, must be agreed upon. 25°C is a good round number and it approximates the temperature of the water and air in a chem lab.

In general, although not always, the solubility of solid substances increases with temperature.

───────────Solubility of Gases───────────

Gases, like solids, vary in their solubility. Of the elemental gases, oxygen and chlorine are the most soluble; the noble gases are the least soluble. Aquatic fauna depend on this dissolved oxygen.

Furthermore, according to Henry's Law, the solubility of a gas is proportional to the pressure of the gas over the solvent in a closed system.

This explains why dissolved carbon dioxide effervesces when the cap—and, therefore, the pressure—is suddenly removed from a softdrink bottle.

210

1. Match the following:

_____ saturated   a. a solution in which additional solute can be dissolved

_____ immiscible   b. noncombination of solutes and solvents

_____ precipitate   c. covalent product of a solution reaction

_____ solution   d. a solution with an abnormally high content of solute

_____ slightly soluble   e. a solid species that dissolves to between 1-10 grams/liter of water

_____ concentrated   f. noncombination of two liquids

_____ mixture   g. a heterogeneous combination of varying proportions

_____ supersaturated   h. a homogeneous combination of fixed proportions

_____ dilute   i. a solution with a high relative proportion of solvent

_____ compound   j. ionic product of a solution reaction

_____ insoluble   k. a solution with a solute/solvent equilibrium

_____ amalgam   l. a solution with a high relative proportion of solute

_____ gas   m. a homogeneous combination of varying proportions

_____ unsaturated   n. an example of a solution of a liquid in a metal

2. Predict the solubility of the compounds at right, using your memory and/or the tabulated information on p. 209. Write in "S" for a soluble compound; "I" for an insoluble compound; and "M" for a slightly soluble (or slightly insoluble) compound:

_____ $BaSO_4$ _____ NH_4CN _____ $LiC_2H_3O_2$

_____ K_2CrO_4 _____ FeS _____ Na_2CO_3 _____ PbI_2

_____ $HgBr_2$ _____ $K_2C_2O_4$ _____ $Ca(OH)_2$

_____ $SnCl_2$ _____ $NaNO_3$ _____ CoI_2 _____ NH_4Br

_____ $CuSO_3$ _____ MgO _____ $Fe(NO_2)_3$

_____ $AgBr$ _____ $(NH_4)_2Cr_2O_7$ _____ HCl

3. Fill in all the squares of this mini-table, using the same symbols and resources as above.

	Al^{3+}	Ag^+	Ba^{2+}	Fe^{3+}	Hg_2^{2+}	K^+	Mg^{2+}	NH_4^+	Ni^{2+}	Zn^{2+}
SO_3^{2-}										
$C_2H_3O_2^-$										
PO_4^{3-}										
Cl^-										
OH^-										
SO_4^{2-}										
NO_3^-										
CrO_4^{2-}										

1. k f j m e l g d i h b n c a

2.

(I) BaSO$_4$ (S) NH$_4$CN   (S) LiC$_2$H$_3$O$_2$

(S) K$_2$CrO$_4$ (I) FeS   (S) Na$_2$CO$_3$ (I) PbI$_2$

(M) HgBr$_2$ (S) K$_2$C$_2$O$_4$ (M) Ca(OH)$_2$

(S) SnCl$_2$ (S) NaNO$_3$ (S) CoI$_2$ (S) NH$_4$Br

(I) CuSO$_3$ (I) MgO   (S) Fe(NO$_2$)$_3$

(I) AgI   (S) (NH$_4$)$_2$Cr$_2$O$_7$ (S) HCl

3. Check your answers against the table on p. 209.

Polar and Nonpolar Solvents

There are two general classes of solvents. Polar solvents are composed of molecules with an asymmetrical, or polar, distribution of charges. They are good solvents for ionic substances because they can surround ions in the surface of an ionic solute as shown (a) with opposite charges and so pull them loose from the ionic lattice (b).

Nonpolar solvents, on the other hand, are more effective with more covalent solutes, which are made up of particles with low or nonexistent polarity. Carbon tetrachloride, which is made of perfectly symmetrical tetrahedral molecules, is a very good nonpolar solvent.

The general rule, then, is that solvents are "homeopathic;" *like dissolves like*, although the "universal solvent," water, can break down innumerable covalent substances in spite of its own fairly pronounced polarity.

Ionic aqueous solutions form whenever ions are chipped off the solute mass and hydrated (as shown at right). These ions do, however, retain their charge, for their companion water molecules are electrically neutral. For this reason, most saline solutions are good conductors.

By another system of classification, solvents are sorted into three categories: aqueous (i. e., water); nonaqueous organic; and everything else.

Solvents

Polar	Nonpolar

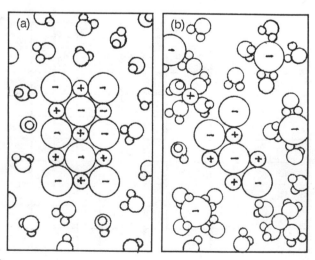

6.3 Solution Concentrations

Concentrations are expressed in several ways to serve a variety of purposes. All are conversion factors. We will "concentrate" only on those with the phrase "moles of solute" in their definitional numerators.

Molarity (M)

This is the most frequently used concentration expression in Chem. 1. It is the number of moles of a substance dissolved in a liter of solution and is thus the quantitative relation of *one component*—the solute—*to the totality of the solution.* A 3.50 molar (3.50M) solution is one in which each liter of the solution contains 3.50 moles of solute.

Molality (m)

This concentration, on the other hand, is the relation of *one component of the solution to the other component*; specifically, the solute to the solvent.

A 8.00 molal (8.00m) solution has eight moles of solute in each kilo of solvent. Note that the solvent is quantified by weight, not by volume.

Normality (N)

Normality will only be mentioned here, for it is beyond our ken at this level. It concerns the *gram-equivalent*, which is the weight (in grams) of an acid that releases a mole of H^+ in solution, or the weight of a hydroxide that releases a mole of OH^-.

A 2.00 normal (2.00N) solution of HCl, for instance, would be 72.9 grams of HCl in a liter of water, for that is the amount that yields two moles of protons.

Additionally, it may be the weight of a reducing agent that releases a mole of electrons in solution, or the weight of an oxidizing agent that picks them up.

Formality (F)

In practice, formality refers specifically to the molarity of an ionic solution; it is thus a subdivision of molarity. Formality has to do with moles of ions in a liter of solution, and so is semantically more precise when we have formula units in mind.

However, while we *must* distinguish formula units from molecules, it is seldom absolutely necessary to distinguish formality from molarity. Any chemist knows that a 1.20 molar solution of ions is really a 1.20 formal (1.20F) without being reminded.

Molarity		
	$M =$	$\dfrac{\text{moles solute}}{\text{liter solution}}$
molality		
	$m =$	$\dfrac{\text{moles solute}}{\text{kilo solvent}}$
Normality		
	$N =$	$\dfrac{\text{equivalents solute}}{\text{liter solution}}$
Formality		
	$F =$	$\dfrac{\text{mole formula units}}{\text{liter solution}}$

6.4 Molarity

$$M = \frac{\text{moles solute}}{\text{liter solution}}$$

As has been pointed out, molarity, along with the other concentration expressions, is a conversion factor.

We use this factor, specifically, to determine what concentration a given quantity of solute will produce in a given volume of solution.

For instance, what will be M for a 500-milliliter solution in which 0.220 mole of $Ni(ClO_3)_2$ is dissolved (convert 500 ml to 0.500 L mentally)?

$$M = \frac{0.220 \text{ mol}}{0.500 \text{ L}} = 0.440$$

This problem is as simple and straightforward as a density problem and, in fact, it is just that: the density of a solute in a liquid (Sects. 1.6 and 5.7 treat density).

In reality, of course, solute samples do not come to us in little packets with the number of moles neatly printed on them. Instead, our solutes will be quantified in the grams we measure them with, and then in the moles that we convert these to. This should be no problem, for by now you will be quite used to molar conversions (Sect. 2.5 and on and on).

Determining molarity from a given weight (usually grams) of solute and a given volume of solution is very easy; the problem contains nothing more than a density-type "calculation" (as in the above example) and a molar conversion factor. There is not so much as even a question to set up. Here is an example: what is the molarity of an 840-milliliter solution with 16.3 grams of NaCl (58.44 g/mol) dissolved in it ?

$$M = \frac{16.3 \text{ g NaCl}}{0.840 \text{ L}} \quad x \quad \frac{\text{mol NaCl}}{58.44 \text{ g NaCl}} = 0.332M$$

Notice that 16.3 g NaCl and 0.840 L (840 ml) are, together, the given density value.

Now, let us consider the preparation of solutions at wanted (in the DA sense) molarities. Suppose that we have to make 750 milliliters of 1.50 molar potassium permanganate solution (1.50M $KMnO_4$). This salt has a molar weight of 158.4. We know that what we will end up with must reach the 750 ml mark on the flask or graduate; this, then, is our given, and 1.50M is only a conversion factor meaning "1.50 moles of solute per 1.00 liter of solution." What we want to find out (the wanted) is how many grams of $KMnO_4$ will provide us with that concentration. This is a conventional dimensional analysis problem:

$$? \text{ grams } KMnO_4 = 0.750 \text{ L} \quad x \quad \frac{1.50 \text{ mols } KMnO_4}{\text{L}} \quad x \quad \frac{158.4 \text{ g } KMnO_4}{\text{mol } KMnO_4} = 178 \text{ g } KMnO_4$$

This type of problem, as you can see, involves no unfamiliar principle, nothing that you have not already seen. Do not be thrown by the mole quantity that is not a whole number; it is not **derived from a formula** and, in any case, molarities necessarily contain decimals (because solutions—unlike compounds—are infinitely variable in their proportions).

214

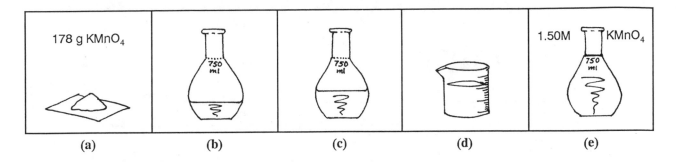

178 g KMnO$_4$				1.50M KMnO$_4$
(a)	(b)	(c)	(d)	(e)

The steps for the preparation of the solution from the previous example are shown above. As soon as we measure out the weight of solute we need (a), we dissolve it in some water (b) that is well below the volume of the solution to be made (c). This done, the proportion of the solute is just right; we need now only to adjust the amount of the solvent by adding more water (d) until we reach the given quantity (e), in this case 750 milliliters.

Molarity can also be used to take us in the other direction. We can determine the number of moles in a given volume of solution, if the molarity is known; conversely, we can determine the volume of solution we will need to get a wanted quantity of moles of solute. This will be very useful in stoichiometric calculations involving solutions, for in the chem lab we initiate many reactions by mixing *solutions of* the reactants.

Such determinations are also quite simple, being miniature DA bridges. Even grams-to-mole conversions are not needed because we are already

dealing with prepared molar solutions; grams are irrelevant. Even labels are nonessential, for it is only a single substance that is in question. Now for some examples.

Suppose 0.360 moles of copper (II) nitrate are required, in solution, for a reaction to take place with another solution. The lab assistant is dispensing solution from a vat labeled 2.00M. What volume must he give you?

$$? \text{L} = 0.360 \text{ mols} \times \frac{\text{L}}{2.00 \text{ mols}} = 1.80 \text{ L}$$

On the other hand, if the volumetric flask is filled to the 500-ml mark with 2.65M sodium sulfate, how many moles are present?

$$? \text{ mols} = 0.800 \text{ L} \times \frac{2.65 \text{ mols}}{\text{L}} = 2.12 \text{ mols}$$

✱ At the top of the page, color the KMnO$_4$ powder black; then color the half-prepared solution in the flask in the middle frame purple, then the finished solution in the last frame, light purple.

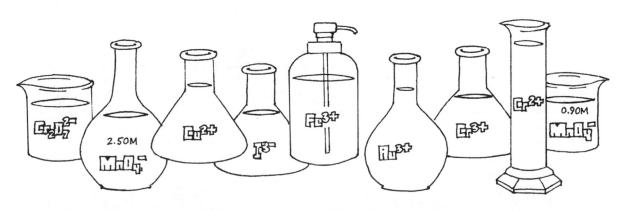

✱ Ionic solutions, especially those with transition-metal ions, are often beautifully colored. Chromium, in fact, comes from the Greek *chroma*, "color." Color the dichromate orange; the copper (II), royal blue; triodide, brown; iron (III), yellow; gold (III), red; chromium (III), green; chromium (II), light blue. The concentrated and dilute permanganate solutions are the same as above.

6.5 Molality

$$m = \frac{\text{mols solute}}{\text{kg solvent}}$$

Your first chemistry course may or may not include a short descriptive unit on *colligative properties*, but you will be hearing about them sooner or later.

They are that set of physical properties—such as the freezing and boiling points of solutions—that vary with the ratio of solute to solvent.

Sea water, for instance, is mainly an impure solution of sodium chloride. It has a lower freezing point than would a more lightly saline solution (with its lower proportion of solute), which would in turn have a freezing point still lower that of pure water; this is why icebergs, though adrift in (and arising from) saltwater oceans are made up of fresh water.

There must be a way, then, to express the concentration of a solute in a solution as a ratio to its solvent; for as the solute-to-solvent ratio changes, so also do the *physical* properties of the solution. There is such a concentration expression, and it is called *molality*. It is different in function from molarity, which is more concerned with *chemical* properties, which are more or less manifest in proportion to the degree of solute.

Now the *molal solute*, like the molar one, is given in grams, so we must include a molar conversion factor in the calculations. The solvent, too, will often be in grams (so, as before, mentally convert to kilograms before you even write it down). You can see, then, that molality is a weight-to-weight relation, for both dimensions—moles and kilograms—represent grams. An example: what molality results if 8.00 grams of fructose (162.1 g/mol) are dissolved in 0.300 kilos of water?

$$m = \frac{8.00 \text{ g C}_6\text{H}_{10}\text{O}_5}{0.300 \text{ kg H}_2\text{O}} \quad \text{x} \quad \frac{\text{mol C}_6\text{H}_{10}\text{O}_5}{162.1 \text{ g C}_6\text{H}_{10}\text{O}_5} = 0.165$$

Does this look familiar? It should. Determining molality is no harder than determining molarity. If you can do the dimensional analysis of one, you can do that of the other, provided that you remember to substitute "kg(*solvent*)" for "L(*solution*)" in the denominator (Note: an unlabeled solvent is understood to be water).

Known molalities, like known molarities, can be used as a conversion factor. With them, we can determine the (wanted) weight of solvent needed to obtain a solution with the desired molality. Or, for that matter, we can determine how much solvent is needed for a given quantity of solute. In all, it takes less time to perform such a calculation than it does to describe it. It is advisable, by the way, to label the solvent in molal expressions.

Let us look at an example: suppose that you must make a 0.400m (the conversion factor) solution using 438 grams of water (the given) with an unknown weight of barium nitrate (the wanted). How much of the salt (261.5 g/mol) is needed?

$$? \text{ grams Ba(NO}_3)_2 = 0.438 \text{ kg H}_2\text{O} \times \frac{0.400 \text{ mol}}{\text{kg H}_2\text{O}} \quad \text{x} \quad \frac{261.5 \text{ g Ba(NO}_3)_2}{\text{mol Ba(NO}_3)_2} = 45.8 \text{ g Ba(NO}_3)_2$$

This type of calculation resembles in every respect its molar counterpart at the bottom of p. 214 except that (again) the denominator of the molal relation is different from that of the molar one. In any case, each is a very simple DA exercise made up of a question, a keystone (M or m), and a molar conversion factor.

1. Match the terms to their definitions:

a. The molar concentration of formula units in a truly ionic solution; also, the adversity between politicians and journalists in most countries.

b. The solution expression concerning equivalents, an equivalent being the amount of a substance that (e.g.) releases a mole of protons in solution.

_____molality

_____formality

c. The quantitative relation between the moles of solute and the volume of solution.

_____morality

d. According to Lewis (C.S., not G.N.), an unwritten Code of law that is universally understood and disobeyed, even by those unfamiliar with its Author.

_____molarity

e. The quantitative relation between the weight of a solution's solvent and the moles of its solute; used when a solution's colligative properties are being considered.

_____normality

(Note: expressions such as "2.40M Na_2SO_4 solution" are redundant and so you will see less of them beyond this problem set. The concentration designation (M, m, etc.) alone indicates an aqueous solution.)

2. If a chunk of cadmium displaces 6.17 cm^3 and weighs 49.0 grams, determine its density (but first, estimate it):

3. What is the density of 48.0 grams of carbon monoxide at standard temperature and pressure (Chaps. 1 and 5)?.

4. What is the molarity of 950 milliliters of a solution containing 90.5 grams of lithium bromide solute (hint: you must have, here and elsewhere in this problem set, molecular weight)?

5. Calculate the molality (m) of a solution made from the dissolution of 83.2 grams of ammonium sulfate in 0.600 kilograms of water:

6. How many grams of the salt iron (II) nitrate are needed to prepare exactly one liter of 3.75M solution?

7. What weight of cobalt (II) chlorate must be dissolved in 1950 grams of water in order to obtain a 750m solution?

8. What is the formality of 450 milliliters of solution containing 31.9 grams of zinc fluoride (which, as with about half of the common fluoride salts, is water-soluble)?

9. How many pounds of sodium hydroxide are required for the preparation of 800 gallons of 2.50m basic solution (gal = 3.79 L; lb = 454 g)?

10. After doing a stoichiometric calculation, you find that you need 1.25 grams of nitric acid (63.08 g/mol) to fully react with another dissolved reactant. How many liters (or milliliters) of 0.700M HNO_3 solution must you use?

11. How many grams of undiluted HNO_3 are dissolved in 16.0 liters of the 0.700M solution mentioned in the foregoing problem?

12. After pulling an A in Chem 1, you get a part-time job as a lab assistant. Your first task is to make 1.40m $KClO_3$ solution. How many grams of salt will you dissolve in 20.0 liters of water?

6.6 Solution Stoichiometry

$\mathcal{S}$toichiometry, to repeat, is a DA process that joins one substance involved in a reaction to another through a keystone (which is still just a conversion factor made by taking a simple whole-number ratio from the balanced equation). In the stoichiometry of solutions, one or both of the substances is in the (aq) state.

In some stoichiometric calculations, such as with two reacting gases at the same T and P, only the keystone in needed. The rest of the time, we just stick on conversion factors until the given dimension and substance become the wanted dimension and substance. The conversions interlock like the pieces of a jigsaw puzzle, yet a stoichiometric jigsaw is only one-dimensional, or linear, and with seldom more than six or seven pieces.

Often, the given in a stoichiometry problem will be a volume of solution at a given molarity. The wanted species will be (1) a solid, (2) a gas, or (3) another solution; therefore, the wanted dimension will be grams, liters, or milliliters at a certain molarity, respectively. Now and then, a gas or a solid may also be the given; but, more often than not, a molar solution will be the given or both the wanted *and* the given. Must you remember all this at once? No. By learning how to use the molarity conversion factor, or M (Sect. 6.4), you will be able to do all this without too much thought.

Now, an example: how many grams, if any, of lead (II) chromate will precipitate if an excess of lead (II) nitrate solution is added to (reacted with) 250 milliliters of 2.00M ammonium chromate? The molarity of the $Pb(NO_3)_2$ solution does not matter, for it is in excess in much the same way as all the other stoichiometry problems you have done in which only one reactant was quantified. In answer to the question implied by "if any", we ask ourselves if $PbCrO_4$ is insoluble. The solubility rules say yes, so a precipitate (entailing grams as the wanted dimension) will form (note the state designations):

$$Pb(NO_3)_2(aq) + (NH_4)_2CrO_4(aq) \rightarrow PbCrO_4(s) + 2NH_4NO_3(aq)$$

? grams $PbCrO_4$ = 0.250 L $(NH_4)_2CrO_4$(aq) $\quad \times \quad \dfrac{2.00 \text{ mols } (NH_4)_2CrO_4}{\text{L } (NH_4)_2CrO_4(aq)} \quad \times \quad \dfrac{\text{mol } PbCrO_4}{\text{mol } (NH_4)_2CrO_4}$

$\times \quad \dfrac{323.2 \text{ g } PbCrO_4}{\text{mol } PbCrO_4} \quad = \quad 162 \text{ g}$

While the length of the formulae and the obligatory "(aq)" make the above bridge look long, it is really pretty much a bread-and-butter stoichiometric calculation. The one real danger is in the labeling, which you must do, and do carefully, because there are in effect three substances in the above bridge and the formulae for two of them still look very much alike: the aqueous and undissolved states of ammonium chromate. You must go from the former to the latter before you can write in the keystone, and this is what molarity, as a conversion factor, does for you. One common way to label them is "$(NH_4)_2CrO_4$ (solute)" and "$(NH_4)_2CrO_4$(sol'n)," but these look too much alike to your author, who prefers to label only the solution, and that with just "(aq)."

In some reactions between solutions, gases form. If the reaction is sufficiently exothermic, a notable quantity of vapor evolves, although this is a physical, rather than a chemical, formation of gas. An example of a chemical formation of gas follows.

If pulverized aluminum is placed in a potassium hydroxide solution, hydrogen is liberated. How many liters of 4.70M KOH solution will be needed to collect 8.00 liters of the gas at STP?

$$2Al(s) + 6KOH(aq) \rightarrow 2K_3AlO_3(aq) + 3H_2(g)$$

$$\text{? liters KOH(aq)} = 8.00 \text{ L } H_2 \times \frac{\text{mol } H_2}{22.4 \text{ L } H_2} \times \frac{6 \text{ mols KOH}}{3 \text{ mols } H_2} \times \frac{\text{L KOH(aq)}}{4.70 \text{ mols KOH}} = 0.152 \text{ L KOH(aq)}$$

You probably recognized the first conversion factor right off: it is our old friend, the molar volume conversion factor (Sect. 5.9). It is present because a gas is involved, and gases, you may recall, are quantified by volume. Note its similarity to the molarity conversion factor on the other side of the keystone: both have L and mol for dimensions. Then note the similarity of the entire calculation to the "basic" stoichiometry bridge that you have been using since Chap. 4. Change L to g, and there is no other difference whatsoever; if you can do one, you can already do the other.

So solution stoichiometry, like other stoichiometries, at worst becomes only lengthier (not harder) with the addition of other conversion factors for things such as nonmetric units or impurities and percentages, or of P and T adjustments. Say, for instance, that in the above example that the wanted and the given were in gallons with the gas was at 784 torr and 27°C. The same calculation as above would look like this:

$$\text{? gallons KOH(aq)} = 2.11 \text{ gals } H_2 \quad \times \quad \frac{3.79 \text{ L } H_2}{\text{gal } H_2} \times \frac{\text{mol } H_2}{22.4 \text{ L } H_2} \times \frac{6 \text{ mols KOH}}{3 \text{ mols } H_2}$$

$$\times \frac{\text{L KOH(aq)}}{4.70 \text{ mols KOH}} \times \frac{\text{gal KOH (aq)}}{3.79 \text{ L KOH(aq)}} \times \frac{273 \text{ K}}{300 \text{ K}} \times \frac{784 \text{ torr}}{760 \text{ torr}} = 0.0376 \ (3.76 \times 10^{-2}) \text{ gals KOH(aq)}$$

And now we will look at the stoichiometric relation between two solutions, the simplest of all. Here is an example: how much 6.50M sodium hydroxide solution will be used to fully precipitate the iron from 400 milliliters of 2.40M iron (III) sulfate solution as iron (III) hydroxide in a new solution of sodium sulfate?

$$6NaOH(aq) + Fe_2(SO_4)_3(aq) \rightarrow 2Fe(OH)_3(s) + 3Na_2SO_4(aq)$$

$$\text{? liters NaOH (aq)} = 0.400 \text{ L } Fe_2(SO_4)_3(aq) \times \frac{2.40 \text{ mols } Fe_2(SO_4)_3}{\text{L } 2.40 \ Fe_2(SO_4)_3 \text{ (aq)}} \times \frac{6 \text{ mols NaOH}}{\text{mol } Fe_2(SO_4)_3} \times \frac{\text{L NaOH(aq)}}{6.50 \text{ mols NaOH}}$$

$$= 0.886 \text{ L NaOH(aq)}$$

1. e   a   d   c   b

2. $\dfrac{49.0 \text{ g}}{6.17 \text{ cm}^3} = 7.94 \text{ g/cm}^3$

3. $\dfrac{28.01 \text{ g}}{22.4 \text{ L}} = 1.25 \text{ g/L}$

4. $\dfrac{90.5 \text{ g LiBr}}{0.950 \text{ L}} \times \dfrac{\text{mol LiBr}}{86.85 \text{ g LiBr}} = 1.10\text{M}$

5. $\text{m} = \dfrac{83.2 \text{ g (NH}_4)_2\text{SO}_4}{0.600 \text{ kg}} \times \dfrac{\text{mol (NH}_4)_2\text{SO}_4}{132.3 \text{ g (NH}_4)_2\text{SO}_4} = 1.05\text{m}$

6. $? \text{ grams Fe(NO}_3)_3 = 1.00 \text{ L} \times \dfrac{3.75 \text{ mols Fe(NO}_3)_3}{\text{L}} \times \dfrac{242.0 \text{ g Fe(NO}_3)_3}{\text{mol Fe(NO}_3)_3} = 908 \text{ g Fe(NO}_3)_3$

7. $? \text{ grams Co(ClO}_3)_2 = 1.95 \text{ kg H2O} \times \dfrac{0.750 \text{ mol Co(ClO}_3)_2}{\text{kg H}_2\text{O}} \times \dfrac{225.8 \text{ g Co(ClO}_3)_2}{\text{mol Co(ClO}_3)_2}$

$= 330 \text{ g Co(ClO}_3)_2$

8. $\text{F} = \dfrac{31.9 \text{ g ZnF}_2}{0.450 \text{ L}} \times \dfrac{\text{mol ZnF}_2}{103.4 \text{ g ZnF}_2} = 0.686\text{F}$

9. $? \text{ pounds NaOH} = 800 \text{ gals} \times \dfrac{3.79 \text{ L}}{\text{gal}} \times \dfrac{2.50 \text{ mols NaOH}}{\text{L}} \times \dfrac{40.00 \text{ g NaOH}}{\text{mol NaOH}} \times \dfrac{\text{lb NaOH}}{454 \text{ g NaOH}}$

$= 668 \text{ lbs NaOH}$

10. $? \text{ liters} = 1.25 \text{ grams HNO}_3 \times \dfrac{\text{mol HNO}_3}{63.08 \text{ g HNO}_3} \times \dfrac{\text{L}}{0.700 \text{ mol HNO}_3} = 2.83 \times 10^{-2} \text{ L}$ (28.3 ml)

11. $? \text{ grams HNO}_3 = 16.0 \text{ L} \times \dfrac{0.700 \text{ mol HNO}_3}{\text{L}} \times \dfrac{63.08 \text{ g HNO}_3}{\text{mol HNO}_3} = 706 \text{ g HNO}_3$

12. $? \text{ grams KClO}_3 = 20.0 \text{ kg H}_2\text{O} \times \dfrac{1.40 \text{ mols KClO}_3}{\text{kg H}_2\text{O}} \times \dfrac{122.6 \text{ g KClO}_3}{\text{mol KClO}_3} = 3.43 \times 10^3 \text{ g KClO}_3$

6.7 Titrations

Quantitative analysis is that branch of chemistry concerned with finding out how much of something is in something else. To make a determination of this sort for aqueous solutions, the titration is the main tool.

At times, we have solutions of unknown concentration, though we know their chemical identity. Some solution concentrations, for instance, do not remain constant over time, and so must be *standardized,* that is, their molarities must be determined or redetermined. To do this, *we take a little bit of it and react it with another solution of known molarity, to see how much of the latter reacts fully with the former.*

As we know how much of the testing solution—that with the known molarity—we used to chemically use up the reactant in the solution of unknown molarity, we have a given with which to start a stoichiometric bridge that will end in the wanted, unknown molarity.

This procedure is a *titration.* The given, titrating substance which we add to the other is the *titrant.* And the thing that tells us that the solution being tested is fully reacted, or that it has reached the *equivalence point,* is the *indicator.*

The indicator is so-called because it will visibly or physically do something to let us know when to *stop adding* the titrant and *begin measuring* it. Most of the the time, the indicator will be a few drops of some chemical that we add to the unknown solution before the titration that, when its time comes, will produce color, or a precipitate, etc. Or the indicator may be a gauge or a lightbulb showing that the solution is suddenly able to conduct electricity. In the first case—the color-or-precipitate one—when the dissolved chemical in the unknown solution is wholly used up, it becomes the indicator's turn to react with the titrant. But we do not allow this; instead, we make a note of how much titrant was used and go straight to our calculation.

There are two main types of titration calculations. One is that corresponding to a *standardization,* or a wanted M (mols/liter). The other is that which only seeks a wanted quantity with a single dimension (e.g., grams of solute in the tested solution). Here is an example of the latter: how many grams of lithium hydroxide are dissolved in solution if 19.6 milliliters of 5.27M sulfuric acid are needed to reach the equivalence point (in this case by neutralizing all of the LiOH)?

$$2LiOH(aq) + H_2SO_4(aq) \rightarrow Li_2SO_4(aq) + 2HOH(l)$$

$$? \text{ g LiOH} = 0.0196 \text{ L titrant} \times \frac{5.27 \text{ mols } H_2SO_4}{\text{L titrant}} \times \frac{2 \text{ mols LiOH}}{\text{mol } H_2SO_4} \times \frac{23.95 \text{ g LiOH}}{\text{mol LiOH}} = 4.95 \text{ g LiOH}$$

The foregoing example was pure stoichiometry, just as it would be if a volume of solution, rather than a weight of solute, were wanted.

The calculation for a standardization, however, is not pure stoichiometry and is tricky, if only slightly, because the last conversion factor—that following the keystone—is *not* joined to the rest of the dimensional analysis bridge with a "polar" dimension. You must be alert to and conscious of this.

Constructing the calculation up through the keystone needs no explanation; but after that a little thinking is required. For example, let us say that we have some sodium chloride solution to be standardized. We take exactly 50.0 ml and add a few drops of a dissolved chromate for an indicator. Then we begin the titration with 4.28M silver nitrate solution. As the the titrant is "tightly-rationed" (precisely metered) into the other solution, white silver chloride precipitates as the NaCl is used up, then suddenly red silver chromate appears, indicating—for that is its job—that the equivalence point has been reached.

Now, to an example based on these conditions: if 47.1 milliliters of titrant are used, what is the molarity?

$$AgNO_3(aq) + NaCl(aq) \rightarrow AgCl(s) + NaNO_3(aq)$$

$$M = 0.0471 \quad \times \quad \frac{4.28 \text{ mols AgNO}_3}{L} \quad \times \quad \frac{\text{mol NaCl}}{\text{mol AgNO}_3} \quad \times \quad \frac{1}{0.0500 \text{ L NaCl(aq)}} = 4.03M$$

This calculation was stoichiometry as usual through the keytsone; getting to that point at least gives you the correct number of moles in the unknown solution. But the wanted is moles (of solute) over liter (of solution), not *just* moles. Remembering this, you will think to use the volume as a divisor—as seen in the last step—and your bridge will be done.

Here is another way to look at it. Since you will not be able (as in other stoichiometric constructions) to connect the last puzzle piece to the keystone with a dimension, link it up instead with the *substance*, which will be found in the only relevant quantity remaining in the problem (in the above case, 500 ml NaCl). You must, afterall, account for it in the calculation, and using it as above is how. It may be even easier, once you have the moles of solute, to just peck that into your calculator and divide it by the liters of solution. You can do this provided you are thinking about the meaning of molarity in the same moment. In any case, a little practice complemented by some lab work will make you all but infallible. Standardizing solutions is not hard.

Changing the subject a little, let us consider what it was, exactly, that took place at the *particle* level during the "tightration" described above.

The process exposed many different types of ions to each other, all swimming about freely. Two of them, sodium ion and nitrate, form no insoluble compounds (at least not here), and so they sit the action out as *spectator ions*. Silver ion, from the titrant, forms insoluble silver chloride until the Cl⁻ is all gone. In this way—by reacting up to the limit of its presence—Cl⁻ signals its own and sodium ion's concentration (and thus, that of NaCl).

At that juncture—the equivalence point—the chromate ions from the indicator (which have been waiting for the chloride to use itself up) kick in and start precipitating out as a second insoluble salt. The chromate, you might say, is unable to compete with chloride in the silver-ion grabbing sweepstakes.

Thus CrO_4^{2-}, while a "weaker" reactant in this sense than Cl⁻, has a much more dramatic flourish, both by precipitating and by producing a bold color.

⊛ Color the Ag_2CrO_4 unit (last frame) red (Note: CrO_4^{2-} is in reality polygamous with Ag^+, but you get the idea).

223

13
Al
26.981

℘rofile: Aluminum

Airplanes are vast samples of impure aluminum.

Though it is by far the most abundant metal, aluminum was elementally unknown until its isolation in 1825 by the Dane Oersted (who is better known for discovering the magnetic effect of electric current). For decades following its discovery aluminum was considered a precious metal. What is now the stuff of beer can pop tabs was once forged into recherché jewelry.

Although minerals with aluminum—granites, feldspars, micah, etc.—are common, it was and still is comparatively costly to remove this somewhat reactive metal from its ores. In the Hall Process, the oxide alumina (Al_2O_3) is separated from silicates and other impurities present with it in the ore (bauxite) and electrolyzed in molten cryolite, which is itself an aluminum-containing mineral. Extraction from nearly every other source is not commercially feasible with current technology.

Aluminum is still precious, but for its versatility rather than its false rarity. With a density one third that of iron, it is the metal (in alloyed form) employed in the construction of aircraft. It is also light, malleable, and conductive enough to be the medium of choice for long-distance power transmissions.

Iron corrodes, as you know, because the hydrate that forms from it (rust) falls away, whereas aluminum protectively coats itself with the same very inert oxide that so strongly resists metallurgical decomposition. Iron, of course, is somewhat stronger. Nevertheless, despite the trade-offs, the two are rivals in many familiar applications. Pots and pans, of course, can be either. Most automobiles have cast-iron engine blocks and aluminum cylinder heads (which dissipate heat more efficiently than iron

ones). Some car marques such as Subaru, Alfa Romeo, and the older Volkswagens and Porsches have all-aluminum engines.

Aluminum, silicon, and oxygen are oligopolic in their share of the Earth's crust, and their many compounds form the bulk of materials in ceramics, porcelains, bricks, slates, and other clay-derivatives (clay being extra-fine sand containing aluminum-bearing minerals).

They are also the stuff of sublimer things. Many gemstones contain all three of these elements, and some of the most familiar gems (see below) are nothing more than crystalline Al_2O_3 colored with impurities of transition-metal ions.

Aluminum does not naturally form part of living tissues and has traditionally been classed as moderately toxic. Of late, however, it is suspected of having a role in Alzheimer's disease. A causality is suggested by aluminum salt concentrations in the most affected area of the patient's brain. Aluminum compounds presumably enter the body by way of topical and oral medications, and through deodorants, most of which contain them.

The sibling element boron is a brittle black solid that resembles its periodic neighbor, carbon, at least a much as its familial one, aluminum. It is a metalloid whose properties lean heavily toward the nonmetals. An important mineral is Borax, a hydrate of sodium borate. It is quarried in Nevada and used as an antiseptic, a water softener, and a fixer for enamels and solders.

Gallium, indium, and thallium are all rather soft metals that melt at low temperatures.

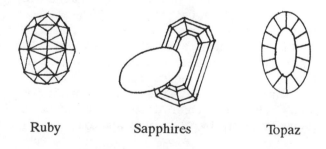

Ruby   Sapphires   Topaz

⊛ Color the topaz yellow-orange or amber; the ruby, red; and the sapphires, one brown and one blue.

224

1. Match:

a. the carefully metered addition of a substance (usually a solution) to determine the concentration of a solution

b. can be a wanted or a given quantity, or a conversion factor

_____spectator

c. a reactant (usually) that does not begin to react until another reactant becomes completely absent from the solution

_____titrant

_____molarity

d. a species that remains in solution, not reacting in it

_____standardization

e. the whole point, or purpose, of doing (a) above

_____titration

f. a solution with a known molarity (or other reactant) that tells us the M of another solution by reacting with it

_____equivalence point

_____indicator

g. the measurement taken between the reactions of (c) and (f)

In problems 2 through 9, you must balance the given equation before doing anything else.

2. What volume of 1.15M HCl solution will be needed to react completely with 218 grams of calcium oxide?

$$HCl(aq) + CaO(s) \rightarrow CaCl_2(aq) + H_2O(l)$$

3. How many grams of barium sulfate will precipitate from the reaction of 3.00 liters of 7.48M barium chlorate solution with excess dissolved potassium sulfate?

$$Ba(ClO_3)_2(aq) + K_2SO_4(aq) \rightarrow KClO_3(aq) + BaSO_4(s)$$

4. If 600 milliliters of 2.20M sulfuric acid solution is reacted with excess elemental aluminum, what volume of hydrogen, at standard temperature and pressure, will evolve?

$$Al(s) + H_2SO_4(aq) \rightarrow Al_2(SO_4)_3(aq) + H_2(g)$$

5. How many gallons of 1.32M silver nitrate solution will cause all of the phosphate ions in 850 milliliters of 2.59M potassium phosphate solution to precipitate out as insoluble salt?

$$AgNO_3(aq) + K_3PO_4(aq) \rightarrow KNO_3(aq) + Ag_3PO_4(s)$$

6. How much 3.54M magnesium iodide solution, as titrant, is needed to reach the equivalence point with 80.0 milliliters of 1.65M ammonium carbonate solution?

$$MgI_2(aq) + (NH_4)_2CO_3(aq) \rightarrow MgCO_3(s) + NH_4I(aq)$$

7. What weight of mercury (II) sulfate will precipitate if a sample of sodium sulfate solution is fully titrated with 7.67 milliliters of 1.95M mercury (II) nitrate solution?

$$Hg(NO_3)_2(aq) + Na_2SO_4(aq) \rightarrow NaNO_3(aq) + HgSO_4(s)$$

8. Standardize a calcium hydroxide solution for which 40.0 milliliters is fully neutralized with 5.6 milliliters of 4.70M phosphoric acid titrant.

$$H_3PO_4(aq) + Ca(OH)_2(aq) \rightarrow Ca_3(PO_4)_2(s) + H_2O(l)$$

9. If it takes 308 milliliters of 2.95M sodium hydrogen carbonate solution (Na+ and HCO⁻ ions) to titrate a 600-milliliter sample of sulfuric acid solution, what is the concentration, in moles per liter, of the acid?

$$NaHCO_3(aq) + H_2SO_4(aq) \rightarrow Na_2SO_4(aq) + H_2O(l) + CO_2(g)$$

(The answers to this problem set are on p. 234)

6.8 Electrolytes

SOME SOLIDS IONIZE IN WATER AND OTHERS DISSOLVE IN IT. WHAT'S THE DIFFERENCE?

ALL THAT IONIZE, DISSOLVE; BUT NOT ALL THAT DISSOLVE IONIZE.

ionizes
dissolves
is solid

Many solids, as you know, are insoluble in water. Others are soluble and, among these, some go a step further and become ions by reacting in their water solvent. These ions may or may not then form ionic hydrates and compounds with the water itself.

Compounds that merely dissolve are covalent. Their crystals dissolve into neutral molecules and nothing more (although they, too, can form hydrates, such as rock candy). As a consequence, a solution of table sugar—which is covalent—is nonelectrolytic; it cannot conduct electricity.

Some covalent compounds, however, and all soluble ionic ones, do break into ions in solution, and their solutions are therefore *electrolytic*. Table salt crystals break into sodium cations and chloride anions (as if you didn't know!). Unlike sugar molecules, they and other salt-forming ions, because they are charged, can carry a current of electricity in solution. It is often said that lightening is "attracted" to water; in fact, it seeks the ions of dissolved salts in the water.

Dissolution, then, is only physical change; but ionization (of which we are now speaking) is both physical (because it entails dissolution) *and* chemical (because new chemical species, in this case ions, are formed).

Electrolytes are those substances which, when dissolved, result in solutions of ions rather than of molecules. Knowing which substances are electrolytic, then, is the key to understanding the chemistry of ionic solutions and predicting their reactions. Think about it.

As with solubility and insolubility, there are gra- dations of difference between electrolytes and nonelectrolytes. You know that many insoluble compounds are in fact slightly soluble. Likewise, many nonelectrolytes are in fact slightly electrolytic. There are even the synonyms "strong electrolyte" for electrolyte and "weak electrolyte" for slightly electrolytic substances. Most of the time, though, we can be satisfied at this level with the subsumation of weak electrolytes— even though they *do* exist—into the category of nonelectrolytes. The truly strong ones we will simply call "electrolytes."

As there are solubility rules, so also are there electrolytic rules; but they are few and can be listed (rather than tabulated).

Electrolyte Rules

I
All common soluble salts are electrolytes.*

II
So are all strong acids.

III
So are all strong bases.

IV
All other compounds are more or less nonelectrolytic. Some—the weak electrolytes—yield a few ions along with their molecules when dissolved in water, but the rest yield only molecules.

*[Exceptions: $Pb(C_2H_3O_2)_2$ and $HgCl_2$]

THERE ARE TENS OF THOUSANDS OF ACIDS ALONE; SOME ARE STRONG, SOME ARE WEAK!

GULP!

?

How much have you learned, by now, of the solution rules from Sect. 6.2?

They have a great deal to do with the electrolyte rules on p. 227.

Consider the first rule: "All soluble salts..." If you know which salts dissolve, you know which (with very few exceptions) are electrolytes.

Skip the second rule for now, and go on to the third: "...all strong bases are electrolytes." These bases are the same as the soluble hydroxides shown in the chart of solubilities. They are—including those not shown—all of the Family 1A hydroxides and some of the family 2A hydroxides.

The fourth rule conveniently excludes everything else from under the electrolyte heading: sugars, insoluble salts, weak acids and bases, metals, gases, organic compounds, etc. are not electrolytes.

And finally—the second rule—there are the strong acids. Almost all of the many thousands of known acids are weak, and we may consider them nonelectrolytes. A great many are, of course, soluble in water, but this solubility is really mere miscibility. No more than seven or eight of them—and the same number of bases—ionize to a significant degree in water. A half-dozen of each are worth learning right away; the remainder are rare or less than fully electrolytic.

There are multiple definitions of acids and bases, and we will get to these in Chap. 9. For now, however, it is enough to say that acids are covalent compounds that, when ionized in aqueous solutions or elsewhere, yield anions—such as Cl^- or $S_2O_3^{2-}$ or CN^- or PO_4^{3-}—and one or more protons (H^+). A strong acid is one that undergoes this change readily and fully or very nearly fully in water, whereas a weak acid remains wholly or largely molecular in water.

A strong base, by parallel definition, is one that readily breaks into metal cations—such as K^+ or Sr^{2+} or Li^+—and hydroxide anions (OH^-). Strong bases are alternatively called alkalis—hence the naming of the two metallic families that furnish these ions.

Strong Acids		Strong Bases	
HCl	HNO_3	LiOH	$Ca(OH)_2$
HBr	H_2SO_4	NaOH	$Sr(OH)_2$
HI	$HClO_4$	KOH	$Ba(OH)_2$

Learn the strong acids by mnemonic cluster: hydrohalogens (HCl, HBr, HI) and the oxyanions; the strong bases are the hydroxides from the alkali metals and those alkaline earths with STRong BAsic CApability).

Do not confuse an acid's or a base's strength with its "meanness" or its reactivity in general. True, these special compounds are quite dangerous to handle (plunge your hand into a beaker of concentrated sulfuric acid—which is only the weakest of these acids—and you will convert it in very short order to a charred black mass). Many other acids, however weak they may be by the above definition, are also dangerous and reactive for other reasons, such as their oxidizing power or their behavior in the presence of substances other than water. Weak hydrocyanic acid is the ether of the gas chamber.

One more thing. The properties associated with these compounds have to do only with their aqueous state. When not dissolved, the hydrohalogens are gases; the other acids are liquids; and the hydroxides are solids. They are thus not only chemically different from their aqueous states, but physically different to boot.

228

6.9 Net Ionic Equations

A salt dissolved in water is less a compound than it is a broth of ions. Consider the following equation:

$$Ba(NO_3)_2(aq) + Na_2SO_4(aq) \rightarrow BaSO_4(s) + 2NaNO_3(aq)$$

This is the reaction of two soluble salts to form the insoluble salt barium sulfate. The other product indicated by the equation, however, does not really form; only its ingredients, so to speak, are present. If we were to remove all the water, we would indeed have some true compound—anhydrous sodium nitrate. Adding back a little water, in varying proportions, would give us the hydrates of this salt. In either case—anhydrous or hydrated—we would have crystals held together by the opposite charges of the ions. But if we add a lot of water, the salt would redissolve into ions.

The two reactants in the equation, being electrolytes, also ionize and do not remain whole compounds in solution. Of the four, then, only $BaSO_4(s)$ is a meaningful expression of a compound. $NaNO_3(aq)$ does not really mean "sodium nitrate"—for *that* is expressed by $NaNO_3(s)$—but rather "water containing Na^+ and NO_3^- ions in the ratio of their source, $NaNO_3(s)$." (Read this again.) The equation can therefore be written as an *ionic equation*:

$$Ba^{2+} + 2NO_3^- + 2Na^+ + SO_4^{2-} \rightarrow BaSO_4\downarrow + 2Na^+ + NO_3^-$$

The ionic equation takes longer to write and is visually sloppy compared to a standard equation, such as the first one, above. It is expedient to use the standard equation for most purposes, with the "(aq)" designation being understood as just explained.

Ionic equations, however, are more accurate in showing what actually takes place in an ionic solution. The above example, for instance, says this: that (a) two salts, barium nitrate and sodium sulfate, break into ions in water and **(b) are** mixed up together. As an insoluble combination of two (of the four possible) ions was present, (c) a precipitate forms; that which was left over could not form an insoluble substance, and so (d) remained in solution.

As noted above, the product other than barium sulfate does not really come into existence, although the solution itself is in some sense a product with its own peculiar properties. Rather, it is only that the parts of this would-be product are just floating around. They were present but inactive before, during, and after the reaction of the barium ions with the sulfate; in other words, they were spectator ions for the whole show. With your pencil, cross out the spectator ions, those on both sides of the equation (this is the mark of a spectator), and write what is left in the blanks below, with the uncrossed-out species as they appear in the ionic equation:

$$\underline{\hspace{2cm}} + \underline{\hspace{1.5cm}} \rightarrow \underline{\hspace{2.5cm}}$$

Does the brief equation you wrote at the bottom of the previous page look something like this?

$$Ba^{2+} + SO_4^{2-} \rightarrow BaSO_4\downarrow$$

If it does, then congratulations; you have just successfully written a net ionic equation (cinchy, was it not?). The writing of a complete ionic equation, or a "gross ionic equation," if you will—such as the one from which you took this net ionic equation— provides us with an "inventory" of all that is present in, or on its way out of, a solution. A solution inventory of, say, dissolved sucrose or the very weak boric acid would only be of $C_{12}H_{22}O_{11}$ and H_3BO_3 molecules and nothing more. An inventory of a relatively (but not absolutely) strong acid, such as oxalic acid, would have a measurable quantity of $C_2O_4^2$

(oxalate) and H^+ ions among its $H_2C_2O_4$ molecules. But solutions of electrolytes—unless they are highly concentrated—are largely or exclusively of ions.

By "taking inventory" of a solution, we will know what reaction, if any, is possible, among the dissolved substances. To write a (gross) ionic equation is to take such an inventory; to write a net ionic one is to isolate only the species that have actually reacted or formed in solution. This same principle applies to each of three major classes of reactions that can occur in solution: metathesis, acid/base, and oxidation /reduction. We will examine each in its turn.

The three equations representing the same reaction—that for the precipitation of barium sulfate of the example that started this section— correspond to the three steps we use to write, or arrive at, a net ionic equation for any aqueous ionic reaction.

Writing Net Ionic Equations

STEP ONE Write the **standard** equation.

STEP TWO Write the **gross ionic** equation by breaking the electrolytes' formulae into their component ions; leave the nonelectrolytes as they are, unbroken.

STEP THREE Write the **net ionic** equation by eliminating the spectator ions (those appearing uncombined on both sides); include only what is left over.

Reactions take place in ionic solutions when the ions form an insoluble compound (precipitate) such as $BaSO_4$ or molecular substances (a gas or other nonelectolyte).

Let us now consider the reaction of elemental copper with sulfuric acid, in which hydrogen gas forms:

STANDARD EQUATION: $Cu(s) + H_2SO_4(aq) \rightarrow CuSO_4(aq) + H_2(g)$

GROSS IONIC EQUATION: $Cu + 2H^+ + SO_4^{2-} \rightarrow Cu^{2+} + SO_4^{2-} + H_2$

NET IONIC EQUATION: $Cu + 2H^+ \rightarrow Cu^{2+} + H_2$

This reaction is of the "replacement" type, a kind of oxidation/reduction, in which electrons are transferred from one species to another; in this instance, from copper to hydrogen ion. Sulfate did nothing by remaining the same species, and so was only a spectator.

There are ten or 12 common gases that form in Chem. 1 solutions, but three of them form when a liquid nonelectrolyte is expected. They are CO_2 and SO_2 from the ionization of carbonate and sulfite (not sul*fate*) salts when reacted with strong acids; and NH_3 when ammonium salts are reacted with strong bases. The compounds expected are H_2CO_3, H_2SO_3, and NH_4OH. The trouble is that "carbonic acid" and "ammonium hydroxide" are of very dubitable existence and sulfurous acid is so short-lived and unstable that it can be classed likewise.

These three nonspecies must be known so that when you begin to write entire equations from only the reactants—that is, to predict reactions—you will not allow these three stooges into your equations.

Here is an example, both of a prediction and of the writing of a net ionic equation in which or three gases just discussed makes an appearance: give the net ionic equation for the reaction of lithium sulfite and nitric acid:

STANDARD EQUATION: $Li_2SO_3(a) + 2HNO_3(aq) \rightarrow 2LiNO_3(aq) + H_2O(l) + SO_2(g)$

GROSS IONIC EQUATION: $2Li^+ + SO_3^{2-} + 2H^+ + 2NO_3^- \rightarrow 2Li^+ + 2NO_3^- + H_2O(l) + SO_2(g)$

NET IONIC EQUATION: $SO_3^{2-} + 2H^+ \rightarrow H_2O + SO_2$

The wrong standard equation would be "$Li_2SO_3 + 2HNO_3 \rightarrow 2KNO_3 + H_2SO_3$." The new salt, whether aqueous or precipitated, can always be predicted in such a reaction; but the nonspecies is divvied into water and a gas.

Neutralization reactions (which belong in the acid/base category) also yield water and a salt (but no gas). The salt may or may not be soluble, but water is always produced, and water, importantly, is a molecular, nonelectrolytic species.

Here is an example of a neutralization: write the net ionic equation for the reaction of hydroiodic acid with potassium hydroxide:

STANDARD EQUATION:

$HI(aq) + KOH(aq) \rightarrow KI(aq) + HOH(l)$

GROSS IONIC EQUATION:

$H^+ + I^- + K^+ + OH^- \rightarrow K^+ + I^- + HOH$

NET IONC EQUATION:

$H^+ + OH^- \rightarrow HOH$

And here is a neat little bonus for the general chemistry student: the formation of water from hydrogen ion and hydroxide is the net ionic equation for any neutralization between an acid and a base, when one or both of them is strong. Try any of the 36 possible combinations from p. 228 and you will see that this is so. If you recognize such a reaction in a problem, then you have only one step: writing "$H^+ + OH^- \rightarrow HOH$."

To repeat, reactions happen in ionic solutions if the components of a precipitate, a gas, or a liquid nonelectrolyte are made available by the dissolution of the reactants. Water belongs to the last of these three groups. Let us go on to another example of the formation of a molecular liquid: give the net ionic equation for the reaction of the salt ammonium nitrite with the strongest acid of all, perchloric:

STANDARD EQUATION: $NH_4NO_2(aq) + HClO_4(aq) \rightarrow HNO_2(aq) + NH_4ClO_4(aq)$

GROSS IONIC EQUATION: $NH_4^+ + NO_2^- + H^+ + ClO_4^- \rightarrow HNO_2 + NH_4^+ + ClO_4^-$

NET IONIC EQUATION: $NO_2^- + H^+ \rightarrow HNO_2$

Nitrous acid (HNO_2), the net product, is a weak acid and, therefore, molecular in solution. You know this because you identified it as (1) an acid but (2) not as a strong one, because you know—or will soon know—the identities of the only six truly strong acids; therefore, you realized that nitrous acid is not among them (unless, of course, you confused it with nitric acid, HNO_3).

By now, you should have a pretty good feel not only for writing net ionic equations from standard ones, but also for predicting metathesis reactions from a given set of dissolved electrolytes.

The essence of ionic solution activity is this: soluble salts, strong acids, and strong bases—the electrolytes—are the reactants in metathesis and ionic solids, molecular liquids, and gases are the products (although a few covalent solids can also precipitate from ionic solution reactions).

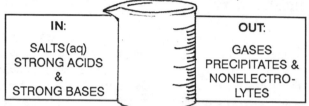

IN:		OUT:
SALTS(aq) STRONG ACIDS & STRONG BASES		GASES PRECIPITATES & NONELECTRO-LYTES

Now let us do a few experiments—those contemplated by the Manchester Quaker to reduce the $Ba(OH)_2$(aq) surplus. Suppose we mix some of it with aluminum sulfate solution. Write the net ionic equation, and use it to predict what will happen. Bypass the standard equation, for when making a prediction you must first have an ionic equation to determine which ions are available. When you know this (from looking at the first half of your gross ionic equation—the given reactants), make what products you can from them and put these on the product side. Then, dump the spectators to get your net ionic equation. As the two ionic equations identify the products, you have your prediction and can thus write a standard equation, in which you will add the state designations and coefficients:

GROSS IONIC EQUATION: $Ba^{2+} + OH^- + Al^{3+} + SO_4^{2-} \rightarrow BaSO_4 + Al(OH)_3$

NET IONIC EQUATION: $Ba^{2+} + OH^- + Al^{3+} + SO_4^{2-} \rightarrow BaSO_4 + Al(OH)_3$

(PREDICTED) STANDARD EQUATION: $3Ba(OH)_2$(aq) $+ Al_2(SO_4)_3$(aq) $+ 3BaSO_4$(s) $+ 2Al(OH)_3$(s)

What is this? The gross and net ionic equations are the same! All the ions reacted, and not one but two insoluble solids precipitated from two soluble ones. No ion spectated, so none of them can be crossed out of the gross equation.

Now, mix some more dissolved barium hydroxide with nickel chlorate. Write the (gross) ionic equation, then cross out the spectators, and predict, by this process of elimination, the product(s):

GROSS IONIC EQUATION: $Ba^{2+} + OH^- + Ni^{2+} + ClO_3^- \rightarrow Ba^{2+} + OH^- + Ni^{2+} + ClO_3^-$

NET IONIC EQUATION: None. All the ions are spectators and so have to be crossed-out.

(PREDICTED) STANDARD EQUATION: Zippo! No reaction takes place; nothing forms.

If the available ions cannot form a product, then no reaction is possible.

A very simple, frequently encountered exercise is the writing of an equation to show the formation of a product from its ions (from any source, but none in particular) with a net ionic equation. It is only a matter of writing the ions on one side and the product on the other.

Consider, as examples, the formation of (a) magnesium hydroxide, (b) calcium phosphate, and (c) hydrogen cyanide gas (dissolved HCN acid).

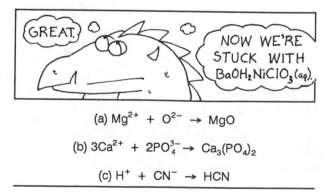

(a) $Mg^{2+} + O^{2-} \rightarrow MgO$

(b) $3Ca^{2+} + 2PO_4^{3-} \rightarrow Ca_3(PO_4)_2$

(c) $H^+ + CN^- \rightarrow HCN$

6.10 Predictions I: Metathesis

Metathesis, a word of Greek derivation ("place beyond"), is the name of the first major category of solution reactions that we have studied. They were introduced back in Sect. 4.2 as exchange, or double-replacement reactions.

Metathesis Reaction

$$AB + CD \rightarrow AC + BD$$

Most of the examples we examined in Sect. 6.9 were of this type. They are easy to predict and, with a few exceptions, conform fully to the "changing partners" pattern shown above. In the laboratory, metathesis reactions are performed by adding a soluble compound to a solution or by mixing two solutions.

Like other solution reactions involving ions, they can only happen if (1) ions from both sources are mutually accessible and (2) combinations of them are present which can form a gas, an insoluble solid, or a nonelectrolyte that remains in solution, miscible with the solvent. If you know the ions (Sects. 2.6 and 2.7) and the solubility and electrolyte rules (Sect. 6.2 and 6.8), you can predict metathesis reactions.

This is done by first writing a full (or "gross") ionic equation: "mentally ionizing" the reactants given in the problem and, from them, writing a product after them. *Do not worry about coefficients in ionic equations*; the purpose of such equations is to show what, if anything, is produced. Balance instead the standard equation that you will write from it later on.

Here is an example. Predict the products, if any, of the reaction of lead (II) acetate solution and hydrochloric acid. Write a balanced standard equation:

IONIC EQUATION: $\qquad Pb^{2+} + C_2H_3O_2^- + H^+ + Cl^- \rightarrow PbCl_2\downarrow + HC_2H_3O_2$

STANDARD EQUATION: $\qquad Pb(C_2H_3O_2)_2(aq) + 2HCl(aq) \rightarrow PbCl_2(s) + 2HC_2H_3O_2$

In this example, the net and gross ionic equations were the same, for there are no spectator species; lead (II) chloride is insoluble and acetic acid is a liquid, a molecular compound, and a weak electrolyte.

The few exceptions to the basic metathesis pattern deviate only slightly from it. They were mentioned on pp. 230-31: carbonates and sulfites with a strong acid, or ammonium salts with a hydroxide solution, all yield (1) another compound, (2) water, and (3) a gas. The key is to recognize the three bogus compounds (H_2CO_3, H_2SO_3, and NH_4OH) and, when they appear in the predictions, to do this: subtract a water molecule from the "molecule" of the nonspecies and the gas molecule will be left over (e.g., $H_2CO_3 - H_2O = CO_2$).

The problem at the top of p. 231 was an example of one of these slightly weird metathesis reactions. Here is another one, in problem form: what will happen if ammonium phosphate—solid or aqueous—is added to lithium hydroxide solution?

IONIC EQUATION: $\qquad NH_4^+ + PO_4^{3-} + Li^+ + OH^- \rightarrow Li_3PO_4\downarrow + NH_4OH$

$$\underline{- H_1OH}$$

(Subtract water to get...) $\qquad NH_3$

STANDARD EQUATION: $\qquad (NH_4)_3PO_4(aq) + 3LiOH(aq) \rightarrow Li_3PO4(s) + NH_3(g) + H_2O(l)$

1. d   f   b   e   a   g   c

2. $2HCl(aq) + CaO(s) \rightarrow CaCl_2(aq) + H_2O(l)$

? liters HCl(aq) = $218 \text{ g CaO} \times \dfrac{\text{mol CaO}}{56.08 \text{ g CaO}} \times \dfrac{2 \text{ mols HCl}}{\text{mol CaO}} \times \dfrac{\text{L HCl (aq)}}{1.15 \text{ mols HCl}} = 6.76 \text{ L HCl}$

3. $Ba(ClO_3)_2(aq) + K_2SO_4(aq) \rightarrow 2KClO_3(aq) + BaSO_4(s)$

? grams BaSO$_4$ = $3.00 \text{ L Ba(ClO}_3)_2(aq) \times \dfrac{7.48 \text{ mols Ba(ClO}_3)_2}{\text{L Ba(ClO}_3)_2(aq)} \times \dfrac{\text{mol BaSO}_4}{\text{mol Ba(ClO}_3)_2} \times \dfrac{233.4 \text{ g BaSO}_4}{\text{mol BaSO}_4}$

$$= 5.24 \times 10^3 \text{ g BaSO}_4 \ (5.28 \text{ kg})$$

4. $2Al(s) + 3H_2SO_4(aq) \rightarrow Al_2(SO_4)_3(aq) + 3H_2(g)$

? liters H$_2$ = $0.600 \text{ L H}_2SO_4(aq) \times \dfrac{2.20 \text{ mols H}_2SO_4}{\text{L H}_2SO_4(aq)} \times \dfrac{3 \text{ mols H}_2}{3 \text{ mols H}_2SO_4} \times \dfrac{22.4 \text{ L H}_2}{\text{mol H}_2} = 29.6 \text{ L H}_2$

5. $3AgNO_3(aq) + K_3PO_4(aq) \rightarrow 3KNO_3(aq) + Ag_3PO_4(s)$

? gallons AgNO$_3$(aq) = $0.850 \text{ L K}_3PO_4(aq) \times \dfrac{2.59 \text{ mols K}_3PO_4}{\text{L K}_3PO_4(aq)} \times \dfrac{3 \text{ mols AgNO}_3}{\text{mol K}_3PO_4} \times$

$\dfrac{\text{L AgNO}_3(aq)}{1.32 \text{ mols AgNO}_3} \times \dfrac{\text{gal AgNO}_3(aq)}{3.79 \text{ L AgNO}_3(aq)} = 1.32 \text{ gals AgNO}_3(aq)$

6. $MgI_2(aq) + (NH4)_2CO_3(aq) \rightarrow MgCO_3(s) + 2NH_4I(aq)$

? liters MgI$_2$(aq) = $0.0800 \text{ L (NH}_4)_2CO_3(aq) \times \dfrac{1.65 \text{ mols (NH}_4)_2CO_3}{\text{L (NH}_4)_2CO_3(aq)} \times \dfrac{\text{mol MgI}_2}{\text{mol (NH}_4)_2CO_3} \times$

$\dfrac{\text{L MgI}_2(aq)}{3.54 \text{ mols MgI}_2} = 0.0373 \text{ L MgI}_2 \text{ (aq)}$

7. $Hg(NO_3)_2(aq) + Na_2SO_4(aq) \rightarrow 2NaNO_3(aq) + HgSO_4(s)$? grams HgSO$_4$ =

$0.0767 \text{ L Hg(NO}_3)_2 \times \dfrac{1.95 \text{ mols Hg(NO}_3)_2}{\text{L HgNO}_3(aq)} \times \dfrac{\text{mol HgSO}_4}{\text{mol Hg(NO}_3)_2} \times$

$\dfrac{296.7 \text{ g HgSO}_4}{\text{mol HgSO}_4} = 44.4 \text{ g HgSO}_4$

8. $2H_3PO_4(aq) + 3Ca(OH)_2(aq) \rightarrow Ca_3(PO_4)_2(s) + 6H_2O(l)$ M = $0.056 \text{ liters H}_3PO_4(aq) \times$

$\dfrac{4.70 \text{ mols H}_3PO_4}{\text{L H}_3PO_4(aq)} \times \dfrac{3 \text{ mols Ca(OH)}_2}{2 \text{ mols H}_3PO_4} \times \dfrac{1}{0.0400 \text{ L Ca(OH)}_2} = 9.9 \text{M (significant figures)}$

9. $2NaHCO_3(aq) + H_2SO_4(aq) \rightarrow Na_2SO_4(aq) + 2H_2O(l) + 2CO_2(g$ M = $0.308 \text{ L NaHCO}_3(aq) \times$

$\dfrac{2.95 \text{ mols NaHCO}_3}{\text{L NaHCO}_3(aq)} \times \dfrac{\text{mol H}_2SO_4}{2 \text{ mols NaHCO}_3} \times \dfrac{1}{0.600 \text{ L H}_2SO_4(aq)} = 0.757 \text{M}$

1. Define these terms by matching them to their examples:

_____ionization	_____weak acids
_____nonelectrolytes	_____dissolution
_____strong bases	_____neutralization
_____metathesis	_____electrolytes
_____nonspecies	, _____strong acids

a. $HClO_4$ HBr

b. $HNO_2(l) \rightarrow HNO_2(aq)$

c. $Fe(NO_3)_3$ HCl

d. H_2CO_3 NH_4OH

e. $WX + YZ \rightarrow WY + XZ$

f. $H^+ + OH^- \rightarrow HOH$

g. $Sr(OH)_2$ KOH

h. $HClO_3$ $HBrO$

i. $HNO_3(l) \rightarrow H^+ + NO_3^-$

j. $HgCl_2$ HF CO_2

2. When placed in water, what types of particles will each of these **substances** release? Answer with the symbols at left.

_____He	_____$Ni_3(PO_4)_2$	_____$Ba(NO_2)_2$	_____CO_2
_____H_3BO_3	_____$C_{12}H_{22}O_{12}$	_____$H_2C_2O_4$	_____$Al(C_2H_3O_2)_3$
_____$(NH_4)_3AsO_4$	_____AgI	_____H_2O	_____H_2SO_4
_____$Mg(OH)_2$	_____Fe_2CO_3	_____$Mn(ClO_3)_2$	_____HIO_3
_____HBr	_____$NaOH$	_____CaI_2	_____Hg_2CrO_4

i (ions)
c (molecules)
b (both)
n (neither)

3. Write a mini net ionic equation showing the formation of these compounds. Do not worry about coefficients (*do* worry about subscripts; Sect. 4.3); you may leave them unbalanced.

a. water	b. cobalt (II) sulfide	c. chlorous acid
d. barium sulfate	e. hydrogen fluoride	f. beryllium hydroxide

235

4. Write a net ionic equation, as applicable, for each of these standard equations. To get it, first write the gross ionic equation.

a. $Ag_2SO_4(aq) + 2KI(aq) \rightarrow 2AgI(s) + K_2SO_4(aq)$

b. $HCl(aq) + NaOH(aq) \rightarrow H_2O(l) + NaCl(aq)$

c. $2NH_4ClO_3(aq) + MgSO_3(aq) \rightarrow (NH_4)_2SO_3(aq) + Mg(ClO_3)_2(aq)$

d. $Na_2CO_3(aq) + 2HNO_3(aq) \rightarrow 2NaNO_3(aq) + CO_2(g) + H_2O(l)$

e. $Zn(C_2H_3O_2)_2(aq) + 2HBr(aq) \rightarrow ZnBr_2(aq) + 2HC_2H_3O_2(aq)$

f. $3Pb(NO_3)_2(aq) + Al_2(SO_4)_3(aq) \rightarrow 3PbSO_4(s) + 2Al(NO_3)_3(aq)$

g. $2(NH_4)_3PO_4(aq) + 3Ba(OH)_2(aq) \rightarrow Ba_3(PO_4)_2(s) + 6NH_3(g) + 6H2O(l)$

5. Predict which of these will take place (yes/no); if yes, give the reason and identify (only) the net product(s). ZnS and Fe_2CO_3, insoluble in water, are dissolved when added to the indicated acids.

a. $ZnS(s) + HCl(aq) \rightarrow$ _____

b. $K_3PO_4(aq) + NH_4C_2H_3O_2(aq) \rightarrow$ _____

c. $Na_2CrO_4(aq) + Ba(C_2H_3O_2)_2(aq) \rightarrow$ _____

d. $Fe_2(CO_3)_3(s) + HNO_3(aq) \rightarrow$ _____

e. $(NH_4)_2SO_3(aq) + Ca(OH)_2(aq) \rightarrow$ _____

f. $HgCl_2(aq) + KClO_3(aq) \rightarrow$ _____

6.11 Chapter Synthesis

THE PROPERTIES BY WHICH MANY SUBSTANCES ARE KNOWN ARE MANIFESTED NOT IN THEIR UNDISSOLVED STATES, BUT IN SOLUTION.

HENCE, THE 4TH STATE!

(aq)

In other words, it is only in solution that many compounds exhibit the behavior they are noted for.

For instance, crystals of the salts $AgNO_3$ and NaBr, even if very finely pulverized and mixed, will not react upon being mixed; but if their solutions are mixed, the reaction proceeds rapidly and without delay. Nor can pure nitric acid, a liquid, turn litmus paper from blue to pink; only in its solution state can it do this.

Most of the reactions performed in general chemistry labs take place in solutions, and water-solvent solutions at that. For this reason, we have in this chapter emphasized the aqueous solution and its most-used expression of concentration, molarity, **from which the other aqueous solution concentration expressions**—save for molality—can be seen to derive. Molarity, as either a given or a wanted dimensional-analysis parameter, or as a conversion factor, is the key quantitative concept in our study, at this level, of solution stoichiometry, concentrations, and titrations. Titrations, in effect, use molarity and the solution reaction as a measuring device.

In understanding these applications of molarity, you have a foundation for understanding the applications of the other concentration expressions (m, N, F) in the future. As a conversion factor, molarity—like any other—is a fraction that equals 1, but in a subjective sort of way: while the molar volume conversion factor is invariable, the numerator in a molarity value can **vary**; but *it always equals 1 in the problem to which it belongs.*

Molarities can also form a familiar symmetry by enclosing a keystone in a stoichiometric calculation.

The second central concept of this chapter is the electrolyte. One must be able to distinguish electrolytes from nonelectrolytes, break them down, and recombine them whenever possible into nonelectrolytes of the three physical states: solids (precipitates); gases; and liquids (dissolved weak electrolytes consisting in molecules). Because of some exceptions, "solids" and "liquids" only roughly correspond, in this context, to "precipitate" and "weak electrolyte."

If you are able, in your head, to "ionize" electrolytes, there is a lot that you can do. For one thing, you can show how electrolytes produced in solution are formed from their component ions. And, by extension, you can write an ionic equation from a standard one, or even from a mere description of a reaction, and then identify the products in an ionic solution. This is the very same thing as making a prediction. With what you have learned in this chapter, you can predict any metathesis reaction, to the extent that you know the solubility rules and are able to look up other solubilities. Some non-metathesis reactions, such as full neutralizations, are also predictable, now that you know about electrolytes.

Apart from their ability to form new compounds by ionizing *in solution* and recombining, electrolytes also have other properties, such as imparting electrical conductivity to their solutions (a consequence of the charged nature of ions). This is why—to return to the starting point of this synthesis—conductivity is a test for mobile ions in a solution; it is this same mobility that makes reactions between electrolytes possible.

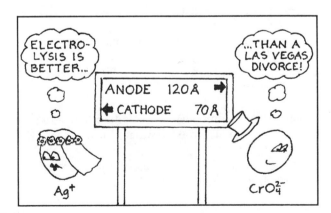

ELECTRO-LYSIS IS BETTER...

...THAN A LAS VEGAS DIVORCE!

ANODE 120Å ➡
⬅ CATHODE 70Å

Ag^+

CrO_4^{2-}

1. i j g e d h b f c a

2.

(n) He   (i) HBr   (n) Fe_2CO_3 (c) H_2O (n) $Al(C_2H_3O_2)_3$

(c) H_3BO_3 (n) $Ni_3(PO_4)_2$ (i) NaOH   (i) $Mn(ClO_3)_6$ (i) H_2SO_4

(i) $(NH_4)_3AsO_4$ (c) $C_{12}H_{22}O_{11}$ (i) $Ba(NO_2)_2$ (i) CaI_2 (c) HIO_3

(n) $Mg(OH)_2$ (n) AgI   (b) $H_2C_2O_4$ (n) CO_2 (n) Hg_2CrO_4

3.

a. $H^+ + OH^- \rightarrow HOH$ b. $Co^{2+} + S^{2-} \rightarrow CoS$ c. $H^+ + ClO_2^- \rightarrow HClO_2$

d. $Ba^{2+} + SO_4^{2-} \rightarrow BaSO_4$ e. $H^+ + F^- \rightarrow HF$ f. $Be^{2+} + OH^- \rightarrow Be(OH)_2$

4.

a. $Ag^+ + I^- \rightarrow AgI\downarrow$

b. $H^+ + OH^- \rightarrow HOH$

c. none; this reaction will not occur

d. $CO_3^{2-} + H^+ \rightarrow CO_2\uparrow + H_2O$

e. $H^+ + C_2H_3O_2^- \rightarrow HC_2H_3O_2$

f. $Pb^{2+} + SO_4^{2-} \rightarrow PbSO_4\downarrow$

g. $NH_4^+ + PO_4^{3-} + Ba^{2+} + OH^- \rightarrow$

$$Ba_3(PO_4)_2\downarrow + NH_3\uparrow + H_2O$$

5.

a. yes; a gas (hydrogen sulfide) form   b. no

c. yes; a precipitate (barium chromate) forms

d. yes; a gas (carbon dioxide) and a nonelectrolyte (water) form

e. yes; a gas (ammonia), a precipitate (calcium sulfate), and a nonelectrolyte (water) form.

f. no; mercury (II) chloride is one of few nonelectrlytic (soluble but covalent) salts

42
Mo
95.94

𝕻𝖗𝖔𝖋𝖎𝖑𝖊: 𝕸𝖔𝖑𝖞𝖇𝖉𝖊𝖓𝖚𝖒

Very complex ions, the polymolybdates, can form in highly acidic solutions

Even for a transition metal, molybdenum shows a great deal of variation in its valencies. This is because all of the electrons in its two uppermost sublevels—five in 4d and one in 5s—can act as valence electrons. All told, molybdenum exhibits valencies of 0 (in some rare covalent compounds), 2+, 3+, 4+, 5+, and 6+.

The principal molybdenum ore is molybdenite, MoS_2. This mineral has physical properties that are identical to graphite, except that it leaves a green streak, rather than a gray one, on paper. There is also a trisulfide, MoS_3.

The ion molybdate, MoO_4^{2-}, is an analog of CrO_4^{2-}. Industrially, it is used to make a series of pigments that are similar to those made with chromium. Zinc molybdate, because it is nontoxic, is the pigment used in the white paint applied to nautical surfaces. The best known molybdate is wulfenite, $PbMoO_4$. Cationic radicals such as molybdenyl, MoO_2^{2+}, are also known.

Of all the trace minerals required by living tissues, molybdenum may be the one needed in the smallest amounts; its biological functions are not well understood, but it is known that molybdenum and somewhat larger quantities of copper must be in balance, such that copper deficiency and molybdenum toxicity are pretty much the same thing, symptomatically speaking.

Molybdenum salts are sometimes found in commercial fertilizers, and from there the ions make their way into legumes, the cabbage family, and feed crops. Toxicity is less likely from eating such foods than from eating higher on the food chain, though it is rare in humans, regardless of their diet. Cattle,

however, sometimes develop a cholera-like disorder called teart, which has been linked to the metal.

Molybdenum containing certain impurities is extremely hard, and has a high melting point to match. Tiny admixtures of it impart some of this hardness and heat resistance to iron, and molybdenum steels are therefore used in cutting and forging tools. In spite of its high melting point, molybdenum burns in air at about 870 K. Pure molybdenum is fairly soft and ductile.

Chromium, the hardest of the household metals, is even more famous for its dye-producing ions. Though it, too, is a necessary trace element—for the metabolism of glucose and lipids—its toxicity is more common. Chromium ions are considered an industrial pollutant of the "heavy-metal" crowd of lead, mercury, and cadmium. Field researchers carry qualitative analysis tests to check for chromium contamination of water supplies.

Tungsten is a very inert and hard metal that does not even react with aqua regia, although it is affected by a mixture of nitric and hydrofluoric acids. Technetium, molybdenum's unusual next-door neighbor, is very radioactive and short-lived and does not exist in nature. It became the first artificially produced element in a modern alchemic transmutation, which used molybdenum as the target nucleus.

Scheele predicted the existence of molybdenum in 1778, and it was isolated four years thence by Hjelm. It is about the fortieth most abundant element in the Earth's crust. There are mines in Colorado dedicated exclusively to its extraction.

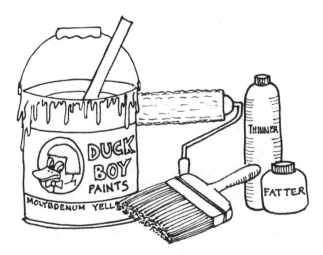

1. 88.0 grams of potassium permanganate (158.0 g/mol) is dissolved to make 652 milliliters of solution. What is its molarity?

2. What weight of zinc iodide (319.2 g/mol) is required to prepare 720 milliliters of 1.33M solution in a 750-milliliter beaker?

3. Determine the molarity of a solution in which 13.7 grams of magnesium acetate (142.4 g/mol) ionizes in 900 milliliters of water.

4. How much cobalt (II) sulfide (91.00 g/mol) will precipitate from the addition of 0.600 liters of 2.00M cobalt (II) bromide (218.7 g/mol) solution with excess 3.55M sodium sulfide solution?

$$CoBr_2(aq) + Na_2S(aq) \rightarrow CoS(s) + 2NaBr(aq)$$

In the next three problems, molar weights are not provided, so you will have to use Avogadro's YOYO system. Further, the word solution is henceforth omitted after molarity values, because it is redundant.

5. How much 0.17M $Ba(OH)_2$ solution must be reacted with 440 mililiters of 2.80M $(NH_4)_3PO_4$ to precipitate all of the phosphate?

$$3Ba(OH)_2(aq) + 2(NH_4)_3PO_4(aq) \rightarrow Ba_3(PO_4)_2(s) + 6NH_3(g) + 6H_2O(l)$$

6. What mass of iron (II) sulfate is ionized in solution if all of it can be removed with 71.9 milliliters of 4.50M potassium carbonate titrant (note: this is a very precise measurement; lab measurements to one less figure will probably be acceptable)?

$$FeSO_4(aq) = K_2CO_3(aq) \rightarrow FeCo_3(s) + K_2SO_4(aq)$$

7. Determine the molarity of 50.0 milliliters of silver nitrate solution if the equivalence point is reached by the addition of 32.4 milliliters of 2.10M AlBr$_3$ titrant.

$$3AgNO_3(aq) + AlBr_3(aq) \rightarrow 3AgBr(s) + Al(NO_3)_3(aq)$$

8. Write the net ionic equation showing the formation of each of these (coefficients optional):

a. silver iodide	b. chromium (II) hydroxide	c. phosphoric acid

9. Write the (gross and) net ionic equations for each of the following (again, coefficients are optional):

a. $NaOH(aq) + HClO_4(aq) \rightarrow NaClO_4(aq) + H_2O(l)$

b. $K_2SO_4(aq) + CuCl_2(aq) \rightarrow 2KCl(aq) + CuSO_4(aq)$

c. $3AgC_2H_3O_2(aq) + (NH_4)_3PO_4(aq) \rightarrow Ag_3PO_4(s) + 3NH_4C_2H_3O_2(aq)$

d. $NiSO_4(aq) + Ca(OH)_2(aq) \rightarrow Ni(OH)_2(s) + CaSO_4(aq)$

e. $Na_2SO_3(aq) + 2HBr(aq) \rightarrow 2NaBr(aq) + SO_2(g) + H_2O(l)$

10. Complete and balance these standard equations, or specify a nonreaction, if that is the case.

a. $HI(aq) + Na_2S(s) \rightarrow$ _____

b. $KOH(aq) + HNO_3(aq) \rightarrow$ _____

c. $FeCl_3(s) + (NH_4)_2SO_4(aq) \rightarrow$ _____

d. $Mn(ClO_3)_2(aq) + MgSO_4(aq) \rightarrow$ _____

e. $Na_2CO_3(aq) + HCl(aq) \rightarrow$ _____

1. $\quad M = \dfrac{88.0 \text{ g KMnO}_4}{0.652 \text{ L KMnO}_4(aq)} \times \dfrac{\text{mol KMnO}_4}{158.0 \text{ g KMnO}_4} = 0.854M$

2. $\quad ? \text{ grams ZnI}_2 = 0.720 \text{ L} \times \dfrac{1.33 \text{ mols ZnI}_2}{L} \times \dfrac{319.2 \text{ g ZnI}_2}{\text{mol g ZnI}_2} = 306 \text{ g ZnI}_2$

3. $\quad m = \dfrac{13.7 \text{ g Mg(C}_2\text{H}_3\text{O}_2)_2}{0.900 \text{ kg}} \times \dfrac{\text{mol Mg(C}_2\text{H}_3\text{O}_2)_2}{142.4 \text{ g Mg(C}_2\text{H}_3\text{O}_2)_2} = 0.107m$

4. $\quad ? \text{ grams CoS} = 0.600 \text{ L CoBr}_2(aq) \times \dfrac{2.00 \text{ mols CoBr}_2}{\text{L CoBr}_2(aq)} \times \dfrac{\text{mol CoS}}{\text{mol CoBr}_2} \times \dfrac{91.00 \text{ g CoS}}{\text{mol CoS}}$
$$= 109.2 \text{ g CoS}$$

5. $\quad ? \text{ liters Ba(OH)}_2(aq) = 0.440 \text{ L (NH}_4)_3\text{PO}_4(aq) \times \dfrac{2.80 \text{ mols (NH}_4)_3\text{PO}_4}{\text{L (NH}_4)_3\text{PO}_4(aq)} \times \dfrac{3 \text{ mols Ba(OH)}_2}{2 \text{ mols (NH}_4)_3\text{PO}_4} \times$

$\quad \dfrac{\text{L Ba(OH)}_2(aq)}{0.17 \text{ mol Ba(OH)}_2} = \textbf{4.8 L Ba(OH)}_2(aq)$

6. $\quad ? \text{ grams FeSO}_4 = 0.0179 \text{ L K}_2\text{CO}_3(aq) \times \dfrac{4.50 \text{ mols K}_2\text{CO}_3}{\text{L K}_2\text{CO}_3(aq)} \times \dfrac{3 \text{ mols FeSO}_4}{\text{mol K}_2\text{CO}_3} \times \dfrac{151.9 \text{ g FeSO}_4}{\text{mol FeSO}_4}$
$$= 36.7 \text{ g FeSO}_4$$

7. $\quad M = 0.0324 \text{ L AlBr}_3(aq) \times \dfrac{2.10 \text{ mols AlBr}_3}{\text{L AlBr}_3(aq)} \times \dfrac{3 \text{ mols AgNO}_3}{\text{mol AlBr}_3} \times \dfrac{1}{0.0300 \text{ L AgNO}_3(aq)} = 6.80 M$

8. a. $Ag^+ + I^- \rightarrow AgI\downarrow$ b. $Cr^{2+} + 2OH^- \rightarrow Cr(OH)_2\downarrow$ c. $3H^+ + PO_4^{3-} \rightarrow H_3PO_4$

9. a. $H^+ + OH^- \rightarrow HOH$
    b. none (a nonreaction)
    c. $3Ag^+ + PO_4^{3-} \rightarrow Ag_3PO_4$
    d. $Ni^{2+} + 2OH^- \rightarrow Ni(OH)_2$
    e. $SO_3^{2-} + 2H^+ \rightarrow SO_2\uparrow + H_2O$

10. a. $2HI(aq) + Na_2S(s) \rightarrow H_2S(g) + 2NaI(aq)$

    b. $KOH(aq) + HNO_3(aq) \rightarrow KNO_3(aq) + H_2O(l)$

    c. $2FeCl_3(aq) + 3(NH_4)_2SO_4(aq) \rightarrow Fe_2(SO_4)_3 + 6NH_4Cl$

    d. none (a nonreaction)

    e. $Na_2CO_3(aq) + 2HCl(aq) \rightarrow 2NaCl(aq) + CO_2(aq) + H_2O(l)$

ARTORIO G. DRAGGININI'S AND FRANCO DI NANARTONI'S SOON-TO-BE FAMOUS FORMULA!

F&D's ORIGINAL VEGETARIAN SPAGHETTI SAUCE

1. EFFECT A ΔT OF 10-12 ML OLIVE OIL IN LG. CAULDRON. 2. ADD 6 LG. FINELY MILLED ONIONS. 3. AGITATE TILL LUSTROUS. 4. DILUTE W/ EXCESS (2.00 L) AQ. SOLVENT. 5. ADD BAY LEAVES. 6. MAINTAIN T OF 100 KELVINS WHILE REACTING WITH 850 G. TOMATO PASTE, TBSP. MUSTARD, FRESH CILANTRO AND 0.5 ML TABASCO. 7. ADD FINELY MILL'D STINKING ROSE AND OREGANO (BOTH TO TASTE). 8. STIR UNTIL DESIRED VISCOSITY IS REACHED (2-3 HRS.). 9. SAVOR GAS PHASE. 10. REACT SOL'N W/ SAUTÉED MIX OF WHOLE-GRAIN PASTA, SHROOMERS, & TEMPEH OR OTHER VEGETABLE VIANDE.

Seven: Concerning Energy and the States

7.1 Liquid Properties

The physical states—solid, liquid, and gas—are called *phases* when we are discussing a specific pure substance.

A heterogeneous sample of combined pure substances is (by definition) a mixture, but the second and fourth samples in the above illustration are heterogeneous (having visibly different parts), though they are obviously not mixtures.

Water is the best example of how a pure substance can be heterogeneous because it is the only such substance that naturally exists widely and visibly in all three phases. If you are near some snow (s) during a thaw and can see both running water (l) and clouds (g), then you are in the simultaneous presence of all three phases of water.

In a laboratory sample of any liquid, a gas phase is present if (in most cases) unseen. This is so because a few molecules—which are what pure liquids (except for ionic solutions and mercury) are wholly made of—manage to absorb enough energy to evaporate and escape the surface. Naturally, if we add more energy to the sample by heating it, more molecules will vaporize within the limits of the container.

As the pressure in the container increases, however, the gas begins to recondense, because pressure has the opposite (if delayed) effect that temperature has. This gas phase, which is present alongside the liquid phase, accounts for the vapor pressure that the *liquid* is said to exert.

Liquid phases, incidentally, are comparatively rare among the four major physical states of matter in the universe, which, in order of increasing energy, are the solids, liquids, gases, and plasmas. This fact is explained by the small range of temperatures (a few thousand kelvins for all substances collectively) at which liquid phases can exist. Everything else, universally speaking, is either frozen stiff or just too hot to be liquid.

Liquids, like gases, are *fluids*: they assume the shape of their container. But unlike gases, liquids do not do so uniformly; gravity causes them to concentrate in the bottom, and intermolecular forces—like those in gases but much stronger—help to keep them there.

Since they are already concentrated, liquids are virtually incompressible. The principles of hydraulics used in braking systems depend both on the property that liquids share with gases (fluidity) and that which they share with solids (incompressibility).

The forces holding molecules together in liquids are collectively known as *Van der Waals Forces*. As you already know from Chap. 5, these phenomena are of little importance in studying the behavior of gases, but for liquids they are paramount (and, consequently, it is in this chapter that we will give them our attention). Van der Waals Forces explain, for instance, why bromine is a liquid at all normal temperatures whereas its sibling, chlorine, is not.

The relative strengths of these forces, from one liquid to the next, are causally related to the following set of properties: vapor pressure, boiling point, viscosity, and surface tension.

Vapor Pressure

In a confined sample of liquid in which the container is not full, the "empty" area, as you know, will be occupied by the gas phase.

Therefore, vapor pressure is higher in liquids with weak Van der Waals Forces because the particles are more able to break free of the liquid phase when they absorb a little energy.

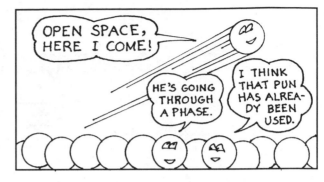

Boiling Point

Some particles are energetic enough at room temperature to evaporate into the gas phase. However, the temperature at which the *average* energy of all the particles is high enough to overcome the intermolecular forces and evaporate is the boiling point.

Obviously, then, boiling points will be higher in liquids with stronger Van der Waals Forces.

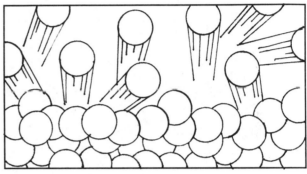

Viscosity

Viscosity is the internal friction of a fluid, or the degree of ease of movement by the particles among themselves. Different grades of motor oil are really of different viscosities, with the higher grades being more viscous.

When the external factors (P and T) are the same for a pair of liquids, the one that has more intermolecular (Van der Waals) attractions will also have the higher viscosity.

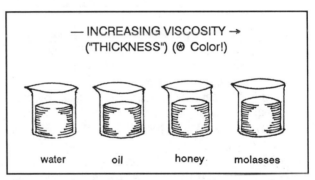

Surface Tension

A molecule beneath the surface of a sample or body of liquid (A) is pulled in all directions at once because it is surrounded by other molecules; one on the surface is mostly just pulled downwards. This pulling increases with the polarity of the molecules, for reasons you can probably understand. It is this *surface tension* that allows water striders and other insects to walk on water.

Surface tension increases with the strength of a liquid's Van der Waals forces.

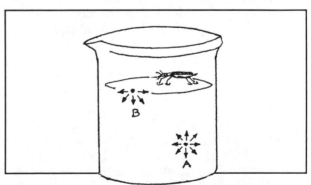

245

7.2 Solid Properties

At room temperature, all gases and pure-substance liquids—excepting Hg(l)—are covalent species, whereas ionic species are favored (for our purposes) in the solution state.

Solids, however, can be ionic as often as covalent. They also include nearly all of the metallically bonded substances, as we know them. But what sets solids apart from the other states is the very strong attractions among the atoms, molecules, or ions that make them up. It is these same forces that give solids their rigidity and mechanical strength.

Three properties that are often indexed for solid materials are (1) electrical conductivity, (2) solubility, and (3) melting point. If you have read the book up to this point, you already know something about the first two.

Apart from certain supercooled substances, only the metals, of all the solids, are good conductors of electricity. Ionic substances, when melted (l) or dissolved (aq) can also conduct, but only because their ions have been made mobile in one of these two ways. Metals conduct well either as solids or liquids because (in effect) their electrons are mobile, whereas covalent substances, even when melted or dissolved, conduct poorly or not at all.

The variations in melting point (and to some degree, solubility) are functions of the same Van der Waals Forces which are usually negligible in gas samples, but critical in liquid ones. In solids, they are even more critical, for they not only hold particles together, but they hold them *in place*.

There are two classes of solids: *crystalline* and *amorphous*. In crystals, the particles are arranged in definite and repeated geometric patterns, whereas in amorphous (Greek, "without form") solids such as rubber, glass, and nylon, there is no such order; particles are held together by bonds of varying lengths and strengths.

For this reason, crystals of all kinds have rather definite melting points, and so tend to melt all at once. Amorphous substances, on the other hand, melt over a range of temperature because they contain bonds having a range of strengths.

All types of crystals can form as suddenly as they break down. *Crystallization*—which is an actual change of state—can take place by the freezing of a liquid or by the seeding of a saturated solution (Sect. 6.1). The generic word for the change of state from liquid to solid—crystalline or amorphous—is *solidification*. Do not confuse this with crystallization.

A few substances can crystallize directly from their vapors, bypassing the liquid phase altogether. Iodine (I_2) is a familiar example of such a substance. This gas-to-solid phenomenon is called *sublimation*.

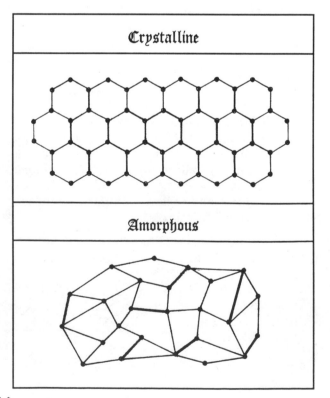

7.3 Crystals

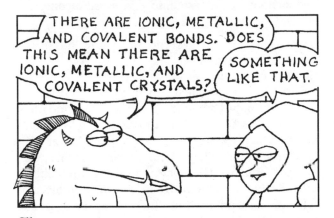

THERE ARE IONIC, METALLIC, AND COVALENT BONDS. DOES THIS MEAN THERE ARE IONIC, METALLIC, AND COVALENT CRYSTALS?

SOMETHING LIKE THAT.

In fact, there are four types of crystals: ionic, metallic, and two classes of covalent: molecular and *macromolecular*.

It is obvious, then, that crystals are not only classified on the basis of what holds them together, but also, in the case of the two covalent types, an important difference in their particle structures. The class to which a given crystal belongs does a lot to explain its solubility, electrical conductivity, and melting point.

The pattern in which particles are arranged in a crystal is its crystal *lattice*. The example on p. 246 is a hexagonal lattice, although only a single plane is represented. Presently, we will look at some representations of three-dimensional models of the six types of lattices.

Two things determine the type of lattice that a crystal will have: (1) the ratio of the different particles to each other (their formulae); and (2) the relative (compared to their neighbors) radii of the particles.

⊛ Color the ammonium dichromate orange-red; the pentahydrate, a deep blue; the penny, copper or brownish; the lead sinker, dark gray; the iodine, purple; the candle, any color you like; the macromolecules can reflect, if you wish, the colors of the other substances.

Ionic

The great majority of salts are ionic, and their crystals have membership in this group. They usually have high to very high melting points and, at least in their solid phases, are nonconductors. Solubility of salts in water, as you already know, varies greatly.

Metallic

Metals can be likened, in one theoretical model, to masses of cations in a bath of mobile, communally shared electrons, and are thus very conductive. Some metal crystals ionize in neutral solution, and melting points range from low (for Hg) to high (for W).

Molecular

Molecular crystals are generally soft, insoluble, and have low melting points. They are nonconductors and make up the softest class of crystals.

Macromolecular

These crystals resemble ionic lattices in that they are not discrete molecules; instead, they are more like "covalent formula units" bonding to every adjacent unit, *but by shared electrons* rather than by charges.

This is possible due the high valencies of nonmetals (e.g., carbon's 4, sulfur's 6) which enable the particles of macromolecular crystals to bond in many directions and to form vast and regular networks, or "giant molecules."

Macromolecular crystals include the hardest substances known, and they also have the highest melting points. They are poor conductors, even when melted, and are highly or completely insoluble, resisting water and other solvents as well.

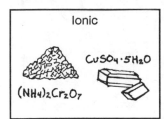

Ionic

$CuSO_4 \cdot 5H_2O$

$(NH_4)_2Cr_2O_7$

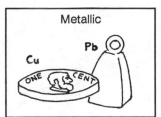

Metallic

Pb

Cu

ONE CENT

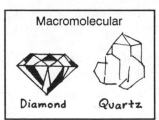

Macromolecular

Diamond   Quartz

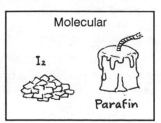

Molecular

I_2

Parafin

247

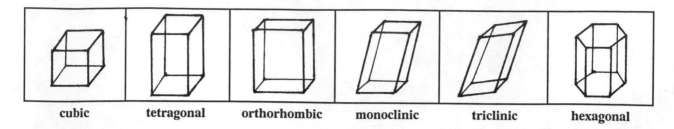

| cubic | tetragonal | orthorhombic | monoclinic | triclinic | hexagonal |

The multitude of crystalline solids exists in many complex forms, but all are variations of the six "systems" shown above. The lattice of a crystal determines which of these shapes it will have. Ionic sodium chloride, macromolecular quartz, and metallic iron, for instance, all have cubic lattices (among others), and so have cubic crystals. Here are descriptions of each system:

Cubic A cube, any cube, has six equal sides.

Tetragonal An elongate box with four equal sides (and two ends).

Orthorhombic A box defined by three axes of unequal length, intersecting at right angles.

Monoclinic A box defined by three axes of unequal length, with one of them not at a right angle to the other two.

Triclinic A box defined by three axes of unequal length, with none at right angles to the others.

Hexagonal An elongate box with six equal sides (and two ends).

Learning these crystal geometries is no big sweat. The cube, tautologically, is cubic. *Tetra*gonal is a sort of misnomer, meaning "four-angled," but you can remember it as the only system with *four* equal sides. A cross-section of the hexagonal form is, what else? A hexagon.

The Latin verb *clinare* ("to lean") is the root of *mono*clinic, which (therefore) means to lean in *one* direction, if stood on end, and *tri*clinic, which means to lean in *three* directions.

Finally, there is the orthorhombic, which means "straight rhombus." If this contradiction is unhelpful, think of the system as having the form of a box of cereal (which it does), such as "Sugar-frosted O'Rhombies."

The tiniest section of a lattice that can be used to show the pattern of a crystal's particles is called a *unit cell*.

Even the simplest system, the cubic, has three possible arrangements. The unit cells of each are themselves cubic. These packing arrangements are governed by the two factors mentioned on p. 247.

For example, some ionic crystals are made up of large anions with small cations filling the holes between them. If the cations are reltively larger (that is, of greater radius), however, the anions must make more room for them by arranging themselves differently. Analogously, in the macromolecular scheme, these anions and cations could be large and small molecules.

In the four unit cell models on this page, the particles are represented as spheres, though in reality, of course, they are not; nor are they all of the same radius (except in elemental lattices, such as diamond).

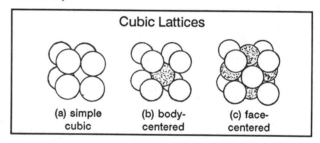

Cubic Lattices

| (a) simple cubic | (b) body-centered | (c) face-centered |

⊛ In (a) above, color the front layer dark green and the layer behind it, light green. In (b), color the four front particles dark blue; the center particle, pink; and what is visible of the four rear particles, light blue. In (c), do the front five, brown; the middle four, yellow; and the back layer, what you can see of it, tan. Then color the alternating layers of (d), below, any two colors of your choice.

248

19
K
39.102

𝕻rofile: 𝕻otassium

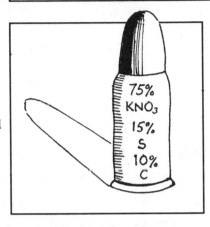

Gunpowder is 75% saltpeter, 15% sulfur, and 10% ground carbon.

75% KNO_3
15% S
10% C

Potassium makes up a fortieth of the Earth's crust and is the most reactive of the common metals. It is a silvery metal so soft that it is easily cut with a dull knife.

If a chunk of it is placed in water, it darts about fitfully while reacting, evolving enough heat to ignite the hydrogen that it removes from the water. A basic (or alkaline) solution results:

$$2K(s) + 2H_2O(l) \rightarrow 2KOH(aq) + H_2(g)$$

The very high activity of the Family 1A metals in general is due to the ease with which the lone s-sublevel electron in the highest Principal Energy Level (n = 4) is surrendered.

The heaviest of the alkali metals, cesium, is the most reactive metal that exists in testable quantities. Lithium, the lightest metal in atomic terms, is also the least dense with a specific gravity only half that of water (0.529); potassium is the next least dense, at 0.870. If these metals did not react with water, they could easily float upon it.

The name has a humble etymology. Potash (a word often used for several potassium salts but most frequently denoting the carbonate) has for centuries been obtained by heating ashes. The salt, or "potash" was and is employed in the manufacture of soap and fertilizer. With the *-ium* affixed, the word means "potash metal."

As potassium compounds are vital to life, farmland must often be enriched with them. Almost all of its salts are water-soluble (although $KClO_4$ is a curious exception), and certain of them are necessary for human metabolism and the conversion of sugars by the liver into glycogen. Potassium supplements can be bought, but the vital salts are abundant in many everyday foods, notably bananas and potatoes. In the latter, it is concentrated just under the peel, so peeled potatoes retain little of it. If you examine a slice of freshly cut potato, you will see the faint "potassium ring" beneath the skin.

Ordinary samples of potassium are somewhat radioactive for a substance not normally thought of as being that way. This is so because of a comparatively high proportion of an unstable isotope, $^{40}_{19}K$. Potassium-40, like carbon-14, is used by scientists to date prehistoric materials, though a controversy is developing over the the reliability of such methods.

Another scientific application for potassium is as a heat-transfer medium in nuclear breeder reactors, in which it is alloyed with sodium (which is much cheaper than potassium).

The primary commercial source of elemental potassium is the mineral sylvite (KCl). The metal is removed from this salt by electrolysis and was in this way first isolated, in 1807, by Davy.

Rubidium takes its name from the red Bunsen flame caused by the heating of its salts. Cesium is used in the production of photoelectric cells. Both were discovered by Bunsen and Kirchoff, circa 1860. Francium is ultra-radioactive and may be the rarest naturally occurring element. It is assumed to have the same chemical properties as its lighter siblings. Most of the other 1A and 2A metals—lithium, sodium, magnesium, calcium, strontium, and barium—were also discovered by Davy in the same way that he found potassium.

1. Match these:

_____ sublimation	a. the transition of a sample from its solid phase to its liquid phase
_____ vapor pressure	b. a state, in the context of a sample's multiple states
_____ crystals	c. the repeated structural pattern of some solids
_____ surface tension	d. the class of solids without predictable particle structures
_____ dissolution	e. the transition of a sample from its liquid phase to its gas phase
_____ melting point	f. that property which makes some liquids pour more slowly than others
_____ lattice	g. something more often had by liquid phases than by solid ones
_____ unit cell	h. substances that melt predictably and all at once
_____ viscosity	i. a way in which some solids and some acids ionize
_____ boiling point	j. the direct conversion of a sample from the gas state to the solid state
_____ amorphous	k. that which is exerted by a liquids's gas phase
_____ phase	l. the smallest indicative portion of a crystal's particle arrangement
_____ conductivity	m. the inward-facing of molecules in a liquid's "top layer"

2. Why is vapor pressure lower in liquids with relatively strong Van der Waals forces?

3. Why is surface tension lower in liquids with relatively weak Van der Waals forces?

4. Fill in, writing "H" for high or usually high; "L" for low or usually low; "V" for variable.

property Xtal type	melting point	solu-bility	conduct-ivity
ionic			
molecular			
metallic			
macromolecular			

5. Identify (label) these crystal models:

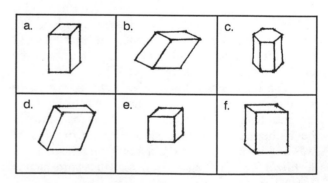

6. What two conditions determine which of the six types of lattices that a crystal will have?

7.4 Heat Dimensions

Metric units belong to a larger international system, the Système International, which is French for you-can-probably-guess-what. All the SI units are in efficient decimal units. They are gradually replacing all other dimensions, first in scientific and engineering endeavors and then in nonscientific applications. There is nowadays an SI unit to measure everything except time.

The units for heat (or energy) are the *joule*, J, and the *kilojoule*, kJ. They are replacing the calorie and the kilocalorie. The latter of these is the actual "calorie" used by dieters. If you told someone that your average daily intake amounted to between two or three million calories, you would in fact be literally correct (though no one would believe you).

Nutritionally speaking, calories are the amount of heat that a quantity of food, if used as fuel, releases in the exothermy of animal metabolism. Most of the food energy consumed by warm-blooded animals goes to the maintenance of their constant temperatures. If such fuel is not used, it is converted by the liver into fat and stored there and elsewhere in the body.

The mathematical relationship between the SI joule and the English calorie is

$$1 \text{ calorie } = 4.184 \text{ joules}$$

Do not, by the way, confuse heat (that is, energy) measurement with temperature measurement.

Here is the difference: a bathtub of tepid water holds more heat (more joules) than a glowing lightbulb filament, by virtue of its far greater mass; but the filament is obviously much hotter (more degrees).

Physically, a joule is defined by two other SI dimensions: it equals one newton of force over one meter of distance.

Change in Heat and Temperature

Now that there is no danger in your confusing heat and temperature measurements (a common error), the algebraic symbols for *change* in both of these parameters can be introduced.

The Greek letter delta, $\triangle$, indicates change in heat or temperature by $\triangle H$ or $\triangle T$, respectively. When chemistry professors speak, for instance, of "delta-T," they are only referring to the difference in temperature of a sample or system before and after some event—such as a reaction—took place. Arithmetically, of course, a difference is only the result of a subtraction operation; in this case, it is the final temperature (T_f) minus the initial one (T_i):

$$T_f - T_i = \triangle T$$

If T_i is higher than T_f (as is usually the case), then $\triangle T$ will be negative (and will therefore indicate an exothermic reation). No matter, this. Delta-T is only a number; *determining it* requires nothing more than subtraction; and *using it* only entails plugging it into equations that are far simpler than some of those you have already mastered if you have come this far.

An example: what is $\triangle T$ if a sample has warmed from 21.5°C to 35.4°C?

$$\triangle T = 21.5 - 35.4 = -13.9°C$$

Now, let us look at an example with $\triangle H$, and one in which an endothermic change is indicated: determine $\triangle H$ if a system's heat was 739J and it is now 255J.

$$\triangle H = 739 - 255 = 484J$$

ANSWERS! GLUG! GLUG!

1. j k h m i a c l f e d b g

2. Because the molecules will need more energy to vaporize, there will be fewer of them in the gas phase.

3. Surface molecules in a low-surface-tension liquid are less oriented towards the rest of the sample than they would be with greater electrostatic forces (a result of molecular polarity, or partial ionic character).

4.   5. (at right)

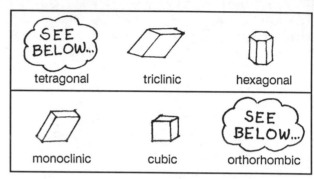

tetragonal   triclinic   hexagonal

monoclinic   cubic   orthorhombic

	melting point	Solu-bility	Conduct-ivity
ionic	H	V	L
molecular	L	L	L
metallic	V	V	H
macromolecular	H	L	L

6. The (1) ratio of one type of particle to the other(s); and (2) the sizes, or radii, of the particles relative to other particles in the lattice.

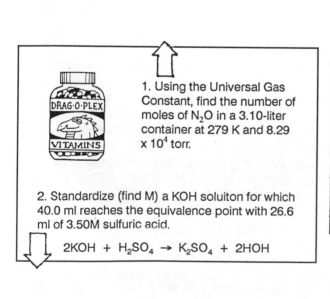

1. Using the Universal Gas Constant, find the number of moles of N_2O in a 3.10-liter container at 279 K and 8.29 x 10^4 torr.

2. Standardize (find M) a KOH soluiton for which 40.0 ml reaches the equivalence point with 26.6 ml of 3.50M sulfuric acid.

$$2KOH + H_2SO_4 \rightarrow K_2SO_4 + 2HOH$$

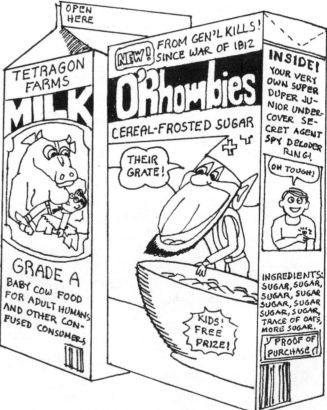

7.5 Change of State

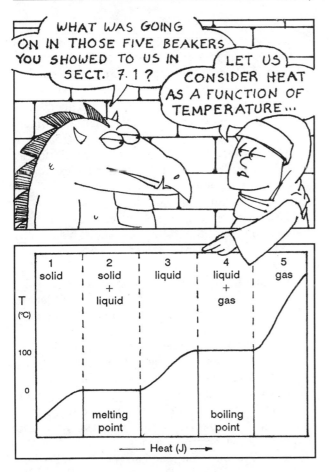

WHAT WAS GOING ON IN THOSE FIVE BEAKERS YOU SHOWED TO US IN SECT. 7.1?

LET US CONSIDER HEAT AS A FUNCTION OF TEMPERATURE...

| 1 solid | 2 solid + liquid | 3 liquid | 4 liquid + gas | 5 gas |

T (°C)

100

0

melting point

boiling point

—— Heat (J) ——▶

The sample in the first beaker (p. 244) is fresh out of the freezer and so is a dry solid. As it sits in a room at ordinary temperatures, its own temperature rises as it absorbs heat (1, in graph at left). The "wetness" of the sample is in fact its inchoate liquid phase.

When the ice reaches the melting point, however, *the temperature stops rising, even though the flow of heat into the sample continues* (2). This is because, in beaker 2, the ice sheds this inflowing heat as a liquid phase rather than absorbing it. The solid phase of water cannot do otherwise at 0°C. In this way, T stays constant; for neither does the liquid phase absorb heat until the solid phase is all gone. Notice, then, that neither the (s) nor the (l) phase absorbs heat while the ice melts. What *does* absorb it? The change itself.

When the change is finally complete, the temperature again starts to rise (3), because the sample must absorb all the energy added to it until so much has been added that the gas phase starts to form, and the temperature levels off a second time.

With water, this happens at 100°C (4). As before, the temperature does not rise, because there is an energy equilibrium as one state converts to another: heat is being *absorbed* by the formation of a higher phase as quickly as it is being *introduced* to the whole sample.

This is why water that has boiled for three seconds is as hot as water that has been boiling all morning long. You can raise the temperature of the liquid phase *to* 100°C, but never *past* it; the continued addition of energy will only result in the whole sample being raised to the gas phase. The liquid phase, then, cannot pass 100°C any more than the solid phase can pass 0°C.

When all the water is vaporized (5), it can again show a rise in T as a Cartesian function (see graph) of the heat it absorbs. It can continue to do so over a very considerable (but not infinite) range. Because the now gaseous H_2O molecules will have to continue absorbing heat for a long time (because **the range is great**), they will become more and more energetic—hotter (higher T)—until they change to the plasmic state.

In Sect. 7.6, we will consider, quantitatively, the increase of T *within* a phase; in Sect. 7.8, we will examine changes *between* phases; and in Sect. 7.9, the culmination: those changes that include both of the above—within *and* between—because they take place over a broader range of temperature—as in the case of the water in beakers 1-5. The qualitative representation of such a change is seen in the above graph (in which the five "subranges" are drawn, though not to scale).

Other substances behave like water, except, of course, that they have their own melting and boiling points, and phase ranges.

⊛ In the graph, color the area below the relation (function) line as follows: the solid region, light blue; that labeled "melting point," light green; liquid, yellow; the "boiling point," orange; and the gas, pink. Primary colors are used for the states and secondary colors for the transitions, or changes, between them.

7.6 Specific Heat

SO HOW IS SPECIFIC HEAT LIKE — OR DIFFERENT FROM — SPECIFIC GRAVITY?

BOTH ARE DIMENSIONLESS AND REFER SPECIFICALLY TO GRAMS OF A SUBSTANCE.

BUT...

FOR A ΔT OF 10% TO TAKE PLACE, THERE MUST BE A 10% GREATER FLOW OF HEAT IN...

150 K   165 K

Q is proportional to ΔT

IT ONLY TAKES ONE TENTH AS MANY JOULES TO WARM YOU UP SHORTY!

(LOGICAL)

Q is proportional to m

Specific *gravity* can be defined as the number of grams that a cubic centimeter of something weighs.

Specific *heat* is the number of joules needed to increase the temperature of a gram of substance by one degree Celsius or one Kelvin. Which degree you use does not matter in delta-T determinations (which, remember are mere subtractions).

For this increase to take place, heat, or energy (the terms are interchangeable in this context) must flow *into* the cubic centimeter of substance. For a decrease, heat must flow *out*.

Like specific gravity, specific heat is a dimensionless mathematical constant (i.e., not a variable) for a substance, and each substance has its own.

Originally, the definition of specific heat (like specific gravity) was based on a gram of water; but in replacing the calorie with the joule, the value for water became 4.184 instead of 1.000. There is, however, a substance (magnesium) that has a specific heat of 1.000 when the value is derived from joules. This means that we have a new standard based on unity, if we want it; but something that is far more important is understanding the meaning and derivation of specific heat from the its three dimensions: joules, grams, and °C.

Heat flow was mentioned above. It is measured in joules and kilojoules and is symbolized in calculations as Q or q. It is a variable that is proportional to two other parameters (for there are two other dimensions, right?).

One of these is temperature change— ΔT. It does not take a genius to understand that, as heat flows into something, its temperature will rise; conversely, if heat flows out, T falls. Even your author was able to comprehend this right off.

The other parameter, mass, is also proportional to Q. A more massive sample needs more heat to warm it up. Again, you do not need to be a potential Nobel Laureate to understand this.

In summary, then, more mass (m) or more increase in temperature (ΔT) means that more heat flow (Q) must take place. Ditto, of course, for less of everything: less mass and/or ΔT equal less Q.

Now that we have looked at the relationships of Q to m and ΔT—which are exactly what common sense would lead us to expect—we can return to specific heat and its own relationship to heat flow.

The physical and chemical properties that are unique to each substance give to every one of them its own value for specific heat which, for algebraic purposes, we represent with the symbol c. Specific heats, of course, can be found in the Handbook. *Each phase of a substance has its own specific heat value.*

Note that liquid water's value is very high; it takes much more heat (Q) to raise the temperature ($\triangle$T) of a gram (m) of water than anything else shown. This high "heat capacity" explains water's ability (1) to regulate body temperature and (2) to limit climactic changes in or near the oceans (those geographic regions farthest from the oceans experience the greatest seasonal variations in temperature).

Q, m, and $\triangle$T, remember, are experimental variables, whereas c is a constant because it is a fixed value for the substance in question.

With any three of these, we can algebraically determine the fourth. In Chem. 1, you are likely to measure or be given both m and $\triangle$T, and you will either have recorded Q or looked up c. Thus, the wanted parameter will be one of these last two.

If Q (heat flow in J or kJ) is sought, the equation will be

$$Q = c \times m \times \triangle T$$

Specific Heats J/g°C			
graphite	0.706	water (s)	2.050
magnesium	1.000	water (l)	4.184
aluminum	0.896	water (g)	2.008
sulfur	0.707		
iron (s)	0.442	methanol	2.510
iron (l)	0.454	ethanol (s)	0.969
nickel	0.444	ethanol (l)	2.453
copper (s)	0.383	ethanol (g)	1.426
copper (l)	0.488	acetone	1.322
cadmium	0.230	benzene	1.736
iodine	0.218	ether	0.547
tungsten	0.145	toluene	0.951
gold (s)	0.130	NaCl (s)	0.882
gold (l)	0.151	NaCl (l)	0.780
lead (s)	0.128	granite	0.803
lead (l)	0.157	olive oil	2.010

At this point, it will be helpful to recall the Universal Gas Constant, R, and how it contained a useful cluster of unnumbered dimensions that allowed you to trash all the unwanted dimensions from the calculation you made to determine P, V, n, or T. The constant c can do the same, although it is somewhat simpler and even easier to learn and use (If you can do one...).

$$R = \frac{(L)(torr)}{(mol)(K)} \qquad c = \frac{(kJ)}{(g)(°C)}$$

Specific heat, however, is not "universal," as is R (which is always 62.4); it varies (1) from one substance to the next and (2) for each phase of a substance.

Nevertheless, both R and c are derived from their dimensions and specific heats and—for purposes of comparison—can be spoken of without dimensions. Those of water and magnesium are worth committing to memory.

So, if you learned how to use R for gas calculations, then mastering c for thermal calculations will be no trick at all. Memorize the arrangement of the dimensions by thinking that since "jewels" are valuable, they are kept on the top shelf (numerator), whether in units (J) or by the thousand (kJ).

This problem is one of substitutions. Mass (m) is given; specific heat (c) is looked up; and $\triangle$T is figured (while Draggin' does so mentally right here, it is advisable to instead do it manually on your calculator).

$$c \times m \times \triangle T = Q$$

$$\frac{0.896\,J}{(g)(°C)} \times 36.0\,g \times 15.2°C = 490\,J$$

With your pencil, cancel out all the unwanted dimensions. Do this now. Only one of them—joules—will remain.

There may be other times when you will have to determine specific heat from the three variables (m, Q, ΔT) because you cannot look it up. In principle, this is similar to proving the Universal Gas Constant, howbeit simpler, as c derives from three variables, not four (now go to the left column).

Since c, not Q, is wanted in this instance, we solve the equation for c:

$$c = \frac{Q}{m \times \Delta T}$$

However, if you do not even wish to do this bit of algebra, you do not have to, for you already (should) know the needed equation, and you have the mnemonic tip from p. 255. It is nothing other than the mathematical definition of specific heat itself:

$$c = \frac{J}{(g)(°C)}$$

Using this equation for a problem, as before with the gases, involves only substitution and a few ordinary calculator operations.

Here is an example: what is the specific heat of silver (s) if a 20.0-gram ingot absorbs 45.1 joules while the temperature changes from 52.0°C to 61.5°C?

$$61.5 - 52.0 = 9.5$$

$$c = \frac{45.1 \text{ J}}{20.0 \text{ g} \times 9.5°C} = 0.237$$

Error Analysis

In your preparatory subtraction to get delta-T, T(final) is written first (as if T "first").

If you should get a negative result from this operation, as in Curie's example on the previous page, drop the (−) from the c- or Q-calculation; ΔT differences are absolute, measuring distance on a number line, so to speak.

1. Match these:

_____ -209 J or -75.4°C	a. specific heat of water (English)
_____ T_f	b. exothermic values
_____ 1.000 calorie	c. specific heat in general
_____ 4.184 joules	d. "before" temperature reading
_____ Q	e. thermal changes
_____ c	f. endothermic values
_____ 209 J or 75.4°C	g. specific heat of magnesium
_____ T_i	h. specific heat of water (SI)
_____ 1.000 joule	i. "after" temperature reading
_____ $\triangle T$ and $\triangle H$	j. that which is proportional to mass

2. Explain why a melting or boiling sample, while undergoing obvious physical change, does not increase in temperature until the change is completed:

3. Why is mass proportional to heat flow?

4. How many joules are in 4.50 ounces of wine if one ounce has 16.2 calories?

5. What is $\triangle T$ if a system has... (a) warmed from 225 K to 1164 K?

(b) cooled from 29.5°C to −19.5°C?

In the following four problems, you will have to begin with a subtraction operation, like those in prob. 5.

The T_i value, you might recall, is always the subtrahend.

6. A 170-gram sample of magnesium increases in temperature to 274 K to 369 K. How much heat did the metal absorb (space for figuring this one is provided on the next page)?

6. (continued)

7. 690 grams of benzene, molar weight 78.1, are cooled from 14.3°C to -14.3°C. What value for Q do you expect your calorimeter (a device used in the lab to measure heat flow) to indicate?

8. What is the specific heat of chloroform, $CHCl_3$, if 1.080 kilojoules of heat are required to increase the temperature of a 71.0-gram sample from 12.1°C to 27.9°C?

9. A 3.75-ounce sample of an unknown metal releases 505 joules as its temperature falls from 61.6°C to 40.9°C. What is its specific heat? Can you identify the metal from its c value (see the table, p. 255)? This problem must be solved in two steps (hint: 1 ounce = 28.3 grams).

(The answers to this problem set are found on p. 266).

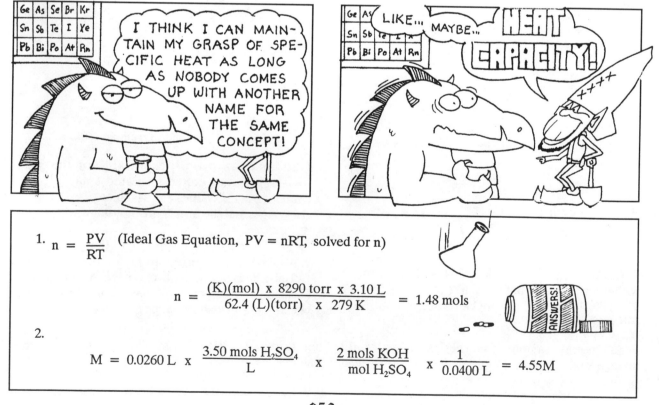

$$1. \quad n = \frac{PV}{RT} \quad \text{(Ideal Gas Equation, } PV = nRT, \text{ solved for n)}$$

$$n = \frac{(K)(mol) \times 8290 \text{ torr} \times 3.10 \text{ L}}{62.4 \text{ (L)(torr)} \times 279 \text{ K}} = 1.48 \text{ mols}$$

2.

$$M = 0.0260 \text{ L} \times \frac{3.50 \text{ mols } H_2SO_4}{L} \times \frac{2 \text{ mols KOH}}{\text{mol } H_2SO_4} \times \frac{1}{0.0400 \text{ L}} = 4.55M$$

The most familiar earthly example of plasmas are neon lights.

Not counting the aqueous state, there are at least eight physical states of matter. The familiar solid, liquid, and gas states are only intermediates in the energy scheme of things.

The most limited is the superfluid state, for which there is only one substance, helium, and even then only below 3 K. The superfluid is paradoxically defined as a "liquid without viscosity." He(sf) fills the bottom of its container, but is also able to creep up the sides, forming a concave surface. It changes state at 3 K, to He(l), and again at 4 K, to He(g).

He(l) is used to bring certain silicon compounds and alloys (e.g., niobium/iridium) to the super-conductor state where, instead of vibrating randomly (as in a solid) or moving about (as in ionic solutions), the particles move together in an orderly fashion, if at all, and thus leave a straight path for the flow of electrons. Recently, however, compounds with superconductive properties at temperatures as high as 93 K have been prepared. This is good news, for it means that cheap $N_2(l)$ instead of He(l) can be used as coolant.

In a superconductor, the particles do not vibrate randomly as in a proper solid; they move (if at all) together in planes or other fixed patterns. This is ideal for a current of electrons, which can pass through unimpeded (that is, without resistance).

In the "sunbelt" of matter, there are, or have been, three other states; Sakharov posited the existence of a fourth. Gases begin ionizing around 10^5 K to form plasma (p), a gaslike mixture of cations and electrons. The ionization results from impacts that are so severe that they knock the electrons free. In neon tubes, noble gases are blasted with electricity to make plasma. The tubes do not overheat because it is only the electrons that are absorbing and re-radiating the energy as photons, rather than the far mor massive ions. The plasmic state extends well into the millions of Kelvins, and stars are mostly H(p) and He(p). At the sun's core the ions are so heated (15 million K) and under such pressure that the nuclei merge; this is the nuclear chemistry, fusion.

Beyond 10 billion K is the free nucleon state. Matter has not so existed since the birth of the universe, when it suddenly cooled to plasma. At the free nucleon level, not even nuclei hold together; the nucleons are free. This state has been achieved in particle accelerators with interestingly, the help of supercooled, superconducting wires, which are needed to deliver the enormous energy punch without resistance, which would instantly melt them.

And finally, beyond 10 trillion K is the quark matter state, where not even the very nucleons can stay in one piece; they are instead quarks. The quark is an enigmatic entity; although believed to have a volume of under one-thousandth that of a nucleon, each nucleon consists in only three quarks. They are held together by a force called gluon. Every quark in the universe is believed to be confined in nuceons. There is, as yet, no way to isolate a quark.

STATE OF MATTER	ESSENTIAL PARTICLE
Quark matter	quarks
Free nucleons	nucleons
(p) Plasmas	ions
(g) Gases	molecules
(l) Liquids	molecules/ions
(s) Solids	molecules/ions/atoms
SF Superconductors	

7.7 Van der Waals Forces

It is true. All three types of Van der Waals Forces are electrostatic attractions between molecules. Molar weight has very little to do with it; gases are not gases because their atoms are "light." For indeed, the mass of phosgene is 99, and that of radon is over 200.

In short, gravity cannot keep substances from being gases instead of liquids. Electrostatic, intermolecular attractions—the Van der Waals Forces—can.

Do not confuse any Van der Waals Force with true chemical (ionic, covalent, metallic) bonds. One of them, however, the *dipole forces*, are very nearly ionic bonds when they are very strong. If they were just a wee bit stronger, they would in fact be actual ionic bonds and cease to be dipole forces.

Another of the three Van der Waals Forces, the so-called "hydrogen bond," is frankly misnamed; so, we will refer to it as the *hydrogen pseudo bond*, so as to clearly distinguish it from the true and simple bond that hydrogen, with its valency of one, forms. This was mentioned and described many times in Chaps. 2 and 3.

1. Dipole Forces

Attractions between the opposite poles of polar molecules—between, specifically, their *dipoles*—are what hold them together. The stronger the dipole attraction within a substance, the more likely it is that the substance will be a solid instead of a liquid, or a liquid instead of a gas, at a given temperature.

For a sample to be transformed from a lower state to a higher one, energy (or heat) must flow in, and if the particles are highly polar—as they are in ionic and macromolecular solids—then the energy needed to overcome them will be higher.

This is why, in comparing two solid substances with approximate molar weights, that the one made up of the more polar molecules will have a higher melting point.

Dipole forces also explain why ionic substances are solids (unless dissolved) and why so many covalent substances can be liquids or even gases at room temperature. They differ from another Van der Waals Force (London) in being an invariable feature of a molecule.

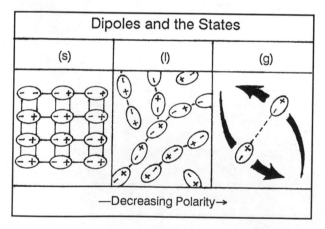

Dipoles and the States

(s)	(l)	(g)

—Decreasing Polarity→

substance	MW grams	molecular geometry	polarity	boiling pt. °C
SiH_4	32	tetragon	NP	−113
PH_3	34	trig. pyramid	P	−85
Br_2	160	linear	NP	59
ICl	162	linear	P	98

260

FAIR ENOUGH. BUT THE HALOGEN MOLECULES, UH, ARE NEUTRAL AND SYMMETRICAL, YET THEY FORM DIFFERENT STATES. SO DO ALKANE MOLECULES, FROM LIGHT GASES TO HEAVY SOLIDS.

WITH AN INCREASE IN SIZE COMETH ALSO AN INCREASE IN ELECTRON-CLOUD DISTORTION.

state	halogen/ alkane	melting Pt. °C	boiling Pt. °C
gas	F_2	−223	−187
	Cl_2	−101	−34.6
	CH_4	−184	−16.1
liquid	Br_2	−7.2	59
	C_8H_{18}	−56.5	125
solid	I_2	113	184
	$C_{40}H_{82}$	81	150

2. London Forces

While atomic weight has little to say in what physical state a substance will be in, atomic size, or radius, has a lot. Very brief and fleeting distortions are thought to take place in electron clouds, imparting *temporary* polarities, even to molecules with symmetric (nonpolar) geometries.

They are called *London,* or dispersion, *forces.* The larger an atom's electron cloud, the greater the potential distortion and, therefore, the temporary poles. These distortions are continual and unceasing, and so collectively influence the overall permanent character of a particle.

Fluorine keeps its electrons on a very tight leash; so does chlorine, though it has one more (if still fairly compact) Principle Energy Level. Without—to a significant degree—the inherent polarity of dipole forces nor the ephemeral polarity of London forces, both elements are gases at room temperature, as are the lighter alkanes and the noble gases, all of which are nonpolar and, on the average, neutral.

Bromine and octane molecules are sufficiently distorted to maintain an every-which-way polarity to keep them in the liquid state; they do not have enough distortion, or strong enough London forces, to form a solid, as in the case of the very big and unwieldy molecules of iodine and the heavier alkanes.

London forces naturally affect polar molecules as well as nonpolar ones, supplementing the effect of dipole forces.

3. Hydrogen Pseudo Bond

A third intermolecular force—perhaps named by Al the Kobold—is the "hydrogen bond." This label confounds some students for they confuse it with the bond that a hydrogen atom forms within a molecule, which is an *intra*molecular phenomenon; hence, it is redubbed in this book (but do not expect scientific journals to follow suit!).

The hydrogen pseudo bond is not inside, but outside, of the molecule proper; it is really nothing more than that same polarity between a hydrogen atom (a positive pole) in one molecule and a nonhydrogen atom (a negative pole) in *another* molecule.

It only makes a difference when hydrogen is bonded with one of the three or four most electronegative elements: nitrogen, oxygen, fluorine, and chlorine (which only barely merits inclusion).

In such a case, the hydrogen atom is left with such a small share of the electron cloud that it is not much more than a bare proton and, therefore, a strong positive pole that is attached to the negative pole of the N, O, or F atom in an adjacent molecule.

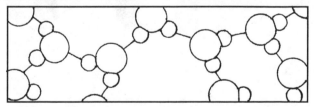

Does this sound familiar? It should: it is the exact same thing explained in Sect. 3.6, in which hydrogen fluoride was our example of a borderline covalent/ionic substance. Another example, water, is diagrammed above. Compare this diagram with that on p. 110 and recognize that the same principle is involved.

The hydrogen pseudo bond is strong enough to keep water in its liquid phase at room temperature (save for the near negligible gas phase). While this Van der Waals force does not prevent HF or NH_3 from being gases at the same temperatures, it does entail higher boiling and melting points for them.

7.8 Energy of Change of State

WHAT'S HEAT OF VAPORIZATION?

1. THE ENERGY NEEDED TO VAPORIZE ONE GRAM OF SOMETHING; 2. THE OPPOSITE OF HEAT OF CONDENSATION.

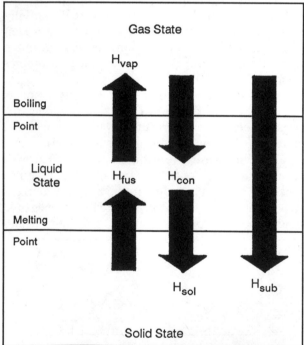

Gas State

H_{vap}

Boiling Point

Liquid State

H_{fus} H_{con}

Melting Point

H_{sol} H_{sub}

Solid State

As you know, in a sample undergoing a change of state, T does not change until the whole sample is in the new state (Sect. 7.5). Nevertheless, heat itself continues to go in or out, as the physical change indicates.

Each change in state, therefore, is a change in a sample's heat flow ($\triangle H$), expressed in calculations as Q. We have five such changes to consider.

One of the two changes in state with a positive value for every substance—positive because it requires heat to flow into the sample to happen—is the *heat of vaporization*, H_{vap}. It is the heat that one (1.00) gram of something must have to vaporize (to pass, not merely reach, its boiling point).

The other positive constant corresponding to a change of state is the *heat of fusion*, H_{fus}. In chemical contexts, fusion means melting; heat of fusion, then, is the energy needed to melt a gram of something, once it has been brought to its melting point (the energy needed to get it there is something apart). H_{vap} is necessarily higher than H_{fus} for any substance, because more heat is required to vaporize a mole of liquid phase than to melt a mole of solid phase.

From one substance to the next, there is a great diversity of melting and boiling points, and of heats of fusion and vaporization as well. And, because each substance has its own set of these four constants, there is considerable overlap, due to differing levels of Van der Waals influence. Helium passes through its boiling point at 4 K, while carbon does not even melt until 4.000×10^3 K.

The opposite—as you are encouraged to think of it—of the heat of vaporization is the *heat of condensation*, H_{con}. Its value will be the negative equivalent of the H_{vap} for any substance, for it represents a loss, or a heat flow *out of* the sample. Specifically, it is the heat that a gram of something must be without to condense, or fall back through the boiling point and into the liquid state.

In the same way, the *heat of solidification*, H_{sol}, is equal but opposite to the heat of fusion. If a gram of liquid at its substance's melting point loses this energy, it solidifies and—if it continues to lose energy—cools. The heats of condensation and solidification are really "negative heats" or "coldnesses."

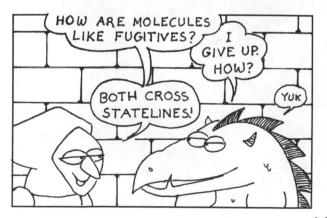

HOW ARE MOLECULES LIKE FUGITIVES?

I GIVE UP. HOW?

BOTH CROSS STATELINES!

YUK

Bob Long Inc.

Some Thermal Constants

Substance	Melting Pt. °C	Boiling Pt. °C	Hfus J/g	Hvap J/g
$H_2O(l)$	0	100	335	2260
$H_2SO_4(l)$	8.6	326	163	510
Al	659	2300	378	1050
Pb	327	1170	247	732
N_2	-210	-196	2.57	20.1
Br_2	-7.2	59	66.9	180
C_2H_5OH	-114	78	105	854
Hg	-39	358	11.7	297
Cu	1083	2595	205	4.81
NaCl	801	1413	519	1617

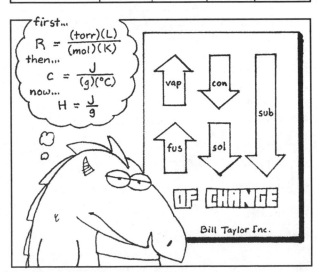

Bill Taylor Inc.

Some substances also have *heat* values—another negative heat. change is that in which a vapor chan crystal (g to s). Too, then, H_{sub} valu

Calculating the heat flow, Q, ne any of the five changes of state determining Q for a sample that is between state changes (Sect. 7.6). The equations you will use are:

$$Q = m \times H_{vap} \quad \text{and} \quad Q = m \times H_{fus}$$

H_{vap} and H_{fus}, as has already been pointed out, are constants, and each substance has its own set. You can find them in the Handbook, in some periodic tables, or in a table of thermal constants such as that at left.

These two constants are defined as joules needed to "fuse" (melt) or vaporize one gram of something that has already been warmed to its melting or boiling temperature, and so is expressed simply as:

$$\frac{J}{g} \quad (\text{or}) \quad \frac{kJ}{g}$$

To get Q, then, we just weigh the sample and multiply it by the constant; it really *is* that easy.

What, for instance, is the heat flow needed to fuse 25.0 grams of lead? Substitute the numbers into the formula:

$$Q = 25.0 \text{ g} \times \frac{247 \text{ J}}{g} = 6.18 \text{ kJ}$$

Here goes another example, one concerning a vaporization: how much energy must be added to 144 grams of ethylene to evaporate it? As before...

$$Q = 144 \text{ g} \times \frac{854 \text{ J}}{g} = 123 \text{ kJ}$$

The pattern, as you can see, is identical.

An alternative way of expressing heats of fusion and vaporization is by the mole of substance, rather than by the gram. Accordingly, the corresponding constants are called *molar heats of fusion* and *vaporization*. Many textbooks and teachers prefer these to the gram-based constants.

If in a problem you must determine Q but are given only a molar constant, you need only to add a molar conversion to the simple dimensional analysis pattern already used. An example follows.

How much heat is needed to change 84.5 grams of water into steam if the molar H_{vap} for water is 40.4 moles?

$$? \text{ kJ} = 84.5 \text{ g} \times \frac{\text{mol}}{18.01 \text{ g}} \times \frac{40.4}{\text{mol}} = 190 \text{ kJ}$$

7.9 Change of State & Temp.

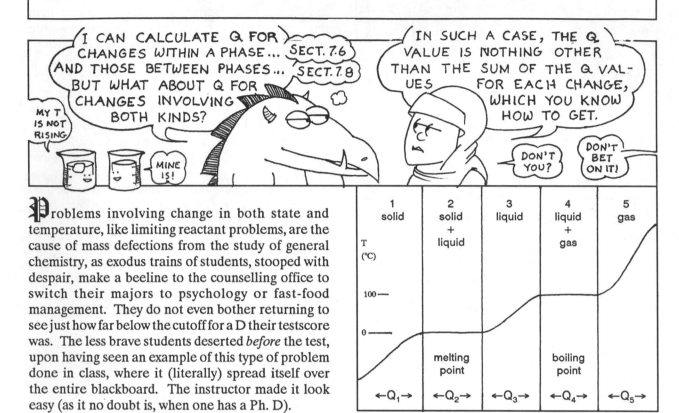

Speech bubbles (left to right):
"I CAN CALCULATE Q FOR CHANGES WITHIN A PHASE... SECT. 7.6 AND THOSE BETWEEN PHASES... SECT. 7.8 BUT WHAT ABOUT Q FOR CHANGES INVOLVING BOTH KINDS?"

"MY T IS NOT RISING"

"MINE IS!"

"IN SUCH A CASE, THE Q VALUE IS NOTHING OTHER THAN THE SUM OF THE Q VALUES FOR EACH CHANGE, WHICH YOU KNOW HOW TO GET."

"DON'T YOU?"

"DON'T BET ON IT!"

$\mathbf{P}$roblems involving change in both state and temperature, like limiting reactant problems, are the cause of mass defections from the study of general chemistry, as exodus trains of students, stooped with despair, make a beeline to the counselling office to switch their majors to psychology or fast-food management. They do not even bother returning to see just how far below the cutoff for a D their test score was. The less brave students deserted *before* the test, upon having seen an example of this type of problem done in class, where it (literally) spread itself over the entire blackboard. The instructor made it look easy (as it no doubt is, when one has a Ph. D).

This is all too bad, because if these students had gained facility in using the two very simple equations that are necessarily covered immediately before change of state and temperature calculations—namely those for state and temperature separately—the only additional skill they would need is fourth-grade addition.

In a qualitative sense, this type of problem is the "addition" (but really the synthesis) of two others:

Change of State   (Sect. 7.5)
Change of Temp.   (Sect. 7.6)
Change of State
          and Temp.

Change of state problems are only a single multiplication operation. Change of temperature includes two multiplications and a division operation; it is like a very simple DA problem. If you can both skip and jump, then you can *alternately* skip and jump; each is a slightly different type of "step."

The final operation—qualitatively and quantitatively—is addition. *There is no trace of even simple algebra anywhere;* it is all simple arithmetic:

subtraction for the T values; multiplication and division in the short equations; and a final addition.

The above table is the same as in Sect. 7.5, except for the bottom margin. Each Q is a step; the last step, the sixth one, is the addition. The steps do not need to be memorized; they follow naturally from each other (note: the arrows could as easily go to the left if the sample were cooling rather than warming).

STEP ONE: $Q_1 = m \times c \times T$

STEP TWO: $Q_2 = m \times H_{fus}$

STEP THREE: $Q_3 = m \times c \times T$

STEP FOUR: $Q_4 = m \times H_{vap}$

STEP FIVE: $Q_5 = m \times c \times T$

LAST STEP: $Q_T = Q_1 + Q_2 + Q_3 + Q_4 + Q_5$

The steps are just alternating applications of two simple equations you by now know. Each can even begin with the sample's mass. You will not always have to do all the steps in such a problem, for the overall change will not include each separate change.

264

Let us say that Curie took another sample of ice from the freezer and then heated it all the way to the gas phase, at which time she collected the steam and heated it further.

If the sample weighed 84.7 grams and was originally at −22°C, and then heated to steam at 130°C, what was the total flow of heat into the sample?

You may find that it is easier to just look up the thermal constants as you go along rather than writing them all down before doing the calculations. There is only one substance involved, in any case; and the constants are often provided in the problems, especially on tests.

The H_2O sample (1) warms, (2) melts, (3) warms, (4) vaporizes, and (5) warms yet a final time, so you will need the melting and boiling points to determine the two delta-Ts. Everything else is mere substitution into the equations.

In the first step, the ice heats up to (but not through) the melting point. ΔT is 22°C [0 − (-22)], so...

$$Q_1 = 84.7g \; x \; \frac{2.050\,J}{(g)(°C)} \; x \; 22°C \; = \; 3.8\,kJ$$

Now, the second step, in which the ice melts:

$$Q_2 \; = \; 84.7\,g \; x \; \frac{335\,J}{g} \; = \; 28.4\,kJ$$

Next, the energy transfer, or heat flow, required to heat the sample through the entire liquid phase; up to (but not through) the boiling point. ΔT is 100 [100 − 0], so...

$$Q_3 \; = \; 84.7\,g \; x \; \frac{4.184\,J}{(g)(°C)} \; x \; 100°C \; = \; 35.4\,kJ$$

Then, determine the energy necessary to vaporize all of it:

$$Q_4 \; = \; 84.7\,g \; x \; \frac{2260\,J}{g} \; = \; 191\,kJ$$

Finally, find the energy added to the gas phase to bring it up to the given 130°C. ΔT is 30 [130 − 100], so...

$$Q_5 \; = \; 84.7\,g \; x \; \frac{2.008\,J}{(g)(°C)} \; x \; 30°C \; = \; 5.1\,kJ$$

Now, just add everything up:

$$Q_T \; = \; 3.8 + 28.4 + 35.4 + 191 + 5.1 \; = \; 264\,kJ$$

With your pencil, cancel out all the unwanted dimensions above; do the same as you read through the next example.

Note, in the language of this problem, the words *cools*, *solidifies*, and *cools*. Each of these represents a step.

The problems in the following sets (and on tests) will not be so explicitly stated; however, your reason will guide you.

Get your constants from the tables on pp. 256 and 263.

In the first step, there is (an absolute) temperature change of 156°C [660 − 816], so...

$$Q_1 \; = \; 320\,g \; x \; \frac{0.488\,J}{(g)(°C)} \; x \; \text{-}156°C \; = \; \text{-}24.4\,kJ$$

Then, for the solidifying (or freezing):

$$Q_2 \; = \; 320 \; g \; x \; \frac{205J}{g} \; = \; \text{-}65.6\,kJ$$

Next, the further cooling (ΔT = -588°C):

$$Q_3 \; = \; 320\,g \; x \; \frac{0.383\,J}{(g)(°C)} \; x \; \text{-}590°C \; = \; \text{-}72.3\,kJ$$

And last of all, the addition:

$$Q_T \; = \; \text{-}24.4 + (\text{-}65.6) + (\text{-}72.3) \; = \; \text{-}162\,kJ$$

1. b   i   a   h   j   c   f   d   g   e

2. During these transitions, the sample is using incoming heat flow to convert itself to the next higher state rather than to increase its temperature. As always, your answer may be phrased much differently than this and yet still be correct.

3. A larger (that is, a more massive) lab sample, house, planet, or pineapple upside-down cake needs more heat flow (joules) to warm it from one given T to another given T than a smaller sample, house, planet, or pineapple upside-down cake needs.

   When cooling, proportionately more heat will have to flow back out if the sample (etc.) is to return to its former temperature.

4. ? joules = 4.50 ounces x $\dfrac{16.2 \text{ cals}}{\text{oz}}$ x $\dfrac{4.184 \text{ J}}{\text{cal}}$ = 305 J (0.305 kJ)

5. (a) 225 − 1164 = $\left|939\right|$ K   (b) 29.5 − (-19.5) = 49°C

6. Q = $\dfrac{1.000 \text{ J}}{(\text{g})(°\text{C})}$ x 170 g x 95°C = 1.62×10^4 (16.2 kJ)

7. Q = $\dfrac{1.74 \text{ J}}{(\text{g})(°\text{C})}$ x 690 g x 28.6°C = 3.43×10^4 (35.5 kJ)

8. c = $\dfrac{1080 \text{ J}}{(71.0 \text{ g})(158.0°)}$ = 0.963 (no dimension)

9. ? grams metal = 3.75 oz x $\dfrac{28.3 \text{ g}}{\text{oz}}$ = 106 g metal

    c = $\dfrac{505 \text{ J}}{(106 \text{ g})(20.7°\text{C})}$ = 0.230 (cadmium)

(The Commutative Property permits the multipliers—m, c, and $\triangle$T—to be written in any order).

266

1. Match:

_____condensation
_____dipole forces
_____fusion
_____H pseudo bond
_____solidification
_____sublimation
_____London forces
_____vaporization

a. attraction between the $(-)$ and $(+)$ regions of particles

b. transitory polarities due to to electron-cloud distortions

c. happens when Van der Waals Forces are all but completely overcome

d. physical disintegration of, for instance, a macromolecular lattice

e. the result of high pressure or low temperature on gases

f. an attraction between bonded protons and negative poles

g. the slowing of particles to a stop, relative to each other

h. state-skipping (in chemistry); manipulation (in advertizing)

Use the tables of constants in Sects. 7.6 and 7.8 as needed to solve all of the following problems...

2. Liquid nitrogen, a coolant for superconductives, is obtained, as you know, by the fractionation of air. The air is cooled to liquid, and slowly rewarmed. The nitrogen is the first to reach its boiling point and so bubbles off, an invisible gas. If collected at this temperature and separately recooled, how much energy will 3.0 grams of $N_2(g)$ lose as it goes back to $N_2(l)$?

3. How many joules are needed to vaporize 13.5 grams of bromine, at its boiling point?

4. Determine Q for the fusion of 799 grams of aluminum:

5. What amount of heat would be evolved by the solidification of 1.00 ton of lead? This problem has two unstated conversion factors.

6. How much energy will be required to convert 6.00 moles of boiling concentrated sulfuric acid, $H_2SO_4(l)$, to its gaseous state?

7. A 4.50-kilogram sample of an alloy with a heat of fusion of 311 J/g is melted. What (a) change in temperature will be recorded? How much (b) heat is necessary for this change (keep in mind that the melted alloy is *not* heated further).

8. Determine the heat flow from 650 grams of molten NaCl at 1710°C as it cools, crystallizes, and falls to room temperature, 28°C:

9. Solid mercury has a specific heat of 0.327, while the liquid's c value is not much different at 0.333. What is Q for the conversion of 24.6 grams of Hg(s) at -49°C to Hg(l) at 49°C?

10. Ethanol (C_2H_5OH) results when sugars are fermented by the action of yeast enzymes. Seventh-day Adventists insist that the wine that Jesus converted from water in his first recorded miracle (John 2:6-9) could not have contained a trace of this substance. How many joules would it take to change 750 grams of ethyl alcohol (its other name) frozen at −160°C to gas at 94°C?

7.10 Enthalpy

The heat content of a set of reactants—that which we have been calling a "chemical system"—is the system's *enthalpy*, H. The heat flow, Q, that takes place as the reactants form a new system by becoming products is the *heat of reaction*, $\triangle H_R$. It is a net gain or loss of heat.

(By definition, a chemical system also includes known values for pressure and temperature. We will not bother with these at this point, save to say that their influences can be worked into a calculation in a similar manner to the P and T adjustment for gases, as explained in Chap. 5.)

[Note: Heat of reaction ($\triangle H_R$) is a specific type of heat flow (variously expressed as $\triangle H$, Q, or q) and is also called net heat of reaction or enthalpy of reaction. In this book, to avoid confusion, Q is our symbol for heat flow in and out of samples and $\triangle H$ is our symbol for heat flow in and out of reactions ($\triangle H_R$) and in the formation of products ($\triangle H_F$).] In all, $\triangle H_R$ is the difference (i.e., a subtraction) between two enthalpies: those of the product and reactant systems.

Specifically, it is a matter of subtracting the reactant system's enthalpy, H_r, from the product system's enthalpy, H_p, to get $\triangle H$ ($H_p - H_r = \triangle H$). In Sect. 4.1, an equation was shown in which 588 kJ evolved:

$$2Hg(l) + H_2SO_4(aq) \rightarrow Hg_2SO_4(s) + H_2(g) + 588\,kJ$$

A mole of mercury sulfate was formed, and 588 kJ was lost from the reaction ($\triangle H = -588\,kJ$). Therefore, the reaction was exothermic.

Heat itself was one of the products of the reaction, and so was lost by it. Yet, as it left the system, it caused a calorimeter to register a positive measurement (it was "positively hot"). However, to indicate delta-H (or Q) apart from the reaction, we would express it as a loss to that reaction as...

$$\triangle H = -588\,kJ$$

The value is negative because, again, heat was lost; it evolved.

Conversely, in an endothermic reaction, heat would be a "reactant" in the same way it was a "product" in the above reaction; this time, the system's surroundings would lose heat, and the system would gain it. A calorimeter would give a negative reading. The photosynthesis of a mole of glucose, for instance, absorbs 2816 kJ of (solar) heat:

$$6H_2O + 6CO_2 \rightarrow C_6H_{12}O_6 + 6O_2 - 2816\,kJ$$

As heat is absorbed by the reactants as they become products, the heat transfer is represented as...

$$\triangle H = +2816\,kJ$$

(The plus sign is optional). The heat of reaction—or heat flow—associated with the formation of a mole of something is its *molar heat of formation*.

269

ENTHALPY! HEAT OF REACTION! HEAT OF FORMATION! SO WHAT'S THE DIFFERENCE?

ONLY THE LATTER TWO ARE DIFFERENCES (ARITHMETICALLY!). BOTH ARE DIFFERENCES BETWIXT PRE- AND POST-REACTION ENTHALPIES.

...and it so happens that these two mathematical differences—$\triangle H_R$ and $\triangle H_F$—are occasionally the same, for reasons that we will presently uncover (they have to do with the Rules for delta-H equations).

Each compound or ionic substance (except H^+) has its own heat of formation. Up to this point, two have been noted:

$$\triangle H = -588 \, kJ \quad \text{mercury (I) sulfate}$$
$$\triangle H = +2816 \, kJ \quad \text{glucose}$$

The first of these values is exothermic (a lowering of enthalpy from before to after) because the reactants lost heat as they *formed* the salt; the second is endothermic, because the sugar produced had more heat content (or enthalpy) than the reactants from which the sugar *was formed*.

Again, the signs (+,−) for heat of formation are opposite those that appear in the equations, though they represent the same value. By convention, the delta-H value is written as a product. This is why, if heat is absorbed as a reactant it is written as a negative product. Instead of being produced, it is used up (actually, it is siloed into the newly forming bonds of the products).

This is endothermy.

Lavoissier had noticed that heat could be a product or a reactant of a chemical reaction, and so he believed that it was also a chemical element. While he was incorrect, his reasoning was sound and defensible.

Your best hope to avoid sign (+, −) problems is by practice and association. On seeing any standard equation showing heat of formation, (a) identify it as endothermic or exothermic and (b) jot down its $\triangle H$ value (heat of formation or of reaction) as a separate mini-equation (like the two in the left column) by taking the $\triangle H$ value from the equation and reversing the signs.

Here is an example: what is the heat of formation for a mole of anhydrous iron (III) oxide?

$$4Fe(s) + 3O_2(g) \rightarrow 2Fe_2O_3 + 164 \, kJ$$

In this case, heat is a "positive" product, so the reaction is exothermic, or heat-evolving. Then, for the mini-equation for the $\triangle H_F$ value, switch the sign: $\triangle H_F = -164 \, kJ$. The negative sign, again, indicates that the heat was lost by the system (and therefore registered positively by the calorimeter gauging the surroundings, which gained).

Now, to another skill: how to determine the heat of *reaction*, $\triangle H_R$, from heats of *formation*, $\triangle H_F$. To do this, we merely subtract the reaction system's total enthalpy from the product system's total enthalpy. Remember that humble equation? ($H_p - H_r = \triangle H$).

Only compounds and ionic species have values; neutral elements are always zero. Thus, a system (reactant or product) that consists only in elements has an enthalpy of zero, as in the reactant systems of the previous two examples, and in the following one:

NO_2 formation is endothermic and (therefore) written $\triangle H = +33.5 \, kJ$:

$$N_2(g) + 2O_2(g) \rightarrow 2NO_2(g) - 67.0 \, kJ$$

Note that different phases of a substance (e.g., NH_3, H_2O) have differing $\triangle H$ values:

Some Heats of Formation (kJ)									
Ag^+	106							NO	90.4
Al_2O_3	-401							NO_2	33.5
Ca^{2+}	-544	Cl^-	-167	FeS	-951	H_2O_2	-186	PCl_3	-306
CH_4	-75.0	$CuCl_2$	-206	H^+	0	H_2S	-21.3	PCl_5	-399
C_2H_5OH	-276	F^-	-329	HCl	-92.5	ICl	17.6	SO_2	-297
C_3H_8	-10.4	$FeCl_2$	-443	HNO_3	-208	K^+	-251	SO_3	-395
C_6H_6	-49.0	Fe_2O_3	-824	$H_2O(l)$	-286	$NH_3(aq)$	-80.8	SO_4^{2-}	-908
CO_2	-393	Fe_3O_4	-1117	$H_2O(g)$	-242	$NH_3(g)$	-42.6	ZnO	-353

270

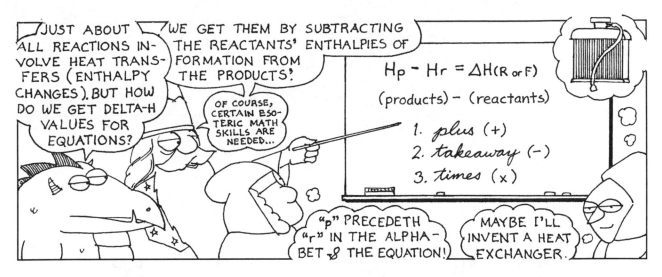

H Equation Rules

I

Neutral elements and H^+ ions have enthalpy of formation values of 0.

II

A compound's value is multiplied by its coefficient.

These two rules are obvious and unforgettable, if you ponder them. Rule 1 is so because H^+ and the neutral elements are *the* elements; they do not form from other substances, as do compounds and ions, and so cannot have heats of formation.

Rule 2 is also self-evident. If two, or three, etc., moles of substance form, it follows that two or three times the heat was transferred than if there were only one mole. In the first example on the previous page, iron (III) oxide has a coefficient of 2, so the ΔH_F shown for the formation is double that shown in the table. Compare the two numbers. As you would for a stoichiometric calculation, just take the coefficients from the balanced equation and use them.

Now, an example: what is the heat of reaction for the decomposition of silver chloride (heat of formation -127 kJ) to silver ion and chloride. Write the given (or looked-up) values below the species in the equation:

$$AgCl(s) \rightarrow Ag^+ + Cl^-$$
$$(-127) \qquad (106) + (-167)$$

(Note: this is a net ionic equation).

The product sum is -61. From it, subtract the reactant sum: $-61 - (-127) = (+)66$. This reaction, therefore, is endothermic, absorbing 66 kJ in the breakdown of each mole of AgCl. The products have more energy than the compound they made up.

Another example: what is ΔH_R for the burning of methane in air?

$$CH_4(g) + O_2(g) \rightarrow CO_2(g) + 2H_2O(g)$$
$$(-75.0) \qquad (0) \qquad (-393) \qquad 2(-286)$$

Notice that the coefficient, 2, was simply plopped in front of the $H_2O(g)$ value. The products' enthalpies add up to -965 kJ. Subtracting from this the reactants' enthalpies (-75.0) gives us -890 kJ for ΔH_R. Heat is lost ($-$), so exothermy is indicated. You would expect this in combustion, which is very rapid oxidation. Heat is released as the bonds in the reacting compounds are broken. If the formation of the new bonds absorbs less energy that the original bonds released, there is a net heat loss; hence, the reaction is exothermic. Conversely, in endothermic reactions, the newly formed bonds hold more heat than the old bonds released; hence, a net gain.

One further example: nitrous oxide reacts with water(l) to form nitric acid and nitric oxide. Determine ΔH_R and state whether exothermic or endothermic:

$$3NO_2(g) + H_2O(l) \rightarrow 2HNO_3(aq) + NO(g)$$
$$3(33.5) \qquad (-286) \qquad 2(-208) \qquad (90.4)$$

The sum of the reactants is -186; that of the products is -326. Subtracting the former from the latter gives us -140 kJ (exothermic).

Error Analysis

Do not confuse heat of reaction, ΔH_R, a value for an equation, with heat of formation, ΔH_F, a value for a species. They can, however, be the same thing if all but one of the heats of formation in a reaction is 0, because zeros do not affect sums. The examples of Fe_2O_3 and NO_2, on p. 270, illustrate this.

Nor must you confuse H_r, enthalpy of reactants, with ΔH_R, the *change* in enthalpy during a reaction.

271

1. e   a   d   f   g   h   b   c

2. $Q = 3.0 \text{ g N}_2 \times \dfrac{2.01 \text{ J}}{\text{g}} = 6.0 \text{ g N}_2$

3. $Q = 13.5 \text{ g Br}_2 \times \dfrac{180 \text{ J}}{\text{g}} = 2.43 \text{ kJ}$

4. $Q = 799 \text{ g Al} \times \dfrac{378 \text{ J}}{\text{g}} = 302 \text{ kJ}$

5. $Q = 1.00 \text{ ton Pb} \times \dfrac{2000 \text{ lbs}}{\text{ton}} \times \dfrac{454 \text{ g}}{\text{lb}} \times \dfrac{-247 \text{ J}}{\text{g}} = (-2.24 \times 10^8 \text{ J}) = -2.24 \times 10^5 \text{ kJ}$

6. $Q = 6.00 \text{ moles H}_2\text{SO}_4 \times \dfrac{98.08 \text{ g H}_2\text{SO}_4}{\text{mol H}_2\text{SO}_4} \times \dfrac{510 \text{ J}}{\text{g}} = 3.00 \times 10^5 \text{ J} = 300 \text{ kJ}$

7. (a) none   (b) $4.50 \text{ kg} \times \dfrac{1000 \text{ g}}{\text{kg}} \times \dfrac{311 \text{ J}}{\text{g}} = 1.40 \times 10^3 \text{ kJ}$

8. $Q_1 = 650 \text{ g} \times \dfrac{0.780 \text{ J}}{(\text{g})(°\text{C})} \times -909°\text{C} = -461 \text{ kJ}$

    $Q_2 = 650 \text{ g} \times \dfrac{-519 \text{ J}}{\text{g}} = -337 \text{ kJ}$

    $Q_3 = 650 \text{ g} \times \dfrac{0.882 \text{ J}}{(\text{g})(°\text{C})} \times -773°\text{C} = -443 \text{ kJ}$

    $Q_T = -461 + (-337) + (-443) = -1241 = -1.24 \times 10^3 \text{ kJ}$

    $[\triangle T = 801 - 1710 = -909]$

    $[\triangle T = 28 - 801 = -773]$

9. $Q_1 = 24.6 \text{ g} \times \dfrac{0.333 \text{ J}}{(\text{g})(°\text{C})} \times 10°\text{C} = 82 \text{ J}$

    $Q_2 = 24.6 \text{ g} \times \dfrac{11.7 \text{ J}}{\text{g}} = 288 \text{ J}$

    $Q_3 = 24.6 \text{ g} \times \dfrac{0.327 \text{ J}}{(\text{g})(°\text{C})} \times 88°\text{C} = 7.1 \times 10^2 \text{ J}$

    $Q_T = 82 + 288 + 7.1 \times 10^2 = 1.08 \times 10^3 \text{ J} = 1.08 \text{ kJ}$

    $[\triangle T = 39 - (-49) = 10]$

    $[\triangle T = 49 - (-39) = 88]$

10. $Q_1 = 750 \text{ g} \times \dfrac{0.969 \text{ J}}{(\text{g})(°\text{C})} \times 56°\text{C} = 40.7 \text{ kJ}$

    $Q_2 = 750 \text{ g} \times \dfrac{105 \text{ J}}{\text{g}} = 788 \text{ kJ}$

    $Q_3 = 750 \text{ g} \times \dfrac{2.453 \text{ J}}{(\text{g})(°\text{C})} \times 192°\text{C} = 353 \text{ kJ}$

    $Q_4 = 750 \text{ g} \times \dfrac{854 \text{ J}}{\text{g}} = 640 \text{ kJ}$

    $Q_5 = 750 \text{ g} \times \dfrac{1.426 \text{ J}}{(\text{g})(°\text{C})} \times 16°\text{C} = 17 \text{ kJ}$

    $Q_T = 41 + 788 + 353 + 640 + 17 = 1.84 \times 10^3 \text{ kJ}$

    $[\triangle T = -114 - (-160) = 56]$

    $[\triangle T = 78 - (-114) = 192]$

    $[\triangle T = 94 - 78 = 16]$

7.11 Thermochemical Stoichiometry

By now you should have no anxiety about stoichiometry, having worked through Sects. 4.4, 4.5, 4.8, 5.3, 5.10, 5.11, 5.14, 6.6, 6.7, and 6.11. We will now consider a new variation of it.

So far, all the stoichiometry we have done has related one substance in a reaction to another using a dimensional-analysis keystone. In thermochemical stoichiometry, however, the relation is between a quantity of substance and a quantity of heat (although Lavoissier would have argued that the keystone relates two substances even here, if that helps you any). Thus, the keystone will have a whole number of moles and a quantity of kilojoules; but both of these come from an equation, like the two parts of any other keystone. The only other link in the stoichiometric bridge is a single molar conversion factor.

Consider the final example in Sect. 7.10, in which the equation, including the enthalpy of reaction, is

$$3NO_2(g) \; + \; H_2O(l) \; \rightarrow \; 2HNO_3(aq) \; + \; NO(g) \; - \; 140 \, kJ$$
$$3(33.5) \qquad (-286) \qquad 2(-208) \qquad (90.4)$$

How much heat (how many kJ or what Q) will evolve in the making of 750 grams of nitric acid? Set it up like any DA problem and solve:

$$? \, kJ \; = \; 750 \, g \, HNO_3 \; \times \; \frac{mol \, HNO_3}{63.08 \, g \, HNO_3} \; \times \; \frac{-140 \, kJ}{2 \, mols \, HNO_3} \; = \; -8.32 \times 10^2 \, kJ$$

All the information for this problem (save for the weight of HNO_3) came from the equation, provided you took the trouble to write the $\triangle H_F$ values under the species and then multiplied them by the coefficients (Rule 2).

Here is a problem asking you to determine $\triangle H_R$ and then predict, stoichiometrically, the heat transfered (in or out): In the reduction of alumina ($\triangle H_F = -401 \, kJ$) with carbon, aluminum and carbon dioxide are the ultimate products. Give $\triangle H_R$ for the preparation (not formation, for it is an element) of 50.0 pounds of aluminum. First, as always, find and write the heats of formation under each species (only one of which is given):

$$2Al_2O_3(s) \; + \; 3C(s) \; \rightarrow \; 4Al(s) \; + \; 3CO_2(g)$$
$$2(-401) \qquad (0) \qquad (0) \qquad 3(-393)$$

Subtracting the sum of the reactant enthalpies from the sum of the product enthalpies gives us − 377 kJ. This is the heat evolved in this clearly exothermic reaction for every four moles of aluminum that are yielded. And so you have from these two quantities—one of moles and the other of kilojoules—a keystone for your stoichiometry. One unstated conversion factor, in addition to the molar one, was called for in this problem:

$$? \, kJ \; = \; 50.0 \, pounds \, Al \; \times \; \frac{454 \, g \, Al}{lb \, Al} \; \times \; \frac{mol \, Al}{26.98 \, g \, Al} \; \times \; \frac{-337 \, kJ}{4 \, mols \, Al} \; = \; -7.93 \times 10^4 \, kJ$$

You may have noticed that molar heats are in kilojoules; this is because samples quantified in moles are somewhat large, and the values that you will be using are for molar heats.

273

1. Distinguish enthalpy in particular from heat of reaction:

2. Explain why endothermic reactions have (+) values and exothermic reactions have (−) values:

3. Distinguish the heat of formation from the heat of reaction:

4. Determine the enthalpies of reaction for the equations below. Use the table in Sect. 7.10 for the heat of formation values that you will write under each substance.

    Then identify each reaction as either exothermic or endothermic.

——————*Error Analysis*——————

Do not neglect the use the signs (−,+) in the calculations; if you add or subtract when you should be doing the inverse, you will obviously get an incorrect result.

    For instance, −367 − (-211) would equal −156 (kJ), and most certainly *not* -578.

a. $2Zn(s) + O_2(g) \rightarrow 2ZnO(s)$

b. $SO_2(g) + 2H_2S(g) \rightarrow 3S(s) + 2H_2O(g)$

c. $Cu(s) + Cl_2(g) \rightarrow CuCl_2(s)$

d. $Fe_3O_4(s) + Zn(s) \rightarrow 3Fe(s) + 4ZnO_2(s)$

e. $PCl_5(g) \rightarrow PCl_3(g) + Cl_2(g)$

f. $C_2H_5OH(l) + 3O_2(g) \rightarrow 2CO_2(g) + 3H_2O(l)$

| a. |
| b. |
| c. |
| d. |
| e. |
| f. |

5. Using equation (b) above, determine how much heat would be absorbed or liberated in the production of 189 grams of sulfur:

6. Determine (a) ΔH_R for the dissociation of 60.0 liters of phosphorus pentachloride, according to the equation (e) from problem 4. Then, (b) state the amount, in liters, of the combined products. Assume that all gases are at STP (a tip: get out the molar volume conversion factor for the stoiciometry part of this problem).

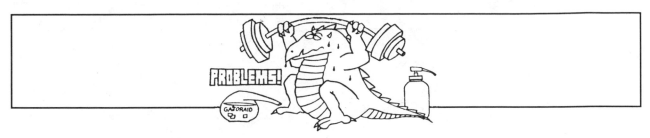

6.

7. Equation (f) from problem 4 describes a combustion reaction, so heat transfer will of course be highly exothermic. How many grams of ethanol would have to be burned to melt one mole of sodium chloride, assuming all the heat reached the salt (a logistical impossibility, but that is beside the point)? Find the molar heat of fusion for NaCl in the table in Sect. 7.8.

Isomerism

Isomers are different compounds that have the same formula. This is possible because fairly large molecules can have different potential arrangements of their component atoms. This is especially so among organic carbon compounds.

The alkanes, for instance, have the general formula C_nH_{2n+2}. Relatively simple butane (C_4H_{10}) has only two isomers; the Lewis diagrams for both are shown here.

(a)

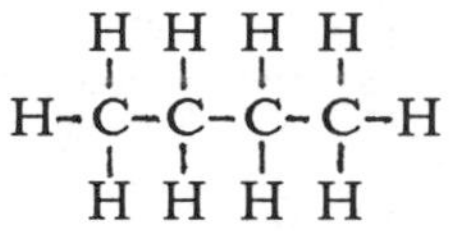

$$H-\overset{\displaystyle H}{\underset{\displaystyle H}{C}}-\overset{\displaystyle H}{\underset{\displaystyle H}{C}}-\overset{\displaystyle H}{\underset{\displaystyle H}{C}}-\overset{\displaystyle H}{\underset{\displaystyle H}{C}}-H$$

$CH_3CH_2CH_2CH$

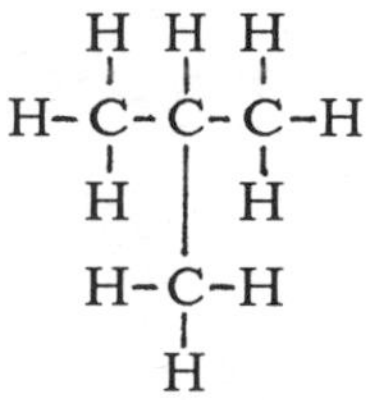

(a) normal butane

(b)

$$H-\overset{\displaystyle H}{\underset{\displaystyle H}{C}}-\overset{\displaystyle H}{\underset{\displaystyle\overset{\displaystyle H-\overset{\displaystyle H}{\underset{\displaystyle H}{C}}-H}{|}}}{C}-\overset{\displaystyle H}{\underset{\displaystyle H}{C}}-H$$

CH_3CHCH_3
　　|
　 CH_3

(b) isobutane

More complex heptane (C_7H_{16}) has five isomers, and decane ($C_{10}H_{22}$), 75. Tetradecane ($C_{40}H_{82}$) has potentially trillions and, as with all heavy alkanes at STP, is solid, due to its very asymmetric geometry and the high level of electron-cloud distortion.

Across

1. To lean (Latin)
6. What Hg methyls make you do
9. Blood chem. types
10. Acid suffix
11. ___glycerine
12. Particle matrix
15. $2 \times 10^3 \times 454$ g
16. 1-2-3 or s-p-d-f
17. Noble gas, to a period
18. Catty-corner 8B metals
19. Suffix: "maker"
20. CH_4 burner
22. Ra___ (a gas)
24. Abbreviated adj. for Chem 1 (maybe)
26. Radioactive nonmetal
27. Malevolent metalloid
28. Oxygen siblings
30. Anode seeker
32. Named for gunpowder inventor
33. Cadmium sulfide
35. Change in 37A
37. Exothermy product
38. $1s^2 2s^2 2p^6 3s^2 3p^6 4s^2 3d^6$
40. Sign gas
41. Wave detector
42. Geothermal, nuclear or hydroelectric

Down

1. 4.184 J (pl.)
2. Mauna _____ (exothermic peak)
3. Oxyanion, part of N_2 cycle
4. Not a base
5. (g) state compared to (s) state
6. Part of success in chem. lab class
7. Generic metal
8. _____ forces, e.g., Scotland Yard
13. Nonmetric unit (pl.)
14. 140.12 g/mol
21. Part of Dutch scientist's name
23. Densest metal
25. Ben___ (a ring)
29. Still state
30. (g) state is as light____
31. Fruit-essence chemical
34. Great _____ (Bohr or canine)
35. See 21D
37. "Hyponitrous acid"
36. Not H_F
39. H_{vap} to H_{con} (abbr.)

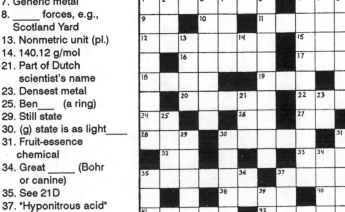

1. Heat of reaction is the change between beginning and ending enthalpies. It is variously called, in a reaction context, simply "heat flow" or "heat transfer."

2. In exothermy, heat is lost (−) by the reactants as they become products; in endothermy, heat is absorbed (+) because the bond energies of the products are higher than those of the reactant, and so require it to form.

3. Heat of formation is the gain/loss (transfer) of heat associated with the formation of a mole of a specific compound, rather than that associated with the reaction as a whole which, of course, is heat of reaction.

4. a. -706 − (0 + 0) = -706 kJ   b. (0 − 484) − (-297 − 42.6) = -144 kJ

    c. -206 − (0 − 0) = -206 kJ   d. (0 − 1412) − (-1117 + 0) = -295 k

    e. -306 − (-399 + 0) = +93 kJ   f. (-786 − 858) − (-276 + 0) = -1368

5. $? kJ = 189\,g\,S \times \dfrac{mol\,S}{32.06\,g\,S} \times \dfrac{-144\,kJ}{3\,mols\,S} = -283\,kJ$

(the 3 in the final conversion factor, which is also the thermal keystone, can be considered as part of a defined relation and so therefore does not affect significant figures).

6. (a) $? kJ = 60.0\,L \times \dfrac{mol\,PCl_5}{22.4\,L\,PCl_5} \times \dfrac{93\,kJ}{mol\,PCl_5} = 2.5 \times 10^2\,kJ$ (b) 120 L

(For every mole of PCl_5, there is a mole of each product, according to the coefficients from the equation).

7. $? g\,eth = 1\,mol\,NaCl \times \dfrac{519\,J}{mol\,NaCl} \times \dfrac{mol\,eth}{-276\,J} \times \dfrac{46.07\,g\,eth}{mol\,eth} = 86.6\,g\,eth$

7.12 Chapter Synthesis

HEAT AND VAN DER WAALS FORCES DETERMINE WHICH STATE OR PHASE A SUBSTANCE WILL BE IN!

WELL SAID! BUT AREN'T THOSE MY LINES?!

This chapter has treated gases, liquids, solids (crystals in particular) and the things which determine to which of these states a substance will belong at a given tempearture.

When we are considering the states as physical varieties of a specific substance, we call them phases, and it is heat that accounts for these variations.

When we are comparing one substance to another, it is intermolecular attractions, of three known sorts, which account for the variations in state when the two substances are being compared under otherwise identical conditions.

In sum, heat determines the phase of a sample, and Van der Waals Forces, its state at a particular P and T. Ponder this for a moment; the relation between the two must be understood. Van der Waals Forces —the electrostatic affinities between molecules—vary from susbtance to substance, but they can be overcome if enough heat is added to a sample. The more heat, the less influence there is from these forces. Still, by their relative strengths, Van der Waals Forces determine how much heat is required for a change of state to occur and, therefore, the melting and boiling points, which are where the *average* molecule has enough energy to change states.

Any two substances will rise in temperature within the same phase at different rates, even if the same amount of heat is flowing in or out of them. The one that is the slower to show a change in temperature is the one with the higher specific heat value. It is for this reason that specific heats are sometimes called "heat capacities." Water, with its rather high specific heat, is therefore highly stable in its T variations. With specific heat's three dimensions in a heat flow equation, we are able to use it to determine the heat flow in or out of a sample.

This Q also depends, obviously, on the mass of the sample (m) and the actual change in temperature ($\triangle T$). Thus, these two parameters are included in heat flow determinations within a phase/state.

The key to understanding a sample that is warming or cooling is that, as heat flows in or out, the sample may either change in temperature or in state; it can do both serially, but never at the same time. For this reason, each temperature change and each state change needs a separate calculation.

Graphically, this means that the temperature curve flattens during a state change, while the heat curve does not. The heat entering or leaving the system at such a time does not, then, change the temperature, but only the phase. These heats are the heats of fusion and vaporization ($\triangle H_{fus}$, $\triangle H_{vap}$) and their inverses. To determine Q at a state change, we just multiply these constants by the mass of the sample (and *not* the change in T, for there is none).

As specific heat is not heat flow itself, neither is enthalpy, which is another type of heat capacity (namely that of the bonds of the substances in a chemical system—reactant or product). If the bonds of the reactants collectively contain more energy than those of the products, the reaction will be exothermic; the heat of reaction, $\triangle H_R$, will be negative, as heat was lost to the surroundings (On the other hand, if the enthalpy of the products were higher...).

Determining $\triangle H_R$, then, is a matter of getting the arithemetical difference between two enthalpies, H_p and H_r. If a single compound is formed from only elements, the $\triangle H_R$ is also the heat of formation, $\triangle H_R$ for that compound, since the elements have a value of 0. If other compounds were in the reaction, the total $\triangle H$ is the heat of reaction.

If we think of heat itself as a substance, as was believed as late as 1800, then it is easy to make a keystone for a stoichiomentric calculation involving heat, because a keystone is a ratio of two substances. The only difference is that we quantify the heat in kilojoules (and the other, truer, substance, in moles).

What makes crystals crystals, liquids liquids, and gases gases, then, is understood in terms of Van der Waals Forces and heat.

277

1. Water has surface tension, whereas carbon tetrachloride does not. How do their molecular geometries explain this?

2. Why do crystals have precise melting points, whereas amorphous solids melt over a range of temperatures?

3. Ionic crystals tend to have rather high melting points, and molecular (not *macro*molecular) crystals have low ones. What does polarity have to do with it?

4. Why are metals good electrical conductors while macromolecular substances conduct very poorly, if they do so at all?

5. Explain the relation between molecular size (as a consequence of atomic radii) and the varying states of the halogens at, say, room temperature:

6. Now, some calculating. How many (kilo)calories are in a 140-grams slice of tofu cheesecake if it has 608 (kilo) joules?

7. Determine ΔT if T_i is -17.5°C and T_f is 24.8°C:

For the remaining problems in this set, refer as needed to the tables in Sects. 7.6, 7.8, and 7.10 for constants that are not provided in the wording of the problems. Be on the lookout for unstated conversion factors and irrelevant data. Pay attention to sigfigs.

8. A 300-gram chunk of zinc (specific heat 0.38) is heated from 28°C to 410°C. Express this heat change as a quantity (do a calculation):

9. What is the specific heat of methanol if a 90.0-gram sample releases 22.16 kilojoules as it cools from 303 K to 205 K?

10. How much energy is required to melt 430 grams of nickel at its melting point, if that melting point is 1776 K and the metal's heat of fusion constant is 312 J/g?

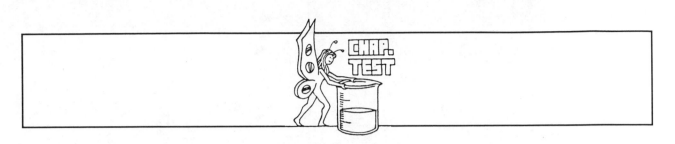

11. A 44.8-gram sample of bromine vapor cooled to its condensation point, 59°C, returns to its liquid state. How much energy will be lost in the change from $Br_2(g)$ and $Br_2(l)$, if no temperature change takes place?

12. How much heat will it take to vaporize 40.0 grams of molten lead at 560 K?

13. How many joules will 277 grams of steam at 123.0°C lose as it is converted to ice at absolute zero?

14. Determine the heats of these reactions and indicate whether they are exothermic or endothermic.

a. $SO_2(g) + H_2O_2(l) \rightarrow SO_3(g) + H_2O(l)$

b. $C_3H_8(g) + 5O_2(g) \rightarrow 3CO_2(g) + 4H_2O(g)$

a.
b.

15. How much heat will result from the reduction of 68.0 grams of hydrochloric acid (68.0 grams of hydrogen chloride dissolved in water) with an excess of pulverized zinc?

$$Zn(s) + 2HCl(aq) \rightarrow H_2(g) + ZnCl_2(aq) + 37.1 \text{ kJ}$$

16. What amount of ammonia, in ounces, will have to be burned to yield 9500 kilojoules?

$$4NH_3(g) + 5O_2(g) \rightarrow 6H_2O(g) + 4NO(g) - 216.8 \text{ kJ}$$

1. Water is bent, and therefore polar, whereas carbon tetrachloride—CCl_4—is a perfect tetrahedron, and so is nonpolar. Water molecules on the surface, then, can be oriented downward (or inward, from the molecule's own perspective) because of this polarity.

2. A crystal's particle structure is regular, so it is held together by bonds that are consistently similar in both length and strength. For this reason, a crystal melts all at once, or at a melting *point*. The amorphous solid, however, has a grab-bag of dissimilar bonds. Thus, a "solid" such as glass melts over a range of temperature.

3. Van der Waals Forces, as a group, are a function of intermolecular polarities. In ionic crystals, these polarities are so strong that they are properly considered ionic bonds; much more heat, therefore, is required to overcome them.

4. Metals, we believe, are like masses of cations sharing a bath of electrons. When the bath tap is on and the drain is open, they flow through the bathtub or system easily. In giant molecules, however, the electrons are locked up in covalent bonds.

5. Large atoms or molecules, which have comparatively many Principal Energy Levels and large radii/volume, have more electron-cloud distortion and therefore more momentary polarities. The small F_2 and Cl_2 molecules are free enough from London forces to be gaseous; medium-sized Br_2 molecules are at least free enough of them to be in the liquid state; but the big I_2 molecules are bound in a molecular lattice.

6. $? \text{ (k)calories} = 608 \text{ kJ} \times \dfrac{\text{kcal}}{4.184 \text{ kJ}} = 145 \text{ kJ}$

7. $24.8 - (-17.5) = 42.3°C \text{ (or K)}$

8. $Q = 300 \text{ g} \times \dfrac{0.38 \text{ J}}{\text{(g)(°C)}} = \times 382°C = 4.4 \times 10^{-1} \text{kJ}$

9. $c = \dfrac{22160 \text{ J}}{(90.0 \text{ g})(98°C)} = 0.25$

10. $Q = 430 \text{ g} \times \dfrac{312 \text{ J}}{\text{g}} = 134 \text{ kJ}$ (the melting point of nickel has nothing to do with the problem)

ΔT FOR PROBLEM 9 WAS -98. SO WHY DID WE DROP THE SIGN WHEN WE PERFORMED THE MATH?

PSST!

BECAUSE WE CARE ONLY ABOUT THE ABSOLUTE VALUE OF THE CHANGE. HEAT FLOW [Q] VALUES CAN BE (−) OR (+) BUT "c" CANNOT.

-98 = |98|

...ONE COULD NOT VERY WELL HAVE NEGATIVE "c" BECAUSE ONE CANNOT INCREASE THE "T" OF A GRAM OF ANYTHING BY 1°C BY REMOVING HEAT FROM IT.

YOU ASK THE DUMBEST QUESTIONS!

BEAT IT!

IMPERTINENT HERPTILE.

11.

$$Q = 44.8 \text{ g} \times \frac{-180 \text{ J}}{\text{g}} = 8.06 \times 10^3 \text{ J} \quad (8.06 \text{ kJ})$$

12.

$$Q_1 = 40.0 \text{ g} \times \frac{0.157 \text{ J}}{(\text{g})(\text{K})} \times 610 \text{ K} = 3.83 \times 10^3 \text{ J} \quad (3.83 \text{ kJ})$$

$$Q_2 = 40.0 \text{ g} \times \frac{732 \text{ J}}{\text{g}} = 29.3 \text{ kJ} \qquad Q_T = 3.8 + 29.3 = 33.1 \text{ kJ}$$

13.

$$Q_1 = 277 \text{ g} \times \frac{2.008 \text{ J}}{(\text{g})(°\text{C})} \times -23.0°\text{C} = -12.8 \text{ kJ} \qquad Q_2 = 277 \text{ g} \times \frac{-2.26 \text{ kJ}}{\text{g}} = -626 \text{ kJ}$$

$$Q_3 = 277 \text{ g} \times \frac{4.184 \text{ J}}{(\text{g})(°\text{C})} \times -100°\text{C} = -1.16 \times 10^2 \text{ kJ} \qquad Q_4 = 277 \text{ g} \times \frac{-335 \text{ J}}{\text{g}} = -92.8 \text{ kJ}$$

$$Q_5 = 277 \text{ g} \times \frac{2.050 \text{ J}}{(\text{g})(°\text{C})} \times -273°\text{C} = -1.55 \times 10^2 \text{ kJ}$$

$$Q_T = -12.8 + (-626) + (-116) + (-92.8) + (-155) = 1.00 \times 10^3 \text{ kJ}$$

14. a. $\triangle H_R = -198 \text{ kJ}$ (exothermic)   b. $\triangle H_R = -2137 \text{ kJ}$ (very exothermic)

15. ? kilojoules $= 68.0 \text{ g HCl} \times \dfrac{\text{mol HCl}}{36.46 \text{ g HCl}} \times \dfrac{37.1 \text{ kJ HCl}}{2 \text{ mols HCl}} = 34.6 \text{ kJ}$

16. ? ounces $NH_3 = 9500 \text{ kJ} \times \dfrac{4 \text{ mols } NH_3}{216.8 \text{ kJ}} \times \dfrac{17.0 \text{ g } NH_3}{\text{mol } NH_3} \times \dfrac{\text{oz } NH_3}{28.3 \text{ g } HN_3} = 105 \text{ oz } NH_3$

281

6
C
12.011

𝕻rofile: 𝕮arbon

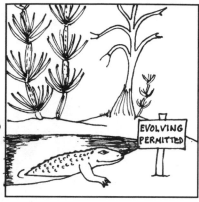

Carboniferous "Era" Vast biomass deposits began the conversion to oil and coal.

Carbon is so central to the study of chemistry that an entire main branch of the discipline is devoted to one class of its compounds: those containing the C-C bond. The reason for this is the seemingly infinite permutability of organic compounds with their carbon "skeletons." Well over 95% of known compounds contain this element, and these occupy the attention of the largest portion of modern professional chemists.

This is surprising on two counts. The first is the apparent low activity of the element. All three allotropes—diamond, graphite, and amorphous (coke, charcoal, soot, coals, etc.) occur in nature as uncombined carbon.

Secondly, carbon is comparatively scarce. It is no more than the twentieth or so most abundant element in the Earth's crust; there is 100 times as much sodium and over 1000 times as much silicon. This underlines the unrenewability of fossil fuels which, in one form or another, are mostly carbon.

Despite this, even uncombined carbon is found in nearly every region of the planet, and biomass and petroleum—two stages of the same thing—are wherever living organisms are or have been.

Carbon has only two electrons in its top sublevel, 2p, but the two electrons in the sublevel just below it, 2s, behave pretty much the same as the 2p electrons such that, while combined carbon *can* show a valency of 2, it is instead almost always 4.

The apparent low activity of carbon is, then, deceptive; for while too many proofs of its reactivity—as compounds—exist to be counted, elemental carbon usually requires relatively high temperatures to combine with something else.

When it is hot enough, however, it bonds to metals and nonmetals alike, and is used extensively in metallurgy.

The carboranes are a class of compounds made from carbon, its physically similar neighbor, boron, and hydrogen. Polymer series based on carboranes have been developed, including some that enhance the catalyctic properties of complexes that also contain metals.

Carbonization, as you know, is the mechanical dissolution of the dioxide in water and beverages (although there are naturally carbonated springs). One can consume any amount of this tired, inert gas without harm (if not to the exclusion of oxygen), so it is not directly dangerous. Some scientists, however, argue that its uncontrolled addition to the atmosphere through combustion is causing a global warming (the greenhouse effect) by permitting the sun's energy to enter the atmosphere as ultraviolet light yet not allowing it to be re-radiated out as infra-red light. An ultimate consequence predicted for this is the rising of the oceans.

Much of this CO_2 forms from the monoxide, which is unstable and quickly afterburns to the dioxide. This is good for us, for if it did not do this, we might well all be dead. CO is poisonous because it bonds, in place of oxygen, with hemoglobin, the blood protein that supplies the body with oxygen. The result is asphyxiation at the cellular level.

The various types of petroleum and coals differ in the nature and content of their impurities. The former is a class of hydrocarbons, while coals are mostly the elemental stuff. The mineral anthracite is a colder burning coal than bituminous coal, but it is freer of pollution-causing impurities such as sulfur.

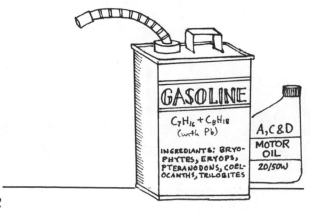

GASOLINE
$C_7H_{16} + C_8H_{18}$
(with Pb)

INGREDIANTS: BRYO-PHYTES, ERYOPS, PTERANODONS, COEL-OCANTHS, TRILOBITES

A,C&D
MOTOR OIL
20/50W

8.1 The Equilibrium Concept

YOU GUYS KEEP MENTIONING THIS EQUILIBRIUM THING WITHOUT SAYING WHAT IT IS. I'M HAVING BAD DREAMS. SO WHAT IS IT?!

THAT WHICH THOU CANNOT MAINTAIN

Equilibrium (pl. *equilibria*) is a word with autonomous meanings in a half dozen of the liberal disciplines. In chemistry alone it has ten or more. Use of the word can seem like so much equivocation when the context is unclear or there is no modifier nearby, but the following umbrella definition is a starting point for all of them. *Equilibrium: an apparent state of rest in which two opposed chemical or physical changes are occuring at exactly the same rate.*

In **chemical equilibria** in general, the two changes are called the *forward reaction* and the *reverse reaction*. In equations for systems in which both are taking place (that is, in systems not going to completion), these reactions are represented by the double arrow (below).

Equilibrium is reached when the proportions of the product(s) and the reactant(s) become constant.

Chemical Equilibrium $A + B \rightleftarrows C + D$

Constant, yes, but not necessarily equal; in fact, very seldom so. There may be 30 times as much product in the system as reactant, or visa-versa; no matter. If the proportions are fixed, then the system is in equilibrium. It is the *rates* of the opposing reactions, then, and not the *concentrations* of the involved substances, that are equalized. In summary, chemical equilibrium means two things: equalized rates and fixed (but unequal) proprtions.

The study of reaction rates is called *kinetics*, a term associated with energy considerations elsewhere, notably in physics. In fact, reaction rates usually do increase with an increase in temperature, but in this book we will assume a constant T in order to emphasize the factor that *always* critically affects reaction rates, namely concentrations (solution proportions).

Solution equilibrium exists between a solvent and a solute, most especially a solid solute. In such a case, the solute is dissolving at the same time that it is recrystallizing, and the solution is therefore saturated; it can dissolve no more of the solute. If the solute also ionizes, we have an **ionic equilibrium** and a true chemical change. Ionic equilibria are those associated with acids, bases, salts, weak electrolytes, and their concentrations.

While metathesis reactions invariably go to completion, acid/base reactions often do not, going only part of the way. If the products in a reacted acid/base system predominate at equilibrium, the forward reaction is said to be "favored"; if the reactants end up as the greater proportion, the reverse reaction is favored. Either way, it is an **acid/base equilibrium**, which is the category of ionic equilibrium with an acid and a base for reactants. Ionic equilibrium is in turn a category of solution equilibrium (for where else in Chem 1 will you have uncombined ions if not in solution?). The two adjectives "aqueous" and "solution" often interchange before the word equilibrium, even though they are not exactly the same thing.

Oxidation/reduction equilibrium is that between an oxidizer and a reducer; more on that in Chap. 10.

Physical equilibria are the other (with chemical equilibria) general category that concerns us. It can refer to solution equilibria in which no chemical change occurs, as in the dissolution of a nonelectrolyte that forms no compounds with water. Equilibria between a substance's phases are also of this type.

One type, **liquid-vapor equilibrium**, as you can well guess, is that between a sample's liquid and gas phases. Vapor pressure (Sect. 7.1) becomes constant when this equilibrium is reached, and the number of molecules condensing from the gas phase equal those vaporizing from the liquid one. Temperature and pressure, of course, are responsible for the proportions of the phases within such a sample.

8.2 Collision Theory

Collision Theory explains—at the particle level—why potential reactions may or may not take place between a pair of reactants. In the first place, particles—be they gaseous or dissolved—must collide if they are to combine or recombine. Two factors determine the success of this potentiality: kinetic energy (speed, basically) and orientation.

The first of these is a true function of temperature, such that as T rises, so also does the frequency and success of collision. The collisions must be effective enough in both of these respects to break the bonds of the reacting particles.

In (a), at right, an iodine and a hydrogen molecule collide with sufficient energy, but not with the right orientation, or what might be thought of as the proper "angle" to overcome the bond energies and combine; therefore, they ricochet off one another.

This is analogous to two cars side-swiping each other at 130 kpm, except that this kind of collision drains the "particles" (cars) of their energy (specifically, their momentum); gas particles and free ions, on the other hand, lose no energy when they collide (Sect. 5.1).

In (b), the collision is "head-on," so the orientation, or angle, is right, but the force of the collision is too low; there is insufficient energy to break the bonds. This time the cars met bumper to bumper, but as each was only going 5 kpm, they just butted each other and disengaged.

In (c), however, the collision is both sufficiently energetic and properly orientated to overcome the bond energies of the reactants. Energy is now re-leased or absorbed (exothermy or endothermy), depending on the reactants; this energy is separate from the activation energy which powered the particles, so to speak. No further elaboration on the two-cars analogy is needed; use your imagination.

⊕ In the frames on this page, color the iodine molecules (only) purple. Do not color HI and H_2.

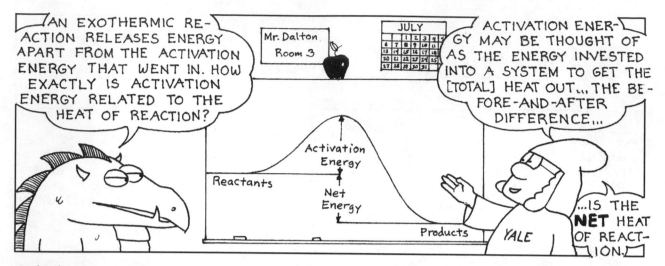

Activation energy, ΔH_{ACT} corresponds to the strength of the bonds in the reactants, *not* to the energy those bonds contain. ΔH_{ACT} is also called a "barrier," and it is important to know why. It is the kinetic minimum needed to overcome the bonds; *minimum* implies requirement; *requirement,* in turn, implies a barrier if it is unconquered. This is the conceptual linkage between the terms *activation energy* and *activation barrier.* Despite appearances, they mean the same thing. At times, it is spoken of as energy (e.g., in the contexts of collisions or heat transfer) and, at other times, as a barrier (predictions or catalysis).

Further, ΔH_{ACT} as is evident from its symbol, is part of the difference (ΔH) between the enthalpies (H_p, H_r), and not the enthalpies themselves, which *do* correspond to the bond energies.

Successful collisions increase with temperature, because there is more motion. Such a collision results first in a transitory activated complex, such as "H_2I_2" from p. 285. As this unstable, ephemeral entity breaks into HI molecules, it loses both the activation energy, ΔH_{ACT} spent by the reactants and the *net energy of reaction,* which is a new name for an old friend from Chap. 7, heat of reaction. Accordingly, it

has at least two symbols, ΔH_R and ΔH_{NET} As we are already familiar with the first, we will stick with it.

This combined loss may be written as delta-H_{TOT} *It is always negative and refers to the total,* not the net, *energy released in a reaction.* As before, ΔH_R is the difference between the enthalpies of the reactant and product systems, and can be negative or positive. In the current example, it is also a heat of formation, ΔH_F because HI is the only species in the reaction that is formed:

$$H_2(g) + I_2(g) = 2HI(g) + kJ$$

We have said that ΔH_{ACT} and ΔH_R, combined, are ΔH_{TOT} However, we are well served by expressing ΔH_{ACT} and ΔH_{TOT} as the addends and ΔH_R as the sum, for this latter value is a *net* one.

$$\Delta H_{ACT} + \Delta H_{TOT} = \Delta H_R$$

Substituting the numbers for this particualr reaction into the equation, we get the determination shown below it. Understand this before reading further.

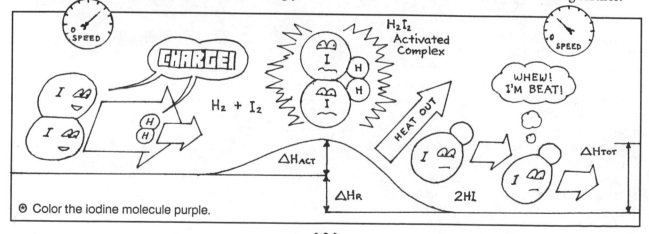

⊕ Color the iodine molecule purple.

I THOUGHT THIS CHAPTER WAS GONNA BE ABOUT EQUILIBRIUM. DIDN'T WE ALREADY STUDY DELTA-H?

AYE— WHICH IS PRECISELY WHY THOU ART NOW READY TO STUDY EQUILIBRIUM.

The newly formed hydrogen iodide molecules will not all remain as such. Because, like the H_2 and I_2 molecules that went into their making, they themselves collide and, in some cases, with sufficient impact to break into H and I atoms. These immediately pair up as H_2 and I_2 molecules. This is the reverse reaction.

The equation from p. 286 (A, below) falsely suggests, with its single forward arrow, that this reaction goes to completion; in fact, an equilibrium results (B):

$$\text{(A) } H_2 + I_2 \rightarrow 2HI$$

$$\text{(B) } H_2 + I_2 \rightleftharpoons 2HI$$

Equation B, then, is truer because it indicates that a point is reached where two reactions are taking place at the same rate, in which one HI molecule forms for every one that breaks apart. They are being made and unmade at the same rate. What this equation does not tell us, however, is that, at this equilibrium, the HI molecules far outnumber the H_2 and I_2 molecules. To show that the forward reaction—that yielding HI—is favored, we would draw the forward arrow longer than the reverse (C). You will see a lot more of this in Chaps. 9 and 10.

$$\text{(C) } H_2 + I_2 \xrightleftharpoons{\hspace{1cm}} 2HI$$

Y'KNOW, I STILL DON'T GET IT 100%. CAN WE LOOK AT ANOTHER EXAMPLE OF HOW $\Delta H_{ACT} + \Delta H_{TOT} = \Delta H_R$? ...AND WITH ANOTHER GRAPHIC ILLUSTRATION OF HOW THE HEAT IS ACCOUNTED FOR?

WE CAN, FORSOOTH! LET US CONSIDER A COMPLEMENTARY ENDOTHERMIC REACTION...

COMPLEMENTARY? COMPLIMENTARY?

O_2 and NO are activated by sunlight (ΔH_{ACT}) to form NO_2, which then retains some of the activation energy, unlike HI (which loses all of its activation energy and more besides).

More heat was absorbed by this reaction than was lost by it (ΔH_{ACT} exceeds ΔH_{TOT}), so the heat of reaction is endothermic ($\Delta H_R = 33.5$ kJ).

$$\Delta H_{ACT} + \Delta H_{TOT} = \Delta H_R$$

$$72 + (-38.5) = 33.5 \text{ kJ}$$

Equilibrium then occurs if NO_2 molecules are in energetic, well-oriented collisions, yielding O_2 and NO molecules:

$$2NO + O_2 \xrightleftharpoons{\hspace{1cm}} 2NO_2$$

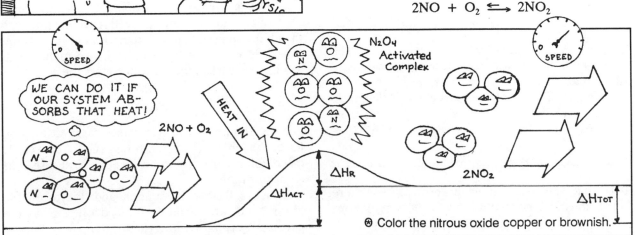

⊕ Color the nitrous oxide copper or brownish.

8.3 Reaction Rates

We will look at four rate-affecting factors.

1. Activation Energy

Activation energy, ΔH_{ACT} as noted, is also a barrier. The potential reactants must have enough of it (as energy) to overcome it (as a barrier). It is a constant for any set of reactants, and it is modifiable (as a barrier) by many variables, of which three are always important, and they will be discussed next. Keep in mind, however, that ΔH_{ACT} corresponds to bond strength, and H_r to the net difference in energy *restored* by the reactants and *stored* by the products.

The activation energy barrier varies from one reactant system to the next, owing to the natures of the particles themselves, and to certain of their properties that make them receptive to reaction with some particles and not with others (this, however, belongs to your future study).

HCl(aq) and zinc (1a) are a combination with a low ΔH_{ACT} requirement, and so they react easily. However, the same acid by itself will not react with gold, because the barrier is too high (1b).

2. Temperature

Temperature, a variable, affects reaction rates. The higher the T, the greater proportion of particles there will be that can overcome the barrier.

A higher T entails faster particles and thus more frequent and violent collisions. The rates for most solutions double for each increase of about 10°C.

3. Concentrations

If the reactants are highly concentrated, then there will obviously be more collisions. When two solutions of high molarity are mixed, the reaction will proceed

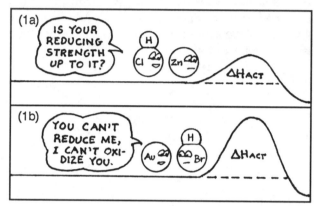

more quickly—and more quickly in both directions at equilibrium—than it will in two dilute solutions.

Likewise, if gases are compressed—and therefore concentrated—they, too, will react more quickly than if they had been in a system with lower pressure. You need not be on the Dean's list to realize that, again, higher frequency of collisions is the cause.

Analogy

Subway commuters in São Paulo and Washington have high tempers (temperatures) and so react easily on colliding with one another, especially at rush hour (concentration).

Such collisions in London and Tokyo, on the other hand, are usually bounced off, due to the particles' peculiar natures (high ΔH_{ACT}).

288

IF WE WANTED TO, COULD WE DO ANYTHING, ASIDE FROM CONCENTRATING OR HEATING A SAMPLE TO ALTER THE CURVE RATE?

YES. BY INTRODUCING A FOURTH FACTOR: CATALYSTS.

4. Catalysis

A catalyst is something that *quickens the rate* of a chemical reaction—or *makes it possible* in the first place—without itself undergoing ultimate change. Yet a catalyst does not affect equilibrium.

It may at some point react, especially if the apparent reaction is really a series of reactions; but by the time the reaction ends, it will have completely recovered itself. Or, it may not chemically participate at any point whatsoever.

Most catalysts are substances; enzymes, as you know, are biological catalysts. Even heat, though, is a technical catalyst, for cooking—in the kitchen or the lab—is catalysis.

The mechanisms of many catalysts are poorly understood, if at all. More important, for our sake, is their effect, which is to lower the activation barrier: to provide a bypass or a shortcut for the reactants.

Oxygen can be slowly gathered by the decomposition of $KClO_3$ (Sect. 4.2), but adding manganese (II) oxide catalyzes (speeds up) the reaction, and is written:

$$2KClO_3 \xrightarrow{\quad MnO_2 \quad} 2KCl + 3O_2$$

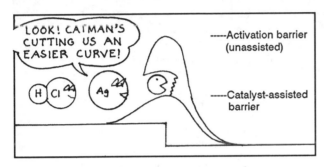

LOOK! CATMAN'S CUTTING US AN EASIER CURVE!

H Cl   Ag

-----Activation barrier (unassisted)

-----Catalyst-assisted barrier

In photosynthesis, the sun catalyzes (makes possible) the reaction:

$$6CO_2 + 6H_2O \xrightarrow{\quad sunlight \quad} C_6H_{12}O_6 + 6O_2$$

Another class of agents are the *inhibitors*, or "negative catalysts". By raising instead of lowering the activation barrier, inhibitors slow reactions or outright preclude them.

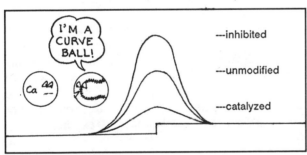

I'M A CURVE BALL!

Ca

---inhibited

---unmodified

---catalyzed

In the above diagram of an endothermic reaction (one in which the forming bonds contain more energy than the old bonds), the curves of inhibited (top) and catalyzed (bottom) reactions are quantitatively compared to an unmodified reaction.

Now, a corollary to the subway analogy: possible catalysts might include doubling the fares or piping in "music" by Black Sabbath. Inhibitors, then, might be along the lines of cutting fares or piping in Brahms.

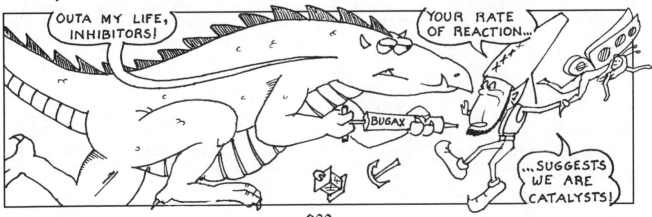

OUTA MY LIFE, INHIBITORS!

YOUR RATE OF REACTION...

...SUGGESTS WE ARE CATALYSTS!

BUGAX

8.4 Reaction Curves

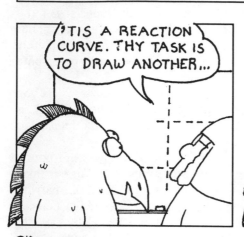

'TIS A REACTION CURVE. THY TASK IS TO DRAW ANOTHER...

While Dalton is taking tea...

YUK

SNICKER

SURE IT'S A REACTION CURVE. WHENEVER I SEE IT, I REACT!

Plotting and drawing a reaction curve is easy to do, although it requires a lot of tabulated data, namely for delta-H (x-axis) and elapsed time (y-axis). We will only consider here the reading of these functions and their relation to the equation from p. 285:

$$\Delta H_{ACTIVATION} + \Delta H_{TOTAL} = \Delta H_{NET}$$

...or, simply, $\Delta H_{ACT} + \Delta H_{TOT} = \Delta H_R$

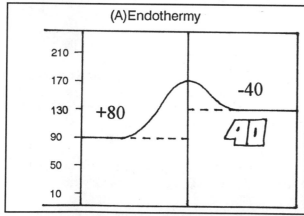

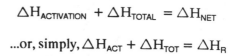

----1. Qualitative Datum----

The first thing to notice about a reaction curve is whether the reaction it represents gained or lost heat. This is indicated by the curve's beginning and ending levels (dotted lines). Both represent an enthalpy. If the curve goes from a lower level to a higher one, the reaction is endothermic (A); if it starts on a higher level and ends up on a lower one, it is exothermic (B).

----2. Quantitative Data----

If you want the values of these heats and losses, use a straightedge or a ruler to determine the "height" of the curve. The climb from the first enthalpy up to the summit is your ΔH_{ACT} value, and the coast down the leeside is your ΔH_{TOT}. Just add them and you have the ΔH_R, which will also be the difference between the two levels.

Application of the equation for the two curves shown on this page are:

(A) 80 kJ + (−40 kJ) = 40 kJ

(B) 175 J + (−750 J) = −575 J

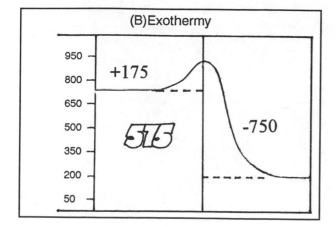

⊕ Color the space between the curves and the enthalpy lines. Use a different color for both sides of the summit-marking locus.

1. Equilibria are dynamic phenomena, yet they appear to be at rest. Explain:

2. What two conditions must be met in a collision between particles for a reaction to take place?

3. Complete: _____ + _____ = (net) heat of reaction

4. Distinguish $\triangle H_{TOT}$ from $\triangle H_R$ (hint: the latter is also written $\triangle H_{NET}$):

5. Why are the products of an exothermic reaction less energetic than are the reactants?

6. What, specifically, can a catalyst do for a set of reactants to increase their speed of chemical change, or make the reaction possible when it otherwise would not take place?

7. Match these equilibrium types to their descriptions:

_____financial

_____chemical

_____biological

_____mythological

_____physical

_____aquiferous

a. an equilibrium that takes place, for example, between phases

b. underground water, moving but always seeking its own level

c. in any population, births exactly equaling deaths

d. neither profit nor loss, but continual cashflow

e. an active standoff between dissimilar substances

f. Hercules' good fortune when the Hydra started growing only one head

    instead of two for each one he lopped off.

8. Keep matching:

_____forward reaction

_____catalyst

_____molarity or density

_____activation energy

_____inhibitor

_____reverse reaction

_____kinetic energy

_____chemical bond

_____activated complex

a. the energy, specifically, needed by a reactant system to react

b. the formation of products from reactants

c. the energy of motion; as it increases, so do reaction rates

d. that which quickens, or makes possible, a reaction

e. the silo of chemical energy

f. an unstable, transitory species in a reaction

g. the formation of reactants from products

h. reaction rates increase in proportion to it

i. that which raises the energy requirement needed to commence a reaction

9. Write a balanced equation for each of the reactions outlined below. Include all the given or implied information. Use state designations. Review Sect. 7.10 as needed.

a. Reactants: nitric oxide and oxygen; products: nitrous oxide; catalyst: sunlight; endothermic; does not go to completion; $\triangle H_R = 70.0kJ$.

b. Reactants: steam, carbon monoxide; products: hydrogen, carbon dioxide; exothermic; does not go to completion; $\triangle H_R = -393$ kJ.

c. Reactant: sucrose ($C_{12}H_{22}O_{11}$); products: water, carbon; catalyst: concentrated (l) sulfuric acid; endothermic; goes to completion; $\triangle H_R = 131$ kJ.

10. Answer true or false: catalysts and inhibitors alter the rate of reaction and the proportions of equilibrium.

Circle one: True False   Now, briefly, explain your answer:

11. The two curves below represent unidentified reactions. Indicate (a) whether they are exothermic or endothermic (circle one); In the blanks provided, write the (b) activation energy; (c) energy of reaction; and (net) heat of reaction. The three quantitative responses will be estimates made using the scales on the charts' y-axes. Do not forget to use the negative sign whenever appropriate; the plus sign is optional. Use a ruler or straightedge.

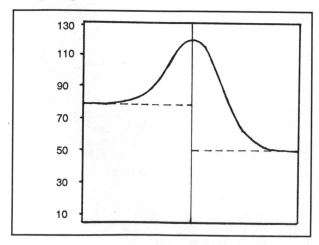

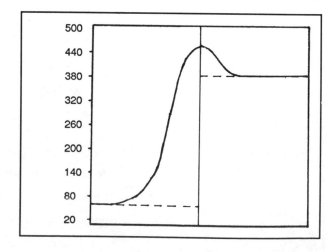

a. exo- endo-   b. H$_{ACT}$_____   a. exo- endo-   b. H$_{ACT}$_____

c. H$_{TOT}$_____ d. H$_R$_____   c. H$_{TOT}$_____ d. H$_R$_____

8.5 Chemical Equilibria

L et us return to the reaction in which hydrogen iodide forms. Were it to go to completion, we would expect two moles of the product from a mole each of the reactants, according to the balanced equation:

$$H_2(g) + I_2(g) \rightarrow 2HI(g)$$

But in fact an equilibrium, rather than a full consumption of the reactants, is the true result.

Team One vaporizes a mole of iodine and reacts it with a mole of hydrogen, under high pressure at about 750 K. The brilliant purple of the iodine vapor fades as it reacts with H_2 to form the invisible hydrogen iodide. It does not fade altogether, but instead to a point where the color stabilizes; equilibrium has been reached. The number (specifically, the concentration) of unreacted iodine molecules is now constant. So, too, are the concentrations of the HI and H_2 (although they, being colorless, give no visible indication of this.)

Team Two takes two moles of HI and subjects it to the same temperature and pressure that Team One is using with its sample. This time, the purple of the iodine seems to mystically appear from "thin air" and it visibly intensifies but, again, only to a point. At that point, the iodine (and hydrogen) molecules are disappearing (visibly) into HI as quickly as they are reappearing as I_2. Once more, equilibrium has been reached, but from a different direction. Still, the concentrations, or proportions, are identical to those of Team One.

With any other set of reactants and conditions, the same thing would occur (unless, of course, the reaction were one of those that by nature go to completion). *Equilibrium, regardless of how it is reached, results in the same proportions,* for a given system of reactants, pressure and temperature.

1. Change is not apparent because no *net* change occurs; rather, two opposite but equal changes continue.

2. Sufficient kinetic energy (speed) and proper orientation.

3. Activation energy (+) total energy (=) (net) heat of reaction.

4. $\triangle H_{TOT}$ is all the energy released in a reaction, and is always negative; $\triangle H_R$ is net energy of the reaction, that which is measured. It is positive if it exceeds $\triangle H_{TOT}$, negative if it does not.

5. The heat lost by the reactants is not retained by the products, and when the products form, the heat is not fully recovered. If it were more than fully recovered, the reaction would by definition be endothermic.

6. It lowers the activation-energy barrier to allow a greater portion of particles to react in less time, or at all.

7. d   e   c   f   a   b

8. b   d   h   a   i   g   c   e   f

9. a. $2NO(g) + O_2(g) \xleftrightarrow{\text{sunlight}} 2NO_2(g) - 70.0 \text{ kJ}$

b. $H_2O(g) + CO(g) \rightleftharpoons H_2(g) + CO_2(g) + 393 \text{ kJ}$

c. $C_{12}H_{22}O_{11}(s) \xrightarrow{H_2SO_4} 11H_2O(l) + 12C(s) + 133 \text{ kJ}$

10. False. While by definition, catalysts and inhibitors can alter the rate of reaction, we have nowhere said that they can alter equilibrium or reactant/product proportions. In its entirety, the statement is therefore untrue.

11. $\triangle H_{ACT} + \triangle H_{TOT} = \triangle H_R$

(left) exothermic $40 + (-70) = -30$ (right) endothermic $400 + (-80) = 320$

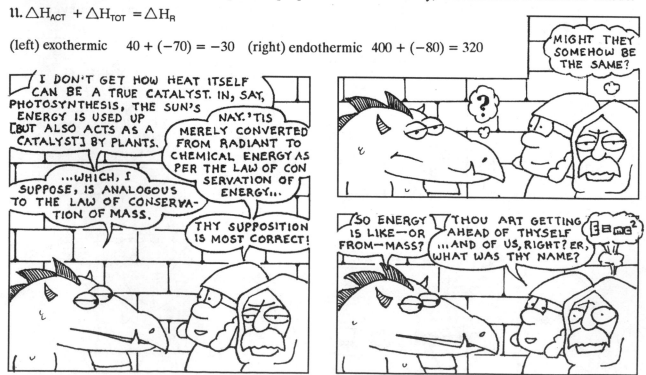

8.6 Equilibrium Constants

SO WE'VE GOT 1.6 MOLES OF PRODUCT AND 0.2 OF EACH REACTANT; WHAT DO WE DO WITH THEM?

EQUILIBRIUM CONSTANT EXPRESSIONS...

If the alchemists had estimated the concentations of the "experiments" (Sect. 8.5) to three, rather than two, significant figures, they would have gotten 1.56 moles for HI and, necessarily, 0.220 moles each for H_2 and I_2 (for the time being, do not worry about where these numbers came from).

In equilibrium calculations, concentrations are represented in brackets. For this particular reaction (and temperature), the concentations are these:

$$[I_2] = 0.220$$
$$[H_2] = 0.220$$
$$[HI] = 1.56$$

These proportions—for indeed that is what they are—can be used to derive a quotient, the equilibrium constant (which, unfortunately, is represented as K).

In Sect. 8.8 we will see how and why it is a constant, but at the moment we are only concerned with the construction of the equilibrium expression (two easy steps) and the derivation of the quotient (a third step). These three steps are not difficult.

STEP ONE Bracket the species in the equation, without the coefficients, and write them as a fraction. The species on the right will make up the numerator; those on the left go to the denominator.

(Mnemonic tip: in writing a fraction, one tends to write the numerator first, so the species on the *right* side of the equation are the *right* ones to begin with. Those on the *left* side are *left* over, and so are put into the fraction last.)

STEP TWO Transfer the coefficients, if any, to the fraction as superscripts. In this way, multipliers become exponents.

STEP THREE Substitute the concentration values of the species for their symbols in the expression, and calculate. That is all.

The last step, the only one that contains any math, is not a problem if you do not screw up the order of calculator operations (exponents then division) and if you know how to raise a number to a power, most commonly a square (x^2) or a cube (x^3); most calculators have keys for these. Coefficients larger than 3 are few.

Here is the general pattern for putting together equilibrium constant expressions from their concentrations, but this time with four, rather than only three, participating species:

$$wA + xB \rightleftarrows yC + zD$$

$$K = \frac{[C]^y[D]^z}{[A]^w[B]^x}$$

...where A and B are reactants, C and D, products, and the lower-case letters, their coefficients *cum* exponents.

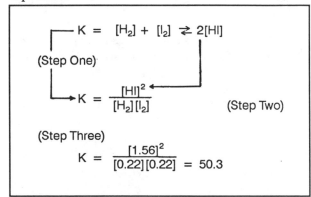

(Step One)
$$K = [H_2] + [I_2] \rightleftarrows 2[HI]$$

(Step Two)
$$K = \frac{[HI]^2}{[H_2][I_2]}$$

(Step Three)
$$K = \frac{[1.56]^2}{[0.22][0.22]} = 50.3$$

I KNOW HOW HI MOLECULES CAN REFORM AFTER THEY BREAK APART.

THEY GO TO "RE-FORM" SCHOOL!

VERY WELL HOW?

Now, for some examples, in which the first two steps will be emphasized.

Construct an equilibrium constant expression (or "mass action expression" as it is also called) for each of the following reactions, all of which involve only substances in their gaseous states:

(a) $N_2 + 3Cl_2 \rightleftarrows 2NCl_3$

(b) $2O_3 \rightleftarrows 3O_2$

(c) $2C_4H_{10} + 13O_2 \rightleftarrows 8CO_2 + 10H_2O$

(d) $2SO_2 + O_2 \rightleftarrows 2SO_3$

(e) $SO_2 + \tfrac{1}{2}O_2 \rightleftarrows SO_3$

(a) $\dfrac{[NCl_3]^2}{[N_2][Cl_2]^3}$	(d) $\dfrac{[SO_3]^2}{[SO_2]^2[O_2]}$
(b) $\dfrac{[O_2]^3}{[O_3]^2}$	(e) $\dfrac{[SO_3]}{[SO_2][O_2]^{1/2}}$
(c) $\dfrac{[CO_2]^8[H_2O]^{10}}{[C_4H_{10}]^2[O_2]^{13}}$	

Examples (a) and (d) are clear enough. The decomposition of ozone (b) into oxygen is the simplest chemical reaction of all, while the burning of propane (c) appears rather more complex. In fact, the same simple procedure is used to construct both; it is perhaps too easy even to bother listing steps for it.

On occasion, though, you may encounter an equation with fractional coefficients (e). Do not algebraically eliminate these by multiplying the coefficients of the equation. Leave them be. Reaction (e), though involving the same species as (d), took place under much different conditions, such that atomic, not molecular oxygen, was involved.

Now, we will examine some examples in which the actual constant is calculated and the favored direction—forward or reverse—is noted. Here goes the first one: a mole of water, as steam, is reacted with a mole of carbon monoxide, resulting in a concentration of 0.120 moles for each reactant and 0.880 for both of the two products. Determine the equilibrium constant.

$$H_2O + CO \rightleftarrows H_2 + CO_2 \text{ (so...) } K = \frac{[H_2][CO_2]}{[H_2O][CO]} = \frac{[0.880][0.880]}{[0.120][0.120]} = 53.8$$

There were no coefficients in this example (that is, they were all 1) so consequently neither were there any exponents in the constant expression. The forward reaction is clearly favored, for there is much more product (H_2, CO_2) than reactant at equilibrium.

In the original example, that which this chapter has so far been built around (HI and components), the equilibrium constant was 50.3. But suppose you had to determine the constant for the same equation, using the same concentrations (which would not be the true ones, but do not mind that), yet with *fractional* coefficients:

$$\tfrac{1}{2}H_2 + \tfrac{1}{2}I_2 \rightleftarrows HI$$

Construct the expression and calculate the quotient/constant:

$$K = \frac{[HI]}{[H_2]^{1/2}[I_2]^{1/2}} = \frac{[1.56]}{[0.220]^{1/2}[0.220]^{1/2}} = 7.09$$

For problems of this sort, your calculator probably has a square-root and a cube-root key. However, the square root of a number times itself (as in the denominator) is, of course, the number.

296

8.7 Solubility Constants

Lead (II) bromide is a salt that is neither particularly soluble nor insoluble; it is in the "slightly soluble" category (Sect. 6.2). As such, its ionization in water leads to equilibrium, whereas truly soluble salts react and ionize to completion, or until the saturation point of the solution. Truly insoluble salts do not produce aqueous ions to any important degree for the simple reason that they do not dissolve to an appreciable extent.

If a pinch of $PbBr_2$ is added to enough water, an ionic solution, $PbBr_2(aq)$, is the result. But with each added pinch, we increase the chances of collision between Pb^{2+} and Br^- ions and, therefore, the re-formation of $PbBr_2$ molecules (this is a molecular salt; check the Pauling Scale, Sect. 3.5). Eventually, this reverse reaction offsets the forward one and the solution is at equilibrium.

If instead of adding a pinch at a time, however, we added an excess of $PbBr_2$ all at once and then shook the system, equilibrium would again be achieved but the undissolved and undissolvable excess would just be dead weight, as far as the equilibrium and its proportions are concerned. The excess would be effectively out of the solution and so out of the expression as well. So, for the reaction

$$PbBr_2(s) \rightleftarrows Pb^{2+}(aq) + 2Br^-(aq)$$

we would *not* write...

$$K = \frac{[Pb^{2+}][Br^-]^2}{[PbBr_2]}$$

...as if the system were a gaseous one, but rather

$$K_{sp} = [Pb^{2+}][Br^-]^2 \quad (= 4.6 \times 10^{-6})$$

because the only concentrations that exist are those of the dissolved ions. Note the "sp" subscript for solubility product, for the *solubility constant* is indeed just that, a product.

K_{sp}, then, is the value representing the extent to which $PbBr_2$ will ionize. The value is the product of the ion concentrations. The less soluble the solid is, the lower will be the concentration of ions it releases into solution; therefore, the K_{sp} value will be lower for insoluble salts and hydroxides and higher for relatively more soluble ones.

Solubility products are also solubility constants because they are always the same, regardless of the proportion of solute or would-be-solute to solvent. Only temperature causes them to vary.

Error Analysis

For one thing, they are arithmetical opposites. Equilibrium constants are *quotients* deriving from the ratios of product and reactant proportions, or relative concentrations. We saw that the constant for the $HI/I_2/H_2$ system at 750 K was about 5×10^2.

Solubility constants, on the other hand, are *products*, although they do also represent equilibria, those between solvent and ions. The word *product*, in this context, refers not to the product of a reaction, but to that of a multiplication operation; specifically, it is the product of the concentrations of the ions in the solution.

Further, solubility constants (or products) are an exclusive province of the (aq) state. The equilibrium constants (or quotients) we have examined in this section are relevant to systems of the (g) state.

One thing that both equilibrium constants (K) and solubility constants (K_{sp}) have in common, however, is that *their significance lies in their magnitude*. Note the following equilibrium constants, to the right of their expressions:

$$\text{(a)} \quad K = \frac{[HI]^2}{[H_2][I_2]} = 5.03 \times 10^3$$

$$\text{(b)} \quad K = \frac{[HCl]^2}{[H_2][Cl_2]} = 2.7 \times 10^{33}$$

$$\text{(c)} \quad K = \frac{[N_2O]}{[N_2][O_2]} = 2.0 \times 10^{-37}$$

Constant (a) is neither an especially big number nor is it particularly small; this is indicated by its low exponent. Such a constant characterizes an equilibrium, because it derives from a ratio of products and reactants in which there is a significant amount (proportion) of both.

Constant (b) is an extremely large number. The high exponent indicates not an equilibrium but rather a reaction that for all practical and impractical purposes has gone to completion. The exponent is positive because the concentration value of the numerator is vastly greater than that of the denominator. In other words, it is high and positive because the the presence of HCl overwhelms that of H_2 and Cl_2 when the reaction is over. The forward reaction was thus favored, although this is an understatement; in the equation, only a single arrow would be used.

Constant (c) is an extremely tiny number; it is far dinkier than (b) is big. But it, too, tells us that there is no equilibrium to speak of, because the exponent, again, is very high (albeit negative). A virtual nonreaction, as a final, net effect, is here indicated; for whatever chemical activity takes place when the reactants meet (the denominator), there will be infinitesimally little N_2O (the numerator) when it is over and done with.

In summary, low exponents (up through positive or negative 4 and 5) indicate an appreciable equilibrium; higher exponents indicate effectively complete reactions; positive exponents mean the forward reaction was favored; negative ones mean the reverse was favored.

Remember that solubility constants, unlike other equilibrium constants, are products, not quotients. Consider the following two:

$$\text{(d)} \quad K_{sp} = [Pb^{2+}][Br^-]^2 = 4.6 \times 10^{-6}$$

$$\text{(e)} \quad K_{sp} = [Ag+]^2[S^-] = 8.0 \times 10^{-42}$$

You already know that lead (II) bromide, our example from p. 298, is a slightly soluble salt. Therefore, more of it will ionize than silver sulfide, which is among the most insoluble salts known. The undissolved Ag_2S units will theoretically outnumber the dissolved ones eight million trillion trillion trillion to one (this is more than Brazil's foreign debt!). The antilog—the first part of the constant—tells us little compared to the exponent in each of constants (d) and (e). Both indicate a favoring of the reverse reaction and the magnitude of equilibrium, *what there is of each*.

Solubility products, then, can only have negative exponents of about 5 or higher. Elsewise, we would have to include the formula of the salt in the expression, for this salt would be constantly breaking down and reforming, to a significant degree, and the expression would be not a solubility constant at all but an equilibrium constant not unlike those for the gaseous systems we looked at above and in Sect. 8.6.

298

78	
Pt	# 𝔓rofíle: 𝔓latínum
195.09	

White gold
is an alloy
of gold, nickel,
zinc, and
platinum.

Platinum is a rather malleable, heavy, and attractive silver-white metal with a bluish tinge. It is the best-known and most commercially important of the so-called "platinum metals."

This group—the bottom six of the 8B family, are among the most unreactive of elements, and for this they are sometimes called the "noble metals." Even fluorine will not attack platinum under some conditions. One of the few substances that will is aqua regia ("royal water")—so named by the alchemists because it dissolved the "king of metals", gold. Still, this mix of nitric and hydrochloric acids cannot act upon most of the other platinum metals. Nor can either acid do so separately. Iridium, or possibly osmium, wears the mantle of Noblest Metal of All.

Canada and Siberia are the leading platinum-producing regions. The metal is obtained from nickel ores and the arsenide, hirtite ($PtAs_2$).

The metal became known to Europeans when the Spanish, who named it *platina* ("little silver"), brought some from the New World. It was not, however, recognized as a chemical element until the 19th century.

The only country ever to mint platinum coins was nineteenth-century Imperial Russia. Tsar Alexander III was so ashamed of the coins, with their humble (non-gold) pedigree that he decreed that they could not be taken outside of his country. Today, however, while its price fluctuates rather freely, platinum is (ironically) much more precious than its periodic neighbor (gold) often by a factor of three or four (so, if your ancestor smuggled a few of those coins out...). As elements go, gold itself is a chemically uninter-

esting dud. Industrially, it is less versatile than most metals, although it is the most malleable; a cubic inch can be drawn into a wire over 65 kilometers long. One gold salt, however, gold (III) chloride, is used to color the red lenses in traffic signals. Poorer countries that cannot afford this substance must make do with orange or pinkish "red" lights. As a legacy of alchemic medical quackery, some people still inject themselves with gold ions to cure certain ailments.

Platinum, on the other hand, is famously useful to chemists. While only a mediocre electrical conductor, it is often used in electrodes in situations where cheaper metals would be chemically affected. Laboratory tools are sometimes plated with a platinum/iridium alloy to take advantage of this inertness. The platinum wire found in glass rods has the same expansion coefficient as the glass, so no cracking results from heating.

The best-known laboratory application of the metal is as a catalyst. By "platinizing" (electroplating with platinum) grains of cheaper material, the surface area and, therefore, the efficiency of the catalyst is enhanced. Catalytic mufflers, installed on cars as pollution-control devices, contain combs coated with platinum and its sibling metal, palladium.

Among the few compounds of platinum are those that are made from its reactions with the help of aqua regia, such as chloroplatinous acid, H_2PtCl_4, chloroplatinic acid, H_2PtCl_6, and the salt, sodium chloroplatinate, Na_2PtCl_6.

44 **Ru** 101.07	45 **Rh** 102.90	46 **Pd** 106.40
77 **Os** 190.21	78 **Ir** 192.22	79 **Pt** 195.09

𝔗he 𝔓latínum 𝔐etals

1. Match:

_____equilibrium constant   a. indicates that a forward reaction was favored at equilibrium

_____high exponent   b. indicates a reaction ending in equilibrium

_____saturation   c. a mathematical product

_____negative exponent   d. indicates that a reaction went to completion

_____low exponent   e. a mathematical quotient

_____solubility constant   f. equilibrium, in a solution

_____positive exponent   g. indicates that a reverse reaction was favored at equilibrium

2. Write equilibrium constants for the following. Equation (i) is an acid/base equilibrium occuring in a solution but, as no species on either side leaves the system, its expression can be constructed in the same manner as those of the gas equilibria in (a) through (h). Water, where it appears, is in the gas state.

a. $2HI(g) \rightleftarrows I_2(g) + H_2(g)$

b. $N_2O_4(g) \rightleftarrows 2NO_2(g)$

c. $PCl_5(g) \rightleftarrows PCl_3(g) + Cl_2(g)$

d. $4H_2(g) + CS_2(g) \rightleftarrows CH_4(g) + 2H_2S(g)$

e. $2NO(g) + Br_2(g) \rightleftarrows 2NOBr(g)$

f. $2Cl_2(g) + 2H_2O(g) \rightleftarrows 4HCl(g) + O_2(g)$

g. $C_4H_{10}(g) + 13/2O_2(g) \rightleftarrows 4CO_2(g) + 5H_2O(g)$

h. $2Hg(g) + O_2(g) \rightleftarrows 2HgO(g)$

i. $H+(aq) + C_2H_3O_2^-(aq) \rightleftarrows HC_2H_3O_2(aq)$

a.	b.	c.
d.	e.	f.
g.	h.	i.

3. Cadmium hydroxide, lead (II) fluoride, nickel chromate, and barium phosphate are all insoluble salts, while calcium sulfate and silver cyanide may be classed as slighly soluble. Use this information to write a solubility-constant *or* an equilibrium-constant expression for each of the following:

a. $Cd(NO_3)_2 + 2NaOH \rightarrow Cd(OH)_2 + 2NaNO_3$

b. $3BaS + 2(NH_4)_3PO_4 \rightarrow 3(NH_4)_2S + Ba_3(PO_4)_2$

c. $ZnF_2 + Pb(ClO_3)_2 \rightarrow Zn(ClO_3)_2 + PbF_2$

d. $CaBr_2 + K_2SO_4 \rightleftarrows 2KBr + CaSO_4$

e. $NiI_2 + MgCrO_4 \rightarrow NiCrO_4 + MgI_2$

f. $Ag^+ + CN^- \rightleftarrows AgCN$

a.	b.
c.	d.
e.	f.

300

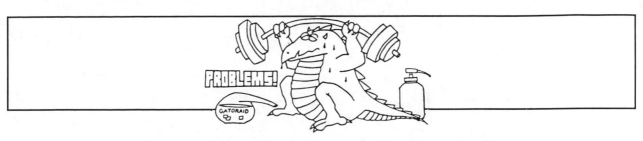

4. A mole each of nitrogen and oxygen are reacted, resulting in concentrations of 0.375 for each reactant and 1.94 for the product, NO(g). For this and the following problem, write (a) a balanced equation, then (b) an equilibrium constant expression. Next, use the expression you have written to (c) calculate K or K_{sp}. Finally, (d) state the favored direction.

5. Some lead (II) iodide is added to water and concentrations of 1.24×10^{-3} for lead (II) ion and 2.48×10^{-3} for iodine result.

6. Write the formulae of the salts listed here in order from the most water-soluble to the least, based on their solubility constants, as given.

Ag_2CrO_4	1.9×10^{-12}	AgI	8.5×10^{-17}
BaF_2	2.4×10^{-5}	CuS	8.0×10^{-32}
$MgCO_3$	3.0×10^{-5}	$PbSO_4$	1.3×10^{-8}

(1)_____ (2)_____ (3)_____ (4)_____ (5)_____ (6)_____

1. An 80.5-gram cube of Au(s) at 27°C is melted. Then, the Au(l) is heated and vaporized, but heated no further. What is Q, if gold melts at 1063°C, vaporizes at 2966°C and has heats of fusion and vaporization of 3.80 J/g and 242 J/g respectively (Note: you must find some missing information before starting.).

2. Determine *m* for a solution in which 300 grams of rubidium nitrate is dissolved in exactly 2.00 kilos of water.

3. Write the electronic notation for arsenic.

1. e d f g b c a

2.

(a) $\dfrac{[I_2][H_2]}{[HI]^2}$	(b) $\dfrac{[NO_2]^2}{[N_2O_4]}$	(c) $\dfrac{[PCl_3][Cl_2]}{[PCl_5]}$
(d) $\dfrac{[CH_4][H_2O]^2}{[H_2][CS_2]}$	(e) $\dfrac{[NOBr]^2}{[NO]^2[Br_2]}$	(f) $\dfrac{[HCl]^4[O_2]}{[Cl_2]^2[H_2O]^2}$
(g) $\dfrac{[CO_2]^4[H_2O]^5}{[C_4H_{10}][O_2]^{13/2}}$	(h) $\dfrac{[HgO]^2}{[Hg]^2[O_2]}$	(i) $\dfrac{[HC_2H_3O_2]}{[H^+][C_2H_3O_2^-]}$

3.

(a) $K_{sp} = [Cd^{2+}][OH^-]^2$	(b) $K_{sp} = [Ba^{2+}]^3[PO_4^{3-}]^2$
(c) $K_{sp} = [Pb^{2+}][F^-]^2$	(d) $\dfrac{[KBr]^2[CaSO_4]}{[CaBr_2][K_2SO_4]}$
(e) $K_{sp} = [Ni^{2+}][CrO_4^{2-}]$	(f) $\dfrac{[AgCN]}{[Ag^+][CN^-]}$

4. $N_2(g) + O_2(g) \rightleftarrows 2NO(g)$

$$K = \frac{[NO]^2}{[N_2][O_2]} = \frac{[1.94]^2}{[0.375][0.375]} = 26.2$$

The forward direction is favored in this reaction, as indicated by the much greater presence of product than of reactant.

5. $PbI_2 \leftarrow Pb^{2+} + 2I^-$

$$K_{sp} = [Pb^{2+}][I^-]^2 = [1.24 \times 10^{-3}][2.48 \times 10^{-3}]^2 = 7.63 \times 10^{-9}$$

In this problem, PbI_2 is omitted from the expression as it is quite insoluble. You knew this when you got the very small number for the solublity product (constant). Perhaps you also remembered that this salt is insoluble, as per the solubility rules (Sect. 6.2).

6. (1) $MgCO_3$ (2) BaF_2 (3) $PbSO_4$ (4) Ag_2CrO_4 (5) AgI (6) CuS

8.8 Le Chatelier's Principle

The equilibrium system that we have so far been using as an example—the $H_2/I_2/HI$ one—is represented by an equation with the molar coefficients 1:1:2. With only this information, and assuming a complete forward reaction, we would expect two moles of hydrogen iodide to form from a mole each of hydrogen and iodine vapor. We now know, of course, that this is not the case; about one fiftieth (at 750°C) would remain reactant.

Suppose, however, that the concentrations (proportions) were not in these same ratios; that is, that one (or more) species were in excess. How would this affect the equilibrium?

The answer is provided by Le Chatelier's Principle, which states that *when a stress is placed on a system in equilibrium*—be it by altering the concentration of a species or by changing the conditions of pressure and/or temperature—*the system will compensate in a manner to relieve it*. This relief takes the form of shifting the equilibrium in one direction or the other. Now, we will consider the major types of "stresses."

Pressure

As only gaseous systems are truly compressible, the effect of pressure is relevant only to equilibria among gaseous products and reactants.

The stress of increased pressure will be partly relieved by a shift in whichever direction results in fewer total molecules because, as you know from Chap. 5, less molecules mean less collisions, which in turn mean less pressure. What kind of molecules they are makes no difference whatsoever.

Decompression, on the other hand, will shift the equilibrium in the direction of more molecules, so as to restore the "lost" pressure.

In the equation for the reaction of H_2 and I_2 to make (two) HI, there are two molecules on either side of the equation, and each exerts the same pressure (as per Gay-Lussac's Law). Therefore, more or less pressure would not affect equilibrium; the molecules are already as few as or as many as they can be. Let us, then, consider a gaseous equilibrium in which there is an inequality—between two sides of the equation—of molecules:

$$COCl_2 \rightleftarrows CO + Cl_2$$

Increased pressure would favor the reverse direction; it would increase the count of phosgene molecules at the expense of carbon monoxide and chlorine. In other words, the system offsets the increase in pressure by creating one pressure-causing molecule ($COCl_2$) from two pressure-causing molecules (CO and Cl_2).

Reduced pressure, conversely, would shift the equilibrium forward, or to the right, for the opposite reason: more molecules can be made from fewer; therefore, more torr are correspondingly "made" from fewer torr as pressure is brought back up by the presence of one CO and one Cl_2 in place of each $COCl_2$.

Catalysis

A catalyst, as you know, can do two things, owing to its ability to lower a reaction's activation energy barrier. It can make a reaction proceed at greater speed, or make that reaction possible in the first place. In equilibrium terms, it can bring a system to equilibrium more quickly.

But *it cannot alter equilibrium itself* (Sect. 8.3); that is, it cannot change the proportions (or ultimate relative concentrations). The same holds true, of course, for an inhibitor. Catalysts and inhibitors, then, are not true stresses.

ONE KEY TO PREDICTING SHIFTS IN THE EQUILIBRIUM IS KNOWING WHICH—OF THE FORWARD OR THE REVERSE—IS EXOTHERMIC AND WHICH IS ENDOTHERMIC.

Temperature

You know that chemical reactions involve heat exchange between the reacting system and its surroundings. One gains heat as the other loses it. If a forward reaction is, say, exothermic, its reverse will be endothermic (and if the forward reaction is endothermic, the reverse one ... figure it out!).

Therefore—keeping Le Chatelier's Principle in mind—if heat is added to the system, it will compensate by shifting the equilibrium in the direction that will absorb heat (the endothermic) and thereby bring the temperature back down. If heat is removed from the system (i.e., it is cooled), equilibrium compensates by shifting in the direction of the exothermic reaction to warm things back up (or at least slow down the cooling).

When hydrogen and iodine vapor react to form hydrogen iodide, heat evolves; the forward reaction ($H_2 + I_2 \rightarrow 2HI$) is exothermic. This automatically entails that the reverse reaction ($H_2 + I_2 \leftarrow 2HI$) is endothermic. So, if we heat it, this equilibrium system "seeks relief" from this stress by shifting somewhat in the endothermic direction. It absorbs some of that added heat by making more H_2 and I_2 molecules from HI molecules. At the new equilibrium, brought on by heat stress, the proportion of the reactants will thus be higher than they were before the stress was added.

Cool this same system and the reverse happens: the lower temperature is met by a shift in the heat-evolving (exothermic) direction and, as a consequence, more HI molecules than in an ustressed system.

Concentration

In Draggin's' "experiment" (p. 303), the excess hydrogen raises the frequency of collisions between H_2 molecules with other H_2 molecules and with I_2 molecules, simply because there is suddenly more H_2 than before this new stress was introduced. These collisions result in more HI molecules until, after awhile, the collisions involve many more HI molecules than were involved before the stressing, because (again) there are now more of them.

When the effect of this second type of collision—that which causes them to break up—equals the effect of the first—that which causes HI molecules to form—equilibrium is re-established, albeit shifted further in the original, forward direction. It thus moves away from hydrogen, which *caused* the stress by being in excess. If iodine vapor instead of H_2 were added, the system would do the exact same thing.

If, on the other hand, some hydrogen (or iodine) were removed (its concentration lowered), the system predictably responds by producing more H_2 molecules (and, concomitantly, more I_2 molecules) from the HI molecules. This time, though, the shift is in the reverse direction. How far would depend on the point at which the forward direction, after its delay, would come around to equaling the change in the reverse. Again, equilibrium and its fixed

SUDDENLY H_2 IS EVERYWHERE.

AND NOW HI IS EVERYWHERE.

concentrations are re-established.

In short, the effect of this stress—changing the concentration of one member of the system—causes equilibrium to shift away from an excess species and towards a scarce one. The "goal" of the system is again restoration; we have also seen how it restores—to a degree, anyway—the original T and P. This time, it works to restore the concentration of the species whose proportion has fallen at the expense of the species whose proportion has increased. We do not often see a *full* restoration of the original conditions in a system's shifting, but we can always predict the direction it will take.

Do not confuse, by the way, a *shift* in the direction (forward or reverse) with a *favoring* of that direction. The more you think about Le Chatelier's Principle, the more it makes sense. Note the analogous response by the system to these three types of stress.

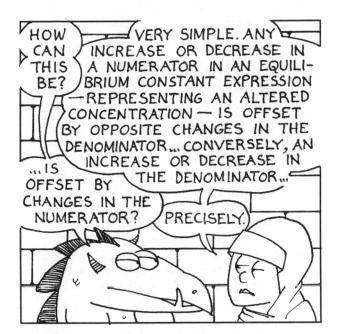

Always remember: an equilibrium expression remains a constant, although its concentrations may be altered. Case in point: the equilibrium of the $H_2/I_2/HI$ system, with the species in their molar ratios is, as you know by now, expressed

$$\frac{[HI]^2}{[H_2][I_2]} = \frac{[1.56]^2}{[0.22][0.22]} = 5.02 \times 10^1$$

...but if we were to triple the hydrogen (add the stress of an increased concentration), we would have...

(stressed system) $\quad \dfrac{[1.56]^2}{[0.66][0.22]}$

Some of this excess hydrogen (along with some of the iodine) would be used make more hydrogen iodide:

(new equilibrium) $\quad \dfrac{[2.11]^2}{[0.59][0.15]} = 5.02 \times 10^1$

Altogether, the three net changes (more H_2, more HI, and less I_2) still equal about 5.02×10^1 or about 50; for this, the expressions are constants. No matter what numbers appear *in* them, the quotient is always the same.

Let us consider a reaction and the effects of the various stresses on its equilibrium. Carbon monoxide reacted with steam yields two other gases and heat. Predict the direction of shift caused by each stress listed.

$$CO + H_2O \rightleftarrows H_2 + CO_2 + 306 \text{ kJ}$$

(a) addition of a catalyst   (d) decrease of [CO]
(b) cooling   (e) decrease of $[CO_2]$
(c) compression   (f) increase of $[H_2]$

Predictions: (a) no shift; (b) forward, because the forward reaction, being exothermic, restores heat; (c) no effect, because there is the same number of molecules on both sides of the equation; (d) reverse, to form more carbon monoxide; (e) forward, so as to make more carbon dioxide; (f) reverse, to use up excess hydrogen.

Some reactions (notably combustions) go to completion because they are so highly exothermic that the products of the reaction are just too "tired" to react in the reverse direction. Put another way, they do not have enough energy—almost all of which evolved as heat—to overcome the activation barrier.

All metathesis reactions, however, and many reactions among the other types (Sect. 4.2) go to completion without necessarily being too highly exothermic; if fact, they do so for a more common circumstance, one that you are already familiar with.

You know that metathesis reactions yield precipitates, gases, or weak electrolytes (do not, however, confuse this *characteristic* of metathesis with its *definition*). When they, or other types of reactions that yield such products—namely those that "escape" the system by their formation—*the particles needed for the reverse reaction become unavailable*. Note the analogy with the above-mentioned preclusive condition (high exothermy). A reverse reaction can be precluded by either a *lack of heat* or a *lack of particles*, whenever one (or both) of these requirements disappears in the forward reaction.

These nonavailabilities are stresses in the form of decreased concentration to zero or an increase up to a point of no return. Below are two examples of the former sort. Ions in solution decrease to a zero-concentration when they form a precipitate (a). When a strong acid reacts with a metal, H_2 escapes. Without all the species needed for the reverse reaction, there can be no equilibrium to halt a complete forward reaction.

(a) $Ba(NO_3)_2 + K_2SO_4 \rightarrow 2KNO_3 + BaSO_4\downarrow$ (b) $Cu + 2HBr \rightarrow CuBr_2 + H_2\uparrow$

305

8.9 Liquid/Vapor Equilibrium

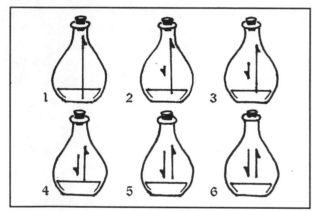

Equilibrium has been mentioned at several points in this work, in a variety of contexts. The principle, however, is always the same: it is the apparent standstill between two opposite changes occuring at the same rate and offsetting each other.

In Sect. 7.1, vapor pressure was identified as a liquid property. In any closed system—such as a stoppered flask—an equilibrium between a liquid sample and its gas phase can be observed (visually, in some cases).

In the Florence flask (Avogadro's favorite type) above, the development of this type of physical (i.e., nonchemical) equilibrium is seen in six stages. Evaporization and its opposite, condensation, are represented by arrows going up and down, respectively.

⊛ Color the "gas area" in flask 2 very slightly blue; then color the same area in the succeeding flasks successively bluer, at barely perceptible gradients. Color the liquid phase dark blue.

Imagine that the flask has just been removed from a storage so cold that no molecules were able to evaporate (form a gas phase). Then, it is left in direct sunlight. At first, there is only evaporation, as the first few molecules that gather enough kinetic energy to enter the gas phase do so (1).

Pretty soon, however, pressure increases with the increasing number of gas molecules. As a result, a few of the airborne particles collide with the surface of the liquid, get stuck, and re-enter the liquid phase (2).

At this point, there are still far fewer molecules returning to the liquid (condensation) than there are leaving it (evaporation). But the former of these two changes continues to increase at the expense of the latter (3, 4, and 5) until they are taking place at the same rate (6). Liquid/vapor equilibrium has been reached: the number of molecules escaping the liquid equals the number being recaptured by it (although the condensation direction can be said to be "favored" for there are far more molecules in the (l) phase.

As with chemical equilibria, temperature and pressure are stresses which can shift the equilibrium in the direction of one or the other of the changes (evaporation or condensation).

An increase in temperature will obviously cause a shift towards evaporation (meaning that a greater number of molecules will evaporate prior to equilibrium).

Simply put, more particles will have the energy they need to overcome the Van der Waals Forces that keep them in the liquid phase. The hotter a pot of soup gets, the more its gas phase will be smelled. Lower temperature, of course, would mean a shift in the direction of condensation (Do you not marvel at your author's grasp of the obvious?).

Pressure affects liquid/vapor equilibria oppositely to temperature's effect. More pressure definitively means more collisions and, in this case, they are collisions between the phases themselves. More recapturing of the evaporated molecules will take place. Less pressure, of course, reduces this colliding and so causes a shift towards evaporation.

Le Chatelier's Principle is not really applicable to *nonchemical* equilibria such as this; however, the Ideal Gas Model (Sect. 5.1) and Kinetic Theory in general are.

GLUG GLUG ANSWERS!

1. Consider the reaction represented by the following equation:

$$XY_2 + Z \rightleftharpoons XZ + 2Y + 47\,J$$

XY_2 and Z may be thought of as reactants and XZ and Y as products that do not leave the system upon forming. Note that the forward reaction is exothermic, but not to a high degree.

At right is a list of possible stresses. Identify the direction in which each one will cause the equilibrium to shift, as per Le Chatelier's Principle: "F" for the forward direction; "R" for the reverse; and "N" if equilibrium is established more quickly or more slowly but without a change in proportions. Do not forget to count the molecules.

_____ heating

_____ catalyst

_____ decreased [Z]

_____ compression

_____ decreased $[XY_2]$

_____ inhibitor

_____ increased [XZ]

_____ decompression

_____ cooling

_____ increased $[Y]^2$

_____ increased [Z]

2. Now consider a second reaction at right :

$$2DE_3 + 3G \rightleftharpoons 2D + 3GE_2$$

Changes in pressure would not affect this equilibrium. Explain why this is so:

_____

3. State which direction the equilibrium will shift (F, R, or N) in each of the following reactions when the stress indicated is introduced to the system.

a. $CO + I_2 \rightleftharpoons COI_2$ increased pressure   a. _____

b. $2SO_2 + O_2 \rightleftharpoons 2SO_3$ decreased $[O_2]$ b. _____

c. $N_2 + O_2 \rightleftharpoons 2NO$ increased $[N_2]$ c. _____

d. $2IBr \rightleftharpoons I_2 + Br_2$ increased pressure   d. _____

e. $CO + 3H_2 \rightleftharpoons CH_4 + H_2O$ decreased $[H_2O]$ e. _____

f. $2NOCl + 2NO + Cl_2$ decreased $[NOCl]^2$ f. _____

g. $3O_2 \rightleftharpoons 2O_3$ decreased pressure   g. _____

4. Each of the following reactions goes to completion; most do so for more than one reason. In the space provided on p. 308, provide at least one explanation for the completeness of the forward reactions (and the nonexistence of reverse reactions). C_7H_{16}, incidentally, is main ingredient in gasoline; let this be a clue in (d).

a. $Zn(s) + 2HBr(aq) \rightarrow ZnBr_2(aq) + H_2(g) + \triangle H$

b. $AgNO_3(aq) + KCl(aq) \rightarrow AgCl(s) + KNO_3(aq) + \triangle H$

c. $NaCN(aq) + HClO_4(aq) \rightarrow NaClO_4(aq) + HCN(aq) + \triangle H$

d. $C_7H_{16}(l) + 4O_2(g) \rightarrow 7CO_2(g) + 8H_2O + \triangle H$

e. $Sr(OH)_2(aq) + 2HBrO_3(aq) \rightarrow Sr(BrO_3)_2 + 2H_2O + \triangle H$

4. (Cont.) answers:

(a)	
(b)	(c)
(d)	(e)

5. Explain the relation between liquid/vapor equilibrium and temperature:

6. Explain the relation between liquid/vapor equilibrium and pressure:

1. (specific heats from table in Sect. 7.6)

$Q_1 = 80.5\text{ g} \times \dfrac{0.130\text{ J}}{(g)(°C)} \times 1036°C = 1.08 \times 10^4\text{ J}$ $[\triangle T = 1063 - 27]$

$Q_2 = 80.5\text{ g} \times \dfrac{3.80\text{ J}}{g} = 3.06 \times 10^2\text{ J}$

$Q_3 = 80.5\text{ g} \times \dfrac{0.151\text{ J}}{(g)(°C)} \times 1903°C = 2.31 \times 10^4\text{ J}$ $[\triangle T = 2966 - 1063]$

$Q_4 = 80.5\text{ g} \times \dfrac{242\text{ J}}{g} = 1.95 \times 10^4\text{ J}$

$Q_T = 5.37 \times 10^4\text{ J}$

2.

$m = \dfrac{300\text{ g RbNO}_3}{2.00\text{KgH}_2O} \times \dfrac{\text{mol RbNO}_3}{147.5\text{ g RbNO}_3} = 1.02m$

3. $1s^2 2s^2 2p^6 3s^2 3p^6 4s^2 3d^{10} 4p^3$

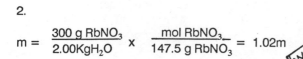

8.10 Chapter Synthesis

An infectious disease begins with a pathogen running unencumbered and multiplying mitotically in the body of its host. If the body's immune system is working, an opposite (and oppositional) reaction will start up with the production of antibodies to check the invasion. An equilibrium is reached when the antibodies are destroying the antigens as quickly as they—the latter—are being introduced into the system. Ideally, this reverse reaction will go all the way to completion, eliminating all but a moribund trace of the enemy.

In a strictly chemical sense, equilibrium always concerns two opposing reactions. Before this equilibrium is reached, however, one of the two reactions—the forward or the reverse—prevails to some proportional degree *before* it is offset by the other; that is, it will be favored at equilibrium. Even at equilibrium, however, both reactions continue to take place, albeit at the same rate. This system, then, is invisibly, if not visibly, dynamic.

A change in the concentration of a species, in temperature or pressure, can shift equilibrium (a catalyst can only bring it about more quickly). The effects of each of these stresses parallels those of all others: when something pertaining to the system is diminished, the system moves in the direction of its restoration; if any of these "somethings"—be they degrees of temperature, torr, or actual chemical species—is augmented, the system shifts towards reducing it.

Chemical equilibria are always established at the same ending proportions, given identical conditions of pressure and temperature; it does not matter whether the reaction begins with "reactants" or "products" as we read them in a linear equation.

Equilibrium constants are constants because the quotient of the species' concentration expression works out to be the same number, despite any changes in the concentrations themselves, which correspond to shifts in equilibrium. Recall that, while equilibrium constants are quotients, solubility constants are (arithmetical) products. In both, however, it is the exponent that contains the important information. A large exponent indicates a complete reaction, whereas a small one indicates equilibrium. The sign $(+,-)$ of the same exponent tells us the favored direction at equilibrium, although all solubility constants (*not* equilibrium constants) are by necessity negative.

Finally, those reactions that do go to completion, instead of to equilibrium, do so only because something required for a reverse reaction is lost from the system. In reactions from which a great deal of heat evolves, this "something", of course, is the heat itself. The rest of the time (and even at the *same* time), the products that are the would-be reactants in the reverse reaction are themselves removed if they are gases, precipitates, or nonelectrolytes.

Recognizing equilibrium in an analogous physical context demonstrates a broader grasp of the principle, which can be extended to further study. The leap from a chemical to a physical understanding, for instance, proceeded late in this chapter when physical processes—condensation and evaporation—took the place of the forward and reverse reactions.

1. R N R R R N R F F R F

2. There is the same number of molecules on either side of this equation; hence, pressure could not be restored or alleviated by a shift.

3. F R F N F R R

4.

	(a) (1) formation of a gas: H_2
(b) (1) formation of a precipitate: AgCl	(c) (1) ionization of a strong electrolyte: $HClO_4$ (2) formation of a weak electrolyte: HCN
(d) (1) formation of two gases: CO_2 and H_2O (2) very high exothermy	(e) (1) ionization of a strong electrolyte: $Sr(OH)_2$ (2) formation of a weak electrolyte: H_2O

Reaction (d), being combustion, loses too much energy for the activation of the reverse reaction to take place. Did you notice, by the way, that (b) and (c) are both metathesis (and so automatically had to go to completion)?

5. Increased temperature shifts a liquid/vapor equilibrium in the direction of more evaporation.

6. Increased pressure shifts the equilibrium in the opposite way that temerature does; there will be more condensation, at increased pressure, before an equilibrium is established.

53
I
126.90

𝕻rofile: 𝕴odine

The thyroid glands are in the neck, and the parathyroids, just above them.

$I_2(s)$ is a dark solid whose color depends on the lighting. Its crystals can sublimate from the richly purple $I_2(g)$. The element's name in fact comes from the Greek word for that color, *ioeides*.

As a halogen, iodine is a rather aggressive element, though much less so than its lighter siblings. A steady lessening of activity is noted from fluorine through chlorine and bromine to iodine, such that iodine is the weakest oxidizer of the group (and, therefore, the strongest reducer).

Iodine is by far the scarcest of the available halogens, yet it is needed in minute quantities by living things. Table salt in most countries is iodized to prevent deficiency, although NaCl taken from the ocean and inland seas such as Utah's Great Salt Lake naturally carries impurities of iodine salts such as NaI and $NaIO_3$. An average human body requires a presence of only about 0.15 mg iodine; significantly larger (but still relatively slight) amounts are poisonous. The element concentrates in the thyroid glands, which use it to synthesize a class of enzymes—biochemical catalysts—called iodothyromines.

Iodine deficiency leads most dramatically to goitre, a severe inflamation of the thyroids, and, systemically, to an impairment of the body's control of the rate of food metabolism, which is the function of the iodothyromines. Kelp, dulse, and other sea vegetables are good sources of dietary iodine; thyroid pills are only used for emergency nutrient restoration and other therapies.

Iodine tincture, in which iod*ide* is dissolved in a water/iodine solution, is the familiar antiseptic that is called by the same name as the element. Iodine, unlike chlorine, is not very soluble by itself, but when iodide (which is) is added, the elemental iodine dissolves. It is the iodide that gives the tincture its voluptuous color.

Iodine is the only halogen that commonly forms positive oxidation states; they are 3+, 5+, and 7+, as seen in the interhalogen compounds ICl_3, IF_5, and IF_7. The iodine atom is so large that when combined, it can accommodate more than an octet of valence electrons; in iodine pentafluoride, it has 10 (five pairs); in the heptafluoride, it is surrounded by 14 (seven pairs). The iodate ion, on the other hand, can reach the 7− state when reacted with a sufficiently strong oxidizer, having the technical formula IO_3^{7-} instead of IO_3^-.

Chlorine and bromine are extremely caustic substances. The former was used in World War I as a chemical weapon and today as an amoebacide in public water supplies, though chloride ions are an essential micronutrient. Bromine, the lone liquid nonmetal, takes its name from a word meaning "stink." The idiom "bromide" is a curious label for a cliché joke or ennui-inducing excuse. Radioactive astatine—produced by bombarding bismuth with alpha particles—is too rare and unstable to be known from natural samples, which probably only amount to a few milligrams in the Earth's crust. Unlike iodine, which is distinctly nonmetallic with a few weakly metallic leanings, astatine must at least be a metalloid.

Iodine was discovered in the chemical watershed year of 1811 and named by Davy, who christened the other halogens as well.

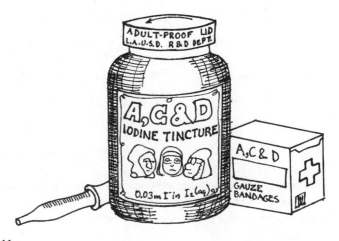

1. Under what two conditions do successful (reaction-making) collisions take place?

2. Briefly, state the correlation between bond strengths and activation energy barriers, as you understand it:

3. For the following stresses, write in "Q" if the stress quickens a reaction rate and "S" if it slows it (for the last one, make an educated guess).

a._____catalyst   c._____decrease in T   e._____increase in the

b._____increase in P   d._____inhibitor   concentration of any reactant

4. Order these equilibrium constants in order from that of the most complete reverse reaction (top) to that of the most complete forward reaction (note: three or four are actual equilibria):

$$1.6 \times 10^{-6} \qquad 4.4 \times 10^{4} \qquad 9.2 \times 10^{27}$$

$$5.1 \times 10^{-23} \qquad 7.8 \times 10^{12} \qquad 8.2 \times 10^{0}$$

$$2.7 \times 10^{1} \qquad 7.8 \times 10^{-42} \qquad 3.5 \times 10^{-1}$$

5. Now, in the other column, order these solulbility constants from most to least soluble:

$$6.7 \times 10^{-4} \qquad 1.3 \times 10^{-7} \qquad 8.1 \times 10^{-96}$$

$$2.2 \times 10^{-13} \qquad 5.4 \times 10^{-9} \qquad 9.8 \times 10^{-7}$$

$$7.5 \times 10^{-35} \qquad 4.5 \times 10^{-26} \qquad 2.0 \times 10^{-13}$$

equilibrium constants	solubility constants

6. For these three gas-system equations, construct an equilibrium constant expression (hint: what is insoluble?):

a. $I_2(g) + 7F_2(g) \rightleftarrows 2IF_7(g)$

b. $C_8H_{18}(g) + 25/2O_2(g) \rightleftarrows 8CO_2(g) + 9H_2O(g)$

c. $3X_2Y_3(g) + 6WZ(g) \rightleftarrows 2X_3W_3(g) + 3Y_3Z_2(g)$

a.	b.	c.

7. Write a constant expression (K or Ksp) for these two solution reactions:

d. $Al_2(SO_4)_3(aq) + 3Mn(C_2H_3O_2)_2(aq)$

$$\rightleftarrows 2Al(C_2H_3O_2)_3(s) + 3MnSO_4(aq)$$

e. $BaCl_2(aq) + 2HgNO_3(aq) \rightleftarrows 2HgCl_2(s) + Ba(NO_3)_2(aq)$

d.	e.

8. Some silver phosphate powder is added to water and concentrations of 1.95×10^{-5} for silver ion and 6.50×10^{-6} for phosphate result. Using the correct formula of this salt, write (a) a balanced equation and (b) an equilibrium constant expression. Then, whip out your calculator and compute K_{sp}.

8. (cont.)

9. The following questions relate to the equation at right. All of the species are gases. Below the equation, write an equilibrium constant expression. Then, in the following five multiple choice problems, circle the correct letter.

$$2XJ_2 + J_2 \rightleftarrows 2XJ_3 + \triangle H$$

10. Compression, in this case, will result in (a) higher $[XJ_3]^2$ (b) higher $[J_2]$ (c) both higher $[J_2]$ and $[XJ_2]^2$ (d) no change in $[XJ_3]^2$ (e) lower $[XJ_3]^2$ (f) none of these

11. An inhibitor will have the effect of (a) increasing $[XJ_3]^2$ (b) decreasing $[XJ_3]^2$ (c) decreasing $[XJ_2]^2$ (d) none of these

12. Increasing $[J_2]$ will (a) somewhat lower $[XJ_3]^2$ (b) raise $[XJ_3]^2$ (c) raise $[XJ_2]^2$ (d) will not affect any other concentration

13. Decompression will (a) increase the equilibrium constant (b) cause a shift in the reverse direction (c) decrease the equilibrium constant (d) shift equilibrium in the forward direction

14. Heating will (a) increase $[J_2]$ (b) result in the shifting of the equilibrium forward (c) increase $[XJ_3]^2$ (d) decrease $[XJ_2]^2$ (e) none of these

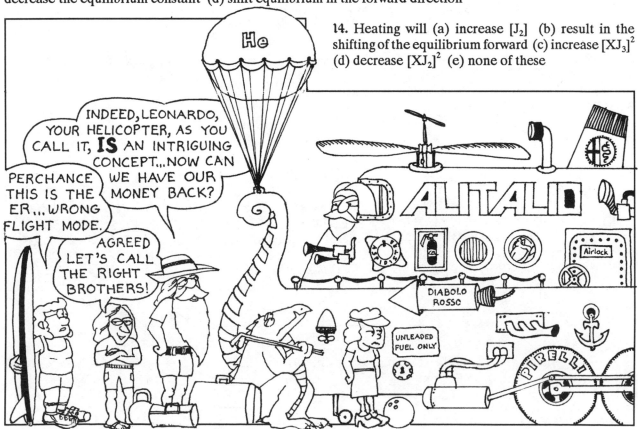

313

1. sufficient energy and proper orientation

2. The stronger the bonds, the greater the activation energy needed to break them.

3. a. Q   b. Q   c. S   d. S   e. Q

4. 7.8×10^{-42} (full reverse reactions)
5.1×10^{-23}
1.6×10^{-6}
3.5×10^{-1}
8.2×10^{0} (chemical equilibria)
2.7×10^{1}
4.4×10^{4}
7.8×10^{12}
9.2×10^{27} (full forward reactions)

5. 6.7×10^{-4} (very slightly soluble)
9.8×10^{-7}
1.3×10^{-7}
5.4×10^{-9}
2.2×10^{-13}
2.0×10^{-13}
4.5×10^{-26}
7.5×10^{-35}
8.1×10^{-96} (extremely insoluble)

6.

(a)	(b)	(c)	(d)	(e)
$\dfrac{[IF_7]^2}{[I_2][F_2]^7}$	$\dfrac{[CO_2]^8[H_2O]^9}{[C_8H_{18}][O_2]^{25/2}}$	$\dfrac{[X_3Y_3]^2[Y_3Z_2]^3}{[X_2Y_3]^3[WZ]^6}$	$K_{sp} = [Mn^{2+}][SO_4^{2-}]$	$K_{sp} = [Ba^{2+}][NO_3^-]^2$

8. $Ag_3PO_4(s) \rightleftharpoons 3Ag^+(aq) + PO_4^{3-}(aq)$ $[Ag^+]^3[PO_4^{3-}] = (7.41 \times 10^{-5})^3(6.50 \times 10^{-6}) = 4.82 \times 10^{-20}$

9. $\dfrac{[XJ_3]^2}{[J_2][XJ_2]^2}$ 10. a   11. d   12. b   13. b   14. a

Nine: Concerning the Acids and Bases

9.1 Acid Nomenclature

In Chap. 2, the nomenclature of ions was discussed. While one must learn—particularly in organic and biochemistry—the names of many very complex acids, there are only three simple but important classes to learn at the Chap. 1 level.

So far our usage of the term *acid* has referred to certain solutions of covalent compounds that, when ionized to some degree in water, yield H^+ (or H_3O^+) and anions—usually oxyanions.

In Sect. 2.2, the "ide" cluster was identified. It is largely with these that the first group—those without oxygen—are associated.

In Sect. 2.6, the commoner oxyanions were discussed. The other two classes of acids correspond to those ions.

You already know the names of some common acids, at least those of the strong acids identified in Sect. 6.8. We will now consider, deductively, the extendible system of naming acids, which parallels the nomenclature of their ionic conjugates.

----------1. Hydro-ic Acids----------

Anions ending in "ide" do not contain oxygen (save for O_2^-, OH^-, O_2^{2-} and some rarer species) and their acids are named using the pattern:

$$hydro + root + ic$$

Note this in the following six:

hydro-	fluor chlor brom iod sulfur cyan	-ic acid

One of these, hydrosulfuric acid, is a little different in that its root (sulfur) is the element's whole name; but in all the other cases, the root is what is left over when the *-ide* suffix is chopped off the name of the ion (fluor-ide, cyan-ide, etc.).

The generalization is that *ide* ions form *hydro-ic* acids.

----------2. Oxyanions----------

The system of affixes used for the oxyanions is extended to the oxyacids. Anions ending in *-ate* become *-ic* acids:

bromate → bromic
(BrO_3^-)   ($HBrO_3$)

...and those ending in *-ite* become the *-ous* acids:

hypobromite → hypobromous acid
(BrO^-)   ($HBrO$)

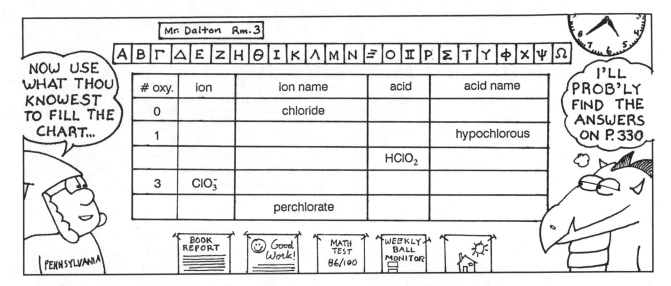

3. Acidic Ions

HNO_3 and H_2SO_4 are strong acids. The former is a *monoprotic* acid, because it can only ionize once, by giving up its lone proton. The latter is *polyprotic*; it can ionize (1) partially, to yield the hydrogen sulfate ion, HSO_4^-, or (2) fully, to yield sulfate, SO_4^{2-}. This phenomenon is called *stepwise ionization*.

The first loss of a proton, that is, the first stepwise ionization, is a relatively easy affair, but the second is not so easy; and the third (if any) is even less so, and so on.

This has an interesting consequence. In Chap. 6, it was noted that strong acids make electrolytic solutions, whereas weak ones, by dissociating less easily, do not. Anions resulting from the partial ionization of polyprotic acids, however, are always weak (because they hold on to their remaining protons more tenaciously), *but they are also electrolytes* (because they have the property of charge). Like any acid, they are internally covalent, but they behave as ions in solution.

It is sometimes noted that sulfuric acid, the only truly strong polyprotic acid, is strong only in its first ionization. This is correct.

Polyprotic acids with more than two protons can yield, as you would expect, more than one hydrogen-containing oxyanion. In naming them, the same prefixes used in their compounds are employed to quantify hydrogen in ionic oxyacids (*mono, di*, etc.).

Below is a table of the acid ions worth learning at this level. Rather than attempting to memorize them, use the clear pattern, and you will be able to name others not shown. Note that the name of each is only "hydrogen" followed by the the name of the "full" ion.

(While sulfurous and carbonic acids do not practically exist, the stepwise ionizations of both form common and important ions. Not having "real" conjugate acids to come from, both ions are usually associated with salts.)

acid	partial ionization	name of acid ion	full ionization
H_2CO	HCO^-	hydrogen carbonate	CO_3^{2-}
H_2S	HS^-	hydrogen sulfide	S^{2-}
H_2SO_4	HSO_4^-	hydrogen sulfate	SO_4^{2-}
H_2SO_3	HSO_3^-	hydrogen sulfite	SO_3^{2-}
$H_2C_2O_4$	$HC_2O_4^-$	hydrogen oxalate	$C_2O_4^{2-}$
H_3PO_4	$H_2PO_4^-$	dihydrogen phosphate	
	HPO_4^{2-}	monohydrogen phosphate	PO_4^{3-}

9.2 Acid/Base Concepts

It has been pointed out that many of the important chemical properties that are associated with certain substances are observable only in their solution state (aq).

While there are, for instance, crystalline solids that can be called acids, our survey will be limited to those that are aqueous solutions.

There are three conceptual models of acids and bases. They are not conflictive; rather, they are complementary and serve as working definitions under different sets of circumstances. Learn to understand them not only from their definitions, but from their differences as well.

――――――― 1. Arrhenius ―――――――

The Arrhenius sense of the words *acid* and *base* is that which has served us so far. It is based on physically observable characteristics of solutions.

A solution is an Arrhenius acid if it contains excess H^+ (in reality, H_3O^+) ions, or a base if it contains excess OH^- ions. These two ions—H^+ and OH^-—each impart a peculiar set of properties to a solution, as we shall presently see.

――――――― 2. Brönsted ―――――――

A Brönsted acid is a substance that "donates" protons to a Brönsted base, a substance which "accepts" protons. In essence, Brönsted theory involves the one-at-a-time transfer of protons. It expands the acid-base concept beyond the Arrhenius definition.

――――――― 3. Lewis ―――――――

A Lewis acid accepts electrons from a Lewis base (which, by definition, donates electrons) to form a covalent bond. This theory has particular relevance to oxidation-reduction-type reactions, into which it further broadens the acid-base idea. The Lewis category, however, is not all-inclusive; a Lewis acid or base is not also a Bronsted species.

A Lewis acid is more appropriately called an oxidizer, and a Lewis acid, a reducer. We will get to these in the next chapter.

318

ARRHENIUS ACIDS...

(1) taste sour;
(2) turn blue litmus paper pink;
(3) neutralize bases;
(4) release H_2 when they react with metals; and
(5) release CO_2 when reacting in carbonate solutions.

ARRHENIUS BASES...

(1) taste bitter;
(2) turn pink litmus paper blue;
(3) neutralize acids;
(4) feel soapy to the touch; and
(5) form insoluble salts in some solutions of metal ions (see Sect. 6.2).

In Sect. 6.7, the definition provided for acids and bases was the Arrhenius one. An Arrhenius acid is a solution with H^+ ions, or one in which H^+ is more abundant than OH^-. When it cedes these protons to something else during a solution reaction, it also qualifies as a Brönsted acid. If an Arrhenius base—a solution with a presence or an excess of OH^-—picks up protons in a solution reaction, then it qualifies as a Brönsted base.

When a strong acid and a strong base meet, a neutralization occurs and the H^+ and OH^- ions form water. As you know, the net ionic and generic equation for all reactions of this sort is $OH^- + H^+ \rightarrow HOH$ (H_2O).

If one or the other is weak, however, a full neutralization (that is, one going to completion) can still happen, as in the following example of a weak acid neutralizing a strong base:

$$KOH(aq) + HC_2H_3O_2(aq) \rightarrow KC_2H_3O_2(aq) + H_2O(1)$$

Strong KOH, as expected, is all but fully ionized while weak $HC_2H_3O_2$ ionizes only slightly, so an excess concentration of OH^- results. This, however, is a stress (Sect. 8.7). As the outnumbered H^+ ions are taken up by OH^- ions, more $HC_2H_3O_2$ ionizes to replace them (as per Le Chatelier's Principle), until it ionizes itself out of independent existence. The reaction is complete.

Arrhenius theory, then, is useful for studying reactions involving water solutions containing significant H^+ or OH^- concentrations. Brönsted's theory is even more general, for it extends the acid-base concept to reactions involving nonaqueous solvents.

In, for instance, the reaction of hydrochloric acid with liquid ammonia, HCl(aq) is an Arrhenius acid because it yields H^+, but this also makes it a Brönsted acid because H^+ is only a proton. The NH_3, however, yields no OH^- and so is not a base in Arrhenius terms. Just the same, the Brönsted theory lets us call it a base, because (1) it picks that proton up to become NH_4^+ (a Brönsted acid) and because (2) in the reverse reaction, some of the ammonium will give the proton back and so return to being ammonia. For the opposite reason, the chloride ion is a base; it accepts protons in the reverse reaction. All this, incidentally, is an acid-base equilibrium:

$$HCl(aq) + NH_3(aq) \rightleftharpoons NH_4^+(aq) + Cl^-(aq)$$

EVEN WATER CAN BE A BRÖNSTED BASE WHEN IT COMBINES WITH H⁺ [RELEASED BY AN IONIZING ACID] TO FORM HYDRONIUM...

...H₃O⁺, OR SIMPLY H⁺ IN MOST NET IONIC EQUATIONS. AFTER ALL, IT IS NOTHING MORE THAN A HYDRATED PROTON...

When a molecule of water accepts a proton (released as a result of an acid ionizing) to become hydronium, it is, by Brönsted's definition, a base; this reaction is nothing more than the hydration of H^+. Note the following reaction:

$$HBr(l) + H_2O(l) \rightleftarrows H_3O^+(aq) + Br^-(aq)$$

Hydronium, *for the sake of the reverse reaction*, is now an acid, and bromide, a base.

In this manner, the acid-base concept is extended from the precise Arrhenius understanding in which acids and bases are only aqueous reactants; in the Brönsted scheme of things, nonsolutions such as $NH_3(g)$ and $HBr(l)$ respectively qualify as an acid and a base, and all the products of the preceding two equations are one or the other.

⊛ In the equation above and in that on the bottom of p. 319, smudge the Brönsted acids pink and the Brönsted bases, light blue. You will smudge every species; each of these equations has two bases and two acids.

OK, LEWIS YOUR TURN...

Lewis, you may remember, put forth the idea that compounds could form not only by transfer of electrons (ionization, Sect. 2.6), but as well by the sharing of electrons (covalency, Sect. 3.6).

A base, in his sense, is one with unused (that is, nonbonding) electrons that it is "willing" to share with one of his acids.

Conversely, the Lewis acid, which is seeking electrons, is that which will attach itself to a Lewis base.

This entails that the identifying characteristic of either will be its valence-electron structure (dot, or Lewis, diagram, Sect. 3.7).

Magnesium oxide, as shown at right, provides the bonding pair that it will share with sulfur dioxide, so it is the Lewis base and the sulfur compound is the Lewis acid (Note: diagram is not fully accurate).

Interestingly, even mere H^+ can qualify as an acid in the Lewis sense of the word, as in the formation of ammonium(box b). Note that the Lewis base, ammonia, is not also a Brönsted base. This is not because it accepts a proton from an acid, but because, according to Lewis, the proton *is* the acid (a) (b). Think about it.

(a) $MgO_2(s) + SO_2(g) \rightarrow MgSO_4(s)$

(b) $H^+(aq) + NH_3(g) \rightleftarrows NH_4^+$

You now have two complementary ways to identify the acid and base species in any equation. The first is the various theories which, from the most finite to the most "stretched", are Arrhenius, Brönsted, and Lewis (note the alphabetical order).

Another way is to recognize conjugates. The conjugate of a base will be an acid, and vice-versa. If, with the theories, you can only identify one acid or base, you can identify its conjugate on the other side of the equation, and then all the other species in the equation, by deduction.

PROBLEMS!

1. Fill in the table .

ion	ion name	acid	acid name	acid ion(s)	acid ion name(s)
CN⁻				N/A	N/A
BO_3^{3-}	borate	H_3BO_3	boric	$H_2BO_3^-$/HBO_2^{2-}	di/monohydrogen borate
		HClO		N/A	N/A
			sulfuric		
IO_4^-				NA	N/A
	fluoride			N/A	N/A
		H_3PO_4			
			acetic	N/A	N/A
NO_2^-				N/A	N/A
		HBr		N/A	N/A
	oxalate				
			hydrosulfuric		

2. Match the following:

_____ Lewis base   a. can be a mere proton looking for an electron pair

_____ Arrhenius base   b. a species that forms covalent bonds with spare electrons

_____ Brönsted acid   c. turns litmus paper blue with hydroxide ions

_____ Arrhenius acid   d. a species with spare protons

_____ Lewis acid   e. a conjugate of a proton-donating species

_____ Brönsted base   f. any solution containing an excess of H⁺ (H₃O⁺) ions

3. In these equations, (⊛) smudge the acids pink and the bases, light blue; or, simply label them A or B. Use your understandings of (1) Brönsted and Lewis concepts, and of (2) conjugates. Smudge any salts you see light violet, or label S (state designations are optional).

a. $H_2SO_4(aq) + OH^-(aq) \rightleftarrows SO_4^{2-}(aq) + H_2O(l)$ b. $BaO(aq) + SO_3(g) \rightleftarrows BaSO_4(s)$

c. $HCO_3^-(aq) + ClO^-(aq) \rightleftarrows CO_3^{2-}(aq) + HClO(aq)$

d. $2NaOH(aq) + H_2PtCl_6(aq) \rightleftarrows 2HOH(l) + NaPtCl_6(aq)$

4. A strong base reacted with a strong acid results in a neutralization, but the reaction can go to completion (not end in equilibrium) even if one of the species is weak. Explain:

1.

ion	ion name	acid	acid name	acid ion(s)	acid ion name(s)
CN^-	cyanide	HCN	hydrocyanic		
BO_3^{3-}	borate	H_3BO_3	boric	$H_2BO_3^-/HBO_3^{2-}$	di/monohydrogen borate
ClO^-	hypochlorate	HClO	hypochlorous		
SO_4^{2-}	sulfate	H_2SO_4	sulfuric	HSO_4^-	hydrogen sulfate
IO_4^-	periodate	HIO_4	periodic		
F^-	fluoride	HF	hydrofluoric		
PO_4^{3-}	phosphate	H_3PO_4	phosphoric	$H_2PO_4^-/HPO_4^{2-}$	di/monohydrogen phosphate
$C_2H_3O_2^-$	acetate	$HC_2H_3O_2$	acetic		
NO_2^-	nitrite	HNO_2	nitrous		
Br^-	bromide	HBr	hydrobromic		
$C_2O_4^{2-}$	oxalate	$H_2C_2O_4$	oxalic	$HC_2O_4^-$	hydrogen oxalate
S^{2-}	sulfide	H_2S	hydrosulfuric	HS^-	hydrogen sulfide

2. b   c   d   f   a   e

4. A weak acid, in this case, would replace the H^+ reacting with the OH^- excess by ionizing until used up; a weak base would do the opposite, releasing OH^- to react with the H^+ surplus.

3. a. $HSO_4^- + OH^- \rightleftarrows SO_4^{2-} + HOH$
   A   B   B   A

b. $BaO + SO_3 \rightarrow BaSO_4$
   B   A   S

c. $HCO_3^- + ClO^- \rightleftarrows CO_3^{2-} + HClO$
   A   B   B   A

d. $2NaOH + H_2PtCl_6 \rightarrow 2HOH + NaPtCl_6$
   B   A   A   S

322

9.3 Relative Acid/Base Strengths

(a)

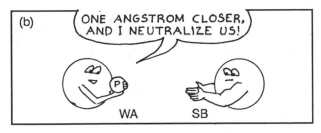

(b)

(c)

(d)

As far back as Sect. 6.8, we have been mentioning strong acids. In the Arrhenius concept, these are species that easily ionize to form a solution of H^+ ion (H_3O^+) and an anion of some kind.

Brönsted's concept proceeds directly from this: the strong acids very readily yield their protons in solution. A strong base is one that ionizes by just as readily dissolving and then capturing protons.

Therefore, as you know, when both or even only one of the two—acid *or* base—is strong, they neutralize each other (see boxes a, b, and c).

A weak acid and a weak base, together, however, do little more than ionize very slightly and form separate equilibria with the *negligible* amount of conjugate that is formed from each as they ionize to a *negligible* degree.

In other words, unless there is a species willing to donate and/or receive a proton, equilibrium, rather than a more or less complete reaction, will be the result (box d).

As you might expect, the favored direction at equilibrium is toward the formation of weak acids and bases, for it is they that are more stable and more unionized in solution.

Polyprotic acids become progressively weaker by several magnitudes with each stepwise ionization.

Below, note the ionizations of phosphoric acid and how they compare with some other weak acids. The third and final stop (monohydrogen phosphate) is an extremely weak acid that hardly ionizes at all.

⊛ Color the bases in the boxes, light blue, and the acids, pink.

——Some Ionization Constants of Acids——

	HIO_4	1.9×10^{-1}
(unionized)	H_3PO_4	1.1×10^{-2}
	$HC_2H_5O_2$	6.6×10^{-5}
(first step)	$H_2PO_4^-$	2.0×10^{-7}
	HCO_3^-	5.9×10^{-14}
(second step)	HPO_4^{2-}	3.6×10^{-23}

...and a *low* exponent indicates a *relatively high* degree of ionization or solubility. The six strong acids, like the many very soluble salts, need no constant, for their change in solution is complete, rather than to a quantifiable degree.

The most important thing to note about the chart of relative strengths is that *the stronger an acid is, the weaker will be its conjugate base,* and visa-versa.

An *amphoteric* species is one which can behave either as an acid or a base, depending on the circumstances (specifically, on the other species that are present). This is particularly true of the acid ions, which are transitions between neutral and fully ionized acids.

In an acid solution, for example, a HSO_4^- particle can gain a proton, and so is a base; in a basic solution, it can lose its remaining proton (second ionization) and so is an acid.

Relative Acid/Base Strengths		
acid name	acid	base
Perchloric	$HClO_4$	ClO_4^-
Hydroiodic	HI	I^-
Hydrobromic	HBr	Br^-
Hydrochloric	HCl	Cl^-
Nitric	HNO_3	NO_3^-
Sulfuric	H_2SO_4	HSO_4^-
Hydronium	H_3O^+	H_2O
Oxalic	$H_2C_2O_4$	$HC_2O_4^-$
H. Sulfate	HSO_4^-	SO_4^{2-}
Phosphoric	H_3PO_4	$H_2PO_4^-$
Hydrofluoric	HF	F^-
Nitrous	HNO_2	NO_2^-
Formic	$HCHO_2$	CHO_2^-
Benzoic	$HC_7H_5O_2$	$C_7H_5O_2^-$
H. Oxalate	$HC_2O_4^-$	$C_2O_4^{2-}$
Acetic	$HC_2H_3O_2$	$C_2H_3O_2^-$
Carbonic	H_2CO_3	HCO_3^-
Hydrosulfuric	H_2S	HS^-
Dih. Phosphate	$H_2PO_4^-$	HPO_4^{2-}
H. Sulfite	HSO_3^-	SO_3^{2-}
Hypochlorous	$HClO$	ClO^-
Boric	H_3BO_3	$H_2BO_3^-$
Ammonium	NH_4^+	NH_3
Hydrocyanic	HCN	CN^-
H. Carbonate	HCO_3^-	CO_3^{2-}
Monoh. Phosphate	HPO_4^{2-}	PO_4^{3-}
H. Sulfide	HS^-	S^{2-}
Water	H_2O	OH^-

(acid column: STRONGER ↑ / WEAKER ↓; base column: WEAKER ↑ / STRONGER ↓)

Perchlorate is the weakest base because its conjugate acid is the strongest acid known; when perchloric acid ionizes, there is virtually no tendency for the resulting ion to accept protons.

The strongest base is hydroxide or (in Arrhenius terms) a solution of one of the few soluble metal hydroxides (those that make up the strong-base club; Sect. 6.8). These species become strong Arrhenius bases because they quickly release, upon dissolution, hydroxide ions which seek protons to form the virtual nonacid, water (at the bottom of the table). Water is the conjugate of hydroxide.

The conjugate pairs in the middle of the table form the truer equilibria.

9.4 Acid/Base Equilibria

You are already aware that strong Arrhenius acids and bases are less stable in water than are weak ones; they ionize fully or near fully, and ionization, by part of its definition, is a *chemical* change.

It is logical to expect, then, that the stabler, weaker acids and bases will prevail in the end over the strong acids and bases simply because the former ionize to a lesser degree.

In short, a proton moves from a stronger acid to a stronger base to form and leave behind the weaker base and weaker acid that are their (respective) conjugates. In this way, the weaker species are favored.

This "favoring" is the same as that spoken of in Sects. 8.6 and 8.7. It refers to the *direction* favored at chemical equilibrium. In the acid/base context, equilibrium is the point at which the stronger acid and the stronger base are re-forming at the same rate they are ionizing to their weaker conjugates. By the time this point is reached, however, the system will be made up mostly of the weaker acid and the weaker base; hence, we say that the weaker species are favored at equilibrium.

The pattern for acid/base equilibria, then, is...

$$\text{SA} + \text{SB} \ \underset{\longleftarrow}{\overset{\longrightarrow}{\rule{2cm}{0pt}}} \ \text{WB} + \text{WA}$$

...where the two species on the left are strong enough, *between* them (p. 319), to transfer a proton by ionizing. SA, and the species that results from it, WB, are a pair of conjugates; so are SB and WA.

The long arrow shows that the weak species are favored, whereas the shorter one indicates that some (and only some) of the reacting stronger species is re-formed. There is more weaker acid and weaker base for no reason more complicated than that these species are stabler in water.

Keep in mind that, as with all equilibria, this type is dynamic; it is always changing, in spite of appearances or other signs to the contrary. In this case, for every trillion and one particles going in one direction, there are a trillion and one going in the opposite direction.

⊛ Color the acid "particles" pink and the base one, light blue.

325

STEP ONE:

STEP ONE   Write a net ionic equation showing the transfer of a single proton (H^+). Why just one?

Recall that the ionization of polyprotic acids is stepwise: one proton at a time. The acids resulting from an ionization will be far weaker than the acid which preceded the ionization, as the chart on p. 324 shows.

STEP TWO   Identify the stronger and the weaker species.

STEP THREE   Aim the longer arrow at the side of the equation in which both the *weaker* species appear.

Here is an example: hydrosulfuric acid ion (hydrogen sulfide) is added to phosphoric acid. What are the products, and which direction is favored? First, write the equation:

STEP ONE:

$$HS^- + H_3PO_4 \rightleftarrows H_2S + H_2PO_4^-$$

Phosphoric acid donates a proton to hydrogen sulfide, which is amphoteric and, in this case, acts as a base (the same is true for another amphoteric species, dihydrogen phosphate). Now, use a chart, such as that on p. 324, to do the other steps:

STEP TWO: SB   SA   WA   WB

STEP THREE: HS^- + H_3PO_4 ⇀↽ H_2S + $H_2PO_4^-$

It is true. Acid solutions dissolve and ionize many salts that are water-insoluble, provided the solution is sufficiently concentrated.

A salt—by one definition—is a compound that, when ionized in water, an acid, or another solvent yields an acid-forming anion and a base-forming cation (indeed, water itself is formed from these in a neutralization).

In general, *if the acid of the ion that it yields is weaker than the acid used in the solvent, the salt will dissolve.*

In this way, solubility can be predicted by comparing acid strengths.

For instance, iron (II) phosphate, a salt of weak phosphoric acid, is not soluble in water, nor is mercury (I) chloride, a salt of hydrochloric acid. What will happen if both of these salts are separately added to concentrated sulfuric acid?

The three acids in question are shown at right, positioned according to their relative strengths. The phosphate salt *will* dissolve because its corresponding acid is weaker than the solvent acid; the chloride *will not* dissolve for the opposite reason.

HCl	(stronger than solvent acid)
H_2SO_4	(solvent acid)
H_3PO_4	(weaker than solvent acid)

9.5 Predictions II Acid/Base

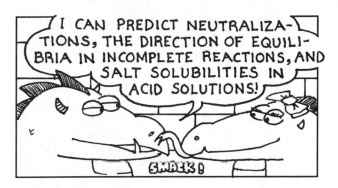

Ⓣhe key to predicting the outcome of acid/base reactions is the relative strengths of the acids and bases.

Apart from knowing the identities of the acids and bases that ionize completely in water (Sect. 6.8), you need not commit to memory the relative strengths of, say, the acids and bases on p. 324; you just look them up. On a test, you are likely to be provided with this information, verbally or (better still) with a table of strengths.

---
1. Neutralizations

A full neutralization is an acid/base reaction that goes to completion. For it to occur, proton transfer must take place until at least one of the reactants is chemically exhausted and changed into something else.

This occurs if either the base or the acid, or both, are strong; not just *relatively* strong, but among those absolutely strong species identified in Sect. 6.8 A complete neutralization will not have the double arrow because it does not result in equilibrium but is instead a one-way chemical change limited only by the quantity of the limiting reactant:

$$Ca(OH)_2(aq) + 2HNO_2(aq) \rightarrow Ca(NO_2)_2(aq) + 2HOH(l)$$

Do not forget that all full neutralizations—no matter what the reactants—have the same net ionic equation:

$$H^+ + OH^- \rightarrow HOH$$

---
2. Equilibria

When truly strong acids and/or bases are not involved, then what happens in a reaction depends on the comparative strengths of the acids and bases that *are* involved. None of the other acids and bases are strong enough to ionize completely (or, in the case of acid ions, to ionize fully to the next step) in aqueous solution, so we compare weak species with those that are even weaker when we want to predict the favored direction. We know this direction when both the weaker acid and the weaker base appear on the same side of the equation. Another, shorter arrow will point to the (relatively) stronger species in the equation that represents the reaction's final state.

(weaker) $\qquad H_3BO_3(aq) + HC_2O_4^-(aq) \rightleftharpoons H_2BO_3^-(aq) + H_2C_2O_4(aq) \qquad$ (stronger)

---
3. Salts and Acids

For a salt that is insoluble in water to dissolve in an acid solution, two conditions must be met.

1. The solution must be sufficiently concentrated (if not, it would be more like ordinary water as far as the salt is concerned).

2. The solvent acid must be stronger than the acid "in" the salt. The dissolution thus follows a familiar pattern: the formation of a weaker acid ahead of a stronger one.

℘rofile: ℜitrogen

Neptune's big moon, Triton, may have volcanoes of N_2 crystals.

The air, as you know, is mostly nitrogen, 78% in fact (when dry). This means that the partial pressure of nitrogen at sea level is about 12 pounds per square inch, for the total pressure is 14.7 lbs/in.^{2} (one atmosphere or 760 torr).

Compared to oxygen, nitrogen is quite inert, requiring high temperatures to form oxides. Two common oxides, nitric oxide (NO) and nitrogen dioxide (NO_2) are pollutants, contributing to smog and acid rain. The third well known oxide, nitrous oxide (N_2O), is a pleasant-smelling light anaesthetic used by surgeons and dentists.

Gaseous ammonia is sometimes injected directly into the soil by farmers, but the sulfate, nitrate, and phosphate salts of ammonia are all fertilizers, as is guano, the nitrogen-rich feces of seabirds. For decades, the Peruvian economy was largely undiversified and based on guano exploitation. Fertilization can also be accomplished by rotating peanuts, beans, alfalfa, etc., with non-nitrogen-fixing crops.

Ammonia can be synthesized with the Haber process and then converted to nitric acid by way of the Ostwald process. Both procedures were developed under the patronage of Kaiser Willhelm II for the sake of Germany's munitions industry. The benzene-ring derivative trinitrotoluene (TNT), dynamite, and guncotton are other nitrogen-based explosives. Gunpowder is about three-fourths saltpeter (KNO_3).

Nitric acid has been commercially important from alchemic times. It is a colorless liquid with a fierce odor (the gas phase burns one's internal membranes). The acid is used not only in the manufacture of fertilizers and explosives, but synthetic fibers (nylon, etc.) and some drugs and dyes. It is an acid-rain former, usually as a result of pollution but it also forms naturally in electrical storms.

Although nitrogen, in this way, has considerable destructive power, it is nevertheless one of the four primary elements of living tissue. Leguminous plants use special bacteria to "fix" nitrogen directly from the air (and, therefore, do not have to depend on the soil for it) to synthesize proteins, a vast class of organic nitrogen compounds. Plants are thus the ultimate source of all proteins, which they synthesize with nitrogen-containing compounds from the soil. The natural composting of plants of and the animals that directly or ultimately consume them is the decomposition, by still yet other specialized bacteria, into ammonia (among other simple compounds), which in turn forms nitrites. The nitrite salts go on to become nitrates and elemental nitrogen, which then return to the atmosphere. This is the nitrogen cycle, a critical ecological mechanism that is impaired by combustion, erosion, and artificial fertilization.

Nitrites are used by the meat industry to disguise the true and unsavory colors of meat that is necessarily decomposed ("aged") for a week or more until it is sufficiently putrefied ("tender") to be sent to the retail market. It is nitrites that help (technically) rotten carrion retain its pink or reddish color while also inhibiting botulism. Cooking, notably frying, catalyzes nitrites into carcinogenic nitrosamines.

Nitrogen was discovered in 1772 by (D.) Rutherford.

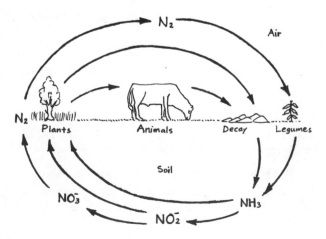

1. Match:

_____proton acceptor that ionizes extensively in water

a. weak base   _____conjugate of a weak base

_____proton donor or acceptor (depending) in water

b. amphoteric   _____proton acceptor that ionizes slightly in water

_____H_2O, HPO_4^{2-}, $H_2BO_3^-$, HS^-, $HC_2O_4^-$, HSO_4^-, etc.

c. strong acid   ———a favored proton donor, in equilibrium

_____proton donor that ionizes extensively in water

d. strong base   _____conjugate of a weak acid

_____proton donor that ionizes only slightly in water

e. weak acid   _____a favored proton acceptor, at equilibrium

2. Complete the following net ionic equations by (a) predicting the species that will appear on the right side of the equation and (b) use arrows to show equilibrium favoring reactants ($\leftarrow\!\!\rightharpoonup$) or products ($\rightleftharpoons\!\!\rightarrow$) or a reaction going to completion ($\rightarrow$). Make use of the table on p. 324.

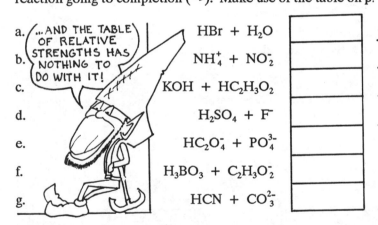

a.
b.
c.
d.
e.
f.
g.

$HBr + H_2O$		
$NH_4^+ + NO_2^-$		
$KOH + HC_2H_3O_2$		
$H_2SO_4 + F^-$		
$HC_2O_4^- + PO_4^{3-}$		
$H_3BO_3 + C_2H_3O_2^-$		
$HCN + CO_3^{2-}$		

3. Circle the salts which will dissolve in concentrated phosphoric acid:

a. $BaCO_3$ b. MnI_2 c. $Fe_2(NO_2)_3$ d. $AgC_2H_3O_2$ e. $PbSO_4$

4. Explain the significance of a high exponent in an ionization constant:

5. The stronger a base (or acid), the weaker its conjugate will be. Why?

6. Rank these bases (the stepwise ionizations of boric acid) in order from the strongest (1) to weakest (3);

_____dihydrogen borate   _____borate   _____monohydrogen borate

329

1. d c b a b e c d e a

2. (a) $HBr + H_2O \rightarrow Br^- + H_3O^+$ (ionization of s strong base in water)

    (b) $NH_4^+ + NO_2^- \rightleftharpoons HNO_2 + NH_3$

    (c) $KOH + HC_2H_3O_2 \rightarrow KC_2H_3O_2(aq) + HOH$ (neutralization of a strong base)

    (d) $H_2SO_4 + F^- \rightarrow HSO_4^- + HF$ (neutralization of a strong acid)

    (e) $HC_2O_4^- + HPO_4^{2-} \rightleftharpoons H_2C_2O_4 + PO_4^{3-}$

    (f) $H_3BO_3 + C_2H_3O_2^- \rightleftharpoons H_2BO_3^- + HC_2H_3O_2$

    (g) $HCN + CO_3^{2-} \rightleftharpoons CN^- + HCO_3^-$

3. (a), (c), and (d) will dissolve because carbonic, nitrous, and acetic acids are all weaker than the solvent acid, phosphoric; (b) and (e) will not dissolve because hydroiodic and sulfuric acids are stronger than the solvent.

4. The higher (that is, the larger) the negative exponent of an ionization constant, the weaker the acid.

5. The species resulting from the ionization of a strong acid or base has little tendency to go back by gaining or losing a proton; the stronger the original species, the weaker will be this tendency.

6. (3) dihydrogen borate (1) borate (2) monohydrogen borate (If these ions had been ranked as acids, the order would have been reversed.)

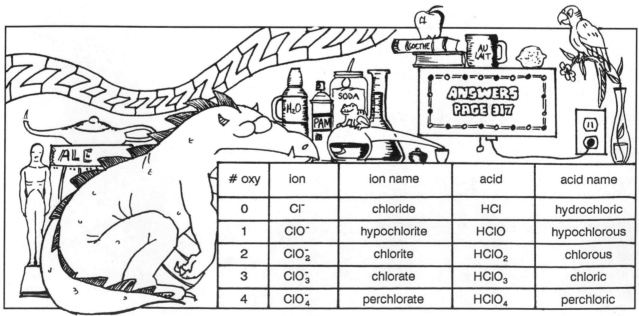

# oxy	ion	ion name	acid	acid name
0	Cl^-	chloride	HCl	hydrochloric
1	ClO^-	hypochlorite	HClO	hypochlorous
2	ClO_2^-	chlorite	$HClO_2$	chlorous
3	ClO_3^-	chlorate	$HClO_3$	chloric
4	ClO_4^-	perchlorate	$HClO_4$	perchloric

9.6 p Numbers

The concentration of H^+ or OH^- ions in solutions can range from very high (1.7×10^{-2}, for example) to infinitesimally low (1.6×10^{-14}). The latter number is less than one trillionth as big as the former. Quantifying concentrations of Arrhenius acids and bases with such articulated numbers can certainly be less than edifying.

Seismologists encountered the same problem with earthquakes, phenomena which occur over a very great range of magnitudes. Their solution was to assign a power of ten to each magnitude, such that, for example, a shaker of the fifth magnitude (a "number five") would be ten times greater than that of the fourth magnitude. This—as any Californian or Nicaraguan past the age of three can tell you—is the Richter Scale.

Chemists solved their problem in similar, if not identical, fashion by substituting ordinary positive integers up to 14 for the messy negative exponential expressions.

(There are, obviously, concentrations of hydrogen ions and hydroxide ions below 1.0×10^{-14}, but these are generally too negligible to be called "concentrations.")

These simple and positive whole numbers and the decimal-containing values between them are called *p numbers*, or *pN*. Specifically, there are two: *pH* and *pOH*.

Strong acids and bases yield H^+ and OH^-, respectively, in proportion to their own concentrations. This is so because they ionize virtually to completion. This means that the p number of a strong species will equal that of the $[H^+]$ or $[OH^-]$ that results from it. The brackets, as you will remember from Chap. 8, indicate concentrations.

Assuming the complete ionization of, say, HCl in a 0.1 molar solution, we would expect a concentration of 0.1 M H^+. A 0.01 M [HCl] solution would likewise be a 0.01 M $[H^+]$ solution; and 0.001 M [HCl] would give us 0.001 M $[H^+]$; and so on. These concentrations, expressed exponentially, are 1.0×10^{-1}, 1.0×10^{-2}, and 1.0×10^{-3}.

However, the p number, as has been pointed out, replaces the whole expression with an integer, and a positive one at that.

In this case, the expressions from the above paragraph, converted to their p values, are simply 1, 2, and 3, with each representing progressively smaller (*not* larger) magnitudes of concentration.

Note this relation in the table below; you will see that the p number, in this instance, pH (for the concentration of H^+) is the number of places to the left of the decimal.

[HCl]	[H$^+$]		pH
0.1	0.1	$= 1.0 \times 10^{-1}$	1
0.01	0.01	$= 1.0 \times 10^{-2}$	2
0.001	0.001	$= 1.0 \times 10^{-3}$	3
0.0001	0.0001	$= 1.0 \times 10^{-4}$	4
0.00001	0.00001	$= 1.0 \times 10^{-5}$	5
0.000001	0.000001	$= 1.0 \times 10^{-6}$	6
0.0000001	0.0000001	$= 1.0 \times 10^{-7}$	7

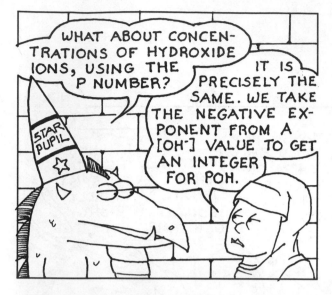

Since sodium hydroxide is a strong base, it ionizes fully, so a concentration of this base [NaOH] of 0.0001 or 0.00001 will give us the same concentration of hydroxide, [OH⁻]. Exponentially, they are 1.0×10^{-4} and 1.0×10^{-5}, but their p numbers are merely 4 and 5. Reread the last two paragraphs on p. 331 and you will see that pH and pOH are identical in principle.

Unlike the Richter Scale, however, *the larger the integer, the smaller the magnitude.* This magnitude, chemically speaking, is the concentration itself.

Basically, getting the pH or the pOH from [H⁺] or [OH⁻] is simply a matter of chucking everything, including the negative sign. Everything, that is, *except* for the exponent itself, which becomes *p*.

Complex solutions, such as those in the chart below, will contain both types of ions, and these will be at equilibrium (unless a reaction is actually going on at the moment).

In equilibrium terms, then, *p numbers refer to the relative concentrations of hydrogen and hydroxide ions in the same solution.* Together, they add up to 14 (which, keep in mind, is an arbitrary maximum chosen because concentrations below 1.0×10^{-14} are deemed unimportant).

The integer 7 is the midpoint between 0 and 14, and so pH = 7 also means p*OH* = 7, because 7 + 7 = 14. A pH (or a pOH) of 7, then, is where neither ion is favored at equilibrium. If pH, however, is 8, then a pOH of 6 is automatically entailed (14 − 8 = 6) and the hydroxide concentration is favored 100-to-one over the hydrogen because 0.000001 (1.0×10^{-6}) is one hundred times greater than 0.00000001 (1.0×10^{-8}).

In the table below, the values in most cases represent approximations or ranges of pH and pOH values. Orange juice can be anywhere from about pH 3.0 to 4.0, but it is always acidic, for its pH is below 7.0 and its pOH (11.0 to 10.0) is always above 7.0. Study the table until you understand the relation between [H⁺], [OH⁻], pH, and pOH.

Solution Liquid	pH	pOH	Sum	[H⁺]	[OH⁻]	Total
lemon juice	2	12	14	1.0×10^{-2}	1.0×10^{-12}	1.0×10^{-14}
vinegar	3	11	14	1.0×10^{-3}	1.0×10^{-11}	1.0×10^{-14}
cola softdrink	3	11	14	1.0×10^{-3}	1.0×10^{-11}	1.0×10^{-14}
orange juice	4	10	14	1.0×10^{-4}	1.0×10^{-10}	1.0×10^{-14}
tomato juice	4	10	14	1.0×10^{-4}	1.0×10^{-10}	1.0×10^{-14}
bovine lactic fluid	6	8	14	1.0×10^{-6}	1.0×10^{-8}	1.0×10^{-14}
human blood	7	7	14	1.0×10^{-7}	1.0×10^{-7}	1.0×10^{-14}
sea water	8	6	14	1.0×10^{-8}	1.0×10^{-6}	1.0×10^{-14}
household ammonia	11	3	14	1.0×10^{-11}	1.0×10^{-3}	1.0×10^{-14}

9.7 pH Calculations

When we have only one of [H⁺], [OH⁻], pH, or pOH, we can (often very easily) determine the other three. You have already seen how to get the p number from the concentration, or the reverse. To get one concentration from the other, just use "equation" (b) above.

Notice that unlike (a), which is an addition operation, (b) is a multiplication one. Or is it? No, it, too, is only addition, thanks to the mathematical principle that states that to multiply numbers raised to a (negative or positive) power of ten, we need only to *add* the exponents. Thus, both concentrations are addends that have 10^{-14} as a sum, *not* a product in the same way that pH and pOH are addends with 14 as a sum. You may already have noticed this in the table on p. 332. Therefore, going from one of the four, as a given, to get the other three requires not much more than the ability to add up to and subtract from 14.

Consider this example: if a solution has a pH of 5.0, determine its other three values. Look at the loop above. Whether you go clockwise or counter clockwise does not matter. If pH is 5, pOH will necessarily be 9; if pOH is 9, then [OH⁻] has to be 1.0×10^{-9}; and if this is so, [H⁺] is 1.0×10^{-5}. Go one step further and you will have come full circle: pH is 5 because [H⁺] is 1.0×10^{-5}.

It is really that easy, provided that the [H⁺] and [OH⁻] values have whole exponents; that is, exponents without mantissas.

Concentration Logarithm

A logarithm is an exponent that is not a whole number.

Sadly, a concentration expression newly converted from a p number (as above) will seldom be "1.0 x ten to the power of a whole number." We do not want that messy logarithm, so we will therefore convert it to an antilogarithm, which is the "big number" that multiplies the ten-to-a-power. So far, the only antilog we have looked at is "1.0." Changing this to another number between one and 10 is our way of converting the logarithm back to a clean, whole-number exponent.

Fortunately, this topic begins with a tidbit of good news.

333

$$[H^+] = 10^{-pH}$$
$$[OH^-] = 10^{-pOH}$$

Here is an example: a solution has a [OH$^-$] of 3.4 x 10^{-5}. What is its [H$^+$]?

Treat the problem as the multiplication of two fractions, or as a very simple DA problem without dimensions or even a set-up. The two numerators are a constant, 1.0 x 10^{-14} and the denominators are the two parts of the given:

$$\frac{1.0}{3.4} \quad x \quad \frac{10^{-14}}{10^{-5}}$$

Now, with your calculator, reduce the first fraction:

$$0.29 \quad x \quad \frac{1.0^{-14}}{10^{-5}}$$

Do not even bother using a calculation for the second fraction; just subtract 5 from 14, and you have a new exponent, 9. Note how similar this is to the first type of determination, above.

$$0.29 \text{ x } 10^{-9}$$

When you get to this point, you are *just about* done with the determination.

1. pH ↔ pOH

Look again at the loop on the previous page. The simplest determination is getting pH from a given pOH, or the other way around. It is always a breeze, requiring only fourth-grade arithmetic.

If one p number is given and the other wanted, it does not matter how many sigfigs are involved, you still have nothing more to do than subtract the given value from 14.

An example: if a solution has a pOH of 5.28, what is its pH? Subtraction provides the answer: 14 − 5.28 = 8.72.

2. [H$^+$] ↔ [OH$^-$]

Instead of subtracting, we subtract the given concentration from this integer's (14) concentration equivalent, 1.0 x 10^{-14}. Since this number is exponential, however, a division is performed, although the exponent part of the calculation is only subtraction (this principle, then, is the inverse of that mentioned on p. 333) (now go the left column).

$$[H^+] = 2.9 \text{ x } 10^{-10}$$

Error Analysis

Scientific notation always begins with such a number ($1 \leq n < 10$). When adjusting your concentration values for this number's sake, adjust the exponent for the correct direction; 10^{-8} would be quite wrong!

334

	0.0	0.1	0.2	0.3	0.4	0.5	0.6	0.7	0.8	0.9
1	.00	.04	.07	.11	.15	.18	.20	.23	.26	.28
2	.30	.32	.34	.36	.38	.40	.41	.43	.45	.46
3	.48	.49	.51	.52	.53	.54	.56	.57	.58	.59
4	.60	.61	.62	.63	.64	.65	.66	.67	.68	.69
5	.70	.71	.72	.72	.73	.74	.75	.76	.76	.77
6	.78	.79	.79	.80	.81	.81	.82	.83	.83	.84
7	.85	.85	.86	.86	.87	.88	.88	.89	.89	.90
8	.90	.91	.91	.92	.92	.93	.93	.94	.94	.95
9	.95	.96	.96	.97	.97	.98	.98	.99	.99	1.00

Use of the Table of Mantissas

(more commonly called a log table)

To get a concentration value from a p value, you need to find the antilogarithm, which, in the example at right, is the 5.5 in the concentration expression. To find it is a cinch: just spot the mantissa in the body of the chart and go "against the logs" (be "anti-log") or, to be technical, towards the axes. Getting your antilog (the last step) is no harder than reading a multiplication table backwards.

On the other hand, if pN is given and [N] is wanted, you will start with the "logs" and end up with the mantissa; that is, now you will read the table in the usual direction. And this time, you will be looking for the mantissa because it is part of the exponent (specifically, the logarithm) which will be in the wanted p[N].

Can you read mileage charts (or times tables)? Can you break logarithms into their two parts and also reassemble them? If you answer *yes* twice, you can do all the math in pN/[N] calculations.

3. pN → [N]

When pH or pOH is given, and one of their respective concentrations wanted, we use (1) the ultra-simple equations shown by Dalton on p. 334 and (2) antilogarithms. There are three steps. Here they are, in an example:

What is the [OH⁻] of a solution with a pOH of 6.26?

STEP ONE Write the p value as a negative exponent of ten in the concentration:

$$pOH = 6.26 \quad (so...) \quad [OH^-] = 1.0 \times 10^{-6.26}$$

You do this exactly as you would do it for a whole-number p value (p. 333).

STEP TWO Get the mantissa, which is the *difference between the exponent and the next negative integer* (here, −7). The mantissa, therefore, is 0.74. The logarithm—6.26—now becomes 0.74 - 7:

$$10^{-6.26} = 10^{0.74-7}$$

The logarithm, then, is made up of two parts: the always positive mantissa (the decimal) and the always negative *characteristic* (the integer).

Now that you have the mantissa...

STEP THREE Use the table. Take *only* the mantissa out of the power-of-ten expression and find it in the table of mantissas. The antilogarithm it provides becomes the new multiplier (and you do nothing whatsoever with the characteristic but leave it where it is):

$$10^{0.74 \, -7} \rightarrow \boxed{\text{ANTILOG}} \rightarrow 5.5 \times \frac{}{5.5 \times 10^{-7}} \quad 10^{-7}$$

And so, [OH⁻] = 5.5×10^{-7}

The steps, then, are (1) write pN as a negative power of ten; (2) get the mantissa; and (3) use it!

The explanation at left is handy if you need help with step three.

335

When the $[H^+]$ or $[OH^-]$ is given and the pH or pOH, respectively, are sought, you do just everything in the reverse of what you did for pN → [N]. The last step, using the table, now becomes the first step but in the opposite direction; thus the order of the steps *and* the steps themselves are both reversed.

The last thing we did in the previous example was to go in the antilog direction (against or towards the logs from the mantissa). This time, we will start with the logs and go towards the mantissa.

In the previous example, we wound up with a result of 5.5×10^{-7} when we converted a p value to its concentration value. Here it is the other way:

STEP ONE Use the table. Take the antilog from the given expression and run it through the table.

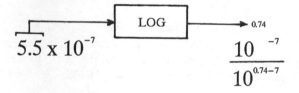

$$5.5 \times 10^{-7} \qquad\qquad \frac{10^{-7}}{10^{0.74-7}}$$

STEP TWO Get the logarithm. This is an assembly step, as contrasted with its inverse, the disassembly into characteristic and mantissa, for the sake of getting the latter.

$$10^{0.74-7} = 10^{-6.26}$$

STEP THREE Finally, write this negative logarithm as a (positive) pOH value; throw away the negative sign and the ten.

$$pOH = 6.26$$

The last step is identical to what you would do if the exponent were a whole number (p. 333), such as −6. But this exponent was a logarithm (it contained a decimal), namely −6.26. All in all, this first/last step is not any harder if the problem has logarithms in place of whole exponents, unless one finds it harder to write "6.26" than "6."

And now, a further example, in which we will go the "whole loop" without introducing any new principle or adding commentary. Make sure that you understand how each line in the worked-out illustration follows from its predecessor.

If a solution has a pOH of 8.38, determine its (a) pH, (b) $[H^+]$, and (c) $[OH^-]$. Then, (d) check your accuracy by closing the circle and redetermining pOH from $[OH^-]$.

(a) $\quad$ pH = 14.00 − 8.38 = 5.62

────────────────────────────

(b) $\quad [H^+] = 1.0 \times 10^{-5.62}$

$\qquad\qquad = 1.0 \times 10^{0.38-6}$

$\qquad\qquad = 2.4 \times 10^{-6}$

────────────────────────────

(c) $\quad [OH^-] = \dfrac{1.0}{2.4} \times \dfrac{10^{-14}}{10^{-6}}$

$\qquad\qquad = 0.42 \times 10^{-8}$

$\qquad\qquad = 4.2 \times 10^{-9}$

────────────────────────────

(d) $\qquad\qquad 1.0 \times 10^{0.62-9}$

$\qquad\qquad = 1.0 \times 10^{-8.38}$

$\quad$ pOH $\quad = 8.38$

When your ending value does not precisely match your beginning value—for instance, 8.37 or 8.39 instead of 8.38—don't sweat it. The last sigfig, you must recall, is just an estimate.

If the given in the previous example were pOH = 8 instead of 8.38, you would still do the same things, less the adjusting for the mantissas:

(a)	pH	=	$14 - 8 = 6$
(b)	$[H^+]$	=	1.0×10^{-6}
(c)	$[OH^-]$	=	1.0×10^{-8}
(d)	pOH	=	8

So, despite their formidable name, doing calculations involving logarithms is really only the application of several simple skills. *If* you can (1) subtract from 14; *if* you can (2) read a mileage chart forwards and backwards; *if* you can (3) understand the significance of negative exponents and—for the sake of those exponents—(4) move a decimal point; and *if* you (5) know the two ridiculously simple "equations" highlighted on p. 334, *then* you can do the more complex calculations, not just for one link, but for the whole loop.

The only possible complication is the appearance of more significant figures. For this, there are tables for use with three-and four-place logarithms, (see the appendices) and even whole books of tables for five-place logs. The mini-table on p. 335 is only for two-placers, but the principle is the same.

Of course, there are calculators, which seem to make log tables (tables of mantissas) obsolete. Some can even bypass all the written steps between, say, a given pH and a wanted $[OH^-]$. Instructors who insist on practice using the tables are not sadists or pedants; in fact, they do their students a service. The precalculator method gives one a more concrete appreciation for the beautiful simplicity of p values and the necessary practicality of concentration values. This a calculator cannot do. Students who learn the "old way," though they habitually use a calculator, have an advantage, for they know better what to look for and expect, and are more immune to the perils of calculator-log-function zombieism.

1. Fill in. In the rightmost column, indicate whether the solution is acidic (A), basic (B), or neutral (N).

pH	[H$^+$]		pOH	[OH$^-$]	A/B
8					
			13		
		.0000001			
			9		
3					
	1.0 x 10^{-10}				
		.01			
13	1.0 x 10^{-13}	.0000000000001	1	1.0 x 10^{-1}	B
				1.0 x 10^{-10}	

2. Using the three-place table of mantissas in the appendices, find an antilog for each mantissa:

.549_____ .981_____ .007_____ .318_____ .117_____ .906_____

3. If pH is 5.1637855, determine the value for pOH to (a) one significant figure; (b) two sigfigs; (c) five sigfigs; and (d) seven sigfigs. Estimate (a) before you arithmetically determine the rest.

(a)_____ (c)_____

(b)_____ (d)_____

4. Do the loop: for a given [OH$^-$] of 1.0 x 10^{-11}, determine, in order, [H$^+$], pH, and pOH; and from pOH, give [OH$^-$] anew.

5. Match these terms to the labelled numerical entities shown to their right:

_____exponent

_____logarithm

_____antilogarithm

_____mantissa

_____characteristic

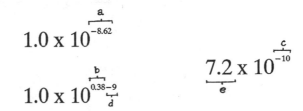

$$1.0 \times 10^{-8.62} \overset{a}{}$$

$$1.0 \times 10^{0.38-9} \underset{d}{\overset{b}{}}$$

$$7.2 \times 10^{-10} \overset{c}{\underset{e}{}}$$

6. Do the loop: for a given pH of 4.72, calculate in order pOH, [OH⁻], and [H⁺]. Then, check your answer by redetermining pH. Again, use the table in the appendices.

Want some more practice? Pick an arbitrary value for any of the four...

pH   pOH   [OH⁻]   [H⁺]

...and calculate your way around the loop. The process, as you know by now, is self-checking.

1.

pH	[H⁺]		pOH	[OH⁻]	A/B
8	1.0×10^{-8}	.00000001	6	1.0×10^{-6}	B
1	1.0×10^{-1}	.1	13	1.0×10^{-13}	A
7	1.0×10^{-7}	.0000001	7	1.0×10^{-7}	N
5	1.0×10^{-5}	.00001	9	1.0×10^{-9}	A
3	1.0×10^{-3}	.001	11	1.0×10^{-11}	B
10	1.0×10^{-10}	.0000000001	4	1.0×10^{-4}	B
2	1.0×10^{-2}	.01	12	1.0×10^{-12}	A
13	1.0×10^{-13}	.0000000000001	1	1.0×10^{-1}	B
4	1.0×10^{-4}	.0001	10	1.0×10^{-10}	A

2.

(.549)	3.54	(.906) 8.06
(.318)	2.08	(.981) 9.57
(.007)	1.02	(.117) 1.31

3.

$$
\begin{array}{r}
14.0000000 \\
-5.1637855 \\
\hline
8.8362145
\end{array}
$$

a. 9   b. 8.8
c. 8.8362
d. 8.836214

4.

$[OH^-] = 1.0 \times 10^{-11}$ (so...)

$[H^+] = 1.0 \times 10^{-3}$ (so...)

$pH = 3$ (and so...)

$pOH = 11$

5. c   a   e   b   d

6.

$pOH = 14.00 - 4.82 = 9.18$

$[OH^-] = 1.0 \times 10^{-9.18}$

$= 1.0 \quad 10^{0.82-10}$

$= 6.6 \quad 10^{-10}$

$[H^+] = \dfrac{1.0}{6.6} \times \dfrac{10^{-14}}{10^{-10}}$

$= 0.15 \times 10^{-4}$

$= 1.5 \times 10^{-5}$

$pH = 1.0 \times 10^{0.18-5}$

$= 1.0 \times 10^{-4.82}$

$= 4.82$

9.8 Chapter Synthesis

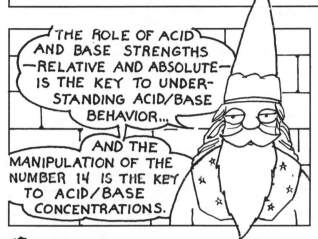

THE ROLE OF ACID AND BASE STRENGTHS —RELATIVE AND ABSOLUTE— IS THE KEY TO UNDERSTANDING ACID/BASE BEHAVIOR...

AND THE MANIPULATION OF THE NUMBER 14 IS THE KEY TO ACID/BASE CONCENTRATIONS.

Common, simple acids are the unionized precursors of the ions you have been familiar with from as far back as Chap. 2. If you understand the nomenclature of ions, you will very easily master that of their corresponding acids.

In Chap. 9, we have been concerned with the two specific definitions for acids and bases. Arrhenius acids and bases are liquid solutions in which either hydronium (hydrated hydrogen ion) or hydroxide is favored at equilibrium. A minority of Arrhenius acids and bases, those of the absolutely strong species, can for all practical purposes be considered not products of equilibria but rather of complete reactions.

A Brönsted acid is any chemical, in or out of solution, that yields a proton in the presence of a proton acceptor, which, by definition, is a Brönsted base.

The more eager the donor or acceptor is, the stronger acid or base it is. In *absolute* terms, there are only a handful each of strong acids and bases, as you have known since Chap. 6. The strong bases are the hydroxides of the most metallic of the elements; they are the only common water-soluble hydroxides. In *relative* terms, the truly strong species are more unstable and ionizing than the weak ones, but within the latter category, some are more weak, so to speak, than others; there are stronger weak acids and weaker weak acids.

These relative strengths are the key to predicting many sorts of reactions involving acids and bases. When one or both of them are strong, a neutralization to completion results, because the whole quantity of the strong species will ionize, liberating H^+ or OH^- in proportion to its molarity.

Among weak acids, equilibrium results, favoring the side of the equation containing both the acid and the base most reluctant to ionize (i.e., the weakest of the weak). Keep in mind that a stronger acid will become its commensurately weaker conjugate base (and the stronger base will become...well, figure it out yourself!). In this way, stronger acids donate protons to stronger bases and wind up as their weaker conjugates (to a degree governed by the strengths of the reacting acid and base). Finally, a salt of a weak acid will usually dissolve in a sufficiently concentrated solution of an acid that is stronger than the acid corresponding to the salt.

Logarithms enable us to express concentrations without using articulated numbers with negative exponents (concentration values). The higher this p number, the lower the concentration, up to 14 magnitudes.

Every p value has a corresponding concentration value. The p value is useful in out-of-the-lab comparisons, reports, written instructions, etc., whereas concentration values are practical in preparing solutions.

If you are going to work both in and out of the lab, knowing how to convert between them is obviously essential.

In equilibria between Arrhenius acids and bases, pH *plus* pOH is 14, and $[H^+]$ *times* $[OH^-]$ is 1.0×10^{-14}. The origin of the p number from the negative exponent is clearly evident.

pH = 7 is also pOH = 7 and a solution with these values is "pH neutral," for the concentration of hydroxide equals that of hydrogen ion.

REALLY? I DIDN'T KNOW WE COULD ORGANIZE!

THEY'RE WEARING THE UNION LABEL!

1. Name the acids (by changing the suffixes) of these ions (even if neither they nor their would-be acids really exist):

a. arsenate _____   e. hypoiodite _____

b. selenate _____   f. arsenide _____

c. hyposelenite _____   g. phlogistonate _____

d. pertellurate _____   h. formate _____

2. At right, fill in the formulae (first column) and names (second column) for the acid ions that would result from the three stepwise ionizations of arsenous acid.

H_3AsO_3	arsenous acid

3. In these two equations, identify the Brönsted acids with "A" or a pink smudge and the Brönsted bases with "B" or a light blue smudge (optional: use the labels WA, WB, SA, and SB):

a. $HS^- + H_2O \rightleftharpoons S^{2-} + H_3O^+$ b. $HS^- + HNO_2 \rightleftharpoons H_2S + NO_2^-$

4. Predict the outcomes of each of these reactions by completing their equations. All of them take place in water solutions. Use arrows for (a) reactions going to completion or (b) to show the favored direction of equilibrium. *If* the reaction goes to completion, give at least one reason for this in the space following the equations, from the possibilities listed at right. Use the tables in Sects. 6.2 and 9.3 as needed [Note: in (a), elemental hydrogen is one of three products; (e) liquid water is one of three products (see Sect. 6.10)].

a. $HClO_4 + NH_4^+$

b. $LiOH(aq)$

c. $H_2PO_4^- + SO_4^{2-}$

d. $HCN + SO_3^{2-}$

e. $Ba(OH)_2 + 2HI$

f. $HCl + Pb(NO_3)_2$

g. $HC_2H_3O_2 + PO_4^{3-}$

h. $K_2CO_3 + 2HBr$

i. $HCO_2 + F^-$

A. Strong acid ionizes

B. Strong base ionizes

G. Gas forms

P. Precipitate forms

W. Weak electrolyte forms

5. For the real or "part-time" (amphoteric) acids that can dissolve CaF_2 (when sufficiently concentrated), answer "yes"; if not, "no."

_____ HSO_4^- _____ HI _____ $HClO$

_____ HCO_3^- _____ $H_2C_2O_4$ _____ H_2O

6. Arrange these hypothetical acids in order from the relatively strongest (1) to the weakest (7) in their first (or only possible) ionization in water, using their solubility constants.

HAb_2	(2.4×10^{-4})	H_2XO_3	(3.9×10^{-7})
HQ^{2-}	(7.7×10^{-14})	$HJbO_4$	(1.4×10^{-9})
HXO_3^-	(5.5×10^{-12})	H_3Q	(9.8×10^{-5})
$H_5Ks_2XCl_{11}$	(6.1×10^{-9})		

(1)_____ (2)_____ (3)_____ (4)_____ (5)_____ (6)_____ (7)_____

7. Do the loop: for a given hydrogen ion concentration of 2.3×10^{-8}, calculate in order (a) hydroxide ion concentration; (b) pOH; and (c) pH. Finally, (d) recalculate the original $[H^+]$ value from the pH value you get from (c). Use Appendix IV.

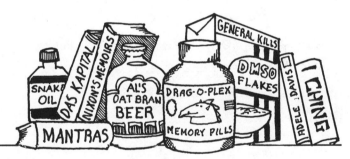

Across

1. Cont. of 6D
3. ___-glycerine
7. Named for Camelot character
9. Element (see 2D)
11. NO_2, in the sky
13. Opposite of cath-
14. Carbohydrate suffix
15. What Brönsted acids do with a proton
18. Exothermic peak in Avo's homeland
20. Dimension (syn.)
21. State where they built Fermi's first reactor
23. Former nuclear bureau (USA)
24. What Brönsted bases do with a proton
27. Named for a prize founder
28. Opposite of pH
29. 2 parts of "planetary sequence"
32. Louis ___ Broglie
34. Often analyzed in this book (verb)
35. Decimal part of a logarithm (pl.)
39. A lanthanide
40. Br^-, O_2^{2-}, or HSO_4^-
43. Taste of bases
44. ...99, 100...

Down

1. See 1A
2. See 9A
3. Z of F, and follower, spelled out
4. Vitamin A unit
5. A lanthanide
6. Fam. 6A lightweights
7. Cringing Matrons Fear ____
8. Fam. 2A middleweights (but out of order)
10. Not acidic
12. Changing partners
16. Z of H (see 3D)
17. ...22, 23...
19. $1s^2 2s^2 2p^6$
22. A quantum number's initials backwards
25. The anion in HI(aq)
26. ___-date. -dite, -dine, or -dide
30. Fam. 1A lightweights
31. pH or pOH
33. Named for $E = mc^2$ formulator
36. Trinitrotoluene
37. Conjugate of WB (see prob. 3)
38. Organic suffix
41. ...8, 9...
42. Normal and Molar

1. a. arsenic   b. selenic   c. hyposelenous   d. pertelluric

e. hypoiodous   f. hydroarsenic   g. phlogistonic   h. formic

2.

H_3AsO_3	arsenous acid
$H_2AsO_3^-$	dihydrogen arsenite
$HAsO_3^{2-}$	monohydrogen arsenite
AsO_3^{3-}	arsenite

3.

a.   WA   WB   SB   SA

$HS^- + H_2O \rightleftharpoons S^{2-} + H_3O^+$

b.   SB   SA   WA   WB

$HS^- + HNO_2 \rightleftharpoons H_2S + H_3O^+$

(Note the amphoteric nature of hydrogen sulfide.)

4.

(a) $HClO_4 + NH_4^+ \rightarrow ClO_4^- + NH_3\uparrow + H_2\uparrow$ (A, G)

(b) $LiOH \rightarrow Li^+ + OH^-$ (B)

(c) $H_2PO_4^- + SO_4^{2-} \rightleftharpoons HPO_4^{2-} + HSO_4^-$

(d) $HCN + SO_3^{2-} \rightleftharpoons CN^- + HSO_3^-$

(e) $Ba(OH)_2 + 2HI \rightarrow BaI_2 + 2H_2O$ (A,B,W)

(f) $2HCl + Pb(NO_3)_2 \rightarrow 2H^+ + 2NO_3^- + PbCl_2\downarrow$ (A,P)

(g) $HC_2H_3O_2 + PO_4^{3-} \rightleftharpoons C_2H_3O_2^- + HPO_4^{2-}$

(h) $K_2CO_3 + 2HBr \rightarrow 2KBr + CO_2\uparrow + H_2O$ (A,G,W)

(i) $HCHO_2 + F^- \rightleftharpoons CHO_2^- + HF$

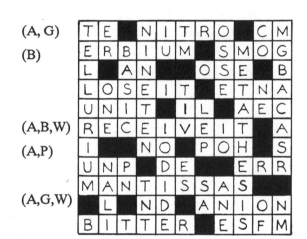

5.   Yes: $H_2C_2O_4$, HI, HSO_4^-

          No: $HClO$, HCO_3^-, H_2O

Water, of course, is never even technically an acid except amphoterically. It is, however, always seen on charts of relative acid/base strengths. This is necessarily so, as the hydroxide ion (the aqueous solutions of the hydroxides of sodium, calcium, barium, etc.) is the strongest of all bases.

    This does not mean, however, that water cannot dissolve other fluoride salts; it can. Fluoride salts follow no pattern as to their solubility.

6.

(1) HAb_2 (2) H_3Q (fairly strong acids)

(3) H_2XO_3 (4) $H_5Ks_2XCl_{11}$

(5) $HJbO_4$ (6) HXO_3^- (7) HQ^{2-}

7.

(a) $[OH^-]$ $= \dfrac{1.0}{2.3} \times \dfrac{10^{-14}}{10^{-8}}$

                $= 0.435 \times 10^{-6}$

                $= 4.35 \times 10^{-7}$

(b)   pOH $= 1.0 \times 10^{0.638-7}$

                $= 1.0 \times 10^{-6.362}$

                $= 6.362$

(c)   pH $= 14.000 - 6.362 = 7.638$

(d) $[H^+]$ $= 1.0 \times 10^{-7.638}$

                $= 1.0 \times 10^{0.362-6}$

                $= 2.3 \times 10^{-8}$

Ten: Concerning Oxidation and Reduction

10.1 Oxidizers and Reducers

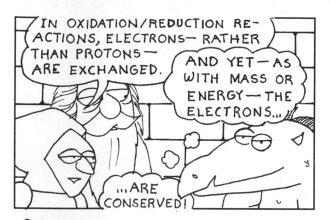

IN OXIDATION/REDUCTION REACTIONS, ELECTRONS—RATHER THAN PROTONS—ARE EXCHANGED.

AND YET—AS WITH MASS OR ENERGY—THE ELECTRONS...

...ARE CONSERVED!

Oxidation/Reduction reactions, nicknamed *redox*, are those in which electrons are transferred from some species to others during chemical change.

Replacement reactions, organic oxidations, and combination reactions (all described in Sect. 4.3) among other types of reactions all fall into this broad category. Neutralizations and acid/base equilibria do not, for they, as you know, involve the transfer not of electrons but protons. Nor do exchange (metathesis) reactions properly belong under the redox heading, for they involve full transfers of neither protons nor electrons.

While Lewis' concept of acids and bases permits us to think of even an electron-transfer as a type of acid/base reaction, it makes better sense, most of the time, to avoid this technical subsumation.

Nevertheless, there are definite similarities between the studies of the acid/base and oxidation/reduction chemistries, and the student is strongly advised to take full and fortuitous advantage of them.

For starters, both redox and acid/base reactions entail the transfer of subatomic particles; as there are proton acceptors and donors, so also are there electron acceptors—*oxidizers*—and donors—*reducers*. As with acids and bases, there are amphoteric species that can be either oxidizers or reducers, depending on conditions (namely, on what other substances are present).

Another parallel is that oxidizers and reducers—alternatively called *oxidizing agents* and *reducing agents*—can be classified as strong or weak, according to the zeal with with which they grab or release electrons. The relative strength of an oxidizer or reducer is the key to its behavior. What is more, a strong oxidizer will have a weak reducer as its conjugate, while a weak oxidizer will have a strong reducer.

And finally, redox reactions that do not go to completion end in a redox equilibrium which favors—as you might expect—the two weaker species (those with greater reluctance to donate or to accept electrons) over the stronger ones (those with a more pronounced capacity to accept or to donate electrons). Does this sounds familiar? Well it should.

Specifically, as you may already have deduced, it is the Brönsted acid/base concept with which there are so many parallels. If you were able to grasp this not very difficult principle (Sect. 9.2) and its implications, you are automatically a long way towards understanding redox basics.

Something needs to be said about the word *oxidation*. Apart from everyday use and misuse of the word (such as a car salesman insisting that a paint job is "oxidation-proof"), there are at least five distinct meanings. Your understanding of a lecture or tutoring session may in fact hinge on your being clear on the *momentary* sense of the word's usage.

(1) Reaction of a substance with oxygen; hence the word's origin.

(2) Reaction of a substance with an oxidizer other than oxygen. Oxidation can occur *without* oxygen. Fluorine, for instance, is an even stronger oxidizer.

(3) Sometimes used as an imprecise synonym for combustion. This is equivocal and sloppy language.

(4) A half-reaction (Sect. 10.2).

(5) As an adjective before *number* or *state* (Sect. 10.3).

⊛ In the chart below, color the base square light blue; the acid, pink; the reducer, orange; and the oxidizer, light green.

particle \ role	donor	acceptor
proton	acid	base
electron	reducer	oxidizer

346

10.2 Redox Half-Reactions

THE ACTIONS OF OXIDIZERS AND REDUCERS ON EACH OTHER ARE IN SOME RESPECTS LIKE AN ACID AND A BASE IN A NEUTALIZATION...

I KINDA THOUGHT SO.

Reducers are so-called because they *reduce* oxidizers, which are so called because they *oxidize* reducers. (Got that?).

Note the transitive force of these two verbs, that they are actions affecting grammatical objects.

Oxidize—like *oxidation*—is used in everyday language in a technically incorrect manner. For instance, stainless steel is said *not* to oxidize, while cast iron does. This suggests a reflexive action by the iron, as if it is somehow doing this on its own. In fact, the iron is not oxidizing itself but reducing (giving electrons to) oxygen from the air. Meanwhile, it is that same oxygen that is doing the real oxidizing (taking electrons from) the iron. Iron reduces and is (therefore) oxidized by oxygen; oxygen oxidizes and is (therefore) reduced by iron.

Why *therefore*? Because oxidation and reduction in this and every other redox reaction are reverse and concomitant processes.

Separately, that which happened to the oxygen (a reduction) and the iron (an oxidation) are *half-reactions*. This term is applicable both for equations and the reactions they represent. Together, the two are an oxidation/reduction, or a redox.

reduction	$2O_2 + 4e^- \rightarrow 2O^{2-}$
oxidation	$2Fe \rightarrow 2Fe^{2+} + 4e^-$
oxidation/reduction	$2Fe + 2O_2 \rightarrow 2Fe^{2+} + 2O^{2-}$

Observe how the half-reactions shown above add up, with only the electrons missing from their "sum." This is because the electrons cancel out. In the above example, the four electrons lost by the iron atoms were picked by the oxygen atoms.

Note, also, that the redox equation is expressed in its net ionic form, so that its relation to its half-reactions, which are also net ionic equations, can be seen. The advantage over the standard equation

$$2Fe + O_2 \rightarrow 2FeO$$

is that it shows, as explained in Sect. 6.9, what really happens. The half-reactions, which are invariably in net ionic form, are necessary for the balancing of all but the simplest oxidation/reductions (which can be performed by inspection, as in Sect. 4.2).

When you have a standard equation, then, you must expand it into net ionic form and then be able to break it into half-reactions (Sect.6.9).

All reactions involving uncombined oxygen are redoxes. Oxygen atoms from the O_2 molecule almost always pick up two electrons and so are said to have an *oxidation number* of 2– (**2 x e⁻ = 2e⁻**). More on oxidation numbers later.

————————Analogy————————

Half-reactions are a double-entry accounting system, but for electrons instead of money. A loss of electrons (reduction) is a debit matched by an equal gain, or credit, elsewhere (oxidation). As in accounting, the electrons can be split among more than one debit or credit.

Redox, though, is simpler than bookkeeping. Its entries are one-figured, whereas the finances for even small businesses run to at least seven figures. Furthermore, the redox "accounts" are juxtaposed rather than hidden from each other in a ledger (so, if your major is business, switch to chemistry!).

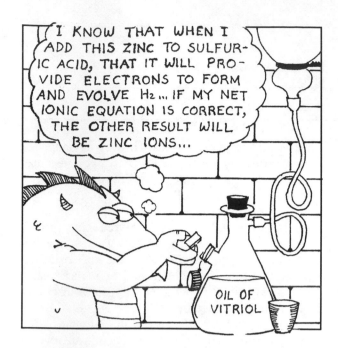

The standard equation for this reaction is:

$$Zn(s) + H_2SO_4(aq) \rightarrow H_2(g)\uparrow + ZnSO_4(aq)$$

To get the net ionic equation, we break up everything we can into ions...

$$Zn + 2H^+ + SO_4^{2-} \rightarrow Zn^{2+} + H_2\uparrow + SO_4^{2-}$$

...and eliminate sulfate because it appears on both sides and so is a spectator. What remains, then, is:

$$Zn + 2H^+ \rightarrow Zn^{2+} + H_2\uparrow$$

This redox reaction, incidentally, will go to completion because one of the products removes itself from the system by evolving as a gas.

In this example, zinc was the reducer (of H^+) and hydrogen ion was the oxidizer (of zinc). Each brought about the chemical alteration of the other.

Oxidizers and reducers are usually elements or elemental ions rather than compounds or compound ions, a fact that simplifies the electron bookkeeping a little. Also—in redox reactions between metals and nonmetals—the metals are always the reducers and the nonmetals, the oxidizers. This, if you recognized it, is due to the higher electronegativity of the nonmentals and is a new expression of a generalization noted on p. 111.

Here, however, is an example of a nonmetal reducer: when chlorine is bubbled into sodium bromide solution, the (very electronegative) chlorine displaces its less active sibling, bromine (which plays the role of reducer):

$$2NaBr(aq) + Cl_2(g) \rightarrow 2NaCl(aq) + Br_2(aq)$$

The net ionic equation for this is:

$$2Br^- + Cl_2 \rightarrow Br_2 + 2Cl^-$$

...and the half-reactions are:

(a) $Cl_2 + 2e^- \rightarrow 2Cl^-$

(b) $\quad\quad 2Br^- \rightarrow Br_2 + 2e^-$

Note that the arrows are "stacked." Canceling the electrons—which is possible in this case only because they balance—and then adding the species gives us the net ionic equation.

Now let us consider a further example, in which a metal oxidizes another metal. This time, though, we will start with the half-reactions and add them up into a net ionic equation.

Nickel ion from a dissolved nickel salt is reduced by tin as tin is oxidized by the nickel ion. Write a combined net ionic equation from the half-reactions:

(O) $\quad\quad\quad Ni^{2+} + 2e^- \rightarrow Ni$

(R) $\quad\quad\quad\quad\quad Sn \rightarrow Sn^{2+} + 2e^-$

_____

Now, with your pencil, cross out the electrons as if they were spectators and add what is left in this space:

Are you left with "nickel ion plus tin yields nickel plus tin (II) ion"?

348

Combining half-reactions is in very deed little more than nonmathematical addition; just put one half-reaction—it does not matter which—over the other, then cancel the electrons and merely copy that which is left over.

It really is that straightforward, unless of course the electrons do not balance; in such a case, you must multiply one or both half-reactions so that they *do* balance. This step is similar to the simple algebraic manipulations you used to balance equations back in Sect. 4.2 and the application of the lowest common multiple in the GamMa Ray and GamMa Delta systems (Sects. 2.9, 4.6) except that here it is even simpler and involves smaller numbers.

Consider, for instance, the oxidation of manganese (II) to manganese (III) by aluminum ion (and, therefore, the concomitant reduction of Al^{3+} by Mn^{2+}), as shown at right. The oxidation shows a transfer of triple the number of electrons that the reduction shows, so we must multiply the coefficients of the latter half-reaction by three (1a, at right) to even them up. With your pencil, cross out the electrons in (1b) and write the combined equation in the space at right (1c).

Often, we have to multiply the coefficients of *both* half-reactions, as in the case of the oxidation of cobalt and the reduction of iodine. The two electrons that iodine will gain and the three that cobalt will lose must be raised by second-grade multiplication (2a) to their lowest common denominator (2b) and only then canceled. Now cross out the electrons and write out the combined redox (2c). After finishing this page, you will have an opportunity to check the answers.

Half-reactions can be more complex when they involve more species (as we will see in later sections); however, balancing them is not that much harder in the same way that a metric/nonmetric conversion factor does not in principle complicate a dimensional analysis problem.

(1a)

$$Al^{3+} + 3e^- \rightarrow Al$$

(3x) $$Mn^{2+} \rightarrow Mn^{3+} + e^-$$

(1b)

$$Al^{3+} + 3e^- \rightarrow Al$$

$$3Mn^{2+} \rightarrow 3Mn^{3+} + 3e^-$$

(1c)

(2a) (3x) $$I_2 + 2e^- \rightarrow 2I^-$$

(2x) $$Co \rightarrow Co^{3+} + 3e^-$$

(2b) $$3I_2 + 6e^- \rightarrow 6I^-$$

$$2Co \rightarrow 2Co^{3+} + 6e^-$$

(2c)

When any solution containing dichromate and hydrogen ions, for example, is reduced with iron(II), we have...

(oxidation) $$Cr_2O_7^{2-} + 14H^+ + 6e^- \rightarrow 2Cr^{2-} + 7H_2O$$

(reduction)   (6x) $$Fe^{2+} \rightarrow Fe^{3+} + e^-$$

We now multiply the entire reduction half-reaction by this six to make the electron counts jive:

(oxidation) $$Cr_2O_7^{2-} + 14H^+ + 6e^- \rightarrow 2Cr^{2+} + 7H_2O$$

(reduction) $$6Fe^{2+} \rightarrow 6Fe^{3+} + 6e^-$$

Now, cancel the "e⁻s" and write the combined redox (3); then check the answers on p. 356.

Profile: Radium

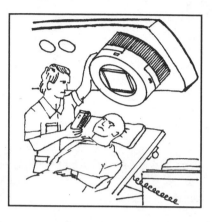

Radium-decay emissions are believed to preferentially damage malignant tissues

When the Curies, in 1896, noticed that the mineral pitchblende (which is mostly triuranium oxide, U_3O_8) was somewhat more radioactive than its uranium component could account for, they undertook a challenge that would become the most celebrated story of perseverance in the history of science.

They surmised, correctly, that the mineral contained traces of an even more radioactive element. The government of Austria-Hungary—which controlled the quarries—agreed to send to Paris whatever quantity of the ore for which the Curies could find the money to cover the shipments. After sifting through tons of pitchblende (and, along the way, demonstrating the existence of three types of radiation, later christened *alpha, beta,* and *gamma rays* by E. Rutherford) they isolated a measurable quantity of polonium (named for her native Poland).

Polonium was, to be sure, many hundred times as radioactive as uranium. But what was this? The pitchblende *without* the polonium was still too radioactive. Additional arduous processing, running from the months into years, led to the discovery of far more minute traces of yet another element, one about a million times as radioactive as uranium: radium.

In any discussion of Curie's accomplishments, the discovery of these two elements is always mentioned first. More important, however, is that she was the first person in history to understand, or offer a largely accurate explanation of, radioactivity, although she was at best only one of several co-discoverers. Many of Curie's distinguished contemporaries had theories of their own; but hers was the right one.

Radium's extreme scarcity is a consequence of this high activity. All of the elements after bismuth (Z = 83) and two before it (Tc, Pm) are radioactive, constantly decaying through the emission of alpha particles (helium nuclei) and beta particles (electrons). Uranium ultimately decays to a stable isotope of lead, but it is briefly radium, an element so unstable that it has a very short half-life and, consequently, is quite rare.

A radium atom results when a thorium atom emits an alpha particle. The radium, in turn, becomes radon by losing another particle and vaporizing from metal (Ra) to gas (Rn).

Radium is not only very active physically, but chemically as well, being the heaviest and most reactive of an already reactive family of metals, the alkaline earths.

Like its siblings, Radium has only the 2+ oxidation number and is a very strong reducer. The chemical and physical activity of radium, however, and of all other radioactive substances, are completely independent of each other.

For its faint blue glow, radium was once used to make fluorescent markings on watch and instrument dials. The hazard was that radium, like its siblings, calcium and strontium-90, concentrates in the bones, from which it bombards the marrow, often leading to leukemia. The great Curie herself finally succumbed to another form of cancer, an almost certain result of decades of exposure, including her work in a mobile X-ray unit during World War I. Ironically, decaying radium is nowadays used in radiotherapy to treat some types of cancer.

$$^{234}_{92}U \rightarrow \alpha$$
$$\downarrow$$
$$^{230}_{90}Th \rightarrow \alpha$$
$$\downarrow$$
$$^{226}_{88}Ra \rightarrow \alpha$$
$$\downarrow$$
$$^{222}_{86}Rn \rightarrow \alpha$$
$$\downarrow$$
$$^{218}_{84}Po \rightarrow \alpha$$
$$\downarrow$$
$$^{214}_{82}Pb \rightarrow \alpha$$

An example of a
Radioative Decay Series

This is the radioactive decay series that shows how uranium can decay naturally to lead by α-particle emission. It can also happen through the emission of β-particles or a combination of both.

10.3 Oxidation Numbers

IN THE LAST EXAMPLE ON PAGE 349, I COULDN'T EASILY DISTINGUISH THE OXIDIZERS FROM THE REDUCERS...

OXIDATION NUMBERS CAN HELP... AND THEY NOT ONLY SHOW WHO LOSES AND WHO GAINS, BUT HOW MUCH IS LOST OR GAINED...

Some oxidation/reduction reactions can be relatively complicated, having several polyatomic species and/or three or more substances on both sides of the equation.

The use of *oxidation numbers*—also called *oxidation states*—makes the electron debiting and crediting clear, not just with respect to ionic reactions (in which the "ownership" of electrons is always obvious) but covalent ones as well (in which we must "arbitrate" electron ownership).

Think of it this way: ions have charges which are, coincidentally, their oxidation numbers as well; but atoms in covalent species have only partial, if any, charges. By giving the covalently bonded atoms their own charge-like oxidation numbers, however, we can pretend, for electron-bookkeeping purposes, that they *do* have charges.

Oxidation numbers, then, are arbitrary *in the case of covalent species*, because the electrons do not belong wholly to one or the other of the atoms between which they form the bond (this is straight from the definition of covalency). In essence, *oxidation numbers allow us to treat covalent species like ionic ones*. A workable definition of oxidation number might therefore be that it is (1) ionic charge—a fact—in ionic species, and (2) "covalent charge"—a convenient fiction—in covalent species.

Like true charge values, oxidation numbers in covalent species are governed by the valency of combined atoms, whether the valency is actual and well-defined (as with an ion) or merely assigned (as with an electron-sharing atom).

There is a set of six simple rules that pertain to discerning oxidation numbers of combined atoms. Some are "redox retreads" of the rules and generalizations from Sects. 2.6 and 3.7.

HERE ARE FIVE OF THE SIX OXIDATION NUMBER RULES, ALONG WITH EXAMPLES...

I.	Any elemental species is 0	N_2, Ag, U, O_3
II.	Combined hydrogen is 1+	$CH_{4\,(x\,1+\,=)}$ 4+
III.	Combined oxygen is 2-	$HNO_{3\,(x\,2-\,=)}$ 6-
IV.	Any ion is its charge	$H_2PO_4^-$ 1-
V.	Any polyatomic species is the sum of the oxidation numbers of its components	$H_2PO_4^-$ $(2+)+(5+)+(8-) =$ 1-

Does this seem like a lot? Maybe it does, if you started reading this book here. Remember the first one by recalling that the heat of formation for elements (an unrelated principle) is also zero. As for the next two, just note that their ionic charges are still their oxidation numbers, even when they are part of covalent configurations. The fourth rule is self-evident, and the last one requires the same fourth-grade addition you have been practicing from as far back as Chap. 2.

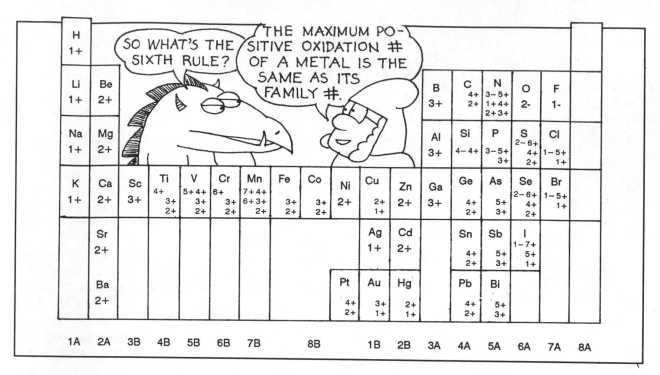

Notice any patterns? More than half of the oxidation numbers shown were introduced as ionic charges in Sect. 2.6. You should already know that manganese, for instance, forms 2+ and 3+ ions, and so has the oxidation numbers 2+ and 3+; but—as you also know—it has others as well, up to the maximum, 7+. Family 1A metals only have the 1+ oxidation number; Family 2A metals only have 2+; and Family 3A metals, only have 3+.

Whereas manganese can form five separate series of ions (and Mn can therefore represent any of five values in a compound's formula) every member of Families 1A, 2A, and 3A (and, for that matter, 3B) is restricted to one oxidation number (or state).

Note that metal ions are exclusively positive (the few exceptions to this are so rare that we may call it a rule). Then, note that highly nonmetallic oxygen and fluorine are exclusively negative; and also that all the other elements in between form a transitional continuum in which many have both negative and positive numbers. Each of these oxidation numbers, as in the case of manganese, corresponds to a separate series of compounds.

The oxidation numbers of rare elements, and the uncommon numbers of familiar elements, are not shown. Further, there are a paltry few exceptions to the six "rules." They include 2+ for copper (reread the sixth rule, as elucidated above by Dalton), 3+ for gold, 1− for hydrogen (in metal hydrides), and 1− and ½− for oxygen (in peroxides and superoxides). The only important exception, for Chem. 1 study, is the copper one.

⊕ Color (in the table) the metals pink; hydrogen, light green; oxygen and fluorine, yellow; and the other nonmetals, orange. Do not color the noble gases.

Oxidation is a loss of electrons for a gain in oxidation number.

Reduction is a gain of electrons for a loss in oxidation number.

Is this confusing? Think of the gain or loss in oxidation numbers as taking place on a number line. Each gain of an electron, or bit of negativeness, necessarily makes the number lower (and visa-versa).

3-	2-	1-	0	1+	2+	3+	4+	5+	6+	7+

(oxidation) $Mn^{3+} - (-4e^-) \rightarrow Mn^{7+}$

$N^{3-} \leftarrow (+3e^-) - N$ (reduction)

Nitrogen, in this case, is the oxidizer and manganese (III), the reducer.

THE OHO SEQUENCE USED IN CHAPTER 4 FOR BALANCING EQUATIONS IS USED IN REVERSE ORDER TO DETERMINE OXIDATION NUMBERS OF ELEMENTS WITHIN A COMPOUND...

OXYGEN
HYDROGEN
OTHER ELEMENTS

NEWTON

In fact, this new flip-flopped OHO sequence is a deductive narrowing, a determination by elimination. If the compound has hydrogen and/or oxygen, the oxidation number of this *remaining* (or Other) element will be that value which *remains* after we take away two for each oxygen atom and/or add one for each hydrogen atom.

If there are more elements than just oxygen, hydrogen, and *one* other, then you can fall back on your knowledge of charges (Sect.2.6), oxidation numbers in general (pp. 351-52) and electronegativities (Sect. 3.5). What does electronegativity have to do with it? Shared electrons can always be counted with the element that, uncombined, would be the more electronegative one.

By using this method, you are, in effect, applying the fifth rule from p. 351 by the *combined* application of the previous four rules which, in sum, equal it (think about this for a moment).

Here is an example, in which we will identify the oxidizers and the reducers by determining the oxidation numbers of every atom in the reaction. These oxidation numbers are multiplied by subscripts or coefficients whenever they appear. An oxide of manganese is added to hydrochloric acid; here is the net ionic equation:

$$\overset{4+\ 4-}{MnO_2}(s) + \overset{4+}{4H^+}(aq) + \overset{2-}{2Cl^-}(aq) \rightarrow \overset{2+}{Mn^{2+}}(aq) + \overset{0}{Cl_2}(g) + \overset{4+\ 4-}{2H_2O}(l)$$

Each atom in the chlorine molecule has an oxidation number of 0 (Rule 1). Each hydrogen ion accounts for 1+; each chloride ion, 1−; each manganese (II) and manganese (IV) ion, 2+ or 4+ (Rule 4). The oxygen atom in the water is 2− (Rule 3); and each hydrogen atom in the water is 1+ (Rule 2). Note that these last two, while they are not charges (for water is covalent), are, nevertheless, oxidation numbers. In the oxide, MnO_2, the two oxygens have a *combined* value of 4−. Therefore, that which makes up the remainder of the compound, the manganese atom, must have a value of 4+ to offset this charge of 4− and, with it, add up to 0 (the oxidation-number sum for any neutral substance, as per Rule 1). Obviously, then, this compound is manganese (IV) oxide. In principle, this material is little different than that presented in Sect. 2.7 (except that at that time, we were limited to ionic charges, not the greater category to which they belong, oxidation numbers).

We can now sort out the oxidizers and reducers in the above example. Manganese (IV) gained electrons (4+ → 2+) and so is an oxidizer (was reduced), whereas chloride—not to be confused with electron-grabbing chlorine—lost electrons (2− → 0) and so is a reducer (was oxidized).

The other reactants (H^+ and O^{2-}) experienced no net gain or loss; so, although they, too, underwent chemical change, they were neither oxidizers nor reducers.

NOW HOW 'BOUT Ba IN BaCl... P IN H_3PO_4... Cr IN $HCr_2O_7^-$ ... AND Sn IN $SnSO_4$...

OXY # RULES

(a) Barium is one of those elements that only has one oxidation number. It is 2+ for each atom in virtually all of its compounds (1 x 2+).

(b) Subtract eight for the four oxygens (4 x 2−); add three for the three hydrogens (3 x 1+); 5− will be left over. This is the oxidation number for the phosphorus.

(c) Subtract 14 for the seven oxygens and add one for the single hydrogen to get 13−. The difference between this and the total ion, which is 1−, is 12. Divvy this number up between the two chromium atoms and you get the sought oxidation number for that element, 6+.

THAT LAST EXAMPLE—THE TIN IN SnSO4—MAY CAUSE YOU SOME CONSTERNATION: IT HAS **TWO** "OTHER" ELEMENTS, EACH WITH MULTIPLE OXIDATION NUMBERS...

YES. I NOTICED.

LUCKILY, IT CONTAINS A "RADICAL" SHORTCUT

1. TIN 2. SULFUR

Recall that a radical (in the slightly modified official definition used in this book) is a cluster of atoms that act as a unit in most reactions.

This translates into a shortcut for the Chem. 1 student who must determine oxidation numbers for givens, such as this tin atom. An ion's charge is also always its oxidation number (Rule 4). As sulfate's is always 2−, the tin will, in this case, necessarily be 2+, or tin (II). The number of the sulfur does not matter, unless the radical itself is going to be broken up. Consider:

(4) oxygen	8−		sulfate	2−
(1) sulfur	6+	(so)	tin	2+
sulfate	2−		tin (II) sulfate	0

In $Sn(SO_4)_2$—as opposed to the $SnSO_4$ of the above example—the oxidation number of the tin would naturally be 4+, to compensate for the two sulfates (2 x 2−). As you can see, there is not much to it. You just have to make the atoms and radicals (which obey Rules 1 through 4 and 6) add up to the correct totals (which obey Rule 5). And finally, the radicals usually let you count two or several elements as one.

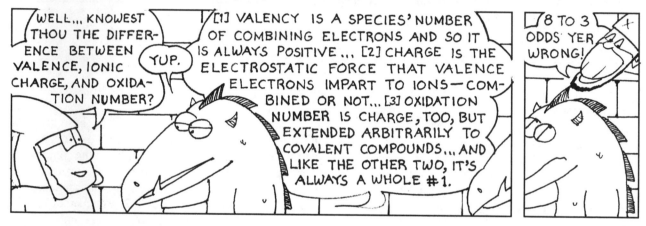

WELL... KNOWEST THOU THE DIFFERENCE BETWEEN VALENCE, IONIC CHARGE, AND OXIDATION NUMBER?

YUP.

[1] VALENCY IS A SPECIES' NUMBER OF COMBINING ELECTRONS AND SO IT IS ALWAYS POSITIVE... [2] CHARGE IS THE ELECTROSTATIC FORCE THAT VALENCE ELECTRONS IMPART TO IONS—COMBINED OR NOT... [3] OXIDATION NUMBER IS CHARGE, TOO, BUT EXTENDED ARBITRARILY TO COVALENT COMPOUNDS... AND LIKE THE OTHER TWO, IT'S ALWAYS A WHOLE #1.

8 TO 3 ODDS YER WRONG!

⸝Fractional Oxidation Numbers⸝

Occasionally, after employing the (now reversed) OHO sequence, and making certain that the more electronegative elements are assigned—arbitrarily or otherwise—their electrons, you will find that the remaining elements cannot evenly divide the remaining electrons among themselves.

For example, the four oxygens in Fe_3O_4 add up to 8−, so the three irons collectively must equal 8+. This entails an oxidation number of $8/3$ for iron.

Fractional values are fairly infrequent, but they certainly help to illustrate the arbitrary nature of covalent oxidation numbers because, in reality, no atom can have 2 ⅔ valence electrons. You may well see fractional oxidation numbers in Chem. 2, but they should present you with no difficulty. It is OK to represent atoms in *covalent* compounds as having "fractional electrons."

⸝Error Analysis⸝

In Sect. 10.1, you were introduced to the problem of semantic confusion that exists around the word *oxidation*. We continue with this here. "Oxidation number" is an unfortunate misnomer; the adjective (oxidation) should be *oxidation-reduction* or, better yet, *redox*, because the term not only refers to the quantities of electrons that an atom can lose (oxidation) but, also, to the number it can gain (reduction).

Additionally, be careful not to confuse oxidation (or reduction), the *process*, with oxidizer, the *agent*. Oxidation describes a loss of electrons *to* the oxidizer. Reduction describes the gain of electrons *from* the reducer. The only way to avoid this pitfall is to be constantly aware that it is just that: a pitfall. Daily rereadings of the definitions of *oxidation, oxidizer, reduction, and reducer* is one thing that often helps.

1. Match:　　　　　_____reduction　　　a. electron gainer

　　　　　　　　　　_____oxidizer　　　　b. electron loser

　　　　　　　　　　_____oxidation　　　c. electron-losing half-reaction

　　　　　　　　　　_____reducer　　　　d. electron-gaining half-reaction

2. Of the following half-reactions, circle the reductions and underline the oxidations:

　　a. $B^{3+} + 3e \rightarrow B$　　　　b. $Au^{1} \rightarrow Au^{3+} + 3e^{-}$　　　c. $F_2 + 2e^{-} \rightarrow 2F^{-}$　　　d. $Se^{6+} + 8e^{-} \rightarrow Se^{2-}$

3. (a) Combine these half-reactions into balanced redoxes and (b) identify them by marking with "O" or "R".

$Ni^{2+} + 2e^{-} \rightarrow Ni$
$Mg \rightarrow Mg^{2+} + 2e^{-}$

$Cl_2 + 2e^{-} \rightarrow 2Cl^{-}$
$Sn^{2+} + 2H_2O \rightarrow SnO_2 + 4H^{+} + 2e^{-}$

4. In these five half-reactions, the number of electrons (*not* number of charge) that are lost or gained (by the species) is not shown. Indicate the *total* number in each case (e.g., +3, −1):

a_____$Zn \rightarrow Zn^{2+}$　　b_____$S^{6+} \rightarrow S^{4+}$　　c_____$2Cl^{-} \rightarrow Cl_2$　　d_____$I^{3-} \rightarrow \frac{1}{2}I_2$　　e_____$Re^{-} \rightarrow Re^{7+}$

5. In each of the following, mark the oxidation number of the italicized atom or ion (*not* of the sum of all the atoms of an element; in other words, the oxidation number, say, of the individual iron atoms in q):

a_____N_2　　b_____CrO_3　　c_____CO　　d_____SiO_2　　e_____KF　　f_____Hg　　g_____Hg^{2+}

h_____TiO_2　　i_____H_2PtCl_4　j_____PH_3　　k_____$FeCO_3$　l_____H_3AsO_4　m_____NO_2^{-}　　n_____NO_3^{-}

o_____NO_3^{-}　　p_____Mn_2O_7　q_____$Fe_2(CO_3)_3$r_____HPO_4^{2-}s_____HPO_3^{2-}　t_____CN^{-}　　u_____$Li_2S_2O_3$

6. In these two redoxes, (a) identify the oxidation number totals of each *atom* on both sides of the equation (except for those in sulfate, because it is not broken up and so stays 2−); and (b) indicate whether a *species* is an oxidizer or a reducer with "O" or "R" or by smudging light green or orange, respectively.

$$2NO_3^{-}(aq) + 8H^{+}(aq) + 3Cu(s) \rightarrow 2NO(g) + 4H_2O(l) + 3Cu^{2+}$$

$$Pb(s) + PbO_2(s) + 4H^{+}(aq) + 2SO_4^{2-}(aq) \rightarrow 2PbSO_4(s) + 2H_2O(l)$$

7. Briefly explain why there is necessarily a reduction with every oxidation (or vice-versa):

1. d   a   c   b

2. a, c, and d are reductions; b is an oxidation

3. $Ni^{2+} + Mg \rightarrow Ni + Mg^{2+}$

   $Cl_2 + Sn^{2+} + 2H_2O \rightarrow 2Cl^- + SnO_2 + 4H^+$

4. (a) −2   (b) +2   (c) −2   (d) −3   (e) −8

ANSWERS PAGE 349

(1c) $Al^{3+} + 3Mn^{2+} \rightarrow Al + 3Mn^{3+}$

(2c) $3I_2 + 2Co \rightarrow 6I^- + 2Co^{3+}$

(3) $Cr_2O_7^{2-} + 14H^+ + 6Fe^{2+} \rightarrow$

   $2Cr^{2-} + 7H_2O + 6Fe^{3+}$

5. (a) 0   (b) 6+   (c) 2+   (d) 4+   (e) 1+   (f) 0   (g) 2+   (h) 2−   (i) 1+   (j) 3−
   (k) 2+   (l) 5+   (m) 3+   (n) 5+   (o) 1−   (p) 7+   (q) 3+   (r) 5+   (s) 3+   (t) 5−   (u) 2+

6.

$$\overset{5+\ 2-}{2NO_3^-}(aq) + \overset{1+}{8H^+}(aq) + \overset{0}{3Cu}(s) \rightarrow \overset{2+\ 2-}{2NO}(g) + \overset{1+\ 2-}{4H_2O}(l) + \overset{2+}{3Cu^{2+}}(aq)$$

(O) nitrate
(R) copper

$$\overset{0}{Pb}(s) + \overset{4+\ 2-}{PbO_2}(s) + \overset{1+}{4H^+}(aq) + \overset{2+}{2SO_4^{2-}}(aq) \rightarrow \overset{2+}{2PbSO_4}(s) + \overset{1+\ 2-}{2H_2O}(l)$$

(O) lead (IV)
(R) lead

7. To conserve (and to account for) the electrons lost and gained by all the involved species in the reaction.

10.4 The Activity Series

Fr
K
Ba
Ca
Na
Mg
Al
Mn
Zn
Cr
Fe
Co
Ni
Sn
Pb
H_2
Sb
Bi
As
Cu
Hg
Ag
Pt
Au
Ir

By now, you know that some metals are chemically busier than others in that they react more quickly and/or with a greater variety of other substances. Cesium (or, theoretically, francium) is the most reactive of all metals; it literally explodes if a chunk of it is dropped into some water. Iridium, on the other hand, is probably the least active of metals; it resists even fluorine and the strong acids.

Aqua regia was used by the alchemists to dissolve gold. Their usual recipe was one part nitric acid to three parts hydrochloric acid, although in modern industrial and metallurgical applications the ratio can range from 1:2 up to 1:4. What really happens when the aqua regia reacts with the metal? Chlorine—a powerful oxidizer—is liberated by the reaction of the two acids with each other and goes on to attack the gold, forming the salt gold (III) chloride (if there is not sufficient chlorine, another gold salt, gold (I) chloride results):

$$3HCl(aq) + HNO_3(aq) \rightarrow NOCl(aq) + 2H_2O(l) + Cl_2(aq)$$

$$2Au(aq) + 3Cl_2(aq) \rightarrow 2AuCl_3(s)$$

This second equation, expressed as its net ionic half-reactions is...

$$2Au \rightarrow 2Au^{3+} + 6e^- \qquad \text{(oxidation)}$$

$$3Cl_2 + 6e^- \rightarrow 6Cl^- \qquad \text{(reduction)}$$

Aqua regia is also used to extract platinum from its ores, first by dissolving the platinum present. The resulting platinum salt is then dissolved and reacted with another metal—a more active one than platinum—and the pure platinum is displaced from the salt.

This discussion of aqua regia is germane to the study of the *Activity Series*, which allows us to predict the reaction of metals with both acids and salts (in the aqueous state, of course). The Series shows the relative positions of the common and the better known metals, plus a metalloid or two, and the "polar extremes" mentioned above. Hydrogen also appears in the Series, but we will come to that very shortly.

⊛ Color H_2 light green; color the metals above it, yellow-orange; and those below it, light purple. Do not color francium or iridium; they are too rare to merit proper inclusion.

(Bugs Bunny and Pals are the intellectual property of Time Warner, Inc. Happy 50th, Bugs!)

1. Acids and Bases

The key to knowing which metals react with acids and which do not is their position in the Activity Series relative to H_2.

Hydrogen, while it is hardly a metal, does have its place in the Series and can be said to stand for acids, in that instead of forming salts with anions, it forms acids. All of the metals above hydrogen are more active than it is, and so they displace it from acids to form salt solutions or salt precipitates (*which of these they form depends on the solubility rules, Sect. 6.2*), whereas the metals below hydrogen do not displace it from acids and so in general are not affected by acids.

Nitric acid is in a class by itself, however, for it reacts not only with metals above the hydrogen cutoff, but with some of those below it, as well. This is not due, however, to its character as a strong acid, but rather to its considerable oxidizing strength.

Arrhenius acids exhibiting exclusively acidic properties (Sect. 9.2) generally react with all the metals above hydrogen but with none of those below it. Comparatively weaker acids can react with some comparatively active metals, mainly those that are the strongest reducers (which happen to be the same metals near the top of the Activity Series). Very weak acids react with few or no metals, but if their solvent is water (which *does* react with many metals), they can appear to do so.

GROUP	REACTS WITH...	EXAMPLES
nitric acid	most metals	HNO_3
other strong acids	all metals above H_2	$HClO_4$ H_2SO_4 HI
some other acids	fewer or no metals	HSO_4^- $HClO_3$ NH_4^+

While there is admittedly much more to this topic than that which is presented here, you will probably not go further than this in Chem. 1. By the time you finish Chem. 3, you will have worked through the details.

2. Salts and Metals

In Sect. 9.4, it was shown that relative acid strengths determine whether or not a salt would dissolve in an acid solution.

We can use the relative "activity strengths" of the metals in the Series in much the same way to determine which of them will react with a given salt solution. Keep in mind that—when we speak of a salt—we are really referring to a compound of an anion (corresponding to an acid) with a metallic cation (or ammonium).

If the metal added to the solution is more active than the metal which forms the cation of the salt, then the former will displace and liberate the latter. If the metal added to the solution is less active than that of the salt, nothing will happen. Unless of course the metal, on its own, can react with the water (as is the case of calcium, sodium, and other metals at the upper end of the Series).

$$Zn(s) + 2HCl(aq) \rightarrow H_2(g) + ZnCl_2(s)$$

$$Zn \rightarrow Zn^{2+} + 2e^-$$

$$2H+ + 2e^- \rightarrow H_2$$

(Chlorine is not seen in the half-reactions because half-reactions are net ionic equations, and this chlorine is a spectator.)

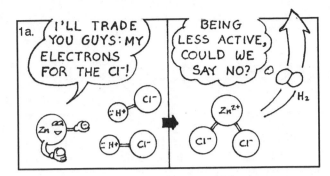

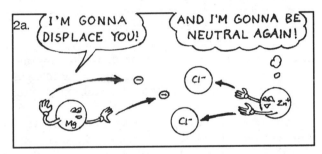

If zinc is placed in an acid solution (1a), it provides the electrons "needed" by the hydrogen ions from the acid, enabling the H^+ to form H_2 gas and evolve. If the solution were dehydrated, the salt zinc cloride would be all that remained.

But when silver is added to the same acid solution (1b), nothing happens, because silver is below hydrogen in the Activity Series; it is a metal that, most of the time, does not react with acids.

Now, let us put magnesium in the zinc chloride solution (2a). Relatively active—compared to zinc, at least—magnesium displaces zinc, such that, as the magnesium is "eaten away," the zinc ions capture its valence electrons and the zinc precipites out as elemental metal, leaving behind an ionic soup of chloride and magnesium ions.

$$Mg \rightarrow Mg^{2+} + 2e^-$$

$$Zn^{2+} + 2e^- \rightarrow Zn$$

$$Zn^{2+}\ Mg \rightarrow Zn + Mg^{2+}$$

To get the magnesium back, we would need an even more active metal.

Sodium, as we can see from the Activity Series, is such a one, and can displace (2b) what is *now* the relatively inactive metal, magnesium, by giving up its electrons to form Na^+ ions (the sodium would meanwhile also be reacting, quite vigorously, with the water to form oxide solution and hydrogen gas, which ignites spontaneously due to the heat of the reaction):

$$(2x)\ Na \rightarrow Na^+ + e^-$$

$$Mg^{2+} + 2e^- \rightarrow Mg$$

$$Mg^{2+} + 2Na \rightarrow Mg + 2Na^+$$

The transfer of electrons in these reactions conclusively puts them in the oxidation-reduction category. In the second equation of prob. 6 in the previous problem set, you can see the electron-transfer reaction that takes place in a "lead-acid" battery, which is responsible for starting a car. Electrons become available through the oxidation of lead and are conducted through a circuit (to the ignition coil and the starter motor), forming lead (II) ions. As the electrons return along the circuit, the lead (IV) ions in the PbO_2 are reduced. Naturally, some electrons are lost over time, so the battery must be "recharged."

There are a few simple patterns that can help you to get a rough feeling for the order of the Series; you need not commit the order to memory—at least at this point—by rote.

One pattern, which applies *only* to transition (B-family) metals, is that the heavier metals, like heavier people, are less active or, if you prefer, more sedentary). For metals in the A-families, the opposite is true.

In another pattern, the A-family elements are more active than the B-family elements. Note, however, that sodium, while we think of it as being more *reactive* than calcium because of some of its observable physical properties and for its being a Family 1A metal, is in fact less *active* than calcium in an oxidation/reduction context.

359

10.5 Relative Redox Strengths

It is a fact. Oxidizers and reducers can be arranged in a table of relative strengths. And, as in the acid/base table in Sect. 9.3, the conjugate of a very strong agent of one type—oxidizer or reducer, in this case—will be a very weak agent of the opposite sort.

Relative Redox Agent Strengths

	oxidizer			reducer	
	F_2	+	$2e^-$	$2F^-$	
	Cl_2	+	$2e^-$	$2Cl^-$	
	$\frac{1}{2}O_2$	+	$2H^+ + 2e^-$	H_2O	
	Br_2	+	$2e^-$	$2Br^-$	
	NO_3^-	+	$4H^+ + 3e^-$	$NO + 2H_2O$	
	Ag^+	+	e^-	Ag	
	Fe^{3+}	+	e^-	Fe^{2+}	
	I_2	+	$2e^-$	$2I-$	
	Cu^{2+}	+	$2e^-$	Cu	
	$2H^+$	+	$2e^-$	H_2	
	Ni^{2+}	+	$2e^-$	Ni	
	Co^{2+}	+	$2e^-$	Co	
	Fe^{2+}	+	$2e^-$	Fe	
	Zn^{2+}	+	$2e^-$	Zn	
	Al^{3+}	+	$3e^-$	Al	
	Na^+	+	e^-	Na	
	Ca^{2+}	+	$2e^-$	Ca	
	K^+	+	e^-	K	

(Left side: STRONGER ↑ / WEAKER ↓ for oxidizer; Right side: WEAKER ↑ / STRONGER ↓ for reducer)

For example, chlorine is one of the strongest oxidizers known, but, when it is ionized, it becomes the proportionately weaker reducer, chloride (you might also recall that Cl^-, in a proton-transfer reaction, is also an extremely weak conjugate of an extremely strong acid, HCl).

The chart of relative acid/base strengths from Chap. 9 shows pairs of species (specifically, pairs of conjugates) that differ by a single proton. However, these redox pairs differ by one *or more* electrons, because oxidation/reduction, unlike acid ionizations, is not necessarily stepwise (but it can be: notice, for instance, that iron (III) can become iron (II) and then elemental iron through stepwise reductions). This means redox reactions are potentially a little more complicated because they can involve the transfer of not only one but two or several electrons at a time, whereas in acid/base reactions we deal with only one proton transfer per step (although there *are* changes with multiple steps and, therefore, multiple proton transfers).

However, if you know a species' oxidation number, you will be safe in this regard. Do you notice, also, that each pair in the chart, if written by itself, is a reduction half-reaction? Write it "backwards" and you would have an oxidation half-reaction.

Note, further, that the order of strong reducers is drawn directly from the Activity Series. Potassium, barium, calcium, and sodium are all so strong that they react immediately with water to yield oxides and hydrogen:

$$2K + H_2O \rightarrow K_2O + H_2\uparrow$$

(R) $$2K + 2e^- \rightarrow 2K^-$$

(O) $$H_2O \rightarrow \frac{1}{2}O_2 + 2H^+ + e^-$$

Notice how in this reaction, water is the reducer, weak as it is. In the chart, its strong oxidizer cognate, oxygen, is written as $\frac{1}{2}O_2$ because each water molecule yields half of an oxygen molecule—an oxygen atom—which is the *true* oxidizing agent in the reverse half-reaction.

"$2H^+$," which is found about midway on the chart, should be understood to mean any strong acid, save for nitric, which is (in redox terms) even somewhat stronger (although it owes this strength to nitrate, which behaves like an elemental oxidizer).

10.6 Redox Equilibrium

ome electron-transfer reactions go all the way, whereas others arrive at and settle into chemical equilibria.

That which you have already learned in the two previous chapters about equilibrium is fortunately applicable to oxidation/reduction reactions.

For one thing, those redox reactions that do go to completion do so for the same reasons that metathesis and some acid/base reactions do: the particles of one or more species leave the system as a gas, precipitate, or weak electrolyte, and so are unavailable for the reverse reaction. Or, the particles

of the products may simply lack the energy to overcome the activation-energy barrier of the reverse reaction (Sect. 8.2). In the combustion of an organic fuel—which is a type of electron-transfer reaction—*both* of these conditions are present to preclude any reverse reaction.

For another thing, reaction equilibria between oxidizers and reducers of varying strengths are parallel in principle to those between acids and bases (Sect. 9.3).

Weaker acids and bases are favored at equilibrium over (comparatively) stronger acids and bases, and the reactions can go all the way if even one of the agents is sufficiently strong. As with acids and bases, a strong reducer donates particles (one or more electrons, in this case) to a strong oxidizer. They become, respectively, a weak oxidizer and a weak reducer.

$$SO + SR \rightleftharpoons WR + WO$$

⊗ Color (in the two frames below, left) the oxidizer "particles" light green, and the reducer ones, orange.

Acids and bases, taken straight from their chart of relative strengths, automatically balance in all equations because all of them transfer (donate or receive) just one particle at a time.

The catch is that while oxidizers and reducers *can* balance automatically, they do not always do so. It is only when each half-reaction transfers the same number of electrons that a redox is balanced.

Recall that the chart of relative strengths on p. 360 is in effect a list of such half-reactions. In it, you can see examples of the transfer of one, two, or three electrons. If the electrons transferred are unequal—between the oxidation and the reduction—a little algebra is needed.

The good news is that by now you know about this kind of balancing (p. 349) and have already practiced it in the first problem set of this chapter.

Let us do some more, but this time using the table of relative redox strengths (Sect. 10.5) to set things up, so to speak (for in the examples in Sect. 10.2, the half-reactions were givens).

What is the net ionic equation for the reaction of aluminum ions and elemental nickel? Go to the table and simply copy the reduction half-reaction as soon as you spot it:

$$Al^{3+} + 3e^- \rightarrow Al$$

And the oxidation half-reaction is just a flip-flop of the reduction half reaction that appears for nickel and its conjugate (left column):

(reduction) $\quad Ni^{2+} + 2e^- \rightarrow Ni \quad$ (so...) $\qquad Ni \rightarrow Ni^{2+} + 2e^- \qquad$ (oxidation)

The electrons are not balanced, but multiplying the coefficients of the aluminum reduction by two and those of the nickel oxidation by three does the trick. This is nothing new; as before (Sects. 2.7, 2.8, 4.2, and 10.3), you find the lowest common multiple. Then, as before, we use the steps from p. 349.

(R) $\qquad 2Al^{3+} + 6e^- \rightarrow 2Al$

(O) $\qquad\qquad 3Ni \rightarrow 3Ni^{2+} + 6e^-$

$$2Al^{3+} + 3Ni \rightarrow 2Al + 3Ni^{2+}$$

According to the table of relative redox strengths on p. 360, nickel is a stronger oxidizer than aluminum ion. Or, for that matter, elemental aluminum is a stronger reducer than elemental nickel. Anyway you choose to look at it, the stronger agents are on the right, so the left, or reverse, direction is the favored one:

$$2Al^{3+} + 3Ni \rightleftarrows 2Al + 3Ni^{2+}$$

Do not confuse the relative activity of metals with the relative activity of oxidizers (p. 360). Aluminum is indeed more active than nickel, but nickel *ions* are more active than aluminum *ions*, in the same way that hydrochloric acid is stronger than oxalic acid, but oxalate is a stronger base than chloride.

Here is another example: write the net ionic equation for the reaction of perchloric acid and iron (II) ion:

First, find the reduction half-reaction in the table, then the oxidation; but be careful, for there are two iron ion reductions; circle them in the table. When you flip-flop them both, you will see that the one you need to use in this problem is the one with iron (II) as a reactant. Now, (Step 1) stack the arrows, (Step 2) put the equations in electronic balance with each other, and then (Step 3) cancel the electrons and add the half-reactions.

This reaction does not result in equilibrium; it goes to completion because a gas, H_2, evolves.

(R) $\qquad 2H^+ + 2e^- \rightarrow H_2$

(O) $\qquad\qquad Fe^{2+} \rightarrow Fe^{3+} + e^-$

$$2H^+ + 2e^- \rightarrow H_2\uparrow$$
$$2Fe^{2+} \rightarrow 2Fe^{3+} + 2e^-$$

$$2H^+ + 2Fe^{2+} \rightarrow H_2\uparrow + 2Fe^{3+}$$

1. Every metal on this chart's x-axis will react with at least one of the compounds in the first column. Indicate the reactive combinations by checking (√).

	K	Co	Au	Pb	Bi	Al	Ca	Hg	Zn
Na_2CrO_4(a0)									
HNO_3(aq)	√	√		√	√	√	√		√
aqua regia									
$Mn(ClO_3)_2$(aq)									
H_2O									
AgF (aq)									
H_2SO_4(aq)									

2. Write each of the following reduction half-reactions (from the chart) as an oxidation half-reaction:

a. $Co^{2+} + 2e^- \rightarrow Co$ _____

b. $I_2 + 2e^- \rightarrow 2I^-$ _____

c. $K^+ + e^- \rightarrow K$ _____

d. $\frac{1}{2}O_2 + 2H^+ + 2e^- \rightarrow H_2O$ _____

e. $Fe^{3+} + e^- \rightarrow Fe^{2+}$ _____

f. $NO_3^- + 4H^+ + 3c^- \rightarrow NO + 2H_2O$ _____

3. Indicate the forward or reverse direction at equilibrium ($\leftrightharpoons$ or $\rightleftharpoons$) or a reaction going to completion ($\rightarrow$):

a.	$Ni + Zn^{2+}$		$Ni^{2+} + Zn$
b.	$2Fe^{3+} + Co$		$2Fe^{2+} + Co^{2+}$
c.	$F_2 + 2Na$		$2F^- + 2Na^+$
d.	$C_7H_{16} + 11O_2$		$7CO_2 + 8H_2O$
e.	$\frac{1}{2}O_2 + 2H^+ Mg$		$H_2O + Mg^{2+}$

4. From these half-reactions, write a balanced net ionic equation, showing the favored direction:

$2Cl^- \rightarrow Cl_2 + 2e^-$ $I_2 + e^- \rightarrow 2I^-$	$Mo^{2+} + 2e^- \rightarrow Mo$ $Al \rightarrow Al^{3+} + 3e^-$

1.

	K	Co	Au	Pb	Bi	Al	Ca	Hg	Zn
Na_2CrO_4(aq)	√						√		
HNO_3(aq)	√	√		√	√	√	√		√
aqua regia	√	√	√	√	√	√	√	√	√
$Mn(ClO_3)_2$(aq)	√					√	√		
H_2O	√						√		
AgF(aq)	√	√		√	√	√	√	√	√
H_2SO_4(aq)	√	√		√		√	√		√

2.

a. $Co \rightarrow Co^{2+} + 2e^-$

b. $I_2 \rightarrow 2I^- + 2e^-$

c. $K \rightarrow K^+ + e^-$

d. $H_2O \rightarrow \frac{1}{2}O_2 + 2H^+ + 2e^-$

e. $Fe^{2+} \rightarrow Fe^{3+} + e^-$

f. $NO + 2H_2O \rightarrow NO_3^- + 4H^+ + 3e^-$

3. a. $\rightleftharpoons$ b. $\rightleftharpoons$ c. $\rightarrow$ d. $\rightarrow$ e. $\rightleftharpoons$

4. $2Cl^- + I_2 \rightleftharpoons Cl_2 + 2I^-$ $3Mo^{2+} + 2Al \rightleftharpoons 3Mo + 2Al^{3+}$

(Note: chlorine, though a gas, is highly soluble and so for all practical purposes does not evolve.)

364

10.7 Redox Ionic Equations

WHY IS THE HALF-REACTION FOR NITRATE SO COMPLEX?

FOR ONE THING THE WATER MOLECULES ARE THERE TO BALANCE THE OXYGEN IN THE NITRATE...

Observed Products:

$NO(g)$
$Co^{2+}(aq)$

BUT THAT'S ALL WE KNOW! WHAT ABOUT THE $2H_2O$, THE $4H^+$ AND THE $3e^-$?

$2H_2O = 2$ oxygens
$4H^+ = 4$ hydrogens
$3e^- = 3$ charges

$NO_3^- + 4H^+ + 3e^- \rightarrow NO + 2H_2O$

ALRIGHT. THE OXIDATION IS EASY TO SEE. BUT I STILL WANNA KNOW EXACTLY HOW WE GOT FROM THERE TO HERE...

THERE : $NO_3^- \rightarrow NO$

HERE :
$NO_3^- + 4H^+ + 3e^-$
$\rightarrow$
$NO + 2H_2O$

$\mathfrak{N}$itrate ion, recall, is a strong oxidizer. It is only so, however, in a solution in which there are four hydrogen ions for every one nitrate. Nitric acid, ionizing in solution, can obviously yield only one H^+ for every HNO_3 molecule, so only one-fourth of the nitrates get to be oxidizers. The other three-fourths only spectate, unless another source of hydrogen ion is added.

If we add a reducer to the solution, then nitric oxide gas evolves. Thus, from observation, we know this much:

$$NO_3^-(aq) \rightarrow NO(g)$$

A system that we will presently introduce for the balancing of redox equations will allow us to use entire water molecules to balance oxygen, such as the three oxygen atoms in nitrate, above. The hydrogen in the water molecules we use to balance the oxygen must itself then be balanced, and for this we use H^+ from the solution. And finally, if the charges are out of balance, we add electrons to the equation.

Let us add cobalt, as our reducer, to the nitric acid solution. As it disappears, it dissolves into cobalt (II) ions and electrons in the following oxidation:

$$Co(s) \rightarrow Co^{2+}(aq) + 2e^-$$

We are going to use the "Look! OOH! Charge!" system.

The first step, the Look! one, is to *look* and see what results from a reaction and to write the two preliminary, partial half-reactions based on observations. We find, visually or otherwise, that cobalt (II) ions and nitric oxide gas are the products and—as it is obvious which reactants each of these products came from—we can write the above two preliminary half-reactions.

The oxidation of elemental cobalt is simple and unambiguous; only a single electron is involved and so the half-reaction is complete as observed in the Look! step.

The reduction of the nitrate, however, is clearly out of balance, both in terms of oxygen atoms and charges. What, then, must be done?

We go to the OOH! Step. We know—from the lab observations from which we were able to write the preliminary (or "look") half-reactions—that nitrate not only disintegrates as a species but that one of its component elements, nitrogen, was reduced (that is, lowered in oxidation number) from 5+ (in NO_3^-) to 2+ (in NO). It is imperative that we balance those elements that have undergone a change in oxidation number first. Cobalt and nitrogen—the Other elements—are already balanced, and as there is no Other element to balance, apart from Oxygen (the second O) and hydrogen (you guessed it, the H), we can then proceed to oxygen, which is out of balance.

There is only one source for the oxygen atoms needed to balance the oxygen in nitrate: the solvent, water. The left side of the half-reaction has *two more* oxygens than does the right side, so we *add two* water molecules to the right:

$$NO_3^- \rightarrow NO\uparrow + 2H_2O$$

Now our problem is that we have hydrogen on the right but not on the left. But there is also a source of *H*ydrogen in the solution: the H^+ ions released by the ionization of the acid. With them, we can balance the *H*ydrogen atoms from the water molecules:

$$4H^+ + NO_3^- \rightarrow NO\uparrow + 2H_2O$$

At this point all the elements are in balance. But are the charges? No, for there are no charges on the right, but the left has a *net* charge of 3+ (4+ from the hydrogens, 1− from the nitrate). Electrons, as you know from Sects. 2.3 and 10.3, impart charge, or bits of negativeness, so we add them as needed to the equation (this is the Charge! Step):

$$3e^- + 4H^+ + NO_3^- \rightarrow NO\uparrow + 2H_2O$$

With this, we have exactly the same same reduction half-reaction that appears in the table of relative strengths (p. 360). Four moles of hydrogen ions are needed for each mole of nitrate to become a mole of nitric oxide gas. The other three moles of nitrate, the excess, would appear on both sides of the *gross* ionic equation (Sect. 6.9) and are therefore only spectators. A gas results, so the reaction goes to completion (to the limit at least, of the limiting reactant, H^+). Now we have correct and balanced half-reactions for both cobalt and nitrate.

As before, we start by (1) stacking the arrows:

$$NO_3^- + 4H^+ + 3e^- \rightarrow NO\uparrow + 2H_2O$$
$$Co \rightarrow Co^{2+} + 2e^-$$

...then (2) we balance the electrons, using algebra...

$$(2x) \quad 2NO_3^- + 8H^+ + 6e^- \rightarrow 2NO\uparrow + 4H_2O$$
$$(3x) \quad\quad\quad\quad\quad 3Co \rightarrow 3Co^{3+} + 6e^-$$

Finally, we (3) cancel the electrons and add the now fully balanced oxidation and reduction half-reactions:

$$2NO_3^- + 8H^+ + 3Co \rightarrow 2NO\uparrow + 4H_2O + 3Co^{2+}$$

It never hurts, after performing this final step, to do a check by inspection (Sect. 4.2): element-by-element, followed by a counting of the charges.

Now, on to another example. This time, though, we will look for the half-reactions in a given, but incomplete net ionic equation, the type you might get on a test or in an exercise. Write a balanced net ionic equation for the reaction of thiosulfate and chlorine, both in aqueous solutions.

$$S_2O_3^{2-} + Cl_2 \rightarrow SO_4^{2-} + Cl^-$$

The Look! OOH! Charge! System Explained

First we write a preliminary half-reaction for both the oxidized species (that containing the oxidized element, if not the element itself, as N in NO_3^-) and the reduced species (ditto) by "looking" (observing a lab result or reading them in a problem). Do not even attempt to balance them at this step; that is the *next* step.

Now balance any Other elements (other than oxygen and hydrogen, that is). At the Chem. 1 level, there will seldom or never be any Others other than those you already wrote down in the Look Step. Then balance Oxygen, if present, with water molecules and, lastly, balance Hydrogen—because it is present in the water molecules just used—with H^+ ions.

Sum up the charge of the ions on both sides (if one side has no ions, then its net charge is, of course, zero). Add electrons to the side with the more positive total—as many as it takes to bring it down to the charge value of the other side of the reaction—and you have a balanced half-reaction. Now, to the current example...

In the Look Step, we wrote preliminary half-reactions for the chlorine (reduced from 0 to 1-) and for the sulfur in thiosulfate (oxidized from 4+ to 6+).

The preliminary reduction half-reaction is easily balanced by the doubling (of the coefficient) of chloride;

the oxidation is dealt with *for the moment* by balancing the sulfur (that is, by adjusting *its* coefficient as well). In this way, the Other elements are taken care of.

After the sulfur is balanced, we see there are no other Others in the still-incomplete oxidation half-reaction, so we go straight to Oxygen. The two sulfates have eight oxygens between them, so we need five water molecules to provide five oxygens, which are added to the three oxygens in thiosulfate. In turn, ten hydrogens are now needed on the other side of the half-reaction to offset those in the five water molecules, and so are added accordingly.

Finally, the charges. The reactants in the oxidation collectively have 2− (2− plus 0) and the reactants 6+ (4− plus 10+). Therefore, we give eight electrons to the reactant-side of the oxidation. Then the electrons are cancelled and the half-reactions added to get the completed half-reaction. Balance the reduction half-reaction by adding two electrons, and the half-reactions are ready to be added.

---
1. Look!

(reduction) $Cl_2 \rightarrow Cl^-$

(oxidation) $S_2O_3^{2-} \rightarrow SO_4^{2-}$

---
2. OOH!

(Others...) $Cl_2 \rightarrow 2Cl^-$

             $S_2O_3^{2-} \rightarrow 2SO_4^{2-}$

(Oxygen...) $5H_2O + S_2O_3^{2-} \rightarrow 2SO_4^{2-}$

(Hydrogen...) $5H_2O + S_2O_3^{2-} \rightarrow 2SO_4^{2-} + 10H^+$

---
3. Charge!

$$5H_2O + S_2O_3^{2-} \rightarrow 2SO_4^{2-} + 10H^+ + 8e^-$$

$$Cl_2 + 2e^- \rightarrow 2Cl^-$$

367

In this example, elemental iodine results from the mixing of iodate and iodide solutions.

1. Look!

| (reduction) | (5+ to 0) | $IO_3^- \rightarrow I_2$ |
| (oxidation) | (1− to 0) | $I^- \rightarrow I_2$ |

2. OOH!

(Other...)	$2IO_3^- \rightarrow I_2$ and	$2I^- \rightarrow I_2$
(Oxygen...)		$2IO_3^- \rightarrow I_2 + 6H_2O$
(Hydrogen...)		$12H^+ + 2IO_3^- \rightarrow I_2 + 6H_2O$

3. Charge!

$$10e^- + 12H^+ + 2IO_3^- \rightarrow I_2 + 6H_2O$$

(5x) $\qquad 2I^- \rightarrow I_2 + 2e^-$

Now, juxtapose the half-reactions (stack the arrows), algebraically adjust the charges, then cancel the electrons and add the equations...

$$10e^- + 12H^+ + 2IO_3^- \rightarrow I_2 + 6H_2O$$
$$10I^- \rightarrow 5I_2 + 10e^-$$

$$12H^+ + 2IO_3^- + 10I^- \rightarrow 6I_2 + 6H_2O$$

...then execute a quick visual inspection, and you are done!

Error Analysis

Although NO_3^-, $S_2O_3^{2-}$, NH_4^+, and other radicals are in a sense redox agents (because they donate or gain electrons while breaking up), it is really an element that is in truth oxidized or reduced. Nevertheless, the whole radical must be in the preliminary equation if it breaks up (for it will not then be a spectator, and half-reactions are net ionic); therefore

$$NO_3^- \rightarrow NO\uparrow$$

(but not...) $\qquad N^{5+} \rightarrow N^{2+}$

In this way, nitrate, not nitrogen, is an oxidizer.

In any oxyanion, this need not result in confusion because oxygen is going to have an oxidation number of 2−, making the value of the oxidation-number-changing element evident.

Notice that in this section's three examples, that one half-reaction from each (the oxidations of Co and I⁻, and the reduction of Cl_2) only required the performance of part of the OOH! Step (you cannot balance oxygen and hydrogen that you do not have).

Future Study

As has been said, redox equations can be quite complex. Those in this book are of the low- and medium-complexity that you will encounter in Chem. 1. There are other ways to write and balance net ionic and redox equations, but they are the province of Chem. 2 and 3.

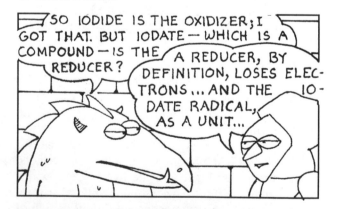

368

10.8 Predictions III: Redox

I CAN PREDICT REACT-IONS OF METALS WITH ACIDS OR SALTS; REDOX EQUILIBRIA; AND REACTIONS BETWEEN STRONG AND/OR WEAK REDOX AGENTS...

As with acids and bases, the key to predicting the outcomes of oxidation/reduction reactions is the relative strengths of the agents.

In highly exothermic redox reactions, such as the combustion of alkanes and other organic fuels, the activation energy barrier (Sect. 8.2) can also affect the result by being so high as to prevent a reverse reaction and, therefore, precluding equilibrium.

Our tools for predicting oxidation/reduction reactions are the Activity Series (Sect. 10.4) and the table of relative redox strengths (Sect. 10.5).

---

1. Acids and Metals

The Activity Series tells us which metals will react with which acids. Such reactions are of the replacement variety (Sect. 4.2) and, as hydrogen is the portion of an acid that some metals can replace and that others cannot, it, too, is part of the Series. Worded in another way, some metals are stronger reducers than hydrogen and, therefore, reduce it as they are being oxidized by it (the metal donates electrons to the hydrogen). Weak reducers, such as mercury or silver, are *below* hydrogen because they do not react with acids.

One strong acid, however—$HNO_3(aq)$—can react with some metals below H_2, and, in combination with a certain other strong acid—$HCl(aq)$—will dissolve even gold or platinum. Weaker acids can also react with some metals, but they do so more slowly and to a lesser degree, for they hold on to their hydrogen (protons) more tightly.

---

2. Saline Solutions

When a metal *does* replace hydrogen, a salt is the product. Depending on its solubility (Sect. 6.2), the salt will (1) precipitate out of the solution, causing the reaction to go to completion, or (2) remain in it, dissolved. The positions of the metals relative to each other (and not only to hydrogen) are also important, for they let us know what metal/salt solution combinations will react at all. A metal can displace any other metal below it by being a more willing donor of electrons. The less active metal of the dissolved salt picks up the electrons and leaves the system as an element, just as hydrogen leaves an acid when it forms and evolves.

---

3. Equilibria

Relative oxidizer and reducer strengths determine the direction of an equilibrium if it—rather than a complete reaction—is the result. As expected, weaker species are favored because they have less tendency to donate or receive electrons and are more stable in solution (in short, they do not chemically change as much, if at all). Stronger agents, on the other hand, have a harder time being themselves in water, so to speak, for they are comparatively eager to chuck or grab electrons and transform themselves into their weaker conjugates.

---

4. Strong Agents

The presence of a very strong oxidizer, reducer, or both, leads to a complete reaction for reasons that parallel the effect of the presence of strong acid/base species in a reaction (Sect. 9.4).

IN THE EXAMPLES IN SECT. 10.7, WHERE DID ALL THOSE IONS COME FROM? AND WHAT ABOUT ALL THE IONS IN THIS PROBLEM SET?

IT WAS NOTED ON PAGE 366 THAT H^+ IONS ARE PRESENT...

...DUE TO THE IONIZATION OF ACID-FORMING COMPOUNDS— SUCH AS $H_2S_2O_3$. THE ANIONS [SUCH AS $S_2O_3^{2-}$] ARE THE OTHER RESULT OF THE IONIZATION. ASSUME THAT EACH OF THE PROBLEMS INCLUDES AN ACID SOLUTION AS ONE OF THE REACTANTS...

...AND THAT THE REMAINING REACTANTS—IONS INCLUDED—ARE (OR ARE FROM) METALS, SALTS, BASIC OR SALINE SOLUTIONS. ...AND THAT THE ACID SOLUTIONS ARE ARRHENIUS ACIDS...SO IT GOES WITHOUT SAYING THAT H^+ IONS ARE PRESENT.

PRECISELY.

WHEW!

For problems 1-7, use the Look! OOH! Charge! System to write a balanced net ionic redox equation from the defective equations given, which, like the first example in Sect. 10.7, are based on experimental observations (indicating only what went into the reaction and what came out without *showing* what happened, which is up to you to do). Include state designations in your final equation (in prob. 3, Pb is oxidized to a Pb ion).

---

1. $Ag + SO_4^{2-} \rightarrow Ag^+ + SO_2\uparrow$

---

2. $Fe^{2+} + Cr_2O_7^{2-} \rightarrow Fe^{3+} + Cr^{3+}$

---

3. $Pb + NO_3^- \rightarrow H_2PbO_3 + NO_2\uparrow$

---

4. $IO_4^- + I^- \rightarrow I_2$

5. $Sb_2O_3 + NO_3^- \rightarrow SbO_4^{3-} + NO\uparrow$

6. $C_2O_4^{2-} + MnO_4^- \rightarrow CO_2\uparrow + Mn^{2+}$

7. $Zn + NO_3^- \rightarrow Zn^{2+} + NH_4^+$

8. Predict (after balancing if needed) whether these reactions will go to completion ($\rightarrow$), result in equilibrium ($\rightleftharpoons$), or not take place at all ($\ominus$) (Note: iron (III) oxalate is soluble):

a.	$Al(s) + Co(ClO_3)_2(aq)$		$Co(s) + Al(ClO_3)_2(aq)$
b.	$Cu(s) + H_2SO_4(aq)$		$CuSO_4(aq) + H_2(g)$
c.	$HNO_3(aq) + Ag(s)$		$H_2(g) + Ag(NO_3)(aq)$
d.	$Fe(s) + ZnC_2O_4(aq)$		$Fe_2(C_2O_4)_3(aq) + Zn(s)$
e.	$H_2SO_4(aq) + Ni(s)$		$NiSO_4(aq) + H_2(g)$
f.	$HBr(aq) + Hg$		$H_2(g) + Hg_2Br_2(s)$

9. For problems 1-7 (above), identify the reductions (R) and the oxidations (O).

371

1.

$$2Ag \rightarrow 2Ag^+ + 2e^- \qquad \text{(O)}$$
$$SO_4^{2-} + 4H^+ + 2e^- \rightarrow SO_2 + 2H_2O \qquad \text{(R)}$$
$$SO_4^{2-}(aq) + 4H^+(aq) + 2Ag(s) \rightarrow SO_2(g) + 2H_2O(l) + 2Ag^+(aq)$$

9. (O)
(R)

2.

$$6Fe^{2+} \rightarrow 6Fe^{3+} + 6e^- \qquad \text{(O)}$$
$$Cr_2O_7^{2-} + 14H^+ + 6e^- \rightarrow 2Cr^{3+} + 7H_2O \qquad \text{(R)}$$
$$Cr_2O_7^{2-}(aq) + 14H^+(aq) + 6Fe^{2+}(aq) \rightarrow 2Cr^{3+}(aq) + 7H_2O(l) + 6Fe^{3+}(aq)$$

3.

$$Pb \rightarrow Pb^{4+} + 4e^- \qquad \text{(O)}$$
$$8H^+ + 4NO_3^- + 4e^- \rightarrow 4NO_2 + 4H_2O \qquad \text{(R)}$$
$$Pb(s) + 8H^+(aq)\ 4NO_3^-(aq) \rightarrow 4NO_2(g) + 4H_2O(l) + Pb^{4+}(aq)$$

4.

$$14I^- \rightarrow 7I_2 + 14e^- \qquad \text{(O)}$$
$$2IO_4^- + 16H^+ + 14e^- \rightarrow I_2 + 8H_2O \qquad \text{(R)}$$
$$14I^- + 2IO_4^-(aq) + 16H^+(aq) \rightarrow 8I_2(s) + 8H_2O(l)$$

5. (*)

$$15H_2O + 3Sb_2O_3 \rightarrow 6SbO_4^{3-} + 30H^+ + 12e^- \qquad \text{(O)}$$
$$4NO_3^- + 16H^+ + 12e^- \rightarrow 4NO + 8H_2O \qquad \text{(R)}$$
$$4NO_3^-(aq) + 16H^+(aq) + 15H_2O(aq) + 3Sb_2O_3(aq) \rightarrow 4NO(g) + 8H_2O(l) + 6SbO_4^{3-}(aq) + 30H^+(aq)$$

6.

$$5C_2O_4^{2-} \rightarrow 10CO_2 + 10e^- \qquad \text{(O)}$$
$$16H^+ + 2MnO_4^- + 10e^- \rightarrow 2Mn^{2+} + 8H_2O \qquad \text{(R)}$$
$$16H^+(aq) + 2MnO_4^-(aq) + 5C_2O_4^{2-}(aq) \rightarrow 2Mn^{2+}(aq) + 10CO_2(g) + 8H_2O$$

7.

$$4Zn \rightarrow 4Zn^{2+} + 8e^- \qquad \text{(O)}$$
$$10H^+ + NO_3^- + 8e^- \rightarrow NH_4^+ + 3H_2O \qquad \text{(R)}$$
$$10H^+(aq) + NO_3^-(aq) + 4Zn(s) \rightarrow NH_4^+(aq) + 3H_2O(l) + 4Zn^{2+}(aq)$$

8.   a. $\rightleftharpoons$ b. $\rightarrow$ c. $\rightarrow$ d. $\ominus$ e. $\rightarrow$ f. $\rightarrow$ (*Net H^+ count is $14H^+$; see note, p. 374, prob. 1)

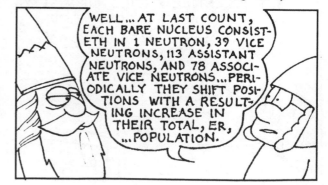

372

10.9 Chapter Synthesis

IN CHEM ONE, WE'RE CONTENT WITH PREDICTING ONLY VERY SIMPLE REACTIONS; BUT WE'VE PRACTICED WRITING BALANCED, NARRATIVE EQUATIONS FOR BOTH SIMPLE AND MEDIUM-COMPLEXITY REACTIONS.

... BASED ON THEIR OBSERVED PRODUCTS.

Oxidation/reduction reactions involve the transfer of electrons from reducers to oxidizers.

Since electrons have negative charges (or may be thought of as little bits of negativeness), the oxidizer falls in oxidation number as it gains electrons, while the reducer goes up in oxidation number by losing them.

As with the acids and bases, oxidizers and reducers have relative strengths; but unlike acids and bases, we can express each agent in its own half-reaction, the doing of which is a necessary step in determining from observable results what really took place.

Redox equations—and, likewise, redox predictions—can be rather more complicated than those we have studied up to this point, but, fortunately, there are special methods for dealing with them that you will learn later on; for the moment, however, you can manipulate many redox equations for reactions taking place in acidic solutions by adding water molecules and hydrogen ions.

Our culmination in Chap. 10, then, has been the writing of correct half-reactions from witnessed or recorded observations, identifying them as oxidations or reductions, and merging them into complete, accurate, and indicative ionic equations. Let us consider a final example:

Solutions of dichromate and ammonium are mixed, liberating nitrogen gas and precipitating solid chromium (III) oxide. Write a "crude" equation to represent these observations, and take it from there:

$$Cr_2O_7^{2-} + NH_4^+ \rightarrow Cr_2O_3\downarrow + N_2\uparrow$$

It is readily obvious what came from what, hence the preliminary or "Look!" reactions (a). Next, balance, if necessary, the Other (than oxygen or hydrogen) elements: chromium (the oxidizer, which goes from 6+ to 3+) and nitrogen (the reducer, going from 3− to 0)(b). Then, balance the oxygen in the reduction, using water from the solution (c) and the hydrogen that is now in both half-reactions using hydrogen ions, also from the solution (this assumes, of course, an Arrhenius acid solution) (d). The total charge of the reactants in the reduction is six less than that of the products, so we add six electrons to the latter. In the oxidation, it is the products' charges that are six below the reactants', so the reactants get six bits of negativeness (e). As the electron adjustment for both is coincidentally six, no algebra is needed. Just cancel the electrons and the H^+ (because, in this case and by definition, it is a spectator), and add the half-reaction to get...

(a)
$$Cr_2O_7^{2-} \rightarrow Cr_2O_3 \quad \text{(reduction)}$$
$$NH_4^+ \rightarrow N_2 \quad \text{(oxidation)}$$

(b)
$$2NH_4^+ \rightarrow N_2$$

(c)
$$Cr_2O_7^{2-} \rightarrow Cr_2O_3 + 4H_2O$$

(d)
$$8H^+ + Cr_2O_7^{2-} \rightarrow Cr_2O_3 + 4H_2O$$
$$2NH_4^+ \rightarrow N_2 + 8H^+$$

(e)
$$8H^+ + Cr_2O_7^{2-} \rightarrow Cr_2O_3 + 4H_2O + 6e^-$$
$$6e^- + 2NH_4^+ \rightarrow N_2 + 8H^+$$

$$Cr_2O_7^{2-}(aq) + NH_4^+(aq) \rightarrow Cr_2O_3(s) + 4H_2O(l) + N_2(g)$$

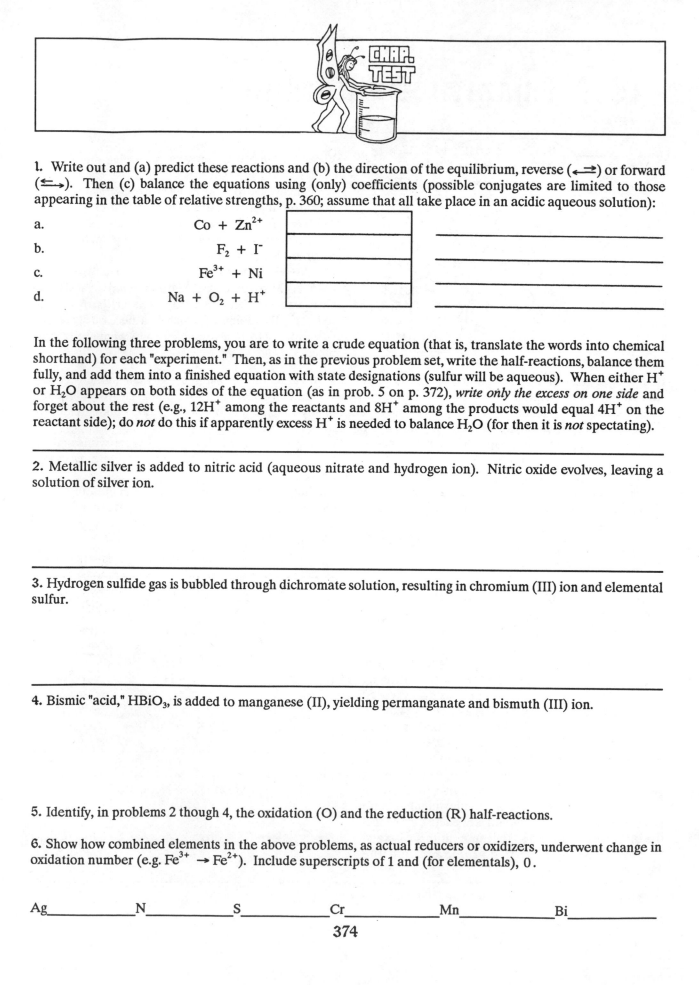

1. Write out and (a) predict these reactions and (b) the direction of the equilibrium, reverse ($\rightleftharpoons$) or forward ($\rightleftharpoons$). Then (c) balance the equations using (only) coefficients (possible conjugates are limited to those appearing in the table of relative strengths, p. 360; assume that all take place in an acidic aqueous solution):

a. $Co + Zn^{2+}$

b. $F_2 + I^-$

c. $Fe^{3+} + Ni$

d. $Na + O_2 + H^+$

In the following three problems, you are to write a crude equation (that is, translate the words into chemical shorthand) for each "experiment." Then, as in the previous problem set, write the half-reactions, balance them fully, and add them into a finished equation with state designations (sulfur will be aqueous). When either H^+ or H_2O appears on both sides of the equation (as in prob. 5 on p. 372), *write only the excess on one side* and forget about the rest (e.g., $12H^+$ among the reactants and $8H^+$ among the products would equal $4H^+$ on the reactant side); do *not* do this if apparently excess H^+ is needed to balance H_2O (for then it is *not* spectating).

2. Metallic silver is added to nitric acid (aqueous nitrate and hydrogen ion). Nitric oxide evolves, leaving a solution of silver ion.

3. Hydrogen sulfide gas is bubbled through dichromate solution, resulting in chromium (III) ion and elemental sulfur.

4. Bismic "acid," $HBiO_3$, is added to manganese (II), yielding permanganate and bismuth (III) ion.

5. Identify, in problems 2 though 4, the oxidation (O) and the reduction (R) half-reactions.

6. Show how combined elements in the above problems, as actual reducers or oxidizers, underwent change in oxidation number (e.g. $Fe^{3+} \rightarrow Fe^{2+}$). Include superscripts of 1 and (for elementals), 0.

Ag_____N_____S_____Cr_____Mn_____Bi_____

114
Rp
(298)

$\mathfrak{Profile: Reptilium}$

In 2009 A.D., Reptilium became the first element to be discovered by a nonsapient being.

In 1982, a team of nuclear chemists at a lab in Darmstadt, Germany claimed the discovery of element number 109. Unfortunately, only one atom—if that—was actually produced, and its existence could only be indirectly inferred from evidence of its near- spontaneous decay.

This find did not come cheap; to make a single atom of "eka-iridium," it is estimated that about 1.0×10^{11} collisions had to take place between an iron nucleus (the ammunition of the particle accelerator) and a bismuth nucleus (the target).

All the elements from Z = 93 to Z = 109 are called *transuranics*. In 1968, the existence in nature of traces of relatively stable transuranics was theorized, but only very small amounts of plutonium (Z = 94) have ever been found (although this element is "bred" in special reactors). Scientists who want to share the distinction of Scheele, Davy, Curie, Ramsey, and Berzelius—all of whom discovered at least two elements—must today pay a very high technological price.

The scarcity or scientific implausibility of transuranics is thought to be due more to the difficulty in producing them—be it by technological or natural means—than to the inherent instability of their nuclei, which nevertheless fates them to a short life.

This instability is in the form of three types of decay: (1) spontaneous fission into simpler nuclei; (2) the emission or capture of electrons (which results in protons or neutrons, respectively); and (3) the emission alpha particles (two neutrons, two protons). The eka-iridium atom (Z = 109) undergoes fission after about three milliseconds.

Would-be element discoverers need not abandon all hope, however. Under principles that are in some ways analogous to the stability of filled electron shells, there are "magic numbers" of protons and neutrons that make up shells of their own within the nucleus.

Beyond element 109, there is a "sea of instability" (indeed, E-109 is a tidepool on its shore), but 114 is a magic number for protons and, with a magic number of neutrons, 184, a relatively stable isotope is predicted (according to the Schrödinger Equation). The isotope $^{298}_{114}Rp$ (its nuclear formula) would have a half-life of several hours. The elements on this far shore—which begin with E-114—are the *supertransuranics*.

Production scenarios follow the pattern for the other transuranics: heavy, fairly stable nuclei such as curium-248 are bombarded with lighter projectiles. Element 114 ("eka-lead") would be a metal but element 118 ("eka-radon") would be, according to the Periodic Law, a noble gas. If elements up through the latter were discovered, we would have seven complete periods.

There are many worthy names for these elements, should they ever be produced: Seaborgium (115), Avogadrium (116), Daltonine (117), and Paulingon (118). The Camelot Primer's name for E-114 is Reptilium, because it will by then be time to honor at least one general chemistry student, in memorial to the millions who have struggled with the subject of general chemistry.

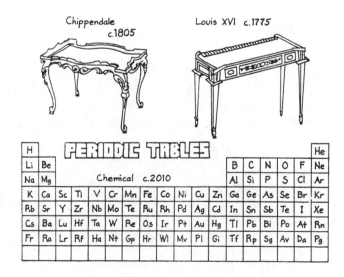

1. (a) $Co + Zn^{2+} \rightleftharpoons Co^{2+} + Zn$

   (b) $F_2 + 2I^- \rightleftharpoons 2F^- + I_2$

   (c) $2Fe^{3+} + Ni \rightleftharpoons 2Fe^{2+} + Ni^{2+}$

   (d) $Na + O_2 + 4H^+ \rightleftharpoons Na + 2H_2O$

2. $Ag + NO_3^- \rightarrow Ag^+ + NO$

$$3Ag \rightarrow 3Ag^+ + 3e^- \qquad \text{5. (O)}$$
$$3e^- + 4H^+ + NO_3^- \rightarrow NO + 2H_2O \qquad \text{(R)}$$
$$4H^+(aq) + NO_3^-(aq) + 3Ag(s) \rightarrow NO(g) + 2H_2O(l) + 3Ag^+(aq)$$

3. $H_2S + Cr_2O_7^{2-} \rightarrow S + Cr^{3+}$

$$3H_2S \rightarrow 3S + 6H^+ + 6e^- \qquad \text{(O)}$$
$$6e^- + 14H^+ + Cr_2O_7^{2-} \rightarrow 2Cr^{3+} + 7H_2O \qquad \text{(R)}$$
$$3H_2S(g) + 8H^+(aq) + Cr_2O_7^{2-}(aq) \rightarrow 3S(aq) + 2Cr^{3+}(aq) + 7H_2O(l)$$

4. $HBiO_3 + Mn^{2+} \rightarrow Bi^{3+} + MnO_4^-$

$$8H_2O + 2Mn^{2+} \rightarrow 2MnO_4^- + 16H^+ + 10e^- \qquad \text{(O)}$$
$$25H^+ + 5HBiO_3 + 10e^- \rightarrow 5Bi^{3+} + 15H_2O \qquad \text{(R)}$$
$$2Mn^{2+}(aq) + 9H^+(aq) + 5HBiO_3(aq) \rightarrow 2MnO_4^-(aq) + 5Bi^{3+}(aq) + 7H_2O(l)$$

6. $Ag^0 \rightarrow Ag^{1+}$ $\quad N^{5+} \rightarrow N^{2+}$ $\quad S^{2-} \rightarrow S^0$ $\quad Cr^{6+} \rightarrow Cr^{3+}$ $\quad Mn^{2+} \rightarrow Mn^{7+}$ $\quad Bi^{5+} \rightarrow Bi^{3+}$

Epilogue:
Concerning the Full Circle

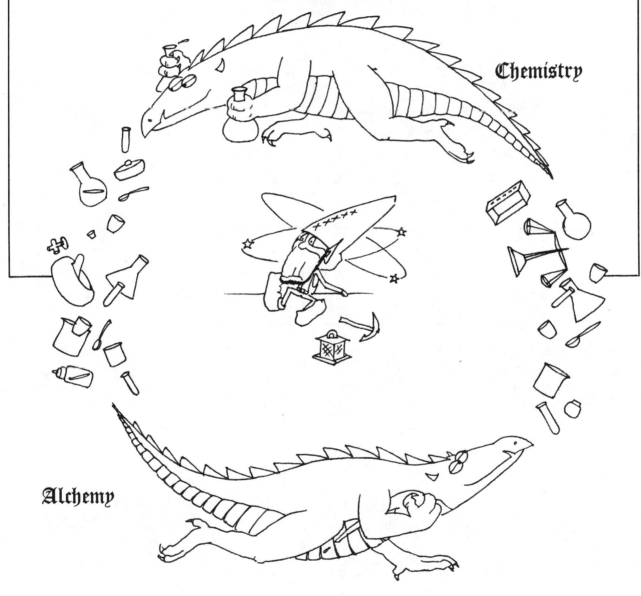

Chemistry

Alchemy

378

381

I FINALLY GOT "AHEAD" OF MYSELF!

WHOA!

OOPS!

DOWN BOY!

FOR THIS YOU SHALL ANSWER WITH YOUR HEADS!

ARREST THAT IMPERDINANT DEPILER OF OUR MOST ROYAL PRESENTS!

...TORTURE HIM WITH THE RACK, THUMBSCREWS, AND HOT IRONS WITH...

HAR-HAR! THE LITTLE CREEP WANTS TO SCARE ME!

... MUSIC BY BLACK SABBATH AND MICHAEL JACKSON...THEN MAKE HIM LISTEN TO A WHOLE READING OF 'THE EGO AND THE ID' AND 'ULYSSES'...

...AND 'MEIN KAMPF' ...THEN HE'LL WATCH 8 SEASONS OF 'THREE'S COMPANY' RERUNS, THE CHECKERS SPEECH, MARGERINE AND BLEACH COMERCIALS...

...THEN, IF HE'S STILL ALIVE, FOOTAGE OF TAMMY FAYE BAKKER CRYING FOR THE CAMERA!

WHAT A WAYDAGO! ...SPEAKING OF WHICH...

CONTRARY TO MASTER DRAGGIN'S CHERISHED BELIEF...

AND DUE TO HIS VIRULENTLY SARDINIAN IDEA OF HUMOR...

RIGHT!

HE'S GONNA LOSE HIS HEAD!

AND, METHINKS, OUR HEADS AS WELL, UNLESS, FORSOOTH, WE KEEP THEM FOR THE MOMENT!

YUKYUK! I TAKE YOUR MEANING, OLD BOY!

MEANTIME, WE CAN AFFORD TO LOSE THIS...

383

Credits

The Camelot General Chemistry Primer

An H.D. Kenndon, U. Peter Krastins & Daniel P. Gould Production

Producer	Antonio Toscana	Concessionaires	Delois Carruth
Director	Shailaja Reddy, J.D.		Ana Valenzuela de G.
Casting Director	Gordon Dean Coop		Angela de Hernández
Asst. Producer	Paty "Poderosa" Aldana		Genevieve Coleman
Asst. Directors	Luz Mayra Contreras	Dubbing	Ruth Hernández
	Barry K. Fortney		Kelly Anne Srnica, Ph.D
Scriptwriter	Dwight Wayne Coop	Sound Mixing	Dick Walden
Set Consultant	Franco Nanartonis	Ushers	Pablo "Buddy" Hernández
Technical Consultant	Jackie Pilcher		Pepe de Leon
Lighting	Mely González		Steven King
Soundroom	Lisa Renée Bogue, J.D.		Jack Funk
Box Office	Elsy Calderón	Reservations	María de León
	Eddy Ruiz Umana		Kathi Fox
Programmes	Robeto Gil Paredes, DDS	Parking Valets	Allen Freedman, Ph.D
	Karen Owsley, Ph.D		Taylor Mack, Ph.D
	Edwin Castellanos, Ph.D.		Ismael González
	Joe Fox		
Doorman	Chuck Leyba, Ph.D		
Proofing	Jefferey Coleman		

The Camelot General Chemistry Primer was originally rehearsed at the Teatro Producciones Laser in the City of Guatemala in the subcontinent of Central America (nowhere near Topeka, Kansas).

Suggested Reading

Books on Chemistry

Coop, Dwight Wayne *The Camelot Allied Health Chemistry Primer*, Available from Kenndon, Krastins & Gould. Another "scientific drama" featuring A.G. Draggin's consort, her half-cousin Spike, with Carver, Pauling, Nightengale, and the villanous Al the Kobald. This is a chemistry primer for majors in nursing, dietetics, etc., incorporating the features of its general chemistry sister. Profiles of nutrients. Due out by late 1993. $22.95

Loebel, Arnold, *Chemical Problem Solving by Dimensional Analysis* (3rd Edition) Best book around that is mainly about DA. Loebel has a strong commitment to his readers, who have helped him improve the book. Very many problems, all fully worked out. Also includes topics such as net ionic equations, colligative properties, sigfigs, pH calculations, and a fine introduction to thermochemistry. This work is equally or very slightly more challenging (if you try the specially marked problems) than the Camelot Primer, and a little more specialized. Priced at about $32.00.

Peters, Edward I., *Problem Solving for Chemistry*, A comprehensive math review makes up the first seven chapters. The remainder of the book teaches math and chemistry side-by-side as they relate to each other. Very many problems, fully worked out. In-depth treatment of all DA topics found in the above books plus sections on buffers, normality, etc. In spite of his own advanced training, Peters has a gift for writing to newcomers to his discipline. $37.00.

Books on Related Topics

Abbott, Edwin, *Flatland: A Romance in Several Dimensions* Available from Kenndon Krastins & Gould A clever and hilarious satire of 19th-century Imperial Britain told in terms of Euclidean Geometry. The reader of this novella is able to see organic connections between apparently unrelated academic disciplines.

Gish, Duane T., Ph. D., *Evolution: the Challenge of the Fossil Record* Available from Kenndon, Krastins & Gould. A noted biochemist examines the theories of evolution and punctuated equilibrium and subjects them to honest epistemological enquiry. Includes discussion of Archaeopterix, Dinosaur aficionados will want to read Dr. Gish's *Dinosaurs: Those Terrible Lizards,* also available from KK&G.

Swann, Howard, and Johnson, John, *Professor E. McSquareds Calculus Primer* (Expanded Intergalactic Edition) Available from Kenndon Krastins & Gould. Most general chemistry students will have to take differential calculus, and this brilliant, fun, and funny work does for precalculus and limits what the Camelot Primers do for chemistry. It was co-written by a mathmetician and a graphic artist.

For more information, write: KK&G Catalog Dept.
B. Hall
Box 732
Temecula CA 92593

Appendices

I. Some Relevant Metric/Nonmetric Conversions

length	angstrom centimeter inch	3.94×10^{-9} inches 3.94×10^{-1} inches 2.54 centimeters 2.54×10^{8} centimeters
mass	gram kilo milligram ounce pound	3.53×10^{-2} ounce 2.20×10^{-3} pound 2.20 pounds 3.53×10^{-5} ounce 28.3 grams 454 grams 0.454 kilo
volume	cm^3 gallon liter milliliter quarts	1.056×10^{-2} quarts 3.785 liters 0.264 gallon 1.056 quarts 1.056×10^{-2} quarts 0.946 liter 946 milliliters
pressure	atmosphere torr	760 torr 1.32×10^{-3} atmosphere
temperature	Celsius Fahrenheit Kelvin	to Fahrenheit: $\times 9. \div 5, +32$ to Kelvin: $+273$ to Celsius: $-32, \times 5, \div 9$ to Celsius: -273
heat	calorie joule kilojoule	4.184 joules 0.239 calorie 239 calories

II. Some Partial Pressures for Water Vapor

T (°C)	P (torr)
15	12.8
16	13.6
17	14.5
18	15.5
19	16.5
20	17.5
21	18.6
22	19.8
23	21.1
24	22.4
25	23.8
26	25.2
27	26.7
28	28.3
29	30.0
30	31.8
31	33.7
32	35.7
33	37.8
34	40.0
35	42.2

III. The Densities of the Elements

Here are the densities for most of the elements. For solid and liquid elements, the value is grams per milliliter; for the gases (italicized), it is grams per liter at STP, and determined with the molar volume conversion factor.

aluminum	2.70	*hydrogen*	*0.05*	*radon*	*9.91*
antimony	6.62	indium	7.31	rhenium	20.95
argon	*1.78*	iodine	4.94	rhodium	12.42
arsenic	5.72	iridium	22.50	rubidium	1.53
barium	3.49	iron	7.86	ruthenium	12.21
beryllium	1.85	*krypton*	*3.74*	scandium	3.02
bismuth	9.81	lanthanum	6.17	selenium	4.79
boron	2.34	lead	11.41	silicon	2.33
bromine	3.12	lithium	0.53	silver	10.49
cadmium	8.65	magnesium	1.74	sodium	0.97
calcium	1.55	manganese	7.43	strontium	2.58
carbon	2.26	mercury	13.59	sulfur	2.07
cesium	1.90	molybdenum	10.18	tellurium	6.24
chlorine	*1.58*	*neon*	*0.90*	thallium	11.85
chromium	7.19	nickel	8.90	tin	7.30
cobalt	8.90	*nitrogen*	*0.63*	titanium	4.51
copper	8.97	osmium	22.62	tungsten	19.31
fluorine	*0.85*	*oxygen*	*0.71*	uranium	19.07
gadolinium	7.89	palladium	12.03	vanadium	6.10
gallium	5.91	phosphorus	1.82	*xenon*	*5.86*
germanium	5.32	platinum	21.38	yttrium	4.47
gold	19.30	potassium	0.86	zinc	7.14
helium	*0.18*	radium	(5.0)	zirconium	6.49

IV. On the Use of Log Tables

The first thing to do when you see a table of mantissas is to figure out whether the given number—that for which you must find a mantissa—begins with the digits along the top of the columns or those on their left edges. The axis with two digits is the one you start with. Usually (but sadly not always) they will contain a decimal. These are the first two digits of your given number. The third is found on the other axis. In the table below, you will start your finger and eye on the side of the column, and stop under the last wanted digit. In the table on p. 335, you go from the top down, stopping when you arrive at the third digit.

	0	1	2	3	4		5	6	7	8	9
1.0	000	004	009	013	017		021	025	029	033	037
1.1	041	045	049	053	057		061	064	068	072	076
1.2	079	083	086	090	093		097	100	104	107	111
1.3	114	117	121	124	127		130	134	137	140	143
1.4	146	149	152	155	158		161	164	167	170	173
1.5	176	179	182	185	188		190	193	196	199	201
1.6	204	207	210	212	215		218	220	223	225	228
1.7	230	233	236	238	240		243	246	248	250	253
1.8	255	258	260	262	265		267	270	272	274	276
1.9	279	281	283	286	288		290	292	294	297	299
2.0	301	303	305	308	310		312	314	316	318	320
2.1	322	324	326	328	330		332	334	336	338	340
2.2	342	344	346	348	350		352	354	356	358	360
2.3	362	364	366	367	369		371	373	375	376	378
2.4	380	382	384	386	387		389	391	393	394	396
2.5	398	400	401	403	405		406	408	410	412	413
2.6	415	417	418	420	422		423	425	426	428	430
2.7	431	433	434	436	438		439	441	442	444	445
2.8	447	449	450	452	453		455	456	458	459	461
2.9	462	464	465	467	468		470	471	473	474	476
3.0	477	479	480	481	483		484	486	487	489	490
3.1	491	493	494	496	497		498	500	501	502	504
3.2	505	506	508	509	510		512	513	514	516	517
3.3	518	520	521	522	524		525	526	528	529	530
3.4	532	533	534	535	537		538	539	540	542	543
3.5	544	545	546	548	549		550	551	553	554	555
3.6	556	558	559	560	561		562	564	565	566	567
3.7	568	569	570	572	573		574	575	576	578	579
3.8	580	581	582	583	584		586	587	588	589	590
3.9	591	592	593	594	596		597	598	599	600	601
4.0	602	603	604	605	606		608	609	610	611	612
4.1	613	614	615	616	617		618	619	620	621	622
4.2	623	624	625	626	627		628	629	630	631	632
4.3	633	634	635	636	637		638	639	640	641	642
4.4	643	644	645	646	647		648	649	650	651	652
4.5	653	654	655	656	657		658	659	660	661	662
4.6	663	664	665	666	666		667	668	669	670	671
4.7	672	673	674	675	676		677	678	678	679	680
4.8	681	682	683	684	685		686	687	687	688	689
4.9	690	691	692	693	694		695	695	696	697	698
5.0	699	700	701	702	702		703	704	705	706	707
5.1	708	708	709	710	711		712	713	713	714	715
5.2	716	717	718	718	719		720	721	722	723	723
5.3	724	725	725	726	727		728	729	730	731	732
5.4	732	733	734	735	736		736	737	738	739	740

	0	1	2	3	4		5	6	7	8	9
5.5	740	741	742	743	743		744	745	746	747	747
5.6	748	749	750	750	751		752	753	754	754	755
5.7	756	757	757	758	759		760	760	761	762	763
5.8	763	764	765	766	766		767	768	769	769	770
5.9	771	772	772	773	774		774	775	776	777	777
6.0	778	779	780	780	781		782	782	783	784	785
6.1	785	786	787	787	788		789	790	790	791	792
6.2	792	793	794	794	795		796	796	797	798	799
6.3	799	800	801	801	802		803	803	804	805	805
6.4	806	807	807	808	809		810	810	811	812	812
6.5	813	814	814	815	816		816	817	818	818	819
6.6	819	820	821	821	822		823	823	824	825	825
6.7	826	827	827	828	829		829	830	831	831	832
6.8	832	833	834	834	835		836	836	837	838	838
6.9	839	839	840	841	841		842	843	843	844	844
7.0	845	846	846	847	848		848	849	849	850	851
7.1	851	852	852	853	854		854	855	855	856	857
7.2	857	858	858	859	860		860	861	861	862	863
7.3	863	864	864	865	866		866	867	867	868	869
7.4	869	870	870	871	872		872	873	873	874	874
7.5	875	876	876	877	877		878	878	879	880	880
7.6	881	881	882	882	883		884	884	885	885	886
7.7	886	887	888	888	889		889	890	890	891	891
7.8	892	893	893	894	894		895	895	896	896	897
7.9	898	898	899	899	900		900	901	901	902	903
8.0	903	903	904	905	905		906	906	907	907	908
8.1	908	909	910	910	911		911	912	912	913	913
8.2	914	914	915	915	916		916	917	917	918	919
8.3	919	920	920	921	921		922	922	923	923	924
8.4	924	925	925	926	926		927	927	928	928	929
8.5	929	930	930	931	931		932	932	933	933	934
8.6	934	935	935	936	936		937	937	938	938	939
8.7	939	940	940	941	941		942	942	943	943	944
8.8	944	945	945	946	946		947	947	948	948	949
8.9	949	950	950	951	951		952	952	953	953	954
9.0	954	955	955	956	956		957	957	958	958	959
9.1	959	959	960	960	961		961	962	962	963	963
9.2	964	964	965	965	966		966	967	967	967	968
9.3	968	969	969	970	970		971	971	972	972	973
9.4	973	974	974	974	975		975	976	976	977	977
9.5	978	978	979	979	979		980	980	981	981	982
9.6	982	983	983	984	984		984	985	985	986	986
9.7	987	987	988	988	989		989	989	990	990	991
9.8	991	992	992	993	993		993	994	994	995	995
9.9	996	996	996	997	997		998	998	999	999	999

V. Some Potentially Confusing Letter Abbreviations

The classical alchemists were never able to standardize a universal system of symbols. Their journals were cryptic by design, because they feared the ecclesiastical authorities, who persecuted not a few of them as sorcerers (which, in fact, some were). These inconsistencies were due to each practitioner having his own system (or *her* own, for there were women alchemists, such as Mary the Jewess). What made things worse was the fact that the alchemists allowed these inconsistencies not only as a group, but *within* their individual work.

As Athena sprung from the head—or the intellect—of Zeus, so sprung chemistry from alchemy. As such, it has established some sensible conventions with regard to symbols (e.g., the elements, the formulae). Unfortunately, there is still some confusion over some symbols, although modern textbook writers seldom have to do time in dungeons. The author of the Camelot Primer has in fact seen a page from an old textbook that has all three meanings for the symbol H on the *same* page; even in context some of the Hs on the page were not immediately clear.

An example of this pitfall was examined in Sects. 7.10 and 8.2. Here are some some letters that suffer the same problem. The list is not exhaustive, but it includes the examples most frequently encountered by the author in his tutoring experience and textbook researches. More important than this list itself is the constant awareness that this type of confusion is still common; expect and anticipate it in this book and elsewhere.

c 1. Specific heat; a unitless constant derived from three dimensions; each phase of every substance has its own value. 2. A constant, the speed of light (3.05×10^5) km/hour.

e 1. Electrolysis, when indicated as a catalyst in an equation. 2a. A quantity of, or informal shorthand for, electrons. 2b. As e^-, the electrons in redox half-reactions.

H 1. The element hydrogen. 2. Ethalpy. 3a. Heat. 3b. Energy.

K 1. The element potassium. 2. The Kelvin, a degree of absolute heat. 3a. The equilibrium constant, the quotient of a system's concentrations. 3b. As K_{sp}, a solubility constant, the product of the small portion of dissolved components from a largely indissoluble solid.

M 1. Molarity, a conversion factor based on one definition of a solution concentration. 2. A common generic symbol for metals in formula, especially transition metals (e.g., $M_2SO_4 = Ni_2SO_4$, Co_2SO_4, Cd_2SO_4, etc.)

m 1. Molality, another solution-related conversion factor. 2. Mass, or weight, normally in grams; an algebraic or a dimensional-analysis parameter.

n 1. A placeholder for a number, usually an integer, in, say, an algebraic construct or a generic formula (e.g., alkenes: C_nH_{2n}). 2. In quantum mechanics, the letters assigned to the integers that identify Principal Energy Levels. 3. An algebraic variable for mole quantities, notably in calculations including other parameters (V, P, T) and related to the physical behavior of gases. 4. A quantity of, or informal shorthand for, neutrons.

p 1. Partial pressure of a gas within a system having more than one gas (p_n). 2. A quantity of, or informal shorthand for, protons.

P 1. The element phosphorus. 2a. Pressure, as a variable in calculations involving one or more gases. 2b. As P_T, the total pressure of a system of gases.

R 1. A unitless and universal constant, applying to all gases, derived from four parameters (P, V, n, T). 2. The molecular weight of two gases in a Graham's Law calculation (R_H and R_L). The letter might as well stand for *Relative*, in the sense that Graham *related* the ability of one gas (to diffuse) to another, based on their molecular weights.

VI. S.I. Prefix System

Some Chem. 1 curricula require the student to learn the S.I. prefixes. Even if you do not have to learn all of them right away, you will be hearing several of them soon enough; you already know at least two. The more important ones are italicized. They are worth learning as soon as possible in the same way that you needed to learn some of the element symbols at the outset and not others.

The S.I. prefixes are of course used only with metric and other S.I. dimensions (grams, liters, meters, seconds, joules, watts, etc.). A millimeter is almost a houshold word, but the nanosecond—a billionth of a second— is an important unit in the physical sciences.

prefix	symbol	magnitude	prefix	symbol	magnitude
atto-	a	10^{-18}	deka-	da	10^1
femto-	f	10^{-15}	hecto-	h	10^2
pico-	p	10^{-12}	*kilo-*	k	10^3
nano-	n	10^{-9}	*mega-*	M	10^6
micro-	μ	10^{-6}	*giga-*	G	10^9
milli-	m	10^{-3}	tera-	T	10^{12}
centi-	c	10^{-2}	peta-	P	10^{15}
deci-	d	10^{-1}	exa-	E	10^{18}

Index

397

XYZ

UV

W

This book is dedicated to
Don and Jennean Coop
for their indefatigable support.